Scott Foresman

CALIFORNIA MATHEMATICS

Authors and Advisors

Jennie Bennett
Charles Calhoun
Mary Cavanagh
Lucille Croom
Stephen Krulik
Robert A. Laing
Donna J. Long
Stuart J. Murphy
Jesse A Rudnick
Clementine Sherman
Marian Small
William Tate

Randall I. Charles
Alma B. Ramirez
Jeanne F. Ramos

Scott Foresman

Editorial Offices: Glenview, Illinois • Parsippany, New Jersey • New York, New York
Sales Offices: Reading, Massachusetts • Duluth, Georgia • Glenview, Illinois
Carrollton, Texas • Ontario, California

ISBN: 0-328-00467-7

4 5 6 7 8 9 10-WC-07 06 05 04 03 02 01

Mathematician Content Reviewers

Roger Howe *Grades K–2*
Professor of Mathematics
Yale University
New Haven, Connecticut

Gary Lippman *Grades 3–6*
Professor of Mathematics and
Computer Science
California State University Hayward
Hayward, California

Edward Barbeau *Grades 3–4*
Professor of Mathematics
University of Toronto
Toronto, Ontario, Canada

David M. Bressoud *Grades 5–6*
DeWitt Wallace Professor of
Mathematics
Macalester College
Saint Paul, Minnesota

California Content Standard Reviewers

Damien Jacotin *Kindergarten*
Los Angeles, California

Jennifer Lozo *Kindergarten*
Lodi, California

Sharon Frost *Grade 1*
Burbank, California

Beth Gould-Golland *Grade 1*
Encinitas, California

Linda Newland *Grade 2*
Santa Clarita, California

Wendy York *Grade 2*
Merced, California

Shakeh Balmanoukian *Grade 3*
Glendale, California

Donna M. Kopenski *Grade 3*
Poway, California

Armine Aghajani *Grade 4*
Tujunga, California

Floyd Flack *Grade 4*
Westminster, California

Donna Crist *Grade 5*
Turlock, California

Jimmy C. Jordan *Grade 5*
La Crescenta, California

Felicia Clark *Grade 6*
Compton, California

Vahe Tcharkhoutian *Grade 6*
Pasadena, California

Contents

CHAPTER 1 Place Value and Money

CHAPTER 2

Addition and Subtraction

CHAPTER 3 Measurement

CHAPTER 4

Multiplication Concepts

CHAPTER 5

Multiplication Facts

CHAPTER 6

Division Concepts

CHAPTER 7

Division Facts

CHAPTER 8

Geometry

CHAPTER 9

Multiplying Greater Numbers

CHAPTER 10

Dividing Greater Numbers

CHAPTER 11

Fractions and Decimals

CHAPTER 12 Data, Graphs, and Probability

California Mathematics Content Standards
Grade 3

By the end of grade three, students deepen their understanding of place value and their understanding of and skill with addition, subtraction, multiplication, and division of whole numbers. Students estimate, measure, and describe objects in space. They use patterns to help solve problems. They represent number relationships and conduct simple probability experiments.

Number Sense

1.0 Students understand the place value of whole numbers:

1.1 Count, read, and write whole numbers to 10,000.

1.2 Compare and order whole numbers to 10,000.

1.3 ( ) Identify the place value for each digit in numbers to 10,000.

1.4 Round off numbers to 10,000 to the nearest ten, hundred, and thousand.

1.5 ( ) Use expanded notation to represent numbers (e.g., $3{,}206 = 3{,}000 + 200 + 6$).

2.0 Students calculate and solve problems involving addition, subtraction, multiplication, and division:

2.1 ( ) Find the sum or difference of two whole numbers between 0 and 10,000.

2.2 ( ) Memorize to automaticity the multiplication table for numbers between 1 and 10.

2.3 ( ) Use the inverse relationship of multiplication and division to compute and check results.

2.4 ( ) Solve simple problems involving multiplication of multidigit numbers by one-digit numbers ($3{,}671 \times 3 =$ ___).

2.5 Solve division problems in which a multidigit number is evenly divided by a one-digit number ($135 \div 5 =$ ___).

2.6 Understand the special properties of 0 and 1 in multiplication and division.

2.7 Determine the unit cost when given the total cost and number of units.

2.8 Solve problems that require two or more of the skills mentioned above.

3.0 Students understand the relationship between whole numbers, simple fractions, and decimals:

3.1 Compare fractions represented by drawings or concrete materials to show equivalency and to add and subtract simple fractions in context (e.g., $\frac{1}{2}$ of a pizza is the same amount as $\frac{2}{4}$ of another pizza that is the same size; show that $\frac{3}{8}$ is larger than $\frac{1}{4}$).

3.2 ( ) Add and subtract simple fractions (e.g., determine that $\frac{1}{8} + \frac{3}{8}$ is the same as $\frac{1}{2}$).

3.3 ( ) Solve problems involving addition, subtraction, multiplication, and division of money amounts in decimal notation and multiply and divide money amounts in decimal notation by using whole-number multipliers and divisors.

3.4 Know and understand that fractions and decimals are two different representations of the same concept (e.g., 50 cents is $\frac{1}{2}$ of a dollar, 75 cents is $\frac{3}{4}$ of a dollar).

Algebra and Functions

1.0 Students select appropriate symbols, operations, and properties to represent, describe, simplify, and solve simple number relationships:

1.1 ( ) Represent relationships of quantities in the form of mathematical expressions, equations, or inequalities.

1.2 Solve problems involving numeric equations or inequalities.

1.3 Select appropriate operational and relational symbols to make an expression true (e.g., if 4 ___ $3 = 12$, what operational symbol goes in the blank?).

1.4 Express simple unit conversions in symbolic form (e.g., ___ inches = ___ feet $\times$ 12).

1.5 Recognize and use the commutative and associative properties of multiplication (e.g., if $5 \times 7 = 35$, then what is 7×5? and if $5 \times 7 \times 3 = 105$, then what is $7 \times 3 \times 5$?).

2.0 Students represent simple functional relationships:

2.1 ( ) Solve simple problems involving a functional relationship between two quantities (e.g., find the total cost of multiple items given the cost per unit).

2.2 Extend and recognize a linear pattern by its rules (e.g., the number of legs on a given number of horses may be calculated by counting by 4s or by multiplying the number of horses by 4).

Measurement and Geometry

1.0 Students choose and use appropriate units and measurement tools to quantify the properties of objects:

1.1 Choose the appropriate tools and units (metric and U.S.) and estimate and measure the length, liquid volume, and weight/mass of given objects.

1.2 ( ) Estimate or determine the area and volume of solid figures by covering them with squares or by counting the number of cubes that would fill them.

1.3 ( ) Find the perimeter of a polygon with integer sides.

1.4 Carry out simple unit conversions within a system of measurement (e.g., centimeters and meters, hours and minutes).

Reproduced from the Mathematics Content Standards for California Public Schools. The symbol (🔑) indicates a key standard as designated by a green oval in the Mathematics Framework for California Public Schools.

2.0 Students describe and compare the attributes of plane and solid geometric figures and use their understanding to show relationships and solve problems:

2.1 (🔑) Identify, describe, and classify polygons (including pentagons, hexagons, and octagons).

2.2 (🔑) Identify attributes of triangles (e.g., two equal sides for the isosceles triangle, three equal sides for the equilateral triangle, right angle for the right triangle).

2.3 (🔑) Identify attributes of quadrilaterals (e.g., parallel sides for the parallelogram, right angles for the rectangle, equal sides and right angles for the square).

2.4 Identify right angles in geometric figures or in appropriate objects and determine whether other angles are greater or less than a right angle.

2.5 Identify, describe, and classify common three-dimensional geometric objects (e.g., cube, rectangular solid, sphere, prism, pyramid, cone, cylinder).

2.6 Identify common solid objects that are the components needed to make a more complex solid object.

Statistics, Data Analysis, and Probability

1.0 Students conduct simple probability experiments by determining the number of possible outcomes and make simple predictions:

1.1 Identify whether common events are certain, likely, unlikely, or improbable.

1.2 (🔑) Record the possible outcomes for a simple event (e.g., tossing a coin) and systematically keep track of the outcomes when the event is repeated many times.

1.3 (🔑) Summarize and display the results of probability experiments in a clear and organized way (e.g., use a bar graph or a line plot).

1.4 Use the results of probability experiments to predict future events (e.g., use a line plot to predict the temperature forecast for the next day).

Mathematical Reasoning

1.0 Students make decisions about how to approach problems:

1.1 Analyze problems by identifying relationships, distinguishing relevant from irrelevant information, sequencing and prioritizing information, and observing patterns.

1.2 Determine when and how to break a problem into simpler parts.

2.0 Students use strategies, skills, and concepts in finding solutions:

2.1 Use estimation to verify the reasonableness of calculated results.

2.2 Apply strategies and results from simpler problems to more complex problems.

2.3 Use a variety of methods, such as words, numbers, symbols, charts, graphs, tables, diagrams, and models, to explain mathematical reasoning.

2.4 Express the solution clearly and logically by using the appropriate mathematical notation and terms and clear language; support solutions with evidence in both verbal and symbolic work.

2.5 Indicate the relative advantages of exact and approximate solutions to problems and give answers to a specified degree of accuracy.

2.6 Make precise calculations and check the validity of the results from the context of the problem.

3.0 Students move beyond a particular problem by generalizing to other situations:

3.1 Evaluate the reasonableness of the solution in the context of the original situation.

3.2 Note the method of deriving the solution and demonstrate a conceptual understanding of the derivation by solving similar problems.

3.3 Develop generalizations of the results obtained and apply them in other circumstances.

CHAPTER 1

Place Value and Money

Diagnosing Readiness

In Chapter 1, you will use these skills:

Ⓐ Place Value to 100

(Gr. 2)

Give the value of the underlined digit.

1. $3\underline{6}$ **2.** $\underline{2}$

3. $\underline{9}0$ **4.** $\underline{1}0$

5. $4\underline{5}$ **6.** $\underline{8}8$

Ⓑ Reading and Writing Numbers to 1,000

(Gr. 2)

Write each number in standard form.

7. 90 + 3

8. eighty-four

9. thirty-six

10. 700 + 60 + 5

11. The average yearly rainfall in Blue Canyon, California, is sixty-eight inches. Write this number in expanded form.

12. There are 365 days in a year. Write this number in expanded form.

C Rounding to the Nearest Ten and Hundred

(Gr. 2)

13. Is 13 closer to 10 or 20?

14. Is 86 closer to 80 or 90?

15. Is 349 closer to 300 or 400?

16. Is 462 closer to 400 or 500?

D Comparing and Ordering Numbers

(Gr. 2)

Use > or < for each ●.

17. 14 ● 18 **18.** 32 ● 28

19. 40 ● 60 **20.** 75 ● 74

Order the numbers from least to greatest.

21. 63, 4, 28, 60, 18

22. 93, 94, 90, 97, 89

E Counting Coins

(Gr. 2)

Use ¢ to write each amount of money.

23. 2 dimes, 2 nickels, 4 pennies

24. 1 quarter, 4 dimes, 3 nickels

25. Matthew has 1 quarter, 3 nickels, and 2 pennies. How much money does he have?

26. Stacy received 2 quarters, 1 dime, and 1 penny in change. How much money did she receive in change?

To the Family and Student

Looking Back	Chapter 1	Looking Ahead
In Grade 2, students learned place value, rounding, and ordering whole numbers to 1,000.	**Place Value and Money** In this chapter, students will learn place value, rounding, and ordering whole numbers through the thousands.	In Grade 4, students will learn place value, rounding, and ordering whole numbers through the millions.

Math and Everyday Living

Opportunities to apply the concepts of Chapter 1 abound in everyday situations. During the chapter, think about how place value, rounding, and ordering whole numbers can be used to solve a variety of real-world problems. The following examples suggest just several of the many situations that could launch a discussion about place value, rounding, and ordering whole numbers.

Math and Shopping
If three sweaters cost $36, $28, and $45, which sweater costs the most?

Math and Collecting
Jake has 80 rocks in his rock collection. Jake's father gave him 10 more. How many rocks does Jake have in his collection?

Math and Sports Kelly and his friends went to a baseball game. The announcer said the game was a sellout with 3,152 fans in attendance. How many fans, rounded to the nearest hundred, were there?

Math and the Internet
Maria was searching the internet for information on stamp collecting. She found a web page that indicated she was visitor number 7,523. Write this number in words.

Math and Transportation
A road sign gives distances in miles to the next city. About how much farther do you have to travel?

Math and Money
Kathryn has 2 five-dollar bills, 4 one-dollar bills, 3 quarters, and 4 dimes. How much money does Kathryn have?

Math at the Zoo
Zoo attendance on Friday was 547 people. About how many people visited the zoo that day?

Math at the Market
Darren is making apple pies, and he is trying to decide between Red Delicious, Golden Delicious, or Granny Smith apples. Which bag of apples will cost the least?

California Content Standards in Chapter 1 Lessons*

	Teach and Practice	Practice
Number Sense		
1.1 Count, read, and write whole numbers to 10,000.	1-1, 1-7	
1.2 Compare and order whole numbers to 10,000.	1-5	
1.3 (🔑) Identify the place value for each digit in numbers to 10,000.	1-1, 1-7	
1.4 Round off numbers to 10,000 to the nearest ten, hundred, and thousand.	1-2, 1-3	
1.5 (🔑) Use expanded notation to represent numbers.	1-1, 1-7	
3.3 (🔑) Solve problems involving addition [and] subtraction . . . of money amounts in decimal notation	1-9	
5.1 (🔑) (Grade 2) Solve problems using combinations of coins and bills.	1-8	
5.2 (🔑) (Grade 2) Know and use the decimal notation and the dollar and cent symbols for money.		1-8
Algebra and Functions		
1.2 Solve problems involving numeric equations or inequalities.		1-1, 1-5, 1-7
1.3 Select appropriate operational and relational symbols to make an expression true.		1-5

	Teach and Practice	Practice
Mathematical Reasoning		
1.0 Students make decisions about how to approach problems.	1-4	
1.1 Analyze problems by identifying relationships . . . [and] . . . sequencing and prioritizing information	1-6	
2.0 Students use strategies, skills, and concepts in finding solutions.		1-1, 1-2
2.3 Use a variety of methods, such as words, numbers, symbols, charts, graphs, tables, diagrams, and models, to explain mathematical reasoning.		1-6, 1-8, 1-9
3.1 Evaluate the reasonableness of the solution in the context of the original situation.		1-6
3.2 Note the method of deriving the solution and demonstrate a conceptual understanding of the derivation by solving similar problems.		1-6

* The symbol (🔑) indicates a key standard as designated in the Mathematics Framework for California Public Schools. Full statements of the California Content Standards are found at the beginning of this book following the Table of Contents.

LESSON 1-1

Reading and Writing Four-Digit Numbers

Warm-Up Review

1. Write eighty-seven as a number.
2. How many tens are in 65?
3. Taylor earned $8 for raking leaves and $15 for mowing the lawn. How much did he earn altogether?

California Content Standards *Number Sense 1.1: Count, read, and write whole numbers to 10,000. Also, Number Sense 1.3 ( ) and Number Sense 1.5 ( ). (See p. 3.)*

Math Link You know how to read and write numbers like 237 and 148. Now you will learn how to read and write numbers like 2,375 and 1,483.

Word Bank

expanded form
standard form
word name

A place-value chart can help you read and write numbers.

thousands	hundreds	tens	ones
2,	3	7	5

The value of the 2 is 2 thousands, or 2,000.

The value of the 3 is 3 hundreds, or 300.

The value of the 7 is 7 tens, or 70.

The value of the 5 is 5 ones, or 5.

You can write the number in three other ways.

expanded form:
2,000 + 300 + 70 + 5

standard form:
2,375

word name:
two thousand, three hundred seventy-five

Example 1

Use the data at the right. Find the value of the 4 in the height of the Petronas Twin Towers.

The 4 is in the hundreds place.

So, the value of the 4 in 1,483 is 400.

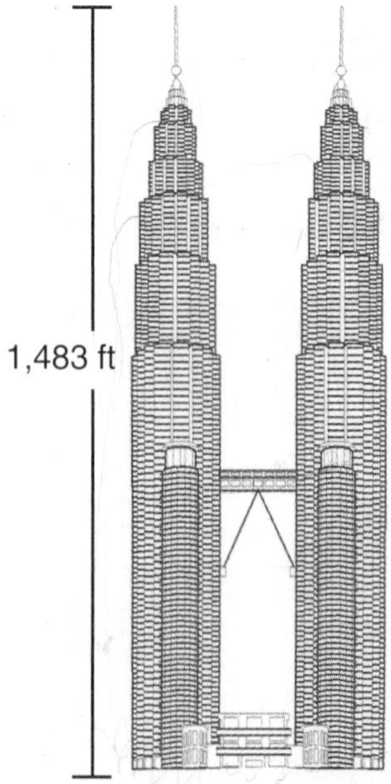

▲ **World's Tallest Buildings**
Petronas Twin Towers in Kuala Lumpur, Malaysia

Example 2

Write the height of the Petronas Twin Towers in expanded form.

First, find the value of each digit.

Then write the number as the sum of the values.

So, the expanded form of 1,483 is 1,000 + 400 + 80 + 3.

Additional Standards: Algebra and Functions 1.2; Mathematical Reasoning 2.0 (See p. 3.)

Guided Practice *For another example, see Set A on p. 30.*

Write each number in standard form.

1. 4,000 + 600 + 20 + 5 **2.** five thousand, forty-eight

Write each number in expanded form.

3. 3,324 **4.** 650 **5.** 1,746 **6.** 9,400

7. Use the digits 5, 0, 9, and 2. Write the greatest possible four-digit number using each of the digits only once.

Independent Practice *For more practice, see Set A on p. 32.*

Write each number in standard form.

8. three thousand, seven hundred five **9.** 8,000 + 500 + 70 +7

10. seven thousand, thirty **11.** 6,000 + 900 + 50

Write each number in expanded form.

12. 2,946 **13.** 335 **14.** 4,806 **15.** 3,006

Write the value of the underlined digit.

16. 5,$\underline{2}$42 **17.** 5$\underline{8}$3 **18.** 9,99$\underline{9}$ **19.** $\underline{4}$,950

20. Write the word name for 2,448. **21.** Write the word name for 5,603.

22. **Algebra** Find the missing number that makes the number sentence true: 8,000 + ■ + 60 + 3 = 8,563.

Mixed Review

23. A school collected 1,351 soup can labels. If they need 2,000 more labels to get a computer, how many labels do they need in all?

24. 7 + 5 **25.** 4 + 8 **26.** 12 − 6 **27.** 17 − 9

Test Prep **Choose the correct letter for each answer.**

28. Complete the pattern.
(Gr. 2)
7, 9, ■, 13, 15

A 10 **C** 12
B 11 **D** 18

29. Randy has 4 dimes and 5 nickels. How much money does he have?
(Gr. 2)

F 9¢ **H** 60¢
G 45¢ **J** 65¢

LESSON 1-2

Rounding to the Nearest Ten and Hundred

California Content Standard *Number Sense 1.4: Round off numbers . . . to the nearest ten [and] hundred . . ..*

Math Link You know how to estimate how many. Now you will learn to estimate by rounding.

Warm-Up Review

1. What number comes between 38 and 40?
2. Is 25 less than or greater than 20?
3. What number is 10 more than 30?
4. There are 8 birds flying. Then 3 birds land. How many birds are still flying?

Word Bank

round

You can **round** numbers to tell about how many.

Example 1

This is how you would round 22, 25, and 28 to the nearest ten using a number line.

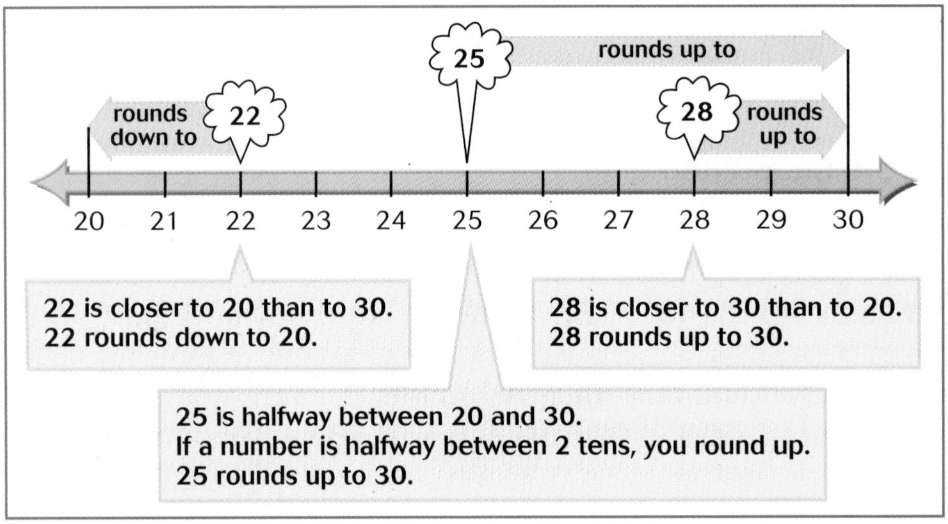

You can also round 22, 25, and 28 to the nearest ten using the rounding rule.

	22	25	28
Find the tens place.	22	25	28
Look at the digit to the right. Then use the rounding rule below.	22	25	28
	rounds to 22 → 20	rounds to 25 → 30	rounds to 28 → 30

If the digit to the right of the tens place is less than 5, round down. If the digit is 5 or greater, round up.

The digit in the tens place stays the same.

The digit in the tens place increases by 1.

Additional Standard: Mathematical Reasoning 2.0 (See p. 3.)

Example 2

This is how you would round 215, 250, and 275 to the nearest hundred using a number line.

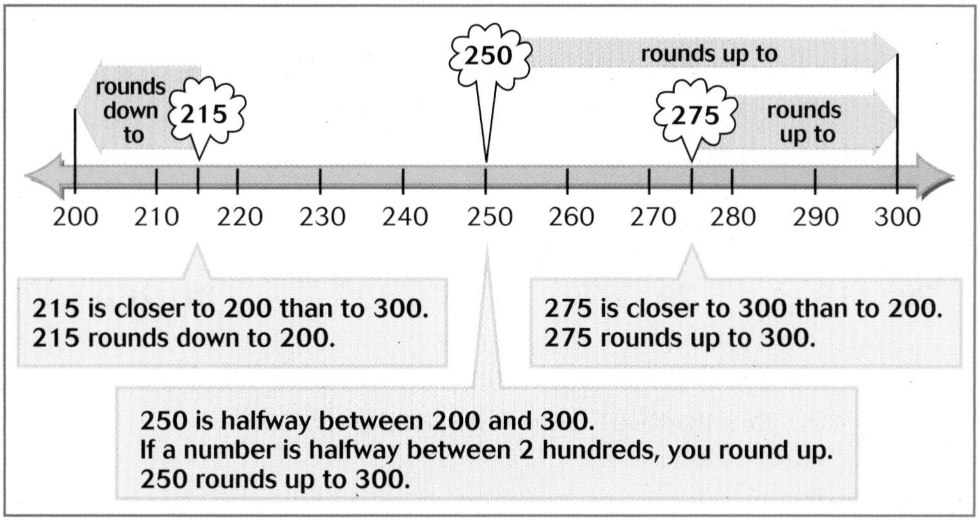

250
rounds up to
rounds down to
215
275
rounds up to
200 210 220 230 240 250 260 270 280 290 300
215 is closer to 200 than to 300.
215 rounds down to 200.
275 is closer to 300 than to 200.
275 rounds up to 300.
250 is halfway between 200 and 300.
If a number is halfway between 2 hundreds, you round up.
250 rounds up to 300.

Now round 215, 250, and 275 to the nearest hundred using the rounding rule.

Find the hundreds place.	215	250	275
Look at the first digit to the right. Then use the rounding rule below.	215	250	275
	rounds to 215 → 200	rounds to 250 → 300	rounds to 275 → 300

If the digit to the right of the hundreds place is less than 5, round down. If the digit is 5 or greater, round up.

The digit in the hundreds place stays the same.

The digit in the hundreds place increases by 1.

Guided Practice *For another example, see Set B on p. 30.*

Round to the nearest ten.

1. 36 **2.** 81 **3.** 75 **4.** 49 **5.** 42

Round to the nearest hundred.

6. 719 **7.** 254 **8.** 648 **9.** 326 **10.** 130

11. Math Reasoning What is the least number that rounds to 500? What is the greatest number that rounds to 500?

Independent Practice *For more practice, see Set B on p. 32.*

Round to the nearest ten.

12. 55 **13.** 34 **14.** 87 **15.** 21 **16.** 19

17. 16 **18.** 93 **19.** 56 **20.** 45 **21.** 73

Round to the nearest hundred.

22. 571 **23.** 749 **24.** 350 **25.** 852 **26.** 442

27. 100 **28.** 418 **29.** 978 **30.** 323 **31.** 260

32. Math Reasoning What is the number halfway between 80 and 90? How can this number help you round 86 to the nearest ten?

33. Mark is driving from Los Angeles to Monterey. He sees the sign at the right as he is leaving Los Angeles. About how many miles is it to Monterey?

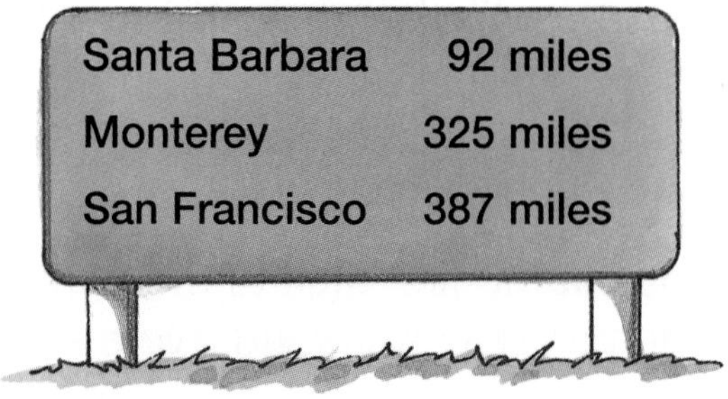

34. Round 999 to the nearest hundred.

Mixed Review

35. The fourth grade collected 3,012 aluminum cans. The third grade collected 3,021 aluminum cans. Write the word name for the number of aluminum cans that the third grade collected.

36. Write 4,650 in expanded form.

37. What is the value of the 5 in 5,723?

Algebra **Find each missing number.**

38. 3 + ■ = 6 **39.** 6 + ■ = 8 **40.** 8 + ■ = 16 **41.** 9 + ■ = 12

Test Prep **Choose the correct letter for each answer.**

42. (1–1) What is the standard form for eight thousand, four hundred twenty-five?

A 84 **C** 8,425
B 825 **D** 8,452

43. (Gr. 2) Name the shape.

F circle **H** square
G triangle **J** rectangle

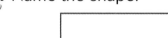

 Use Homework Workbook 1-2.

TEST PREP

Multiple-Choice Cumulative Review

Choose the correct letter for each answer.

1. Kayla kept track of the insects she saw while on a walk. She wrote them in the table below.

Insects	
Ladybug	𝍸
Beetle	III
Cricket	𝍸 II
Grasshopper	IIII

How many beetles did she see?

A 3 beetles
B 4 beetles
C 5 beetles
D 7 beetles

2. Cole has 1 quarter, 4 dimes, 2 nickels, and 3 pennies. How much money does he have?

F 68¢
G 78¢
H 88¢
J 98¢

3. Becky takes the bus home from school. The bus leaves at 2:00 P.M. The bus drops Becky off at 2:30 P.M. How much time does Becky spend riding the bus?

A 5 min
B 15 min
C 25 min
D 30 min

4. Raul scored 394 points in a game. Estimate the total number of points he scored.

F About 200 points
G About 300 points
H About 400 points
J About 500 points
K NH

5. A dress costs $54. How much does the dress cost rounded to the nearest ten dollars?

A $40
B $50
C $60
D $100
E NH

6. Which number is the same as four hundred thirty-seven?

F 430
G 437
H 473
J 4,073
K NH

7. What is the value of the digit 8 in 4,806?

A 8
B 80
C 800
D 8,000

LESSON 1-3

Rounding Larger Numbers

Warm-Up Review

Round to the nearest ten.

1. 55 **2.** 19 **3.** 82

Round to the nearest hundred.

4. 413 **5.** 370 **6.** 956

7. Tia jogged 4 miles on Sunday. She jogged 3 miles on Monday and 5 miles on Tuesday. How many miles did she jog in all?

California Content Standard *Number Sense 1.4: Round off numbers to 10,000 to the nearest ten, hundred, and thousand.*

Math Link You know how to round numbers to 1,000. Now you will learn how to round numbers to 10,000.

Example 1

Round 1,265 to the nearest thousand.

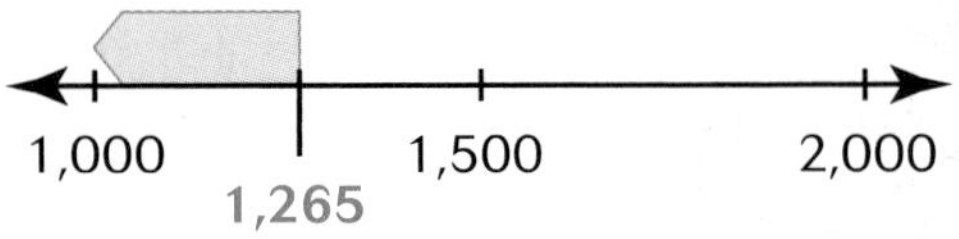

Find the thousands place. 1,265

Look at the first digit to the right. 1,265

Since 2 is less than 5, round down. 1,265 rounds to 1,000.

To the nearest thousand, 1,265 rounds to 1,000.

Example 2

Round 1,265 to the nearest hundred.

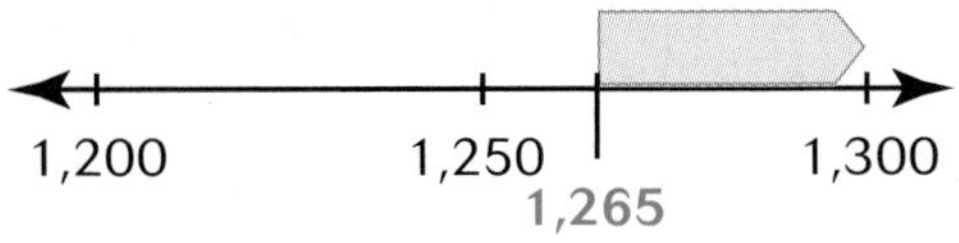

Find the hundreds place. 1,265

Look at the first digit to the right. 1,265

Since 6 is greater than 5, round up. 1,265 rounds to 1,300.

To the nearest hundred, 1,265 rounds to 1,300.

Example 3

Round 1,265 to the nearest ten.

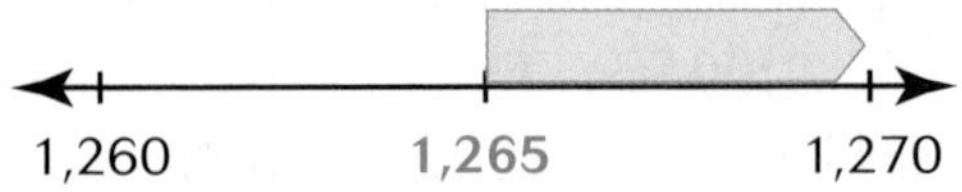

Find the tens place. 1,265

Look at the digit to the right. 1,265

Since the digit is 5, round up. 1,265 rounds to 1,270.

To the nearest ten, 1,265 rounds to 1,270.

Guided Practice *For another example, see Set C on p. 30.*

Round each number to the nearest thousand, hundred, and ten.

1. 5,387 **2.** 6,743 **3.** 1,190 **4.** 9,500

5. The library lent 1,256 books during March. To the nearest hundred, how many books were lent during March?

Independent Practice *For more practice, see Set C on p. 32.*

Round each number to the nearest thousand.

6. 4,573 **7.** 1,220 **8.** 7,234 **9.** 9,119

Round each number to the nearest hundred.

10. 1,876 **11.** 5,329 **12.** 3,400 **13.** 6,985

Round each number to the nearest ten.

14. 8,078 **15.** 4,007 **16.** 2,481 **17.** 9,999

Use the data at the right for Exercises 18 and 19.

18. To the nearest ten, what was the zoo attendance on Saturday?

19. To the nearest thousand, hundred, and ten, what was the zoo attendance on Friday?

Mixed Review

20. There were 6,532 people at the concert last night. Write this number in expanded form.

21. Algebra What is the missing number? 5 + ■ = 4 + 5

22. Round 87 to the nearest ten. **23.** Round 349 to the nearest hundred.

Test Prep **Choose the correct letter for each answer.**

24. Find the sum of 13 and 6.
(Gr. 2)

A 7 **D** 19
B 9 **E** NH
C 17

25. 27 − 10 =
(Gr. 2)

F 7 **J** 37
G 17 **K** NH
H 27

LESSON 1-4

Understand
Plan
Solve
Look Back

Problem-Solving Skill:

Exact Numbers or Estimates

Warm-Up Review

Round to the nearest ten.

1. 68 **2.** 42 **3.** 25

Round to the nearest hundred.

4. 423 **5.** 840 **6.** 596

7. Julie is 9 years old. Mike is 11 years old. Lee is 3 years older than Mike. How much older is Mike than Julie?

California Content Standard *Mathematical Reasoning 1.0: Students make decisions about how to approach problems.*

Read for Understanding

Emma has more than 500 stamps in her stamp collection. She has almost 40 flower stamps. She also has 22 bird stamps and 12 stamps from foreign countries.

1. How many stamps does Emma have?
2. How many flower stamps does she have?
3. How many stamps from foreign countries does she have?
4. Emma bought a 1998 U.S. first-class bird stamp. How much did it cost?

U.S. Stamp Rates (first class)

Year (rate became effective)	Cost
1988	25¢
1991	29¢
1995	32¢
1999	33¢

Think and Discuss

MATH FOCUS

Exact Numbers or Estimates

Estimates are not exact numbers. Words like *more than, almost,* and *about* can tell you that numbers are estimated, not exact.

Reread the paragraph at the top of the page.

5. Does Emma have exactly 40 flower stamps? If not, does she have more or fewer? How can you tell?
6. Does Emma have exactly 12 stamps from foreign countries? If not, does she have more or fewer? How can you tell?
7. When might the number 30 stand for an exact amount? When might it be an estimate?

Use the information below for Exercises 1–3.

> **SPECIAL NOTICE**
>
> For a limited time, we are offering Customers an electronic coupon worth $20 to use on all orders more than $75.

Guided Practice

1. There are two numbers used in the Special Notice. How many of the numbers are exact amounts?

- **a.** two of the numbers
- **b.** one of the numbers
- **c.** none of the numbers

2. Which words help you know that $75 is an estimate?

- **a.** electronic coupon
- **b.** all orders
- **c.** more than

3. Which sentence tells how much the coupon is worth?

- **a.** The coupon is worth exactly $20.
- **b.** The coupon is worth almost $20.
- **c.** The coupon is worth less than $20.

Independent Practice

Use the ad at the right for Exercises 4–7.

> **STAMP IT!**
>
> **Open 6 Days a Week**
>
> More than 700 stamps available!
> Over 30 kinds to choose from!
>
> **Only 10¢ each!**

4. There are 4 numbers in the ad. How many of the numbers are estimates?

- **a.** two of the numbers
- **b.** three of the numbers
- **c.** all of the numbers

5. How much would 4 stamps cost altogether?

- **a.** less than 40¢
- **b.** more than 40¢
- **c.** exactly 40¢

6. Which of the following could be the number of stamps available?

- **a.** 700 stamps
- **b.** 697 stamps
- **c.** 720 stamps

7. **Math Reasoning** Explain how you can tell which numbers in the ad are estimates and which numbers are exact.

LESSON 1-5

Comparing and Ordering Numbers

Warm-Up Review

Write the value of the underlined digit.

1. 182 2. 405

3. 7,641 4. 2,933

5. Joe brings 4 sandwiches to the picnic. Bonnie brings 8 more. How many sandwiches are there in all?

California Content Standard *Number Sense 1.2: Compare and order whole numbers to 10,000.*

Math Link You know how to compare and order numbers to 1,000. Now you will learn how to compare and order numbers to 10,000.

Remember when you compare numbers, you can use the symbols at the right.

< means "is less than."
> means "is greater than."

Example 1

Use the data at the right. Which tortoise can live longer—a Box tortoise or a Marion's tortoise?

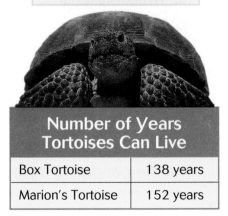

Number of Years Tortoises Can Live	
Box Tortoise	138 years
Marion's Tortoise	152 years

To find out, compare 138 and 152.

138 ● 152 The hundreds digits are the same.

138 ● 152 3 tens is less than 5 tens.

$138 < 152$ So, 138 is less than 152.

A Marion's tortoise can live longer than a box tortoise.

Example 2

Compare 3,167 and 3,136.

3,167 ● 3,136 The thousands digits are the same.

3,167 ● 3,136 The hundreds digits are the same.

3,167 ● 3,136 6 tens is greater than 3 tens.

$3,167 > 3,136$ So, 3,167 is greater than 3,136.

Example 3

Compare 726 and 7,265.

726 ● 7,265 Since all 3-digit numbers are less than all 4-digit numbers, there is no need to compare the digits.

$726 < 7,265$ So, 726 is less than 7,265.

Additional Standards: Algebra and Functions 1.2, 1.3 (See p. 3.)

Example 4

Order these numbers from *least* to *greatest*.

5,364 4,536 5,464

Write the numbers with the ones digits lined up. Then compare the numbers digit by digit starting with the greatest place value.

Compare the thousands digits.

5,364	Since 4 thousands is less than
4,536	5 thousands, 4,536 is the
5,464	least number.

Since 5,364 and 5,464 have the same thousands digit, compare the hundreds digits.

5,364	Since 4 hundreds is greater than 3 hundreds,
5,464	5,464 is the greatest number.

The order of the numbers from *least* to *greatest* is:

4,536 5,364 5,464

Guided Practice *For another example, see Set D on p. 31.*

Compare. Write >, <, or =.

1. 366 ● 336 **2.** 2,531 ● 253 **3.** 7,091 ● 8,541

Write the numbers in order from least to greatest.

4. 448 232 238 **5.** 3,012 3,168 319

6. Sergio has 139 shells. Kara has 187 shells. Carl has 10 more shells than Sergio. Who has the most shells?

Independent Practice *For more practice, see Set D on p. 33.*

Compare. Write >, <, or =.

7. 482 ● 487 **8.** 899 ● 899 **9.** 672 ● 756

10. 1,305 ● 135 **11.** 492 ● 4,032 **12.** 9,999 ● 9,998

13. 1,467 ● 1,567 **14.** 4,929 ● 4,930 **15.** 6,954 ● 6,945

Write the numbers in order from least to greatest.

16. 642 602 649

17. 784 748 7,182

18. 4,002 4,200 4,020

19. 6,475 6,457 646

Algebra **Replace the ■ with a digit that makes the comparison true.**

20. 721 > 72■

21. 47■ > 478

22. 3,836 < 3,83■

23. Use the table at the right. Order the countries where television was first broadcast from the earliest date to the latest date.

When Television Was First Broadcast	
Cuba	1950
England	1936
United States	1939

24. Risa has 1,247 stamps in her collection. Miguel has 1,439 stamps in his collection. Who has more stamps?

Mixed Review

25. Round 3,823 to the nearest ten.

26. Round 455 to the nearest hundred.

27. Round 9,805 to the nearest thousand, hundred, and ten.

28. What is the value of the underlined digit in 1,4<u>6</u>7?

29. 80 + 10

30. 50 + 30

31. 60 − 40

32. 90 − 70

33. 200 + 600

34. 300 + 700

35. 900 − 600

36. 5,000 − 1,000

Test Prep **Choose the correct letter for each answer.**

37. *(Gr. 2)* What part of the figure is shaded?

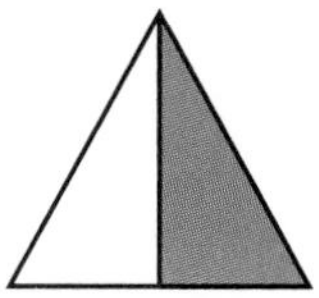

A $\frac{1}{5}$

B $\frac{1}{4}$

C $\frac{1}{3}$

D $\frac{1}{2}$

38. *(Gr. 2)* What time does the clock show?

F 10:30

G 9:30

H 9:15

J 9:00

Diagnostic Checkpoint

Write each number in standard form.

1. three thousand, six *(1-1)*

2. 7,000 + 700 + 7 *(1-1)*

3. 6,000 + 300 + 50 + 2 *(1-1)*

4. five thousand, four hundred ten *(1-1)*

5. nine thousand, four hundred eight *(1-1)*

6. 8,000 + 80 + 3 *(1-1)*

Round to the nearest ten.

7. 45 *(1-2)*

8. 37 *(1-2)*

9. 63 *(1-2)*

10. 29 *(1-2)*

Round to the nearest hundred.

11. 875 *(1-2)*

12. 357 *(1-2)*

13. 208 *(1-2)*

14. 911 *(1-2)*

Round to the nearest thousand.

15. 6,643 *(1-3)*

16. 3,937 *(1-3)*

17. 5,555 *(1-3)*

18. 3,829 *(1-3)*

Compare. Write $>$, $<$, or $=$.

19. 347 ● 374 *(1-5)*

20. 182 ● 179 *(1-5)*

21. 1,107 ● 1,170 *(1-5)*

22. 1,354 ● 1,354 *(1-5)*

23. 2,000 ● 2,010 *(1-5)*

24. 9,035 ● 9,029 *(1-5)*

Write the numbers in order from least to greatest.

25. 126 114 128 *(1-5)*

26. 3,019 337 324 *(1-5)*

27. 4,242 4,232 4,223 *(1-5)*

Read the paragraph below to answer Exercises 28 and 29.

Suzanne read more than 12 books over the summer vacation. Brent read less than 10 books. Lauren read 7 books. Altogether the friends read almost 30 books!

28. *(1-4)* Is 30 books used as an exact amount or an estimate? Explain.

29. *(1-4)* How many of the numbers in the paragraph above are exact?

LESSON 1-6

Understand
Plan
Solve
Look Back

Problem-Solving Strategy:

Use Logical Reasoning

Warm-Up Review

Tell whether each number is even or odd.

1. 50 **2.** 19 **3.** 42

Compare. Write >, <, or =.

4. 155 ● 185

5. 299 ● 300

6. A number is greater than 76, but less than 80. It is even. What is the number?

California Content Standard *Mathematical Reasoning 1.1: Analyze problems by identifying relationships . . . [and] sequencing and prioritizing information . . ..*

Sam and Leah are lining up four model cars in a row. Leah puts the red car in front of the blue car. Sam puts the yellow car between the blue car and the red car. Leah puts the purple car next to the red car but not next to the yellow car. What is the order of the cars?

Understand

What do you need to find?

You need to find how Sam and Leah are lining up the four model cars.

Plan

How can you solve the problem?

You can **use logical reasoning** to help you organize the facts. As you read each sentence of the problem, start listing the order of the cars. Adjust your list each time you find new information.

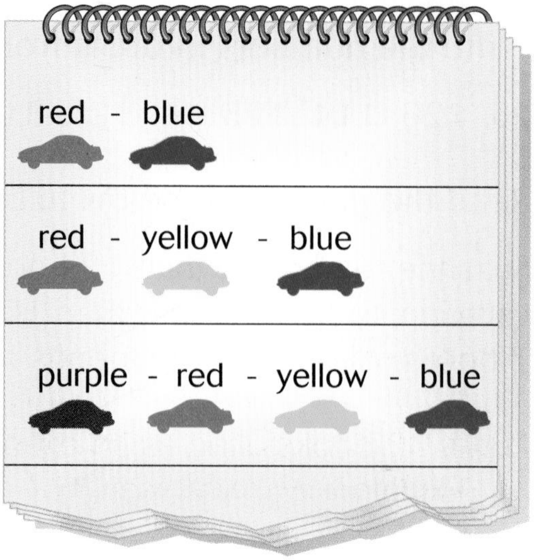

Solve

The order of the cars is purple, red, yellow, and blue.

Look Back

Compare your answer with the facts in the problem. Does your answer match the facts?

Additional Standards: Mathematical Reasoning 2.3, 3.1, and 3.2 *(See p. 3.)*

Guided Practice

1. Julie has 4 glass horses lined up on a shelf. The black horse is between the brown horse and the silver horse. The brown horse is fourth. The red horse is first. What is the color of the third horse in line?

Independent Practice

2. Aaron gave Melinda a hint about the number of trucks in his collection. He said, "It is an odd number less than 20 and greater than 10. The sum of the digits in the number is 6." How many trucks are in Aaron's collection?

3. Stacy, Marc, Jordan, and Letisha each buy a red, blue, green, or yellow T-shirt. Letisha buys a blue T-shirt. Jordan does not buy a red or yellow T-shirt. Stacy does not buy a red or green T-shirt. If they each buy a different color T-shirt, which color T-shirt did each person buy?

4. Mary is thinking of an even number that uses the digits 0, 1, 2, and 3. The number is greater than 2,000 but less than 3,000. There is a 3 in the tens place. What is the number?

Mixed Review

Try these or other strategies to solve each problem. Tell which strategy you used.

Problem-Solving Strategies

- *Write a Number Sentence*
- *Use Logical Reasoning*
- *Find a Pattern*
- *Draw a Picture*

5. Jeff arranges fall leaves around the bulletin board in the order: brown, green, red, and yellow. If he continues the pattern, what color will the 16th leaf be?

6. Josh has 6 lines to say in each act of a play. There are 2 acts. He has learned 3 of his lines. How many more lines does he need to learn?

Use Homework Workbook 1-6.

LESSON 1-7

Extending Place-Value Concepts

Warm-Up Review

Write each number in words and expanded form.

1. 4,216 **2.** 7,006 **3.** 5,938

4. Write 8,000 + 200 + 7 in standard form.

5. Tomas has 29 stickers. Beth has 35 stickers, and Julie has 18 stickers. Who has the most stickers?

California Content Standards *Number Sense 1.1: Count, read, and write whole numbers to 10,000. Also, Number Sense 1.3 ( ) and Number Sense 1.5 ( ). (This lesson extends place value to 5- and 6-digit numbers.)*

Math Link You know how to read and write numbers like 1,368 and 9,208. Now you will learn how to read and write numbers like 13,684 and 920,835.

Place-value can help you understand larger numbers.

hundred thousands	ten thousands	thousands	hundreds	tens	ones
9	2	0,	8	3	5

expanded form: 900,000 + 20,000 + 800 + 30 + 5
standard form: 920,835
word name: nine hundred twenty thousand, eight hundred thirty-five

Example 1

Find the value of the 1 in 13,684.

The 1 is in the ten thousands place of 13,684.

So, the value of the 1 in 13,684 is 10,000.

Example 2

Write 706,451 in expanded form.

First, find the value of each digit.

Then write 706,451 as the sum of the values.

So, the expanded form of 706,451 is 700,000 + 6,000 + 400 + 50 + 1.

Guided Practice *For another example, see Set E on p. 31.*

Write the value of the underlined digit.

1. $611{,}06\underline{5}$ **2.** $34{,}6\underline{5}2$ **3.** $\underline{2}43{,}507$ **4.** $47\underline{5}{,}422$ **5.** $19{,}\underline{6}97$

Write each number in expanded form.

6. 32,191 **7.** 932,124 **8.** 57,492 **9.** 66,504 **10.** 264,830

 Additional Standard: Algebra and Functions 1.2 (See p. 3.)

11. A store has 10,000 blue marbles, 3,000 green marbles, and 80 red marbles. How many marbles does the store have in all?

Independent Practice *For more practice, see Set E on p. 33.*

Write the value of the underlined digit.

12. $30\underline{9},041$ **13.** $7\underline{2}9,467$ **14.** $80,\underline{1}93$ **15.** $72,43\underline{6}$ **16.** $\underline{5}5,641$

17. $44,5\underline{6}0$ **18.** $854,\underline{2}08$ **19.** $94\underline{7},913$ **20.** $1\underline{3},071$ **21.** $\underline{5}69,302$

Write each number in expanded form.

22. 61,504 **23.** 79,415 **24.** 543,078 **25.** 10,405 **26.** 336,523

27. Complete the pattern.

12,100, 12,200, 12,300, 12,400 ■, ■, ■

28. Algebra Find the missing number that makes the number sentence true: 30,000 + ■ + 900 + 2 = 34,902.

29. Suppose a museum has a collection of 354,000 clay marbles. If another 10,000 marbles are brought to the museum, how many marbles will be in the collection?

Mixed Review

Compare. Write >, <, or =.

30. 759 ● 7,588 **31.** 4,146 ● 4,132

Use the table at the right for Exercises 32 and 33.

32. Which bird is fastest? Which bird is slowest?

33. Round the speed of the falcon to the nearest hundred.

Speeds of Birds	
Eagle	120 miles per hour
Swift	106 miles per hour
Falcon	168 miles per hour

Test Prep **Choose the correct letter for each answer.**

34. Round 3,562 to the nearest hundred.
(1–3)

A 3,500 **C** 3,600
B 3,560 **D** 4,000

35. What is the standard form for 5,000 + 80 + 9?
(1–1)

F 5,089 **H** 5,809
G 5,098 **J** 5,890

LESSON 1-8 Counting Coins and Bills

Warm-Up Review

Use ¢ to write the amount of money.

1. 2 dimes, 5 pennies
2. seventy-four cents
3. 1 quarter, 1 dime, 2 nickels
4. 3 quarters, 2 dimes
5. Sue has 4 dimes, 1 nickel, and 1 penny in her pocket. How many more pennies does she need to make 50¢?

California Content Standard *Number Sense 5.1 (key), Grade 2: Solve problems using combinations of coins and bills.*

Math Link When you buy something, you need to count the money you have and then check the change you receive. In this lesson, you will count groups of coins and bills.

Example 1

Find the total value of the group of coins and bills.

When you count the money, start with the bill of greatest value and end with the coin of least value.

Count: \$5.00, \$6.00, \$6.25, \$6.50, \$6.75, \$6.85, \$6.95, \$6.96

The total value of the group of bills and coins is \$6.96.

Use a dollar sign and decimal point to write money.

Example 2

Find the total value of the group of coins and bills.

Count: \$1.00, \$2.00, \$2.25, \$2.50, \$2.60, \$2.65, \$2.70, \$2.75, \$2.76, \$2.77

The total value of the group of coins and bills is \$2.77.

 Additional Standards: Number Sense 5.2 (key), Grade 2; Mathematical Reasoning 2.3 *(See p. 3.)*

Guided Practice *For another example, see Set F on p. 31.*

Find the total value of each group of coins and bills.

1.

2.

3. Tania said, "I lost a coin! I had $2.30. Now I have only 1 one-dollar bill and 5 quarters." What coin did Tania lose?

Independent Practice *For more practice, see Set F on p. 33.*

Find the total value of each group of coins and bills.

4.

5.

6. five-dollar bill, one-dollar bill, 2 quarters, 2 dimes, and 1 nickel

7. ten-dollar bill, 1 dime, 1 nickel, and 2 pennies

8. Math Reasoning Tom needs change for a five-dollar bill. A friend gives him 4 one-dollar bills, 2 quarters, 3 dimes, and 2 nickels. Is this a fair trade? Explain.

Mixed Review

Write the numbers in order from least to greatest.

9. 1,837 2,078 1,999

10. 4,357 434 4,350

Test Prep Choose the correct letter for each answer.

11. (Gr. 2) **Algebra** Find the missing number: 18 − ■ = 9.

A 8 **C** 10
B 9 **D** 27

12. (1–7) What is the value of the underlined digit in $23{,}0\underline{5}7$?

F 5 **H** 500
G 50 **J** 5,000

LESSON 1-9

Understand
Plan
Solve
Look Back

Problem-Solving Application:
Using Money

California Content Standard *Number Sense 3.3 (🔑): Solve problems involving addition [and] subtraction . . . of money amounts in decimal notation . . ..*

Warm-Up Review

Find the total value of the money in each group.

1. 3 quarters, 3 nickels
2. 2 one-dollar bills, 3 dimes, 1 nickel, 3 pennies
3. 1 five-dollar bill, 2 quarters, 3 dimes

Use the data at the right. Shaun bought a package of insect stickers. He paid with a \$5 bill. How much change should he receive?

Understand

What do you need to find?

You need to find how much change Shaun should receive.

Plan

How can you solve the problem?

You can count up from the cost of the stickers to find the correct change.

Solve

Start with the cost of the stickers and count up to \$5. The money you add to count up to \$5 will be the correct change.

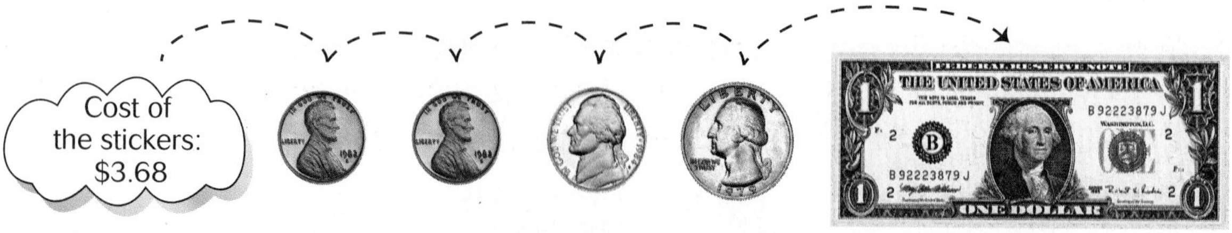

\$3.68 ⟶ \$3.69 → \$3.70 → \$3.75 → \$4.00 ⟶ \$5.00

The change Shaun should receive is \$1.32.

Look Back

How could you check that this is the correct change?

Additional Standard: Mathematical Reasoning 2.3 *(See p. 3.)*

Guided Practice

1. Cam buys Safari Fun animal stickers that cost $3.31. She gives the clerk $5.00. Cam's change includes 4 pennies, 2 quarters, 1 one-dollar bill, and 2 other coins. What are the other 2 coins Cam receives?

2. Suppose you spend $1.36 on panda stickers and $1.10 on tiger stickers. You give the clerk $2.50. What is your change?

Independent Practice

3. Kit spends $2.46 on lion stickers. Brian buys a hippo sticker for $0.99 and zebra stickers for $1.45. They each pay with three $1 bills. Who gets more change? How much more?

4. Maya spends $8.79 on a sticker album. She pays the clerk with a $10 bill. List the fewest coins and bills the clerk could give Maya as change.

Complete the chart to show the change that each person should receive.

	Name of Friend	Sticker Package	Amount of Money Given	Cost of Sticker Package	Change
5.	Bill	Package A	$1.00	$0.72	
6.	Sue	Package B	$5.00	$4.33	
7.	Cindy	Package C	$10.00	$8.97	

Mixed Review

8. Shannon made 6 baskets and committed 2 fouls on Friday. On Saturday, she made 3 more baskets than she did on Friday. How many baskets did she make on Saturday?

9. Each class has 30 minutes to play basketball. Mrs. Thorpe's class has played for 23 minutes. How many minutes do they have left to play?

10. Martin needs to put away his toys. Make a list to find all the ways he can put 6 different toys in 2 toy boxes.

Use Homework Workbook 1-9.

Diagnostic Checkpoint

Complete. For Exercises 1–3, use the words from the Word Bank.

Word Bank
expanded form
standard form
word name
round

1. (1-2) When an exact number is not needed, you can ____________ a number to the nearest ten, hundred, or other place value.

2. (1-1) _______________ is a way to write numbers that shows the place value of each digit.

3. (1-1) 4,651 is written in _______________.

Write the value of the underlined digit.

4. (1-7) 15,$\underline{7}$90

5. (1-7) 68,3$\underline{7}$8

6. (1-7) 5$\underline{7}$0,020

7. (1-7) $\underline{2}$87,002

Find the total value of each group of coins and bills.

8. (1-8)

9. (1-8)

10. (1-9) Rodney buys a key chain for $2.79. He pays with three one-dollar bills. What is his change?

11. (1-6) Fran, Mike, Jeff, and Tia are waiting in line. Tia is standing between Fran and Mike. Jeff is the last person in line. Fran is not first in line. List the order in which the four friends are standing in line from first to last.

12. (1-6) Kohei is thinking of a number that is less than 45, greater than 35, and the sum of the digits is 7. What is the number?

Chapter 1 Test

Write each number in standard form.

1. seven thousand, sixty-seven

2. four thousand, one hundred

3. 60,000 + 4,000 + 300 + 7

4. 1,000 + 400 + 30 + 2

Write the value of the underlined digit.

5. $8{,}2\underline{3}9$

6. $\underline{2}{,}054$

7. $5{,}68\underline{5}$

8. $1\underline{3}6{,}712$

Round to the nearest hundred.

9. 645

10. 554

11. 5,193

12. 1,407

Compare. Write >, <, or =.

13. 5,047 ● 5,046

14. 8,670 ● 8,750

15. 9,348 ● 9,328

Find the total value of each group of coins and bills.

16.

17.

18. Marcus has 44 stickers. He has more than 25 animal stickers and about 10 airplane stickers. Is 44 stickers an exact amount or an estimate? Explain.

19. Allison buys a poster for $7.48. She pays with a $10 bill. What is her change?

20. John, Brent, Rosa, and Valerie each take a different snack from a bowl of apples, pears, bananas, and oranges. Valerie takes a banana. Rosa does not eat oranges. Brent does not eat oranges or pears. Which type of fruit does each person choose?

TEST PREP

Multiple-Choice Chapter 1 Test

Choose the correct letter for each answer.

1. What is the value of the 9 in 390,048?

A 90
B 900
C 9,000
D 90,000
E NH

2. Which of the following numbers is between 8,406 and 8,416 on a number line?

F 8,400
G 8,410
H 8,420
J 8,430
K NH

3. Which of the following numbers rounds to 4,000?

A 3,000
B 3,499
C 4,499
D 4,500
E NH

4. What is 46,702 in expanded form?

F 4,000 + 600 + 70 + 2
G 46,000 + 700 + 20
H 40,000 + 6,000 + 700 + 20
J 40,000 + 6,000 + 700 + 2
K NH

5. What number is the standard form for two thousand, fifty?

F 250
G 2,005
H 2,500
J 20,500
K NH

The table shows the price of four different bicycle models. Use the table for Questions 6 and 7.

Bicycles

Model	Price
Hare	$345
Deer	$410
Fox	$360
Lynx	$455

6. Order the models from least price to greatest price.

A Deer, Hare, Lynx, Fox
B Lynx, Deer, Fox, Hare
C Fox, Lynx, Hare, Deer
D Hare, Fox, Deer, Lynx

7. Which bicycle models have the same price when rounded to the nearest hundred?

F Deer and Fox
G Hare and Fox
H Deer and Lynx
J Hare and Deer

Use the following paragraph for Questions 8 and 9.

> Dylan finished the race in 54 seconds. Macy finished in less than 60 seconds. Austin came in last with a time of 76 seconds.

8. How many numbers in the paragraph above are estimates?

F three of the numbers
G two of the numbers
H one of the numbers
J none of the numbers

---

9. Which of the following could be Macy's race time?

A 76 seconds
B 70 seconds
C 60 seconds
D 58 seconds

---

10. If Nolan pays $7.64 for a model airplane with a ten-dollar bill, which combination of bills and coins could he receive as change?

F two one-dollar bills, 1 quarter, 1 dime, 1 penny
G two one-dollar bills, 1 quarter, 2 nickels, 4 pennies
H two one-dollar bills, 2 quarters, 1 dime, 1 penny
J two one-dollar bills, 2 quarters, 2 dimes, 4 pennies

11. Bethany has a one-dollar bill, 4 quarters, 2 dimes, and 1 nickel. How much money does she have?

A $1.25
B $1.55
C $2.25
D $2.75
E NH

---

12. Roma buys a turkey sandwich for $3.25 and a juice box for $0.49. She pays with a $5 bill. What is her change?

F $0.96
G $1.06
H $1.16
J $1.26

---

13. There are 4 taxicabs waiting in a line at the airport curb. The red taxi is between the blue taxi and the white taxi. The blue taxi is not last in line. The green taxi is first in line. What is the order of taxicabs from first to last in line?

A Green, Blue, Red, White
B White, Red, Blue, Green
C Green, Red, Blue, White
D White, Blue, Red, Green

Reteaching

Set A (pages 4–5)

Write 3,146 in expanded form.

A place-value chart can help you read and write numbers.

thousands	hundreds	tens	ones
3,	1	4	6

Write the number as the sum of the values of each digit.

3,000 + 100 + 40 + 6

Write two thousand, eighty-five in standard form.

2,085 ← standard form

Remember a four-digit number in standard form is written with a comma between the hundreds digit and the thousands digit.

Write each number in expanded form.

1. 405 **2.** 1,390

3. 5,065 **4.** 7,889

Write each number in standard form.

5. three hundred twelve

6. one thousand, seventy-nine

7. 4,000 + 900 + 20 + 3

Set B (pages 6–8)

Round 742 to the nearest hundred.

1. Find the hundreds place.
2. Look at the digit to the right.
3. Since 4 is less than 5, round down.

So, 742 rounds to 700.

Remember if the digit to the right of the rounding place is greater than or equal to 5, you round up.

Round to the nearest ten.

1. 56 **2.** 31

Round to the nearest hundred.

3. 128 **4.** 499

Set C (pages 10–11)

Round 2,512 to the nearest thousand.

1. Find the thousands place.
2. Look at the digit to right.
3. Since the digit is 5, round up.

So, 2,512 rounds to 3,000.

Remember if the digit to the right of the rounding place is less than 5, round down.

Round each number to the nearest thousand, hundred, and ten.

1. 3,537 **2.** 2,450

3. 6,831 **4.** 7,500

Set D (pages 14–16)

Compare. Write >, <, or =.

4,348 ● 4,365

The thousands digits are the same.

The hundreds digits are the same.

Since 4 tens is less than 6 tens, 4,348 is less than 4,365.

So, 4,348 < 4,365.

Remember < means "is less than" and > means "is greater than."

Compare. Write >, <, or =.

1. 412 ● 420 **2.** 1,094 ● 1,940

3. 3,650 ● 3,605 **4.** 8,320 ● 8,322

5. 740 ● 7,400 **6.** 9,480 ● 9,480

Set E (pages 20–21)

Find the value of the underlined digit in 1<u>3</u>5,461.

The 3 is in the ten thousands place of 135,461.

So, the value of the 3 in 135,461 is 30,000.

Remember a place-value chart can help you read and write larger numbers.

Write the value of the underlined digit.

1. 1<u>9</u>,648 **2.** 53,4<u>6</u>1

3. <u>1</u>29,609 **4.** 348,<u>6</u>33

5. 4<u>5</u>5,000 **6.** 907,01<u>1</u>

Set F (pages 22–23)

Find the total value of the group of coins and bills below.

When you count money, start with the bill of greatest value and end with the coin of least value.

Count: $5.00, $6.00, $6.25, $6.50, $6.60, $6.61, $6.62

Remember use a dollar sign and decimal point to write money.

Find the total value of each group of coins and bills.

1.

2.

More Practice

Set A *(pages 4–5)*

Write each number in standard form.

1. one thousand, twenty

2. three thousand, four hundred

3. 8,000 + 700 + 9

4. 9,000 + 900 + 10 +1

Write the value of the underlined digit.

5. $1\underline{1}7$

6. $1,\underline{3}70$

7. $4,03\underline{8}$

8. $\underline{3},509$

9. Write the word name for 3,072.

10. Write the word name for 8,006.

Set B *(pages 6–8)*

Round to the nearest ten.

1. 42

2. 68

3. 51

4. 98

Round to the nearest hundred.

5. 514

6. 956

7. 658

8. 730

9. Round the number of pizzas sold for each month to the nearest hundred. After rounding, which two months had the same number of pizzas sold?

Month	Pizzas Sold
June	438
July	466
August	502

Set C *(pages 10–11)*

Round each number to the nearest thousand.

1. 3,611

2. 4,299

3. 6,400

4. 8,512

Round each number to the nearest hundred.

5. 1,081

6. 4,566

7. 2,400

8. 8,709

Round each number to the nearest ten.

9. 3,096

10. 5,001

11. 7,544

12. 9,686

13. The museum had 3,461 visitors in November and 3,012 visitors in December. To the nearest hundred, how many people visited the museum in December?

Set D (pages 14–16)

Compare. Write >, <, or =.

1. 332 ● 3,200 **2.** 1,980 ● 1,900 **3.** 607 ● 607

4. 3,675 ● 3,657 **5.** 410 ● 4,001 **6.** 9,000 ● 9,500

Write the numbers in order from least to greatest.

7. 342 323 351 **8.** 4,100 4,001 410 **9.** 5,393 5,933 5,333

10. Rachel earned $112 in May, $102 in June, and $121 in July delivering newspapers. In which month did she earn the most money? the least money?

Set E (pages 20–21)

Write the value of the underlined digit.

1. 30,1$\underline{3}$0 **2.** $\underline{4}$6,512 **3.** 65$\underline{4}$,344 **4.** 703,$\underline{4}$00

Write each number in expanded form.

5. 32,045 **6.** 68,411 **7.** 654,309 **8.** 703,488

9. A library has 31,258 books. If the library purchases another 200 books, how many books will the library have?

Set F (pages 22–23)

Find the total value of each group of coins and bills.

1.

2.

3. Emilio paid for a sweater with 2 ten-dollar bills, 1 five-dollar bill, 2 quarters, 3 dimes, and 2 pennies. How much did he pay for the sweater?

TEST PREP

Problem Solving: Preparing for Tests

Choose the correct letter for each answer.

1. **Four students each pulled one of the numbers shown below out of a bag. The student with the smallest number that had ALL even digits won a prize. Which was the winning number?**

A 317
B 420
C 638
D 842

Tip
In this problem you can eliminate two of the answer choices because the numbers have digits that are not even.

2. **Kate earns between \$6 and \$8 an hour baby-sitting. Which of these is reasonable for the amount of money Kate could make in 3 hours?**

F Less than \$10
G Between \$10 and \$18
H Between \$18 and \$24
J Greater than \$24

Tip
Find the least and greatest amounts of money Kate could make.

3. **Pedro had 2 dimes, 3 nickels, and 4 pennies. Then he bought an apple that cost 25¢. How much money does he have now?**

A 9¢
B 14¢
C 30¢
D 39¢

Tip
Use the strategy *Draw a Picture* to solve the problem.

4. At the store, Michael spent 49¢ on cards and 39¢ on stickers. *About* how much money did Michael spend at the store?

F 10¢
G 60¢
H 80¢
J 90¢

---

5. The house numbers on Alicia's block are all the even numbers between 70 and 84. Which list shows all the house numbers?

A 72, 73, 76, 78, 82
B 72, 74, 76, 78, 80, 82
C 70, 72, 74, 76, 78, 80
D 72, 74, 76, 78, 80, 82, 83

---

6. Simone had 46¢. She spent 30¢ on stickers. How much money does Simone have left?

F 6¢
G 16¢
H 70¢
J 76¢

---

7. Patti drew 8 flowers and crossed out 3 of them. Which number sentence could you use to show what Patti did?

A $3 + 8 = 11$
B $8 - 3 = 5$
C $3 \times 8 = 24$
D $11 - 3 = 8$

---

8. Willy bought 3 books that each cost between $5 and $10. Before tax is added, which is reasonable for the total cost of all 3 books?

F Less than $15
G Between $15 and $30
H Between $30 and $35
J Greater than $35

---

9. A missing number is greater than 173 *and* less than 197. Which number could it be?

173		197

A 170
B 172
C 182
D 199

---

10. The table below shows prices for baseball caps. If Jill buys 1 small plain cap and 2 large caps with logos, how much will she spend?

Baseball Caps

	Small	Large
Plain	$4	$6
With Logo	$5	$8

F $12
G $16
H $20
J $24

Multiple-Choice Cumulative Review

Choose the correct letter for each answer.

Number Sense

1. What number is the same as three thousand, two hundred nine?

- **A** 329
- **B** 3,029
- **C** 3,209
- **D** 3,290
- **E** NH

2. Which number is between 981 and 1,011?

- **F** 891
- **G** 901
- **H** 1,001
- **J** 1,110
- **K** NH

3. What is the value of the 5 in 15,004?

- **A** 50
- **B** 500
- **C** 5,000
- **D** 50,000
- **E** NH

4. What fraction of the figure is shaded?

- **F** $\frac{4}{5}$
- **G** $\frac{3}{4}$
- **H** $\frac{1}{3}$
- **J** $\frac{1}{4}$
- **K** NH

5.

$$\begin{array}{r} 51 \\ +\ 8 \\ \hline \end{array}$$

- **A** 59
- **B** 58
- **C** 43
- **D** 13
- **E** NH

6. Mark had the money shown below. Then he spent 40¢ to buy a snack. How much money did he have left?

- **F** 30¢
- **G** 25¢
- **H** 20¢
- **J** 10¢

7. Find the difference between 12 and 9.

- **A** 21
- **B** 13
- **C** 8
- **D** 3
- **E** NH

8. Karen has 12 crayons. She gave 3 to her sister. Which number sentence shows how many crayons she has now?

- **F** $12 + 3 = 15$
- **G** $12 - 3 = 9$
- **H** $12 + 12 = 24$
- **J** $12 + 6 = 18$

Measurement and Geometry

9. **What time is shown on the clock?**

A 4:07

B 4:30

C 4:35

D 7:20

10. **What temperature is shown on the thermometer?**

F 50°F

G 55°F

H 60°F

J 65°F

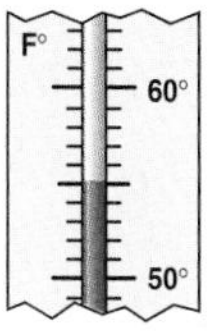

11. **What shape should NOT be grouped with the others?**

A 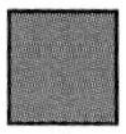

C 

B 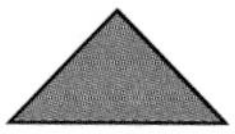

D 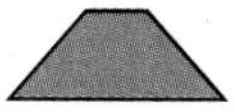

12. **Which clock shows 2 hours before 5 o'clock?**

F 

H 

G 

J 

Algebra and Functions

13. **Which names the same number as 24 + 46?**

A 46 − 24

B 46 + 24

C 20 + 46

D 2 + 40 + 6

14. **What is the missing number in the number pattern?**

12, 18, ■, 30, 36, 42

F 24 H 26

G 25 J 27

15. **What is the missing number in the number sentence?**

5 + ■ = 9

A 3 C 9

B 4 D 14

16. **What is the missing number in the number sentence?**

1,000 + ■ + 9 = 1,209

F 0 H 100

G 20 J 200

CHAPTER 2

Addition and Subtraction

Diagnosing Readiness

In Chapter 2, you will use these skills:

A Addition Facts

(Grade 2)

1. $\begin{array}{r} 9 \\ +\ 2 \\ \hline \end{array}$

2. $\begin{array}{r} 4 \\ +\ 7 \\ \hline \end{array}$

3. $\begin{array}{r} 3 \\ +\ 6 \\ \hline \end{array}$

4. $\begin{array}{r} 7 \\ +\ 5 \\ \hline \end{array}$

5. $5 + 8$

6. $8 + 6$

7. Shari saw 4 puppies playing and 5 puppies sleeping. How many puppies did she see in all?

B Subtraction Facts

(Grade 2)

8. $\begin{array}{r} 14 \\ -\ 7 \\ \hline \end{array}$

9. $\begin{array}{r} 12 \\ -\ 4 \\ \hline \end{array}$

10. $\begin{array}{r} 11 \\ -\ 8 \\ \hline \end{array}$

11. $\begin{array}{r} 16 \\ -\ 7 \\ \hline \end{array}$

12. $9 - 3$

13. $18 - 9$

14. Fifteen ducks are swimming in the pond. Seven fly away. How many are left?

C Missing Addends

(Grade 2)

15. 8 + ■ = 9 **16.** ■ + 7 = 12

17. 4 + ■ = 8 **18.** ■ + 5 = 11

19. ■ + 2 = 10 **20.** 3 + ■ = 5

21. Juan saw some deer in a meadow. After 2 deer joined them, he counted 7 deer. How many deer were there to start with?

D Adding and Subtracting Multiples of 10 and 100

(Grade 2)

22. $\begin{array}{r} 40 \\ +\ 50 \\ \hline \end{array}$ **23.** $\begin{array}{r} 60 \\ -\ 20 \\ \hline \end{array}$

24. $\begin{array}{r} 50 \\ +\ 30 \\ \hline \end{array}$ **25.** $\begin{array}{r} 80 \\ -\ 40 \\ \hline \end{array}$

26. $\begin{array}{r} 300 \\ -\ 100 \\ \hline \end{array}$ **27.** $\begin{array}{r} 700 \\ +\ 600 \\ \hline \end{array}$

E Reading and Writing Four-Digit Numbers

(pages 4–5)

Write the value of each underlined digit.

28. 8,$\underline{2}$47 **29.** 7,6$\underline{3}$0

30. $\underline{4}$,011 **31.** 5,0$\underline{4}$9

Write the standard form for each number.

32. three thousand, eight hundred fifty-six

33. one thousand, nine hundred forty-one

F Rounding

(pages 10–11)

Round each number to the nearest hundred.

34. 426 **35.** 574

36. 2,108 **37.** 6,251

Round each number to the nearest thousand.

38. 3,594 **39.** 7,601

To the Family and Student

Looking Back	Chapter 2	Looking Ahead
In Grade 2, students learned how to add and subtract up to three-digit numbers. $235 + 531 = 766$	**Addition and Subtraction** In this chapter, students will learn how to add and subtract up to four-digit numbers. $3{,}527 + 6{,}321 = 9{,}848$	In Grade 4, students will learn how to add and subtract greater numbers and decimals. $12{,}521 - 10{,}792 = 1{,}729$

Math and Everyday Living

Opportunities to apply the concepts of Chapter 2 abound in everyday situations. During the chapter, think about how addition and subtraction can be used to solve a variety of real-world problems. The following examples suggest just several of the many situations that could launch a discussion about addition and subtraction.

Math at the Grocery Store This week you spent $62.25 at the grocery store. Last week you spent $84.57. How much money did you spend altogether?

Math at the Library Your library has 5,024 books, and 1,268 books are checked out. How many books are left in the library?

Math at the Amusement Park The merry-go-round has 108 horses. If 99 horses have riders, how many horses do not have riders?

Math at the Zoo One afternoon, 2,621 people visited the zoo. The next afternoon, 4,286 people visited the zoo. About how many people visited the zoo in all?

Math and Sports A professional baseball player is aiming for a record of 3,000 hits. He currently has 2,641 hits. How many more hits does he need to reach 3,000?

Math in the City Bus fare is 55 cents. You have 87 cents. How can you determine mentally how much money you will have left after paying the bus fare?

Math at the Mall You bought a calendar on sale for $7.85. The calendar usually costs $8.98. How much money did you save?

Math at the Movie Theater Two movies are playing at the theater. The first movie is 128 minutes long. The second movie is 119 minutes long. How much longer is the first movie than the second one?

Math and Fund-Raisers Marlo received $165 in pledges for a charity walkathon. Her goal is to gather $200 in pledges. How much more pledge money does she need to meet her goal?

California Content Standards in Chapter 2 Lessons*

	Teach and Practice	Practice
Number Sense		
2.1 (🔑) (Grade 2) Understand and use the inverse relationship between addition and subtraction . . . to solve problems and check solutions.	2-1	
2.1 (🔑) Find the sum or difference of two whole numbers between 0 and 10,000.	2-4, 2-5, 2-8, 2-9, 2-10, 2-11	
3.3 (🔑) Solve problems involving addition, subtraction, multiplication, and division of money amounts in decimal notation and multiply and divide money amounts in decimal notation by using whole-number multipliers and divisors.	2-5, 2-9, 2-10	
Algebra and Functions		
1.1 (🔑) Represent relationships of quantities in the form of mathematical expressions, equations, or inequalities.	2-13, 2-14	2-1, 2-5, 2-9
1.2 Solve problems involving numeric equations or inequalities.	2-14	2-5, 2-9
1.3 Select appropriate operational and relational symbols to make an expression true (e.g., if 4 ___ 3 = 12, what operational symbol goes in the blank?).		2-1

	Teach and Practice	Practice
Mathematical Reasoning		
1.1 Analyze problems by identifying relationships, distinguishing relevant from irrelevant information, sequencing and prioritizing information, and observing patterns.	2-2	2-3, 2-4, 2-14
1.2 Determine when and how to break a problem into simpler parts.		2-1
2.1 Use estimation to verify the reasonableness of calculated results.	2-3, 2-7	2-4, 2-5, 2-8, 2-9, 2-10
2.3 Use a variety of methods, such as words, numbers, symbols, charts, graphs, tables, diagrams, and models, to explain mathematical reasoning.	2-6, 2-12	2-14
2.4 Express the solution clearly and logically by using the appropriate mathematical notation and terms and clear language; support solutions with evidence in both verbal and symbolic work.		2-11
2.5 Indicate the relative advantages of exact and approximate solutions to problems and give answers to a specified degree of accuracy.	2-3, 2-7	
3.2 Note the method of deriving the solution and demonstrate a conceptual understanding of the derivation by solving similar problems.		2-6

* The symbol (🔑) indicates a key standard as designated in the Mathematics Framework for California Public Schools. Full statements of the California Content Standards are found at the beginning of this book following the Table of Contents.

LESSON 2-1

Relating Addition and Subtraction

California Content Standard *Number Sense 2.1(key), Grade 2: Understand and use the inverse relationship between addition and subtraction . . . to solve problems and check solutions.*

Math Link You are familiar with the operations of addition and subtraction. Now you will learn more about how these operations are related.

Example 1

Use the data at the right. Find how many pounds of the alpaca's wool are left after making a sweater. Then check your answer.

8	−	3	=	■
pounds of wool		pounds used		pounds left

So, 5 pounds of wool are left.

Since addition and subtraction are **inverse operations,** you can write a related addition sentence to check your answer.

related addition sentence: $5 + 3 = 8$

<u>*Check*</u> Since $5 + 3 = 8$, you know that $8 - 3 = 5$.

Example 2

Find $6 + 9$ and then check your answer by writing a related subtraction sentence.

$6 + 9 = 15$

related subtraction sentence: $15 - 9 = 6$

<u>*Check*</u> Since $15 - 9 = 6$, you know that $6 + 9 = 15$.

Warm-Up Review

1. $4 + 5$
2. $6 + 3$
3. $6 + 7$
4. $9 + 5$
5. $6 + 6$
6. $4 + 8$
7. Meg sold 122 tickets. Larry sold 98 tickets, and Max sold 108 tickets. Who sold the least number of tickets?

Word Bank

inverse operations

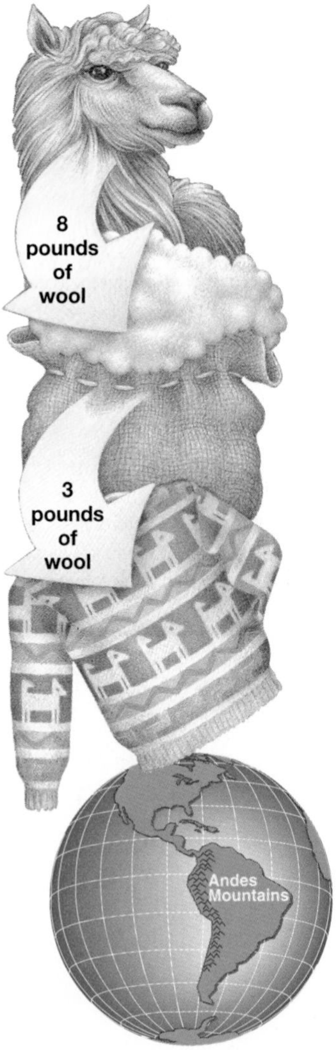

▲ The alpaca is related to the camel. It lives in the Andes Mountains in South America.

Additional Standards: Algebra and Functions 1.1(key), 1.3; Mathematical Reasoning 1.2 (See p. 41.)

Guided Practice For another example, see Set A on p. 78.

Write a related addition or subtraction sentence.

1. 12 − 8 = 4
■ + ■ = 12

2. 5 + 9 = 14
■ − ■ = 5

3. 10 − 3 = 7
■ + ■ = 10

4. 8 + 5 = 13
■ − ■ = 8

5. Suppose a weaver makes 13 blankets to sell at the market. If 7 blankets are sold, how many are left?

Independent Practice For more practice, see Set A on p. 81.

Write a related addition or subtraction sentence.

6. 7 + 2 = 9
■ − ■ = 7

7. 6 + 4 = 10
■ − ■ = 6

8. 12 − 3 = 9
■ + ■ = 12

9. 11 − 7 = 4
■ + ■ = 11

Add or subtract. Write a related sentence to check your answer.

10. $\begin{array}{r} 8 \\ -\ 6 \\ \hline \end{array}$

11. $\begin{array}{r} 5 \\ +\ 1 \\ \hline \end{array}$

12. $\begin{array}{r} 7 \\ -\ 3 \\ \hline \end{array}$

13. $\begin{array}{r} 17 \\ -\ 9 \\ \hline \end{array}$

14. $\begin{array}{r} 7 \\ +\ 7 \\ \hline \end{array}$

Algebra Replace each ● with + or −.

15. 12 ● 5 = 7 7 ● 5 = 12

16. 6 ● 8 = 14 14 ● 8 = 6

17. Math Reasoning Marcy has 9 shells. A friend gives her 5 shells. Then Marcy gives 5 shells to her brother. How many shells does Marcy have left? Explain.

Mixed Review

18. Alisa has 2 one-dollar bills, 3 quarters, 3 dimes, and 3 pennies in her wallet. How much money does she have in all?

19. Write 374,501 in expanded form.

20. What is the value of the 2 in 12,189?

Test Prep Choose the correct letter for each answer.

21. (1–1) What is the standard form for six thousand, three hundred?

A 6,003
B 6,030
C 6,300
D 6,333

22. (1–5) Which number is the greatest?

F 3,000
G 2,399
H 399
J 3,001

LESSON 2-2

Understand
Plan
Solve
Look Back

Problem-Solving Skill: Too Much or Too Little Information

Warm-Up Review

1. 2 + 9 2. 3 + 7
3. 8 + 6 4. 10 − 4
5. 14 − 7 6. 16 − 9
7. A toad caught 8 flies, 3 grasshoppers, and 2 mosquitoes with its sticky tongue. How many insects did it catch altogether?

California Content Standard *Mathematical Reasoning 1.1: Analyze problems by identifying relationships, distinguishing relevant from irrelevant information . . ..*

Read for Understanding

Jenny visits a horse farm. She learns that the height of a horse is measured in hands. She sees a Shetland pony that is 8 hands high. She sees 4 Welsh ponies. One of the Welsh ponies is shown in the photograph at the right.

▲ This Welsh pony is 12 hands high.

1. How many Welsh ponies does Jenny see?
2. How tall is the Welsh pony in the photograph?

Think and Discuss

MATH FOCUS

Too Much or Too Little Information

Before you solve a problem, you need to decide whether you have too much or too little information.

Reread the paragraph at the top of the page.

3. Do you have enough information to find the total number of ponies at the horse farm? Why or why not?
4. Do you have enough information to find how much taller the Welsh pony in the photograph is than the Shetland pony? Why or why not?
5. What information in the paragraph is needed to solve Problem 4? What information is *not* needed?

Guided Practice

Pedro visited a horse farm. In the barn, he saw 2 Arabian horses and 8 Morgan horses. Out in the field, he saw 3 Shetland ponies and 7 Arabian horses. How many Arabian horses did he see in all?

1. What information is *not* needed to solve the problem?

a. Pedro saw 2 Arabian horses in the barn.

b. Pedro saw 8 Morgan horses in the barn.

c. Pedro saw 7 Arabian horses in the field.

2. What information do you need to solve the problem?

a. Pedro saw 2 Arabian horses in the barn.

b. Pedro saw 7 Arabian horses in the field.

c. Both of the above.

3. Which number sentence could you use to solve the problem?

a. $2 + 7 = \blacksquare$

b. $7 - 2 = \blacksquare$

c. $8 + 7 = \blacksquare$

Independent Practice

There are 4 horseback riding trails near the horse farm. One group of 9 people is riding on the blue trail. Another group of 5 people is riding on the red trail. Suppose the two groups join each other. How many people will be riding together?

4. What information do you need to solve the problem?

a. the number of people riding on the yellow trail

b. the number of people riding on the red trail

c. the number of trails

5. What other information do you need to solve the problem?

a. the number of trails

b. the number of people visiting the horse farm

c. the number of people riding on the blue trail

6. Math Reasoning Is there enough information to find how many more people are riding on the blue trail than are riding on the red trail? Explain.

Use Homework Workbook 2-2.

LESSON 2-3

Estimating Sums

California Content Standards *Mathematical Reasoning 2.1: Use estimation to verify the reasonableness of calculated results. Also, Mathematical Reasoning 2.5 (See p. 41.)*

Warm-Up Review

1. 7 + 2
2. 9 + 5
3. 50 + 40
4. 60 + 20
5. 100 + 600
6. 800 + 300
7. Ann used 5 yellow beads, 3 orange beads, and 13 white beads to make a bracelet. How many more white beads than yellow beads did she use?

Math Link You know how to round numbers. In this lesson, you will learn how to use rounding to estimate sums.

Example 1

Jiro got a sum of 119 when he added 54 and 65. To check that his answer of 119 is reasonable, you can use estimation.

Round 54 and 65 to the nearest ten to get numbers you can add mentally.

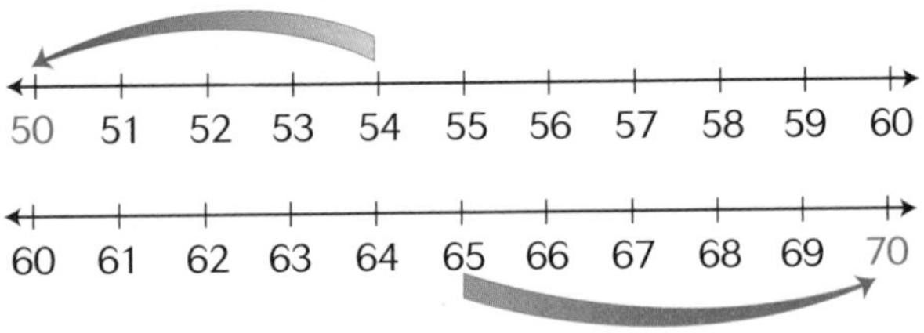

Add the rounded numbers.

54 + **65**
rounds to / rounds to
50 + **70** = **120**

The answer is reasonable because 119 is close to 120.

Example 2

Estimate 450 + 326.

Round 450 and 326 to the nearest hundred to get numbers you can add mentally.

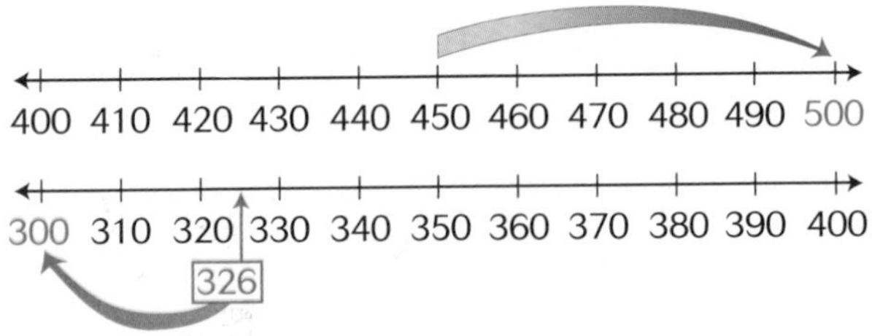

Add the rounded numbers.

450 + **326**
rounds to / rounds to
500 + **300** = **800**

450 + 326 is *about* 800.

Guided Practice

For another example, see Set B on p. 78.

Estimate by rounding to the nearest ten.

1. 62 + 38 **2.** 45 + 72 **3.** 96 + 28 **4.** 74 + 76

 Additional Standard: Mathematical Reasoning 1.1 (See p. 41.)

Estimate by rounding to the nearest hundred.

5. 421 + 680 **6.** 945 + 312 **7.** 495 + 786 **8.** 297 + 503

9. There are 39 boys and 42 girls swimming in the pool. About how many children are swimming?

Independent Practice *For more practice, see Set B on p. 81.*

Estimate by rounding to the nearest ten.

10. 57 + 36 **11.** 24 + 37 **12.** 51 + 65 **13.** 98 + 21

Estimate by rounding to the nearest hundred.

14. 495 + 384 **15.** 206 + 918 **16.** 717 + 850 **17.** 521 + 649

18. 481 + 253 **19.** 690 + 280 **20.** 718 + 531 **21.** 927 + 463

Use the table at the right for Exercises 22 and 23.

Food	Amount	Calories
Hamburger	3 oz	385
Pizza	1 slice	345
Fruit Salad	1 cup	85
Roll	1 roll	120
Orange Juice	1 cup	120
Whole Milk	1 cup	150

22. Clare had pizza, fruit salad, and a cup of whole milk for lunch. About how many calories did she eat at lunch?

23. Which food has about 400 calories?

Mixed Review

24. Find 13 − 6. Write two addition sentences that you could use to check your answer.

Write each amount.

25. five-dollar bill, 2 one-dollar bills, 3 dimes, 4 nickels

26. 4 one-dollar bills, 1 quarter, 2 dimes, 3 pennies

Test Prep **Choose the correct letter for each answer.**

27. (1–9) Joe buys a book for $3.75. He pays with a $5 bill. What is his change?

A $2.25 **C** $1.25

B $1.75 **D** 25¢

28. (1–3) Round 1,499 to the nearest thousand.

F 1,000 **J** 2,000

G 1,400 **K** NH

H 1,500

LESSON 2-4

Adding Two- and Three-Digit Numbers

California Content Standard *Number Sense 2.1 (key): Find the sum or difference of two whole numbers between 0 and 10,000.*

Warm-Up Review

1. 30 + 40
2. 90 + 50
3. 600 + 100
4. 500 + 700
5. A matinee at the movies costs $5.00. Regular price is $8.00. How much will you save by seeing a matinee instead of paying regular price?

Math Link You know how to find 50 + 30 and 500 + 300. Now you will learn how to add any two- and three-digit numbers.

Example 1

Use the data at the right. A visitor climbs part of the way up a Mayan pyramid, rests, and then continues to the top. How many steps does the visitor climb to the top of the pyramid?

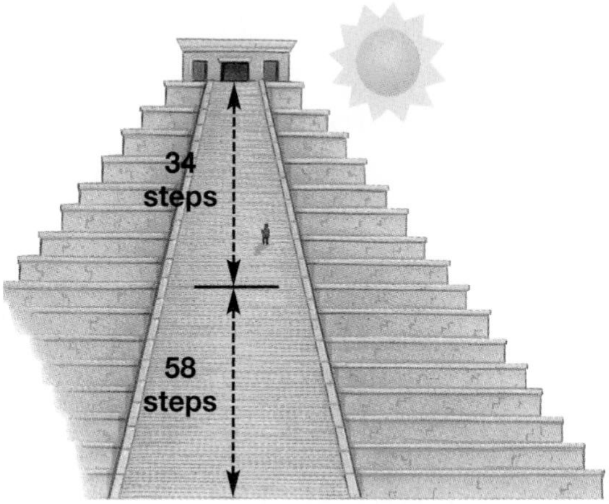

Step 1
Add the ones.
Regroup as needed.

$$\begin{array}{r} {}^{1} \\ 58 \\ +\ 34 \\ \hline 2 \end{array}$$

Regroup 12 ones as 1 ten 2 ones.

Step 2
Add the tens.

$$\begin{array}{r} {}^{1} \\ 58 \\ +\ 34 \\ \hline 92 \end{array}$$

Check by estimating. 60 + 30 = 90. Since 92 is close to 90, the answer is reasonable. The visitor climbed 92 steps.

Here's WHY It Works

Write each number in expanded notation. Then use the grouping property.

$$58 + 34 = 50 + 8 + 30 + 4$$
$$= 80 + 8 + 4$$
$$= 80 + 12$$
$$= 92$$

Example 2

Find 797 + 278.

Step 1
Add the ones.
Regroup as needed.

$$\begin{array}{r} {}^{1} \\ 797 \\ +\ 278 \\ \hline 5 \end{array}$$

Step 2
Add the tens.
Regroup as needed.

$$\begin{array}{r} {}^{1\,1} \\ 797 \\ +\ 278 \\ \hline 75 \end{array}$$

Step 3
Add the hundreds.

$$\begin{array}{r} {}^{1\,1} \\ 797 \\ +\ 278 \\ \hline 1{,}075 \end{array}$$

Check by estimating. 800 + 300 = 1,100. Since 1,075 is close to 1,100, the answer is reasonable.

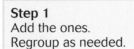

Additional Standards: Mathematical Reasoning 1.1, 2.1 (See p. 41.)

Guided Practice *For another example, see Set C on p. 78.*

1. $\begin{array}{r} 14 \\ +\ 93 \\ \hline \end{array}$ 2. $\begin{array}{r} 32 \\ +\ 88 \\ \hline \end{array}$ 3. $\begin{array}{r} 204 \\ +\ 35 \\ \hline \end{array}$ 4. $\begin{array}{r} 842 \\ +\ 193 \\ \hline \end{array}$ 5. $\begin{array}{r} 647 \\ +\ 965 \\ \hline \end{array}$

6. Last week 156 elementary students wrote letters for a time capsule. This week 106 middle school students added their letters. How many letters were put in the capsule?

Independent Practice *For more practice, see Set C on p. 81.*

7. $\begin{array}{r} 47 \\ +\ 6 \\ \hline \end{array}$ 8. $\begin{array}{r} 71 \\ +\ 46 \\ \hline \end{array}$ 9. $\begin{array}{r} 29 \\ +\ 32 \\ \hline \end{array}$ 10. $\begin{array}{r} 64 \\ +\ 87 \\ \hline \end{array}$ 11. $\begin{array}{r} 52 \\ +\ 98 \\ \hline \end{array}$

12. $\begin{array}{r} 212 \\ +\ 505 \\ \hline \end{array}$ 13. $\begin{array}{r} 403 \\ +\ 256 \\ \hline \end{array}$ 14. $\begin{array}{r} 608 \\ +\ 765 \\ \hline \end{array}$ 15. $\begin{array}{r} 312 \\ +\ 98 \\ \hline \end{array}$ 16. $\begin{array}{r} 718 \\ +\ 390 \\ \hline \end{array}$

17. 56 + 13 + 600 **18.** 27 + 274 + 99 **19.** 125 + 361 + 75

20. Mental Math Find 245 + 30. **21. Mental Math** Find 674 − 200.

22. Mental Math How can you find 23 + 39 + 7 mentally?

23. Abby read one book with 291 pages. She read a second book with 98 pages, and a third book with 275 pages. How many pages did she read in all?

24. A large pottery bowl costs $63, and a small bowl costs $49. How much would 2 small bowls cost?

Mixed Review

25. It took Nick 36 minutes to hike up to the waterfall and 22 minutes to hike down. About how long did Nick hike?

Algebra Replace each ● with + or −.

26. 7 ● 6 = 13 13 ● 6 = 7 **27.** 15 ● 9 = 6 6 ● 9 = 15

Test Prep Choose the correct letter for each answer.

28. (1–1) What is the value of the 5 in 4,562?

A 5 **C** 500
B 50 **D** 5,000

29. (1–1) What is the standard form for 8,000 + 600 + 30?

F 863 **H** 8,603
G 8,063 **J** 8,630

LESSON 2-5

Adding Greater Numbers

California Content Standard *Number Sense 2.1 (🔑): Find the sum . . . of two whole numbers between 0 and 10,000. Also, Number Sense 3.3 (🔑) (See p. 41.)*

Math Link You know how to add two- and three-digit numbers. Now you will learn how to add four-digit numbers.

Warm-Up Review

1. 20 + 60
2. 700 + 400
3. 55 + 34
4. 298 + 345
5. What is the value of the 3 in 3,982?
6. Lyle read 8 books. Sue read 2 fewer books than Lyle. Bob read 3 more books than Sue. How many books did Bob read?

Example 1

Find 1,985 + 1,270.

Step 1 Add the ones. Regroup as needed.	Step 2 Add the tens. Regroup as needed.	Step 3 Add the hundreds. Regroup as needed.	Step 4 Add the thousands.
1,985 + 1,270 5	¹ 1,985 + 1,270 55	¹ ¹ 1,985 + 1,270 255	¹ ¹ 1,985 + 1,270 3,255

Check by estimating. 2,000 + 1,000 = 3,000. Since 3,255 is close to 3,000, the answer is reasonable.

Example 2

Find $23.96 + $45.67.

When you add money, line up the decimal points and add the way you would whole numbers.

Step 1	Step 2	Step 3	Step 4
¹ $23.96 + 45.67 3	¹ ¹ $23.96 + 45.67 .63	¹ ¹ $23.96 + 45.67 9.63	¹ ¹ $23.96 + 45.67 $69.63

Remember to show the dollar sign and decimal point in the sum.

Check by estimating. $20.00 + $50.00 = $70.00. Since $69.63 is close to $70.00, the answer is reasonable.

Guided Practice

For another example, see Set D on p. 78.

1. 4,836 + 3,053
2. 5,241 + 6,593
3. $14.08 + 2.96
4. 6,394 + 5,735
5. $37.95 + 84.98

Additional Standards: Algebra and Functions 1.1 (🔑), 1.2; Mathematical Reasoning 2.1 (See p. 41.)

6. One month, 3,642 people went rafting. The next month 4,396 people went rafting. How many people went rafting in the two months?

Independent Practice

For more practice, see Set D on p. 81.

7. 2,614 + 7,210 **8.** 3,025 + 65 **9.** $86.20 + 5.49 **10.** 1,316 + 4,802 **11.** 5,062 + 8,761

12. $62.24 + 16.40 **13.** 8,627 + 499 **14.** 9,999 + 225 **15.** $54.69 + 32.75 **16.** $23.65 + 58.77

17. 129 + 2,009 + 4,675 **18.** 87 + 3,506 + 450

Use the table at the right for Exercises 19 and 20.

19. How much would it cost to buy a small life vest and a large life vest?

20. How much would it cost to buy 2 medium life vests?

21. Algebra What is the missing number?

5,621 + 3,891 = 3,891 + ■

Summer SALE

small life vest	$34.99
medium life vest	$50.99
large life vest	$93.95

Mixed Review

22. Bernard collected 38 pounds of newspapers to be recycled. Dorothy collected 47 pounds. About how many pounds did they collect altogether?

23. Round 4,455 to the nearest 10. **24.** Estimate 34 + 89.

25. 17 − 8 **26.** 14 − 7 **27.** 302 + 896 **28.** 26 + 417

Test Prep Choose the correct letter for each answer.

29. (2–1) Which of the following is a related addition sentence for 12 − 8 = 4?

A 8 − 4 = 4
B 8 + 4 = 12
C 9 + 3 = 12
D 12 + 8 = 20

30. (2–4) Stamps come in rolls of 100 stamps and as single stamps. Mrs. Ross bought 9 single stamps and 2 rolls. How many stamps did she buy?

F 11 stamps **H** 92 stamps
G 29 stamps **J** 209 stamps

LESSON 2-6

Understand
Plan
Solve
Look Back

Problem-Solving Strategy:
Make a Table

California Content Standard *Mathematical Reasoning 2.3: Use a variety of methods, such as words, numbers, symbols, charts, graphs, tables, diagrams, and models, to explain mathematical reasoning.*

Warm-Up Review

1. 7 + 7 **2.** 9 + 9

3. 15 + 15 **4.** 56 + 56

5. 28 + 37 **6.** 92 + 65

7. Angie bought an eraser for 59¢. She gave the clerk 3 quarters. How much change did she receive?

One day a miner finds 3 gold nuggets. Each day after that he finds twice as many nuggets as he found the day before. If this pattern continues, how many gold nuggets will he find on the fifth day?

Understand

What do you need to know?

You need to know that the miner finds 3 gold nuggets on the first day. Then you need to know that he always finds twice as many nuggets as he found the day before.

Plan

How can you solve the problem?

You can **make a table** like the one at the right.

Day	Number of Gold Nuggets Found
First	3
Second	6
Third	12
Fourth	24
Fifth	48

Solve

List the number of gold nuggets the miner finds each day.

Remember to double the number each day.

The miner finds 48 gold nuggets on the fifth day.

Look Back

Why is using a table helpful?

Additional Standard: Mathematical Reasoning 3.2 (See p. 41.)

Guided Practice

Make a table to solve Exercise 1.

1. Max's teacher gives him 5 stickers each week he completes his homework. If Max turns in his homework every week, how many stickers will he have after 4 weeks?

Independent Practice

Make a table to solve Exercises 2–4.

2. In 1848, many people traveled west on wagons hoping to find gold. Suppose each wagon was pulled by 4 oxen. How many oxen would be needed to pull 5 wagons? 8 wagons? 10 wagons?

3. Eight wagons are on the trail. Two wagons stop to give their oxen water. How many oxen still need to get water?

4. **Math Reasoning** Suppose 4 wagons are packed and ready to travel west. If there are 13 oxen, are there enough oxen to pull all the wagons? Why or why not?

Mixed Review

Try these or other strategies to solve each problem. Tell which strategy you used.

Problem-Solving Strategies

- *Find a Pattern*
- *Make a Table*
- *Use Logical Reasoning*
- *Write a Number Sentence*

5. One gold nugget is worth more than $37 but less than $40. If the amount is an odd number, how much is the gold nugget worth?

6. Use the data at the right. Mia buys a small and a large popcorn. How much does she spend in all?

7. Four children are standing in line. Joshua is behind Mary. Sue is between Mary and Cal. Cal is in the front. In what order are the children standing?

Diagnostic Checkpoint

Write a related addition or subtraction sentence.

1. (2-1) 10 − 6 = 4
■ + ■ = 10

2. (2-1) 7 + 5 = 12
■ − ■ = 5

3. (2-1) 8 − 3 = 5
■ + ■ = 8

4. (2-1) 6 + 5 = 11
■ − ■ = 6

5. (2-1) 8 + 4 = 12
■ − ■ = 8

6. (2-1) 14 − 3 = 11
■ + ■ = 14

7. (2-1) 9 + 6 = 15
■ − ■ = 6

8. (2-1) 17 − 8 = 9
■ + ■ = 17

Estimate by rounding to the nearest ten.

9. (2-3) 53 + 28

10. (2-3) 36 + 81

11. (2-3) 73 + 19

12. (2-3) 98 + 39

Estimate by rounding to the nearest hundred.

13. (2-3) 296 + 323

14. (2-3) 727 + 432

15. (2-3) 680 + 215

16. (2-3) 578 + 332

Find each sum.

17. (2-4) 59 + 28

18. (2-4) 86 + 73

19. (2-4) 24 + 17

20. (2-4) 812 + 46

21. (2-4) 508 + 325

22. (2-4) 836 + 648

23. (2-5) 2,156 + 4,618

24. (2-5) 3,422 + 2,465

25. (2-5) 1,687 + 7,432

26. (2-5) 6,283 + 8,256

27. (2-5) 2,039 + 5,296

28. (2-5) 9,825 + 7,443

Copy and complete the table to solve Exercise 29.

29. (2-6) If John buys 5 lunch tickets each week, how many tickets will he have bought after 4 weeks?

Week	Number of Lunch Tickets Bought
First	5
Second	
Third	
Fourth	

30. (2-2) A store received 85 soccer balls and 28 softballs one week. The next week the store received 36 softballs. How many softballs did the store receive in all?

LESSON 2-7

Estimating Differences

Warm-Up Review

1. 60 − 30 **2.** 80 − 20

3. Round 942 to the nearest ten.

4. Mrs. Burke awarded 16 blue ribbons and 24 red ribbons to the walkathon winners. How many ribbons did she award?

California Content Standards *Mathematical Reasoning 2.1: Use estimation to verify the reasonableness of calculated results. Also, Mathematical Reasoning 2.5 (See p. 41.)*

Math Link You know how to estimate sums. Now you will learn how to estimate differences.

Example 1

Use the data at the right. About how much longer is the brachiosaurus than the tyrannosaurus?

Since you want to know *about* how much longer, you do not need an exact answer. You can round to estimate the difference.

Round 82 and 39 to the nearest ten.

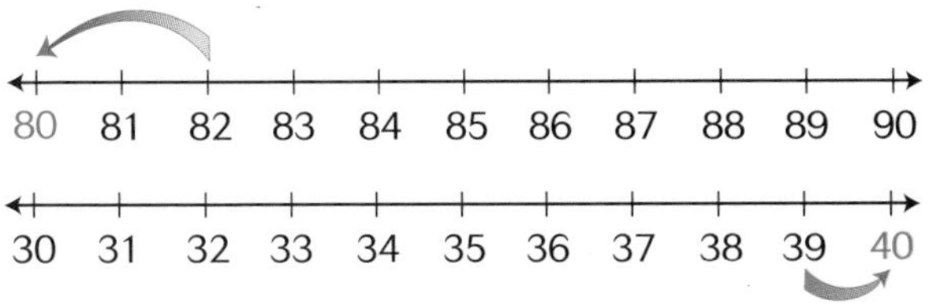

Then subtract the rounded numbers.

82 − **39**
rounds to / rounds to
80 − **40** = **40**

The brachiosaurus is about 40 feet longer.

Example 2

Is 283 a reasonable answer for 750 − 467? Estimate to check.

Round 750 and 467 to the nearest hundred.

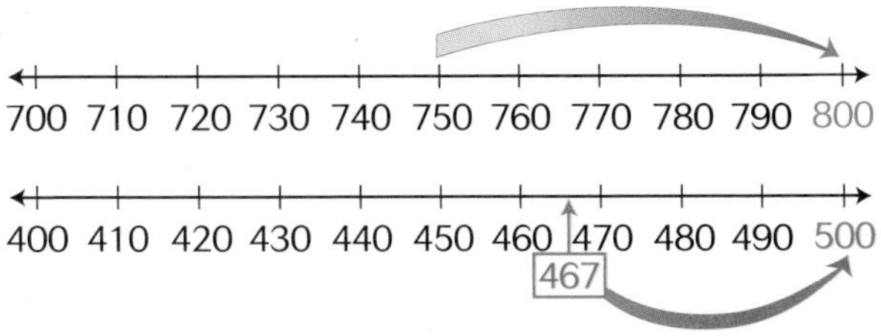

Then subtract the rounded numbers.

750 − **467**
rounds to / rounds to
800 − **500** = **300**

The answer is reasonable because 283 is close to 300.

You can estimate differences by rounding.
You can also estimate differences by using **front-end estimation.**

Example 3

Use front-end estimation to estimate 76 − 47.

Look at the front digit of each number.

Use zeros for all the other digits.

Then subtract.

76 − 47
↓ ↓
70 − 40 = 30

76 − 47 is *about* 30.

Example 4

Use front-end estimation to estimate 562 − 159.

Look at the front digit of each number.

Use zeros for all the other digits.

Then subtract.

562 − 159
↓ ↓
500 − 100 = 400

562 − 159 is *about* 400.

Guided Practice *For another example, see Set E on p. 79.*

Estimate by rounding to the nearest ten.

1. 62 − 37 **2.** 43 − 15 **3.** 71 − 32 **4.** 97 − 28

Estimate by rounding to the nearest hundred.

5. 715 − 109 **6.** 351 − 237 **7.** 187 − 118 **8.** 971 − 163

Estimate by using front-end estimation.

9. 65 − 48 **10.** 766 − 218 **11.** 52 − 38 **12.** 836 − 494

13. A tour takes 60 minutes. If you have been on the tour for 24 minutes, about how much longer is the tour?

Independent Practice *For more practice, see Set E on p. 82.*

Estimate by rounding to the nearest ten.

14. 52 − 13 **15.** 68 − 39 **16.** 93 − 18 **17.** 72 − 49

Estimate by rounding to the nearest hundred.

18. 881 − 253 **19.** 620 − 416 **20.** 732 − 541 **21.** 990 − 735

Estimate by using front-end estimation.

22. 31 − 17 **23.** 72 − 46 **24.** 34 − 15 **25.** 85 − 27

26. 981 − 405 **27.** 578 − 392 **28.** 631 − 467 **29.** 951 − 164

30. In ten computer classes, there are 85 girls and 66 boys. About how many more girls than boys are in the classes?

31. When Juan computed 733 − 318, he got a difference of 415. Show how you would estimate to check if his answer is reasonable. Use rounding to estimate.

32. Math Reasoning How would you use front-end estimation to estimate 416 + 829? Explain.

Mixed Review

33. Algebra What digit will make the statement true? 12■ > 128

34. 23 + 56 **35.** 1,289 + 494 **36.** $13.57 + $52.89

Test Prep **Choose the correct letter for the answer.**

37. (1–1) If 100 more people decided to move to Forest City, what would be the population of Forest City?

A 4,316 people
B 4,216 people
C 3,226 people
D 3,116 people
E NH

38. (2–4) Kayla read the three books below. How many pages did she read altogether?

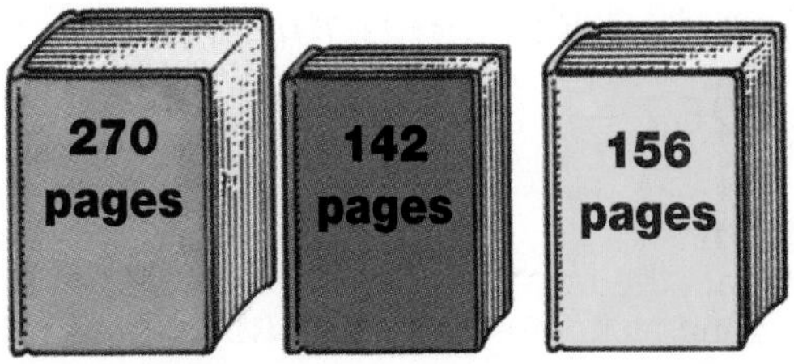

F 468 pages
G 568 pages
H 578 pages
J 668 pages
K NH

LESSON 2-8

Subtracting Two- and Three-Digit Numbers

California Content Standard *Number Sense 2.1 (🔑): Find the sum or difference of two whole numbers between 0 and 10,000.*

Warm-Up Review

1. 15 − 8
2. 12 − 5
3. 60 − 50
4. 900 − 700
5. A number is between 300 and 400. The ones digit in the number is 4. The tens digit is 3 less than the ones digit. What is the number?

Math Link You know how to find 50 − 30 and 500 − 300. In this lesson, you will learn how to subtract any two- and three-digit numbers.

Example 1

Find 62 − 39.

Step 1
Subtract the ones.
Regroup as needed.

$$\begin{array}{r} {}^{5}\not{6}{}^{12}\not{2} \\ -\ 39 \\ \hline 3 \end{array}$$

Regroup 6 tens 2 ones as 5 tens 12 ones.

Step 2
Subtract the tens.

$$\begin{array}{r} {}^{5}\not{6}{}^{12}\not{2} \\ -\ 39 \\ \hline 23 \end{array}$$

Here's WHY It Works

62 = 60 + 2
= 50 + 10 + 2
= 50 + 12
= 5 tens 12 ones

39 = 30 + 9
= 3 tens 9 ones

62	→	5 tens	12 ones
− 39	→	− 3 tens	9 ones
23		2 tens	3 ones

Check by using rounding to estimate. 60 − 40 = 20. Since 23 is close to 20, the answer is reasonable.

Subtracting three-digit numbers is like subtracting two-digit numbers, only now you may need to regroup a hundred.

Example 2

Find 267 − 186.

Step 1
Subtract the ones.
Regroup as needed.

$$\begin{array}{r} 267 \\ -\ 186 \\ \hline 1 \end{array}$$

Step 2
Subtract the tens.
Regroup as needed.

$$\begin{array}{r} {}^{1}\not{2}{}^{16}\not{6}7 \\ -\ 186 \\ \hline 81 \end{array}$$

Step 3
Subtract the hundreds.

$$\begin{array}{r} {}^{1}\not{2}{}^{16}\not{6}7 \\ -\ 186 \\ \hline 81 \end{array}$$

Check by using front-end estimation. 200 − 100 = 100. Since 81 is close to 100, the answer is reasonable.

Additional Standard: Mathematical Reasoning 2.1 *(See p. 41.)*

Guided Practice

For another example, see Set F on p. 79.

1. $89 - 56$
2. $52 - 5$
3. $57 - 38$
4. $137 - 118$
5. $358 - 297$

6. William H. Harrison was President of the United States for only 32 days in 1841. James Garfield was President for 199 days in 1881. How many more days was Garfield President?

Independent Practice

For more practice, see Set F on p. 82.

7. $95 - 14$
8. $45 - 31$
9. $71 - 6$
10. $42 - 25$
11. $82 - 39$
12. $321 - 111$
13. $255 - 36$
14. $357 - 293$
15. $688 - 379$
16. $565 - 474$

17. **Mental Math** Find $85 - 30$.

18. **Mental Math** Find $948 - 200$.

Use the data at the right for Exercises 19–21.

	EARTH WEIGHT (in pounds)	MOON WEIGHT (in pounds)
Mrs. Kay	144	24
Ali	90	15
Joey	78	13

19. Did you know that you weigh less on the moon than on Earth? How much more does Joey weigh on Earth than on the moon?

20. How much more does Mrs. Kay weigh on Earth than on the moon?

21. On Earth, how much more does Mrs. Kay weigh than Ali?

Mixed Review

22. Estimate $562 - 346$ using rounding. Then estimate the difference using front-end estimation.

23. $541 + 6{,}036$

24. $7{,}652 + 1{,}788$

25. $43 + 9{,}079$

Test Prep **Choose the correct letter for each answer.**

26. Which is the hundreds digit in 8,903? (1–1)

A 0 **C** 8
B 3 **D** 9

27. **Algebra** What is the missing number? (1–1)
$5{,}000 + 700 + 90 + \blacksquare = 5{,}791$

F 0 **H** 10
G 1 **J** 100

LESSON 2-9

Subtracting Greater Numbers

Warm-Up Review

1. 70 − 30
2. 900 − 600
3. 46 − 23
4. 824 − 511
5. Round 3,599 to the nearest thousand.
6. You have 2 quarters, 2 dimes, 6 nickels, and 7 pennies. How much money do you have?

California Content Standard *Number Sense 2.1 (key): Find the sum or difference of two whole numbers between 0 and 10,000. Also, Number Sense 3.3 (key)* *(See p. 41.)*

Math Link You know how to subtract two- and three-digit numbers. Now you will learn how to subtract four-digit numbers.

Example 1

Find 8,264 − 5,312.

Step 1 Subtract the ones. Regroup as needed.	Step 2 Subtract the tens. Regroup as needed.	Step 3 Subtract the hundreds. Regroup as needed.	Step 4 Subtract the thousands.
$\begin{array}{r} 8{,}264 \\ -\ 5{,}312 \\ \hline 2 \end{array}$	$\begin{array}{r} 8{,}264 \\ -\ 5{,}312 \\ \hline 52 \end{array}$	$\begin{array}{r} \scriptstyle 7\ 12 \\ \not{8}{,}\not{2}64 \\ -\ 5{,}312 \\ \hline 952 \end{array}$	$\begin{array}{r} \scriptstyle 7\ 12 \\ \not{8}{,}\not{2}64 \\ -\ 5{,}312 \\ \hline 2{,}952 \end{array}$

Check by using rounding to estimate. 8,000 − 5,000 = 3,000. Since 2,952 is close to 3,000, the answer is reasonable.

Example 2

Find 7,473 − 2,198.

Step 1 Subtract the ones. Regroup as needed.	Step 2 Subtract the tens. Regroup as needed.	Step 3 Subtract the hundreds. Regroup as needed.	Step 4 Subtract the thousands.
$\begin{array}{r} \scriptstyle 6\,13 \\ 7{,}4\not{7}\not{3} \\ -\ 2{,}198 \\ \hline 5 \end{array}$	$\begin{array}{r} \scriptstyle 16 \\ \scriptstyle 3\ \not{6}\,13 \\ 7{,}\not{4}\not{7}\not{3} \\ -\ 2{,}198 \\ \hline 75 \end{array}$	$\begin{array}{r} \scriptstyle 16 \\ \scriptstyle 3\ \not{6}\,13 \\ 7{,}\not{4}\not{7}\not{3} \\ -\ 2{,}198 \\ \hline 275 \end{array}$	$\begin{array}{r} \scriptstyle 16 \\ \scriptstyle 3\ \not{6}\,13 \\ 7{,}\not{4}\not{7}\not{3} \\ -\ 2{,}198 \\ \hline 5{,}275 \end{array}$

Check by using front-end estimation. 7,000 − 2,000 = 5,000. Since 5,275 is close to 5,000, the answer is reasonable.

More Examples

A. $\begin{array}{r} \scriptstyle 8\ 12 \\ \$4\not{9}.\not{2}8 \\ -\ \ 3.74 \\ \hline \$45.54 \end{array}$

B. $\begin{array}{r} \scriptstyle 11\ 12 \\ \scriptstyle 4\ \not{1}\ \not{2}16 \\ \$\not{5}\not{2}.\not{3}\not{6} \\ -\ 14.59 \\ \hline \$37.77 \end{array}$

Remember to show the dollar sign and decimal point in the answer.

Additional Standards: Algebra and Functions 1.1 (key), 1.2; Mathematical Reasoning 2.1 *(See p. 41.)*

Guided Practice *For another example, see Set G on p. 79.*

1. 4,687 − 1,346

2. 9,247 − 162

3. \$81.63 − 24.18

4. 6,431 − 5,928

5. 7,342 − 2,658

6. In June, 1,838 CDs were sold. In July, 1,967 CDs were sold, and in August, 2,134 CDs were sold. How many more CDs were sold in July than in June?

Independent Practice *For more practice, see Set G on p. 82.*

7. 5,329 − 3,107

8. 9,999 − 4,322

9. \$42.93 − 1.60

10. 7,318 − 6,093

11. \$93.18 − 64.03

12. 3,162 − 2,428

13. 8,284 − 96

14. 6,308 − 1,127

15. 7,410 − 2,854

16. \$52.14 − 36.99

17. Mental Math Find 3,465 − 20.

18. Mental Math Find 5,918 − 300.

Use the data at the right for Exercises 19 and 20.

Carol's Fabulous Toys
Wind-up duck $11.20
Beak mask $ 1.60
Finger puppet $ 6.50
Jumping spider $ 2.75
Fake bug $ 0.75

19. How much more does a wind-up duck cost than a finger puppet?

20. Ted bought a jumping spider and a fake bug. How much money did he spend?

21. Algebra What are the missing digits?

3,■35
− ■2■
2,114

Mixed Review

22. What is the least number that you can write using the digits 8, 0, 3, and 9?

23. Estimate 75 − 38.

24. Estimate 845 − 236.

25. 56 + 37

26. 25 + 99

27. 319 − 205

28. 234 − 165

Test Prep Choose the correct letter for each answer.

29. 436 + 56 + 924 =
(2–3)

A 1,416 **C** 1,516
B 1,506 **D** 1,920

30. Round 550 to the nearest hundred.
(1–2)

F 1,000 **H** 560
G 600 **J** 500

LESSON 2-10

Subtracting Across Zeros

California Content Standard *Number Sense 2.1 (🔑): Find the . . . difference of two whole numbers between 0 and 10,000. Also, Number Sense 3.3 (🔑) (See p. 41.)*

Warm-Up Review

1. 732 − 225
2. 8,234 − 641
3. Write 4,307 in expanded form.
4. George had 980 tulip bulbs and 520 iris bulbs. He sold 300 tulip bulbs. How many tulip bulbs did he have left?

Math Link You know how to find differences like 546 − 341 and 9,124 − 7,678. Now you will learn how to find differences like 500 − 341 and 9,004 − 7,678.

Example 1

Use the table at the right. How much higher is Yuba Pass than Sagehew Pass?

6,701 − 5,556 = ■
feet feet feet higher

California Mountain Passes

Mountain Pass	Height (feet)
Tioga	9,941
Sherwin	7,000
Yuba	6,701
Sagehew	5,556

Step 1 You need more ones and tens to subtract.	**Step 2** First regroup 7 hundreds as 6 hundreds 10 tens.	**Step 3** Then regroup 10 tens 1 one as 9 tens 11 ones.	**Step 4** Subtract.
6,701 − 5,556	6 10 6,701 − 5,556	9 6 10 11 6,701 − 5,556	9 6 10 11 6,701 − 5,556 1,145

Check by estimating. 7,000 − 6,000 = 1,000. Since 1,145 is close to 1,000, the answer is reasonable. Yuba pass is 1,145 feet higher than Sagehew Pass.

Example 2

Find 300 − 124.

Step 1 You need more ones and tens to subtract.	**Step 2** First regroup 3 hundreds as 2 hundreds 10 tens.	**Step 3** Then regroup 10 tens 0 ones as 9 tens 10 ones.	**Step 4** Subtract.
300 − 124	2 10 300 − 124	9 2 10 10 300 − 124	9 2 10 10 300 − 124 176

Check by estimating. 300 − 100 = 200. Since 176 is close to 200, the answer is reasonable.

Additional Standard: Mathematical Reasoning 2.1 (See p. 41.)

Example 3

Find $20.00 − $6.14.

Step 1	Step 2	Step 3	Step 4	Step 5
	110	9 1 10 10	9 9 1 10 10 10	9 9 1 10 10 10
$20.00	$20.00	$20.00	$20.00	$20.00
− 6.14	− 6.14	− 6.14	− 6.14	− 6.14
				$13.86

Check by estimating. $20.00 − $6.00 = $14.00. Since $13.86 is close to $14.00, the answer is reasonable.

More Examples

A.	B.	C.
9 5 10 13	9 1 10 10	9 4 10 10
603	2,004	$75.00
− 275	− 1,521	− 4.29
328	483	$70.71

Guided Practice *For another example, see Set H on p. 79.*

1. 703 − 659
2. 600 − 348
3. 8,078 − 4,291
4. 5,002 − 2,411
5. $40.00 − 23.60

6. Use the data on p. 62. How much higher is Sherwin Pass than Yuba Pass?

Independent Practice *For more practice, see Set H on p. 82.*

7. 307 − 158
8. 502 − 279
9. 200 − 58
10. 600 − 419
11. $9.00 − 3.49
12. 7,012 − 2,940
13. $25.00 − 12.69
14. 6,020 − 4,340
15. 8,000 − 2,854
16. 4,000 − 2,056

Mental Math Use mental math to find each difference.

17. 500 − 80
18. 7,000 − 1,600
19. $9.00 − $1.50

20. Use the data on p. 62. How much higher is Sherwin Pass than Sagehew Pass?

21. Mrs. Chan bought a new lamp for $48. She paid for it with a $100 bill. How much change did she get?

22. In 1996, astronaut Shannon Lucid spent 188 days in space. Cosmonaut Valery Polyakov spent 439 days in space. How many more days did Polyakov spend in space than Lucid?

23. The attendance at a conference is 4,007 students. If 2,794 of these students are from the United States, how many are from other countries?

Mixed Review

Use the data at the right for Exercises 24–26.

24. How much higher is the elevation of Los Angeles than San Francisco?

25. How much higher is the elevation of Los Angeles than Sacramento?

26. Write the elevation of Los Angeles in expanded form.

27. The highest point in Atlanta, Georgia, is 1,050 feet above sea level. The highest point in Denver, Colorado, is 4,230 feet higher. How high is the highest point in Denver?

28. 674 − 550

29. 8,789 − 6,300

30. 1,456 − 1,328

Algebra Replace each ● with + or −.

31. 11 ● 4 = 7

32. 45 ● 25 = 70

33. 95 ● 25 = 70

Test Prep Choose the correct letter for each answer.

34. (2-7) Some students need to wash 380 cars to raise money for a school trip. They have washed 168 cars. About how many more cars do they need to wash?

A About 200

B About 300

C About 400

D About 500

35. (2-4) Last year there were 753 students in Elm School. There are 191 more students this year. How many students are in Elm School this year?

F 562 students

G 844 students

H 944 students

J 954 students

LESSON 2-11

Mental Math Strategies

California Content Standard *Number Sense 2.1 (🔑): Find the sum or difference of two whole numbers between 0 and 10,000.*

Math Link You know how to add and subtract numbers with up to four digits. In this lesson, you will learn how to use some mental math strategies that can help you add and subtract.

Breaking apart is a method you can use to add and subtract numbers mentally.

Warm-Up Review

1. 9 + 6
2. 12 − 8
3. 40 − 20
4. 700 + 100
5. 66 − 32
6. 329 + 206
7. A sweater costs $43, and a shirt costs $35. The sweater is on sale for $14 off. What is the sale price of the sweater?

Word Bank

breaking apart
compensation

Example 1

Find 53 + 39 by breaking apart the numbers in the problem.

Think: 50 + 30 = 80	Add the tens in both numbers.
3 + 9 = 12	Add the ones in both numbers.
80 + 12 = 92	Add the sums of the tens and ones.

So, 53 + 39 = 92.

Example 2

Find 756 − 205 by breaking apart the numbers in the problem.

Think: 700 − 200 = 500	Subtract the hundreds in both numbers.
50 − 0 = 50	Subtract the tens in both numbers.
6 − 5 = 1	Subtract the ones in both numbers.
500 + 50 + 1 = 551	Add the sums of the hundreds, tens, and ones.

So, 756 − 205 = 551.

More Examples

A. 430 + 267 = ■

Think: 400 + 200 = 600
30 + 60 = 90
0 + 7 = 7
600 + 90 + 7 = 697

So, 430 + 267 = 697.

B. 89 − 15 = ■

Think: 80 − 10 = 70
9 − 5 = 4
70 + 4 = 74

So, 89 − 15 = 74.

Additional Standard: Mathematical Reasoning 2.4 (See p. 41)

Compensation is another method you can use to add and subtract numbers mentally.

Example 3

Find 125 + 98 by using compensation.

98 + 2 ↓ 125 + 100 = 225	Add 2 to 98 to make 100. 100 is easier to use.
225 − 2 = 223	Subtract 2 from the sum to compensate for adding 2.

So, 125 + 98 = 223.

Example 4

Find 65 − 19 by using compensation.

19 + 1 ↓ 65 − 20 = 45	Add 1 to 19 to make 20. 20 is easier to use.
45 + 1 = 46	Add 1 to the difference to compensate for subtracting 1 extra.

So, 65 − 19 = 46.

More Examples

A. 59 + 34 = ■

Think: 60 + 34 = 94
94 − 1 = 93

So, 59 + 34 = 93

B. 471 − 195 = ■

Think: 471 − 200 = 271
271 + 5 = 276

So, 471 − 195 = 276

Guided Practice *For another example, see Set I on p. 80.*

Add or subtract mentally. Use breaking apart.

1. 52 + 35 **2.** 37 − 12 **3.** 663 + 128 **4.** 792 − 441

Add or subtract mentally. Use compensation.

5. 47 − 18 **6.** 64 + 39 **7.** 238 + 495 **8.** 276 − 198

9. Sam's book has 52 pages. He has read 19 pages. How many pages does he have left to read?

Independent Practice *For more practice, see Set I on p. 83.*

Add or subtract mentally. Use breaking apart.

10. 49 − 16 **11.** 56 + 43 **12.** 96 − 23 **13.** 34 + 68

14. 566 + 103 **15.** 454 + 312 **16.** 947 − 35 **17.** 783 − 261

Add or subtract mentally. Use compensation.

18. 68 + 29 **19.** 72 − 19 **20.** 92 − 45 **21.** 74 + 28

22. 834 − 199 **23.** 690 − 57 **24.** 514 + 79 **25.** 468 + 295

26. On Friday, 253 adults and 124 children saw the display. How many people saw the display altogether?

27. Math Reasoning Nathan says, "I can find 160 − 59 by adding 1 to 59 and then subtracting to get 100." What did Nathan do wrong? Explain.

Mixed Review

Use the data at the right for Exercises 28–31.

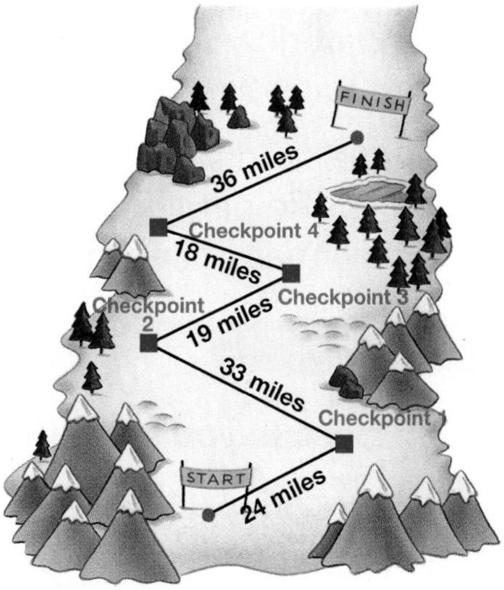

28. Kipanik and his dog are in a sled-dog race. They only make it as far as Checkpoint 3. How far did they go?

29. How far is it from Checkpoint 3 to Finish?

30. How far is it from Start to Finish?

31. The shortest section of the race is from Checkpoint 3 to Checkpoint 4. Which section of the race is the longest?

32. 7,123 − 3,517 **33.** 4,008 − 1,355 **34.** 6,000 − 2,945

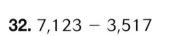

Test Prep **Choose the correct letter for the answer.**

35. (1–6) The United States has 50 states. Rhode Island is the smallest state. How many states are larger than Rhode Island?

F 1 state **G** 48 states **H** 49 states **J** 50 states

LESSON 2-12

Understand
Plan
Solve
Look Back

Problem-Solving Application:

Using a Bar Graph

Warm-Up Review

1. 8 + 6 **2.** 14 + 5

3. Compare: 23 ● 13

4. Order the numbers from least to greatest: 18, 7, 17, 12, 20

5. Rob is 13 years old, Megan is 6 years old and Liz is 9 years old. Who is oldest?

California Content Standard *Mathematical Reasoning 2.3: Use a variety of methods, such as words, numbers, symbols, charts, graphs, tables, diagrams, and models to explain mathematical reasoning.*

The bar graph at the right shows the number of animals Lucy's class saw on their trip to the zoo. How many more turtles than lizards did the class see?

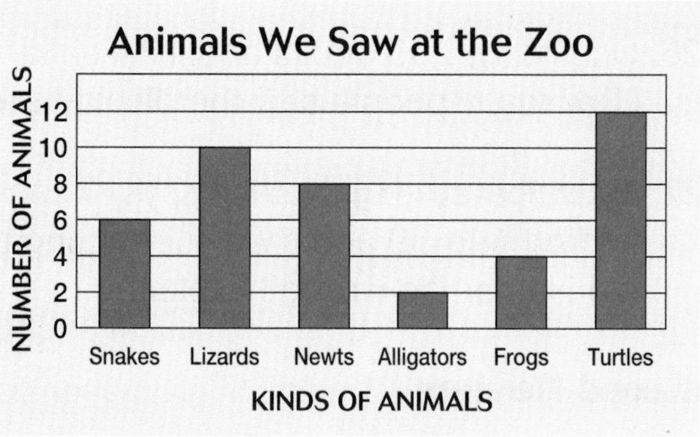

Understand

What do you need to know?

You need to know that you can use the numbers on the side of the graph and the height of the bars to tell how many of each kind of animal the class saw.

Plan

How can you solve the problem?

You can use the bar graph to compare how many turtles and how many lizards the class saw.

Solve

The class saw 12 turtles and 10 lizards.

12 − 10 = 2 turtles

The class saw 2 more turtles than lizards.

Look Back

How many turtles and lizards did the class see altogether?

Use the graph on page 68 to help you solve Exercises 1–9.

Guided Practice

1. Which kind of animal did the class see the least on their trip to the zoo?

2. How many more lizards than snakes did the class see?

Independent Practice

3. Which kind of animal did the class see the most on their trip to the zoo?

4. How many more turtles than frogs did the class see?

5. How many lizards and snakes did the class see altogether?

6. What is the total number of animals the class saw on their trip to the zoo?

7. List the animals the class saw in order from the least animals seen to the most animals seen.

8. **Math Reasoning** Sarah said she saw two large snakes, a green sea turtle and a painted turtle. Can you tell for certain if this is true by looking at the graph? Tell why or why not.

9. **Math Reasoning** Henry said he saw a bullfrog, a grass frog, a toad frog, and a red-eyed tree frog. Look at the graph. Could this be true? Tell why or why not.

Mixed Review

10. Use the chart at the right. If the pattern continues, how many houses will be sold in August?

11. Talia told how many tomatoes she had grown. "I grew an even number between 40 and 50. I grew more than 45, but I did not grow 46." How many tomatoes did she grow?

Month	Number of Houses Sold
March	7
April	14
May	21

LESSON 2-13

Expressions with Addition and Subtraction

Algebra

Warm-Up Review

1. 23 + 5
2. 75 − 9
3. 13 + 47
4. 81 − 15
5. 59 + 21
6. 67 − 36
7. Wheels Galore made 2,083 scooters in January and 1,809 in February. How many more scooters should they make to meet a goal of 9,500?

California Content Standard *Algebra and Functions 1.1 (🔑): Represent relationships and quantities in the form of mathematical expressions . . ..*

Math Link You can find sums and differences like 18 + 3 and 45 − 9. Now you will learn about expressions like 18 + ■ and 45 − ■.

Word Bank

expression

18 + ■ is an **expression.** It has a number, an operation, and a ■. The ■ stands for a number.

Example 1

Give three numbers that make this statement true:
18 + ■ is greater than 30.

Use a number line.

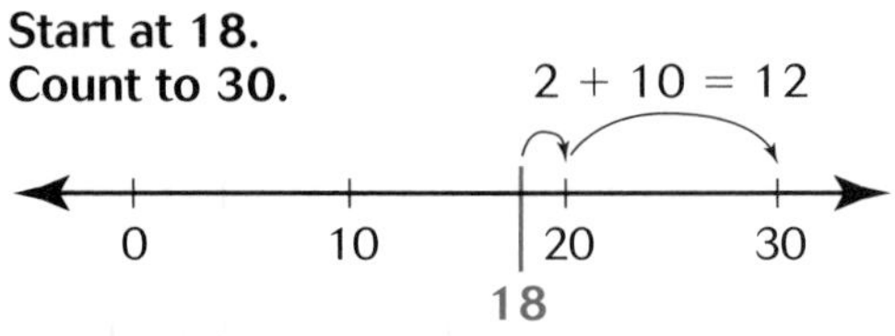

You know that 18 + 12 is 30.

So, 18 + 13 must be greater than 30.

Therefore, three numbers that make the statement true are 13, 14, and 15.

<u>Check</u> 18 + 13 = 31; 18 + 14 = 32; and 18 + 15 = 33.
Since each sum is greater than 30, the answer checks.

Example 2

Give three numbers that make this statement true:
45 − ■ is less than 20.

Use a number line.

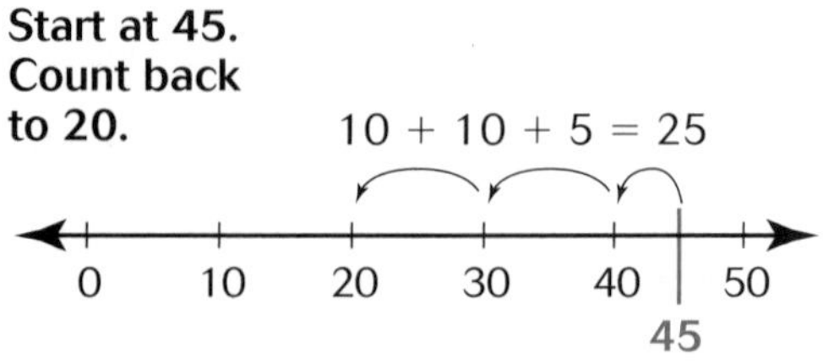

You know that 45 − 25 is 20.

So, 45 − 26 must be less than 20.

Therefore, three numbers that make the statement true are 26, 27, and 28.

<u>Check</u> 45 − 26 = 19; 45 − 27 = 18; and 45 − 28 = 17.
Since each difference is less than 20, the answer checks.

Guided Practice *For another example, see Set J on p. 80.*

Give three numbers that make each statement true.

1. 9 + ■ is greater than 14.

2. 9 + ■ is less than 14.

3. 15 − ■ is greater than 10.

4. 15 − ■ is between 5 and 10.

5. List all the whole numbers that make the following statement true: 44 + ■ is less than 51.

Independent Practice *For more practice, see Set J on p. 83.*

Give three numbers that make each statement true.

6. 10 + ■ is greater than 23.

7. 10 + ■ is less than 23.

8. 16 + ■ is less than 20.

9. 16 + ■ is between 20 and 30.

10. 20 − ■ is less than 5.

11. 20 − ■ is between 5 and 15.

12. 54 − ■ is less than 40.

13. 54 − ■ is greater than 40.

14. The missing length is less than 11 cm. What are two possibilities for this length?

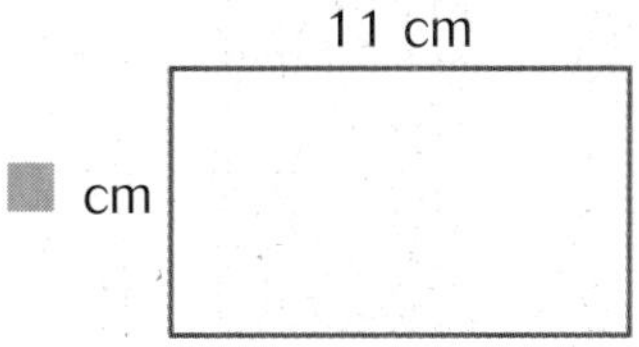

15. List all the whole numbers that make the following statement true: 78 − ■ is greater than 72.

Mixed Review

16. Fancy scooters cost $200. Jan has saved $85. How much more money does she need to buy the scooter?

17. Mental Math Find 57 − 29.

18. Mental Math Find 323 + 506.

Test Prep **Choose the correct letter for each answer.**

19. (2–5) A museum has a collection of 1,407 shells. A donor gives the museum 345 shells. How many shells does the museum have now?

A 1,753 shells **C** 1,742 shells

B 1,752 shells **D** 752 shells

20. (1–8) How much money is shown below?

F $1.36 **H** $5.36

G $5.31 **J** $5.46

Use Homework Workbook 2-13.

LESSON 2-14

Equations with Addition and Subtraction

Algebra

Warm-Up Review

1. 15 + 7
2. 27 + 6
3. 20 − 8
4. 42 − 3
5. 68 + 31
6. 36 − 20
7. Maple school has 426 students. 197 of the students are boys. How many students are girls?

California Content Standard *Algebra and Functions 1.1 (key): Represent relationships and quantities in the form of mathematical . . . equations . . . Also, Algebra and Functions 1.2 (See p. 41.)*

Word Bank

equation

Math Link You have learned about expressions like 5 + ■ and 34 − ■. Now you will learn how to find missing numbers in equations like 5 + ■ = 22 and 34 − ■ = 15.

5 + ■ = 22 is an **equation.** It has numbers, an operation, a ■, and an equal sign.

Example 1

Find the missing number in this equation:
5 + ■ = 22.

Use a number line.

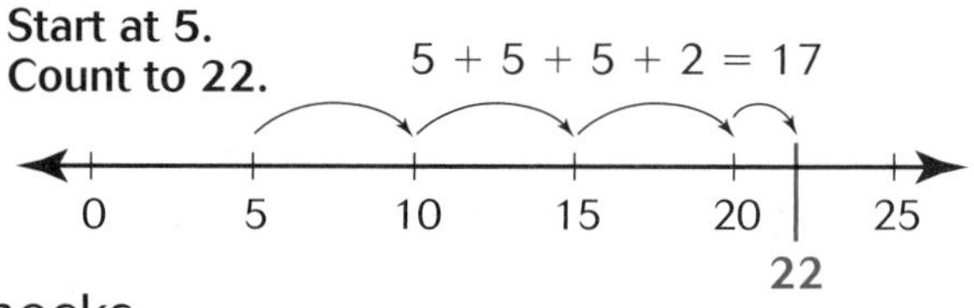

So, ■ = 17.

<u>*Check*</u> Since 5 + 17 = 22, the answer checks.

Example 2

Find the missing number in this equation:
43 − ■ = 25

Use a number line.

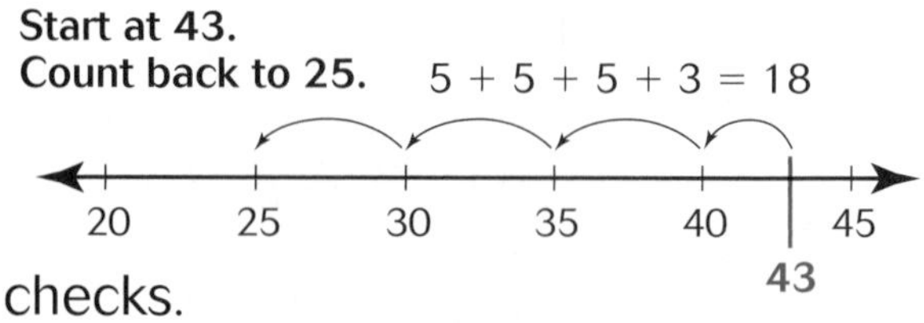

So, ■ = 18.

<u>*Check*</u> Since 43 − 18 = 25, the answer checks.

Guided Practice *For another example, see Set K on p. 80.*

Find each missing number.

1. 9 + ■ = 14
2. 10 + ■ = 30
3. 17 − ■ = 8
4. 46 − ■ = 26
5. Lana bought 93 marbles for $7.60. She gave 76 marbles away. How many marbles did she have left?

Additional Standards: Mathematical Reasoning 1.1, 2.3 (See p. 41.)

Independent Practice *For more practice, see Set K on p. 83.*

Find each missing number.

6. 5 + ■ = 11 **7.** 9 + ■ = 13 **8.** 10 − ■ = 4 **9.** 14 − ■ = 7

10. 8 + ■ = 18 **11.** 4 + ■ = 21 **12.** 19 − ■ = 6 **13.** 23 − ■ = 9

14. 21 + ■ = 28 **15.** 34 + ■ = 46 **16.** 39 − ■ = 34 **17.** 57 − ■ = 23

18. Polly had 42 stickers. Her friend gave her 14 more. How many stickers did she have then?

19. Math Reasoning Is the missing number in ■ + 3 = 15 the same as the missing number in 3 + ■ = 15? Explain.

Mixed Review

20. Dan sold 247 tickets for main floor seats and 583 tickets for the balcony. About how many tickets did he sell in all?

21. Mental Math Find 72 + 28.

22. Mental Math Find 506 − 199.

Algebra **Give three numbers that make each statement true.**

23. 12 + ■ is less than 20.

24. 40 − ■ is greater than 15.

Test Prep **Choose the correct letter for each answer.**

25. (2–8) Liam's album for his baseball cards holds 256 cards. Liam has 392 cards. How many cards will not fit in his album?

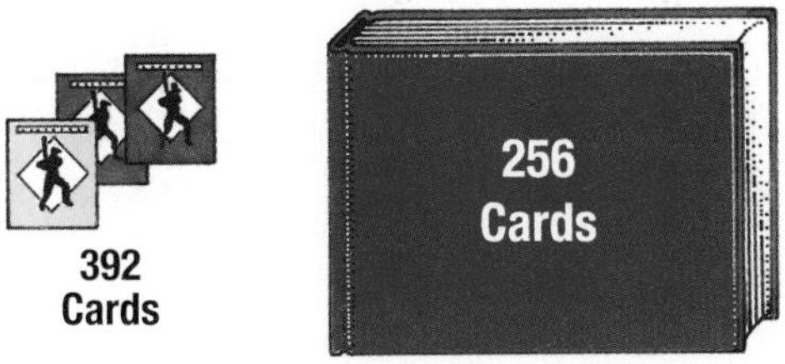

A 126 cards
B 136 cards
C 146 cards
D 648 cards
E NH

26. (2–10) Nathaniel bought the video game Roadster Rally and paid with two $50 bills. How much change should he get back?

Video Game	Price
Roadster Rally	$64
Turbo Charger	$59
My Quest	$39

F $164
G $46
H $36
J $34
K NH

Diagnostic Checkpoint

Complete. For Exercises 1–4, use the words from the Word Bank.

Word Bank
inverse operations
compensation
expression
equation

1. (2-11) One method you can use to add and subtract mentally is ________________.

2. (2-13) 12 + ■ is an ________________. It has a number, an operation, and a ■.

3. (2-14) 7 + ■ = 11 is an ________________. It has a number, an operation, a ■, and an equal sign.

4. (2-1) Addition and subtraction are ________________.

Estimate by using front-end estimation.

5. (2-7) 74 − 25 **6.** (2-7) 82 − 48 **7.** (2-7) 615 − 208 **8.** (2-7) 890 − 372

Subtract.

9. (2-8) $46 - 25$ **10.** (2-8) $817 - 645$ **11.** (2-10) $6.08 − $4.59 **12.** (2-9) 2,211 − 1,788 **13.** (2-10) $25.01 − 10.75

Add or subtract mentally. Use breaking apart.

14. (2-11) 43 + 25 **15.** (2-11) 38 − 26 **16.** (2-11) 552 + 136 **17.** (2-11) 884 − 323

Give three numbers that make each statement true.

18. (2-13) 15 + ■ is greater than 32. **19.** (2-13) 35 − ■ is less than 30.

Find each missing number.

20. (2-14) 6 + ■ = 16 **21.** (2-14) 16 − ■ = 7 **22.** (2-14) 25 + ■ = 38 **23.** (2-14) 47 − ■ = 20

Use the sign at the right for Exercises 24 and 25.

24. (2-9) Ayla bought a pair of basketball shoes on sale. How much did she save?

25. (2-5) Marcus bought two pairs of basketball shoes on sale. How much did he spend?

Chapter 2 Test

Estimate by rounding to the greatest place value.

1. 45 + 39 **2.** 71 − 58 **3.** 282 + 729 **4.** 782 − 275

Find each sum.

5. 26 + 78

6. 541 + 306

7. $3.05 + 6.48

8. 7,356 + 4,732

9. $81.33 + 15.69

Find each difference.

10. 80 − 44

11. $4.39 − 2.47

12. 6,202 − 5,347

13. $30.00 − 25.98

14. 5,682 − 4,391

Find each missing number.

15. 8 + ■ = 17 **16.** 20 + ■ = 50 **17.** 14 − ■ = 5 **18.** 25 − ■ = 8

Give three numbers that make each statement true.

19. 20 − ■ is less than 8. **20.** 15 + ■ is between 30 and 34.

21. Write a related addition sentence. 12 − 5 = 7
■ + ■ = ■

22. Subtract 314 − 199 mentally. Use compensation.

23. Tom bought a jacket on sale for $36.99 and a pair of pants for $24.00. If the original price for the jacket was $75.00, how much did Tom save? What information is not needed to solve the problem?

24. Jack's neighbor gives him $4 each day to walk the dog. If Jack walks the dog for 5 days, how much will he earn in all? (Copy and complete the table to solve.)

Day	Total Amount Paid
1st	$4
2nd	
3rd	
4th	
5th	

25. Suppose you made a bar graph from the data in the table you made in Exercise 24. Which day would have the longest bar on the graph?

TEST PREP

Multiple-Choice Chapter 2 Test

Choose the correct letter for each answer.

1. Which is a related addition sentence for 12 − 7 = 5?

   A 12 + 5 = 17
   B 12 + 7 = 19
   C 5 + 7 = 12
   D 5 + 0 = 5

2. Estimate by rounding to the nearest ten.

   47 + 64

   F 90
   G 100
   H 110
   J 120
   K NH

3. Find 507 + 756.

   A 249
   B 1,200
   C 1,253
   D 1,363
   E NH

4. Find 4,857 + 3,162.

   F 7,019
   G 7,919
   H 8,019
   J 8,756
   K NH

5. Kim has 327 trading cards. Her sister Katie has 461 trading cards. Their brother Ron has 390 trading cards. What information is *not* needed to find out how many more cards Katie has than Kim?

   A Kim has 327 trading cards.
   B Ron has 390 trading cards.
   C Katie has 461 trading cards.
   D All of the above

6. Estimate by using front-end estimation.

   86 − 38

   F 50
   G 60
   H 70
   J 90

7. The Eiffel Tower in Paris is 984 feet tall. The Washington Monument in Washington, D.C., is 555 feet tall. How much taller is the Eiffel Tower?

   A 1,539 feet
   B 431 feet
   C 429 feet
   D 428 feet

8. **Find the 6,338 − 4,119.**

F 2,219
G 2,221
H 2,229
J 3,479
K NH

9. **Mark had $40.25. He spent $26.59 on a skateboard. How much money did Mark have left?**

A $13.41
B $13.66
C $24.76
D $66.84

10. **To add 35 + 42 using breaking apart, Sean started by finding that 30 + 40 = 70 and 5 + 2 = 7. What should he do next?**

F Add 42 and 7.
G Add 35 and 7.
H Subtract 7 from 70.
J Add 70 and 7.

11. **Find 4,060 − 1,273.**

A 2,787 **D** 3,897
B 3,213 **E** NH
C 3,787

12. **Estimate 779 + 1,273 by rounding to the nearest 100.**

F 1,100 **H** 2,100
G 1,700 **J** 2,200

13. **Tim bought a game on sale for $8.50. The regular price was $9.95. How much did he save?**

A $0.45
B $1.45
C $1.55
D $18.45

14. **Use the table below. If each book costs the same amount, how much will Juanita pay for 2 books?**

Number of Books	1	2	3
Cost	$5		$15

F $6
G $10
H $11
J $15

15. **Which number makes the statement true?**

3 + ■ is greater than 14

A 8
B 9
C 10
D 12

16. **Find the missing number.**

4 + ■ = 18

F 12
G 13
H 14
J 22

Reteaching

Set A *(pages 42–43)*

Write a related addition sentence for 10 − 6 = 4.

A related sentence uses the same three numbers: 10, 6, and 4.

Related additon sentence:
4 + 6 = 10

Remember addition and subtraction are inverse operations.

Write a related addition or subtraction sentence.

1. 17 − 9 = 8
■ + ■ = ■

2. 8 + 5 = 13
■ − ■ = ■

Set B *(pages 46–47)*

Estimate 255 + 549 by rounding to the nearest hundred.

255	+	549	
rounds to		rounds to	
300	+	500	= 800

255 + 549 is about 800.

Remember to round each number, and then add.

Estimate by rounding to the nearest hundred.

1. 226 + 728 **2.** 378 + 529

3. 417 + 656 **4.** 184 + 359

Set C *(pages 48–49)*

Find 48 + 66.

Step 1	Step 2
$\begin{array}{r} ^{1} \\ 48 \\ +\ 66 \\ \hline 4 \end{array}$	$\begin{array}{r} ^{1} \\ 48 \\ +\ 66 \\ \hline 114 \end{array}$

Remember you can regroup 10 ones as 1 ten and 10 tens as 1 hundred.

1. 42 + 88 **2.** 54 + 37

3. 75 + 399 **4.** 278 + 486

Set D *(pages 50–51)*

Find 2,649 + 1,824.

$$\begin{array}{r} ^{1\ \ 1} \\ 2{,}649 \\ +\ 1{,}824 \\ \hline 4{,}473 \end{array}$$

Remember you can regroup 10 hundreds for 1 thousand.

1. $\begin{array}{r} 1{,}279 \\ +\ 2{,}647 \\ \hline \end{array}$ **2.** $\begin{array}{r} 6{,}298 \\ +\ 2{,}543 \\ \hline \end{array}$

3. $\begin{array}{r} 5{,}921 \\ +\ 3{,}485 \\ \hline \end{array}$ **4.** $\begin{array}{r} 4{,}825 \\ +\ 1{,}743 \\ \hline \end{array}$

Set E (pages 55–57)

Use front-end estimation to estimate 793 − 248.

$$\begin{array}{ccc} 793 & - & 248 \\ \downarrow & & \downarrow \\ 700 & - & 200 = 500 \end{array}$$

700 − 200 is *about* 500.

Remember to look only at the front digit of each number when using front-end estimation.

Estimate using front-end estimation.

1. 89 − 17 **2.** 62 − 34

3. 563 − 473 **4.** 754 − 422

Set F (pages 58–59)

Find 85 − 16.

Step 1	Step 2
$\begin{array}{r} {\scriptstyle 7\ 15} \\ \not{8}\not{5} \\ -\ 16 \\ \hline 9 \end{array}$	$\begin{array}{r} {\scriptstyle 7\ 15} \\ \not{8}\not{5} \\ -\ 16 \\ \hline 69 \end{array}$

Remember you can regroup 1 ten as 10 ones or 1 hundred as 10 tens.

1. $\begin{array}{r} 48 \\ -\ 29 \\ \hline \end{array}$ **2.** $\begin{array}{r} 82 \\ -\ 44 \\ \hline \end{array}$

3. $\begin{array}{r} 817 \\ -\ 645 \\ \hline \end{array}$ **4.** $\begin{array}{r} \$4.39 \\ -\ \$2.47 \\ \hline \end{array}$

Set G (pages 60–61)

Find 3,824 − 1,468.

$$\begin{array}{r} {\scriptstyle 11} \\ {\scriptstyle 7\ \not{1}\ 14} \\ 3,\not{8}\not{2}\not{4} \\ -\ 1,468 \\ \hline 2,356 \end{array}$$

Remember you can regroup 1 thousand as 10 hundreds.

1. $\begin{array}{r} 5,682 \\ -\ 4,391 \\ \hline \end{array}$ **2.** $\begin{array}{r} 8,975 \\ -\ 3,437 \\ \hline \end{array}$

3. $\begin{array}{r} 4,826 \\ -\ 2,914 \\ \hline \end{array}$ **4.** $\begin{array}{r} 7,259 \\ -\ 3,576 \\ \hline \end{array}$

Set H (pages 62–64)

Find 904 − 258.

$$\begin{array}{r} {\scriptstyle 9} \\ {\scriptstyle 8\ \not{10}\ 14} \\ \not{9}\not{0}\not{4} \\ -\ 258 \\ \hline 646 \end{array}$$

Remember to estimate to check if your answer is reasonable.

1. $\begin{array}{r} 608 \\ -\ 459 \\ \hline \end{array}$ **2.** $\begin{array}{r} 6,202 \\ -\ 5,347 \\ \hline \end{array}$

3. \$38.06 − \$13.47

Reteaching (continued)

Set I *(pages 65–67)*

Find 253 − 197 by using compensation.

197 + 3
↓
253 − 200 = 53

53 + 3 = 56

So, 253 − 197 = 56.

Remember you can add mentally by breaking apart or using compensation.

Add or subtract mentally.

1. 64 − 19
2. 43 + 25
3. 674 − 399
4. 295 + 403
5. 332 + 198
6. 572 − 241

Set J *(pages 70–71)*

Give three numbers that make this statement true:
54 − ■ is less than 20.

Start at 54. Count back to 20.

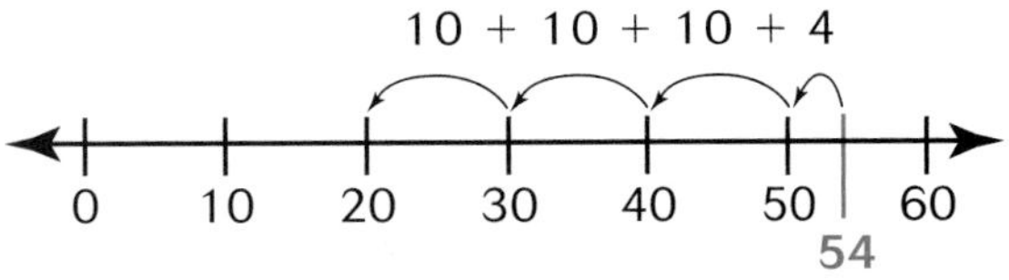

You know that 54 − 34 is 20.

So, three numbers that make the statement true are 35, 36, and 37.

Remember you can check your answer by substituting.

Give three numbers that make each statement true.

1. 25 + ■ is greater than 40.
2. 15 + ■ is less than 20.
3. 46 − ■ is less than 10.
4. 20 − ■ is greater than 10.

Set K *(pages 72–73)*

Find the missing number.
42 − ■ = 18

Start at 42. Count back to 18.

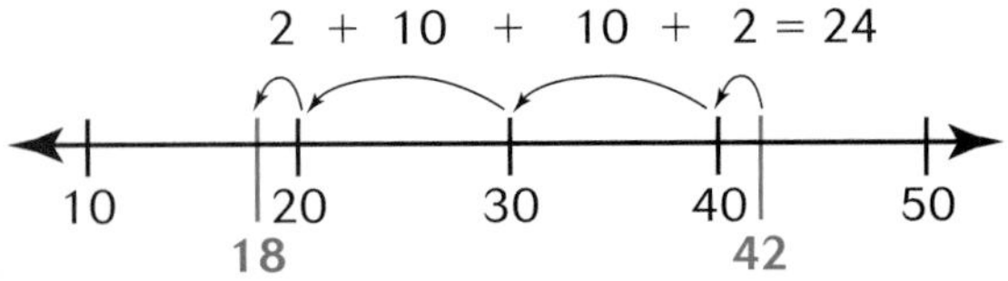

So, ■ = 24.

Remember you can check your answer by substituting.

Find each missing number.

1. 8 + ■ = 15
2. 6 + ■ = 21
3. 27 + ■ = 45
4. 17 − ■ = 5
5. 26 − ■ = 14
6. 57 − ■ = 39

More Practice

Set A *(pages 42–43)*

Write a related addition or subtraction sentence.

1. $9 - 6 = 3$
■ + ■ = ■

2. $5 + 6 = 11$
■ − ■ = ■

3. $15 - 8 = 7$
■ + ■ = ■

4. $6 + 9 = 15$
■ − ■ = ■

5. There are 13 students in the school library. If 5 students go back to class, how many students are left in the library?

Set B *(pages 46–47)*

Estimate by rounding to the nearest hundred.

1. 263 + 388 **2.** 595 + 405 **3.** 812 + 279 **4.** 973 + 285

5. Lucy has 124 U.S. coins and 288 Canadian coins in her collection. About how many coins does she have in all?

Set C *(pages 48–49)*

1. 57 + 35 **2.** 36 + 45 **3.** 47 + 38 **4.** 27 + 68

5. 305 + 472 **6.** 813 + 345 **7.** 234 + 897 **8.** 989 + 625

9. The second grade class collected 348 cans, and the third grade class collected 386 cans for recycling. How many cans did the two grades collect together?

Set D *(pages 50–51)*

1. $\begin{array}{r} 8{,}712 \\ +\ 1{,}286 \\ \hline \end{array}$ **2.** $\begin{array}{r} 1{,}989 \\ +\ 7{,}053 \\ \hline \end{array}$ **3.** $\begin{array}{r} 3{,}509 \\ +\ 8{,}799 \\ \hline \end{array}$ **4.** $\begin{array}{r} \$22.17 \\ +\ 44.93 \\ \hline \end{array}$

5. One school district has 1,812 students. The neighboring school district has 1,449 students. How many students would be in a new district that combines the two districts?

More Practice (continued)

Set E *(pages 55–57)*

Estimate by using front-end estimation.

1. 94 − 49 **2.** 54 − 37 **3.** 434 − 147 **4.** 541 − 306

5. On Saturday, Joe and Dan washed cars to raise money for their school. Joe washed 52 cars, and Dan washed 35 cars. About how many more cars did Joe wash than Dan?

Set F *(pages 58–59)*

1. $\begin{array}{r} 78 \\ -\ 22 \\ \hline \end{array}$ **2.** $\begin{array}{r} 61 \\ -\ 28 \\ \hline \end{array}$ **3.** $\begin{array}{r} 92 \\ -\ 74 \\ \hline \end{array}$ **4.** $\begin{array}{r} 48 \\ -\ 29 \\ \hline \end{array}$ **5.** $\begin{array}{r} 98 \\ -\ 71 \\ \hline \end{array}$

6. 782 − 275 **7.** 750 − 610 **8.** 817 − 296 **9.** 648 − 305

10. In the 15 swim classes, there are 165 boys and 146 girls. How many more boys than girls are in the classes?

Set G *(pages 60–61)*

1. $\begin{array}{r} 1{,}989 \\ -\ 268 \\ \hline \end{array}$ **2.** $\begin{array}{r} 7{,}343 \\ -\ 4{,}829 \\ \hline \end{array}$ **3.** $\begin{array}{r} 5{,}276 \\ -\ 1{,}849 \\ \hline \end{array}$ **4.** $\begin{array}{r} 6{,}524 \\ -\ 2{,}627 \\ \hline \end{array}$

5. Jill paid $17.98 for a CD and $12.84 for a cassette tape. How much more did she spend on the CD than on the cassette tape?

Set H *(pages 62–64)*

1. $\begin{array}{r} 408 \\ -239 \\ \hline \end{array}$ **2.** $\begin{array}{r} \$25.06 \\ -\ 19.28 \\ \hline \end{array}$ **3.** $\begin{array}{r} 4{,}072 \\ -1{,}885 \\ \hline \end{array}$ **4.** $\begin{array}{r} \$30.00 \\ -\ 25.98 \\ \hline \end{array}$

5. Last week 1,031 children signed up for softball. So far, 386 of the children have received their team shirts. How many children still need to receive their shirts?

Set I (pages 65–67)

Add or subtract mentally. Use breaking apart.

1. 78 + 11 **2.** 135 + 263 **3.** 65 − 32 **4.** 587 − 241

Add or subtract mentally. Use compensation.

5. 43 + 58 **6.** 345 + 199 **7.** 84 − 38 **8.** 628 − 295

9. Joe wants to buy a baseball that costs $8.43 and a bat that costs $11.49. How much do these cost altogether?

Set J (pages 70–71)

Give three numbers that make each statement true.

1. 6 + ■ is greater than 10.

2. 6 + ■ is less than 10.

3. 34 − ■ is less than 10.

4. 34 − ■ is greater than 10.

5. 5 + ■ is between 10 and 15.

6. 60 − ■ is between 25 and 30.

7. List all the numbers that make the following statement true: 52 − ■ is greater than 47.

8. List all the numbers that make the following statement true: 38 + ■ is less than 45.

Set K (pages 72–73)

Find each missing number.

1. 7 + ■ = 16 **2.** 20 + ■ = 36 **3.** 36 + ■ = 48 **4.** 22 + ■ = 41

5. 14 − ■ = 8 **6.** 30 − ■ = 12 **7.** 46 − ■ = 22 **8.** 53 − ■ = 37

9. Carolyn had 24 cans of juice. Two weeks later there were only 9 cans left. How many cans did she drink?

10. Javier had 18 colored pencils. His mother gave him 8 more. How many pencils did he have then?

TEST PREP

Problem Solving: Preparing for Tests

Choose the correct letter for each answer.

---

1. Ted has 8 baseball cards and 6 football cards. Bob has 9 baseball cards and 4 football cards. How many baseball cards do they have altogether?

A 1 card
B 13 cards
C 14 cards
D 17 cards
E NH

Tip
Sometimes extra information is given in a problem. Start by deciding what information is needed in order to answer the question.

---

2. Ken is drawing pictures of a row of 4 different kinds of trees. He puts the elm between the oak and the pine. The oak is fourth. The first tree is a maple. What is the third tree?

F Elm
G Oak
H Pine
J Maple

Tip
Use one of these strategies to solve the problem.
- Draw a Picture
- Make a List

---

3. On Tuesday, Ursula saw 15 birds in a pet store window. Each day after that, there were 2 fewer birds. How many birds were there on Friday?

A 9 birds
B 11 birds
C 13 birds
D 17 birds

Tip
Try making a table to show how many birds there are on Wednesday, Thursday, and Friday.

4. **There were 3 squirrels and 8 birds in the backyard. Then 2 more squirrels joined the others. Which number sentence shows the number of squirrels in the backyard now?**

F $8 + 2 = \blacksquare$
G $3 + 2 = \blacksquare$
H $3 - 2 = \blacksquare$
J $3 + 8 + 2 = \blacksquare$

---

5. **Lynn is 3 years older than Tim. Angie is 3 years younger than Tim. Which of the following is true?**

A Tim is older than Lynn.
B Angie is older than Lynn.
C Lynn is older than Angie.
D Angie is older than Tim.

---

6. **Nan spent $1.50 on pens and more than $2.00 on markers. Which is a reasonable amount that Nan might have spent in all?**

F $1.70 **H** $3.50
G $2.20 **J** $3.75

---

7. **Patricia has 29 red hearts and 42 blue hearts in her sticker collection. About how many red and blue hearts does Patricia have?**

A 10
B 20
C 40
D 70

---

8. **The table below shows prices at a restaurant. Julie buys a small shake and a large milk. How much does she pay?**

Drink Prices

	Milk	Juice	Shake
Small	$0.75	$0.80	$1.75
Large	$0.95	$1.10	$2.20

F $2.50 **H** $2.95
G $2.70 **J** $3.15

Use the graph for Questions 9 and 10.

This graph shows the number of pets that the students in Karen's class have.

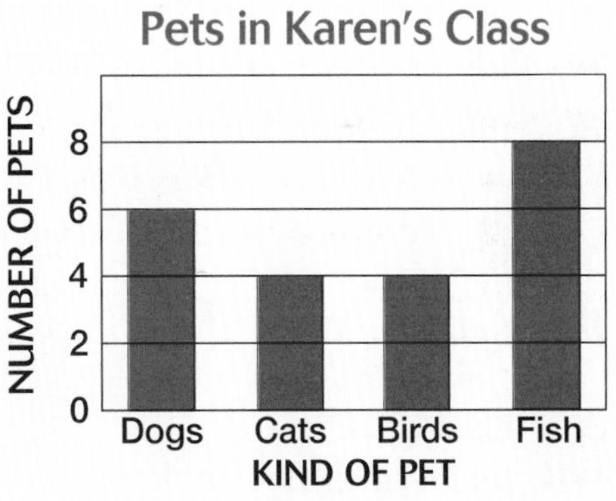

9. **How many fish do the students in Karen's class have?**

A 4 fish **C** 8 fish
B 6 fish **D** 9 fish

---

10. **How many more dogs than cats do the students in Karen's class have?**

F 2 more dogs
G 3 more dogs
H 6 more dogs
J 10 more dogs

TEST PREP

Multiple-Choice Cumulative Review

Choose the correct letter for each answer.

Number Sense

1. **Tina spent $2.88 on a calculator and $3.99 on a notebook. About how much money did she spend?**

- **A** $3.00
- **B** $5.00
- **C** $7.00
- **D** $17.00

2.

$$\begin{array}{r} 486 \\ -\ 97 \\ \hline \end{array}$$

- **F** 389
- **G** 399
- **H** 411
- **J** 583
- **K** NH

3. **Will has 41¢ in his pocket. His Aunt Mary gave him the money below. How much money does he have now?**

- **A** 14¢
- **B** 86¢
- **C** 92¢
- **D** 96¢

4. **What is the value of the 3 in 134,007?**

- **F** 300
- **G** 3,000
- **H** 30,000
- **J** 300,000

5. **Find the numeral that means six thousand, seven hundred thirty-four.**

- **A** 3,467
- **B** 6,734
- **C** 6,743
- **D** 7,643

6. **Cara is reading a book that has 99 pages. Last week she read 47 pages. How many more pages does she have to read to finish the book?**

- **F** 48 pages
- **G** 52 pages
- **H** 132 pages
- **J** 142 pages

7. **Meg has 16 books. She has read 7 of them. Which number sentence could be used to find how many books she has NOT read?**

- **A** $16 + 7 = \blacksquare$
- **B** $7 + 16 = \blacksquare$
- **C** $16 - 7 = \blacksquare$
- **D** $7 + 7 = \blacksquare$

Algebra and Functions

8. **Which number makes this sentence true?**

41 + ■ = 45

F 3 **H** 5

G 4 **J** 6

9. **What is the missing number in the number pattern?**

48, 44, 40, ■, 32, 28

A 36 **C** 38

B 37 **D** 42

10. **Which names the same number as 12 + 14 + 16?**

F 12 + 14 − 16

G 12 + 16 + 14

H 12 + 14 + 1 + 6

J 12 + 1 + 4 + 6

11. **One sticker costs 6¢. Two stickers cost 12¢. Three stickers cost 18¢. How much would 4 stickers cost?**

A 20¢

B 24¢

C 30¢

D 36¢

12. 85
+22

F 107 **J** 17

G 117 **K** NH

H 63

Geometry and Measurement

13. **How many sides does this shape have?**

A 3 sides

B 4 sides

C 5 sides

D 6 sides

14. **Which number is inside the rectangle and outside the triangle?**

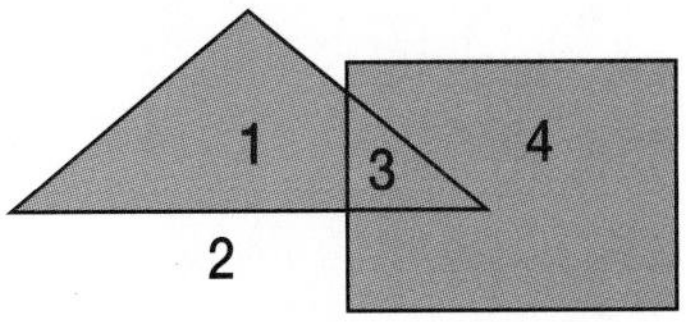

F 1 **H** 3

G 2 **J** 4

15. **Which object is shaped like a cone?**

A 

C 

B 

D 

16. **Which space shape could you use to draw a circle?**

F 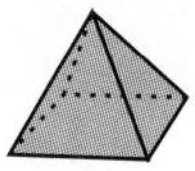

H 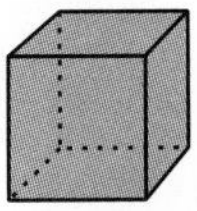

G 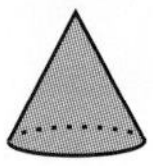

J 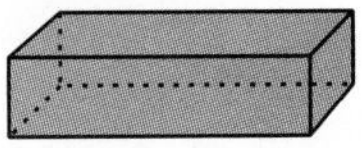

CHAPTER 3

Measurement

Diagnosing Readiness

In Chapter 3, you will use these skills:

Ⓐ Telling Time

(Grade 2)

Write the time.

1. 

2. 

3. 

4. 

5. Caroline started playing the piano at 11:00 A.M. She played for 30 minutes. What time was it then?

Ⓑ Adding

(Grade 2)

6. 12 + 12

7. 100 + 100 + 100

8. 3 + 3 + 3 + 3

9. 1,000 + 1,000

10. Elena has $16. Nathaniel has the same amount as Elena. How much money do they have altogether?

C Missing Numbers

(Grade 2)

Find each missing number.

11. $3 + ■ = 9$

12. $■ + 7 = 13$

13. $16 - ■ = 8$

14. $■ + 5 = 14$

15. $11 - ■ = 6$

D Comparing Numbers

(Grade 2)

Compare. Write >, <, or =.

16. 10 ● 100

17. 78 ● 77

18. 40 ● 39

19. 315 ● 31

20. The plant was 15 inches tall. Then the plant grew 3 inches. How tall is the plant now?

E Measurement

(Grade 2)

Measure each line to the nearest inch.

21. ————————

22. ——————————————————

23. Would you measure the length of your finger in inches or feet?

24. Would you measure the length of a car in centimeters or meters?

25. Does a feather weigh more or less than one pound?

26. Does a spoon hold more or less than one liter?

27. Is a paintbrush heavier or lighter than one kilogram?

To the Family and Student

Looking Back

In Grade 2, students use standard and nonstandard units to measure length. They explore concepts of weight, capacity, and temperature using metric and customary units.

Chapter 3

Measurement

In this chapter, students measure length to the nearest $\frac{1}{2}$ inch, $\frac{1}{4}$ inch, and one centimeter. They expand their understanding of customary and metric units used to measure weight, capacity, and temperature.

Looking Ahead

In Grade 4, students review customary and metric units of measure.

Math and Everyday Living

Opportunities to apply the concepts of Chapter 3 abound in everyday situations. During the chapter, think about how an understanding of units of measure is needed in a variety of real-world problems. The following examples suggest just several of the many situations that could launch a discussion about using units of measurement.

Math and Hobbies Fabric is sold by the yard. A quilt pattern calls for 3 yards of fabric. How many feet are in 3 yards?

Math and the Weather The meteorologist forecasts tomorrow's high temperature to be 82°F. Do you plan to wear shorts or a sweater?

Math and Transportation Your father stops at a gas station to fill up the family car with gasoline. What unit of measure would be used for the gasoline?

Math and Science You are doing a science experiment where you must add small quantities of a liquid to a test tube. Would you use milliliters or liters to measure the liquid?

Math at Home A bread recipe calls for 12 ounces of flour. You have a 5-pound sack of flour. Do you have enough flour to make the recipe? How do you know?

Math at School It's only 10:45 A.M. and you're hungry! Lunch is at 12:15 P.M. How much longer is it until lunch time?

Math and Exercise You buy one liter of water for you and a friend to drink after you finish jogging. If you each drink the same amount of water, how many milliliters will you each drink?

California Content Standards in Chapter 3 Lessons*

	Teach and Practice	Practice
Algebra and Functions		
1.4 Express simple unit conversions in symbolic form (e.g., __ inches = __ feet × 12).	3-3, 3-4	3-7
Measurement and Geometry		
1.0 Students choose and use appropriate units and measurement tools to quantify the properties of objects.	3-10	
1.1 Choose the appropriate tools and units (metric and U.S.) and estimate and measure the length, liquid volume, and weight/mass of given objects.	3-3, 3-4, 3-5, 3-7, 3-8, 3-9	
1.4 Carry out simple unit conversions within a system of measurement (e.g., centimeters and meters, hours and minutes).	3-3, 3-4	3-7, 3-8, 3-9
1.5 (Grade 2) Determine the duration of time intervals in hours (e.g., 11:00 a.m. to 4:00 p.m.).	3-1	

	Teach and Practice	Practice
Mathematical Reasoning		
1.0 Students make decisions about how to approach problems.	3-2	
1.1 Analyze problems by identifying relationships, distinguishing relevant from irrelevant information, sequencing and prioritizing information, and observing patterns.	3-6, 3-11	3-1, 3-3, 3-4, 3-5, 3-10
1.2 Determine when and how to break a problem into simpler parts.		3-6
3.2 Note the method of deriving the solution and demonstrate a conceptual understanding of the derivation by solving similar problems.		3-6

* The symbol (🔑) indicates a key standard as designated in the Mathematics Framework for California Public Schools. Full statements of the California Content Standards are found at the beginning of this book following the Table of Contents.

LESSON 3-1

Elapsed Time

California Content Standard *Measurement and Geometry 1.5, Grade 2: Determine the duration of time intervals in hours . . .. (This lesson extends elapsed time to 5-minute intervals.)*

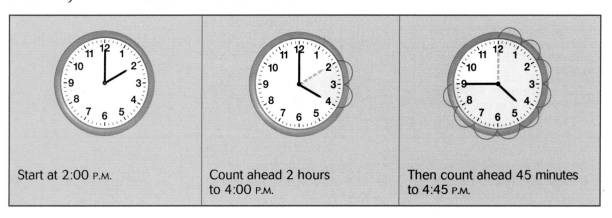

Math Link You know how to tell time. Now you will learn how to find how much time has passed.

Warm-Up Review

Write the time shown.

1. 

2. 1 hour = ▪ minutes

3. The soccer game begins at 10:45 A.M. Is this time closer to 10:00 A.M. or 11:00 A.M.?

Example 1

Little League baseball is popular all over the world. Suppose a game starts at 2:00 P.M. It lasts two hours and forty-five minutes. When does it end?

Start at 2:00 P.M.

Count ahead 2 hours to 4:00 P.M.

Then count ahead 45 minutes to 4:45 P.M.

The game ends at 4:45 P.M.

Example 2

Look at the pair of times. Find how much time has passed.

Start 12:35 P.M.
End 1:45 P.M.

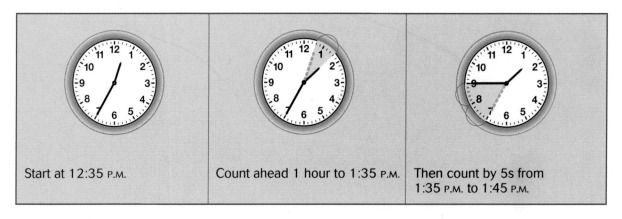

Start at 12:35 P.M.

Count ahead 1 hour to 1:35 P.M.

Then count by 5s from 1:35 P.M. to 1:45 P.M.

1 hour and 10 minutes has passed between times.

Additional Standard: Mathematical Reasoning 1.1 *(See p. 91.)*

Guided Practice *For another example, see Set A on p. 122.*

Look at each pair of times. Find how much time has passed.

1. Start 10:50 P.M.
End 11:50 P.M.

2. Start 7:35 A.M.
End 8:00 A.M.

3. Start 3:25 P.M.
End 6:40 P.M.

4. The game begins at 11:00 A.M. It lasts 2 hours and 30 minutes. When does it end?

Independent Practice *For more practice, see Set A on p. 125.*

Look at each pair of times. Find how much time has passed.

5. Start 1:10 P.M.
End 1:15 P.M.

6. Start 2:20 P.M.
End 3:50 P.M.

7. Start 8:25 A.M.
End 10:00 A.M.

Write the time each clock will show in 50 minutes.

8. 

9. 

10. 

11. 

12. **Math Reasoning** The swimming pool is open from 9:15 A.M. to 12:15 P.M. and from 1:00 P.M. to 5:30 P.M. each day. How long is the pool open each day?

Mixed Review

13. **Algebra** Give three numbers that make the following statement true: 3 + ■ is less than 10.

Algebra Find each missing number.

14. 19 − ■ = 5

15. ■ + 2 = 11

16. 25 − ■ = 18

Test Prep Choose the correct letter for each answer.

17. What is the value of the digit 8 in the number 7,863?
(1-7)

A 8 **B** 80 **C** 800 **D** 8,000

18. Mandy had $13.50. Her mom gave her another $2.35. How much does she have now?
(2-5)

F $11.15 **G** $14.70 **H** $15.75 **J** $15.85 **K** NH

LESSON 3-2

Understand
Plan
Solve
Look Back

Problem-Solving Skill:

Exact Numbers or Estimates

Warm-Up Review

Estimate each sum.

1. 37 + 28 **2.** 91 + 63

3. 45 + 31 **4.** 27 + 87

5. The bus left school at 8:35 A.M. and arrived at the museum at 9:25 A.M. How long was the bus ride?

California Content Standard *Mathematical Reasoning 1.0: Students make decisions about how to approach problems.*

Read for Understanding

In an exciting soccer game yesterday the Eagles beat the Hornets. Over 120 fans watched the game, which lasted about 90 minutes. After the game, Coach Ramos and 4 parents treated the winning team to popcorn.

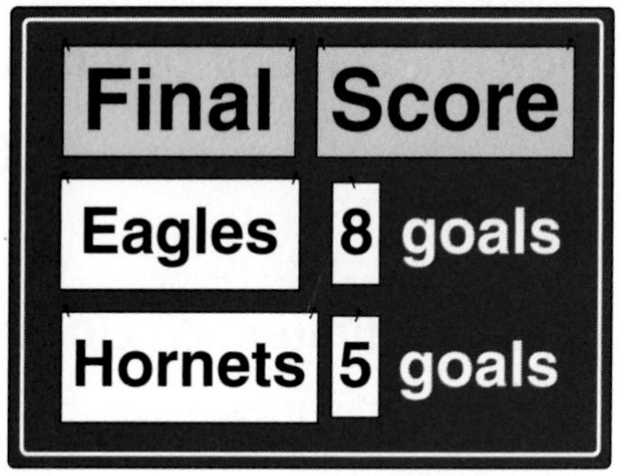

1. How many goals did the Eagles score?
2. How long did the game last?
3. Who treated the players to popcorn?

Think and Discuss

MATH FOCUS

Exact Numbers or Estimates

Estimates are not exact numbers. Words like *about, over, less than,* and *almost* can tell you that numbers are estimated, not exact.

Reread the paragraph at the top of the page.

4. Can you tell exactly how many fans there were? Why or why not?
5. How many people treated the winning team to popcorn? Is your answer an exact number or an estimate? Explain how you know.
6. Why is it important to be able to know if numbers are exact or if they are estimates?

Guided Practice

Cara played in a soccer game for almost 15 minutes. Her team scored 2 goals in that time. Then a rainstorm stopped the game for over 30 minutes. About 25 fans left the game during the storm. Two of them returned when the rain stopped.

1. How long was the game stopped by rain?

a. Exactly 30 minutes

b. Less than 30 minutes

c. More than 30 minutes

2. How many people returned to the game when the rain stopped?

a. 2 people

b. 25 people

c. 30 people

3. Which of these numbers is *not* an estimate?

a. 15 minutes

b. 2 goals

c. 30 minutes

4. Which of these words tells you that 25 fans is an estimate?

a. game

b. about

c. left

Independent Practice

One Eagles game played during a light rain lasted for over 50 minutes. About 40 people watched the game. Only 8 people had umbrellas. The Eagles won 2 goals to 1.

5. How many people might have watched the game?

a. 42 people

b. 20 people

c. 73 people

6. How many people at the game had umbrellas?

a. 8 people

b. More than 8 people

c. Fewer than 8 people

7. Which number below is used as an estimate?

a. 2 goals

b. 8 people

c. 50 minutes

8. Which of these words tells you that 50 minutes is an estimate?

a. about

b. over

c. only

9. How do you know that your answer to Exercise 7 is an estimate?

Use Homework Workbook 3-2.

LESSON 3-3

Using Customary Units of Length

California Content Standard *Measurement and Geometry 1.1: Choose the appropriate tools and units . . . and estimate and measure the length . . . of given objects. Also, Algebra and Functions 1.4 and Measurement and Geometry 1.4 (See p. 91.)*

Warm-Up Review

1. 3 + 3
2. 12 + 12 + 12
3. Lacy's paper airplane flew 12 feet. Darci's plane flew 10 feet. Ted's plane flew 8 feet. How much farther did Lacy's plane fly than Ted's plane?

Math Link You know how to measure length to the nearest inch. Now you will learn to measure length to the nearest $\frac{1}{2}$ inch and $\frac{1}{4}$ inch.

Word Bank

inch (in.)
foot (ft)
yard (yd)
mile (mi)

Inches are used to measure short lengths. **Feet, yards,** and **miles** are units used to measure longer lengths.

A small paper clip is about 1 **inch** long.

A football is about 1 **foot** long.

A baseball bat is about 1 **yard** long.

Most people can walk 1 **mile** in about 25 minutes.

Customary Units of Length
1 ft = 12 in.
1 yd = 3 ft
1 yd = 36 in.
1 mi = 1,760 yd
1 mi = 5,280 ft

Example 1

Would you use *inches*, *feet*, *yards*, or *miles* to measure the length of a paper clip?

Think: The paper clip is longer than 1 inch. The paper clip is much shorter than 1 foot, 1 yard, and 1 mile.

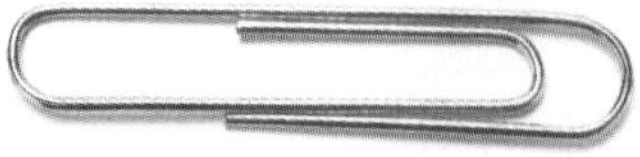

So, inches would be used to measure the length of a paper clip.

Example 2

Find the missing number.

■ ft = 2 yd

Since there are 3 feet in 1 yard, there are 3 feet + 3 feet, or 6 feet, in 2 yards.

So, 6 ft = 2 yd.

 Additional Standard: Mathematical Reasoning 1.1 (See p. 91.)

Example 3

How long are the stamps to the nearest $\frac{1}{2}$ inch?

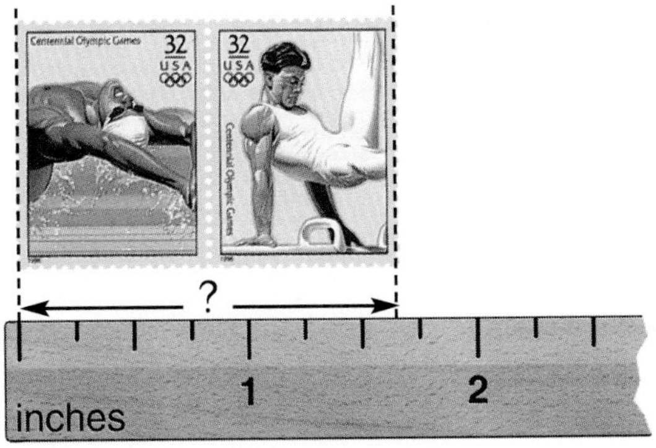

The stamps are closer to $1\frac{1}{2}$ inches long than to 2 inches long.

So, the stamps are $1\frac{1}{2}$ inches long to the nearest $\frac{1}{2}$ inch.

Example 4

How long is the stamp to the nearest $\frac{1}{4}$ inch?

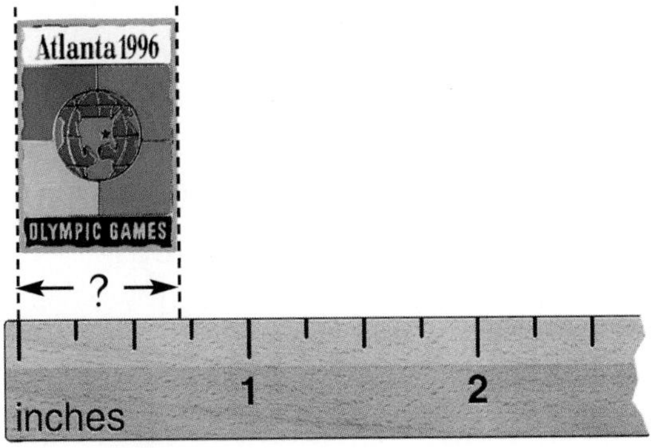

The stamp is closer to $\frac{3}{4}$ inch long than to $\frac{1}{2}$ inch long.

So, the stamp is $\frac{3}{4}$ inch long to the nearest $\frac{1}{4}$ inch.

When you measure, remember to line up the first mark on the ruler with the left side of the object that you are measuring.

Guided Practice

For another example, see Set B on p. 122.

Estimate each length. Then measure to the nearest $\frac{1}{2}$ inch.

1.

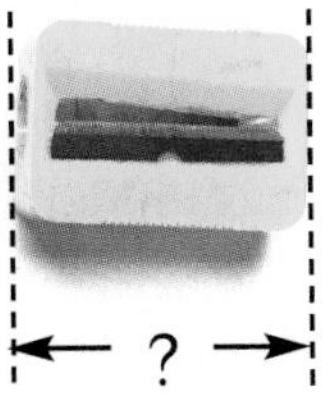

2.

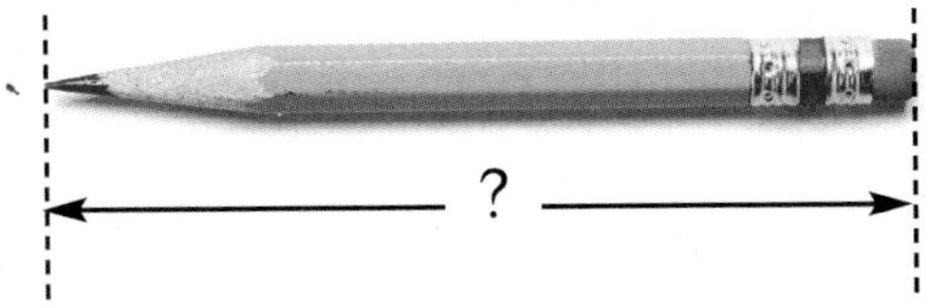

3. Mrs. O'Brien's class made a poster that measures 2 feet long. How long is the poster in inches?

Independent Practice

For more practice, see Set B on p. 125.

Estimate each length. Then measure to the nearest $\frac{1}{2}$ inch.

4.

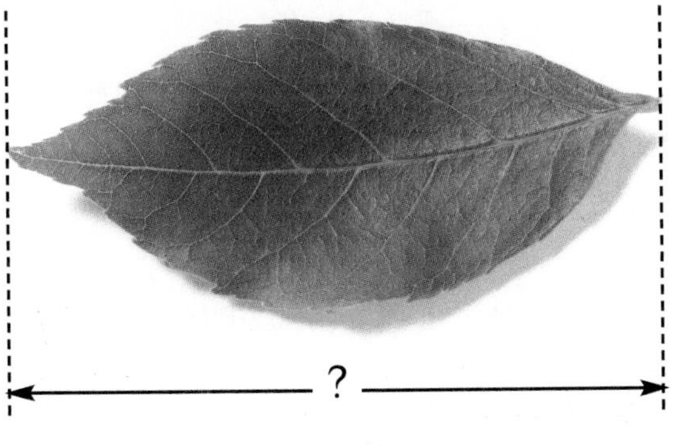

5.

Estimate each length. Then measure to the nearest $\frac{1}{4}$ inch.

6.

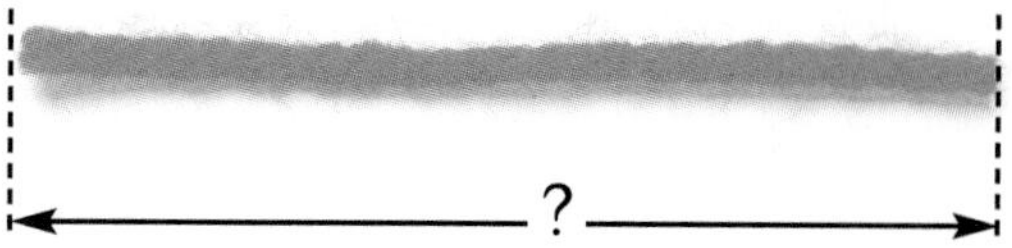

7.

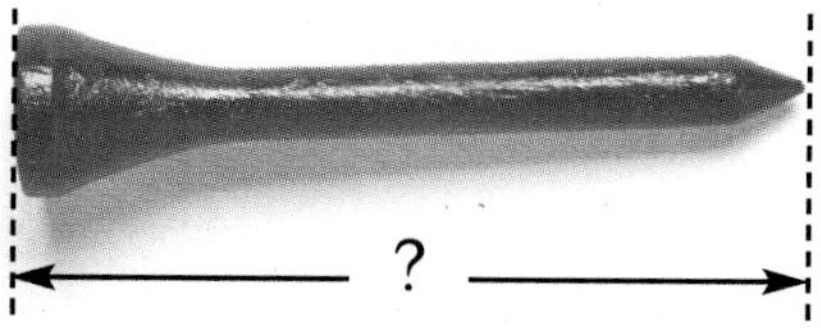

Which unit would you use to measure each item? Write *inch, foot, yard,* or *mile.*

8. length of a marker

9. distance between two towns

Find each missing number.

10. 1 ft = ■ in.

11. ■ ft = 1 mi

12. ■ yd = 1 mi

13. 36 in. = ■ yd

14. 36 in. = ■ ft

15. ■ ft = 3 yd

16. Mrs. Wilson's class made a banner that is 7 feet long. About how many yards long is the banner?

17. Math Reasoning Would it make sense to measure the length of a swimming pool with a ruler?

Mixed Review

18. Frank's party started at 5:30 P.M. It was over at 7:15 P.M. How long did the party last?

Algebra Find each missing number.

19. ■ + 8 = 15

20. 18 − ■ = 9

21. 6 + ■ = 11

Find how much time has passed.

22. Start 8:10 A.M.
End 8:55 A.M.

23. Start 7:30 P.M.
End 10:00 P.M.

24. Start 6:15 A.M.
End 10:45 A.M.

Test Prep **Choose the correct letter for each answer.**

25. 126 − 29 =
(2-8)

A 96 **B** 97 **C** 103 **D** 193 **E** NH

26. Which of these times come between 11:40 A.M. and a quarter after noon?
(3-1)

F 11:15 A.M. **G** 11:35 A.M. **H** 12:10 P.M. **J** 12:20 P.M. **K** NH

Use Homework Workbook 3–3.

Multiple-Choice Cumulative Review

Choose the correct letter for each answer.

1. Choose the clock that displays a half hour after 12:05.

A

C

B

D

2. Lola needs to be home by 5:30 P.M. It takes her 15 minutes to ride her bike from her friend's house to the post office and another 10 minutes to ride from the post office home. How can you find the time Lola needs to leave her friend's house?

F Start at 5:30 P.M. and subtract 25 minutes.

G Start at 5:30 P.M. and add 25 minutes.

H Start at 5:30 P.M. and subtract 5 minutes.

J Start at 5:30 P.M. and add 15 minutes then subtract 10 minutes.

3. How many inches are in 3 feet?

A 12 inches
B 18 inches
C 24 inches
D 36 inches
E NH

4. What is the value of the digit 3 in the number 4,038?

F 3
G 30
H 300
J 3,000
K NH

5. Tanita has 84¢. She buys one sticker for 13¢. How much money does she have left?

A 61¢
B 71¢
C 79¢
D 97¢
E NH

6.

$$\begin{array}{r} 156 \\ +\ 37 \\ \hline \end{array}$$

F 173
G 183
H 193
J 203
K NH

7. Round 37,605 to the nearest thousand.

A 30,600
B 36,000
C 37,600
D 38,000
E NH

LESSON 3-4

Using Customary Capacity

Warm-Up Review

Find each missing number.

1. ■ ft = 12 in.
2. 1 yd = ■ in.
3. ■ ft = 1 yd
4. Tia has 5 dolls, May has 8 dolls, and Leah has 4 more dolls than Tia. Who has the most dolls?

California Content Standards *Measurement and Geometry 1.1: Choose the appropriate tools and units . . . and estimate and measure . . . liquid volume . . .. Also, Algebra and Functions 1.4 and Measurement and Geometry 1.4 (See p. 91.)*

Math Link In the previous lesson, you learned about some units used to measure length. Now you will learn about some units used to measure how much liquid a container holds.

Word Bank

capacity
cup (c)
pint (pt)
quart (qt)
gallon (gal)

The amount of liquid a container holds is called its **capacity**.

Units used to measure capacity include **cups**, **pints**, **quarts**, and **gallons**.

The chart below shows how these units of capacity are related.

2 cups = 1 pint

4 cups = 2 pints = 1 quart

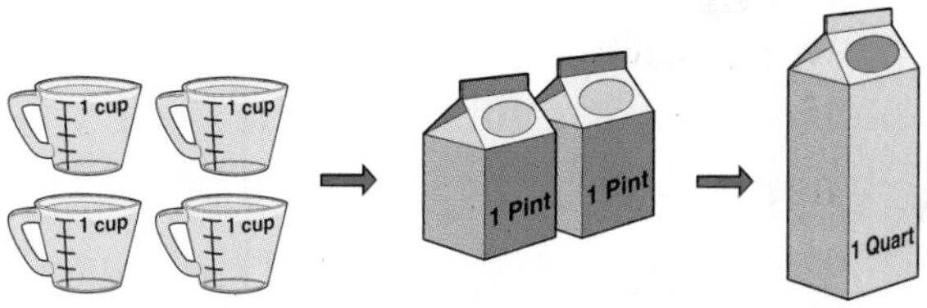

16 cups = 8 pint = 4 quarts = 1 gallon

Example

Find the missing number.

■ c = 1 qt

The chart above shows that there are 4 cups in 1 quart.

So, 4 c = 1 qt.

 Additional Standard: Mathematical Reasoning 1.1 (See p. 91.)

Guided Practice *For another example, see Set C on p. 122.*

Find each missing number.

1. 1 pt = ▒ c

2. 1 gal = ▒ qt

3. ▒ pt = 1 qt

4. Adults should drink about 8 cups of water per day to help them stay healthy. How many quarts is that?

Independent Practice *For more practice, see Set C on p. 125.*

Find each missing number.

5. ▒ c = 1 gal

6. 4 c = ▒ qt

7. 8 pt = ▒ qt

Choose the better estimate for each container.

8.

1 c or 1 gal

9.

1 c or 1 qt

10.

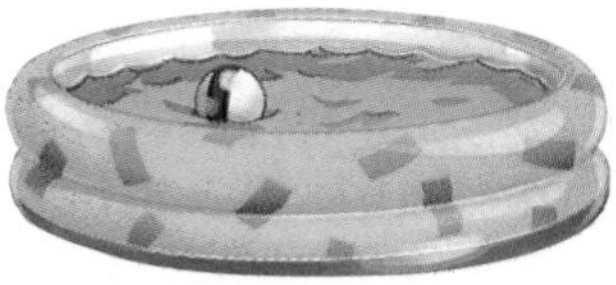

50 c or 50 gal

11. Math Reasoning Suppose you want to take 25 cups of water to a track meet. What is the least number of gallon containers you should take?

Mixed Review

12. Bonita read a book with 103 pages. Then she read a book with 119 pages. How many pages did she read in all?

Estimate each length. Then measure to the nearest $\frac{1}{4}$ inch.

13.

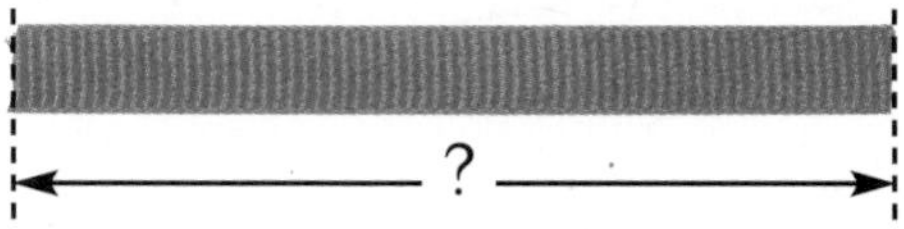

14.

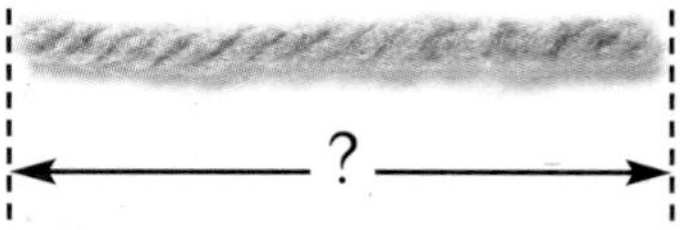

Test Prep **Choose the correct letter for each answer.**

15. Which number could you subtract from 23 without regrouping?
(2-8)

A 2 **B** 4 **C** 6 **D** 8

16. Suppose it is 4:25 P.M. What time was it 60 minutes ago?
(3-1)

F 5:25 P.M. **G** 4:00 P.M. **H** 3:35 P.M. **J** 3:25 P.M.

LESSON 3-5

Using Ounces and Pounds

California Content Standard *Measurement and Geometry 1.1: Choose the appropriate tools and units . . . and estimate and measure the . . . weight/mass of given objects.*

Warm-Up Review

Compare. Write >, <, or =.

1. 1 ft ● 10 in.
2. 1 c ● 1 pt
3. Tim bought 1 pound of cheese, 2 pounds of sausage, and 5 pounds of hamburger. How many pounds of meat did he buy?

Math Link You know that weight can be measured in pounds. Now you will learn the unit of measure used for objects that weigh less than a pound.

Word Bank

ounce (oz)
pound (lb)

Ounces and **pounds** are units used to measure weight.

An **ounce** is a unit of weight that is less than a pound.

16 ounces = 1 pound

About 1 pound

Example 1

Compare. Write >, <, or =.

13 oz ● 1 lb

You know that there are 16 ounces in 1 pound.

Since 13 ounces is less than 16 ounces, 13 ounces is less than 1 pound.

So, 13 oz < 1 lb.

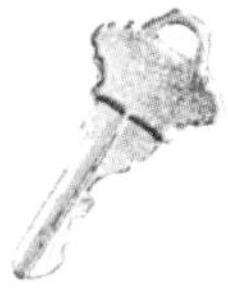

About 1 ounce

Example 2

Would 1 ounce or 1 pound be a better estimate for the weight of a loaf of bread?

Think: A loaf of bread weighs much more than a key. A loaf of bread could weigh the same as a football.

So, 1 pound is a better estimate.

Additional Standard: Mathematical Reasoning 1.1 (See p. 91.)

Guided Practice *For another example, see Set D on p. 123.*

Compare. Write >, <, or =.

1. 16 oz ● 1 lb **2.** 34 oz ● 2 lb **3.** 3 lb ● 50 oz

4. Adam bought a 15-ounce steak. Luis bought a 1-pound steak. How much heavier is Luis' steak than Adam's steak?

Independent Practice *For more practice, see Set D on p. 126.*

Compare. Write >, <, or =.

5. 1 oz ● 1 lb **6.** 32 oz ● 2 lb **7.** 1 lb ● 18 oz

Choose the better estimate.

8. 
2 lb or 2 oz

9. 
1 lb or 1 oz

10. 
8 lb or 8 oz

11. 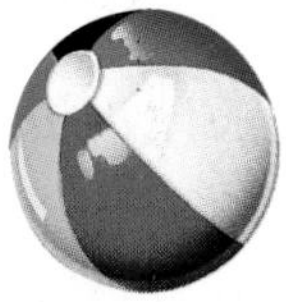
3 oz or 3 lb

12. A tennis racket weighs about 12 ounces. A tennis ball weighs about 2 ounces. How much heavier is a tennis racket than 4 tennis balls?

Mixed Review

13. Suppose you spend $3.15 on a book and $1.58 on crayons. You give the clerk $5.00. What is your change?

Estimate each length. Then measure to the nearest $\frac{1}{2}$ inch.

14. 

15. 

Test Prep Choose the correct letter for each answer.

16. (2-4)

$$\begin{array}{r} 362 \\ +\ 58 \\ \hline \end{array}$$

A 310 **D** 530
B 420 **E** NH
C 520

17. (3-4) What is the missing number?

1 gal = ■ qt

F 2 **J** 8
G 4 **K** NH
H 6

LESSON 3-6

Understand
Plan
Solve
Look Back

Problem-Solving Strategy:
Work Backward

California Content Standard *Mathematical Reasoning 1.1: Analyze problems by identifying relationships . . . [and] sequencing and prioritizing information . . ..*

Warm-Up Review

1. $1.25 + $3.50
2. $10.00 − $8.25
3. Find how much time has passed.
   Start 8:15 A.M.
   End 9:45 A.M.
4. The movie started at 2:15 P.M. It was 1 hour and 30 minutes long. When did the movie end?

Leah and Dan hiked from the lake to Hippo Rock. It took 1 hour and 5 minutes to hike from the lake to Cave Shelter. Then it took 25 minutes to get from Cave Shelter to Hippo Rock. They arrived at Hippo Rock at 2:45 P.M. At what time did they leave the lake?

Understand

What do you need to find?

You need to find the time that the hikers left the lake.

Plan

How can you solve the problem?

You can **work backward** from the time the hikers reached Hippo Rock. Subtract the time it took to hike from Cave Shelter to Hippo Rock. Then subtract the time it took to hike from the lake to Cave Shelter.

Solve

Start at 2:45 P.M.	Subtract 25 minutes.	Subtract 1 hour and 5 minutes.
This is the time the hikers reached Hippo Rock.	This is the time it took to get from Cave Shelter to Hippo Rock.	This is the time it took to get from the lake to Cave Shelter.

Leah and Dan left the lake at 1:15 P.M.

Look Back

How can you check if your answer is reasonable?

Additional Standards: Mathematical Reasoning 1.2, 3.2 (See p. 91.)

Guided Practice

1. Phil bought 2 toy cars for $3 each and a yo-yo for $1.25. His change was $0.75. How much money did he give the clerk?

Independent Practice

Item	Cost
trail mix	$2.75
bottled water	$1.75
map	$2.50

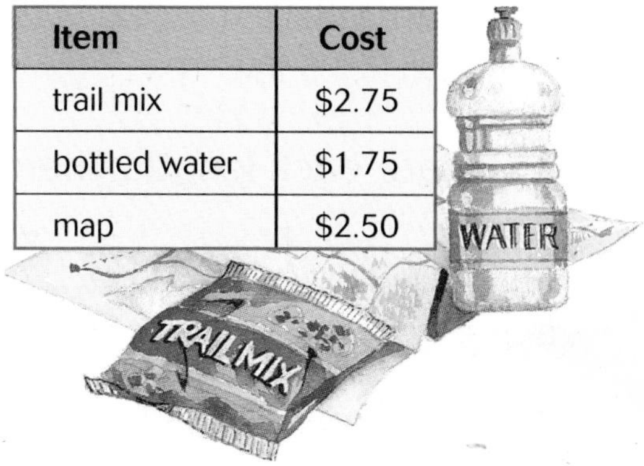

2. Use the data at the right. Beth's change was $15.75 when she bought a map and a bottle of water. How much money did she give the clerk?

3. Leah goes on a hike every other month. She went on her fourth hike in October. In what month did Leah go on her first hike?

4. The park is 12 blocks from Maggie's house. When Maggie leaves her house she first walks to the fire station. Then she walks 2 more blocks to the post office, then another 5 blocks to the park. How many blocks is it from her house to the fire station?

Mixed Review

Try these or other strategies to solve each problem. Tell which strategy you used.

Problem-Solving Strategies

- *Make a Table*
- *Use Logical Reasoning*
- *Draw a Picture*
- *Write a Number Sentence*

5. Bob, Joan, and Pat are hiking on a trail in the woods. Joan is in front of Bob. Pat is between Joan and Bob. Who is first in line? Who is last in line?

6. A bag of mixed nuts and raisins costs $1.25. How many bags can you buy with $5.00?

7. Walt drank 2 cups of water during the first hour of his hike. If his water bottle holds 8 cups, how many cups of water does he have left?

Use Homework Workbook 3–6.

Diagnostic Checkpoint

Look at each pair of times. Write how much time has passed.

1. (3-1) Start 1:30 P.M.
End 2:15 P.M.

2. (3-1) Start 11:55 A.M.
End 12:05 P.M.

3. (3-1) Start 5:25 P.M.
End 6:50 P.M.

Estimate each length. Then measure to the nearest $\frac{1}{2}$ inch.

4. (3-3) 

5. (3-3) 

Choose the best estimate.

6. (3-3) the length of an earthworm
3 in. or 1 ft

7. (3-3) the length of a skateboard
30 yd or 30 in.

8. (3-4) the capacity of a fish tank
2 c or 2 gal

9. (3-5) the weight of a large dog
75 lb or 75 oz

Find each missing number.

10. (3-4) ■ c = 1 pt

11. (3-4) 1 qt = ■ c

12. (3-4) ■ gal = 4 qt

Compare. Write >, <, or =.

13. (3-5) 1 lb ● 1 oz

14. (3-5) 24 oz ● 1 lb

15. (3-5) 2 lb ● 32 oz

16. (3-2) Jamie catches the school bus at 7:55 A.M. School begins at 8:35 A.M. Is it reasonable to think that Jamie could spend 30 minutes on the bus? Explain.

17. (3-6) Rick has $3.00 left after buying a ticket for $4.50 and popcorn for $2.50 at the movie theater. How much money did Rick bring with him to the movie theater?

18. (3-6) Amy cuts 36 in. of a board to make a shelf. Then she cuts the rest of the board into 4 equal sections. Each section is 9 in. long. How long was the original board?

LESSON 3-7

Using Metric Units of Length

California Content Standard *Measurement and Geometry 1.1: Choose the appropriate tools and units . . . and estimate and measure the length . . . of given objects.*

Math Link You know how to estimate and measure length using inches, feet, yards, and miles. Now you will learn how to estimate and measure lengths using metric units.

Warm-Up Review

Find each missing number.

1. ■ ft = 12 inches
2. 1 mile = ■ yd
3. 6 feet = ■ yd
4. Jane jumped 1 foot off the ground. Sam jumped 10 inches. Who jumped higher? How much higher?

Centimeters and **decimeters** are units used to measure shorter lengths. **Meters** and **kilometers** are units used to measure longer lengths.

Word Bank

centimeter (cm)
decimeter (dm)
meter (m)
kilometer (km)

A **centimeter** is about the width of your finger.

A **decimeter** is about the length of a craft stick.

A **meter** is about the width of a door.

A **kilometer** is about the distance you walk in 15 minutes.

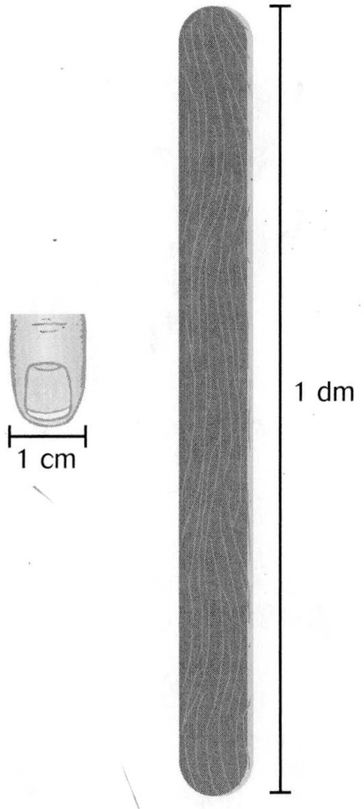

Metric Units of Length
1 dm = 10 cm
1 m = 100 cm
1 km = 1,000 m

Example 1

Would you use *centimeters, decimeters, meters,* or *kilometers* to measure the length of a classroom?

Think: The length of a classroom is much longer than a centimeter or decimeter. It is much shorter than a kilometer. It is most likely several meters long.

So, meters would be used to measure the length of a classroom.

*Additional Standards: Algebra and Functions 1.4; Measurement and Geometry 1.4 (**See p. 91.**)*

Example 2

Find the length of each golf tee to the nearest centimeter.

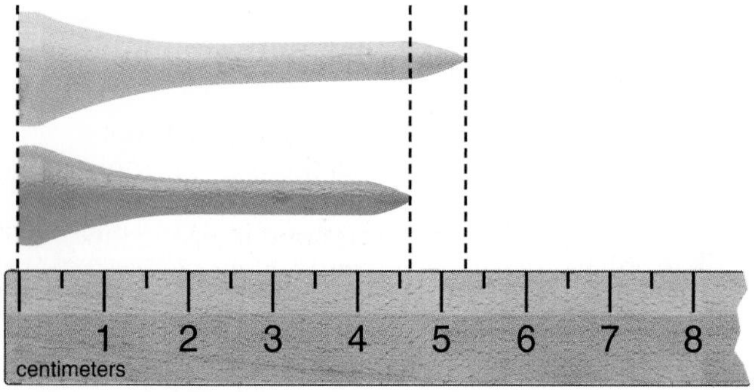

The yellow golf tee is longer than 5 centimeters, but closer to 5 centimeters than 6 centimeters.

The orange golf tee is shorter than 5 centimeters, but closer to 5 centimeters than 4 centimeters.

To the nearest centimeter, each golf tee measures 5 centimeters long.

Guided Practice *For another example, see Set E on p. 123.*

Estimate each length. Then measure to the nearest centimeter.

1. 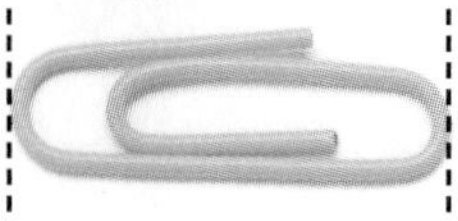

2. 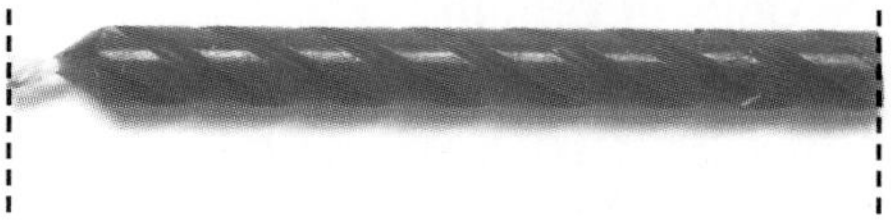

3. A shoelace measures 3 decimeters. How many centimeters long is it?

Independent Practice *For more practice, see Set E on p. 126.*

Estimate each length. Then measure to the nearest centimeter.

4. 

5. 

What unit would you use to measure each item? Write *centimeter, decimeter, meter,* or *kilometer.*

6. length of your foot

7. length of a paper clip

8. distance between cities

9. length of a playground

Choose the better estimate.

10. length of a skateboard
7 cm or 70 cm

11. length of your math book
28 cm or 28 km

Find each missing number.

12. 100 cm = ■ m

13. 1 km = ■ m

14. ■ cm = 2 m

The map shows the route of a park path. Use the map for Exercises 15–17.

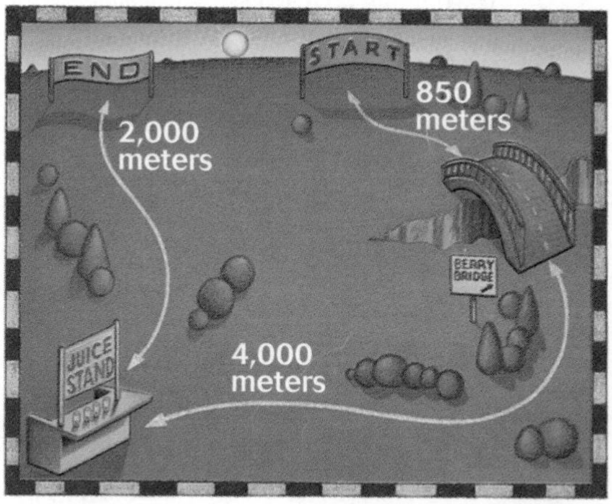

15. Is the distance from Start to Berry Bridge more or less than 1 kilometer?

16. How many kilometers is the distance from Berry Bridge to the juice stand?

17. Is the distance from the juice stand to the end of the path less than, more than, or the same as the distance from Start to Berry Bridge?

Mixed Review

18. Suppose a kitten weighs 2 pounds. How many ounces does it weigh?

Compare. Write >, <, or =.

19. 1 qt ● 1 pt

20. 1 pt ● 2 c

21. 12 oz ● 1 lb

Test Prep **Choose the correct letter for each answer.**

22. (Gr. 2) Which number is NOT an odd number?

A 77 **C** 91
B 80 **D** 105

23. (2-14) **Algebra** What number belongs in the box?

16 + ■ = 21

F 4 **H** 6
G 5 **J** 37

LESSON 3-8

Using Milliliters and Liters

California Content Standard *Measurement and Geometry 1.1: Choose the appropriate tools and units . . . and estimate . . . liquid volume . . ..*

Warm-Up Review

List the units from smallest to largest.

1. pint, gallon, cup, quart
2. meter, centimeter, kilometer, decimeter
3. Marty is 8 years old. Curtis is 14 years old and Ben is 4 years older than Marty. How much older is Curtis than Ben?

Math Link You know that you can use cups, pints, quarts, and gallons to measure capacity. Now you will learn some metric units that you can use to measure capacity.

A **liter** and a **milliliter** are metric units used to measure capacity.

Word Bank

liter (L)
milliliter (mL)

1,000 mL = 1 L

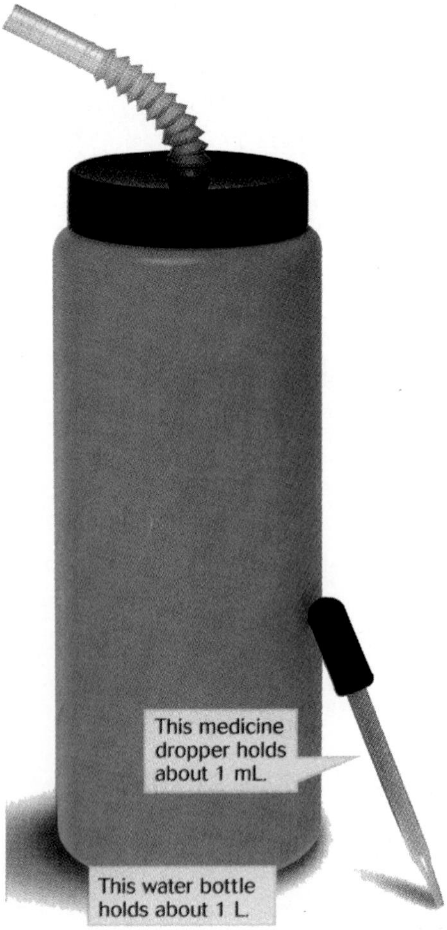
This medicine dropper holds about 1 mL.
This water bottle holds about 1 L.

Example 1

Marsha wants to find out how much liquid a teacup holds. Should she measure the amount of liquid the teacup holds in milliliters or liters?

Think: A teacup holds more than a medicine dropper, but less than a sports bottle.

So, Marsha should measure the amount of liquid a teacup holds in milliliters.

Example 2

Would 2 milliliters or 2 liters be a better estimate for the amount of liquid a tea kettle can hold?

Think: A tea kettle holds much more than 2 medicine droppers. It could hold as much as 2 sports bottles.

So, 2 liters is a better estimate.

 Additional Standard: Measurement and Geometry 1.4 *(See p. 91.)*

Guided Practice *For another example, see Set F on p. 123.*

Choose a unit to measure the capacity of each item. Write *liters* or *milliliters*.

1. bathtub　　**2.** car gasoline tank　　**3.** drinking glass

4. How many milliliters are in a 2 liter container?

Independent Practice *For more practice, see Set F on p. 127.*

Choose a unit to measure the capacity of each item. Write *liters* or *milliliters*.

5. soup can　　**6.** spoon　　**7.** swimming pool

Choose the better estimate.

8.

1 L or 150 mL

9.

250 mL or 25 L

10.

40 mL or 40 L

11. Suppose you drank 650 milliliters of water after running a race. How many more milliliters would you need to drink to equal 1 liter?

Mixed Review

Estimate each length. Then measure to the nearest centimeter.

12.

13.

Compare. Write >, <, or =.

14. 1 dm ● 1 cm　　**15.** 1 lb ● 1 oz　　**16.** 16 oz ● 1 lb

Test Prep **Choose the correct letter for the answer.**

17. Ed got home at 7:45 P.M. He left the restaurant 20 minutes before that. At what time did he leave the restaurant?
(3-1)

A 7:25 P.M.　　**B** 7:20 P.M.　　**C** 6:45 P.M.　　**D** 6:25 P.M.　　**E** NH

LESSON 3-9

Using Grams and Kilograms

California Content Standard *Measurement and Geometry 1.1: Choose the appropriate tools and units . . . and estimate and measure the . . . weight/mass of given objects.*

Math Link You know that weight can be measured using pounds and ounces. You can also measure how heavy an object is using metric units.

Grams and **kilograms** are metric units used to measure how heavy an object is.

One large paper clip is about 1 gram.

A baseball bat is about 1 kilogram.

1,000 grams = 1 kilogram

Example 1

Compare. Use >, <, or =.

800 g ● 1 kg

You know that there are 1,000 grams in 1 kilogram.

Since 800 grams is less than 1,000 grams, 800 grams is less than 1 kilogram.

So, 800 g < 1 kg.

Example 2

Would 30 grams or 30 kilograms be a better estimate for how heavy an eraser is?

Think: An eraser is heavier than a paper clip, but much lighter than a baseball bat.

So, 30 grams is a better estimate.

Warm-Up Review

Compare. Write >, <, or =.

1. 1,200 ● 2,300
2. 5,000 ● 5,000
3. 1,000 ● 650
4. The red string is 5 cm long. The orange string is 8 cm long. The purple string is 7 cm longer than the red string. How much string is there altogether?

Word Bank

gram (g)
kilogram (kg)

Additional Standard: Measurement and Geometry 1.4 *(See p. 91.)*

Guided Practice *For another example, see Set G on p. 124.*

Compare. Write >, <, or =.

1. 1,000 g ● 1 kg **2.** 1 kg ● 100 g **3.** 3 kg ● 3,000 g

4. A school cafeteria uses 450 grams of salt per week. How many grams does it use in 2 weeks?

Independent Practice *For more practice, see Set G on p. 127.*

Compare. Write >, <, or =.

5. 1 g ● 1 kg **6.** 1 kg ● 10,000 g **7.** 2 kg ● 200 g

Choose the better estimate.

8. 

8 g or 800 g

9. 

1 kg or 1 g

10. 

1 g or 1 kg

11. A cook has 400 grams of apples. How many more grams of apples does he need for a recipe that calls for 2 kilograms of apples?

Mixed Review

12. Jason has 3 pints of milk. Martin has 1 quart. Who has more? How much more?

Estimate each length. Then measure to the nearest centimeter.

13. 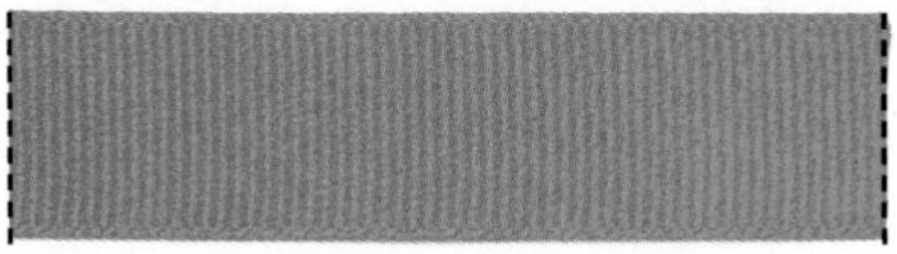

14. 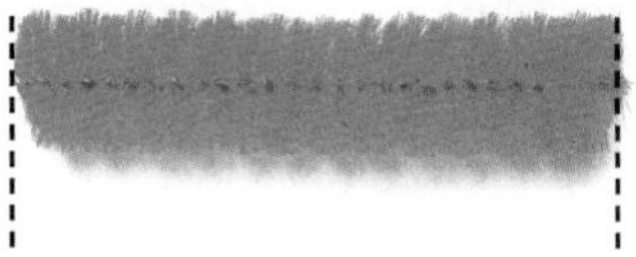

Test Prep **Choose the correct letter for each answer.**

15. (3-8) Suppose a pitcher holds 2 liters. How many milliliters does it hold?

A 200 mL **C** 2,000 mL

B 1,000 mL **D** 10,000 mL

16. (3-1) Heather's piano lesson begins at 2:30 P.M. It lasts 45 minutes. When does her lesson end?

F 3:15 P.M. **H** 2:45 P.M.

G 3:00 P.M. **J** 1:45 P.M.

LESSON 3-10

Temperature

California Content Standard *Measurement and Geometry 1.0: Students choose and use appropriate units and measurement tools to quantify the properties of objects.*

Warm-Up Review

Complete with $>$, $<$, or $=$.

1. 57 ● 73 **2.** 96 ● 95

3. Jamie has \$6. Mica has \$5. Katrina has \$2 less than the amount Jamie and Mica have together. How much money does Katrina have?

Math Link You know that a thermometer is used to measure how hot or cold something is. Now you will learn how to estimate temperature and read a thermometer.

Temperature can be measured in **degrees Celsius (°C)** and **degrees Fahrenheit (°F)**.

Word Bank

degrees Celsius (°C)
degrees Fahrenheit (°F)

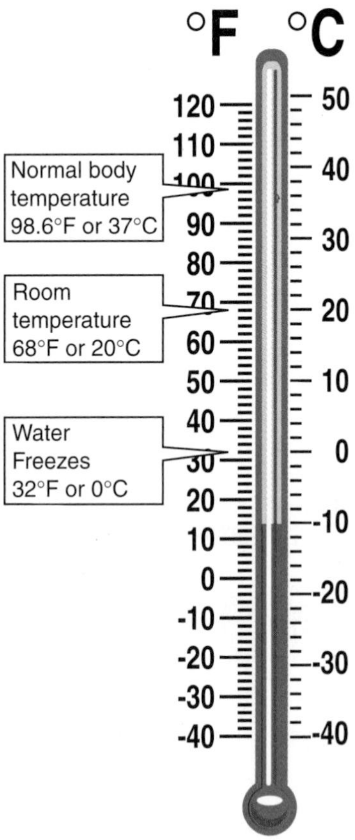

Example 1

Which is the better estimate for the temperature of the activity shown below?

30°F or 60°F

You know that water freezes at 32°F. 60°F is well above 32°F, but 30°F is very close to 32°F.

So, the better estimate is 30°F.

Example 2

Look at the thermometer at the left. What is the temperature in degrees Fahrenheit?

Step 1 Find the Fahrenheit side of the thermometer. Notice that on the thermometer the marks go up by 2s.

Step 2 Start at 10°F. Then count by 2s to where the mercury stops.
12°F, 14°F

So, the temperature is 14°F.

Additional Standard: Mathematical Reasoning 1.1 *(See p. 91.)*

Guided Practice *For another example, see Set H on p. 124.*

Choose the better estimate for the outdoor temperature of each activity.

1. flying a kite
32°F or 68°F

2. snow skiing
25°F or 75°F

3. swimming
35°C or 98°C

4. hiking
18°C or 55°C

5. In the morning the temperature was 18°C. By 2 o'clock, the temperature was 29°C. How many degrees had the temperature risen?

Independent Practice *For more practice, see Set H on p. 127.*

Choose the better estimate for the temperature

6. inside a freezer.
0°C or 32°C

7. of drinking water.
7°C or 27°C

8. inside a classroom.
20°F or 70°F

9. of hot chocolate.
70°F or 170°F

Write each temperature.

10.
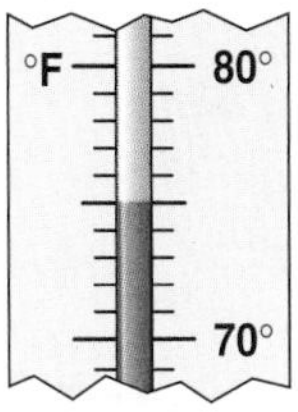

11.
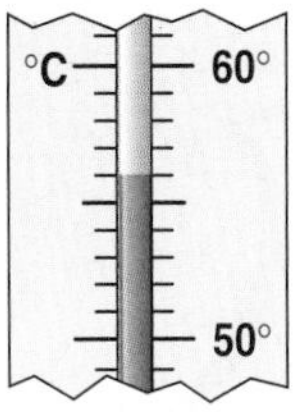

12.
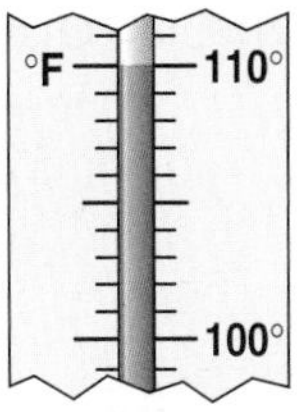

13.
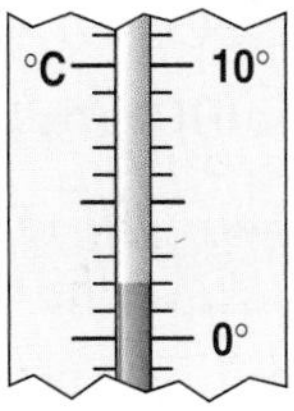

14. Math Reasoning Suppose the temperature in your home freezer is 30°F. Can you make ice? Explain why or why not.

Mixed Review

15. Round 2,389 to the nearest hundred.

16. 468 + 203

17. 3,009 − 156

18. 4,775 + 2,806

19. 1 mL ● 1 L

20. 1,000 mL ● 1 L

21. 100 g ● 1 kg

Test Prep **Choose the correct letter for the answer.**

22. Susan needs to measure the amount of milk needed in a muffin recipe. Which measurement tool should she use?
(3-4)

A ruler **B** measuring cup **C** thermometer **D** scale

LESSON 3-11

Understand
Plan
Solve
Look Back

Problem-Solving Application:
Using Measurement

California Content Standard *Mathematical Reasoning 1.1: Analyze problems by identifying relationships, distinguishing relevant from irrelevant information, sequencing and prioritizing information, and observing patterns.*

Warm-Up Review

Find each missing number.

1. 1 ft = ▒ in.
2. 1 qt = ▒ c
3. 1 min = ▒ sec
4. Tyson's rope is 16 inches long. Reese's rope is 1 foot long. Sam's rope is 6 inches longer than Reese's rope. Whose rope is the longest?

Ginny's class is planning a field day. Her teacher, Mr. Nelson, gives her 100 meters of rope. He asks Ginny to make a rectangle on the playground that is 40 meters long and 25 meters wide. Does Ginny have enough rope?

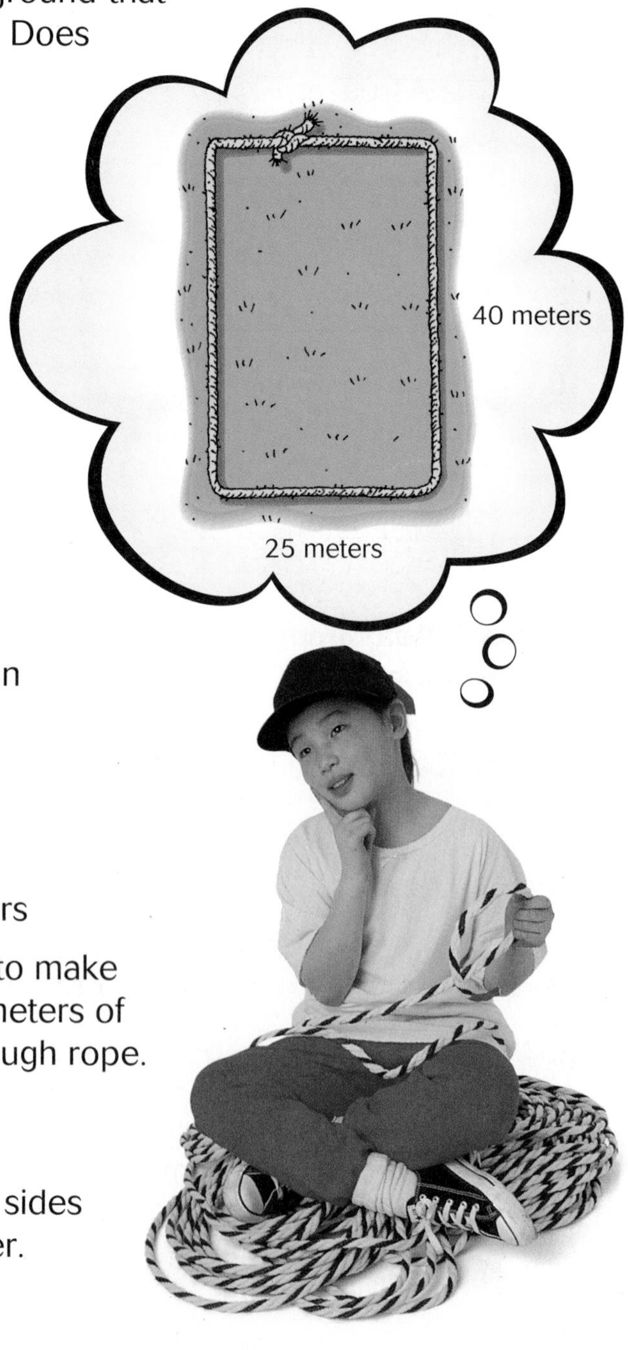

Understand

What do you need to find?

You need to find the distance around the rectangle. You also need to know how much rope Ginny has.

Plan

How can you solve the problem?

You can add the lengths of each side of the rectangle. Then you can compare that sum with the length of the rope.

Solve

$40 + 40 + 25 + 25 = 130$ meters

Ginny needs 130 meters of rope to make the rectangle. She only has 100 meters of rope, so Ginny does *not* have enough rope.

Look Back

Check your answer by adding the sides of the rectangle in a different order.

Guided Practice

1. In the jumping contest, Kamara jumped 2 feet 4 inches. Gwen jumped 3 feet 2 inches. How much farther did Gwen jump?

2. Ginny hopped the 50-meter sack race in 3 minutes. Suppose she hopped at the same speed in a 100-meter sack race. How many minutes would it take her to finish the race?

Independent Practice

3. In one game, Nat's team had to fill a gallon jug with water using a measuring cup. Nat went last. The jug was 3 quarts full. How many more cups did Nat have to add?

4. The 3-kilometer race started at 1:55 P.M. Jed finished the race at 2:10 P.M. How many minutes did Jed run?

Use the chart below to answer Exercises 5 and 6.

Race Results		
Runner	**50-Meter Race**	**200-Meter Race**
Jake	14 seconds	54 seconds
Scott	15 seconds	52 seconds
Latanya	12 seconds	50 seconds

5. Write the order in which the three runners finished the 50-meter race.

6. Rachel also ran in the 50-meter race. If she was 4 seconds slower than the winner, what was her time?

Mixed Review

7. How much money would you spend if you bought 2 T-shirts and a pair of socks?

8. Nadia buys a T-shirt. She pays the clerk with a $10 bill. List the fewest coins and bills the clerk could give Nadia as change.

9. You buy a pair of socks. You pay with 2 one-dollar bills. What is your change?

Diagnostic Checkpoint

Complete. For Exercises 1–4, use the words from the Word Bank.

Word Bank
Fahrenheit
capacity
foot
gram
liter
yard
gallon
pound
decimeter
degrees

1. (3-10) We can use degrees __________ to measure temperature.

2. (3-9) A kilogram is equal to 1,000 ________ (s).

3. (3-3) A customary unit of length about as long as a baseball bat is a ________.

4. (3-4) We can use cups to measure the ________ of a container.

What unit would you use to measure each item? Write *centimeters, decimeters, meters,* or *kilometers.*

5. (3-7) length of an eraser

6. (3-7) length of swimming pool

Choose a unit to measure the capacity of each item. Write *liters* or *milliliters.*

7. (3-8) kitchen sink

8. (3-8) mug

9. (3-8) eye dropper

Compare. Write >, <, or =.

10. (3-9) 1 kg ● 900 g

11. (3-9) 10 g ● 1 kg

12. (3-9) 2 kg ● 2,100 g

Choose the better estimate for the temperature

13. (3-10) of boiling water.
0°C or 100°C

14. (3-10) of a warm day.
32°F or 92°F

15. (3-11) Colleen's running shoes weigh 20 oz. Kurt's running shoes weigh 1 lb 7 oz. Whose running shoes weigh less?

16. (3-8) Tammy needs 1 liter of orange juice to make some punch. She has 750 milliliters of orange juice. How many more milliliters of orange juice does she need?

Chapter 3 Test

Look at each pair of times. Write how much time has passed.

1. 8:10 A.M. and 11:10 A.M.

2. 6:05 P.M. and 7:00 P.M.

Estimate the length. Then measure to the nearest $\frac{1}{2}$ inch.

3. 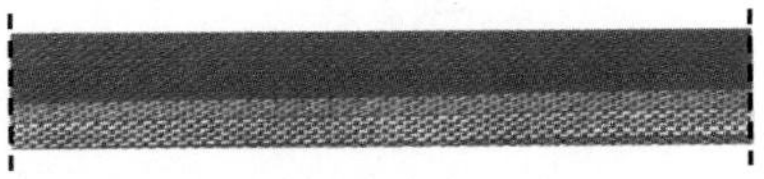

4. 

Estimate the length. Then measure to the nearest centimeter.

5. 

Find each missing number.

6. ■ c = 1 pt

7. 1 lb = ■ oz

8. 1 L = ■ mL

9. 1m = ■ cm

10. 3 ft = ■ yd

11. ■ kg = 1,000 g

Choose the better estimate for each.

12. weight of an ear of corn
8 lb or 8 oz

13. capacity of a soup ladle
160 mL or 160 L

14. outdoor temperature for sledding
30°F or 60°F

15. outdoor temperature for a picnic
30°C or 80°C

16. It takes Lily more than 35 minutes to get home. If she leaves at 4:25 P.M., can she be home by 5:00 P.M.? Explain why or why not.

17. The temperature at noon was 74°F. At night, the temperature was 58°F. How much colder was the temperature at night?

18. Bob lost some money. He has $3.50 now. Yesterday he spent $2.50. He started with $10. How much money did Bob lose?

Multiple-Choice Chapter 3 Test

TEST PREP

Choose the correct letter for each answer.

1. A hockey game started at 6:45 P.M. and lasted 1 hour and 10 minutes. Which clock shows the time at the end of the game?

A 

C 

B 

D 

2. The skating rink is open from 3:30 P.M. to 6:00 P.M. and from 7:00 P.M. to 10:30 P.M. each day. How long is the skating rink open each day?

F 5 hours

G 5 hours 30 minutes

H 6 hours

J 6 hours 30 minutes

3. Brett finishes his paper route at 6:15 P.M. each day. It takes him 40 minutes to deliver all the newspapers. How can you find the time Brett starts delivering newspapers?

A Take 6:15 P.M. and subtract 40 minutes.

B Take 6:15 P.M. and add 40 minutes.

C Take 6:15 P.M., add 40 minutes, and then subtract 15 minutes.

D Take 6:15 P.M., subtract 40 minutes, and then add 15 minutes.

4. Which number makes the statement true?

■ in. = 2 ft

F 1

G 16

H 12

J 24

5. Use a ruler. Measure the piece of string to the nearest $\frac{1}{4}$ inch.

A $1\frac{1}{2}$ inches

B $1\frac{3}{4}$ inches

C 2 inches

D $2\frac{3}{4}$ inches

6. A pudding recipe calls for 1 quart of milk. How many cups is that?

F 2 cups

G 4 cups

H 6 cups

J 8 cups

K NH

7. Which unit of measurement would be best to use to measure the capacity of a bathtub?

A cups

B pints

C quarts

D gallons

8. **Laura's backpack weighs 12 pounds 3 ounces. Stephanie's backpack weighs 6 ounces more than Laura's. How much does Stephanie's backpack weigh?**

F 12 lb 9 oz
G 12 lb 12 oz
H 13 lb 9 oz
J 13 lb 12 oz

9. **Cora's puppy weighs 2 pounds. How many ounces is that?**

A 16 oz C 24 oz
B 20 oz D 32 oz

10. **Mike needs to measure the length of his desk. Which measurement tool should he use?**

F thermometer
G scale
H ruler
J measuring cup

11. **Choose the best estimate for the length of a pencil.**

A 15 cm C 15 m
B 15 dm D 15 km

12. **Which number makes the statement true?**

1 km = ▒ m

F 10 H 1,000
G 100 J 10,000

13. **Which of these units would you use to measure the capacity of a car's gasoline tank?**

A liters C kilograms
B meters D miles

14. **Choose the best estimate for the capacity of a teaspoon.**

F 5 mL H 5 L
G 500 mL J 500 L

15. **Which number makes the statement true?**

▒ g = 2 kg

A 20 C 1,000
B 200 D 2,000

16. **The forecast predicts a high temperature of 27°C. What article of clothing would be most appropriate for the weather conditions?**

F snowsuit
G heavy coat
H sweater
J bathing suit

17. **Clarence ran 3 laps around a 150-meter track. How many meters did he run?**

A 300 m D 450 m
B 350 m E NH
C 400 m

Reteaching

Set A (pages 92–93)

Elena worked in her garden from 1:15 P.M. until 1:50 P.M. How long did Elena work in her garden?

Start at 1:15 P.M. Count by 5s to 1:50 P.M. So, Elena worked in her garden for 35 minutes.

Remember the hour hand goes around an analog clock twice each day. It goes around once for A.M. hours and a second time for P.M. hours.

Look at each pair of times. Write how much time has passed.

1. Start 3:20 P.M.
End 4:20 P.M.

2. Start 10:25 A.M.
End 11:00 A.M.

3. Start 12:05 P.M.
End 2:20 P.M.

4. Start 10:30 A.M.
End 1:30 P.M.

Set B (pages 96–98)

Measure the length of the string to the nearest $\frac{1}{4}$ inch.

The string is about $1\frac{3}{4}$ inches long.

Remember to line up the first mark on the ruler with the left side of the object that you are measuring.

Estimate the length. Then measure to the nearest $\frac{1}{4}$ inch.

1. 

2. 

3. How many feet are in 1 yard?

Set C (pages 100–101)

Mrs. Lyndon's pitcher holds 1 quart of water. How many cups of water is this?

Since 1 quart = 4 cups, her pitcher holds 4 cups of water.

Remember the amount of liquid a container holds is called its capacity.

Find each missing number.

1. 2 pt = ■ qt

2. ■ c = 1 gal

3. 2 c = ■ pt

4. 2 qt = ■ c

Set D (pages 102–103)

Would you measure the weight of a bicycle in ounces or pounds?

An ounce is a smaller unit of measure than a pound.

Since a bicycle weighs much more than one pound, you would use pounds.

Remember that there are 16 ounces in 1 pound.

Choose a unit to measure each item. Write *ounces* or *pounds*.

1. horse
2. toothpick
3. slice of cheese
4. bag of flour

Set E (pages 107–109)

How long is the paper clip to the nearest centimeter?

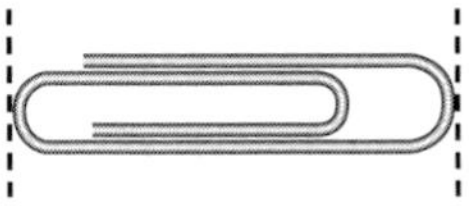

The paper clip is about 3 cm long.

Remember centimeters and decimeters are units used to measure shorter lengths. Meters and kilometers are units used to measure longer lengths.

Estimate each length. Then measure to the nearest centimeter.

1. 

2. 

Set F (pages 110–111)

Would you use liters or milliliters to measure the capacity of a soup bowl?

A milliliter is a smaller unit of measure than a liter.

Since a soup bowl holds less than a liter, you would use milliliters.

Remember that there are 1,000 milliliters in 1 liter.

Choose a unit to measure the capacity of each item. Write *milliliters* or *liters*.

1. swimming pool
2. test tube
3. baby bottle
4. mop bucket

Reteaching (continued)

Set G (pages 112–113)

Choose the better estimate.

Watermelon

2g or 2 kg

A watermelon is much heavier than 2 g, so 2 kg would be a better estimate.

Remember grams are units used to measure smaller weights. Kilograms are units used to measure larger weights.

Choose the better estimate.

1. Brick
1 g or 1 kg

2. Can of soup
300 g or 300 kg

3. Hamburger
200 g or 200 kg

4. Car
1,500 g or 1,500 kg

Set H (pages 114–115)

Ryan wants to check the temperature of the swimming pool. What is the temperature in degrees Fahrenheit?

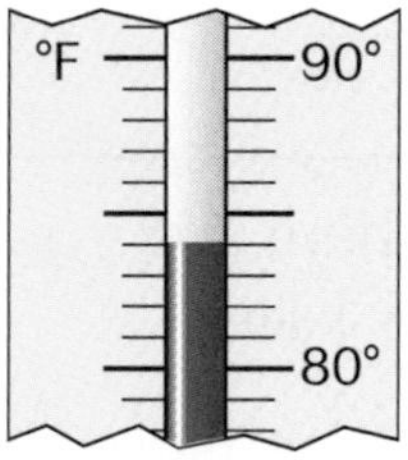

Step 1 Notice that the thermometer shows temperature in degrees Fahrenheit..

Step 2 Notice that the marks on the thermometer go up by 1s. Start at 80°F. Then count up to 84°F.

The temperature of the water in the swimming pool is 84°F.

Remember to find whether the thermometer shows degrees Fahrenheit or degrees Celsius.

1.
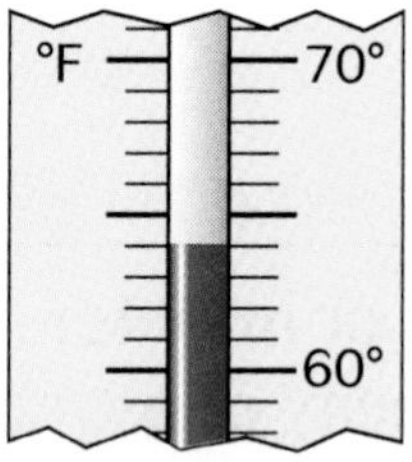

2.
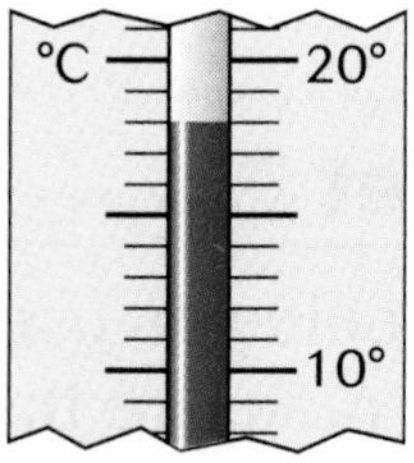

3.
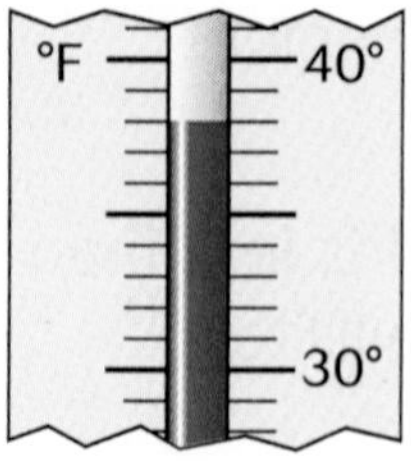

4.
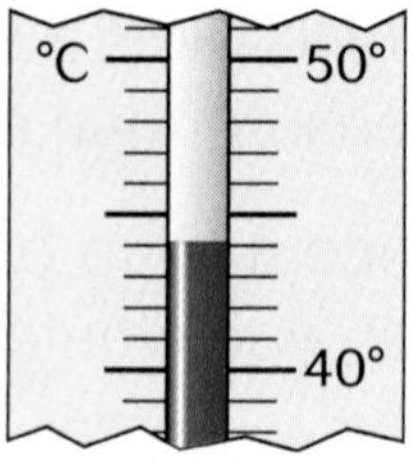

More Practice

Set A (pages 92–93)

Look at each pair of times. Write how much time has passed.

1. Start 4:15 P.M.
   End 5:30 P.M.
2. Start 10:05 A.M.
   End 10:10 A.M.
3. Start 9:10 P.M.
   End 11:15 P.M.
4. Start 2:45 P.M.
   End 6:00 P.M.
5. Start 5:35 A.M.
   End 7:10 A.M.
6. Start 11:20 A.M.
   End 12:00 P.M.
7. The zoo closes in 2 hours and 50 minutes at 5:30 P.M. What time is it now?

Set B (pages 96–98)

Find each missing number.

1. 24 in. = ■ ft
2. 3 ft = ■ yd
3. ■ ft = 1 mi
4. 1 ft = ■ in.
5. 1,760 yd = ■ mi
6. 1 yd = ■ in.

Estimate the length. Then measure to the nearest $\frac{1}{2}$ inch.

7. 

8. To get a first down, a football team must move the ball 2 more yards. How many feet is this?

Set C (pages 100–101)

Find each missing number.

1. 1 qt = ■ pt
2. 4 c = ■ qt
3. ■ pt = 1 gal

Choose the better estimate for the capacity of each container.

4. tea kettle
   2 qt or 2 gal
5. water glass
   1 c or 1 qt
6. A recipe for hot chocolate calls for 4 cups of milk. You have a gallon of milk. How many cups of milk will you have left over?

More Practice (continued)

Set D (pages 102–103)

Choose a unit to measure each item. Write *ounces* or *pounds*.

1. a baby
2. a baseball
3. a hamster
4. a dog
5. an egg
6. a watermelon

Compare. Write >, <, or =.

7. 24 oz ● 2 lb
8. 3 lb ● 30 oz
9. 16 oz ● 1 lb

10. Henry wants to make macaroni salad for a class picnic. His recipe calls for 1 pound of macaroni. Macaroni comes in 8-ounce boxes. How many boxes does he need?

11. A car weighs 2,800 pounds. Maria's mother weighs 125 pounds and Maria weighs 55 pounds. If Maria and her mother go to the store in the car, how much does the car weigh with its passengers ?

Set E (pages 107–109)

What unit would you use to measure each item?
Write *centimeters, decimeters, meters,* or *kilometers*.

1. length of a toothpick
2. height of a mountain
3. height of a flagpole

Find each missing number.

4. 200 cm = ■ m
5. 1 km = ■ m
6. ■ cm = 1 dm

Estimate the length. Then measure to the nearest centimeter.

7. 

8. 

9. The distance between Emily's house and Kendra's house is 10 kilometers. How many kilometers is it from Emily's house to Kendra's house and back?

Set F (pages 110–111)

Choose a unit to measure the capacity of each item. Write *liters* or *milliliters*.

1. medicine dropper **2.** car's gas tank **3.** drinking glass

Choose the better estimate for the capacity of each item.

4. carton of milk
2 L or 2 mL

5. washing machine
80 L or 80 mL

6. Raymond needs 2 liters of water to boil some pasta. How many milliliters is this?

Set G (pages 112–113)

Compare. Write >, <, or =.

1. 1 kg ● 1 g **2.** 2 kg ● 2,000 g **3.** 10 g ● 10 kg

Choose a unit to measure each item. Write *grams* or *kilograms*.

4. dog **5.** zebra **6.** goldfish

7. boat **8.** cracker **9.** pencil

10. Nathaniel's cat weighs 1 kg. Laura's cat weighs 650 grams. How much more does Nathaniel's cat weigh than Laura's cat?

Set H (pages 114–115)

Write each temperature.

1.
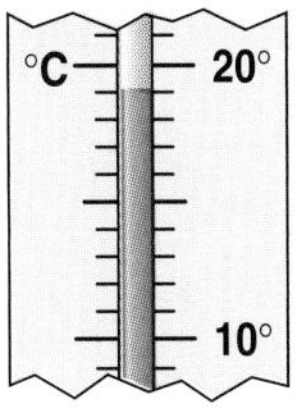

2.
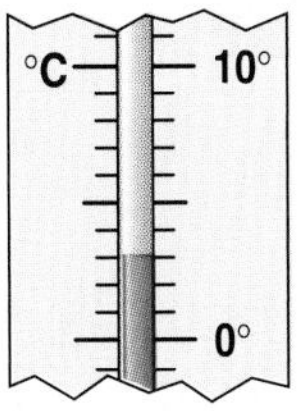

3.
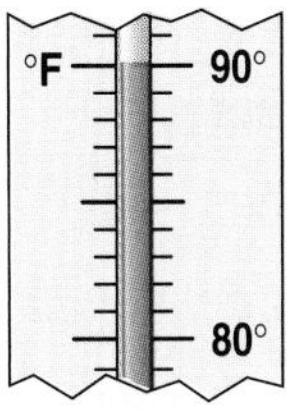

4. The temperature fell 15°F from a temperature of 65°F. What is the new temperature?

TEST PREP

Problem Solving: Preparing for Tests

Choose the correct letter for each answer.

---

1. Phil left home in the morning at the time shown on the clock below. He got back three and one-half hours later. What time did Phil get home?

A 1:50 A.M.

B 1:50 P.M.

C 2:20 A.M.

D 2:20 P.M.

Tip

Sometimes you can eliminate some answer choices. Why can you eliminate Choices A and C?

---

2. Over the weekend, 239 people went to the school play on Saturday and 178 people went on Sunday. What is the best way to estimate the total number of people who went to the play in all?

F 200 + 100

G 200 + 20

H 200 + 200

J 300 + 200

Tip

Start by rounding each number to the nearest hundred.

---

3. Jim is fencing in a play area for his dog. He has 75 feet of wire fencing. If he only needs 56 feet of fencing for the play area, how much fencing will Jim have left?

A 19 feet

B 21 feet

C 29 feet

D 131 feet

Tip

You can use the *Draw a Picture* strategy to help you solve this problem.

4. Mary Beth played soccer for 38 minutes in one game and 42 minutes in another game. About how many minutes did she play in the two games?

F 50 minutes
G 60 minutes
H 80 minutes
J 90 minutes

5. Mark's dog weighs 57 pounds. Jane's dog weighs 42 pounds. Which number sentence would be best to use to estimate the difference in weights?

A $60 - 50 = \blacksquare$
B $60 - 40 = \blacksquare$
C $60 - 30 = \blacksquare$
D $50 - 30 = \blacksquare$

6. Gil and Ben collect toy cars. If they combined their collections they would have 14 cars. Ben has 4 more cars than Gil. How many cars does Gil have?

F 4 cars
G 5 cars
H 9 cars
J 10 cars

7. If today is July 3, what will the date be in 3 weeks?

A July 19
B July 20
C July 21
D July 24

8. Will bought a calculator that cost $8 and a battery to go with it. The total cost of his purchase was less than $10. Which is reasonable for the cost of the battery?

F Between $1 and $2
G Between $2 and $3
H Between $3 and $4
J More than $4

Use the chart for Questions 9–10.

Playing Time	
Activity	**Minutes**
Basketball	55
Kickball	20
Skating	30

9. You start skating at 3:30 P.M. What time will you finish?

A 3:00 P.M.
B 3:45 P.M.
C 4:00 P.M.
D 4:30 P.M.

10. Basketball practice starts at 2:25 P.M. and ends 55 minutes later. The bus will pick up the basketball team 20 minutes after basketball practice ends. What time will the bus pick up the team?

F 2:45 P.M.
G 3:20 P.M.
H 3:30 P.M.
J 3:40 P.M.

Multiple-Choice Cumulative Review

Choose the correct letter for each answer.

Measurement and Geometry

1. Which is the best estimate for the length of a toothpick?

A 2 in.
B 2 ft
C 2 yd
D 2 mi

2. Tonya's soccer game starts at 4:00 P.M. and ends at 5:15 P.M. How long does it last?

F 45 minutes
G 1 hour 5 minutes
H 1 hour 15 minutes
J 1 hour 45 minutes

3. Look at the thermometer. If the temperature goes down by 4°F, how warm will it be?

A 72°F
B 78°F
C 80°F
D 82°F

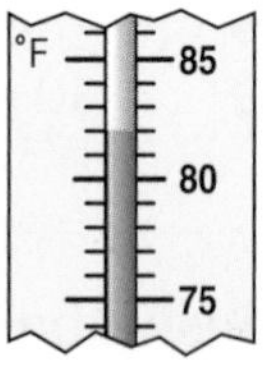

4. A party began at 2:30 P.M. It lasted 2 hours 20 minutes. Which clock shows what time the party ended?

F

H

G

J

5. How many sides does this shape have?

A 4
B 6
C 7
D 8

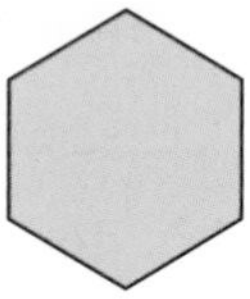

6. How many centimeters are in a meter?

F 5 cm
G 10 cm
H 100 cm
J 1,000 cm

7. How many corners does a square have?

A 6
B 5
C 4
D 3

8. John needs to find the weight of his dog. Which measurement tool should he use?

F ruler
G measuring cup
H thermometer
J scale

Number Sense

9. What is the value of the digit 1 in the number 1,256?

A 1
B 10
C 100
D 1,000

---

10. Which number is the same as five thousand, one hundred three?

F 5,301
G 5,130
H 5,103
J 513

---

11. Which group of numbers is in order from *greatest* to *least*?

A 4,832 3,930 2,749 2,184
B 4,832 2,749 3,930 2,184
C 2,284 2,749 3,930 4,832
D 2,749 2,184 4,832 3,930

---

12. Which shaded region represents $\frac{3}{4}$ of the figure?

F
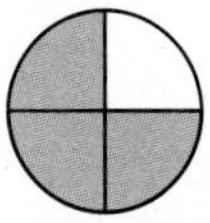

H
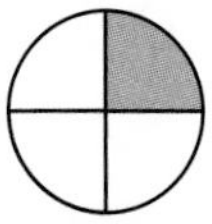

G
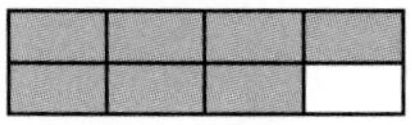

J
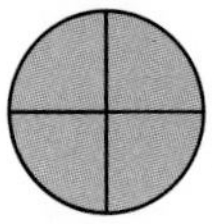

Statistics, Data Analysis, and Probability

13. Use the chart below. How many people chose red as their favorite color?

Favorite Color	
Green	III
Blue	𝍸 𝍸
Red	𝍸 II

A 2
B 3
C 7
D 10

Use the graph for Questions 14 and 15.

Bushels of Apples Sold Each Day
Friday
Saturday
Sunday

Each  means 2 bushels of apples.

14. On which day were the most apples sold?

F Friday
G Saturday
H Sunday
J Monday

---

15. How many more bushels were sold on Saturday than on Sunday?

A 1 more bushel
B 2 more bushels
C 4 more bushels
D 5 more bushels

CHAPTER 4

Multiplication Concepts

Diagnosing Readiness

In Chapter 4, you will use these skills:

Ⓐ Multiplying by 2

(Gr. 2)

1. There are 4 pairs of shoes in Tracy's closet. How many shoes are there altogether?

2. Each basket has 7 apples in it. How many apples are there altogether?

Ⓑ Multiplying by 5

(Gr. 2)

3. Ray put his rock collection into 4 groups of 5 rocks. How many rocks are in his rock collection?

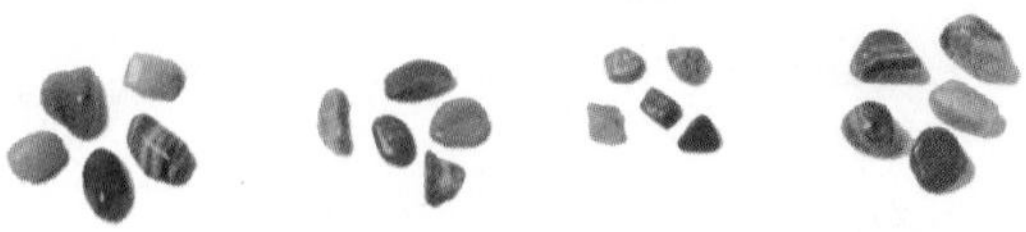

C Multiplying by 10

(Gr. 2)

4. 3×10 **5.** 10×2

6. 10×4 **7.** 7×10

8. 10×5 **9.** 6×10

10. Toby has 8 stacks of newspapers to deliver. Each stack has 10 newspapers. How many newspapers must he deliver?

D Adding

(Gr. 2)

11. $2 + 2 + 2 + 2$

12. $3 + 0$

13. $6 + 1$

14. $5 + 5 + 5$

15. $3 + 3 + 3 + 3$

16. $0 + 7$

17. Heather has 3 boxes of pennies. Each box has 7 pennies. How many pennies does she have altogether?

E Patterns

(Gr. 2)

Find the next two numbers for each pattern.

18. 2, 4, 6, 8, ■, ■, . . .

19. 3, 6, 9, 12, ■, ■, . . .

20. Micah is building a tower. She uses 24 blocks for the first level, 20 for the second, and 16 for the third. If the pattern continues, how many blocks will be on the fourth level?

F Using Money

(Gr. 2)

Find the total value of the group of coins and bills.

21.

22. Suppose you spend $3.46 on lunch. You give the cashier a $5 bill. What is your change?

To the Family and Student

Looking Back	Chapter 4	Looking Ahead
In Grade 2, students learned to multiply by 2, 5, and 10.	**Multiplication Concepts** In this chapter, students will learn the multiplication facts for 0 though 5.	In Chapter 5, students will learn the multiplication facts for 6 through 10.

Math and Everyday Living

Opportunities to apply the concepts of Chapter 4 abound in everyday situations. During the chapter, think about how multiplication can be used to solve a variety of real-world problems. The following examples suggest just several of the many situations that could launch a discussion about multiplication.

Math and Transportation
If 5 cars can hold 4 passengers each, how many passengers can ride in the cars?

Math at Home If you have 6 pairs of shoes, how many shoes do you have?

Math and Cooking If a recipe calls for 3 cups of flour, how much flour is needed to double the recipe?

Math at the Grocery Store
At $2 per pound, what would it cost to buy 4 pounds of butter?

Math and Exercise If you swim 4 laps in a pool that is 10 yd long, how many yards did you swim?

Math and Nutrition You are going to eat 5 servings from the fruit-and-vegetable food group each day. After 3 days, how many servings have you eaten?

Math in the City An apartment building has 4 apartments. Each apartment has 3 windows. How many windows are there altogether?

Math and Games You and a friend play a game where each captured game piece is worth 3 points. You have captured 7 game pieces, how many points do you have?

Math and School You are a member of the Glee Club at school. Your club meets twice each week to practice for the spring recital. How many times will your club meet in the 5 weeks?

California Content Standards in Chapter 4 Lessons*

	Teach and Practice	Practice
Number Sense		
2.2 (🔑) Memorize to automaticity the multiplication table for the numbers between 1 and 10.	4-4, 4-5, 4-6, 4-7	4-2
2.6 Understand the special properties of 0 and 1 in multiplication.	4-9	
2.8 Solve problems which combine the skills above.		4-3, 4-7, 4-11
3.1 (Grade 2) Use repeated addition, arrays, and counting by multiples to do multiplication.	4-1	
Algebra and Functions		
1.2 Solve problems involving numeric equations.		4-2
1.3 Select appropriate operational and relational symbols to make an equation true.		4-9
1.5 Recognize and use the commutative property of multiplication.	4-2	4-4, 4-7
2.1 (🔑) Solve simple problems involving a functional relationship between two quantities.	4-11	4-5, 4-6
2.2 Extend and recognize a linear pattern by its rules.	4-10	4-5, 4-6

	Teach and Practice	Practice
Mathematical Reasoning		
2.0 Students use strategies, skills, and concepts in finding solutions.		4-3, 4-8, 4-11
2.1 Use estimation to verify the reasonableness of calculated results.		4-1
2.2 Apply strategies and results from simpler problems to more complex problems.		4-9
2.3 Use a variety of methods such as words, numbers, symbols, charts, graphs, tables, diagrams, and models to explain mathematical reasoning.	4-8	4-1, 4-3
2.4 Express the solution clearly and logically by using the appropriate mathematical notation and terms and clear language; support solutions with evidence in both verbal and symbolic work.		4-2, 4-4, 4-5, 4-6
2.6 Make precise calculations and check the validity of the results from the context of the problem.		4-3, 4-11
3.1 Evaluate the reasonableness of the solution in the context of the original situation.	4-3	
3.2 Note the method of deriving the solution and demonstrate a conceptual understanding of the derivation by solving similar problems.		4-8
3.3 Develop generalizations of results obtained and apply them in other circumstances.		4-9

* The symbol (🔑) indicates a key standard as designated in the Mathematics Framework for California Public Schools. Full statements of the California Content Standards are found at the beginning of this book following the Table of Contents.

LESSON 4-1

Relating Multiplication and Addition

Warm-Up Review

1. 2 + 2 + 2
2. 5 + 5 + 5 + 5
3. 4 + 4 + 4
4. 3 + 3 + 3 + 3 + 3
5. Pam has 2 boxes of pencils. Each box has 8 pencils. How many pencils does she have?

California Content Standard *Number Sense 3.1 (Grade 2): Use repeated addition . . . to do multiplication.*

Math Link You know how to add more than two numbers. Now you will learn how to relate addition and multiplication.

Word Bank

factor
product

Example 1

Each of the four shelves in this bookcase holds 8 books. How many books are in the bookcase?

You can use repeated addition to find out.

$8 + 8 + 8 + 8 = 32$

Whenever you use repeated addition, you can also multiply.

$8 + 8 + 8 + 8 = 32$

4 groups of 8 = 32

So $4 \times 8 = 32$

(4 and 8: factors; 32: product)

There are 32 books in the bookcase.

The numbers you multiply are called **factors**. The answer you get when you multiply is called the **product**.

More Examples

A.

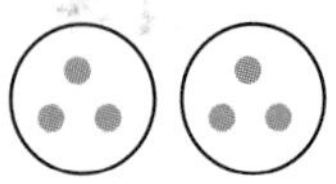

$3 + 3 = 6$

2 groups of 3 = 6

$2 \times 3 = 6$

B.

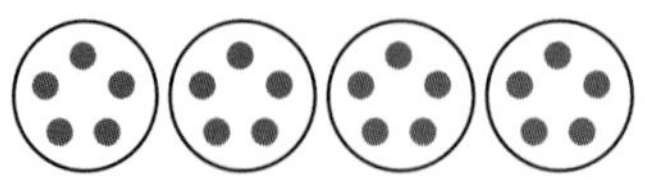

$5 + 5 + 5 + 5 = 20$

4 groups of 5 = 20

$4 \times 5 = 20$

 Additional Standards: Mathematical Reasoning 2.1, 2.3 *(See p.135.)*

Guided Practice *For another example, see Set A on p. 166.*

Write an addition sentence and a multiplication sentence for each set of pictures.

1. 

2. 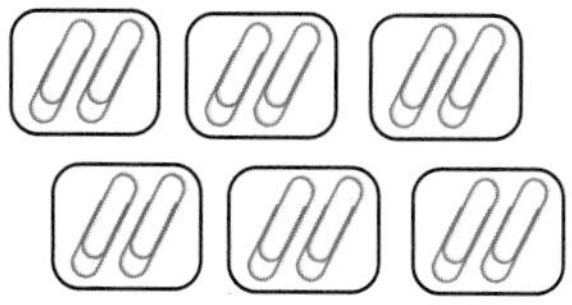

3. 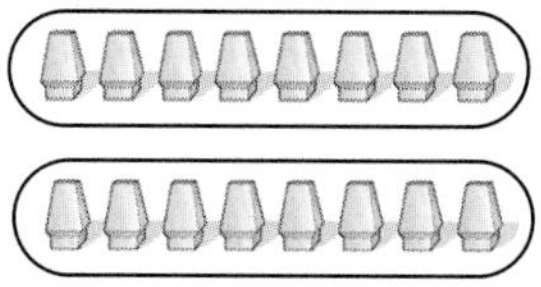

4. Nathan has 3 bags of oranges. Each bag has 6 oranges. How many oranges does Nathan have?

Independent Practice *For more practice, see Set A on p. 168.*

Write an addition sentence and a multiplication sentence for each set of pictures.

5. 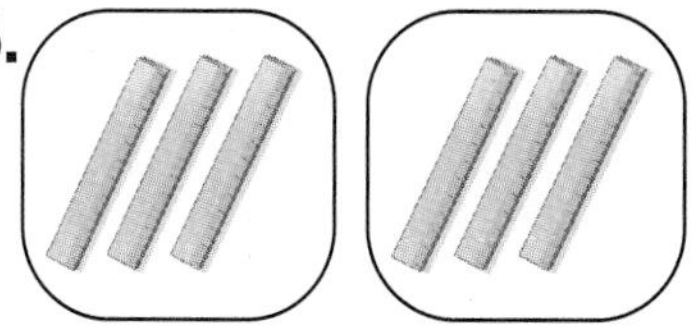

6. 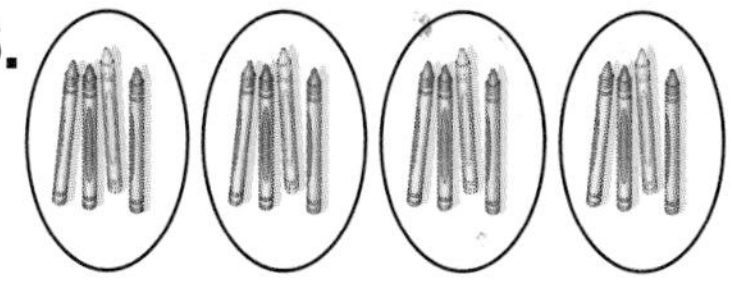

7. 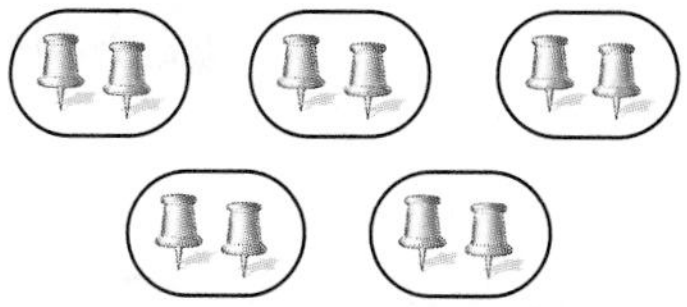

8. 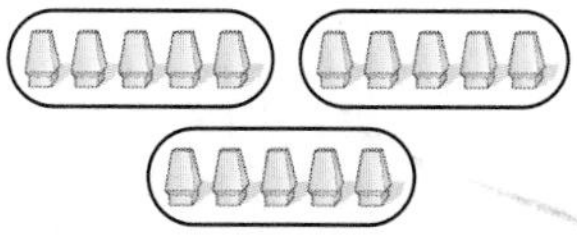

9. 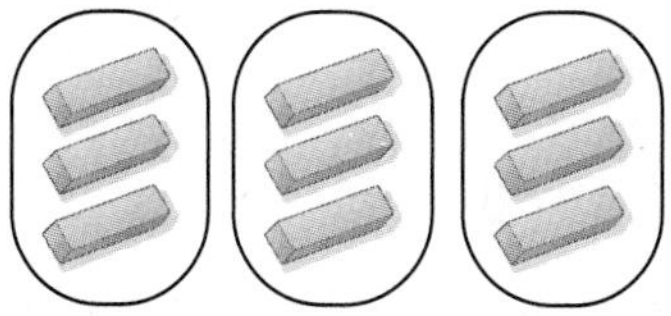

10. 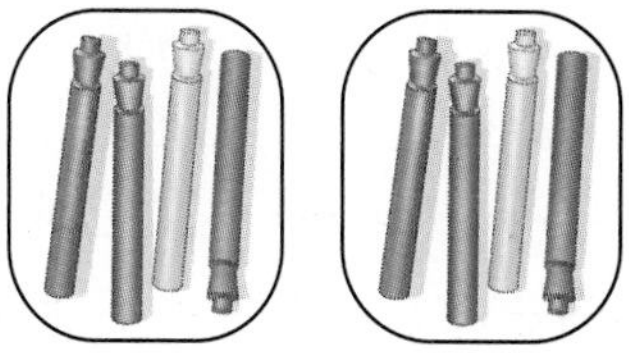

Write a multiplication sentence for each addition sentence.

11. $2 + 2 + 2 + 2 = 8$

12. $9 + 9 + 9 = 27$

13. $7 + 7 + 7 + 7 + 7 = 35$

14. $1 + 1 + 1 + 1 = 4$

15. $8 + 8 = 16$

16. $5 + 5 + 5 = 15$

17. $3 + 3 + 3 + 3 + 3 + 3 = 18$

18. $7 + 7 + 7 = 21$

Use the chart for Exercises 19–21.

19. How much do 4 comic books cost?

20. Which costs less, 9 comic books or 9 picture books?

21. Math Reasoning Suppose you had \$27. Would it be reasonable to say you can buy 6 storybooks? Explain your reasoning.

22. Math Reasoning Explain why you cannot multiply to find the number of pencils in the picture.

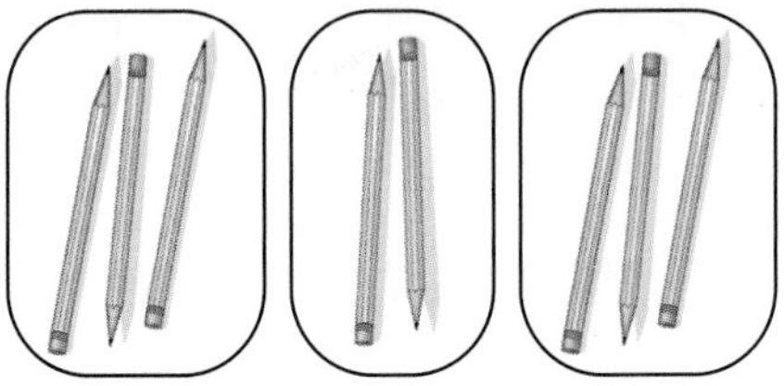

Mixed Review

23. The temperature in the morning is 35°F. By lunch it has risen 15°F. Then it drops 8°F. What temperature is it then?

Write each temperature.

24.

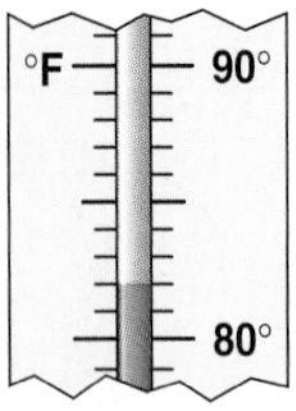

25.

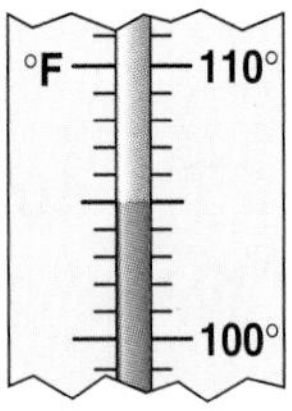

26.

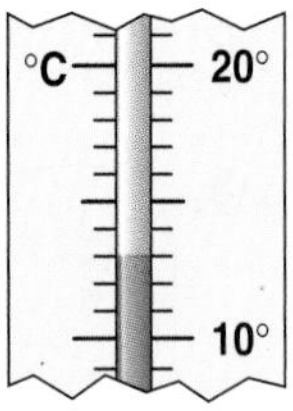

27.

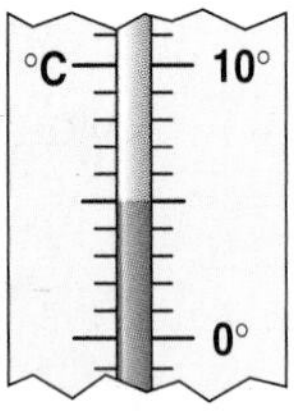

Compare with $<$, $>$, or $=$.

28. 50 g ● 1 kg **29.** 3,000 g ● 3 kg **30.** 400 g ● 4 kg

Test Prep Choose the correct letter for each answer.

31. What is the value of the 3 in the number 3,572?
(1-1)

A 3 **B** 30 **C** 300 **D** 3,000

32. Algebra Find the missing number.
(2-14)

15 − ■ = 9

F 4 **G** 5 **H** 6 **J** 7

LESSON 4-2

Using Arrays

Algebra

California Content Standard *Algebra and Functions 1.5: Recognize and use the commutative property . . . of multiplication . . ..*

Math Link You know that 4 + 8 and 8 + 4 have the same sum. Now you will learn that expressions like 4 × 8 and 8 × 4 have the same product.

Warm-Up Review

Complete the pattern.

1. 2, 4, 6, 8, ____, ____.
2. 5, 10, 15, ____, ____.
3. 10, 20, 30, ____, ____.
4. Erasers cost 9¢ at the bookstore. Pencils cost 25¢. How much does one eraser and one pencil cost?

Word Bank

array

Example 1

It's United Nations Day! You are putting up a display of flags from around the world on your classroom wall. How many flags are in the display?

Wait! Before you start counting, look at how the flags are placed.

The flags form an **array**. An array shows objects in rows and columns.

There are 3 columns.

There are 6 rows.

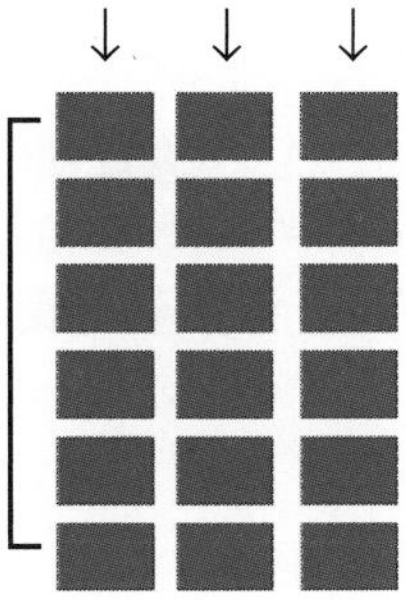

Since an array is made up of equal groups, you can multiply to find how many objects are in it.

There are 6 rows.
There are 3 flags in each row.
6 × 3 = 18

There are 18 flags in the display.

Additional Standards: Number Sense 2.2 (🔑); Algebra and Functions 1.2; Mathematical Reasoning 2.4 *(See p. 135.)*

Example 2

If the display was turned sideways, would there still be 18 flags?

Compare the two arrays.

How many rows?
How many flags in each row?
How many in all?
$6 \times 3 = 18$

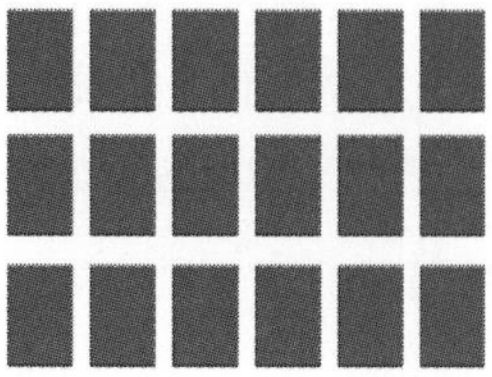

How many rows?
How many flags in each row?
How many in all?
$3 \times 6 = 18$

Yes, both arrays have 18 flags.

The order in which you multiply factors does not change the product.

More Examples

A.

$4 \times 2 = 8$

$2 \times 4 = 8$

B.

$5 \times 3 = 15$

$3 \times 5 = 15$

Guided Practice *For another example, see Set B on p. 166.*

Write a multiplication sentence for each array.

1. 

2. 

3. 

4. Mr. Knoke's class planted bean seeds for a science project. There are 8 rows. There are 5 seeds in each row. How many bean seeds did the class plant?

Independent Practice *For more practice, see Set B on p. 168.*

Write a multiplication sentence for each array.

5. 

6. 

7. 

Draw an array for each multiplication expression. Then find the product.

8. 3×4 **9.** 4×3 **10.** 2×5 **11.** 5×2

Algebra Write the number that belongs in each ■.

12. $4 \times 6 = 24$, so $6 \times 4 =$ ■ **13.** $7 \times 4 = 28$, so ■ $\times 7 = 28$

14. Math Reasoning Is the product of 8×3 the same as the product of 3×8? Explain.

15. A flag store has many flags displayed in an array. There are 3 rows of state flags and 3 rows of flags from other countries. If there are 8 flags in each row, how many flags are on display?

Mixed Review

16. Beau is 4 feet 1 inch tall. Dillon is 4 feet 5 inches tall. How much taller is Dillon?

Write a multiplication sentence for each addition sentence.

17. $6 + 6 + 6 + 6 = 24$ **18.** $3 + 3 + 3 + 3 + 3 + 3 + 3 = 21$

Which temperature is colder?

19. 40°F or 50°F **20.** 49°F or 39°F **21.** 0°C or 32°C

Test Prep **Choose the correct letter for each answer.**

22. *(1-8)* There are 5 nickels on the table. How much money is on the table?

A 5¢ **C** 25¢

B 10¢ **D** 50¢

23. *(1-7)* What is the least number you can write using the digits 2, 6, 9, 3, and 4?

F 96,432 **J** 23,469

G 32,694 **K** NH

H 24,369

LESSON 4-3

Understand
Plan
Solve
Look Back

Problem-Solving Skill: Reasonable Answers

Warm-Up Review

1. 4 + 4 2. 24 − 5

3. 36 + 4 4. 28 + 2

5. 4, 8, 12, 16, ____, ____

6. 4 groups of 5 is ____.

7. Jason had 15 marbles. He found 3 more on the playground. Then he gave 8 to Dillon. How many did he have left?

California Content Standard *Mathematical Reasoning 3.1: Evaluate the reasonableness of the solution in the context of the original situation.*

Read for Understanding

Ms. Morgan's class is going on a field trip to the science museum. She is putting students in groups of 4. There are 8 groups of students. One adult volunteer will stay with each group.

1. How many groups are there?
2. How many students are in each group?
3. How many adult volunteers will there be on the trip?

Think and Discuss

MATH FOCUS

Reasonable Answers

Whenever you answer a question, always check that your answer is reasonable. Look at the facts that are given. Then make sure your answer makes sense compared with those facts.

Reread the paragraph at the top of the page.

4. Would it be reasonable to say that 8 students are going on the trip? Explain why or why not.
5. How many people (including Ms. Morgan) are going on the trip? Would 32 people be a reasonable answer?
6. What should you do if your answer is not reasonable?

Additional Standards: Number Sense 2.8; Mathematical Reasoning 2.0, 2.6 *(See p. 135.)*

Guided Practice

The students visit the Rock and Mineral Exhibit, where they see a rock collection. The rocks are arranged in 6 rows with 4 rocks in each row. Four of the rocks are green.

1. How could you find the number of rocks that are *not* green?
   a. Find the total number of rocks.
   b. Find the total number of rocks. Then add 4.
   c. Find the total number of rocks. Then subtract 4.

2. If someone wanted to know how many rocks are *not* green, would 24 be a reasonable answer?
   a. Yes, because there are 24 rocks in all.
   b. No, the answer must be greater than 24.
   c. No, the answer must be less than 24.

Independent Practice

The Electricity Exhibit shows 6 videos every day. Five of the videos are each 3 minutes long. The other video is 7 minutes long.

3. How could you find the total number of minutes it would take to watch all the 3-minute videos?
   a. Find $5 + 3$.
   b. Find 5×3.
   c. Find 6×3.

4. What could you do to find the total number of minutes it would take to watch all the videos?
   a. Find $7 + 3$. Then multiply by 6.
   b. Find 5×3. Then add 7.
   c. Find 6×3. Then add 7.

5. **Math Reasoning** Would it be reasonable to say that it takes 15 minutes to watch all 6 of the videos? Why or why not?

LESSON 4-4

Multiplying by 2

California Content Standard *Number Sense 2.2 (🔑): Memorize to automaticity the multiplication table for numbers between 1 and 10.*

Warm-Up Review

1. 2 + 2	**2.** 3 + 3
3. 4 + 4	**4.** 5 + 5
5. 6 + 6	**6.** 7 + 7
7. 8 + 8	**8.** 9 + 9

9. Mr. Marks bought a tire for $79. He paid for it with a $100 bill. How much change did he receive?

Math Link You know how to skip count by 2s. Now you will learn how to multiply by 2.

Example 1

The music assembly is starting! Your class has 7 pairs of maracas to use in the show. How many maracas does your class have?

$7 \times 2 = \blacksquare$ or $\begin{array}{r} 7 \\ \times\ 2 \\ \hline \blacksquare \end{array}$

You can skip count by 2s to help you find the product.

$2 + 2 + 2 + 2 + 2 + 2 + 2 = 14$

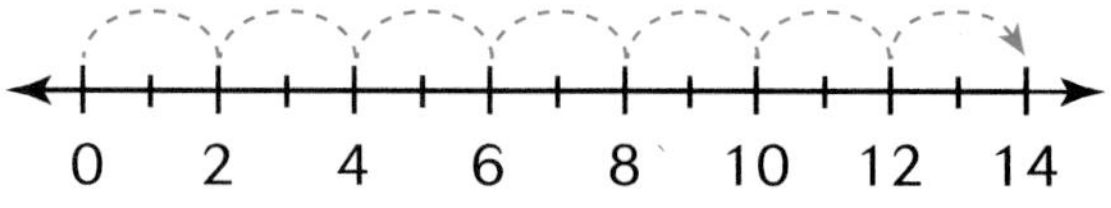

Count by 2s until you have said 7 numbers.
2, 4, 6, 8, 10, 12, 14

Your class has 14 maracas.

Example 2

Find 4×2.

You can skip count by 2s to help you find the product.

$2 + 2 + 2 + 2 = 8$

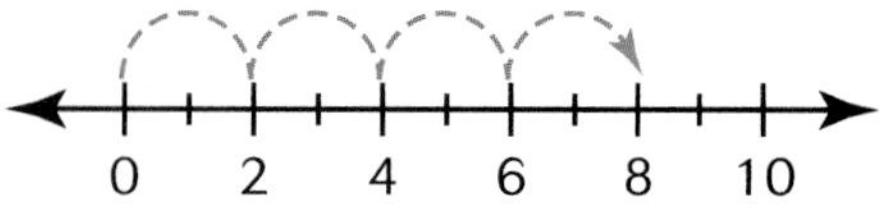

Count by 2s until you have said 4 numbers.
2, 4, 6, 8

So, $4 \times 2 = 8$.

Additional Standards: Algebra and Functions 1.5; Mathematical Reasoning 2.4 *(See p.135.)*

Guided Practice *For another example, see Set C on p. 166.*

1. 6×2 **2.** 2×8 **3.** 9×2 **4.** 8×2 **5.** 2×4

6. Mario buys 2 packages of pencils. Each package has 5 pencils. How many pencils does Mario buy?

Independent Practice *For more practice, see Set C on p. 168.*

7. 2×1 **8.** 2×2 **9.** 2×3 **10.** 2×9 **11.** 7×2 **12.** 5×2

13. Math Reasoning A tape of the music assembly is on sale for $2. Is $13 enough to buy 6 tapes? Explain.

14. One class learned how to play tabla drums for the assembly. If the class has 3 pairs of drums, how many drums do they have in all?

Mixed Review

15. The lunch room displayed milk cartons in an array. There are 5 rows. There are 5 cartons in each row. How many cartons of milk are there?

Write an addition sentence and a multiplication sentence for each set of pictures.

16.
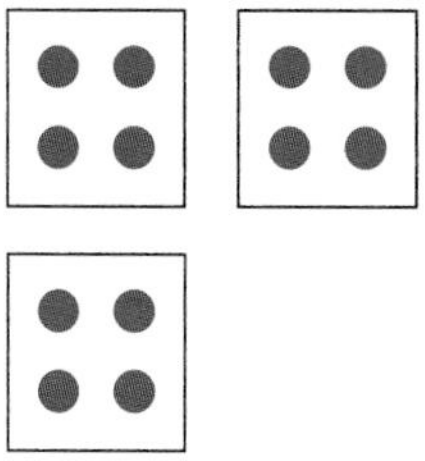

17.
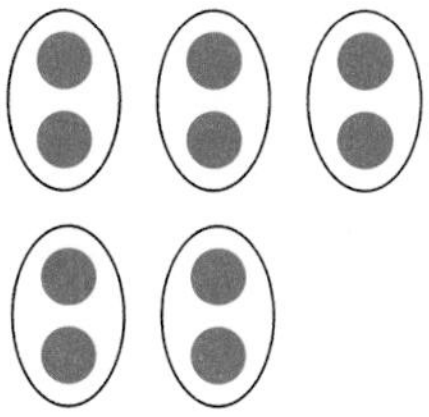

18.
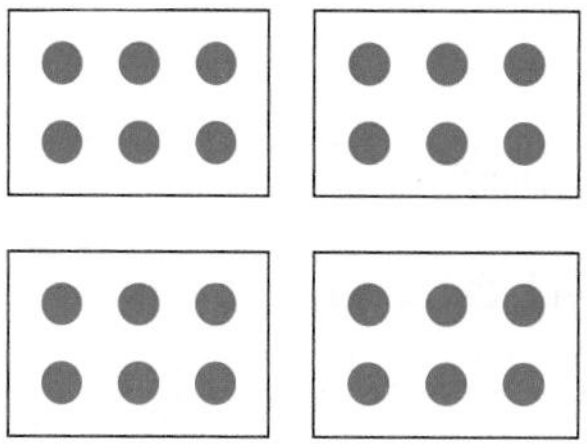

Test Prep **Choose the correct letter for each answer.**

19. (1-3) Which of the following numbers, when rounded to the nearest thousand, does not round to 8,000?

A 7,498 **C** 8,365

B 7,802 **D** 8,499

20. (3-5) Which is the best estimate for the weight of an apple?

F 7 pounds **H** 7 ounces

G 2 pounds **J** 2 ounces

LESSON 4-5

Multiplying by 5

Warm-Up Review

1. 5 + 5
2. 2×5
3. 5, 10, 15, 20, ____, ____
4. 5 + 5+ 5+ 5+ 5
5. Antonio ordered 2 pizzas. Each pizza had 6 slices. How many slices did Antonio get in all?

California Content Standard *Number Sense 2.2(🔑): Memorize to automaticity the multiplication table for numbers between 1 and 10.*

Math Link You know how to multiply by 2. Now you will learn how to multiply by 5.

Example 1

You are getting paint ready for art class. There are 4 groups of students. Each group needs 5 different colors of paint. How many dishes of paint do you need?

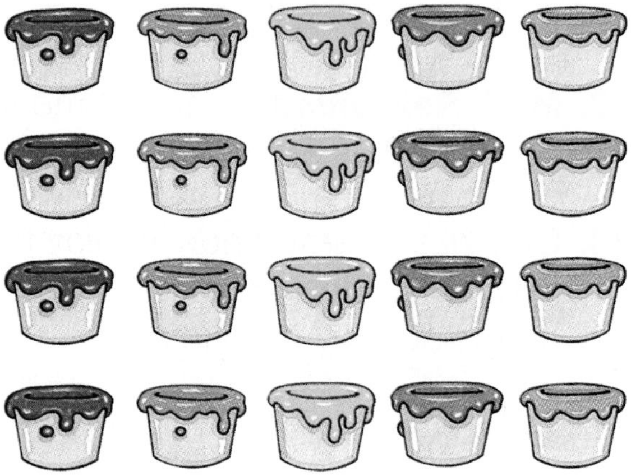

$4 \times 5 = ■$ or $\begin{array}{r} 4 \\ \times\ 5 \\ \hline ■ \end{array}$

You can skip count by 5s to help you find the product.

5 + 5 + 5 + 5 = 20

Count by 5s until you have said 4 numbers.
5, 10, 15, 20

You need 20 dishes of paint.

Example 2

Find 5×6.

You can skip count by 5s to help you find the product.

5 + 5 + 5 + 5 + 5 + 5 = 30

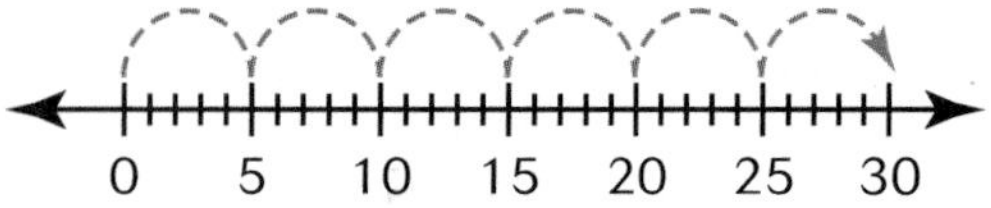

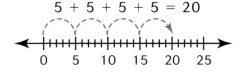

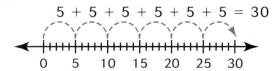

Count by 5s until you have said 6 numbers.
5, 10, 15, 20, 25, 30

So, $5 \times 6 = 30$.

Additional Standards: Algebra and Functions 2.1(🔑), 2.2; Mathematical Reasoning 2.4 (See p.135.)

Guided Practice *For another example, see Set D on p. 166.*

1. 5×3 **2.** 7×5 **3.** 2×5 **4.** 4×5 **5.** 5×1

6. Olivia has 5 sheets of puppy stickers and 2 sheets of kitten stickers. Each sheet has 5 stickers. How many puppy stickers does Olivia have?

Independent Practice *For more practice, see Set D on p. 169.*

7. 1×5 **8.** 5×3 **9.** 9×5 **10.** 5×2 **11.** 5×5 **12.** 7×5

13. 5×1 **14.** 5×5 **15.** 5×8 **16.** 5×3 **17.** 5×9 **18.** 5×10

19. Michael drinks 5 glasses of water per day. How many glasses of water does he drink in a week?

20. Nara makes banjos in her shop. Each banjo has 5 strings. How many strings does she need for 4 banjos?

21. **Math Reasoning** If you know the product of 7×5, how can you use it to find 8×5?

Mixed Review

22. Makayla had 296 stickers in her sticker collection. She gave 113 stickers to her friend in exchange for 15 rocks for her rock collection. How many stickers does Makayla have now?

23. 2×7 **24.** 3×2 **25.** 4×2 **26.** 2×9

27. **Algebra** What is the missing number? $6 \times 3 = 18$, so ■ $\times 6 = 18$

Test Prep **Choose the correct letter for each answer.**

28. (2-7) Henry wants to buy a bicycle that costs $295. He has saved $98. About how much more does he need to save?

A $100 **C** $300
B $200 **D** $400

29. (1-5) Compare 6,050 and 6,500. Choose the correct symbol.

6,050 ● 6,500

F + **J** =
G > **H** <

Diagnostic Checkpoint

Write a multiplication sentence for each picture.

1. *(4-1)*

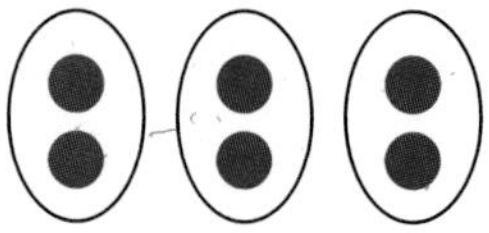

2. *(4-1)*

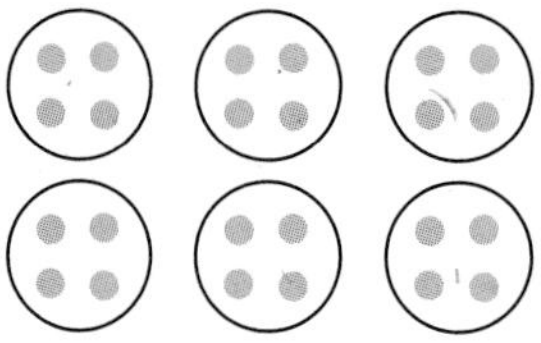

3. *(4-1)*

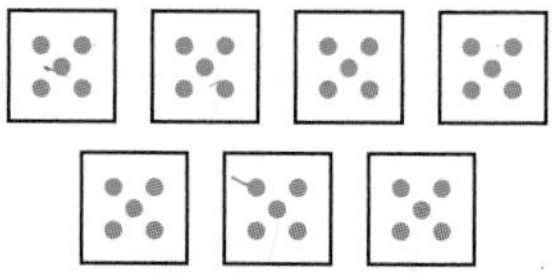

Write a multiplication sentence for each addition expression.

4. *(4-1)* 2 + 2 + 2 + 2 + 2

5. *(4-1)* 7 + 7 + 7

6. *(4-1)* 5 + 5 + 5 + 5

7. *(4-1)* 9 + 9 + 9 + 9

8. *(4-1)* 6 + 6

9. *(4-1)* 4 + 4 + 4 + 4 + 4 + 4

Write a multiplication sentence for each array.

10. *(4-2)*

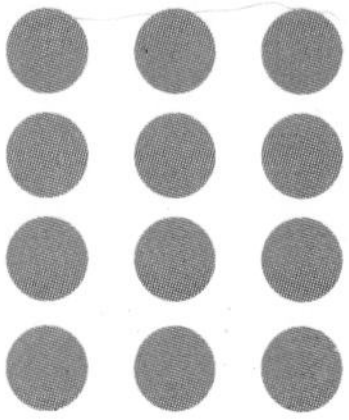

11. *(4-2)*

12. *(4-2)*

Draw an array for each multiplication expression.

13. *(4-2)* 2 × 5

14. *(4-2)* 4 × 3

15. *(4-2)* 2 × 2

Find each product.

16. *(4-4)* 2 × 7

17. *(4-4)* 4 × 2

18. *(4-5)* 6 × 5

19. *(4-5)* 9 × 5

20. *(4-5)* 5 × 3

21. *(4-5)* 4 × 5

22. *(4-4)* 6 × 2

23. *(4-4)* 7 × 2

24. *(4-4)* 2 × 9

25. *(4-5)* 5 × 7

26. *(4-3)* It takes 15 minutes to walk to the park. Would 30 minutes be a reasonable amount of time to walk to the park and back? Explain.

27. *(4-3)* You have 20 students in your class. Would 30 cookies be a reasonable number of cookies to buy if you were going to give each student 2 cookies? Explain.

TEST PREP

Multiple-Choice Cumulative Review

Choose the correct letter for each answer.

1. **What number is equal to six hundred seven?**

   A 607
   B 670
   C 676
   D 677
   E NH

2. **Which expression could be used to find the sum of 9 and 12?**

   F 9 + 21
   G 21 − 12
   H 9 − 12
   J 9 + 12

3. **The table shows the number of each type of bagel sold in June.**

Bagel	Number Sold
Sesame	599
Raisin	407
Honey Wheat	544
Blueberry	660

   Which type of bagel was sold most often?

   A Sesame
   B Raisin
   C Honey Wheat
   D Blueberry

4. **If Tomeka answered the phone at 4:15 P.M. and talked until 5:03 P.M., how long did her phone conversation last?**

   F 44 min
   G 48 min
   H 1 hr 4 min
   J 1 hr 15 min

5. **Robert swims 5 laps every day. How many laps does he swim in 1 week?**

   A 5 laps
   B 10 laps
   C 30 laps
   D 35 laps

6. **Thomas and Ronny are playing a board game. Thomas has 16 points. Ronny has 14 points. On Ronny's next turn, he loses 3 points. How many points does Ronny have now?**

   F 11 points
   G 13 points
   H 17 points
   J 19 points

7. **What number belongs in the box?**
   16, 18, ■, 22, 24

   A 18　　**C** 20
   B 19　　**D** 21

LESSON 4-6

Multiplying by 3

Warm-Up Review

1. 2 × 5 2. 5 × 2
3. 3, 6, 9, 12, ____, ____.
4. 3 + 3 + 3 + 3 + 3
5. Michael has 9 packages of erasers. Each package has 2 erasers. How many erasers does Michael have in all?

California Content Standard *Number Sense 2.2(🔑): Memorize to automaticity the multiplication table for numbers between 1 and 10.*

Math Link You know how to multiply by 2 and 5. Now you will learn how to multiply by 3.

Example 1

It's time for recess! There are only 4 jump ropes. If 3 students share each jump rope, how many students can play jump rope at one time?

$4 \times 3 = ■$ or $\begin{array}{r} 4 \\ \times\ 3 \\ \hline ■ \end{array}$

You can skip count by 3s to help you find the product.

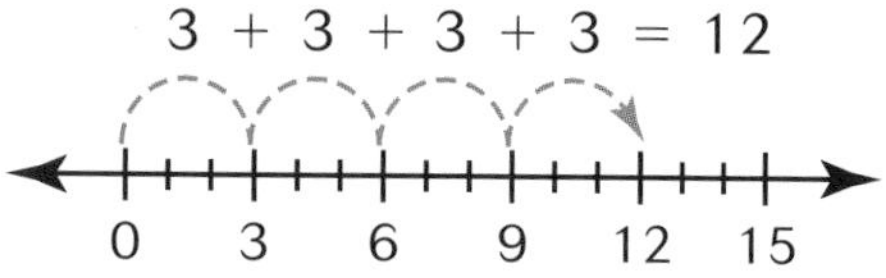

Count by 3s until you have said 4 numbers.
3, 6, 9, 12

12 students can play jump rope at one time.

Example 2

Find 3 × 3.

You can skip count by 3s to help you find the product.

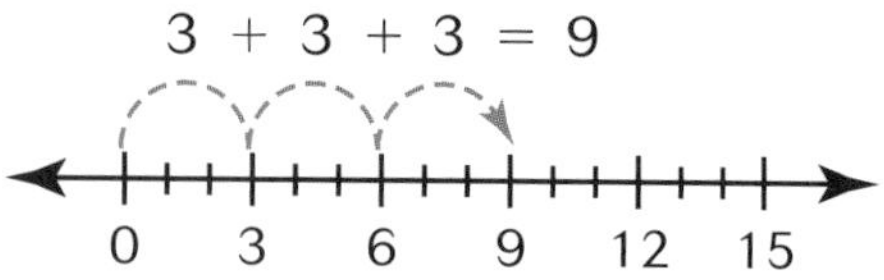

Count by 3s until you have said 3 numbers.
3, 6, 9

So, 3 × 3 = 9.

Additional Standards: Algebra and Functions 2.1 (🔑); 2.2; Mathematical Reasoning 2.4 *(See p. 135.)*

Guided Practice *For another example, see Set E on p. 167.*

1. 5×3 **2.** 3×1 **3.** 4×3 **4.** 3×6 **5.** 3×9

6. Jennifer has 4 dolls. Each doll has 3 outfits. How many outfits does Jennifer have for her dolls?

Independent Practice *For more practice, see Set E on p. 169.*

7. 2×3 **8.** 3×8 **9.** 6×3 **10.** 3×7 **11.** 3×3 **12.** 9×3

13. Algebra Complete the pattern.

9, 12, 15, ■, ■, 24, ■, 30

14. Janice needs 12 jump ropes for her class. She already has 4 jump ropes. New jump ropes cost $3 each. How much must she spend on new jump ropes?

15. Math Reasoning Kendra says, "To find 3×8, I can find 2×8 and add one more group of 3." What's wrong?

Mixed Review

16. On Monday, 4,692 books were checked out at the library. On Tuesday, 3,289 books were checked out. How many books were checked out in the two days?

17. 5×8 **18.** 5×4 **19.** 9×5 **20.** 2×6 **21.** 7×2

Test Prep Choose the correct letter for each answer.

22. Which multiplication sentence shows how many stars in all?
(4-2)

A $3 \times 3 = 9$
B $3 \times 4 = 12$
C $3 \times 5 = 15$
D $3 \times 6 = 18$

23. What time is shown on the clock?
(Gr. 2)

F 7:12
G 7:53
H 10:07
J 11:35
K NH

LESSON 4-7

Multiplying by 4

Warm-Up Review

1. 2 × 2
2. 3 × 6
3. 5 × 3
4. 6 × 5
5. 4, 8, 12, 16, ____, ____
6. Doris made 24 muffins. She ate 2 muffins and her brother ate 3 muffins. How many muffins were left?

California Content Standard *Number Sense 2.2(🔑): Memorize to automaticity the multiplication table for numbers between 1 and 10.*

Math Link You know how to multiply by 2, 3, and 5. Now you will learn how to multiply by 4.

Example 1

Your school has a new computer lab. There are 5 rows of computers. There are 4 computers in each row. How many computers are there in the computer lab?

5 × 4 = ■ or

$$\begin{array}{r} 5 \\ \times\ 4 \\ \hline ■ \end{array}$$

You can skip count by 4s to help you find the product.

4 + 4 + 4 + 4 + 4 = 20

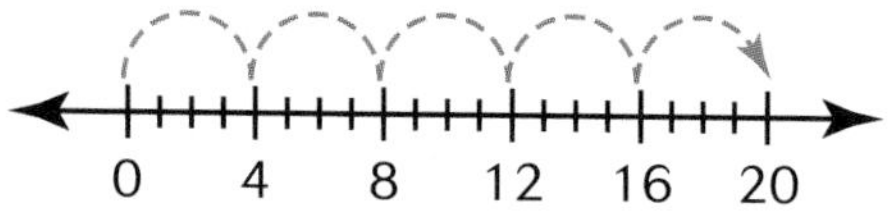

Count by 4s until you have said 5 numbers.
4, 8, 12, 16, 20

There are 20 computers in the lab.

Example 2

Find 3 × 4.

You can skip count by 4s to help you find the product.

4 + 4 + 4 = 12

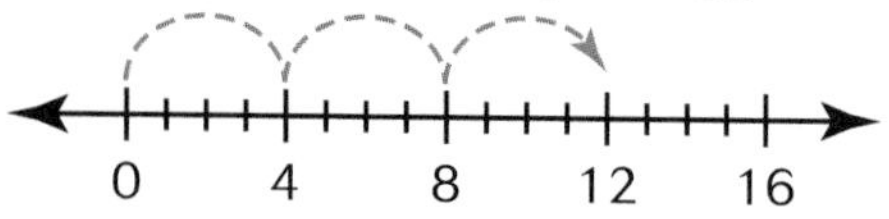

Count by 4s until you have said 3 numbers.
4, 8, 12

So, 3 × 4 = 12.

Additional Standards: Number Sense 2.8; Algebra and Functions 1.5 *(See p. 135.)*

Guided Practice *For another example, see Set F on p. 167.*

1. 4×3 **2.** 6×4 **3.** 1×4 **4.** 7×4 **5.** 4×9

6. Melvin buys 4 CDs. Each CD has 8 songs. How many songs are on Melvin's CDs?

Independent Practice *For more practice, see Set F on p. 169.*

7. 4×8 **8.** 4×1 **9.** 9×4 **10.** 4×7 **11.** 8×4 **12.** 1×4

13. 4×4 **14.** 3×4 **15.** 4×5 **16.** 4×6 **17.** 2×4

18. Algebra If $5 \times 4 = 20$, then $4 \times ■ = 20$.

19. Four groups of students use the class computer each day. Two students work on the computer at a time. How many students use the computer each day?

20. The computer teacher had 49 CD-ROMs. She bought 3 more boxes of CD-ROMs. Each box has 4 CD-ROMs in it. How many CD-ROMs does she have now?

Mixed Review

21. The school store is open from 8:00 A.M. to 8:30 A.M. and from 11:45 A.M. to 12:30 P.M. each day. How long is the school store open?

22. 3×8 **23.** 1×3 **24.** 5×6 **25.** 5×5 **26.** 6×3

Test Prep **Choose the correct letter for each answer.**

27. (3-7) Which is the best estimate for the height of a cat?

A About 30 centimeters
B About 30 yards
C About 30 meters
D About 30 miles

28. (2-13) What is the missing number that completes the number sentence?

$■ + 15 = 23$

F 7
G 8
H 9
J 10

LESSON 4-8

Understand
Plan
Solve
Look Back

Problem-Solving Strategy:
Make a List

Warm-Up Review

1. $3.04 + $8.97
2. $15.32 − $9.61

Put these numbers in order from least to greatest.

3. 18, 23, 11, 6, 35
4. 9, 25, 3, 16, 30
5. Mitch has 5 red marbles, 9 blue marbles, and 11 cars. How many marbles does Mitch have?

California Content Standard *Mathematical Reasoning 2.3: Use a variety of methods, such as words, numbers, symbols, charts, graphs, tables, diagrams, and models, to explain mathematical reasoning.*

Mr. Weaver is taking a picture of Jenny, Liza, and Ryan for the class scrapbook. He asks them, "In how many different ways could you three students stand in a line?"

First	Second	Third
Jenny	Liza	Ryan
Jenny	Ryan	Liza
Liza	Ryan	Jenny
Liza	Jenny	Ryan
Ryan	Jenny	Liza
Ryan	Liza	Jenny

Understand

What do you need to know?

You need to know that any of the students can be first, second, or third.

Plan

How can you solve the problem?

You can **make a list** to help you find all the different ways. Choose one student to be first and another to be second. The last one will be third.

Solve

When you make your list, you will notice that there are 2 ways for Jenny to be first, 2 ways for Liza to be first, and 2 ways for Ryan to be first.

So, there are 6 ways that the students could stand in line.

Look Back

How is making a list helpful when you want to know if you covered all the ways?

 Additional Standards: Mathematical Reasoning 2.0, 3.2 *(See p. 135.)*

Guided Practice

Make a list to help you solve the problem.

1. Rudy must decide what to wear for his school picture. He has a blue shirt and a yellow shirt. He has black pants and brown pants. What are the ways Rudy could choose a shirt and pair of pants to wear?

Independent Practice

2. Students get to pick the background for their school pictures. They can choose blue, green, or tan. The color can be solid or striped. List all the different background choices that the students have.

3. Jan, Carl, and Peter are standing in line to get their picture taken. What are all the different ways they can stand in line?

4. Tim can sit or stand for his photo. He also has a choice of a blue or black background. What ways can he have his picture taken?

Mixed Review

Try these or other strategies to solve each problem. Tell which strategy you used.

Problem-Solving Strategies

- *Make a List*
- *Use Logical Reasoning*
- *Work Backward*
- *Make a Table*

5. Jeff is taller than Alan. Sue is shorter than Alan. Gayle is taller than Jeff. The school photographer wants the 4 students to stand in line from tallest to shortest. In what order should they stand?

6. Joan had $2.05 when she got home from school. She had paid $14.95 for her school pictures. She also bought a new pen at the school store for $3.00. How much money did Joan have to start with?

Use Homework Workbook 4–8.

LESSON 4-9

Multiplying by 1 or 0

Algebra

Warm-Up Review

1. 3 + 1 **2.** 3 + 0

3. 9 + 1 **4.** 9 + 0

5. 1 + 1 **6.** 0 + 0

7. 8 + 1 **8.** 8 + 0

9. Heather had 15 stamps. She gave them all away. How many stamps did she have left?

California Content Standard *Number Sense 2.6: Understand the special properties of 0 and 1 in multiplication.*

Math Link You know how to add with 1 or 0. Now you will learn how to multiply by 1 or 0.

Example 1

It's lunchtime! There are 4 plates on the counter. Each plate has 1 hamburger on it. How many hamburgers are there?

4 × 1 = ■

4 × 1 = 4

There are 4 hamburgers.

When you multiply any number by 1, the product is that same number.

Example 2

There are 3 plates on another counter. There are no salads on any of the plates. How many salads are there?

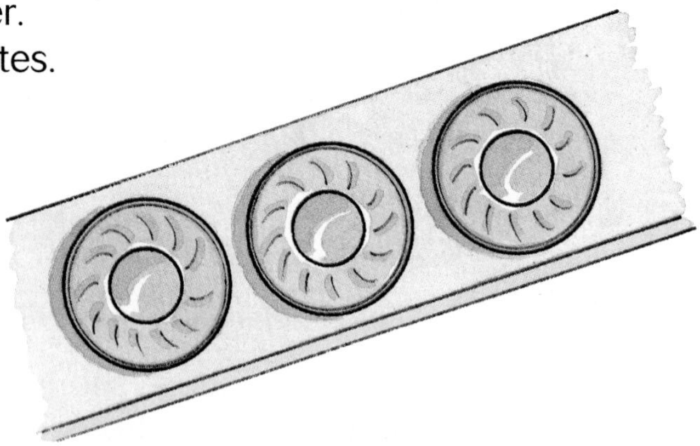

3 × 0 = ■

3 × 0 = 0

There are 0 salads.

When you multiply any number by 0, the product is 0.

Example 3

Brian buys 5 pencils at the student store for $1 each. How much money did he spend altogether?

5 × 1 = ■

5 × 1 = 5

Brian spent $5.

 Additional Standards: Algebra and Functions 1.3; Mathematical Reasoning 2.2, 3.3 (See p. 135.)

Guided Practice *For another example, see Set G on p. 167.*

1. 1 × 8 **2.** 0 × 8 **3.** 3 × 1 **4.** 6 × 1 **5.** 0 × 9

6. There are 5 plates on the table. There are no sandwiches on any of the plates. How many sandwiches are there?

Independent Practice *For more practice, see Set G on p. 169.*

7. 1 × 6 **8.** 9 × 0 **9.** 1 × 7 **10.** 2 × 0 **11.** 1 × 0 **12.** 5 × 0

13. 8 × 1 **14.** 0 × 6 **15.** 4 × 1 **16.** 3 × 1 **17.** 0 × 4

Algebra Write × or + in each ●.

18. 6 ● 1 = 6 **19.** 6 ● 0 = 0 **20.** 6 ● 0 = 6 **21.** 6 ● 1 = 7

Use the menu to solve Exercises 22–23.

22. How much do 7 tacos cost?

23. You don't buy any super salads. How much money do you spend on super salads?

24. Write 7 as the product of two factors.

25. Math Reasoning Is it easier to multiply 3 × 1 than it is to multiply 345 × 1? Explain.

Mixed Review

26. Sonny has a blue car, a red car, and a green car. In how many ways can Sonny line up his cars?

27. 4 × 4 **28.** 6 × 4 **29.** 3 × 3 **30.** 9 × 3 **31.** 8 × 4

Test Prep **Choose the correct letter for each answer.**

32. (1-7) Which is 7,000 + 800 + 70 in standard form?

A 787
B 7,087
C 7,870
D 7,800,070
E NH

33. (1-2) What is 847 rounded to the nearest hundred?

F 850
G 800
H 900
J 1,000
K NH

LESSON 4-10

Input/Output Tables

Algebra

California Content Standard *Algebra and Functions 2.2 Extend and recognize a linear pattern by its rules. . . .*

Warm-Up Review

1. 3×4 **2.** 4×6

3. 2×8 **4.** 5×8

5. 0×5 **6.** 1×7

7. 5×3 **8.** 3×9

9. Each student has 3 markers and 2 pencils. If there are 5 students, how many markers do they have altogether?

Math Link You know how to find patterns. In this lesson, you will use patterns to complete tables and find rules.

Example 1

The table at the right is called an input/output table. The rule for an input/output table describes what to do to the input number to get the output number.

What is the rule for this table? Look for a pattern. If you look closely, you will see that the inputs are all related in the same way to the outputs.

Rule: ___?___

Input	Output
1	2
2	4
3	6
4	8

$1 \times 2 = 2$

$2 \times 2 = 4$

$3 \times 2 = 6$

$4 \times 2 = 8$

The rule is multiply by 2.

Example 2

Complete the table.

Rule: Add 3.

Input	Output
0	3
1	4
■	5
3	■

$2 + 3 = 5$

$3 + 3 = 6$

The missing input is 2.

The missing output is 3.

Example 3

Complete the table.

Rule: Subtract 4.

Input	Output
10	6
8	■
6	2
4	■

$8 - 4 = 4$

$4 - 4 = 0$

The missing outputs are 4 and 0.

Guided Practice *For another example, see Set H on p. 167.*

Complete each table.

1. Rule: Multiply by 2.

Input	Output
5	10
6	
7	
8	

2. Rule: Multiply by 3.

Input	Output
2	6
4	
	18
8	

3. Rule: Add 4.

Input	Output
0	4
4	
	10
8	

4. The rule for a table is multiply by 5. If an input is 8, what is the output?

Independent Practice *For more practice, see Set H on p. 169.*

Write the rule. Then complete the table.

5. Rule: ____________

Input	Output
20	15
16	11
12	7
8	
5	

6. Rule: ____________

Input	Output
2	8
5	
6	24
8	
9	36

7. Rule: ____________

Input	Output
2	10
4	12
7	
10	
13	21

Mixed Review

8. Lance has black pants, blue pants, and tan pants. He has a white shirt and a red shirt. List all the different ways Lance could choose a shirt and a pair of pants to wear.

9. 0×1 **10.** 8×1 **11.** 7×0 **12.** 4×9 **13.** 2×4

Test Prep Choose the correct letter for each answer.

14. Find 3,904 − 2,895.
(2-10)

A 1,009
B 1,109
C 1,191
D 6,799
E NH

15. Compare: 1500 mL ● 1 L
(3-8)

F +
G <
H >
J =
K NH

LESSON 4-11

Understand
Plan
Solve
Look Back

Problem-Solving Application: Using Data

Algebra

California Content Standard *Algebra and Functions 2.1 (🔑): Solve simple problems involving a functional relationship between two quantities. . ..*

Warm-Up Review

1. 4 × 6 **2.** 3 × 8

3. 85¢ − 13¢

4. $25.00 − $17.75

5. Mia bought 6 pieces of gum for 50¢. Tiana bought 12 pieces of gum for $1.00. Mia also bought a candy bar for 65¢. How much money did the girls spend on gum?

Example

Lisa is going to the school store to buy some pencils. Lisa decides to buy 5 pencils. How much money does she save? Use the data at the right.

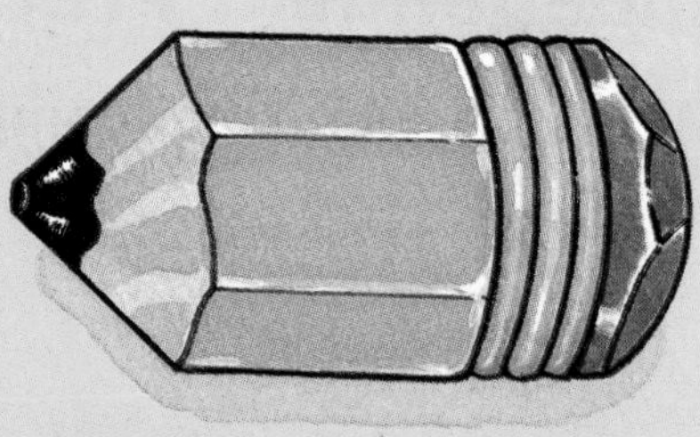

School Store Sale
Regular price: 24¢ each
Sale price: Buy 4 or more pencils and save 6¢ each!

Understand

What do you need to know?

First, you need to know how many pencils Lisa is buying. If she is buying 4 or more pencils, you need to know that she saves 6¢ on each pencil she buys.

Plan

How can you solve the problem?

You can **write a number sentence.** Since Lisa is buying more than 4 pencils, you can multiply 6¢ by 5 to find how much money she saves.

Solve

5	×	6¢	=	30¢
↑		↑		↑
Number of Pencils		Savings for 1 Pencil		Total Savings

Lisa saves 30¢.

Look Back

How could you use addition to check your answer?

Use repeated addition. Since 6 + 6 + 6 + 6 + 6 = 30¢, the answer checks.

Additional Standards: Number Sense 2.8; Mathematical Reasoning 2.0, 2.6; (See p. 135.)

Use the information below to answer Exercises 1–6.

Guided Practice

1. How much money will Tamara pay for an eraser and 2 pens?

2. Maya buys 4 note pads on sale. How much money does she save?

Independent Practice

3. How much do 2 pens and 3 stickers cost?

4. Paul and Karen each need 2 erasers. They decide to buy the erasers together. How much money will each of them save?

5. Which costs more, 10 pens or 10 notepads?

6. **Math Reasoning** You have $1 to spend at the school store. You buy a notepad. Do you have enough money left to buy 4 stickers? How do you know?

Mixed Review

7. Fred buys a sandwich for $1.89 and an apple for 80¢. He pays with a $5 bill. What is his change?

8. Juanita spends $8.88 on a vegetable pizza. She pays the clerk with a $10 bill. List the fewest coins and bills the clerk could give Juanita as change.

9. The first night, Ollie learned 6 spelling words. By the second night, he had learned 12 words. By the third night, he had learned 18 words. If the pattern continues, in how many more nights will he have learned 60 words?

Diagnostic Checkpoint

Complete. For Exercises 1–3, use the words from the Word Bank.

Word Bank
array
count by 5s
factors
input/output tables
product

1. (4-1) The numbers you multiply are called __________.

2. (4-2) A(n) __________ shows objects in rows and columns.

3. (4-1) The answer you get when you multiply is called the __________.

Find each product.

4. (4-6) 2 × 3 **5.** (4-7) 4 × 5 **6.** (4-6) 6 × 3 **7.** (4-7) 9 × 4 **8.** (4-7) 4 × 4

9. (4-7) 4 × 6 **10.** (4-6) 3 × 3 **11.** (4-9) 7 × 0 **12.** (4-7) 7 × 4 **13.** (4-9) 1 × 9

14. (4-6) 3 × 5 **15.** (4-7) 4 × 8 **16.** (4-9) 6 × 1 **17.** (4-6) 3 × 7 **18.** (4-6) 9 × 3

19. (4-9) 2 × 0 **20.** (4-7) 4 × 7 **21.** (4-7) 6 × 4 **22.** (4-9) 0 × 4 **23.** (4-9) 1 × 7

Algebra Complete each table.

24. (4-10) Rule: Multiply by 5.

Input	Output
3	
5	
	35
9	

25. (4-10) Rule: Subtract 9.

Input	Output
15	
	13
27	
32	

26. (4-10) Rule: Add 15.

Input	Output
5	
16	
27	
38	

27. (4-8) Three groups of students go to the computer lab each Friday. The group names are Red, Blue, and Green. Each group can go either first, second, or last. What are all the different ways the groups can go to the lab?

28. (4-11) Use the table to the right. There are 3 children and 2 adults in Dan's family. How much will it cost his family to go to the movies?

Movie Prices	
Children	$3.00
Adult	$5.00

Chapter 4 Test

Write a multiplication sentence for each addition sentence.

1. 4 + 4 + 4 = 12

2. 6 + 6 + 6 + 6 + 6 + 6 = 36

3. 5 + 5 + 5 + 5 = 20

4. 7 + 7 + 7 + 7 + 7 = 35

Draw an array for each multiplication expression.

5. 9 × 3

6. 7 × 5

Find each product.

7. $\begin{array}{r} 3 \\ \times\ 4 \\ \hline \end{array}$

8. $\begin{array}{r} 5 \\ \times\ 6 \\ \hline \end{array}$

9. $\begin{array}{r} 5 \\ \times\ 9 \\ \hline \end{array}$

10. $\begin{array}{r} 2 \\ \times\ 6 \\ \hline \end{array}$

11. $\begin{array}{r} 4 \\ \times\ 9 \\ \hline \end{array}$

12. 0 × 9

13. 1 × 5

14. 9 × 1

Algebra **Write the number that belongs in each ■.**

15. 3 × 5 = 15, so 5 × 3 = ■

16. 7 × 2 = 14, so 2 × 7 = ■

Complete each table.

17. Rule: Multiply by 3.

Input	Output
4	
1	
5	

18. Rule: Multiply by 0.

Input	Output
9	
6	
3	

Use the table to answer Exercises 19 and 20.

19. In the cafeteria you can buy any bagel with or without cream cheese. What are the different ways you can buy a bagel?

20. Mark has $2. He says he can buy two bagels, each with cream cheese, and a juice. Is Mark correct? Explain.

TEST PREP

Multiple-Choice Chapter 4 Test

Choose the correct letter for each answer.

1. Find the product of 4 × 8.

A 4
B 12
C 32
D 36
E NH

2. Find the product of 5 × 9.

F 14
G 45
H 54
J 59
K NH

3. Which number belongs in the ■?
3 × 7 = 21, so
7 × ■ = 21

A 2
B 3
C 7
D 14
E NH

4. What has the same product as 0 × 6.

F 1 × 6
G 2 × 3
H 3 × 3
J 9 × 0
K NH

5. What is the rule for the table?

Input	Output
2	8
3	12
5	20
7	28

A Add 4.
B Multiply by 4.
C Add 6.
D Multiply by 6.

6. There are 4 bagels in a bag. How many bagels are there in 6 bags?

F 10 bagels
G 12 bagels
H 20 bagels
J 24 bagels

7. Each of Tandra's swimming lessons lasts 2 hours. She goes to swimming lessons 4 times per week. How many hours each week does Tandra have swimming lessons?

A 2 hours
B 4 hours
C 6 hours
D 8 hours

8. Which means the same as $8 + 8 + 8 + 8 + 8$?

F 1×8
G 2×8
H 4×8
J 5×8
K NH

9. Latrisha, Shelly, and Mickey need to line up for the spelling bee. In how many different ways can they stand in line?

A 3 ways
B 6 ways
C 8 ways
D 9 ways

10. Each of 4 students has 5 notebooks. How many notebooks do the students have altogether?

F 5 notebooks
G 9 notebooks
H 15 notebooks
J 20 notebooks

11. Jill has $10 to spend at the gift shop. Cards cost $2 each, balloons cost $3 each, and roses cost $4 each. Which gift purchase would NOT be reasonable?

A 2 cards and 1 balloon
B 2 roses and 1 card
C 3 roses and 1 card
D 1 card, 1 rose, and 1 balloon

12. How much money will Darnell pay for 4 binders and 2 packages of pens?

School Supplies	
Package of pencils	$1
Package of pens	$2
Notebook paper	$1
Binder	$4

F $6
G $8
H $16
J $20

13. Find the product 8×2.

A 4
B 6
C 10
D 14
E NH

14. Which describes the array?

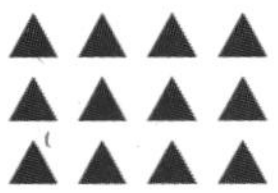

F 2×3
G 3×3
H 3×4
J 4×4
K NH

Reteaching

Set A (pages 136–138)

Each of the three spiders below has 8 legs each. How many legs are there altogether?

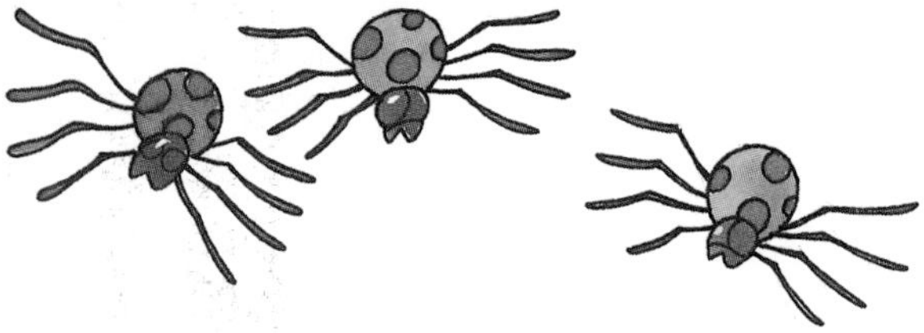

8 + 8 + 8 = 24
3 groups of 8 = 24
So, 3 × 8 = 24.

There are 24 spider legs altogether.

Remember whenever you add the same number again and again, you can also multiply.

Write an addition sentence and a multiplication sentence for the number of leaves below.

1.

Set B (pages 139–141)

Write a multiplication sentence for the array.

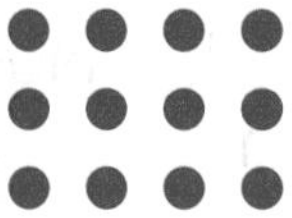

There are 3 rows of 4 dots.
So, 3 × 4 = 12.

Remember the order in which you multiply factors does not change the product.

Write a multiplication sentence for each array.

1. 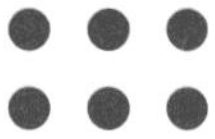

2. 

Set C (pages 144–145)

Find 2 × 8.

2 × 8 means 2 groups of 8, or 8 + 8. Since 8 + 8 = 16, 2 × 8 = 16 and 8 × 2 = 16.

Remember the numbers you multiply are called factors. When you multiply, the answer is called the product.

1. 5 × 2 **2.** 7 × 2

Set D (pages 146–147)

Find 5 × 8.

Count by 5s until you have said 8 numbers.
5, 10, 15, 20, 25, 30, 35, 40
5 × 8 = 40

Remember you can skip count to find a product.

1. 5 × 9 **2.** 5 × 5

Set E (pages 150–151)

Find 3 × 5.

Skip count by 3s to find the product.

3 + 3 + 3 + 3 + 3 = 15

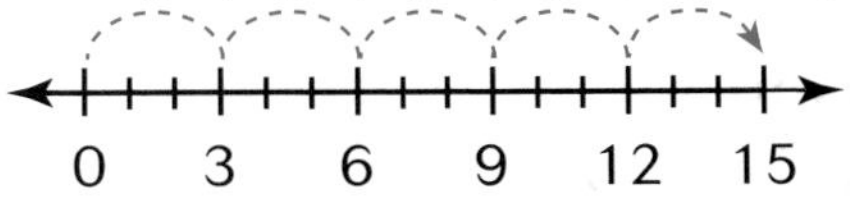

So, 3 × 5 = 15.

Remember you can skip count by 3s to find a product.

1. 3 × 4 **2.** 3 × 7

3. 1 × 3 **4.** 9 × 3

Set F (pages 152–153)

Find 6 × 4.

Skip count by 4s to find the product.

4 + 4 + 4 + 4 + 4 + 4 = 24

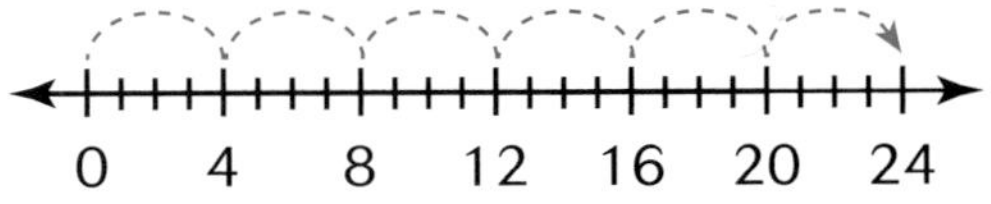

So, 6 × 4 = 24.

Remember you can skip count by 4s to find a product.

1. 4 × 1 **2.** 4 × 5

3. 7 × 4 **4.** 9 × 4

Set G (pages 156–157)

Find 6 × 0.

When 0 is a factor, the product is always 0.

6 × 0 = 0

Remember when 1 is a factor, the product is always the same as the other factor.

1. 4 × 0 **2.** 1 × 6

3. 0 × 7 **4.** 9 × 1

Set H (pages 158–159)

Complete the table.

Rule: Multiply by 2.

Input	Output	
1	2	1 × 2 = 2
2	4	2 × 2 = 4
	6	3 × 2 = 6
4		4 × 2 = 8

The missing input is 3.
The missing output is 8.

Remember to use the rule on the number in the input column.

Complete each table.

1. Rule: Subtract 5.

Input	Output
6	
8	
	5
12	

2. Rule: Add 7.

Input	Output
	8
5	
7	
9	

More Practice

Set A *(pages 136–138)*

Write an addition sentence and a multiplication sentence for each set of pictures.

1. 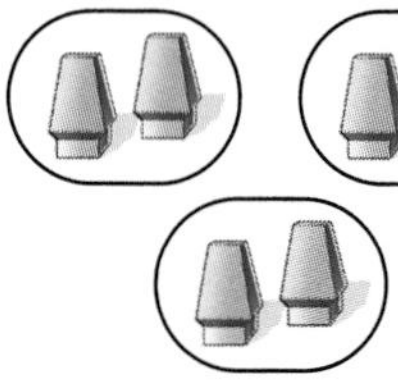

2. 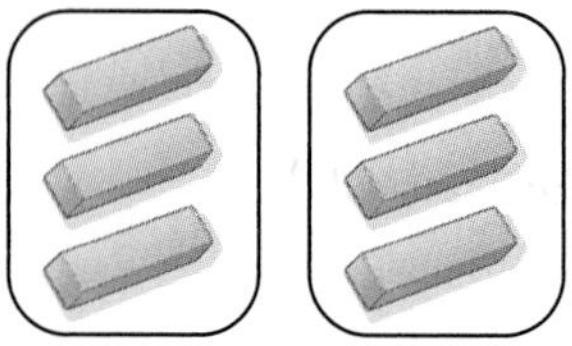

3. 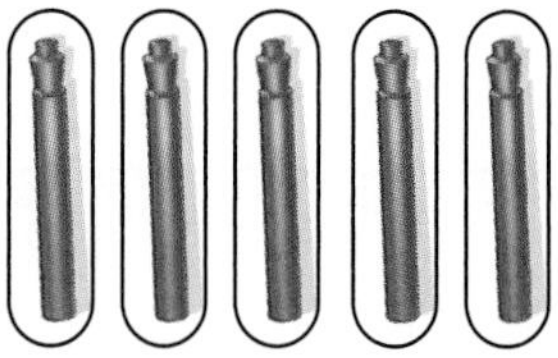

Write a multiplication sentence for each addition sentence.

4. 8 + 8 + 8 = 24
5. 6 + 6 + 6 + 6 = 24
6. 1 + 1 + 1 = 3
7. One book costs $4. How much will 5 of these books cost?

Set B *(pages 139–141)*

Write a multiplication sentence for each array.

1. 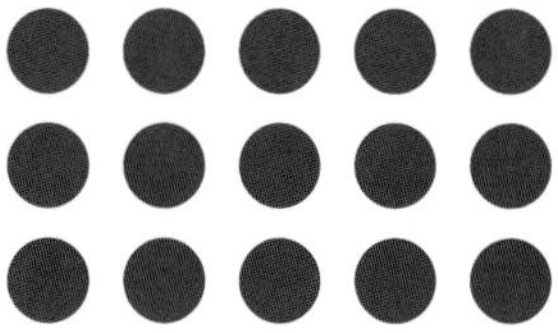

2. 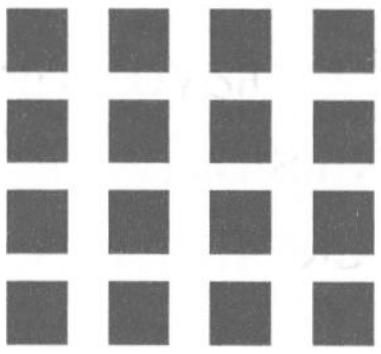

3. 

Draw an array to show each multiplication problem. Then find the product.

4. 1 × 6
5. 7 × 4
6. 2 × 3
7. In the gym there are 4 rows of mats. There are 8 mats in each row. How many mats are there?

Set C *(pages 144–145)*

1. 2 × 4
2. 2 × 3
3. 2 × 9
4. 2 × 8
5. 2 × 6
6. 7 × 2
7. The computer lab received 7 new computer games. Two people are needed to play each game. How many people can play at one time?

Set D (pages 146–147)

1. 5×6 **2.** 2×5 **3.** 5×4 **4.** 5×1 **5.** 3×5 **6.** 7×5

7. A teacher can put 5 paintings on each bulletin board. He has enough paintings to fill 4 bulletin boards. How many paintings can the teacher put up?

Set E (pages 150–151)

1. 3×2 **2.** 5×3 **3.** 3×8 **4.** 4×3 **5.** 3×3 **6.** 6×3

7. There are 3 relay teams. There are 7 students and 2 teachers on each team. How many students are there in all?

Set F (pages 152–153)

1. 8×4 **2.** 6×4 **3.** 2×4 **4.** 4×4 **5.** 5×4 **6.** 7×4

7. There are 4 buckets of balls on the playground. Each bucket has 7 balls. Kari takes 4 balls out of one bucket. How many balls are left in the buckets?

Set G (pages 156–157)

1. 3×0 **2.** 7×1 **3.** 1×2 **4.** 0×6 **5.** 5×1 **6.** 9×0

7. There are 7 bags. Each bag has 1 orange in it. How many oranges are there?

Set H (pages 158–159)

Complete each table.

1. Rule: Subtract 2.

Input	Output
3	1
5	
	5
9	

2. Rule: Multiply by 3.

Input	Output
2	6
3	
6	
	27

3. Rule: Add 6.

Input	Output
6	12
9	
14	
	24

Problem Solving: Preparing for Tests

Choose the correct letter for each answer.

1. **Use the ticket prices given below. Bob is buying 6 tickets for a car show. Which of these is reasonable for the amount of money Bob will spend on the tickets?**

A Less than $13

B Less than $30

C Between $30 and $48

D More than $48

> **Tip**
> Start by finding out the least and most money Bob could spend on tickets.

2. **A store has a stuffed animal display. There are 31 animals in the back row, 27 in the next row, 23 in the next row, and 19 in the next row. If the pattern continues, how many animals are in the next 4 rows?**

F 18, 17, 16, 15

G 16, 13, 10, 7

H 15, 11, 7, 3

J 11, 9, 7, 3

> **Tip**
> Use the *Find a Pattern* strategy to help you solve this problem. Start by subtracting to find out how the numbers are decreasing.

3. **Sadie drew 2 groups of butterflies with 2 butterflies in each group. She also drew 4 groups of flowers with 3 flowers in each group. Which number sentence shows the number of flowers Sadie drew?**

A $4 + 3 = 7$

B $4 \times 3 = 12$

C $3 + 3 + 3 = 9$

D $2 \times 2 = 4$

> **Tip**
> Use one of the strategies below to solve this problem.
> - *Draw a Picture*
> - *Write a Number Sentence*

4. In a contest, Ann guessed there were 493 beans in a jar. Her guess was 112 beans too few. Which is the best estimate for the number of beans in the jar?

F About 400

G About 500

H About 600

J About 700

---

5. Small baskets cost $6.00 and large baskets cost $8.00. How much would you pay if you bought 5 small baskets?

A $2.00 **C** $14.00

B $30.00 **D** $40.00

---

6. Jill and Isaac are stamping 4 birds on each greeting card they make. So far, Jill has made 8 cards and Isaac has made 5 cards. How many more birds has Jill stamped than Isaac?

F 3 more birds

G 12 more birds

H 20 more birds

J 32 more birds

---

7. Jerry and his 3 friends each have 2 dogs. Which shows the total number of dogs they have?

A 3×2

B 4×2

C $3 + 2$

D $2 + 2 + 2 + 3$

8. Amy had 91¢. She gave 48¢ to a friend. About how much money does Amy have left?

F About 30¢ **H** About 40¢

G About 90¢ **J** About $1.40

Use the graph for Questions 9–10.

The graph below shows the favorite kinds of exercise of a group of students.

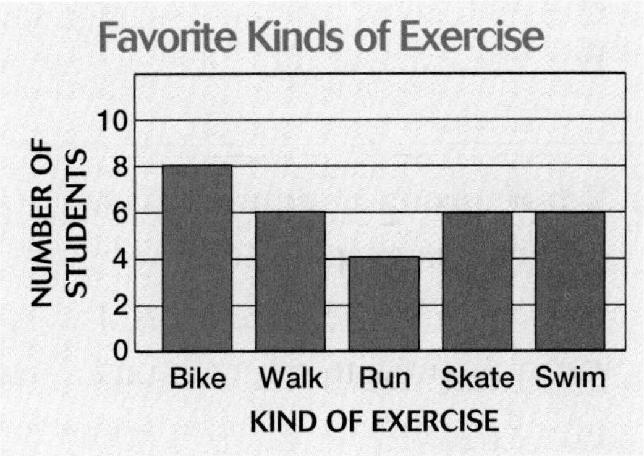

9. How many more students chose biking than skating?

A 1 more student

B 2 more students

C 3 more students

D 12 more students

---

10. Which number sentence shows the number of students who like to bike, run, or swim?

F $8 + 4 + 6$

G $8 + 4 + 4$

H $6 + 4 + 6$

J $8 + 4 + 8$

TEST PREP

Multiple-Choice Cumulative Review

Choose the correct letter for each answer.

Number Sense

1. Which number is between 667 and 776?

667		776

A 570 C 777
B 704 D 966

2. Which group of numbers is in order from *greatest* to *least?*

F 1,000 1,134 1,279 1,621
G 1,621 1,279 1,134 1,000
H 1,621 1,134 1,279 1,000
J 1,279 1,134 1,000 1,621

3. Which shaded region does NOT represent $\frac{1}{4}$ of the figure?

A 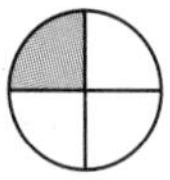
C 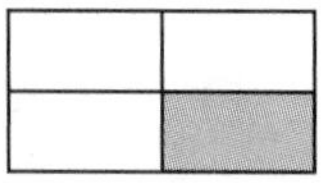
B 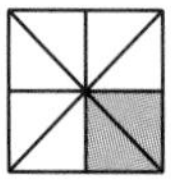
D 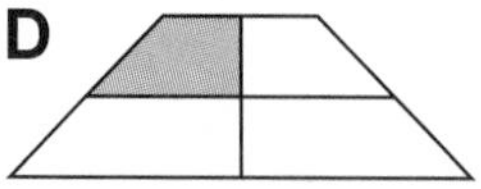

4. Which is a set of even numbers?

F	4	6	7	12
G	6	10	12	17
H	8	12	14	18
J	4	10	13	17

5. A puzzle book costs $3. A storybook costs $5. How much do 3 puzzle books cost?

A $8 C $11
B $9 D $15

6. Meg worked 3 hours on Friday, 6 hours on Saturday, and 4 hours on Sunday. How many more hours did Meg work on Saturday than Sunday?

F 1 hour H 10 hours
G 2 hours J 13 hours

7. Tyler had 20 stamps. He sent out 4 letters that needed 2 stamps each. How many stamps does he have left?

A 12 C 16
B 14 D 18

8. Which number sentence describes this picture?

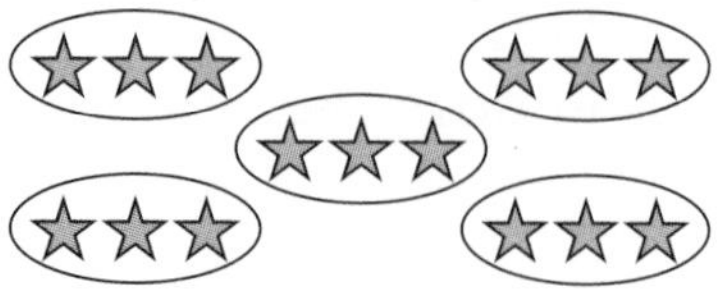

F $5 \times 3 = 15$
G $10 + 5 = 15$
H $5 + 3 = 8$
J $15 - 5 = 10$

Algebra and Functions

9. A piece of taffy costs 4¢. Two pieces of taffy cost 8¢. Three pieces of taffy cost 12¢. How much would seven pieces of taffy cost?

A 18¢ **C** 28¢
B 24¢ **D** 32¢

---

10. What shape goes in the empty space?

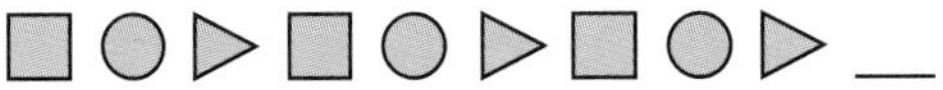

F  **H** 

G  **J** 

---

11. What is the rule for this table?
Rule: ______

Input	Output
3	0
5	0
7	0
9	0

A Multiply by 0. **C** Subtract 3.
B Multiply by 1. **D** Add 3.

---

12. What is the missing number in the number pattern?

12, 18, 24, ■, 36, 42

F 30 **H** 33
G 32 **J** 34

Measurement and Geometry

13. What is the missing number?
1 ft = ■ inches

A 3 **C** 6
B 12 **D** 36

---

14. What temperature does the thermometer show?

F 22°C
G 26°C
H 31°C
J 34°C

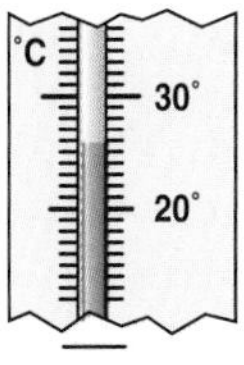

---

15. Measure the paper clip. About how long would 4 paper clips in a row be?

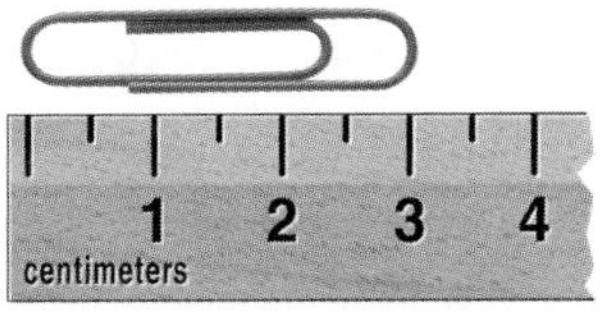

A 4 cm **C** 12 cm
B 8 cm **D** 16 cm

---

16. What time will the clock show in 1 hour?

F 3:03 **H** 4:11
G 3:15 **J** 4:21

CHAPTER 5

Multiplication Facts

Diagnosing Readiness

In Chapter 5, you will use these skills:

Ⓐ Using Arrays

(pages 139–141)

Draw an array for each multiplication sentence.

1. 2×4 **2.** 4×2

3. 4×5 **4.** 1×3

Ⓑ Multiplying by 3

(pages 150–151)

5. 3×8 **6.** 7×3

7. 9×3 **8.** 3×1

9. $\begin{array}{r} 3 \\ \times\ 3 \\ \hline \end{array}$ **10.** $\begin{array}{r} 5 \\ \times\ 3 \\ \hline \end{array}$

11. $\begin{array}{r} 3 \\ \times\ 2 \\ \hline \end{array}$ **12.** $\begin{array}{r} 4 \\ \times\ 3 \\ \hline \end{array}$

13. Complete the pattern.
12, 15, 18, ■, ■, 27, ■

14. Rebecca wants to buy 6 cans of tennis balls. Each can costs $3. How much money does she need?

C Multiplying by 4

(pages 152–153)

15. 4×1

16. 3×4

17. 9×4

18. 4×2

19. 4×4

20. 5×4

21. Trudy swims 6 laps each day. How many laps does she swim in 4 days?

D Multiplying by 0, 1, 2, or 5

(pages 144–147, 156–157)

22. 9×0

23. 8×1

24. 7×2

25. 6×5

26. 9×2

27. 7×5

28. Ms. Grant passes out 1 sticker to each of her 9 students. How many stickers did she hand out?

E Equations with Addition and Subtraction

(pages 72–73)

Find each missing number.

29. $10 + ■ = 20$

30. $32 - ■ = 10$

31. $26 - ■ = 7$

32. $12 + ■ = 27$

33. Jon had 12 pencils. His friend Sue gave him more pencils, so now he has 20 pencils. How many pencils did Sue give Jon?

F Comparing Numbers

(pages 14–16)

Compare. Write >, <, or =.

34. 156 ● 165

35. 918 ● 917

36. 699 ● 701

37. 401 ● 401

38. Mel has 124 pennies. Ana has 112 pennies. Ashley has 10 more pennies than Ana. Who has the most pennies?

To the Family and Student

Looking Back	Chapter 5	Looking Ahead
In Chapter 4, students learned how to multiply by 0, 1, 2, 3, 4, and 5.	**Multiplication Facts** In this chapter, students will learn how to multiply by 6, 7, 8, 9, and 10.	In Chapter 9, students will learn to multiply two-digit numbers.

Math and Everyday Living

Opportunities to apply the concepts of Chapter 5 abound in everyday situations. During the chapter, think about how multiplication can be used to solve a variety of real-world problems. The following examples suggest just several of the many situations that could launch a discussion about multiplication.

Math at the Store You want to buy 8 gallons of orange juice for a school party. Each gallon costs $3. How much money will you need?

Math and Reading If you read 6 books per month for 2 months, how many books would you have read?

Math at Home If you recycle 8 aluminum cans each day for 1 week, how many cans will you recycle?

Math and Sports In football, a touchdown with an extra point kick counts for 7 points. If a team scores 4 touchdowns with extra point kicks, how many points is that?

Math and Architecture A capitol building has 10 columns of windows. Each column has 5 windows. How many windows are there all together?

Math and Recreation You and your friend each have a pair of 4-wheel roller skates. How many wheels are there in all?

Math and Communication If it costs 7¢ per minute to call Boston, how much does a 9-minute phone call cost?

Math and Travel If you and your family spend 3 weeks exploring Europe, how many days long is your trip?

Math and Transportation People and cars sometimes travel by ferry boat between destinations separated by water. If there are 6 rows of 8 seats on the ferry, how many passengers can ride the ferry?

California Content Standards in Chapter 5 Lessons*

	Teach and Practice	Practice
Number Sense		
2.1 (🔑) Find the sum or difference of two whole numbers between 0 and 10,000.		5-5, 5-12
2.2 (🔑) Memorize to automaticity the multiplication table for numbers between 1 and 10.	5-1, 5-2, 5-3, 5-5, 5-6, 5-7	5-9, 5-10, 5-11, 5-12, 5-13
2.8 Solve problems that require two or more of the skills mentioned above.		5-1, 5-5, 5-7
Algebra and Functions		
1.1 (🔑) Represent relationships of quantities in the form of mathematical expressions, equations, or inequalities.	5-10, 5-11	5-1, 5-12
1.2 Solve problems involving numeric equations or inequalities.	5-12	5-1, 5-11
1.3 Select appropriate operational and relational symbols to make an expression true (e.g., if 4 ___ 3 = 12, what operational symbol goes in the blank?).	5-12	
1.5 Recognize and use the commutative and associative properties of multiplication. (e.g., if 5 × 7 = 35, then what is 7 × 5? And if 5 × 7 × 3 = 105, then what is 7 × 3 × 5?)	5-9	5-3
2.1 (🔑) Solve simple problems involving a functional relationship between two quantities.		5-2, 5-8
2.2 Extend and recognize a linear pattern by its rules.		5-3, 5-11

	Teach and Practice	Practice
Mathematical Reasoning		
1.1 Analyze problems by identifying relationships, distinguishing relevant from irrelevant information, sequencing and prioritizing information, and observing patterns.	5-4	5-1, 5-5, 5-6, 5-7, 5-8
1.2 Determine when and how to break a problem into simpler parts.		5-8
2.2 Apply strategies and results from simpler problems to more complex problems.		5-8
2.3 Use a variety of methods such as words, numbers, symbols, charts, graphs, tables, diagrams, and models to explain mathematical reasoning.	5-13	5-8
3.2 Note the method of deriving the solution and demonstrate conceptual understanding of the derivation by solving similar problems.	5-8	5-13

* The symbol (🔑) indicates a key standard as designated in the Mathematics Framework for California Public Schools. Full statements of the California Content Standards are found at the beginning of this book following the Table of Contents.

LESSON 5-1

Making Arrays

California Content Standard *Number Sense 2.2 (🔑): Memorize to automaticity the multiplication table for numbers between 1 and 10.*

Warm-Up Review

1. 6 × 3 **2.** 7 × 4

3. 4 × 4 **4.** 5 × 3

5. Four families were at the park. Three of the families had 5 people each. The other family had four people. How many people were at the park?

Math Link You know how to use equal groups to solve a multiplication problem. Now you will make arrays to solve multiplication problems.

Word Bank

square number

Example 1

How many arrays can you make using 8 tiles? Complete the table to show the arrays and multiplication sentences you found.

Array	Number of Rows	Number in Each Row	Multiplication Sentence
	1	8	$1 \times 8 = 8$
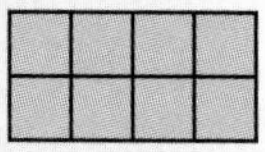	2	4	$2 \times 4 = 8$
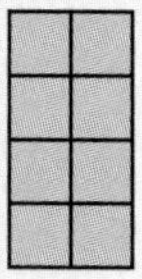	4	2	$4 \times 2 = 8$
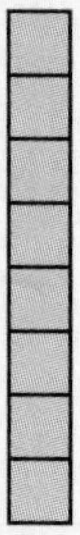	8	1	$8 \times 1 = 8$

There are 4 arrays that show all the factors of 8. Each array is shaped like a rectangle.

Additional Standards: Number Sense 2.8; Algebra and Functions 1.1 (🔑), 1.2; Mathematical Reasoning 1.1 *(See p. 177.)*

Example 2

Look at the arrays at the right. One of them is a square. Look at its factors. What do you notice about the factors?

When both factors in a multiplication sentence are the same, the product is called a **square number**.

So 9 is a square number, since $3 \times 3 = 9$.

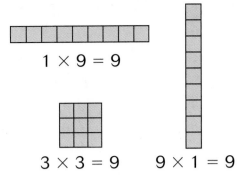

$1 \times 9 = 9$

$3 \times 3 = 9$

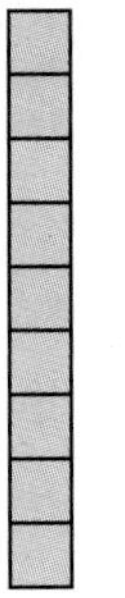

$9 \times 1 = 9$

Guided Practice *For another example, see Set A on p. 212.*

Write a multiplication sentence for each array.

1. 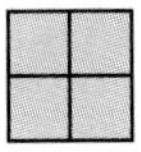

2. 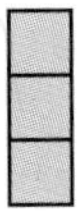

3. 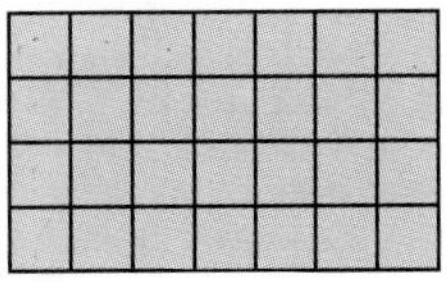

4. 

5. 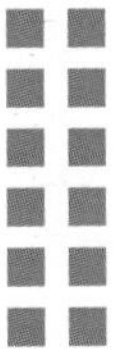

6. 

7. Mariah planted 5 rows of tulips. Each row had 4 tulips. How many tulips did Mariah plant?

Independent Practice *For more practice, see Set A on p. 215.*

Write a multiplication sentence for each array.

8. 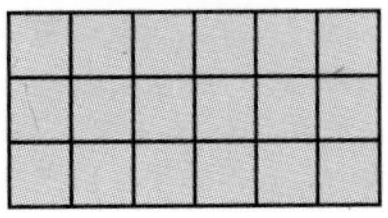

9. 

10. 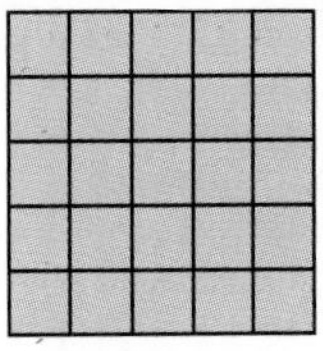

11. 

12. 

13. 

14. Look at the arrays in Exercises 1–6 and 8–13. Which products are square numbers?

Draw as many arrays as you can for each number shown.
Record your work in charts like the ones below.

6

	Drawing	Multiplication Sentence
		1 × 6 = 6
15.		2 × ■ = ■
16.		3 × ■ = ■
17.		6 × ■ = ■

15

	Drawing	Multiplication Sentence
18.		1 × 15 = 15
19.		■ × ■ = ■
20.		■ × ■ = ■
21.		■ × ■ = ■

22. Look back at your charts. Do you see any square numbers? Explain.

23. There are 8 rows of parking spaces with 5 spaces in each row. There are only 3 spaces left open. How many cars are already parked?

Mixed Review

24. Meredith bought a sheet of 400 stickers. Courtney bought a sheet of 300 stickers. How many stickers are there in all?

Algebra **Follow the rule to complete the table.**

25. Rule: Multiply by 3.

Input	Output
5	
	21

26. Rule: Multiply by 1.

Input	Output
6	
	3

Test Prep **Choose the correct letter for each answer.**

27. Add: 3,567 + 1,927
(2-5)

A 1,640
B 4,484
C 5,494
D 5,594
E NH

28. Hal has 5 marble bags. Each bag is empty. How many marbles are there in all?
(4-9)

F 5 marbles
G 4 marbles
H 1 marble
J 0 marbles
K NH

 Use Homework Workbook 5-1.

TEST PREP

Multiple-Choice Cumulative Review

Choose the correct letter for each answer.

1. Which of the following multiplication sentences can be used to describe the array?

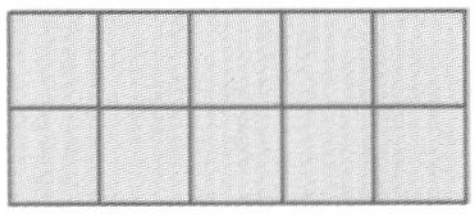

A $4 \times 5 = 20$
B $2 \times 5 = 10$
C $2 \times 10 = 20$
D $5 \times 10 = 50$

2. What is the value of the digit 7 in the number 370,428?

F 7 hundred
G 7 thousand
H 70 thousand
J 700 thousand

3. Which is the best estimate for the capacity of a bathtub?

A 5 cups
B 50 pints
C 5 quarts
D 50 gallons

4. Choose the next four numbers that continue the pattern.

4, 8, 12, 16, ■, ■, ■, ■...,

F 18, 20, 24, 26
G 20, 24, 28, 32
H 20, 28, 32, 40
J 26, 30, 36, 40

5. What is the value of the bills and coins?

A \$1.40
B \$2.28
C \$2.40
D \$2.55

6.

$$\begin{array}{r} 200 \\ -\ 136 \\ \hline \end{array}$$

F 64
G 164
H 74
J 274

7. It takes Sara 20 minutes to get to her swimming lesson. If she leaves her house at 5:13 P.M., at what time will she arrive at the pool?

A 4:53 P.M.
B 5:23 P.M.
C 5:33 P.M.
D 6:03 P.M.

8. Which group of numbers is in order from least to greatest?

F 3,842; 2,648; 2,011; 4,790
G 3,842; 2,011; 2,648; 4,790
H 2,011; 2,648; 3,842; 4,790
J 4,790; 3,842; 2,648; 2,011

LESSON 5-2

Multiplying by 6

Warm-Up Review

1. 4×3 **2.** 2×9

3. 8×3 **4.** 5×3

5. Mario had 7 marbles. Chris had three times as many. How many more marbles did Chris have than Mario?

California Content Standard *Number Sense 2.2 (🔑): Memorize to automaticity the multiplication table for numbers between 1 and 10.*

Math Link You know how to multiply by 3. Now you will learn to multiply by 6 by doubling the 3s fact.

Example 1

Find the product of 4×6.

Think: Find 4×3 and double to find 4×6.

$4 \times 3 = 12$

↓ ↓

$4 \times 6 = 24$

Doubling one factor doubles the product.

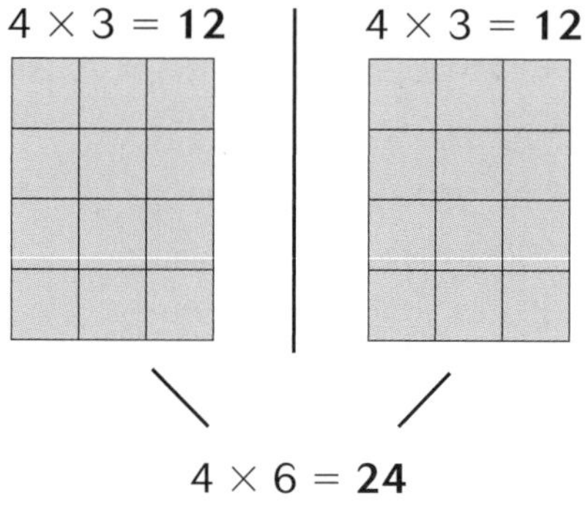

Example 2

Find 3×6.

Think: Use doubles.

$3 \times 3 = 9$

↓ ↓

$3 \times 6 = 18$

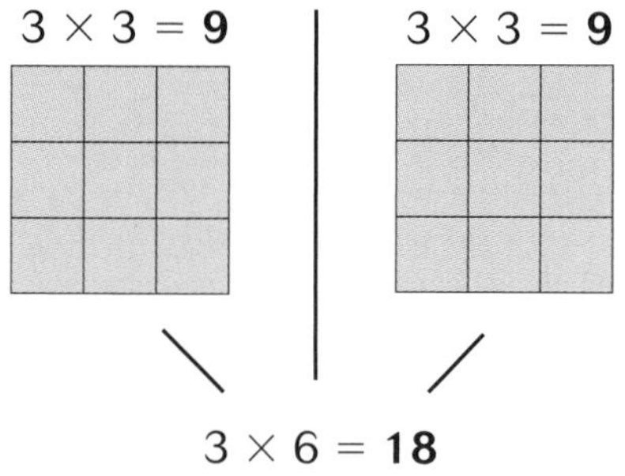

Guided Practice *For another example, see Set B on p. 212.*

Use the first fact to help you multiply the second fact.

1. $6 \times 3 = $ ■ $6 \times 6 = $ ■

2. $9 \times 3 = $ ■ $9 \times 6 = $ ■

3. $2 \times 3 = $ ■ $2 \times 6 = $ ■

4. $7 \times 3 = $ ■ $7 \times 6 = $ ■

5. Seven students are in each of 6 hot-air balloons. How many students are in the hot-air balloons?

 Additional Standard: Algebra and Functions 2.1 (🔑) (See p. 177.)

Independent Practice *For more practice, see Set B on p. 215.*

For Exercises 6–9, use the first fact to help you multiply the second fact.

6. $3 \times 3 = \blacksquare$
$3 \times 6 = \blacksquare$

7. $8 \times 3 = \blacksquare$
$8 \times 6 = \blacksquare$

8. $10 \times 3 = \blacksquare$
$10 \times 6 = \blacksquare$

9. $5 \times 3 = \blacksquare$
$5 \times 6 = \blacksquare$

10. 9×6 **11.** 6×0 **12.** 7×6 **13.** 6×5 **14.** 6×4

15. 6×1 **16.** 3×6 **17.** 2×6 **18.** 6×6 **19.** 6×8

20. Six hot-air balloons are each carrying 9 students. How many students are in the hot-air balloons?

21. A hot-air balloon pilot gives 6 rides per day. How many rides does she give in 3 days?

22. **Math Reasoning** What is one way to write 12 as the product of two numbers? What is another way?

Mixed Review

23. **Algebra** Give three numbers that make the statement true.
$12 + \blacksquare$ is less than 18.

Write a multiplication sentence for each array.

24. 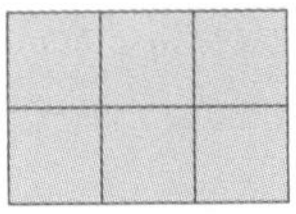

25. 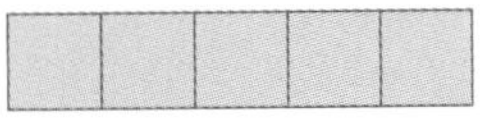

26. 

27. Tom puts an 8 in a multiplication machine that has the rule to multiply by 4. What is the output?

Test Prep **Choose the correct letter for each answer.**

28. (4-5) Misty has 3 nickels. Donna has twice as many nickels as Misty. How much money does Donna have?

A 10¢ **C** 25¢
B 15¢ **D** 30¢

29. (1-1) What missing number would make this number sentence true?
$4,000 + \blacksquare + 7 = 4,107$

F 1 **J** 1,000
G 10 **K** NH
H 100

LESSON 5-3

Multiplying by 8

Warm-Up Review

1. 2×4
2. 6×4
3. 9×4
4. 5×4
5. Danielle had four times as many fish as Erin had. Erin had 3 fish. How many fish did they have together?

California Content Standard *Number Sense 2.2 (🔑): Memorize to automaticity the multiplication table for numbers between 1 and 10.*

Math Link You know how to multiply by 4. Now you will learn to multiply by 8 by doubling the 4s fact.

Example 1

Find the product of 5×8.

Think: Find 5×4 and double to find 5×8.

$5 \times 4 = 20$

↓ ↓

$5 \times 8 = 40$

Doubling one factor doubles the product.

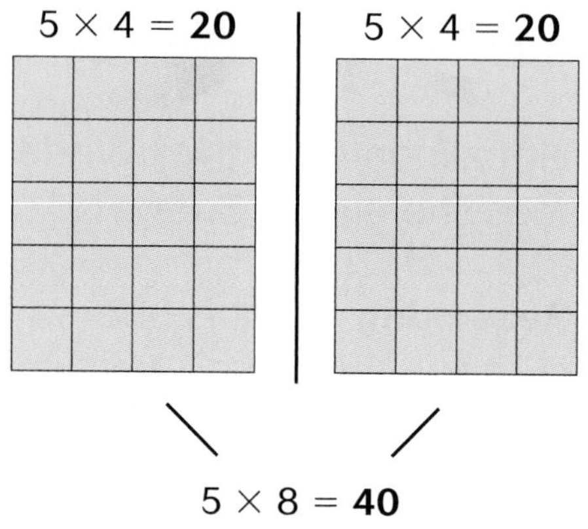

Example 2

Find 3×8.

Think: Use doubles.

$3 \times 4 = 12$

↓ ↓

$3 \times 8 = 24$

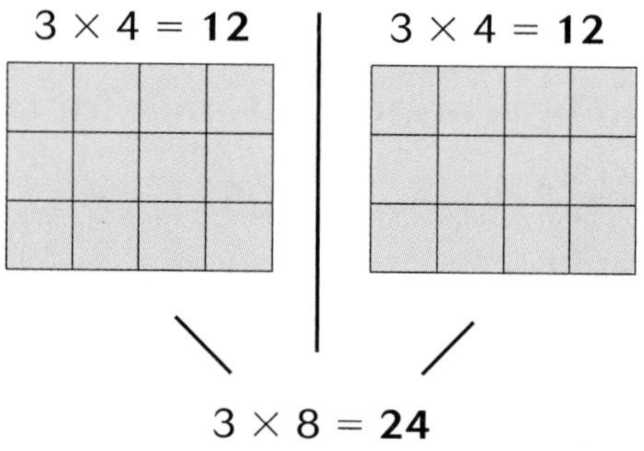

Guided Practice *For another example, see Set C on p. 212.*

Use the first fact to help you multiply the second fact.

1. $4 \times 4 = ■$
   $4 \times 8 = ■$
2. $10 \times 4 = ■$
   $10 \times 8 = ■$
3. $2 \times 4 = ■$
   $2 \times 8 = ■$
4. $1 \times 4 = ■$
   $1 \times 8 = ■$
5. Howard reads 8 books every week. How many books would he read in 6 weeks?

 Additional Standards: Algebra and Functions 1.5, 2.2 (See p. 177.)

Independent Practice *For more practice, see Set C on p. 215.*

For Exercises 6–9, use the first fact to help you multiply the second fact.

6. $8 \times 4 = \blacksquare$ $8 \times 8 = \blacksquare$

7. $7 \times 4 = \blacksquare$ $7 \times 8 = \blacksquare$

8. $6 \times 4 = \blacksquare$ $6 \times 8 = \blacksquare$

9. $9 \times 4 = \blacksquare$ $9 \times 8 = \blacksquare$

Find each product.

10. 8×9 **11.** 8×4 **12.** 8×8 **13.** 2×8 **14.** 3×8 **15.** 0×8

16. 8×1 **17.** 6×8 **18.** 8×3 **19.** 9×8 **20.** 8×5 **21.** 8×4

22. Algebra What is the missing number? $8 \times 9 = \blacksquare \times 8$

23. A class writes letters to a school in Mexico. They write 8 letters each week for 3 weeks. How many letters do they write?

24. Suppose the class above wrote only 4 letters per week. How many letters would the class have written?

Mixed Review

25. The Bay School computer lab has 9 tables. There are 5 computers on each of 6 tables. How many computers are in the lab?

26. 6×7 **27.** 3×6 **28.** 6×5 **29.** 6×6 **30.** 1×6

Test Prep **Choose the correct letter for each answer.**

31. *(3-1)* Look at the clock. What time will it be in 15 minutes?

A 12:40
B 12:35
C 11:35
D 11:40

32. *(4-7)* Whitney scored four points in each of the four quarters of the game. How many points did she make?

F 4 points
G 8 points
H 16 points
J 100 points
K NH

LESSON 5-4

Understand
Plan
Solve
Look Back

Problem-Solving Skill:
Too Much or Too Little Information

Warm-Up Review

1. 2×8
2. 0×7
3. 5×4
4. 6×6
5. Misha weighs 67 pounds and James weighs 79 pounds. How much more does James weigh than Misha?

California Content Standard *Mathematical Reasoning 1.1: Analyze problems by identifying relationships, distinguishing relevant from irrelevant information, sequencing and prioritizing information, and observing patterns.*

Read for Understanding

The Cole family is taking a 30-minute taxi ride to the airport. Look at their route to the right. Mr. Cole will take a taxi home after saying good-bye to his family. There is a toll on the way to the airport. There is no toll on the way home.

1. How long is the taxi ride to the airport?
2. How much is the toll on the way to the airport?
3. Is there a toll on the way home from the airport?

Think and Discuss

MATH FOCUS

Too Much or Too Little Information

Sometimes word problems contain too much or too little information. If there is too much, you need to choose what you need to solve the problem. If there is too little information, you cannot solve the problem.

Reread the paragraph at the top of the page.

4. Do you have enough information to find the total cost for the toll? Why or why not?
5. How much will the taxi ride cost? Is there too much or too little information to solve the problem?
6. What information in the paragraph is needed to solve Problem 5?

Guided Practice

Look at the picture to the right. A taxi driver charges different prices for trips to the bus station and the airport. How much money does she charge for 3 trips to the airport?

1. What information do you *not* need to solve the problem?

a. the number of trips to the airport

b. the charge for one trip to the bus station

c. the charge for one trip to the airport

2. Which number sequence could you use to solve the problem?

a. $\$9 + \$5 = ■$

b. $3 \times \$9 = ■$

c. $3 \times \$5 = ■$

Independent Practice

A taxi driver gave rides to 60 people on Monday, 48 people on Tuesday, and 54 people on Wednesday. He did not drive the taxi on Thursday or Friday. How many more people rode with him on Monday than on Tuesday?

3. What information do you *not* need to solve the problem?

a. the number of people who rode on Monday

b. the number of people who rode on Tuesday

c. the number of people who rode on Wednesday

4. **Math Reasoning** Is there enough information to solve the problem? Why or why not? If not, what else do you need to know to solve the problem?

5. **Math Reasoning** Is there enough information to tell how much money the taxi driver collected on Monday and Tuesday? Why or why not?

Use Homework Workbook 5-4.

LESSON 5-5

Multiplying by 7

Warm-Up Review

1. 2 × 8 2. 5 × 6
3. 6 × 8 4. 4 × 5
5. Abraham has 8 bags of oranges. Each bag has 4 oranges. How many oranges does Abraham have?

California Content Standard *Number Sense 2.2 (🔑): Memorize to automaticity the multiplication table for numbers between 1 and 10.*

Math Link You know how to multiply by 0, 1, 2, 3, 4, 5, 6, and 8. Now you will use these facts to help you multiply by 7.

Example 1

Find the product of 3 × 7.

You know that 7 × 3 = 21.

You can use the commutative property to find that 3 × 7 = 21.

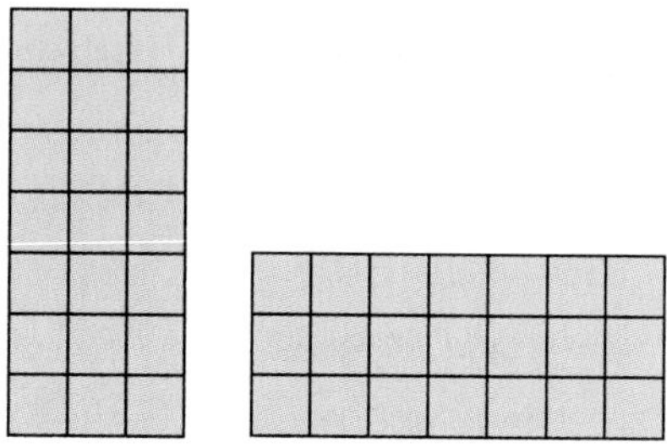

7 × 3 = 3 × 7

Example 2

After using facts you know, you still don't know 7 × 7, 9 × 7, and 10 × 7.

You can use a facts chart to find these missing facts. Each product increases by 7.

Add 7 to the product of 6 × 7 to find **7 × 7**. 42 + 7 = **49**.

Add 7 to the product of 8 × 7 to find **9 × 7**. 56 + 7 = **63**.

Add 7 to the product of 9 × 7 to find **10 × 7**. 63 + 7 = **70**.

7s Facts
6 × 7 = 42
7 × 7 = **49**
8 × 7 = 56
9 × 7 = **63**
10 × 7 = **70**

Guided Practice

For another example, see Set D on p. 213.

For Exercises 1–4, use the first fact to help you multiply the second fact.

1. $\begin{array}{r}7\\ \times 6\\ \hline\end{array}$ $\begin{array}{r}6\\ \times 7\\ \hline\end{array}$ **2.** $\begin{array}{r}7\\ \times 2\\ \hline\end{array}$ $\begin{array}{r}2\\ \times 7\\ \hline\end{array}$ **3.** $\begin{array}{r}7\\ \times 0\\ \hline\end{array}$ $\begin{array}{r}0\\ \times 7\\ \hline\end{array}$ **4.** $\begin{array}{r}7\\ \times 1\\ \hline\end{array}$ $\begin{array}{r}1\\ \times 7\\ \hline\end{array}$

5. Myra bought 5 bags of apples. Each bag had 7 apples. How many apples did Myra buy?

Additional Standards: Number Sense 2.1 (🔑), 2.8; Mathematical Reasoning 1.1 (See p. 177.)

Independent Practice *For more practice, see Set D on p. 216.*

For Exercises 6–9, use the first fact to help you multiply the second fact.

6. 7×2 $\quad 2 \times 7$

7. 7×5 $\quad 5 \times 7$

8. 7×4 $\quad 4 \times 7$

9. 7×8 $\quad 8 \times 7$

10. 7×0 **11.** 7×5 **12.** 7×3 **13.** 7×7 **14.** 7×4 **15.** 7×6

16. 3×7 **17.** 10×7 **18.** 5×7 **19.** 1×7 **20.** 6×7 **21.** 7×9

22. A group of travelers spends 8 weeks exploring the Amazon River. How many days is their trip?

23. Math Reasoning Three boats are each 7 feet long. The dock is 4 feet longer than all the boats placed end to end. How long is the dock?

Mixed Review

24. When the field day began, the temperature was 73°F. At noon it was 8°F hotter. By 2:00 P.M., the temperature was 2°F hotter than it was at noon. What was the temperature at 2:00 P.M.?

25. 4×8 **26.** 7×8 **27.** 5×8 **28.** 9×6 **29.** 7×6

Test Prep **Choose the correct letter for each answer.**

30. Which lists the weights from least to greatest?
(1-5)

A Dog, Ferret, Cat, Rabbit
B Ferret, Rabbit, Cat, Dog
C Ferret, Cat, Rabbit, Dog
D Rabbit, Cat, Ferret, Dog

Weights of Pets

Pet	Pounds
Dog	47 lb
Ferret	2 lb
Cat	14 lb
Rabbit	6 lb

31. Algebra What is the missing number that completes the number sentence?
(2-14)

40 − ■ = 25

A 25 **B** 20 **C** 15 **D** 5 **E** NH

LESSON 5-6

Multiplying by 9

Warm-Up Review

1. 8×3
2. 5×7
3. 7×6
4. 6×6
5. Edurado has $6. Trisha has $4 more than Edurado, and Mike has $2 less than Trisha. How much does Mike have?

California Content Standard *Number Sense 2.2 (🔑): Memorize to automaticity the multiplication table for numbers between 1 and 10.*

Math Link You know the multiplication facts for the factors 0 through 8. Now you will use these facts to learn the 9s facts.

Example 1

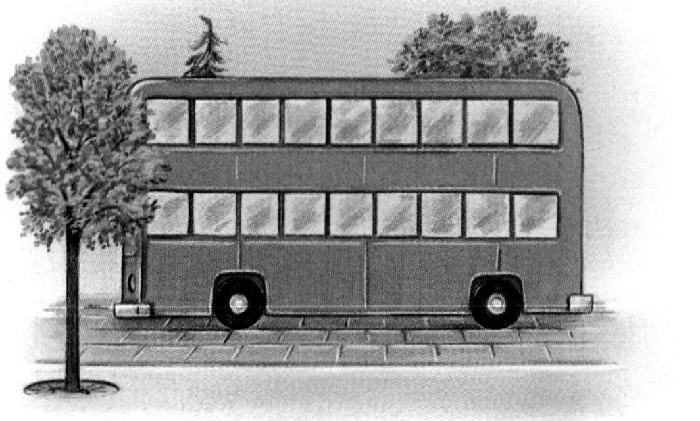

One of the best seats on a double-decker bus is a window on top. How many windows are there on one side of this bus?

$2 \times 9 = ■$ or $\begin{array}{r} 2 \\ \times 9 \\ \hline ■ \end{array}$

Find the product by changing the order of the factors.

If you know $9 \times 2 = 18$,
then you know $2 \times 9 = 18$.

There are 18 windows on one side.

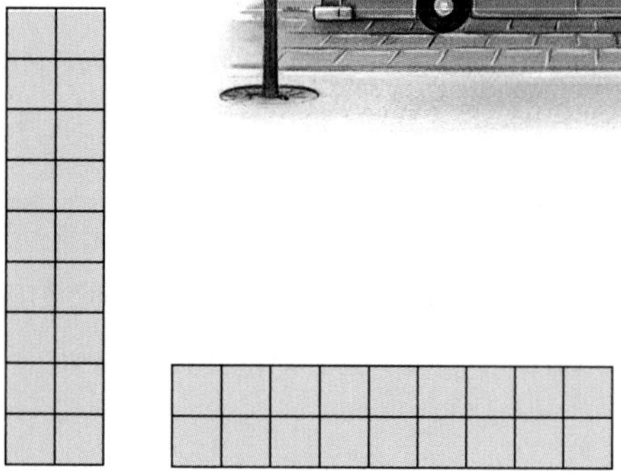

$9 \times 2 = 2 \times 9$

Example 2

After using the facts you know, you still don't know 9×9 and 10×9.

To find 9×9, add an extra 9 to 8×9.

$8 \times 9 = 72$
$9 \times 9 =$ **72 + 9**

So, $9 \times 9 =$ **81.**

To find 10×9, add an extra 9 to 9×9.

$9 \times 9 = 81$
$10 \times 9 =$ **81 + 9**

So, $10 \times 9 =$ **90.**

Guided Practice

For another example, see Set E on p. 213.

Use the first fact to help you multiply the second fact.

1. 9×4 — 4×9
2. 9×6 — 6×9
3. 9×1 — 1×9
4. 9×3 — 3×9
5. Erin has 5 basketball games per week. How many games does she play in 9 weeks?

 Additional Standard: Mathematical Reasoning 1.1 (See p. 177.)

Independent Practice *For more practice, see Set E on p. 216.*

For Exercises 6–9, use the first fact to help you multiply the second fact.

6. 9×0 / 0×9 **7.** 9×7 / 7×9 **8.** 9×5 / 5×9 **9.** 9×8 / 8×9

10. 2×9 **11.** 9×9 **12.** 10×9 **13.** 1×9 **14.** 9×5

15. 6×9 **16.** 9×0 **17.** 8×9 **18.** 9×3 **19.** 4×9

Math Reasoning Look at the examples. Then write *even* or *odd* for each sentence.

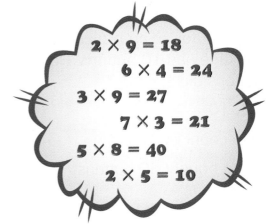

$2 \times 9 = 18$
$6 \times 4 = 24$
$3 \times 9 = 27$
$7 \times 3 = 21$
$5 \times 8 = 40$
$2 \times 5 = 10$

20. If you multiply 2 odd numbers, the product is __?__.

21. If you multiply 2 even numbers, the product is __?__.

22. If you multiply an even number and an odd number, the product is __?__.

23. Math Reasoning James travels 9 miles to school by bus. How many miles does he travel to school and home again in 2 days?

Mixed Review

24. The second-grade students collected 1,978 cans. The third-grade students collected 2,129 cans. How many more cans did the third-grade students collect?

25. 6×7 **26.** 3×7 **27.** 6×8 **28.** 2×8 **29.** 7×8

Test Prep Choose the correct letter for each answer.

30. (1-1) **Algebra** What is the missing number?
$6{,}000 + \blacksquare + 80 + 9 = 6{,}589$

A 5,000 **D** 5
B 500 **E** NH
C 50

31. (3-10) What is the temperature in °C shown on this thermometer?

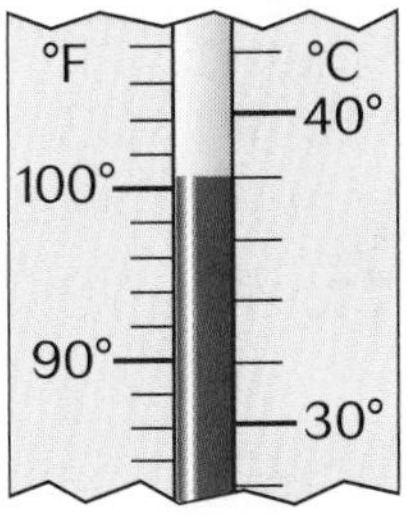

F 28°C **H** 38°C
G 31°C **J** 90°C

LESSON 5-7

Multiplying by 10

California Content Standard *Number Sense 2.2 (🔑): Memorize to automaticity the multiplication table for numbers between 1 and 10.*

Math Link You know how to skip count by 10s. Now you will learn how to use that information to multiply with 10 as a factor.

Warm-Up Review

1. 10 + 10 + 10 + 10
2. 10 + 10 + 10 + 10 + 10 + 10
3. 10 + 10 + 10
4. Liza has 3 dimes, 5 nickels, and 4 dollars in her pocket. How much more money does she need to make $5?

Example 1

Jillian bought the buttons shown to the right for an art project. Each package had 10 buttons. How many buttons did she buy?

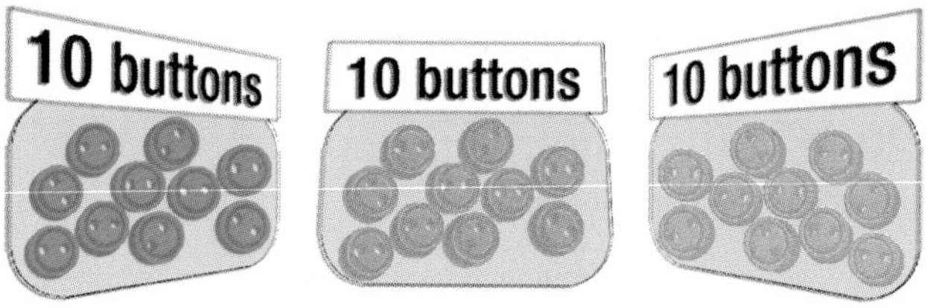

10, 20, 30

3 × 10 = ■

Skip count by 10s.

Jillian bought 30 buttons.

Example 2

Find 5 × 10.

Skip count by 10s.

5 × 10 = 50.

10 + 10 + 10 + 10 + 10 = 50

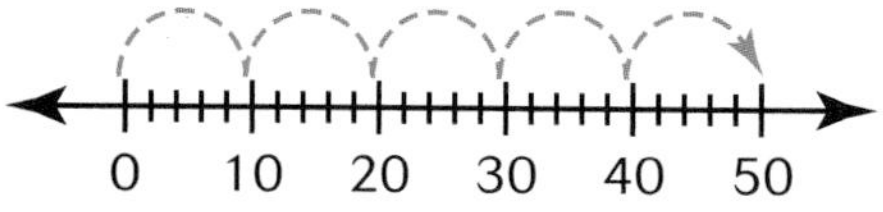

Guided Practice

For another example, see Set F on p. 213.

1. 6 × 10 **2.** 9 × 10 **3.** 2 × 10 **4.** 10 × 7

5. Mike invited 10 friends to his party. Each friend brought 8 toy cars to play with. How many toy cars did they have together?

Independent Practice

For more practice, see Set F on p. 216.

6. 10 × 3 **7.** 8 × 10 **8.** 3 × 10 **9.** 10 × 10 **10.** 9 × 10

11. 4 × 10 **12.** 1 × 10 **13.** 10 × 2 **14.** 10 × 0 **15.** 10 × 7

Additional Standards: Number Sense 2.8; Mathematical Reasoning 1.1 (See p.177.)

Write a multiplication sentence for each addition expression.

16. 10 + 10 + 10 + 10 **17.** 10 + 10 + 10 + 10 + 10 + 10 **18.** 10 + 10

Use the chart for Exercises 19–22.

School Supplies	Price
Small note pad	\$2
Medium note pad	\$3
Large note pad	\$4
Small box of crayons	\$3
Medium box of crayons	\$4
Large box of crayons	\$5

19. How much money would 10 large notepads cost?

20. How much do 10 small notepads and 10 small boxes of crayons cost?

21. How much more money would it cost to buy 10 large boxes of crayons than 10 small boxes of crayons?

22. Mrs. Nelson needs to buy 10 medium boxes of crayons for her son's party. Will \$30 be enough? Explain.

Mixed Review

23. Ryan bought 6 bags of dog food. Each bag weighed 5 pounds. How many pounds of dog food did Ryan buy?

24. 3×9 **25.** 2×7 **26.** 4×9 **27.** 7×7 **28.** 9×9

29. $\begin{array}{r} 9 \\ \times\ 8 \\ \hline \end{array}$ **30.** $\begin{array}{r} 6 \\ \times\ 5 \\ \hline \end{array}$ **31.** $\begin{array}{r} 8 \\ \times\ 6 \\ \hline \end{array}$ **32.** $\begin{array}{r} 9 \\ \times\ 5 \\ \hline \end{array}$ **33.** $\begin{array}{r} 6 \\ \times\ 7 \\ \hline \end{array}$

Test Prep **Choose the correct letter for each answer.**

34. (2-7) Which of these estimates shows the answer is reasonable?

$$\begin{array}{r} 723 \\ -\ 382 \\ \hline 341 \end{array}$$

A 700 − 300 = 400

B 700 − 400 = 300

C 800 − 300 = 500

D 800 − 400 = 400

35. (2-13) **Algebra** What are two numbers that make this statement true?

10 + ■ is less than 16

F 3; 6

G 3; 7

H 4; 5

J 4; 6

Diagnostic Checkpoint

Write a multiplication sentence for each array.

1. (5-1)
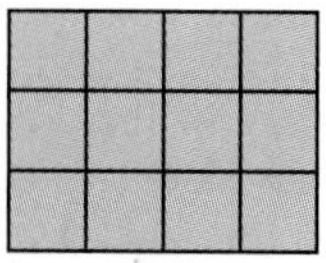

2. (5-1)
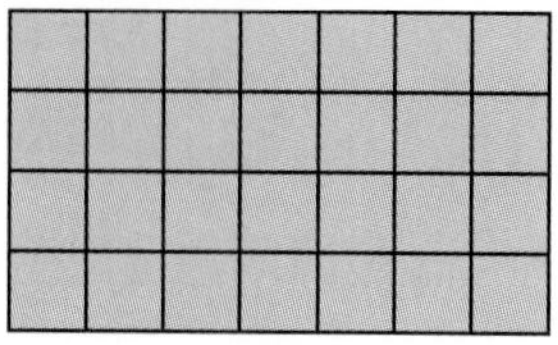

3. (5-1)
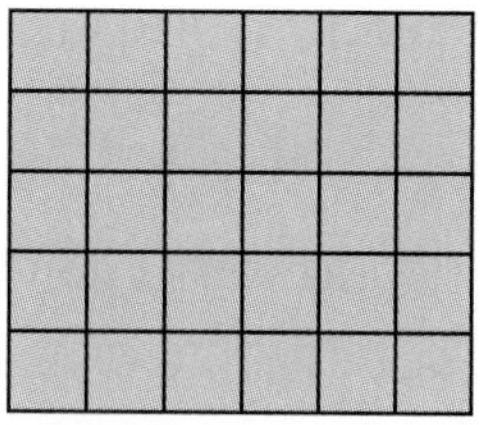

4. (5-1)
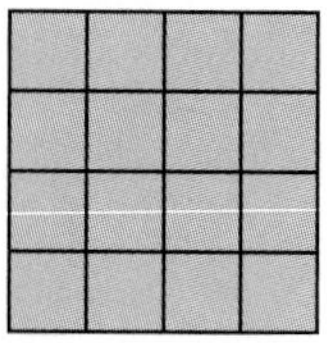

5. (5-1)
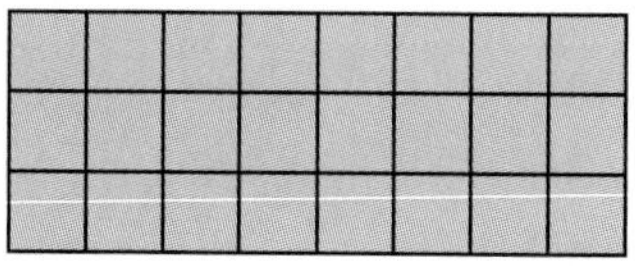

6. (5-1)
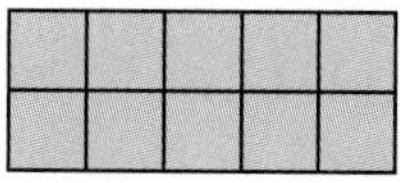

Use the first fact to help you multiply the second fact.

7. (5-2) 2×3; 2×6

8. (5-2) 6×3; 6×6

9. (5-2) 9×3; 9×6

10. (5-3) 5×4; 5×8

11. (5-3) 4×4; 4×8

12. (5-3) 3×4; 3×8

Find the product.

13. (5-2) 4×6

14. (5-2) 6×8

15. (5-7) 10×6

16. (5-3) 8×2

17. (5-7) 10×3

18. (5-3) 8×5

19. (5-5) 4×7

20. (5-3) 0×8

21. (5-5) 8×7

22. (5-6) 3×9

23. (5-6) 6×9

24. (5-5) 7×3

25. (5-7) 10×4

26. (5-5) 7×6

27. (5-3) 1×8

28. (5-2) 0×6

29. (5-7) 10×10

30. (5-3) 3×8

31. (5-4) Tanita is rollerblading to the park. The park is 3 miles from her house. The park is 5 miles from the school. How many miles is it from Tanita's house to the park and back?

32. (5-4) Gabriel delivered 38 newspapers on Monday, 40 on Friday, and 49 on Sunday. How many more newspapers did he deliver on Friday than on Monday?

TEST PREP

Multiple-Choice Cumulative Review

Choose the correct letter for each answer.

1. Jordan bought eggs that come in cartons of 6. If Jordan bought 4 cartons, how many eggs did she buy?

A 10
B 12
C 20
D 24
E NH

2. Complete the pattern.

30, 36, 42, ■, ■, ■

F 48, 54, 60
G 46, 52, 66
H 36, 30, 24
J 44, 48, 52

3. Michael baked 8 tins of muffins. Each muffin tin holds 6 muffins. How many muffins did Michael bake?

A 68
B 66
C 46
D 48
E NH

4. Complete the multiplication sentence.

$7 \times 8 = ■$

F 46
G 56
H 65
J 78
K NH

5. There are 24 balloons at a hot-air balloon festival. Six balloons are in a race. Each balloon carries 2 people. How many people are in the race?

A 12
B 18
C 32
D 48
E NH

6. Which of the following has the greatest product?

F 4×8
G 0×10
H 6×9
J 7×7

7. Complete the conversion.

3,000 mL = ■ L

A 3
B 30
C 300
D 30,000

8. Carter spends $8.32 on a yo-yo. He gives the clerk a $10 bill. What is his change?

F $1.78
G $2.78
H $2.68
J $1.68
K NH

LESSON 5-8

Understand
Plan
Solve
Look Back

Problem-Solving Strategy:
Choose a Strategy

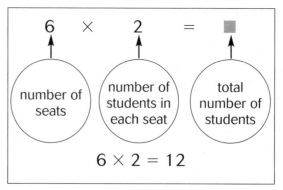

Warm-Up Review

1. 4×6 2. 6×5

3. 7×5 4. 2×3

5. Joan has a red shirt, a blue shirt, and a white shirt. She wants to wear the blue shirt on Friday. She wants to wear the red shirt 2 days after she wears the blue shirt. What day will she wear the red shirt?

California Content Standard *Mathematical Reasoning 3.2: Note the method of deriving the solution and demonstrate a conceptual understanding of the derivation by solving similar problems.*

Some students are exploring a streetcar at the transportation museum. They sit in 6 seats. Each seat holds 2 people. How many students are sitting on the streetcar?

Understand

What do you need to find?

You need to find the total number of students sitting on the streetcar.

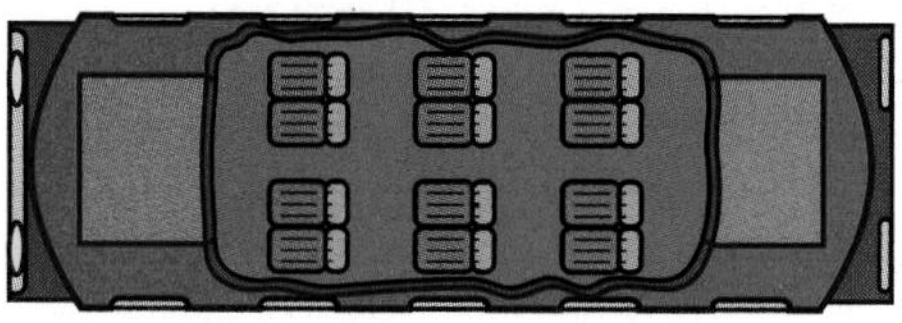

Plan

How can you solve the problem?

You can often use more than one strategy. For this problem, you could **draw a picture** or **write a number sentence.**

Solve

Draw a Picture	Write a Number Sentence
• Draw 6 dashes to stand for the seats. • Draw 2 Xs on each dash. Then count the Xs. <u>XX</u> <u>XX</u> <u>XX</u> <u>XX</u> <u>XX</u> <u>XX</u>	$6 \times 2 = ■$ 6 ↑ number of seats; 2 ↑ number of students in each seat; ■ ↑ total number of students $6 \times 2 = 12$

There are 12 students sitting on the streetcar.

Look Back

Can you think of another way to solve the problem?

Additional Standards: Algebra and Functions 2.1 (key); Mathematical Reasoning 1.1, 1.2, 2.2, 2.3 *(See p.177.)*

Guided Practice

Try these or other strategies to solve each problem. Tell which strategy you used.

Problem-Solving Strategies

- *Use Logical Reasoning*
- *Make a Table*
- *Make a List*
- *Work Backward*
- *Use Operations*
- *Write a Number Sentence*

1. The museum has 5 rows of train pictures and 3 rows of airplane pictures. How many more rows of train pictures are there?

2. You put 14 model train cars down on a track. Your friend picks up 4 cars. You put down 5 cars. Your friend picks up 6 cars. Then you put down 3 cars. How many cars are on the track now?

Independent Practice

3. You are putting together 6 model trucks. Each truck needs 6 wheels. How many wheels do you need to put together all 6 trucks?

4. There are 7 tables where students can make model cars. If 4 students work at each table, how many students can make model cars?

5. **Math Reasoning** In front of the museum, a model streetcar moves around a tiny town. The streetcar can travel 100 feet in 2 minutes. How long does it take to travel 1,000 feet?

Mixed Review

6. Ben, Dan, and Will wrote their names on cards. They put the cards in a hat. Then they each took out one card. No one had his own name. Ben picked Dan. What name did Will pick?

7. When Nora got to the museum, she looked at cars for 1 hour. Next, she watched a 30-minute movie about trains. The movie ended at 1:15 P.M. When did Nora get to the museum?

Use Homework Workbook 5-8.

LESSON 5-9

Multiplying Three Numbers

Algebra

California Content Standard *Algebra and Functions 1.5: Recognize and use the commutative and associative properties of multiplication (e.g., If 5 × 7 = 35, then what is 7 × 5? And if 5 × 7 × 3 = 105, then what is 7 × 3 × 5?)*

Warm-Up Review

1. 3×9
2. 4×2
3. 8×5
4. 7×6
5. 0×1
6. 5×5
7. Boyd has a dozen pencils. Ronnie also has a dozen pencils. How many pencils do they have together?

Math Link You know how to multiply with 2 factors. Now you will learn to multiply with 3 factors.

Example 1

Each of 3 skaters is wearing 2 skates. Count the wheels on each skate to the right. How many wheels are there in all?

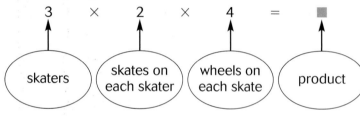

$3 \times 2 \times 4 = \blacksquare$

- 3 → skaters
- 2 → skates on each skater
- 4 → wheels on each skate
- $\blacksquare$ → product

Word Bank

grouping property

Grouping property: You can change the grouping of factors, and the product will be the same.

Solve using grouping symbols ( ). Grouping symbols tell which factors to multiply first.

Step 1 Group the first two factors.	**Step 2** Multiply the grouped factors.	**Step 3** Multiply the remaining factors.
$(3 \times 2) \times 4 = \blacksquare$	$(3 \times 2) \times 4 = \blacksquare$ $6 \times 4 = \blacksquare$	$6 \times 4 = 24$

There are 24 wheels in all.

Example 2

Find $3 \times 2 \times 4$ by grouping the last two factors.

Step 1 Group the last two factors.	**Step 2** Multiply the grouped factors.	**Step 3** Multiply the remaining factors.
$3 \times (2 \times 4) = \blacksquare$	$3 \times (2 \times 4) = \blacksquare$ $3 \times 8 = \blacksquare$	$3 \times 8 = 24$

$3 \times 2 \times 4 = 24$

Additional Standard: Number Sense 2.2 (key) (See p.177.)

Guided Practice *For another example, see Set G on p. 214.*

1. 9 × (1 × 7) = ■ **2.** (2 × 3) × 3 = ■ **3.** 5 × (6 × 1) = ■

4. Kim, Kaycee, and Katie each have 2 rings on each hand. How many rings are there?

Independent Practice *For more practice, see Set G on p. 216.*

5. 8 × (0 × 9) = ■ **6.** (3 × 3) × 2 = ■ **7.** 3 × (2 × 4) = ■

8. (4 × 2) × 3 = ■ **9.** 1 × (7 × 9) = ■ **10.** (2 × 1) × 4 = ■

11. (2 × 2) × 4 = ■ **12.** (1 × 5) × 3 = ■ **13.** 2 × (6 × 1) = ■

14. Elbow pads are on sale for $5 each. How much would it cost to buy 4 pairs of elbow pads?

15. Your mom, dad, and two grandparents each have a pair of 5-wheel skates. How many wheels is that in all?

16. Write 12 as the product of three factors.

17. Write 20 as a product of three factors.

Mixed Review

18. **Algebra** What is the missing number?
6,781 + 2,124 = 2,124 + ■

19. 6 × 10 **20.** 4 × 10 **21.** 8 × 9 **22.** 4 × 9 **23.** 6 × 9

Test Prep Choose the correct letter for each answer.

24. (2-3) The table shows how many students attended the third-grade class play. About how many students attended the play in all?

A About 40 students **C** About 80 students
B About 60 students **D** About 100 students

Class	Number of Students
First Grade	21
Second Grade	19
Third Grade	39

25. (1-1) What number does the model show?

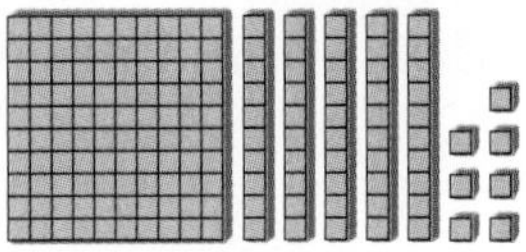

F 157 **J** 1,570
G 175 **K** NH
H 1,507

LESSON 5-10

Expressions with Multiplication

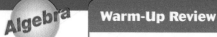

Algebra

Warm-Up Review

1. 3×8 **2.** 9×8

3. 6×4 **4.** 7×6

5. 2×7 **6.** 5×3

7. Rose had 2 sets of markers, and Jack had 3 sets of markers. Each set had 8 markers. How many markers did they have?

California Content Standard *Algebra and Functions 1.1 ( ): Represent relationships of quantities in the form of mathematical expressions, equations, or inequalities.*

Math Link You can find products like 4×8 and 7×4. Now you will learn about expressions like $3 \times$ ■ and $5 \times$ ■.

Example 1

Give three numbers that make this statement true:
$4 \times$ ■ is greater than 15.

Think: List all the 4s facts to find products greater than 15.

4s Facts	
$4 \times 0 = 0$	$4 \times 4 = 16$
$4 \times 1 = 4$	$4 \times 5 = 20$
$4 \times 2 = 8$	$4 \times 6 = 24$
$4 \times 3 = 12$	$4 \times 7 = 28$

4×3 is less than 15 and
4×4 is greater than 15.

So, three numbers that make the statement true are 4, 5, and 6.

Check: $4 \times 4 = 16$; $4 \times 5 = 20$; and $4 \times 6 = 24$.
Since each product is greater than 15, the answer checks.

Example 2

Give three numbers that make this statement true:
$6 \times$ ■ is less than 18.

Think: List all the 6s facts to find products less than 18.

6s Facts
$6 \times 0 = 0$
$6 \times 1 = 6$
$6 \times 2 = 12$
$6 \times 3 = 18$

So, three numbers that make the statement true are 0, 1, and 2.

Check: $6 \times 0 = 0$; $6 \times 1 = 6$; and $6 \times 2 = 12$.
Since each product is less than 18, the answer checks.

Additional Standard: Number Sense 2.2 ( ) *(See p.177.)*

Guided Practice *For another example, see Set H on p. 214.*

Give three numbers that make each statement true.

1. 9 × ■ is greater than 18.

2. 5 × ■ is less than 42.

3. 3 × ■ is between 10 and 20.

4. 4 × ■ is greater than 8.

5. List all the numbers that make the following statement true: 2 × ■ is less than 17.

Independent Practice *For more practice, see Set H on p. 217.*

Give three numbers that make each statement true.

6. 7 × ■ is less than 55.

7. 2 × ■ is between 3 and 19.

8. 8 × ■ is greater than 20.

9. 5 × ■ is greater than 15.

10. 3 × ■ is less than 20.

11. 9 × ■ is between 20 and 80.

12. 10 × ■ is less than 88.

13. 6 × ■ is greater than 30.

14. List all the numbers that make the following statement true: 4 × ■ is less than 10.

15. Molly has nickels and pennies in her pocket. If she has between 13¢ and 28¢, how many nickels could she have?

Mixed Review

16. Michelle makes $9 for cutting grass on a small lawn and $12 for a large lawn. If she mows 4 small lawns, how much money will she get?

17. 6 × 10 **18.** 3 × 10 **19.** 3 × 1 × 5 **20.** 4 × 2× 6 **21.** 3 × 3× 3

Test Prep **Choose the correct letter for each answer.**

22. (2-5) Cal wants to buy a CD for $17.88 and a T-shirt for $10.38. How much money does he need?

A $7.50
B $27.16
C $28.26
D $30.00
E NH

23. (3-4) Rolonda bought 2 quarts of orange juice. How many pints is that?

F 1 pint
G 2 pints
H 4 pints
J 6 pints
K NH

LESSON 5-11

Missing Factors

Algebra

Warm-Up Review

1. 6×7
2. 3×9
3. 9×8
4. 5×5
5. A student mails 4 envelopes to friends. Each envelope contains 8 pictures. How many pictures did the student send?

California Content Standard *Algebra and Functions 1.1 (Key): Represent relationships of quantities in the form of mathematical expressions, equations, or inequalities.*

Math Link You know all the basic multiplication facts. Now you will use the facts to help you solve problems that have missing factors.

Example 1

Twenty-eight people wait on the helicopter pad. Seven people can fit in each helicopter. How many helicopters are needed?

Write: $\blacksquare \times 7 = 28$.

Think: List 7s facts to find the missing factor.

7s Facts	
$0 \times 7 = 0$	$3 \times 7 = 21$
$1 \times 7 = 1$	$4 \times 7 = 28$
$2 \times 7 = 14$	

Since $4 \times 7 = 28$, the number 4 is the missing factor.

So, 4 helicopters are needed for 28 people.

Example 2

Find the missing factor for $6 \times \blacksquare = 30$.

Think: List 6s facts to find the missing factor.

6s Facts	
$6 \times 0 = 0$	$6 \times 3 = 18$
$6 \times 1 = 6$	$6 \times 4 = 24$
$6 \times 2 = 12$	$6 \times 5 = 30$

Since, $6 \times 5 = 30$, the number 5 is the missing factor.

Guided Practice

For another example, see Set I on p. 214.

Find each missing factor.

1. $8 \times \blacksquare = 24$
2. $\blacksquare \times 7 = 56$
3. $6 \times \blacksquare = 30$
4. Sixty-three students are waiting to get on the school vans. How many vans are needed if 7 students can fit in each van?

Additional Standards: Number Sense 2.2 (Key); Algebra and Functions 1.2, 2.2 (See p. 177.)

Independent Practice *For more practice, see Set I on p. 217.*

Find each missing factor.

5. 9 × ■ = 63

6. 5 × ■ = 45

7. ■ × 4 = 28

8. 1 × ■ = 6

9. 2 × ■ = 12

10. 9 × ■ = 36

Write a multiplication sentence to solve each problem.

11. A company has 2 pilots for each helicopter it owns. If there are 14 pilots, how many helicopters does the company own?

12. If 3 people can ride in each helicopter, how many helicopters are needed for 15 people?

13. Math Reasoning How do you know that the missing factor in 4 × ■ = 12 is more than 2?

Algebra Find the rule. Then complete each table.

14. Rule: ________

Input	Output
2	8
9	36
7	
4	16
	24

15. Rule: ________

Input	Output
9	81
3	27
6	
	72
2	18

16. Rule: ________

Input	Output
9	63
7	49
6	
3	21
	56

Mixed Review

17. Every hour a helicopter pilot gives 4 rides. How many rides does she give in 8 hours?

18. Algebra List all the numbers that make the following statement true: 3 × ■ is less than 13.

Test Prep Choose the correct letter for each answer.

19. Find the product of 6 × 4 × 2.
(5-9)

A 24 **C** 64
B 48 **D** 252

20. (2-10)

$$\begin{array}{r} 6{,}003 \\ -\ 3{,}215 \\ \hline \end{array}$$

F 2,787 **J** 9,218
G 2,789 **K** NH
H 3,212

LESSON 5-12

Inequalities

Algebra

California Content Standard Algebra and Functions 1.2: Solve problems involving numeric equations or inequalities. Also, Algebra and Functions 1.3 (See p. 177.)

Warm-Up Review

Compare. Write >, <, or =.

1. 36 ● 40 **2.** 19 ● 18

3. 24 ● 22 **4.** 66 ● 36

5. Marion has 1 brother and 2 sisters. Steve has twice as many brothers, but 1 less sister than Marion. How many brothers and sisters does Steve have?

Math Link You know how to compare numbers to 10,000. Now you will learn how to compare addition, subtraction, and multiplication expressions.

Example 1

Use the data at the right. Which combination of packages gives you the most pieces of fruit— 3 packages of apples or 2 packages of oranges?

Fruit	Number in Each Package
Bananas	5
Oranges	8
Kiwi	4
Strawberries	20
Apples	6

To find out, compare 3×6 and 2×8.

3×6 ● 2×8 **Multiply each expression.**

18 16

$3 \times 6 > 2 \times 8$ **Since 18 is greater than 16, 3 × 6 is greater than 2 × 8.**

So, 3 packages of apples would give you more pieces of fruit.

Example 2

Compare $12 + 18$ and 5×7.

$12 + 18$ ● 5×7 **Find the value of each expression.**

30 35

$12 + 18 < 5 \times 7$ **Since 30 is less than 35, 12 + 18 is less than 5 × 7.**

Guided Practice

For another example, see Set J on p. 214.

Compare. Write >, <, or = for each ●.

1. $24 - 8$ ● 2×8 **2.** $28 - 9$ ● $16 + 3$ **3.** 6×7 ● 9×5

4. 5×6 ● $41 - 12$ **5.** 5×7 ● 8×4 **6.** 3×6 ● $12 + 6$

7. Bonnie bought 4 packages of kiwi and 3 packages of bananas. Of which fruit did she buy more?

Additional Standards: Number Sense 2.1 (🔑), 2.2; Algebra and Functions 1.1 (🔑) (See p. 177.)

Independent Practice *For more practice, see Set J on p. 217.*

Compare. Write >, <, or = for each ●.

8. 6×3 ● $46 - 17$

9. $19 + 36$ ● 9×6

10. $58 + 19$ ● 8×8

11. $81 - 26$ ● 6×8

12. 4×7 ● $44 - 16$

13. $20 + 30$ ● 6×10

14. 3×8 ● 16

15. 3×4 ● 24

16. 16 ● 4×4

17. 4×3 ● 3×4

18. 1×2 ● 9×0

19. 4×8 ● 5×8

20. $(2 \times 3) \times 2$ ● 14

21. $4 \times (1 \times 5)$ ● 20

22. $(3 \times 3) \times 4$ ● 9×4

23. $2 \times (3 \times 3)$ ● 2×3

Algebra **Replace the ■ with a digit to make the number sentence true.**

24. $16 = 4 \times$ ■

25. $5 \times$ ■ > 18

26. $18 >$ ■ $\times 6$

Mixed Review

27. A hot-air balloon is covered with colored stripes. The stripes appear in this order: red, white, blue, white. If this pattern repeats 6 times, how many white stripes are on the balloon?

Find each missing factor.

28. ■ $\times 3 = 21$

29. $9 \times$ ■ $= 54$

30. $8 \times$ ■ $= 0$

Give three numbers that make each statement true.

31. $4 \times$ ■ is less than 25.

32. $5 \times$ ■ is between 18 and 42.

Test Prep **Choose the correct letter for each answer.**

33. (5-11) Which number goes in the box to make the sentence true?

$4 \times$ ■ $\times 2 = 56$

A 4 **C** 6

B 5 **D** 7

34. (2-8) Mr. Capo's third-grade class has 24 students. Eleven of them are boys. How many girls are in the class?

F 11 **J** 35

G 12 **K** NH

H 24

LESSON 5-13

Understand
Plan
Solve
Look Back

Problem-Solving Application:

Using a Pictograph

California Content Standard *Mathematical Reasoning 2.3: Use a variety of methods, such as . . . graphs, . . . to explain mathematical reasoning.*

Warm-Up Review

1. 5×5
2. 2×3
2. 4×4
4. 6×2
5. Five boys ate tuna sandwiches. Three girls ate tuna sandwiches. Five adults ate tuna sandwiches. How many children ate tuna sandwiches?

Suppose a train makes three stops going from Miami to Jacksonville. The pictograph shows how many people board the train at each stop. How many people get on at Orlando?

People Boarding the Train	
Miami	🚶🚶🚶🚶🚶🚶
Ft. Lauderdale	🚶🚶🚶🚶🚶
West Palm Beach	🚶🚶🚶🚶🚶🚶🚶🚶
Orlando	🚶🚶🚶🚶🚶🚶🚶
Jacksonville	🚶🚶🚶🚶
Each 🚶 stands for 5 people.	

Understand

What do you need to know?

First you need to know which row shows the people getting on at Orlando. Then you need to know how many people each 🚶 stands for.

Plan

How can you solve the problem?

Count the pictures in the row for Orlando. Then look at the key to see how many people each 🚶 stands for. Then multiply the two numbers.

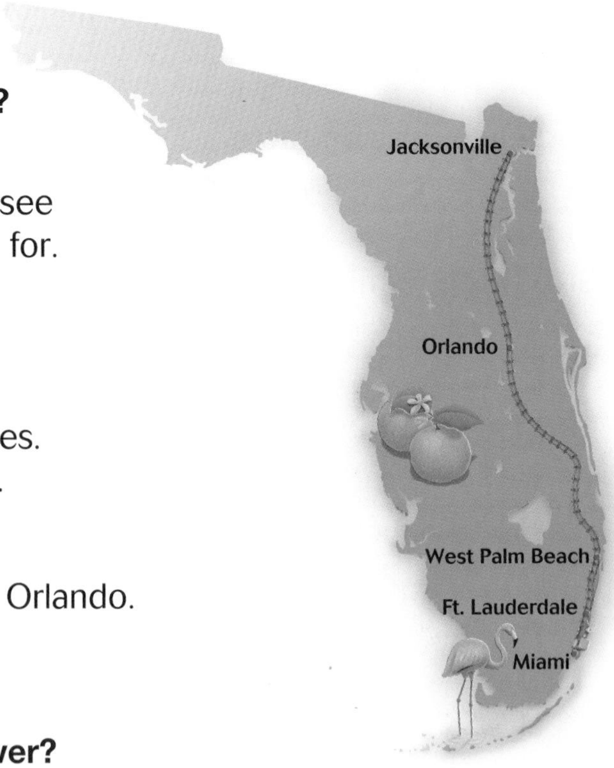

Solve

The row for Orlando has 7 pictures. Each picture stands for 5 people.

$7 \times 5 = 35$ people

So, 35 people got on the train at Orlando.

Look Back

How could you check your answer?

Use repeated addition. $5 + 5 + 5 + 5 + 5 + 5 + 5 = 35$ people. The answer checks.

Additional Standards: Number Sense 2.2 (🔑); Mathematical Reasoning 3.2 *(See p. 177.)*

Use the pictograph at the right to answer Exercises 1–7.

The pictograph at the right shows the number of people sitting in each section of a dining car.

Number of People in One Dining Car	
Section 1	
Section 2	
Section 3	
Section 4	
Each  stands for 4 people.	

Guided Practice

1. Which section has the greatest number of people?

2. Which section has the least number of people?

Independent Practice

3. How many people are sitting in Section 3?

4. Which section has half as many people as Section 2?

5. Each section of the dining car can seat 24 people. A group of 8 more people come in. They want to sit together. In which sections could they sit?

6. Suppose 4 people moved from Section 2 to Section 3. How many people would there be in Section 3 then?

7. **Math Reasoning** How can you tell, without counting, if there is an even or odd number of people in the dining car altogether?

Mixed Review

8. You give the cashier a one-dollar bill and a quarter to buy two drinks. She gives you back a dime and a nickel as change. What did you buy?

9. You have 4 quarters and a dime. What money would you use to pay for 2 cartons of milk? What would your change be?

10. The race started at 12:50 P.M. Marvin finished the race at 1:15 P.M. How many minutes did it take Marvin to finish?

Diagnostic Checkpoint

Complete. For Exercise 1, use the words from the Word Bank.

Word Bank
square number
product
array
multiply

1. The product is a(n) ______ when both factors are the same.
(5-1)

Multiply.

2. $2 \times 1 \times 8$ (5-9)

3. $(2 \times 3) \times 3$ (5-9)

4. $(2 \times 1) \times 7$ (5-9)

5. $4 \times (2 \times 4)$ (5-9)

6. $8 \times 7 \times 0$ (5-9)

7. $6 \times 1 \times 8$ (5-9)

Give three numbers that make each statement true.

8. 6 × ■ is greater than 25. (5-10)

9. 4 × ■ is less than 30. (5-10)

10. 7 × ■ is between 20 and 50. (5-10)

11. 8 × ■ is less than 62. (5-10)

Find each missing factor.

12. ■ × 6 = 18 (5-11)

13. 7 × ■ = 21 (5-11)

14. 8 × ■ = 56 (5-11)

15. 9 × ■ = 81 (5-11)

16. ■ × 5 = 45 (5-11)

17. ■ × 9 = 72 (5-11)

Compare. Use >, <, or =.

18. 8 × 4 ● 54 − 21 (5-12)

19. 19 + 28 ● 6 × 9 (5-12)

20. 96 − 34 ● 10 × 6 (5-12)

Solve.

21. Danielle rode 2 miles in her first bike race. Every race after that she rode 2 miles more than she rode in the race before. How many miles did she ride in her fifth race? Tell which strategy you used to solve the problem. Then solve.
(5-8)

22. A water taxi makes 4 trips each day. On the right is a pictograph that shows the number of passengers for each trip. How many more passengers were on trip 4 than trip 3?
(5-13)

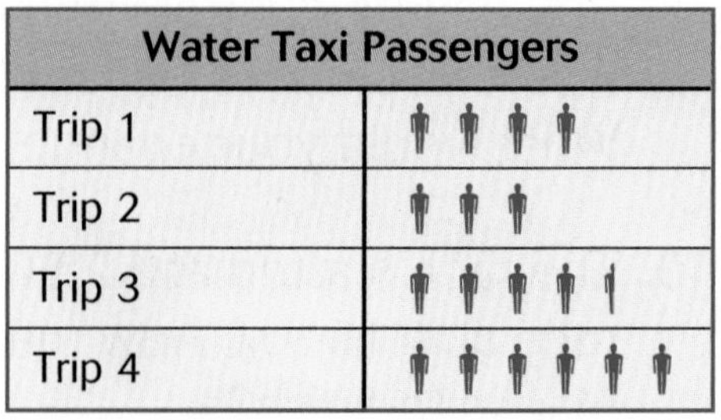

Each 🯅 stands for 10 passengers.

Chapter 5 Test

Write a multiplication sentence for each array.

1. 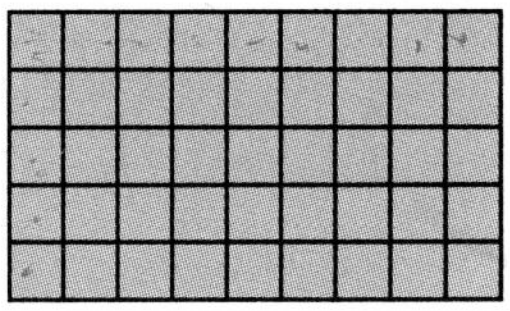

2. 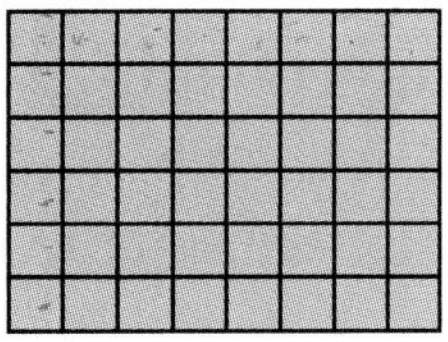

Multiply.

3. 3×9

4. 3×8

5. 6×7

6. 9×5

7. 7×7

8. 10×4

9. $2 \times 1 \times 9$

10. $3 \times 2 \times 4$

11. $3 \times 9 \times 1$

Find the missing factor.

12. 7 × ■ = 56

13. ■ × 6 = 54

14. ■ × 8 = 72

15. 3 × ■ = 21

16. ■ × 4 = 28

17. 9 × ■ = 81

Give three numbers that make each statement true.

18. 6 × ■ is less than 44.

19. 8 × ■ is between 41 and 79.

Compare. Use >, <, or =.

20. 5 × 6 ● 4 × 8

21. 9 × 7 ● 99 − 25

22. 3 × (5 × 2) ● 5 × 7

23. Jill read 15 pages on Monday, 17 pages on Tuesday, and 16 pages on Wednesday. She reads for 20 minutes each day. How many pages did she read in all three days?

24. Three skiers fit on one chair of a chair lift. How many skiers can fit on 9 chairs?

25. How many more trees were planted at Birch Park than at Redwood Park?

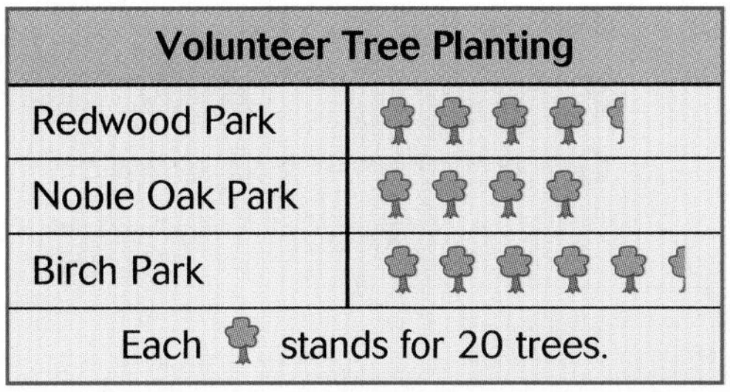

Volunteer Tree Planting
Redwood Park
Noble Oak Park
Birch Park
Each stands for 20 trees.

TEST PREP

Multiple-Choice Chapter 5 Test

Choose the correct letter for each answer.

1. Daria planted 8 rows of tulips. Each row has 4 tulips. How many tulips did Daria plant altogether?

   A 24 tulips
   B 30 tulips
   C 32 tulips
   D 42 tulips
   E NH

2. $$\begin{array}{r} 6 \\ \times\, 9 \\ \hline \end{array}$$

   F 54
   G 45
   H 36
   J 18
   K NH

3. Choose a multiplication sentence for the addition expression.
   10 + 10 + 10 + 10 + 10 + 10

   A $5 \times 10 = 50$
   B $6 \times 10 = 60$
   C $10 \times 10 = 100$
   D $1 \times 10 = 10$

4. Bob is putting tricycles together. He has 12 handle bars, 18 wheels, and 9 seats. How many tricycles can he put together?

   F 4
   G 6
   H 9
   J 18

5. Choose the multiplication sentence that describes the array.

   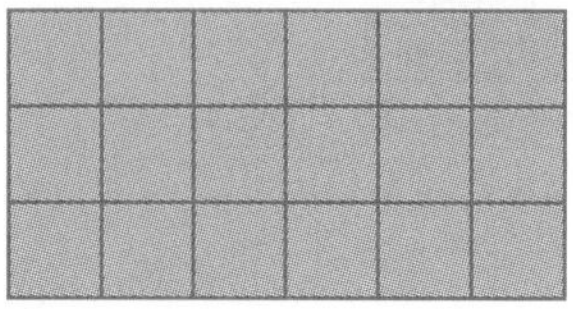

   A $3 \times 5 = 15$
   B $3 \times 6 = 18$
   C $6 \times 4 = 24$
   D $6 \times 6 = 36$

6. It costs $3 to mail a videocassette. An audiocassette costs $1 to mail. It costs $8 to mail a camcorder. How much money does it cost to mail 9 videocassettes?

   F $8
   G $9
   H $27
   J $72

7. Allie runs 4 miles every day. How many miles does she run in 1 week?

   A 4 miles
   B 16 miles
   C 24 miles
   D 28 miles
   E NH

8. Complete the pattern.
   18, 27, 36, ■, ■, ■, . . . ,

   F 27, 18, 9
   G 36, 27, 18
   H 44, 52, 60
   J 45, 54, 63

9. $3 \times (4 \times 2) = \blacksquare$

A 9
B 14
C 18
D 24
E NH

Use the table for Questions 10–11.

Flavor	Bagels Sold
Plain	
Sesame	
Raisin	
Blueberry	
 stands for 10 bagels.	

10. **How many plain bagels did Fred sell?**

F 6 bagels
G 30 bagels
H 55 bagels
J 60 bagels

11. **How many more raisin bagels did Fred sell than blueberry?**

A 10 more
B 15 more
C 20 more
D 25 more
E NH

12. **Choose a digit to make the number sentence true.**

$8 \times \blacksquare$ is less than 35

F 4
G 6
H 7
J 8

13. **If 4 people can ride in a cart, how many carts are needed for 24 people?**

A 3 carts
B 6 carts
C 8 carts
D 12 carts

14. **Choose a set of three numbers that make the statement true.**

$7 \times \blacksquare$ is greater than 40

F 5, 6, 7
G 3, 4, 5
H 6, 7, 8
J 4, 5, 6

15.
$$\begin{array}{r} 9 \\ \times\ 8 \\ \hline \end{array}$$

A 54
B 69
C 72
D 78
E NH

16. **Which of the statements is *not* true?**

F $8 \times 8 > 7 \times 9$
G $25 + 5 = 6 \times 5$
H $40 - 9 < 9 \times 3$
J $4 \times 6 = 8 \times 3$

17. **You and three friends each have a pair of roller skates. How many wheels is that in all if each skate has 4 wheels?**

A 10 wheels
B 12 wheels
C 18 wheels
D 32 wheels
E NH

Reteaching

Set A *(pages 178–180)*

Write a multiplication sentence for the array formed by the marbles.

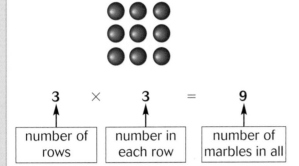

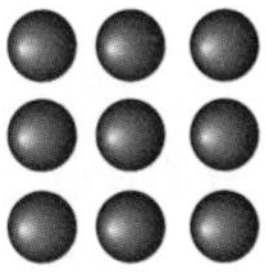

3 × 3 = 9

- 3: number of rows
- 3: number in each row
- 9: number of marbles in all

Remember when both factors in a multiplication sentence are the same, the product is called a **square number.**

Write a multiplication sentence for each array.

1. 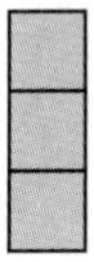

2. 

Set B *(pages 182–183)*

Find the product using doubles.

5 × 6 = ■ or

$$\begin{array}{r} 5 \\ \times\ 6 \\ \hline ■ \end{array}$$

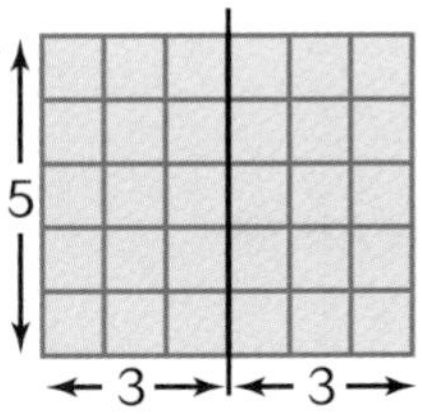

Since 5 × 3 = 15,

Then 5 × 6 = 30.

Remember when you double one factor, the product doubles.

Use the first fact to help you multiply the second fact.

1. 1 × 3 = ■
1 × 6 = ■
2. 4 × 3 = ■
4 × 6 = ■
3. 7 × 3 = ■
7 × 6 = ■
4. 10 × 3 = ■
10 × 6 = ■

Set C *(pages 184–185)*

A basketball player made 8 baskets worth 2 points each. How many points did he score?

2 × 8 = ■

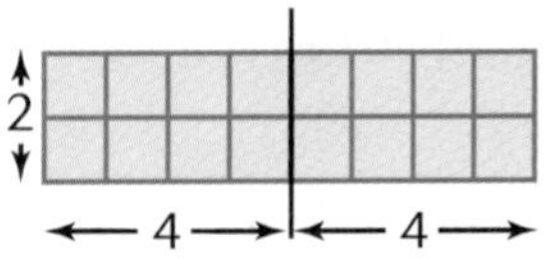

2 × 4 = 8,

2 × 8 = 16.

The basketball player scored 16 points.

Remember you can use doubles to find a product.

1. $\begin{array}{r} 3 \\ \times\ 8 \\ \hline \end{array}$
2. $\begin{array}{r} 8 \\ \times\ 4 \\ \hline \end{array}$
3. $\begin{array}{r} 8 \\ \times\ 2 \\ \hline \end{array}$
4. $\begin{array}{r} 5 \\ \times\ 8 \\ \hline \end{array}$
5. $\begin{array}{r} 10 \\ \times\ 8 \\ \hline \end{array}$
6. $\begin{array}{r} 6 \\ \times\ 8 \\ \hline \end{array}$
7. $\begin{array}{r} 8 \\ \times\ 7 \\ \hline \end{array}$
8. $\begin{array}{r} 8 \\ \times\ 8 \\ \hline \end{array}$
9. $\begin{array}{r} 9 \\ \times\ 8 \\ \hline \end{array}$

Set D *(pages 188–189)*

Find 2 × 7.

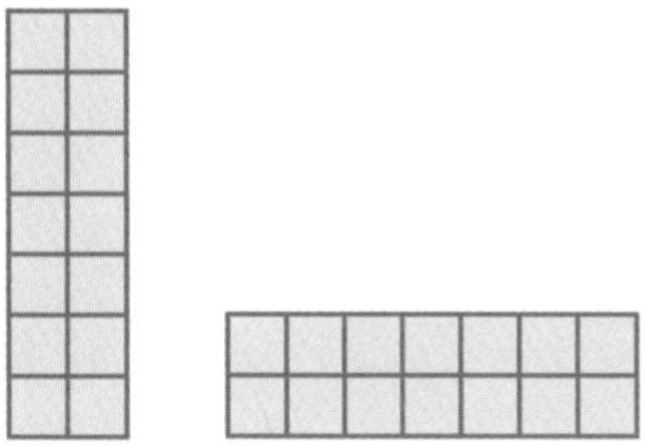

$7 \times 2 = 2 \times 7$

If you know $7 \times 2 = 14$, you know that $2 \times 7 = 14$.

Remember you can find the product by changing the order of the factors.

1. 7×6 **2.** 5×7 **3.** 3×7

4. 8×7 **5.** 7×4 **6.** 7×9

7. 7×1 **8.** 0×7 **9.** 4×7

Set E *(pages 190–191)*

A photo album has space for 4 photographs on each page. Simon has completely filled 9 pages. How many photographs does Simon have?

$4 \times 9 = ■$

If you know $9 \times 4 = 36$, then you know $4 \times 9 = 36$.

Simon has 36 photographs.

Remember you can use the first fact to help you multiply the second fact.

1. 9×2
2×9

2. 9×8
8×9

3. 9×5
5×9

4. 9×6
6×9

5. 9×7
7×9

6. 9×4
4×9

Set F *(pages 192–193)*

Emilie bought 4 bags of beads, each with 10 beads. How many beads did she buy?

$4 \times 10 = ■$

$10 + 10 + 10 + 10 = 40$

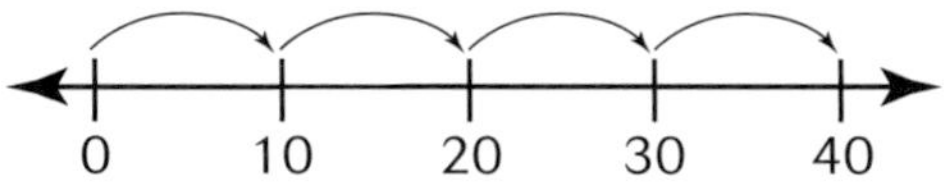

Count by 10s until you have said 4 numbers.

10, 20, 30, 40

Emilie bought 40 beads.

Remember you can skip count by 10s to find a product.

1. 10×2 **2.** 9×10

3. 3×10 **4.** 10×0

5. 8×10 **6.** 10×5

7. 7×10 **8.** 10×6

Reteaching (continued)

Set G (pages 198–199)

Find 2 × 3 × 4.

$(2 \times 3) \times 4 = \blacksquare$ Multiply the first two factors.

$6 \times 4 = 24$ Multiply remaining factors.

Remember you can change the grouping of factors.

1. $(7 \times 1) \times 6 = \blacksquare$
2. $4 \times (5 \times 2) = \blacksquare$
3. $(3 \times 1) \times 8 = \blacksquare$

Set H (pages 200–201)

Give three numbers that make the statement true:

3 × ■ is less than 8.

0, 1, and 2 make the statement true.

3s facts
$3 \times 0 = 0$
$3 \times 1 = 3$
$3 \times 2 = 6$
$3 \times 3 = 9$

Remember to check answers by using each solution in the statement.

Give three numbers that make each statement true.

1. $7 \times \blacksquare$ is greater than 25.
2. $10 \times \blacksquare$ is between 45 and 75.

Set I (pages 202–203)

Find the missing factor.

$2 \times \blacksquare = 6$.

3 is the missing factor.

2s facts
$2 \times 0 = 0$
$2 \times 1 = 2$
$2 \times 2 = 4$
$2 \times 3 = 6$

Remember to use fact tables to find missing factors.

Find each missing factor.

1. $9 \times \blacksquare = 45$
2. $\blacksquare \times 6 = 42$
3. $\blacksquare \times 4 = 32$
4. $5 \times \blacksquare = 20$

Set J (pages 204–205)

Compare 16 + 12 and 3 × 9.

$16 + 12$ ● 3×9 Solve each.

28 ● 27

$28 > 27$

So, $16 + 12 > 3 \times 9$.

Remember to solve each expression first. Then, compare solutions.

Compare. Use >, <, or =.

1. 3×7 ● 20
2. $67 - 28$ ● 5×9
3. 6×4 ● $52 - 28$

More Practice

Set A *(pages 178–180)*

Write a multiplication sentence for each array.

1. 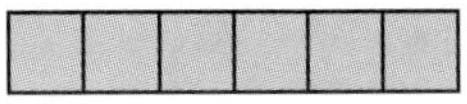

2. 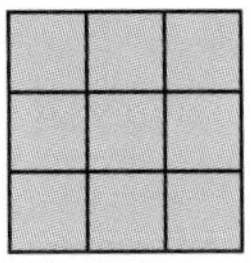

3. 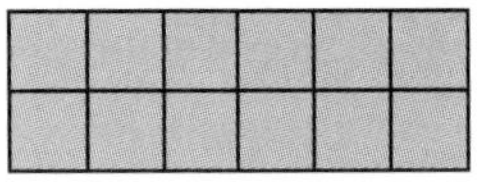

4. 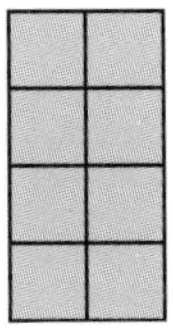

5. 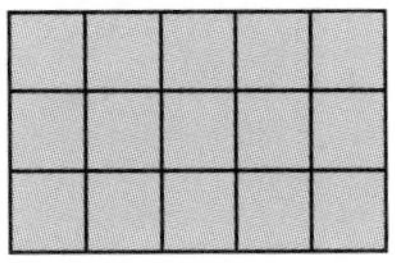

6. 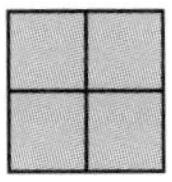

7. There are 6 rows in Mel's parking lot. He can park 8 cars in each row. If all the rows are filled, how many cars are parked in his lot?

Set B *(pages 182–183)*

Multiply.

1. $\begin{array}{r} 6 \\ \times\ 2 \\ \hline \end{array}$ **2.** $\begin{array}{r} 6 \\ \times\ 8 \\ \hline \end{array}$ **3.** $\begin{array}{r} 4 \\ \times\ 6 \\ \hline \end{array}$ **4.** $\begin{array}{r} 3 \\ \times\ 6 \\ \hline \end{array}$ **5.** $\begin{array}{r} 6 \\ \times\ 9 \\ \hline \end{array}$ **6.** $\begin{array}{r} 0 \\ \times\ 6 \\ \hline \end{array}$

7. Your father has bought 3 packs of amusement ride tickets. There are 6 tickets in each pack. How many tickets are there in all?

Set C *(pages 184–185)*

Multiply.

1. $\begin{array}{r} 8 \\ \times\ 8 \\ \hline \end{array}$ **2.** $\begin{array}{r} 3 \\ \times\ 8 \\ \hline \end{array}$ **3.** $\begin{array}{r} 8 \\ \times\ 9 \\ \hline \end{array}$ **4.** $\begin{array}{r} 5 \\ \times\ 8 \\ \hline \end{array}$ **5.** $\begin{array}{r} 2 \\ \times\ 8 \\ \hline \end{array}$ **6.** $\begin{array}{r} 8 \\ \times\ 6 \\ \hline \end{array}$

7. $\begin{array}{r} 8 \\ \times\ 4 \\ \hline \end{array}$ **8.** $\begin{array}{r} 7 \\ \times\ 8 \\ \hline \end{array}$ **9.** $\begin{array}{r} 8 \\ \times\ 1 \\ \hline \end{array}$ **10.** $\begin{array}{r} 10 \\ \times\ 8 \\ \hline \end{array}$ **11.** $\begin{array}{r} 9 \\ \times\ 8 \\ \hline \end{array}$ **12.** $\begin{array}{r} 8 \\ \times\ 0 \\ \hline \end{array}$

13. There are 5 vans leaving for Fresno. Each van holds 8 people. If all the vans are full except for 2 empty seats, how many people are leaving for Fresno?

More Practice (continued)

Set D *(pages 188–189)*

Multiply.

1. $\begin{array}{r} 7 \\ \times 1 \\ \hline \end{array}$ **2.** $\begin{array}{r} 4 \\ \times 7 \\ \hline \end{array}$ **3.** $\begin{array}{r} 9 \\ \times 7 \\ \hline \end{array}$ **4.** $\begin{array}{r} 7 \\ \times 8 \\ \hline \end{array}$ **5.** $\begin{array}{r} 10 \\ \times 7 \\ \hline \end{array}$ **6.** $\begin{array}{r} 7 \\ \times 5 \\ \hline \end{array}$

7. Mrs. Lee rides a subway to and from work 4 days per week. Each ride is 7 miles long. How many miles does she travel each week?

Set E *(pages 190–191)*

Multiply.

1. $\begin{array}{r} 3 \\ \times 9 \\ \hline \end{array}$ **2.** $\begin{array}{r} 9 \\ \times 8 \\ \hline \end{array}$ **3.** $\begin{array}{r} 9 \\ \times 4 \\ \hline \end{array}$ **4.** $\begin{array}{r} 5 \\ \times 9 \\ \hline \end{array}$ **5.** $\begin{array}{r} 10 \\ \times 9 \\ \hline \end{array}$ **6.** $\begin{array}{r} 9 \\ \times 1 \\ \hline \end{array}$

7. Can 37 people row across a lake in 9 rowboats that hold 4 people each? Explain your answer.

Set F *(pages 192–193)*

Multiply.

1. 10×7 **2.** 3×10 **3.** 6×10 **4.** 10×8 **5.** 10×10 **6.** 2×10

7. 1×10 **8.** 10×4 **9.** 5×10 **10.** 7×10 **11.** 10×0 **12.** 10×9

13. Mr. Peterson is preparing for a trip in his hot-air balloon. Each day for a week he travels 10 miles in the balloon. How many miles does he travel?

Set G *(pages 198–199)*

Multiply.

1. $8 \times 1 \times 5$ **2.** $3 \times 3 \times 3$ **3.** $5 \times 3 \times 1$ **4.** $1 \times 2 \times 9$

5. $9 \times 0 \times 5$ **6.** $3 \times 2 \times 4$ **7.** $2 \times 3 \times 3$ **8.** $2 \times 3 \times 1$

9. Amy, Ron, and Chris each bought 1 pair of 5-wheel skates. They counted all the wheels. How many wheels did they count?

Set H (pages 200–201)

Give three numbers that make each statement true.

1. 2 × ■ is less than 11.
2. 5 × ■ is between 29 and 43.
3. 7 × ■ is greater than 48.
4. 6 × ■ is between 37 and 57.
5. 4 × ■ is greater than 25.
6. 3 × ■ is greater than 19.
7. 9 × ■ is less than 50.
8. 10 × ■ is less than 66.
9. Trey pays for his lunch and receives some change. If he receives between 21¢ and 45¢, how many dimes could he receive?

Set I (pages 202–203)

Find each missing factor.

1. 5 × ■ = 40
2. 7 × ■ = 42
3. 9 × ■ = 27
4. ■ × 6 = 30
5. 4 × ■ = 32
6. ■ × 8 = 48
7. ■ × 7 = 56
8. ■ × 9 = 81
9. ■ × 4 = 36
10. ■ × 5 = 45
11. 3 × ■ = 21
12. 4 × ■ = 24
13. Forty-eight people need to ride in helicopters to the airport. Each helicopter can hold 8 people. How many helicopters are needed?

Set J (pages 204–205)

Compare. Use >, <, or =.

1. 6 × 4 ● 18 + 13
2. 64 − 31 ● 5 × 6
3. 48 + 37 ● 9 × 9
4. 6 × 7 ● 96 − 54
5. 32 + 24 ● 5 × 10
6. 6 × 9 ● 7 × 8
7. (3 × 2) × 9 ● 6 × 10
8. (3 × 2) × 4 ● 3 × 8
9. Kelly and Gloria collect stamps in albums. Kelly has filled 6 pages of her album, and each page has 8 stamps on it. Gloria has filled 5 pages of her album, and each page has 9 stamps on it. Who has more stamps?

TEST PREP

Problem Solving: Preparing for Tests

Choose the correct letter for each answer.

---

1. **For an art project, Larry cut a sheet of paper into 4 equal strips. Then he cut 2 of the strips into 3 equal parts. How many pieces of paper does Larry have now?**

A 7
B 8
C 9
D 12

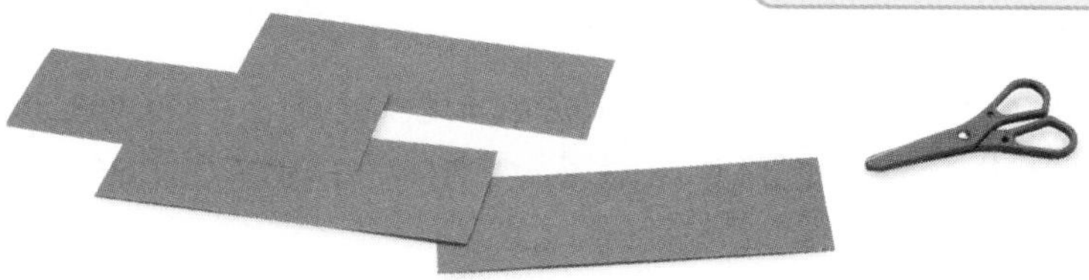

Tip

Try the strategy *Draw a Picture* to solve this problem.

---

2. **Students at a picnic drank 123 bottles of orange juice, 189 bottles of apple juice, and 168 bottles of water. Which is the best estimate for the number of bottles of juice drunk at the picnic?**

F 200
G 300
H 500
J 600

Tip

Read the question carefully. Choose only the numbers you need. Then round these numbers to the nearest hundred.

---

3. **There are 8 colored markers in each box of markers. Pete bought 4 boxes, and Sue bought 6 boxes. How many colored markers did they buy in all?**

A 20
B 32
C 48
D 80

Tip

When more than one step is needed to solve a problem, you must decide both *what* to do and in what *order* you should do it.

4. **Sharon, Linda, and 4 of their friends each read 5 books for a school project. Which number sentence shows the total number of books they read?**

F $4 + 2 = \blacksquare$

G $4 \times 5 = \blacksquare$

H $5 \times 5 = \blacksquare$

J $6 \times 5 = \blacksquare$

5. **A store has different kinds of jackets for sale. This table shows how many of each kind of jacket the store has.**

Jackets for Sale			
	Plain	Stripes	Checks
Red	80	60	115
Blue	125	35	55
Green	75	105	40

How many plain red jackets and striped blue jackets does the store have?

A 205

B 140

C 115

D 45

6. **Kenny's mom bought 5 concert tickets that are all in a row. One ticket has been lost. The other ticket numbers are A28, A32, A30, and A24. Which ticket is lost?**

F A20 **H** A26

G A22 **J** A34

7. **Paul makes a banner that is 41 inches long. Keshawn makes a banner that is 32 inches long. About how much longer is Paul's banner than Keshawn's banner?**

A 5 in. **C** 30 in.

B 10 in. **D** 70 in.

8. **It takes Joan 15 minutes to walk to the library. She leaves for the library at 11:20 A.M. She must be back home by 2:15 P.M. How much time can Joan spend in the library?**

F 2 h 15 min

G 2 h 25 min

H 3 h 15 min

J 2 h 55 min

9. **George made 8 large cookies. He put 5 or 6 raisins on the top of each cookie. Which of these is reasonable for the total number of raisins George used?**

A Fewer than 11

B Between 11 and 30

C Between 40 and 48

D More than 50

10. **Ed has 7 games and 4 puzzles. His friend Min has 2 puzzles and 5 games. Which number sentence shows the total number of puzzles they have?**

F $7 + 4$ **H** $4 + 2$

G $2 + 5$ **J** $7 + 5$

TEST PREP

Multiple-Choice Cumulative Review

Choose the correct letter for each answer.

Number Sense

1. Which group of numbers is in order from *least* to *greatest*?

   A 6,400 4,254 4,524 4,600
   B 4,254 4,600 4,524 6,400
   C 6,400 4,524 4,254 4,600
   D 4,254 4,524 4,600 6,400

2. Find the number that goes in the empty box.

15		25	30	35

   F 17 **H** 40
   G 20 **J** 45

3. Which number sentence is NOT correct?

   A $42 < 85$ **C** $85 < 57$
   B $85 > 42$ **D** $42 > 29$

4. Which picture shows $\frac{1}{3}$ of the circles shaded?

   F 

   G 

   H 

   J 

5. Cindy had 95¢. She spent 40¢ on a drink. How much money did she have then?

   A 50¢ **C** 99¢
   B 55¢ **D** $1.35

6. Stacy has 4 hats. Each hat has 2 bows on it. How many bows are there in all?

   F 2 bows **H** 8 bows
   G 6 bows **J** 12 bows

7. Find the difference.

   $485 - 297 = ■$

   A 161 **C** 206
   B 188 **D** 782

8. There are 6 rows of seats at a concert. Each row has 8 seats. All but 4 of the seats are taken. How many people are seated?

   F 18 people
   G 44 people
   H 48 people
   J 52 people

Algebra and Functions

9. **What is the rule for this table?**

In	3	4	5	6
Out	12	16	20	24

A Add 9
B Multiply by 3.
C Multiply by 4.
D Add 12.

---

10. **Which number sentence is in the same family of facts as 6 + 8 = 14?**

F $6 \times 8 = 48$
G $8 + 6 = 14$
H $48 \div 8 = 6$
J $48 - 6 = 42$

---

11. **Which number makes this sentence true?**

6 × ▇ = 42

A 6 **C** 36
B 7 **D** 48

---

12. **Which has a greater product than 6 × 8?**

F 7×7
G 8×6
H 9×5
J 10×4

Measurement and Geometry

13. **How many sides does this shape have?**

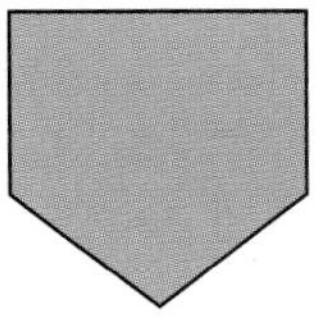

A 2
B 3
C 4
D 5

---

14. **Which figure best represents a square?**

F 

H 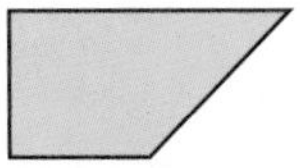

G 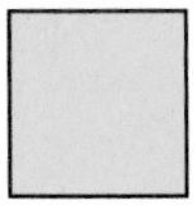

J 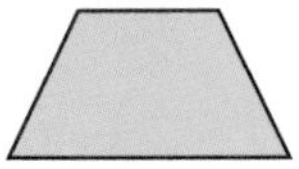

---

15. **Which space shape could you use to draw a rectangle?**

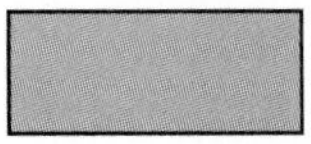

A 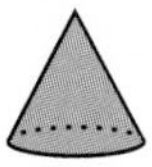

C 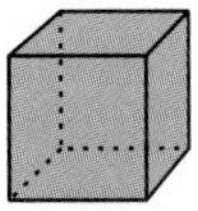

B 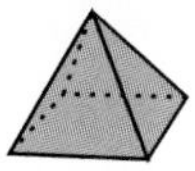

D 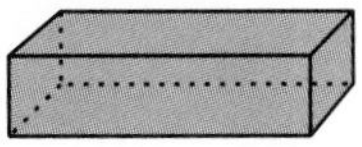

CHAPTER 6

Division Concepts

Diagnosing Readiness

In Chapter 6, you will use these skills:

A Multiplying by 2

(pages 144–145)

1. 2×3

2. 2×6

3. 2×0

4. 5×2

5. 1×2

6. 9×2

7. $\begin{array}{r} 4 \\ \times 2 \\ \hline \end{array}$

8. $\begin{array}{r} 2 \\ \times 7 \\ \hline \end{array}$

9. Richard has 2 packages of corn seeds. Each package has 8 seeds in it. How many corn seeds does Richard have?

B Multiplying by 3

(pages 150–151)

10. 3×7

11. 3×2

12. 1×3

13. 9×3

14. 4×3

15. 0×3

16. $\begin{array}{r} 5 \\ \times 3 \\ \hline \end{array}$

17. $\begin{array}{r} 3 \\ \times 6 \\ \hline \end{array}$

18. Alberto read 10 pages in a book each day for 3 days. How many pages did Alberto read?

C Multiplying by 4

(pages 152–153)

19. 4×4

20. 6×4

21. 4×7

22. 9×4

23. 4×2

24. 3×4

25. $\begin{array}{r} 5 \\ \times\ 4 \\ \hline \end{array}$

26. $\begin{array}{r} 4 \\ \times\ 0 \\ \hline \end{array}$

27. Toby has 8 bags of marbles. Each bag has 4 marbles in it. How many marbles does Toby have in all?

D Multiplying by 5

(pages 146–147)

28. 5×0

29. 7×5

30. 5×9

31. 5×5

32. 8×5

33. 6×5

34. $\begin{array}{r} 3 \\ \times\ 5 \\ \hline \end{array}$

35. $\begin{array}{r} 10 \\ \times\ 5 \\ \hline \end{array}$

36. A building has 4 rows of 5 windows. How many windows are there altogether?

E Using Arrays

(pages 139–141)

Write a multiplication sentence for each array.

37. 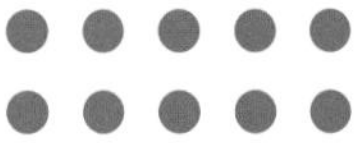

38. 

F Using Money

(pages 24–25)

39. $10 + $25

40. $36 + $12

41. $7.00 + $3.50

42. $10.00 − $4.25

43. $6.25 + $3.60

44. $5.00 − $2.49

45. Beatrice had $15. She bought a paint set for $4 and 2 packages of paper for $3 each. She also bought a paintbrush for $1. How much money did she spend?

To the Family and Student

Looking Back	Chapter 6	Looking Ahead
In Grade 2, students were introduced to the concept of division.	**Division Concepts** In this chapter, students will learn how to divide by 1, 2, 3, 4, and 5.	In Chapter 7, students will learn how to divide by 6, 7, 8, 9, and 10.

Math and Everyday Living

Opportunities to apply the concepts of Chapter 6 abound in everyday situations. During the chapter, think about how division can be used to solve a variety of real-world problems. The following examples suggest just a few of the many situations that could launch a discussion about division.

Math at the Store You have $6 to spend on carrots for a school cooking project. Each bunch of carrots costs $2. How many bunches of carrots can you buy?

Math and Reading You are reading a book that has 50 pages. If you read 5 pages each day, how many days will it take you to finish the book?

Math at Home A recipe calls for 4 eggs. If you have one dozen eggs, how many times can you make the recipe?

Math and Games The game of checkers has a game board with 64 squares arranged in 8 rows. How many columns of squares are there?

Math and Money Jack has 16 quarters. He wants to put them in stacks of 4 so that he can count how many dollars he has. How many stacks of quarters can he make?

Math and Art Your box of paints has 24 different colors. There are 4 rows of colors with the same number in each row. How many colors are in each row?

Math and Sports You play in an after-school basketball league. There are 35 players in all. How many basketball teams of 5 players can be formed?

Math and the Market At the farmers' market, apples are selling at $3 for 2 pounds. You need 6 pounds to make applesauce. How much will this cost?

Math and Transportation A bus can seat 32 people. There are 4 seats in each row. How many rows of seats are there?

Math and Dining Out A restaurant can seat 36 people. Four people can sit at each table. How many tables are there in the restaurant?

Math and Gardening Thomas planted 18 cucumber plants. He put 3 in each row. How many rows of cucumber plants did he plant?

Math at School The bike racks at school hold 50 bikes altogether. Each bike rack holds 5 bikes. How many bike racks are there?

California Content Standards in Chapter 6 Lessons*

	Teach and Practice	Practice
Number Sense		
2.0 Students calculate and solve problems involving addition, subtraction, multiplication, and division.		6-7
2.2 (key) Memorize to automaticity the multiplication table for numbers between 1 and 10.		6-1
2.3 (key) Use the inverse relationship of multiplication and division to compute and check results.	6-1, 6-2, 6-3, 6-5, 6-6	
2.6 Understand the special properties of 0 and 1 in multiplication and division.	6-8	
2.8 Solve problems that require two or more of the skills mentioned above.	6-4	6-9
3.3 (key) Solve problems involving addition, subtraction, multiplication, and division of money amounts in decimal notation and multiply and divide money amounts in decimal notation by using whole-number multipliers and divisors.	6-9	
Algebra and Functions		
1.2 Solve problems involving numeric equations		6-1, 6-2, 6-3, 6-5, 6-6
2.2 Extend and recognize a linear pattern by its rules		6-6

	Teach and Practice	Practice
Mathematical Reasoning		
1.1 Analyze problems by identifying relationships, distinguishing relevant from irrelevant information, sequencing and prioritizing information, and observing patterns.		6-7, 6-9
1.2 Determine when and how to break a problem into simpler parts.	6-4	6-2, 6-5, 6-6, 6-7, 6-9
2.2 Apply strategies and results from simpler problems to more complex problems.		6-4, 6-5, 6-6
2.3 Use a variety of methods, such as words, numbers, symbols, charts, graphs, tables, diagrams, and models, to explain mathematical reasoning.		6-1, 6-3
2.4 Express the solution clearly and logically by using the appropriate mathematical notation and terms and clear language; support solutions with evidence in both verbal and symbolic work.	6-7	
3.2 Note the method of deriving the solution and demonstrate a conceptual understanding of solving similar problems.		6-7, 6-8

* The symbol (key) indicates a key standard as designated in the Mathematics Framework for California Public Schools. Full statements of the California Content Standards are found at the beginning of this book following the Table of Contents.

LESSON 6-1

Relating Multiplication and Division

Warm-Up Review

1. 4×8 **2.** 6×7

3. 2×6 **4.** 5×6

5. Whitney made dinner rolls. Each pan had 4 rows with 6 rolls in each row. She made 2 pans of rolls. How many rolls did she make?

California Content Standard *Number Sense 2.3 ( ): Use the inverse relationship of multiplication and division to compute and check results.*

Math Link You know how to multiply with basic facts. Now you will use what you know about multiplication to help you divide.

Word Bank

dividend
divisor
quotient

Example 1

The school band is marching in the parade.

There are 2 rows with 4 drummers in each row. How many drummers are marching?

Multiply. Find 2×4.

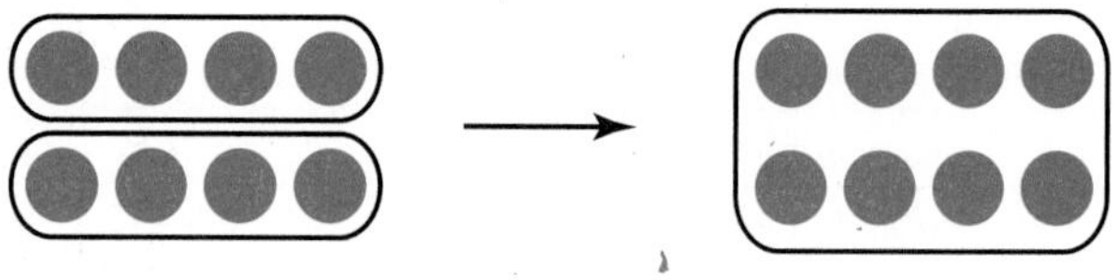

$2 \times 4 = 8$

2 — factor; 4 — factor; 8 — product

There are 8 drummers marching.

There are 8 drummers marching in 2 equal rows. How many drummers are in each row?

Divide. Find $8 \div 2$.

Think: $2 \times 4 = 8$

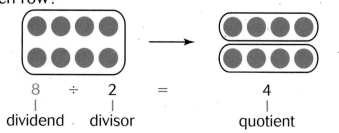

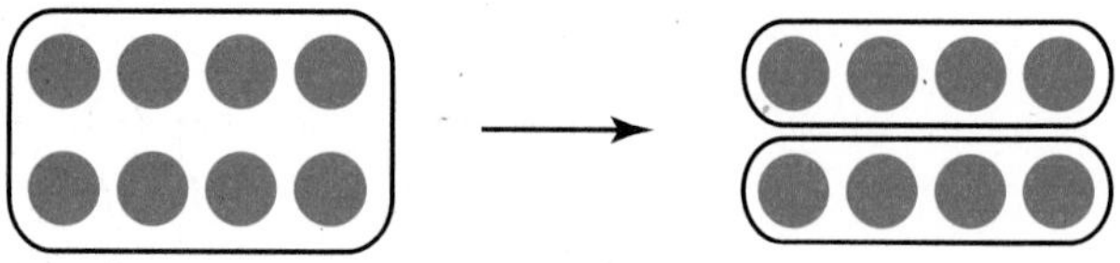

$8 \div 2 = 4$

8 — dividend; 2 — divisor; 4 — quotient

There are 4 drummers in each row.

The **dividend** is the number being divided.

The **divisor** is the number by which you divide the dividend.

The **quotient** is the answer in a division problem.

Additional Standards: Number Sense 2.2 ( ); Algebra and Functions 1.2; Mathematical Reasoning 2.3 *(See p. 225.)*

Example 2

There are 21 horn players in 3 rows. Each row has the same number of players. How many players are in each row?

21	÷	3	=	■
number in all		number of rows		number of players in each row

Use a multiplication fact to help you divide.

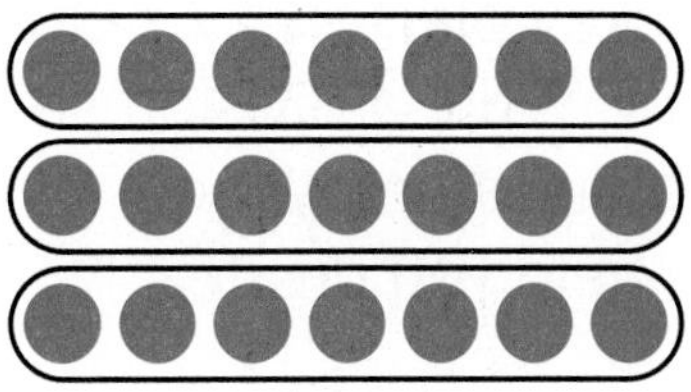

Think: 3 times what number equals 21?

$3 \times 7 = 21$

So, $21 \div 3 = 7$.

There are 7 horn players in each row.

Guided Practice *For another example, see Set A on p. 252.*

Algebra **Use the array to complete each sentence.**

1. 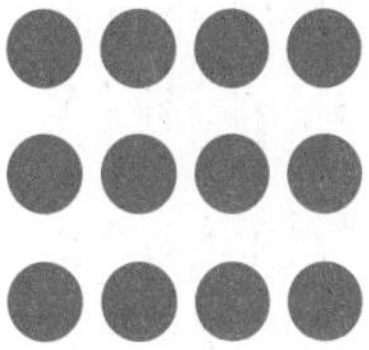

3 × ■ = 12
12 ÷ 3 = ■

2. 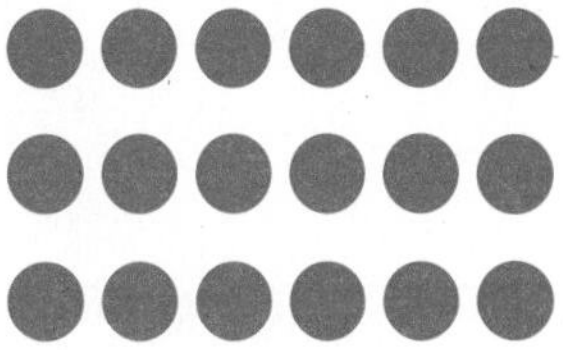

3 × ■ = 18
18 ÷ 3 = ■

3. 

4 × ■ = 16
16 ÷ 4 = ■

4. The school band has 48 members. They march in rows with 6 people in each row. Write a division sentence to show how many rows of marchers there are.

Independent Practice *For more problems, see Set A on p. 254.*

Algebra **Use the array to complete each sentence.**

5. 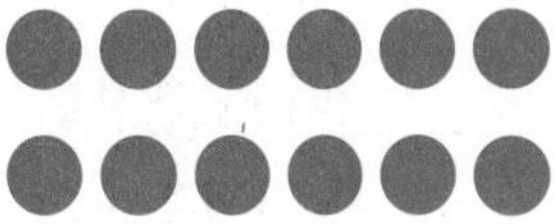

2 × ■ = 12
12 ÷ 2 = ■

6. 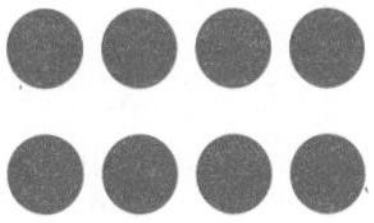

2 × ■ = 8
8 ÷ 2 = ■

7. 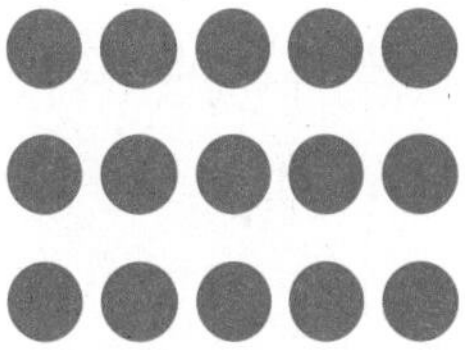

3 × ■ = 15
15 ÷ 3 = ■

Complete each number sentence.

8. $4 \times \blacksquare = 12$
$12 \div 4 = \blacksquare$

9. $3 \times \blacksquare = 9$
$9 \div 3 = \blacksquare$

10. $4 \times \blacksquare = 36$
$36 \div 4 = \blacksquare$

11. $7 \times \blacksquare = 28$
$28 \div 7 = \blacksquare$

12. $5 \times \blacksquare = 25$
$25 \div 5 = \blacksquare$

13. $6 \times \blacksquare = 42$
$42 \div 6 = \blacksquare$

14. $8 \times \blacksquare = 64$
$64 \div 8 = \blacksquare$

15. $9 \times \blacksquare = 54$
$54 \div 9 = \blacksquare$

16. Rickey planted 27 petunias. He put 9 petunias in each row. Write a division sentence to show how many rows of petunias he planted. What multiplication fact did you use to help you divide?

17. Janna helped her friend set up 40 chairs for a meeting. They set up the chairs in 5 equal rows. Write a division sentence to show the number of chairs in each row. What multiplication fact did you use to help you divide?

18. **Math Reasoning** Write two division sentences you could solve using the multiplication fact $5 \times 6 = 30$.

Mixed Review

19. Keith paid $4.59 for a calendar. Larry's calendar cost $1.40 more than Keith's calendar. How much did Larry's calendar cost?

Algebra **Find each missing number.**

20. $\blacksquare \times 5 = 35$ **21.** $6 \times \blacksquare = 48$ **22.** $\blacksquare \times 3 = 21$

Algebra **Compare. Write >, <, or =.**

23. $6 \times 4 \bigcirc 96 - 59$ **24.** $5 \times 3 \bigcirc 6 \times 2$ **25.** $(3 \times 8) \times 1 \bigcirc 24$

Test Prep **Choose the correct letter for each answer.**

26. (2-13) What two numbers make the statement true?
$3 + \blacksquare$ is less than 9.

A 0; 12 **C** 3; 6
B 2; 5 **D** 5; 9

27. (5-9) Which has the same product as 6×4?

F $8 \times 3 \times 0$ **J** $2 \times 4 \times 3$
G $3 \times 3 \times 7$ **K** NH
H $2 \times 6 \times 4$

 Use Homework Workbook 6-1.

TEST PREP

Multiple-Choice Cumulative Review

Choose the correct letter for each answer.

1. **Choose a number that makes the sentence true.**

6 × ▩ is greater than 45.

A 5 **C** 7
B 6 **D** 8

2.
$$\begin{array}{r} 7 \\ \times\ 8 \\ \hline \end{array}$$

F 42 **J** 72
G 54 **K** NH
H 56

3. **Choose a related division sentence for the multiplication sentence.**

3 × 9 = 27

A $9 \div 3 = 3$
B $9 \div 9 = 1$
C $27 \div 9 = 3$
D $27 \div 1 = 27$

4. **Choose a multiplication sentence that describes the array.**

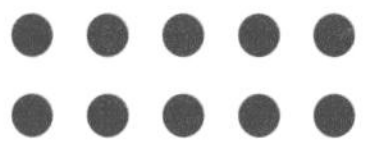

F $2 \times 5 = 10$
G $2 \times 2 = 4$
H $5 \times 5 = 25$
J $5 \times 4 = 20$

5. **Which number is the same as four thousand, six hundred two?**

A 4,062 **C** 4,612
B 4,602 **D** 4,620

6. **The length of a pencil is about**

F 16 centimeters.
G 16 decimeters.
H 16 meters.
J 16 kilometers.

7.
$$\begin{array}{r} 3{,}416 \\ +\ 1{,}712 \\ \hline \end{array}$$

A 4,118
B 4,128
C 5,128
D 6,118
E NH

8. **A band performance began at 7:00 P.M. and ended at 9:30 P.M. There were no intermissions. How long did the concert last?**

F 1 hour and 30 minutes
G 2 hours
H 2 hours and 30 minutes
J 3 hours
K NH

LESSON 6-2

Dividing by 2

California Content Standard *Number Sense 2.3 (🔑): Use the inverse relationship of multiplication and division to compute and check results.*

Warm-Up Review

1. 2×8
2. 3×2
3. 6×2
4. 2×5
5. 9×2
6. 2×4
7. Rosie had 5 markers. Will had 3 markers and Jada had twice as many markers as Will. How many markers did they have altogether?

Math Link You know how to double numbers by multiplying by 2. Now you will learn to find half of a number by dividing by 2.

Example 1

The spoon-and-egg relay race is starting! Ten people form two teams. Each team has the same number of people. How many people are on each team?

Divide 10 by 2 to find out.

10	÷	**2**	=	$\blacksquare$
number of people		number of teams		number of people on each team

Think: $2 \times \blacksquare = 10$

$2 \times 5 = 10$

So, $10 \div 2 = 5$

dividend (10), divisor (2), quotient (5)

When you divide a number by 2, you find half of that number. Half of 10 is 5.

There are 5 people on each team.

More Examples

A. Find $18 \div 2$.

Think: $2 \times \blacksquare = 18$

$2 \times 9 = 18$

So, $18 \div 2 = 9$.

B. Find $8 \div 2$.

Think: $2 \times \blacksquare = 8$

$2 \times 4 = 8$

So, $8 \div 2 = 4$.

Additional Standards: Algebra and Functions 1.2; Mathematical Reasoning 1.2 *(See p. 225.)*

Guided Practice *For another example, see Set B on p. 252.*

Algebra Find the missing factor. Use it to help you divide.

1. $2 \times \blacksquare = 4$ $4 \div 2 = \blacksquare$

2. $2 \times \blacksquare = 6$ $6 \div 2 = \blacksquare$

3. $2 \times \blacksquare = 16$ $16 \div 2 = \blacksquare$

4. $2 \times \blacksquare = 18$ $18 \div 2 = \blacksquare$

5. Each box of spoons has 18 spoons. Half are red and half are blue. How many red spoons are in 3 boxes?

Independent Practice *For more practice, see Set B on p. 254.*

Algebra Find the missing factor. Use it to help you divide.

6. $2 \times \blacksquare = 10$ $10 \div 2 = \blacksquare$

7. $2 \times \blacksquare = 8$ $8 \div 2 = \blacksquare$

8. $2 \times \blacksquare = 14$ $14 \div 2 = \blacksquare$

9. $2 \times \blacksquare = 12$ $12 \div 2 = \blacksquare$

10. A festival lasts 8 hours. After the first 4 hours, a band begins to play. If the band plays for half the time that is left, how long does it play?

11. A dozen eggs are arranged in a carton in 2 equal rows. How many eggs are in each row?

Mixed Review

12. Jim made a flag with 32 stars. He put 8 in each row. Write a division sentence to show how many rows of stars he made. What multiplication fact did you use to help you divide?

Algebra Compare. Write >, <, or =.

13. $40 + 27 \bullet 9 \times 6$ **14.** $27 \bullet 3 \times 9$ **15.** $6 \times (1 \times 9) \bullet 55$

Test Prep **Choose the correct letter for each answer.**

16. (5-3) Each table in the lunchroom seats 8 students. There are 8 tables. What is the greatest number of students that can eat lunch at one time?

A 16 students

B 32 students

C 56 students

D 64 students

17. (4-10) **Algebra** What is the rule for this table?

Input	Output
2	10
8	16
5	13
0	8

F Add 8.

G Subtract 8.

H Multiply by 8.

J Divide by 8.

LESSON 6-3

Dividing by 3

California Content Standard *Number Sense 2.3 (🔑): Use the inverse relationship of multiplication and division to compute and check results.*

Warm-Up Review

1. 2×3
2. 3×8
3. 4×3
4. 5×3
5. 3×7
6. 3×9
7. Drew had 3 packages of pencils. Each package contained 8 pencils. How many pencils does Drew have in all?

Math Link You know how to multiply by 3. In this lesson, you will learn to divide by 3.

Example 1

At a craft booth, 12 wooden animals are displayed on pieces of kente cloth. There are 3 animals on each piece of cloth. How many pieces of kente cloth are there?

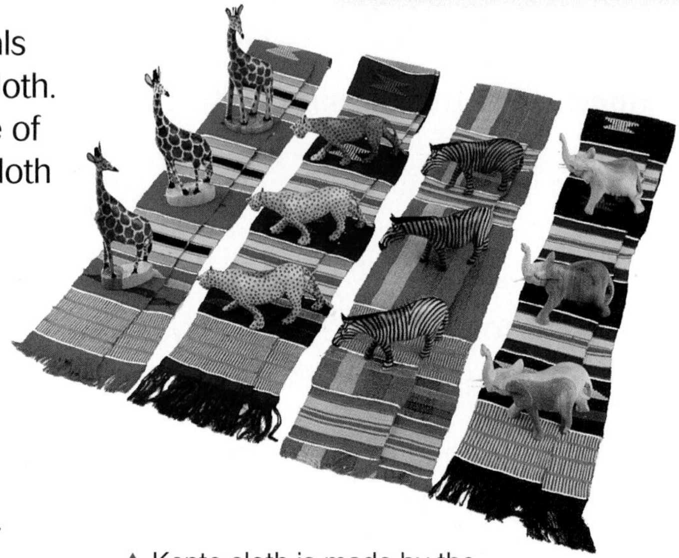

▲ Kente cloth is made by the Ashanti people of Ghana.

Find $12 \div 3$.

Think: $3 \times ■ = 12$
$3 \times 4 = 12$

So, $12 \div 3 = 4$.

There are 4 pieces of kente cloth.

More Examples

A. Find $18 \div 3$.

Think: $3 \times ■ = 18$
$3 \times 6 = 18$

So, $18 \div 3 = 6$.

B. Find $27 \div 3$.

Think: $3 \times ■ = 27$
$3 \times 9 = 27$

So, $27 \div 3 = 9$.

Guided Practice *For another example, see Set C on p. 252.*

Algebra Find the missing factor. Use it to help you divide.

1. $3 \times ■ = 15$
   $15 \div 3 = ■$
2. $3 \times ■ = 24$
   $24 \div 3 = ■$
3. $3 \times ■ = 21$
   $21 \div 3 = ■$
4. Jason has a dozen roses. He gave 1 rose to his mother and 2 roses to his grandmother. He split the remaining roses equally between his 3 sisters. How many roses did each sister get?

Additional Standards: Algebra and Functions 1.2; Mathematical Reasoning 2.3 *(See p. 225.)*

Independent Practice *For more practice, see Set C on p. 254.*

Algebra **Find the missing factor. Use it to help you divide.**

5. $3 \times \blacksquare = 12$
$12 \div 3 = \blacksquare$

6. $3 \times \blacksquare = 9$
$9 \div 3 = \blacksquare$

7. $3 \times \blacksquare = 18$
$18 \div 3 = \blacksquare$

8. $3 \div 3$ **9.** $27 \div 3$ **10.** $6 \div 3$ **11.** $15 \div 3$

12. $24 \div 3$ **13.** $30 \div 3$ **14.** $21 \div 3$ **15.** $16 \div 2$

16. An artist has 9 wooden animals to pack in boxes. If each box holds 3 animals, how many boxes does she need?

17. Math Reasoning Suppose you have 15 wooden animals and 4 pieces of kente cloth. You want to display 3 animals on each cloth. Do you have enough pieces of kente cloth to display all the animals? Explain.

Mixed Review

18. Jackson has 16 trading cards. He wants to share them equally with his friend Antonio. How many cards should Jackson give to Antonio?

19. $14 \div 2$ **20.** $6 \div 2$ **21.** $4 \div 2$ **22.** $18 \div 2$

Write two related division sentences for each multiplication sentence.

23. $5 \times 2 = 10$ **24.** $3 \times 6 = 18$ **25.** $4 \times 7 = 28$ **26.** $5 \times 8 = 40$

Test Prep **Choose the correct letter for each answer.**

27. (5-6) Each desk in the school library has space for 4 students. There are 9 desks in all. What is the greatest number of students that can work at all the desks?

A 15 students
B 27 students
C 32 students
D 36 students

28. (1-3) Which of the following numbers, when rounded to the nearest thousand, does **not** round to 5,000?

F 4,480
G 4,890
H 4,950
J 5,450

LESSON 6-4

Understand
Plan
Solve
Look Back

Problem-Solving Skill:
Multistep Problems

Warm-Up Review

1. 16 ÷ 2 **2.** 18 ÷ 3

3. 4 ÷ 2 **4.** 9 ÷ 3

5. 6 ÷ 2 **6.** 27 ÷ 3

7. Chanell has 15 muffins. She puts 3 muffins in each bag. How many bags did Chanell have?

California Content Standard *Number Sense 2.8 (🔑): Solve problems that require two or more of the skills mentioned above. Also, Mathematical Reasoning 1.2 (See p. 225.)*

Read for Understanding

The 4-H Club grew 16 outdoor plants and 12 houseplants. They sold half of the outdoor plants at the community fair. They only sold 3 of the houseplants. After the fair, they donated all the leftover plants to a local hospital.

1. How many houseplants did the 4-H Club grow?
2. How many houseplants were sold?
3. How many outdoor plants did the 4-H Club grow?

Think and Discuss

MATH FOCUS

Multistep Problem

Sometimes more than one step is needed to solve a problem. To solve the problem you must decide not only *what* to do, but in what *order* you should do it.

Reread the paragraph at the top of the page.

4. What information do you need in order to find out how many plants the 4-H Club donated?
5. How many plants did the 4-H Club donate? Write number sentences to show the steps you used to find the answer.
6. Look back at your answer to Exercise 5. Could you have done the steps in a different order? Why or why not?

 Additional Standard: Mathematical Reasoning 2.2 (See p. 225.)

Guided Practice

A club planted a neighborhood vegetable garden. They had 4 rows of tomato plants and 2 rows of bean plants. They put 8 plants in each row. How many more tomato plants than bean plants were there?

1. Which would you do first to solve the problem?
   - **a.** Find the total number of tomato plants.
   - **b.** Subtract the number of bean plants from the number of tomato plants.
   - **c.** Add the number of tomato plants to the number of bean plants.

2. What else do you need to find in order to solve the problem?
   - **a.** the number of bean plants
   - **b.** the total number of rows
   - **c.** the total number of plants

3. What is the final step you need to do to solve the problem?
   - **a.** Find 4×8.
   - **b.** Find $32 - 16$.
   - **c.** Find 2×8.

Independent Practice

Scott, Allison, and Miles are working on a cleanup project. They have volunteered to fill 15 bags with trash. So far they have filled 3 bags with trash. If they each want to fill the same number of the remaining bags, how many bags does each person need to fill?

4. Which number sentence tells how many bags there are left to fill?
   - **a.** $15 - 3 = 12$ bags
   - **b.** $15 + 3 = 18$ bags
   - **c.** $15 - 12 = 3$ bags

5. Which number sentence tells how many bags there are left for each person to fill?
   - **a.** $3 \div 3 = 1$ bag
   - **b.** $18 \div 3 = 6$ bags
   - **c.** $12 \div 3 = 4$ bags

6. **Math Reasoning** Suppose the 3 students had volunteered to fill 21 bags with trash. Would the steps needed to solve the problem change?

Use Homework Workbook 6-4.

Diagnostic Checkpoint

Algebra Use the array to complete each sentence.

1. (6-1)

$3 \times ■ = 15$
$15 \div 3 = ■$

2. (6-1)

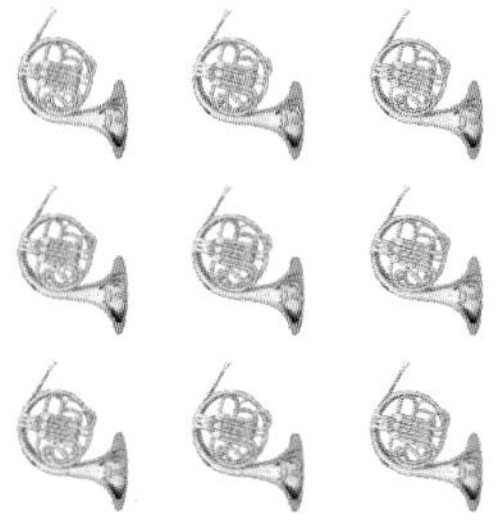

$3 \times ■ = 9$
$9 \div 3 = ■$

3. (6-1)

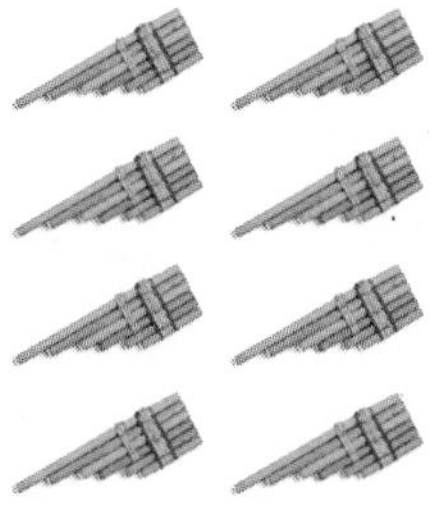

$4 \times ■ = 8$
$8 \div 4 = ■$

Algebra Find the missing factor. Use it to help you divide.

4. (6-3) $3 \times ■ = 18$
$18 \div 3 = ■$

5. (6-2) $2 \times ■ = 8$
$8 \div 2 = ■$

6. (6-3) $3 \times ■ = 12$
$12 \div 3 = ■$

7. (6-2) $2 \times ■ = 12$
$12 \div 2 = ■$

8. (6-3) $3 \times ■ = 27$
$27 \div 3 = ■$

9. (6-2) $2 \times ■ = 6$
$6 \div 2 = ■$

Find each quotient.

10. (6-2) $4 \div 2$

11. (6-3) $9 \div 3$

12. (6-3) $21 \div 3$

13. (6-3) $24 \div 3$

14. (6-2) $16 \div 2$

15. (6-2) $10 \div 2$

16. (6-3) $15 \div 3$

17. (6-2) $14 \div 2$

18. (6-3) $27 \div 3$

19. (6-2) $12 \div 2$

20. (6-2) $18 \div 2$

21. (6-3) $18 \div 6$

22. (6-3) During the parade, 18 clowns hand out balloons. If the clowns walk in groups of 3, how many groups are there?

23. (6-4) The Music Club float leads the parade. There are 25 members in the club, but 4 of the members were not able to be in the parade. There are 3 platforms on the float with an equal number of club members standing on each platform. How many club members are standing on each platform? What steps did you take to solve the problem?

Multiple-Choice Cumulative Review

TEST PREP

Choose the correct letter for each answer.

1. Balloons are sold in packages of 4. Jan buys 9 packages of balloons. How many balloons does she buy?

A 32 balloons
B 36 balloons
C 40 balloons
D 45 balloons
E NH

2. Which of the following has the smallest product?

F 3×9
G 8×4
H 4×7
J 5×6

3. $12 \div 2 = ■$

A 3
B 4
C 5
D 6
E NH

4.

$$\begin{array}{r} 3{,}004 \\ -\ 1{,}588 \\ \hline \end{array}$$

F 1,412
G 1,416
H 1,512
J 1,516
K NH

5. What is the missing number?

■ oz = 1 lb

A 10
B 12
C 16
D 32
E NH

6. What is the value of the underlined digit?

$\underline{7}$,034

F 70
G 700
H 7,000
J 70,000

7. Choose the rule for the input/output table.

Input	Output
3	18
9	54
4	24
7	42

A Multiply by 6.
B Divide by 6.
C Add 15.
D Subtract 15.

Dividing by 4

California Content Standard *Number 2.3 (🔑): Use the inverse relationship of multiplication and division to compute and check results.*

Warm-Up Review

1. 4×6 **2.** 5×4

3. 9×4 **4.** 2×4

5. 4×3 **6.** 4×7

7. John is meeting 3 friends at the skating rink. Each of his friends is bringing 2 of their friends. How many people will John be meeting?

Math Link You know how to multiply by 4. Now you will use these multiplication facts to help you divide by 4.

Example 1

Here come the clowns! There are 12 balloons and 4 clowns. Each clown has the same number of balloons. How many balloons does each clown have?

You can show 12 divided by 4 by writing $12 \div 4 = ■$.

You can also show $12 \div 4$ by writing:

$$\begin{array}{r} ■ \\ 4\overline{)12} \end{array}$$

■ ⟵ quotient

divisor ⟶ $4\overline{)12}$ ⟵ dividend

Now solve $12 \div 4 = ■$.

Think: $4 \times ■ = 12$
$4 \times 3 = 12$

So, $12 \div 4 = 3$ or $\begin{array}{r} 3 \\ 4\overline{)12} \end{array}$.

Each clown has 3 balloons.

More Examples

A. Find $32 \div 4$.

Think: $4 \times ■ = 32$
$4 \times 8 = 32$

So, $32 \div 4 = 8$.

You can also write $\begin{array}{r} 8 \\ 4\overline{)32} \end{array}$.

B. Find $20 \div 4$.

Think: $4 \times ■ = 20$
$4 \times 5 = 20$

So, $20 \div 4 = 5$.

You can also write $\begin{array}{r} 5 \\ 4\overline{)20} \end{array}$.

Additional Standards: Algebra and Functions 1.2; Mathematical Reasoning 1.2, 2.2 *(See p. 225.)*

Guided Practice *For another example, see Set D on p. 253.*

Algebra Find the missing factor. Use it to help you divide.

1. $4 \times ■ = 36$
$36 \div 4 = ■$

2. $4 \times ■ = 24$
$24 \div 4 = ■$

3. $4 \times ■ = 28$
$28 \div 4 = ■$

4. Elton has $16. He needs to share the money equally among his brother, 2 sisters, and himself. How much money will each person get?

Independent Practice *For more practice, see Set D on p. 255.*

Algebra Find the missing factor. Use it to help you divide.

5. $4 \times ■ = 12$
$12 \div 4 = ■$

6. $4 \times ■ = 20$
$20 \div 4 = ■$

7. $4 \times ■ = 16$
$16 \div 4 = ■$

8. $4\overline{)4}$　**9.** $4\overline{)36}$　**10.** $4\overline{)16}$　**11.** $4\overline{)32}$　**12.** $4\overline{)8}$

13. $40 \div 4$　**14.** $28 \div 4$　**15.** $24 \div 4$　**16.** $32 \div 4$

17. Balloons are sold in bunches of 8 at the fair. If 4 friends share 1 bunch equally, how many balloons will each person get?

18. Suppose the friends buy 2 more bunches to share equally. How many balloons would each person get altogether?

Mixed Review

19. Movie tickets cost $5 for adults and $3 for children. How much will it cost for the Cunningham family to go to the movies if there are 2 adults and 3 children?

20. $16 \div 2$　**21.** $18 \div 3$　**22.** $6 \div 2$　**23.** $15 \div 3$

Test Prep **Choose the correct letter for each answer.**

24. (3-4) William drank 4 pints of water. How many cups is that?

A 2 cups　**C** 6 cups
B 4 cups　**D** 8 cups

25. (5-7) $10 \times 6 =$

F 6　**J** 600
G 60　**K** NH
H 66

LESSON 6-6

Dividing by 5

California Content Standard *Number Sense 2.3 (🔑): Use the inverse relationship of multiplication and division to compute and check results.*

Math Link You know how to multiply by 5. Now you will learn how to divide by 5.

Warm-Up Review

1. 5×3
2. 6×5
3. 8×5
4. 5×5
5. Robin had 5 feet of rope. Cody had 3 times as much rope as Robin, but then he gave 4 feet of rope to Josh. How much rope does Cody have now?

Example 1

Firefighters are giving children rides on an old fire truck. Twenty children want a ride. If 5 children can ride at a time, how many trips will the fire truck make?

Find $20 \div 5 = ■$ or $5\overline{)20}$ with ■ as the quotient.

Think: $5 \times ■ = 20$
$5 \times 4 = 20$

So, $20 \div 5 = 4$ or $5\overline{)20}$ with 4 as the quotient.

The fire truck will make 4 trips.

More Examples

A. Find $35 \div 5$.

Think: $5 \times ■ = 35$
$5 \times 7 = 35$

So, $35 \div 5 = 7$.

B. Find $45 \div 5$.

Think: $5 \times ■ = 45$
$5 \times 9 = 45$

So, $45 \div 5 = 9$.

Guided Practice *For another example, see Set E on p. 253.*

Algebra Find the missing factor. Use it to help you divide.

1. $5 \times ■ = 25$
   $25 \div 5 = ■$
2. $5 \times ■ = 15$
   $15 \div 5 = ■$
3. $5 \times ■ = 10$
   $10 \div 5 = ■$
4. Marian bought a package of 20 pencils. She divided them equally among 4 friends and herself. She then gave one of her pencils to her brother. How many pencils did Marian end up with?

 Additional Standards: Algebra and Functions 1.2, 2.2; Mathematical Reasoning 1.2, 2.2 (See p. 225.)

Independent Practice *For more practice, see Set E on p. 255.*

Algebra **Find the missing factor. Use it to help you divide.**

5. 5 × ■ = 45
45 ÷ 5 = ■

6. 5 × ■ = 20
20 ÷ 5 = ■

7. 5 × ■ = 30
30 ÷ 5 = ■

8. $5\overline{)20}$ **9.** $5\overline{)5}$ **10.** $5\overline{)25}$ **11.** $5\overline{)40}$ **12.** $5\overline{)50}$

13. $5\overline{)45}$ **14.** $5\overline{)30}$ **15.** $5\overline{)10}$ **16.** $5\overline{)15}$ **17.** $5\overline{)35}$

Algebra **Complete each table.**

Rule: Divide by 4.

	Input	Output
	28	7
18.	8	
19.	16	
20.	32	

Rule: Divide by 5.

	Input	Output
	30	6
21.	10	
22.	35	
23.	40	

Rule: Divide by 3.

	Input	Output
	27	9
24.	18	
25.		4
26.		8

27. The firefighters sound the siren every 5 minutes. How many times does the siren sound in a half hour? What strategy did you use to solve the problem?

28. Math Reasoning Anne has 25 pennies and 2 dimes. Dylan has the same amount of money, but he has only nickels. How many nickels does Dylan have?

Mixed Review

29. Casey and his 3 sisters each have \$5. If they put all their money together, could they buy an \$18 game? Explain.

30. $3\overline{)21}$ **31.** $4\overline{)24}$ **32.** $4\overline{)36}$ **33.** $3\overline{)15}$ **34.** $4\overline{)20}$

Test Prep **Choose the correct letter for each answer.**

35. (1-5) Compare. Choose the correct symbol.

3,563 ● 3,653

A +
B >
C <
D =
E NH

36. (3-1) Martin's music class lasts 35 minutes. If class starts at 1:50 P.M., when will it end?

F 1:15 P.M.
G 2:15 P.M.
H 2:25 P.M.
J 2:35 P.M.

LESSON 6-7

Understand
Plan
Solve
Look Back

Problem-Solving Strategy:

Write a Number Sentence

Warm-Up Review

1. $18 \div 3$ **2.** $24 \div 4$

3. $30 \div 5$ **4.** $6 \div 2$

5. Tara has 3 red crayons, 5 green crayons, and 3 purple crayons. She also has 3 red markers and 2 purple markers. How many more red coloring tools does she have than purple coloring tools?

California Content Standard *Mathematical Reasoning 2.4: Express the solution clearly and logically by using the appropriate mathematical notation and terms and clear language.*

Bike Safety booklets are free at the Community Day Fair. Twenty-one booklets have been put into 3 equal groups. How many booklets are in each group?

Understand

What do you need to know?

You need to know that there are 21 booklets and that they are divided into 3 equal groups.

Plan

How can you solve the problem?

You can **write a number sentence** to solve the problem. Write a division sentence to divide the booklets into 3 equal groups.

Solve

21	÷	3	=	7
number of booklets in all		number of groups		number of booklets in each group

There are 7 booklets in each group.

Look Back

Explain another strategy you could use to solve the problem.

Additional Standards: Number Sense 2.0; Mathematical Reasoning 1.1, 1.2, 3.2 *(See p. 225.)*

Write a number sentence to solve each problem.

Guided Practice

1. Tracey helps out at the bike safety table. She fills 2 boxes with helmets. She puts the same number of helmets in each box. There are 16 helmets in all. How many helmets are in each box?

2. A bicycle shop has donated 27 bike horns for the Bike Safety table. Each horn is red, gold, or black. There are the same number of each color horn. How many gold horns were donated?

Independent Practice

3. Peter spends $12 for mirrors and $3 for lights. How much money does Peter spend?

4. Mrs. Kane buys 2 reflectors for each of her 3 children. How many reflectors does she buy?

5. There were 40 reflectors for sale on the Bike Safety Table. The volunteers sold 16 by noon, and 12 more by the end of the day. How many reflectors were sold?

Mixed Review

Try these or other strategies to solve each problem. Tell which strategy you used.

Problem-Solving Strategies

- *Make a List*
- *Use Logical Reasoning*
- *Make a Table*
- *Write a Number Sentence*

6. Eduardo is training for a bike race. The first week he rides 4 miles. Then each week for the next 2 weeks he doubles the number of miles he rides. How many miles does Eduardo ride in the third week?

7. Mary wants to buy a bike helmet. Helmets come in pink, green, or blue. Each color comes in small, medium, and large sizes. What are her choices?

Use Homework Workbook 6-7.

LESSON 6-8

0 and 1 in Division

Warm-Up Review

1. 8×1
2. 0×4
3. 9×0
4. 3×1
5. 5×1
6. 0×1
7. Devin has 8 bags. He puts 1 box of tissues in each bag. How many boxes of tissues are there in all?

California Content Standard *Number Sense 2.6: Understand the special properties of 0 and 1 in multiplication and division.*

Math Link You know how to multiply by 0 and 1. Now you will learn how to divide with 0 and 1.

Example 1

Divide 4 into 1 group.
How many are in the group?

$4 \div 1 = \blacksquare$
$4 \div 1 = 4$

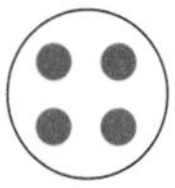

When you divide a number by 1, the answer is that number.

Example 2

Divide 4 into 4 groups.
How many are in each group?

$4 \div 4 = \blacksquare$
$4 \div 4 = 1$

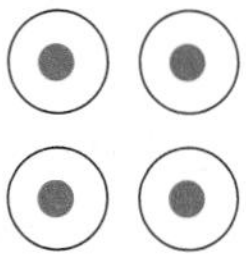

When you divide any number except zero by itself, the answer is 1.

Example 3

Divide 0 into 4 groups.
How many are in each group?

$0 \div 4 = \blacksquare$
$0 \div 4 = 0$

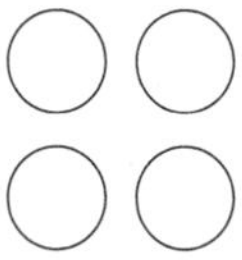

When you divide 0 by any number except 0, the answer is 0.

Example 4

Try to divide 4 into 0 groups.
It's not possible!

$4 \div \not{0} = \blacksquare$

You cannot divide a number by 0.

Guided Practice

For another example, see Set F on p. 253.

1. $0 \div 5$
2. $3 \div 3$
3. $2 \div 1$
4. $0 \div 4$
5. $7 \div 1$
6. $6\overline{)0}$
7. $2\overline{)2}$
8. $1\overline{)4}$
9. $8\overline{)0}$
10. $6\overline{)6}$
11. Five of Mr. Jackson's students went to the library. Each student checked out the same number of books. Five books were checked out. How many books did each student check out?

Additional Standard: Mathematical Reasoning 3.2 (See p. 225.)

Independent Practice *For more practice, see Set F on p. 255.*

12. $1\overline{)3}$ **13.** $2\overline{)0}$ **14.** $5\overline{)5}$ **15.** $7\overline{)0}$ **16.** $1\overline{)1}$

17. $1\overline{)5}$ **18.** $7\overline{)7}$ **19.** $9\overline{)0}$ **20.** $1\overline{)9}$ **21.** $3\overline{)0}$

22. $4 \div 4$ **23.** $0 \div 6$ **24.** $8 \div 8$ **25.** $6 \div 1$ **26.** $3 \div 3$

27. At the end of the fair, a total of 7 prizes were given to 7 people. Each person got the same number of prizes. How many prizes did each person get?

28. Zack has 6 apples. He puts 1 apple into each lunch bag. How many bags can he fill with apples?

29. **Math Reasoning** Look at the division sentences at the right. Explain how you could use the division rules on page 244 to complete them.

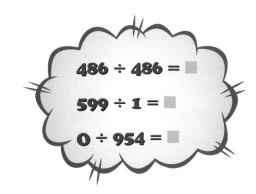

$486 \div 486 = \blacksquare$

$599 \div 1 = \blacksquare$

$0 \div 954 = \blacksquare$

Mixed Review

30. Margaret writes 7 letters a week to friends. How many letters does she write in 5 weeks?

31. Bobbi planted 30 rosebushes. She put 3 in each row. Write a division sentence to find how many rows she planted. What multiplication fact did you use?

32. $28 \div 4$ **33.** $16 \div 4$ **34.** $35 \div 5$ **35.** $15 \div 5$ **36.** $36 \div 4$

Test Prep Choose the correct letter for each answer.

37. (1-7) Which is the number in standard form?

sixty-four thousand, three hundred one

A 6,431
B 64,031
C 64,301
D 64,310

38. (2-13) **Algebra** Which gives *all* the numbers that make the statement true?

$23 - \blacksquare$ is less than 11.

F 9, 10, 11
G All numbers greater than 12
H All numbers less than 12
J 13, 14, 15

LESSON 6-9

Understand
Plan
Solve
Look Back

Problem-Solving Application:
Using Money

Warm-Up Review

1. $9 + $3.25
2. $10 − $5.25
3. $9 × 8
4. Danica had $20. She bought 3 comic books for $2 each. She also bought 2 pens that were on sale for 4 for $8. How much did she spend?

California Content Standard *Number Sense 3.3 (key): Solve problems involving addition, subtraction, multiplication, and division of money amounts in decimal notation and multiply and divide money amounts in decimal notation by using whole-number multipliers and divisors.*

3-D puzzles are popular at the fair! Look at the price tag of a large puzzle to the right. If Carly and her two sisters want to share the cost of a large puzzle equally, how much money will each girl need?

Understand

What do you need to know?

First you need to know the cost of the puzzle. Then you need to know how many girls are sharing the cost.

Plan

How can you solve the problem?

Divide $18 by 3 to find how much money each girl needs to buy the puzzle.

Solve

$18	÷	3	=	$6
cost of the puzzle		number of people sharing the cost		cost for each person

Each girl needs $6 to buy the puzzle.

Look Back

Write a number sentence to show how you could check your answer by multiplying.

Additional Standards: Number Sense 2.8; Mathematical Reasoning 1.1, 1.2 *(See p. 225.)*

Guided Practice

1. John bought a cap for $6 and a picture for $8.50. How much money does he have left if he started with $20?

2. James has $12. He wants to buy as many key chains as he can. Each key chain costs $2.99. Is it reasonable to say that he could buy 5 key chains? Explain your reasoning.

Independent Practice

3. You can buy 2 rings for $3.00. If Kamara spent $12.00 for rings, how many rings did she buy?

4. Meg made 8 potholders to sell at the fair. If she sells each one for $2, how much money will she earn?

5. Nelson spent $16 on 4 bags of marbles. If each bag costs the same amount, how much did each bag of marbles cost?

Mixed Review

Use the pictograph at the right to answer Exercises 6–9.

Parade Marchers	
Police Officers	● ● ●
Firefighters	● ● ◖
Music Club	● ◖
Drama Club	● ◖
4-H Club	●

Each ● stands for 10 people.

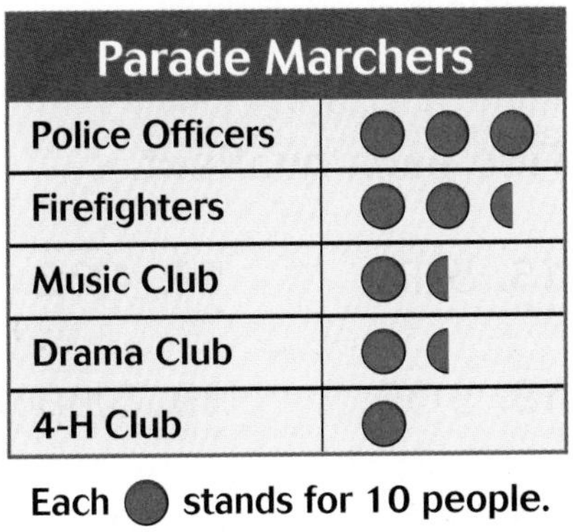

6. Which is the largest group in the parade?

7. How many 4-H Club members are in the parade?

8. How many more firefighters are there than Music Club members?

9. What is the total number of marchers in the parade?

10. Asia spends $8.69 on a craft kit. She pays the clerk with a $10 bill. List the fewest coins and bills the clerk could give Asia as change.

11. Max is 4 feet 2 inches tall. His father is 6 feet 1 inch tall. How much taller is Max's father than Max?

Diagnostic Checkpoint

Complete. For Exercises 1–3, use the words from the Word Bank.

Word Bank
dividend
divisor
quotient

1. (6-1) The number by which another number is divided is called the ________.

2. (6-1) The answer in division is called the ________.

3. (6-1) The number to be divided is called the ________.

Algebra **Complete each table.**

Rule: Divide by 4.

	Input	Output
	36	9
4. (6-5)	16	
5. (6-5)		1
6. (6-5)	24	

Rule: Divide by 5.

	Input	Output
	20	4
7. (6-6)	25	
8. (6-6)		9
9. (6-6)	15	

Rule: Divide by 2.

	Input	Output
	8	4
10. (6-2)		9
11. (6-2)	6	
12. (6-2)		5

Find each quotient.

13. (6-6) $5\overline{)15}$ **14.** (6-5) $4\overline{)32}$ **15.** (6-8) $1\overline{)6}$ **16.** (6-5) $4\overline{)24}$ **17.** (6-5) $4\overline{)20}$

18. (6-6) $5\overline{)35}$ **19.** (6-6) $5\overline{)30}$ **20.** (6-8) $8\overline{)8}$ **21.** (6-6) $5\overline{)10}$ **22.** (6-5) $4\overline{)12}$

23. (6-5) $8 \div 4$ **24.** (6-8) $5 \div 5$ **25.** (6-8) $8 \div 1$ **26.** (6-8) $0 \div 1$ **27.** (6-8) $4 \div 4$

28. (6-7) John and 3 friends want to ride on the merry-go-round. Each person needs 4 tickets for the ride. If John has 16 tickets, will they have enough tickets for the ride? Write a number sentence to solve the problem.

29. (6-9) You can buy 4 flowers for $5.00. If Kelsey spent $15 for flowers, how many flowers did she buy?

Chapter 6 Test

Write a multiplication and a division sentence for each array.

1. 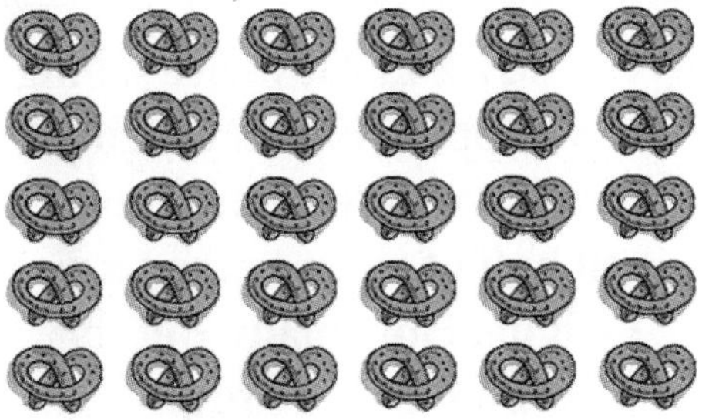

2. 

Find each quotient.

3. $4\overline{)36}$ **4.** $5\overline{)45}$ **5.** $3\overline{)21}$ **6.** $2\overline{)16}$ **7.** $1\overline{)8}$

8. $40 \div 5$ **9.** $18 \div 2$ **10.** $0 \div 7$ **11.** $18 \div 3$

Algebra **Complete each table.**

Rule: Divide by 3.

	Input	Output
	21	7
12.	15	
13.	27	
14.	9	

Rule: Divide by 4.

	Input	Output
	8	2
15.	12	
16.	28	
17.	20	

Rule: Divide by 1.

	Input	Output
	6	6
18.	8	
19.		5
20.		3

21. Mrs. Baird is canning peaches. She has filled 3 jars already and has 6 more to fill. If she cans 45 peaches altogether and each jar has the same number of peaches, how many peaches are in each jar?

22. The flag bearers march in 9 rows with 5 people in each row. Each person is carrying a flag. Write a number sentence to show how many flags there are.

23. Katrina spent $28 on party favors. Each party favor cost $4. How many party favors did Katrina buy?

Multiple-Choice Chapter 6 Test

TEST PREP

Choose the correct letter for each answer.

1. Choose the division sentence that describes the array.

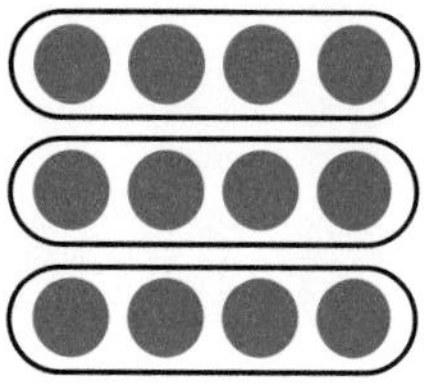

A $16 \div 4 = 4$
B $20 \div 4 = 5$
C $12 \div 3 = 4$
D $10 \div 2 = 5$

2. Jarod's friends left their shoes by the front door. If there are 10 shoes by the door, how many pairs of shoes are there?

F 5 pairs of shoes
G 2 pairs of shoes
H 10 pairs of shoes
J 20 pairs of shoes
K NH

3. $27 \div 3 = \blacksquare$

A 9
B 7
C 8
D 6
E NH

4. $18 \div 2 = \blacksquare$

F 6
G 7
H 8
J 9
K NH

5. Cassidy and Alexa are selling rolls of wrapping paper. Cassidy has 9 rolls and Alexa has 7 rolls. They sell half of them to the Ladies League. How many rolls of wrapping paper are left?

A 7 rolls
B 8 rolls
C 9 rolls
D 16 rolls
E NH

6. Choose a related division sentence for the multiplication sentence.

$$5 \times 8 = 40$$

F $40 \div 10 = 4$
G $40 \div 4 = 10$
H $45 \div 5 = 9$
J $40 \div 5 = 8$

7. Barrett has 12 balloons. He wants to tie them together in bunches of 3 balloons. How many bunches of balloons can he make?

A 3 bunches
B 4 bunches
C 6 bunches
D 12 bunches
E NH

8. **Kristen has $12. She wants to buy as many rings as she can. If 2 rings cost $3, how many rings can she buy?**

- **F** 4 rings
- **G** 6 rings
- **H** 9 rings
- **J** 8 rings
- **K** NH

9. **A food booth sells a basket with 28 pieces of fruit. There is an equal number of oranges, pears, apples, and bananas in the basket. How many apples are there?**

- **A** 7 apples
- **B** 6 apples
- **C** 5 apples
- **D** 4 apples
- **E** NH

10. $45 \div 5 = \blacksquare$

- **F** 3
- **G** 5
- **H** 7
- **J** 9
- **K** NH

11. **Mrs. Licata bought 2 muffins for each of her 6 breakfast guests. Which number sentence describes how many muffins Mrs. Licata bought in all?**

- **A** $6 + 2 = 8$
- **B** $12 - 2 = 10$
- **C** $6 \times 2 = 12$
- **D** $12 \div 6 = 2$

12. **Shannon sold a total of 4 cakes to 4 people. Each person bought the same number of cakes. How many cakes did each person buy?**

- **F** 1 cake
- **G** 4 cakes
- **H** 8 cakes
- **J** 16 cakes
- **K** NH

13. $4\overline{)36}$

- **A** 8
- **B** 4
- **C** 9
- **D** 12
- **E** NH

14. **The 35 baton twirlers from Jefferson High School march in a parade. There are 5 twirlers in each row. How many rows of twirlers are there?**

- **F** 5 rows
- **G** 6 rows
- **H** 7 rows
- **J** 8 rows
- **K** NH

15. $0 \div 9 = \blacksquare$

- **A** 0
- **B** 1
- **C** 9
- **D** 90
- **E** NH

Reteaching

Set A *(pages 226–228)*

Find 12 ÷ 3.

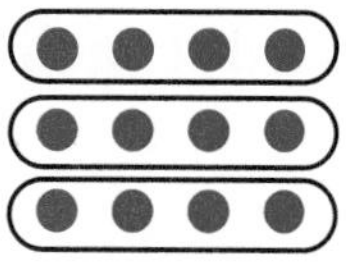

Use a multiplication fact to help you divide.

Think: 3 times what number equals 12?

$3 \times 4 = 12$

So, $12 \div 3 = 4$.

Remember you can use a multiplication fact to help you divide.

Use the array to complete each sentence.

1.

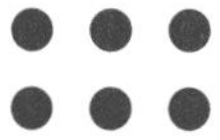

$2 \times$ ■ $= 6$

$6 \div 2 =$ ■

2.

$4 \times$ ■ $= 20$

$20 \div 4 =$ ■

Set B *(pages 230–231)*

Find 16 ÷ 2.

Think: $2 \times$ ■ $= 16$

$2 \times 8 = 16$

So, $16 \div 2 = 8$.

Remember when you are dividing by two, it is the same as finding half of a number.

1. $18 \div 2$ **2.** $12 \div 2$

3. $10 \div 2$ **4.** $4 \div 2$

5. $6 \div 2$ **6.** $8 \div 2$

7. $16 \div 2$ **8.** $14 \div 2$

Set C *(pages 232–233)*

Find 21 ÷ 3.

Think: $3 \times$ ■ $= 21$

$3 \times 7 = 21$

So, $21 \div 3 = 7$.

Remember the number you are dividing by is called the divisor.

1. $9 \div 3$ **2.** $27 \div 3$

3. $18 \div 3$ **4.** $24 \div 3$

5. $6 \div 3$ **6.** $12 \div 3$

7. $15 \div 3$ **8.** $21 \div 3$

Set D (pages 238–239)

Find 20 ÷ 4.

Think: $4 \times \blacksquare = 20$

$4 \times 5 = 20$

So, $20 \div 4 = 5$.

Remember the answer in division is called the quotient.

1. $16 \div 4$

2. $36 \div 4$

3. $24 \div 4$

4. $12 \div 4$

5. $4\overline{)8}$

6. $4\overline{)28}$

7. $4\overline{)32}$

8. $4\overline{)20}$

Set E (pages 240–241)

Find 45 ÷ 5.

Think: $5 \times \blacksquare = 45$

$5 \times 9 = 45$

So, $45 \div 5 = 9$.

Remember the number being divided is called the dividend.

1. $20 \div 5$

2. $15 \div 5$

3. $5 \div 5$

4. $40 \div 5$

5. $5\overline{)25}$

6. $5\overline{)10}$

7. $5\overline{)35}$

8. $5\overline{)30}$

Set F (pages 244–245)

Find $5\overline{)0}$.

Think: The rule says, "Zero divided by any number (except 0) equals 0."

So, $5\overline{)0}$ with quotient 0

<u>*Check*</u>: $5 \times \blacksquare = 0$

$5 \times 0 = 0$

Remember any number divided by 1 equals that number. Any number divided by itself equals 1.

1. $9 \div 9$

2. $0 \div 8$

3. $3 \div 3$

4. $6 \div 6$

5. $0 \div 7$

6. $9 \div 1$

7. $4\overline{)4}$

8. $1\overline{)8}$

9. $1\overline{)5}$

10. $3\overline{)0}$

More Practice

Set A *(pages 226–228)*

Algebra Use the array to complete each sentence.

1. 

$5 \times \blacksquare = 20$
$20 \div 5 = \blacksquare$

2. 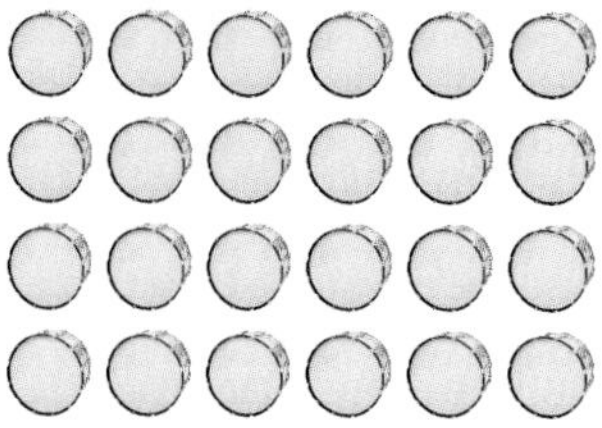

$4 \times \blacksquare = 24$
$24 \div 4 = \blacksquare$

3. 

$3 \times \blacksquare = 12$
$12 \div 3 = \blacksquare$

4. The school band has 36 members. They are sitting in 4 equal rows. How many band members are in each row?

Set B *(pages 230–231)*

Algebra Find the missing factor. Use it to help you divide.

1. $2 \times \blacksquare = 6$
   $6 \div 2 = \blacksquare$
2. $2 \times \blacksquare = 18$
   $18 \div 2 = \blacksquare$
3. $2 \times \blacksquare = 10$
   $10 \div 2 = \blacksquare$
4. $4 \div 2$
5. $8 \div 2$
6. $12 \div 2$
7. $14 \div 2$
8. At a food booth, Jason has 14 jars of homemade jelly to sell. He displays the jars in 2 equal rows. How many jars are in each row?

Set C *(pages 232–233)*

Algebra Find the missing factor. Use it to help you divide.

1. $3 \times \blacksquare = 12$
   $12 \div 3 = \blacksquare$
2. $3 \times \blacksquare = 27$
   $27 \div 3 = \blacksquare$
3. $3 \times \blacksquare = 15$
   $15 \div 3 = \blacksquare$
4. $6 \div 3$
5. $21 \div 3$
6. $9 \div 3$
7. $24 \div 3$
8. Cassie makes costumes. She has 15 beads to glue on 3 costumes. If she divides the beads equally, how many beads can she glue on each costume?

Set D (pages 238–239)

Algebra **Find the missing factor. Use it to help you divide.**

1. $4 \times ■ = 32$
   $32 \div 4 = ■$

2. $4 \times ■ = 8$
   $8 \div 4 = ■$

3. $4 \times ■ = 20$
   $20 \div 4 = ■$

4. $4\overline{)28}$　　5. $4\overline{)36}$　　6. $4\overline{)24}$　　7. $4\overline{)16}$　　8. $4\overline{)32}$

9. At a craft booth you can make a sand painting for $4. If you have $12, how many sand paintings can you make?

Set E (pages 240–241)

Algebra **Complete each table.**

Rule: Divide by 3.

	Input	Output
	9	3
1.	21	
2.	15	
3.	12	

Rule: Divide by 4.

	Input	Output
	12	3
4.	24	
5.	20	
6.	36	

Rule: Divide by 5.

	Input	Output
	45	9
7.		3
8.		8
9.	30	

10. $5\overline{)25}$　　11. $5\overline{)15}$　　12. $5\overline{)20}$　　13. $5\overline{)10}$　　14. $5\overline{)5}$

15. Kyla is selling muffins at the bakery booth. She puts 5 muffins in each package. How many packages can she make with 30 muffins?

Set F (pages 244–245)

1. $1\overline{)5}$　　2. $1\overline{)9}$　　3. $6\overline{)0}$　　4. $3\overline{)3}$　　5. $2\overline{)0}$

6. $0 \div 1$　　7. $8 \div 8$　　8. $2 \div 1$　　9. $9 \div 9$　　10. $0 \div 8$

11. The 4-H Club is having a bake sale. Roger sells 9 loaves of banana bread. How many bags does he use if he puts 1 loaf of bread in each bag?

TEST PREP

Problem Solving: Preparing for Tests

Choose the correct letter for each answer.

---

1. Lucinda drove 132 miles on Friday, 237 miles on Saturday, and 186 miles on Sunday. Which is the best estimate of the distance she drove on the last two days?

A 200 miles
B 400 miles
C 500 miles
D 550 miles

Tip
Start by choosing the numbers you need. Then round each number to the nearest hundred.

---

2. Jen is older than Arnie. Paul is older than Jen. Which of these is a reasonable conclusion?

F Arnie is older than Paul.
G Paul is older than Arnie.
H Paul is younger than Jen.
J Jen is younger than Arnie.

Tip
Read the four answer choices. Then compare each choice with the information given until you find the correct answer.

---

3. Ruth packed 24 games into the boxes below. She put an equal number of games into each box. Which shows the number of games Ruth packed in each box?

A $3 + 24$
B 3×24
C $24 \div 3$
D $24 \div 4$

Tip
Start by choosing the operation you need. Then place the given information in the correct places.

4. **On a walk in the woods, Vicky saw 8 raccoons, 13 deer, and more than 25 squirrels. Which of these is reasonable for the total number of animals Vicky saw?**

F Fewer than 36
G Between 36 and 40
H Between 40 and 45
J More than 46

5. **Beth saved 419 nickels. Her sister saved 288 nickels. Which is the best way to estimate the total number of nickels they have?**

A 400 + 300
B 500 + 300
C 500 + 200
D 400 + 400

6. **Look at the graph. Smith School collected bags of clothing. How many more bags did the fifth grade collect than the fourth grade?**

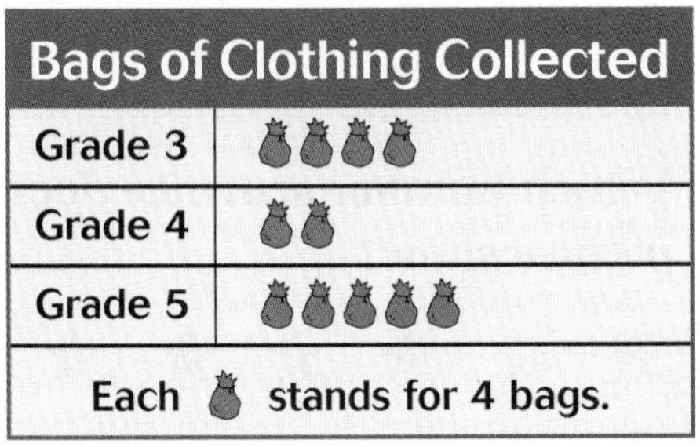

F 3 bags
G 6 bags
H 12 bags
J 24 bags

7. **Dave raked leaves for two and one-half hours. He stopped raking at 2:15 P.M. When did he begin?**

A 11:30 A.M. **C** 4:30 P.M.
B 11:45 A.M. **D** 4:45 P.M.

8. **Tom divided 16 boxes of raisins equally among 4 friends. How could you find the number of boxes of raisins each friend got?**

F Subtract 4 from 16.
G Multiply 4 times 16.
H Divide 16 by 4.
J Add 16 and 4.

9. **Jason is fixing window shades. He needs 39 feet of cord to fix the shades. How much cord will he have left if he buys a package with 45 feet of cord?**

A 4 ft **C** 10 ft
B 6 ft **D** 16 ft

10. **Look at the graph. How many more adventure books were sold than history books in January?**

F 150 **H** 350
G 200 **J** 600

Multiple-Choice Cumulative Review

Choose the correct letter for each answer.

Number Sense

1. Look at the base-ten blocks.

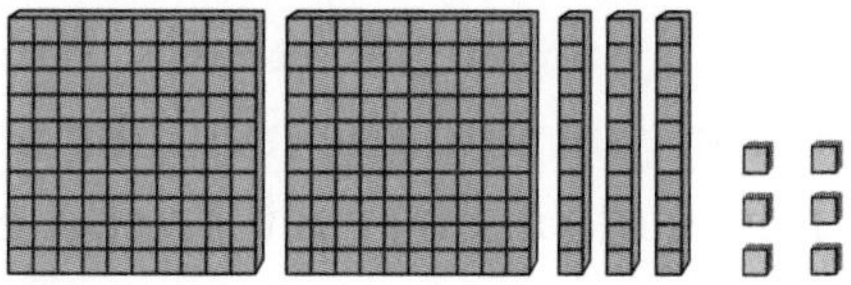

If 3  are taken away from the tens group, what number will be shown?

A 206   **C** 266
B 216   **D** 536

2. What number is the same as five thousand, one hundred three?

F 531   **H** 5,130
G 5,103   **J** 51,003

3. What is the value of the 9 in 391,654?

A 9 hundred
B 9 thousand
C 90 thousand
D 900 thousand

4. Which is a set of odd numbers?

F 5, 7, 9, 12
G 3, 6, 9, 12
H 1, 3, 4, 7
J 3, 7, 9, 11

5. Jody has 12 movie tickets. How many *pairs* of tickets does she have?

A 2 pairs
B 4 pairs
C 6 pairs
D 8 pairs
E NH

6. Dean has 46 car stamps and 94 animal stamps in his collection. He bought 22 more car stamps. How many car stamps does he have now?

F 68 car stamps
G 116 car stamps
H 140 car stamps
J 162 car stamps
K NH

7. Which number sentence does this picture show?

A $12 \div 3 = 4$
B $2 \times 6 = 12$
C $2 \times 5 = 10$
D $12 \times 1 = 12$

Algebra and Functions

8. What is the missing number?

■ + 24 = 35

F 59 H 11
G 13 J 9

---

9. Which two numbers make the statement true?

6 × ■ is less than 20.

A 2; 3 C 4; 5
B 3; 4 D 6; 7

---

10. What is the rule for the table?

Input	Output
10	5
15	10
12	7
6	1

F Divide by 2.
G Subtract 5.
H Add 5.
J Multiply by 2.

---

11. Which names the same number as 6 × 8?

A $6 + 8$
B 8×6
C $8 + 6$
D $8 \div 6$

Measurement and Geometry

12. How long is the crayon?

F $1\frac{1}{2}$ in. H $2\frac{1}{2}$ in.
G 2 in. J 3 in.

---

13. What is the temperature shown on the thermometer?

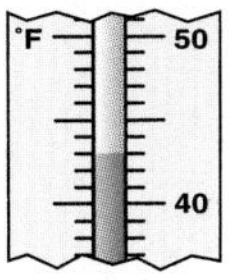

A 43° F
B 46° F
C 52° F
D 57° F

---

14. A concert begins at 7:30 P.M. It lasts 1 hour and 25 minutes. Which clock shows what time the concert ends?

F

G

H

J

CHAPTER 7

Division Facts

Diagnosing Readiness

In Chapter 7, you will use these skills:

Ⓐ Multiplying by 6

(pages 182–183)

1. 3×6

2. 6×2

3. 6×7

4. 0×6

5. $\begin{array}{r} 6 \\ \times\ 6 \\ \hline \end{array}$

6. $\begin{array}{r} 6 \\ \times\ 5 \\ \hline \end{array}$

7. Mr. Boursin made 5 rows of 6 desks in his classroom. How many desks are in Mr. Boursin's classroom?

Ⓑ Multiplying by 7

(pages 188–189)

8. 6×7

9. 7×9

10. 3×7

11. 7×7

12. $\begin{array}{r} 8 \\ \times\ 7 \\ \hline \end{array}$

13. $\begin{array}{r} 10 \\ \times\ 7 \\ \hline \end{array}$

14. The new library has 5 rows of windows across the front of it. Each row has 7 windows. How many windows are on the front of the library?

C Multiplying by 8

(pages 184–185)

15. 8×1

16. 7×8

17. 8×6

18. 2×8

19. $\begin{array}{r} 10 \\ \times 8 \\ \hline \end{array}$

20. $\begin{array}{r} 5 \\ \times 8 \\ \hline \end{array}$

21. Carson earns $7 a week watering lawns. How much will he earn in 8 weeks?

D Multiplying by 9

(pages 190–191)

22. 9×3

23. 5×9

24. 0×9

25. 4×9

26. $\begin{array}{r} 8 \\ \times 9 \\ \hline \end{array}$

27. $\begin{array}{r} 9 \\ \times 1 \\ \hline \end{array}$

28. $\begin{array}{r} 9 \\ \times 9 \\ \hline \end{array}$

29. $\begin{array}{r} 7 \\ \times 9 \\ \hline \end{array}$

30. Jack made 9 spiders for a diorama. Each spider has 8 legs. How many legs are on all the spiders?

E Multiplying by 10

(pages 192–193)

31. 3×10

32. 6×10

33. 10×9

34. 0×10

35. $\begin{array}{r} 10 \\ \times 7 \\ \hline \end{array}$

36. $\begin{array}{r} 10 \\ \times 1 \\ \hline \end{array}$

37. Kayla picked 4 flowers. Each flower has 10 petals. How many petals are on all the flowers?

F Missing Factors

(pages 202–203)

38. $3 \times ■ = 15$

39. $6 \times ■ = 36$

40. $■ \times 9 = 0$

41. $7 \times ■ = 28$

42. $■ \times 2 = 18$

43. $8 \times ■ = 64$

44. $6 \times ■ = 60$

45. If 4 students and 1 adult can ride in a car, how many cars are needed to transport 32 students to the science museum?

To the Family and Student

Looking Back	Chapter 7	Looking Ahead
In Chapter 6, students learned how to divide by 1, 2, 3, 4, and 5.	**Division Facts** In this chapter, students will learn how to divide by 6, 7, 8, 9, and 10.	In Chapter 10, students will learn how to divide two- and three-digit numbers.

Math and Everyday Living

Opportunities to apply the concepts of Chapter 7 abound in everyday situations. During the chapter, think about how division can be used to solve a variety of real-world problems. The following examples suggest just several of the many situations that could launch a discussion about division.

Math at the Symphony An orchestra has 24 violinists who sit in 3 rows. If the same number of violinists sit in each row, how many violinists are in each row?

Math and Sports You attend a sports camp for 7 days. There are 35 different sports activities to choose from. You must choose an equal number of activities in which to participate each day. How many sports activities can you choose for each day?

Math and Advertising During a 1 hour television show, 6 minutes are used for 6 commercials of equal length. How long is each commercial?

Math at the Park This Friday, 100 people are expected to attend an outdoor play. There is room for 10 seats in a row. How many rows of seats are needed?

Math at the Market Jaron has $6 to spend at the farmers market. Cucumbers are $2 per pound. How many pounds of cucumbers can he buy?

Math and Money Jack has 70 dimes. He wants to put them in stacks of 10 so that he can count how many dollars he has. How many stacks of dimes can he make?

Math at the Museum A museum exhibit has 24 paintings in it. The museum curator wants to hang an equal number of paintings on each of 4 walls. How many paintings can he hang on each wall?

Math at Home Marta's parents have 24 crackers to split evenly among herself and her 3 brothers. How many crackers does each child get?

Math at School There are 18 lockers in a hallway. They are arranged in two equal rows. How many lockers are in each row?

Math and Theater A costume designer is making 8 beaded headbands. She only has 72 beads to work with. How many beads can she use to make each headband?

Math and Time Steven has 1 week to read the last 63 pages of a book. If he reads the same number of pages each day, how many pages will he need to read each day to finish the book?

California Content Standards in Chapter 7 Lessons*

	Teach and Practice	Practice
Number Sense		
2.3 (🔑) Use the inverse relationship of multiplication and division to compute and check results.	7-1, 7-2, 7-4, 7-5, 7-6	7-8
2.8 Solve problems that require two or more of the skills mentioned above.		7-1, 7-2, 7-4, 7-5, 7-6, 7-9
Algebra and Functions		
1.1 (🔑) Represent relationships of quantities in the form of mathematical expressions, equations, or inequalities.	7-8	
1.2 Solve problems involving numeric equations		7-1, 7-2, 7-4, 7-5, 7-6, 7-8
1.3 Select appropriate operational and relational symbols to make an expression true (e.g., if 4 ___ 3 = 12, what operational symbol goes in the blank?).	7-3	7-4
2.1 (🔑) Solve simple problems involving a functional relationship between two quantities.		7-6
2.2 Extend and recognize a linear pattern by its rules.		7-5

	Teach and Practice	Practice
Mathematical Reasoning		
1.1 Analyze problems by identifying relationships, distinguishing relevant from irrelevant information, sequencing and prioritizing information, and observing patterns.	7-3	7-6
1.2 Determine when and how to break a problem into simpler parts.		7-2, 7-3, 7-4, 7-5, 7-6
2.0 Students use strategies, skills, and concepts in finding solutions.	7-9	
2.2 Apply strategies and results from simpler problems to more complex problems.		7-1, 7-4, 7-5
2.3 Use a variety of methods, such as words, numbers, symbols, charts, graphs, tables, diagrams, and models, to explain mathematical reasoning.	7-7	7-9
3.2 Note the method of deriving the solution and demonstrate a conceptual understanding of the derivation by solving similar problems.		7-3, 7-7
3.3 Develop generalizations of the results obtained and apply them in other circumstances.	7-7	7-8

* The symbol (🔑) indicates a key standard as designated in the Mathematics Framework for California Public Schools. Full statements of the California Content Standards are found at the beginning of this book following the Table of Contents.

LESSON 7-1

Dividing by 6

California Content Standard *Number Sense 2.3 (🔑): Use the inverse relationship of multiplication and division to compute and check results.*

Warm-Up Review

1. 6×2
2. 6×4
3. 6×8
4. 6×9
5. Macy walked 3 blocks east, twice as many blocks north, and then another block east. How far did Macy walk?

Math Link You know how to multiply with 6 as a factor. Now you will learn to divide by 6.

Example 1

There are 18 cellos in 6 groups of equal size. How many cellos are in each group?

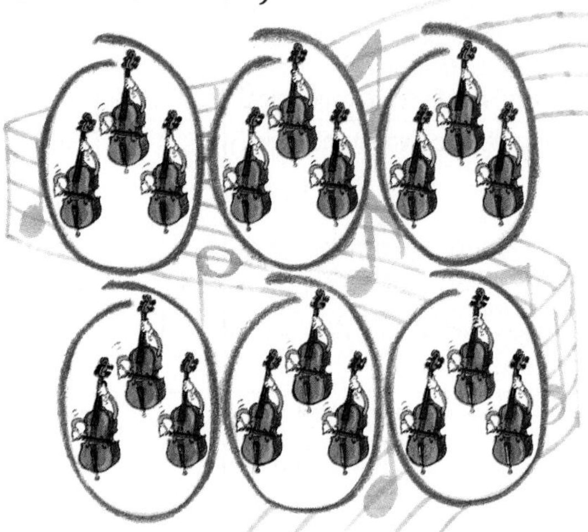

$18 \div 6 = \blacksquare$ or $\begin{array}{r} \blacksquare \\ 6\overline{)18} \end{array}$

Think: $6 \times \blacksquare = 18$

$6 \times 3 = 18$

So, $18 \div 6 = 3$, or $\begin{array}{r} 3 \\ 6\overline{)18} \end{array}$.

There are 3 cellos in each group.

More Examples

A. Find $42 \div 6$.

Think: $6 \times \blacksquare = 42$

$6 \times 7 = 42$

So, $42 \div 6 = 7$.

B. Find $6\overline{)30}$.

Think: $6 \times \blacksquare = 30$

$6 \times 5 = 30$

So, $\begin{array}{r} 5 \\ 6\overline{)30} \end{array}$.

Guided Practice *For another example, see Set A on p. 288.*

Algebra Find each missing factor. Use it to help you divide.

1. $6 \times \blacksquare = 12$

$12 \div 6 = \blacksquare$

2. $6 \times \blacksquare = 6$

$6 \div 6 = \blacksquare$

3. $6 \times \blacksquare = 36$

$36 \div 6 = \blacksquare$

4. Dillon had 28 baseballs. He gave 4 baseballs to the second graders and he divided the rest between 6 third-grade teams. How many baseballs will each team get?

Additional Standards: Number Sense 2.8; Algebra and Functions 1.2; Mathematical Reasoning 2.2 (See p. 263.)

Independent Practice *For more practice, see Set A on p. 290.*

Algebra **Find each missing factor. Use it to help you divide.**

5. $6 \times ■ = 24$
$24 \div 6 = ■$

6. $6 \times ■ = 48$
$48 \div 6 = ■$

7. $6 \times ■ = 54$
$54 \div 6 = ■$

8. $6\overline{)6}$ **9.** $6\overline{)12}$ **10.** $6\overline{)36}$ **11.** $6\overline{)24}$ **12.** $6\overline{)30}$

13. $6 \div 6$ **14.** $30 \div 6$ **15.** $18 \div 6$ **16.** $42 \div 6$

17. $24 \div 6$ **18.** $48 \div 6$ **19.** $36 \div 6$ **20.** $54 \div 6$

21. An orchestra has 18 violinists who sit in 6 rows. If the same number of violinists sit in each row, how many violinists are in each row?

22. Suppose 1 violinist leaves and 7 new violinists come. How many violinists would be in each row then?

23. **Math Reasoning** If you know that $24 \div 4 = 6$, how could that help you find $24 \div 6$?

Mixed Review

24. Cody bought 3 roses for his mother. He spent $9 on the roses. How much did each rose cost?

25. $9 \div 9$ **26.** $5 \div 1$ **27.** $0 \div 3$ **28.** $5\overline{)35}$ **29.** $5\overline{)30}$

Test Prep Choose the correct letter for each answer.

30. (2-4) What is the greatest possible sum using 3 of these numbers?

358 431 112 528 385

A 1,317 **B** 1,334 **C** 1,344 **D** 1,354 **E** NH

31. (3-1) The clock on the wall is shown at the right. Mia has been at piano practice for 35 minutes. What time did her practice begin?

F 11:50 **H** 1:00
G 12:55 **J** 4:28

LESSON 7-2

Dividing by 7

California Content Standard Number Sense 2.3 (🔑): *Use the inverse relationship of multiplication and division to compute and check results.*

Math Link You know how to multiply by 7. Now you will use those basic multiplication facts to learn to divide by 7.

Warm-Up Review

1. 7×2
2. 7×5
3. 7×7
4. 7×9
5. Liza had 15 animal stickers and 9 sports stickers. She stuck them on 3 pages. How many stickers did she put on each page if she put the same number on each page?

Example 1

The Top Hat dancers have gone on stage! There are 14 dancers in the group. They dance in rows of 7. How many rows are there?

$14 \div 7 = \blacksquare$ or $7\overline{)14}$ (quotient $\blacksquare$)

Think: $7 \times \blacksquare = 14$

$7 \times 2 = 14$

So, $14 \div 7 = 2$, or $7\overline{)14}$ with quotient 2.

There are 2 rows of dancers.

More Examples

A. Find $56 \div 7$.

Think: $7 \times \blacksquare = 56$

$7 \times 8 = 56$

So, $56 \div 7 = 8$.

B. Find $7\overline{)21}$.

Think: $7 \times \blacksquare = 21$

$7 \times 3 = 21$

So, $7\overline{)21}$ with quotient 3.

Additional Standards: Number Sense 2.8; Algebra and Functions 1.2; Mathematical Reasoning 1.2 (See p. 263.)

Guided Practice *For another example, see Set B on p. 288.*

Algebra **Find each missing factor. Use it to help you divide.**

1. $7 \times ■ = 42$ $\quad 42 \div 7 = ■$

2. $7 \times ■ = 56$ $\quad 56 \div 7 = ■$

3. $7 \times ■ = 35$ $\quad 35 \div 7 = ■$

4. Tad went to baseball camp. He was there for a week. During that week he hit 49 singles. If he hit the same number each day, how many singles did he hit each day?

Independent Practice *For more practice, see Set B on p. 290.*

Algebra **Find each missing factor. Use it to help you divide.**

5. $7 \times ■ = 49$ $\quad 49 \div 7 = ■$

6. $7 \times ■ = 21$ $\quad 21 \div 7 = ■$

7. $7 \times ■ = 63$ $\quad 63 \div 7 = ■$

8. $7\overline{)35}$ **9.** $7\overline{)0}$ **10.** $7\overline{)42}$ **11.** $7\overline{)7}$ **12.** $7\overline{)21}$

13. There are 21 tap dancers on stage. They dance in groups of 7. How many groups of dancers are there?

14. Backstage there are 20 red hats and 15 blue hats hung in 7 equal rows. How many hats are in each row?

Mixed Review

15. Doug emptied all the money from his piggy bank. He had 1 \$10 bill, 2 \$5 bills, 3 quarters, 5 dimes, and 17 pennies. How much money did he have?

16. $1\overline{)7}$ **17.** $6\overline{)54}$ **18.** $6\overline{)36}$ **19.** $4\overline{)0}$ **20.** $6\overline{)12}$

Test Prep **Choose the correct letter for each answer.**

21. *(1-2)* Chandra has 352 stamps in her collection. What is 352 rounded to the nearest ten?

A 300 **B** 350 **C** 360 **D** 400

22. *(5-2)* Bottled water comes in packs with 6 bottles in each pack. Lila bought 5 packs of bottled water. How many bottles of water did she buy?

F 11 bottles **G** 25 bottles **H** 28 bottles **J** 30 bottles

LESSON 7-3

Understand
Plan
Solve
Look Back

Problem-Solving Skill:

Choose the Operation

California Content Standard *Mathematical Reasoning 1.1: Analyze problems by identifying relationships, distinguishing relevant from irrelevant information, sequencing and prioritizing information, and observing patterns. Also, Algebra and Functions 1.3* *(See p. 263.)*

Warm-Up Review

1. $47 + 28$ **2.** $83 - 27$

3. 6×8 **4.** $20 \div 5$

5. Hailey has 3 dolls, 5 stuffed animals, and 4 trucks. If Hailey gave away 2 of the toys, how many toys will she have left?

Read for Understanding

The Division Street Theater is getting ready for the next play. Six people are making costumes. They need to make a total of 24 costumes. The different scenes being painted for the play are shown to the right. Three people are painting each scene.

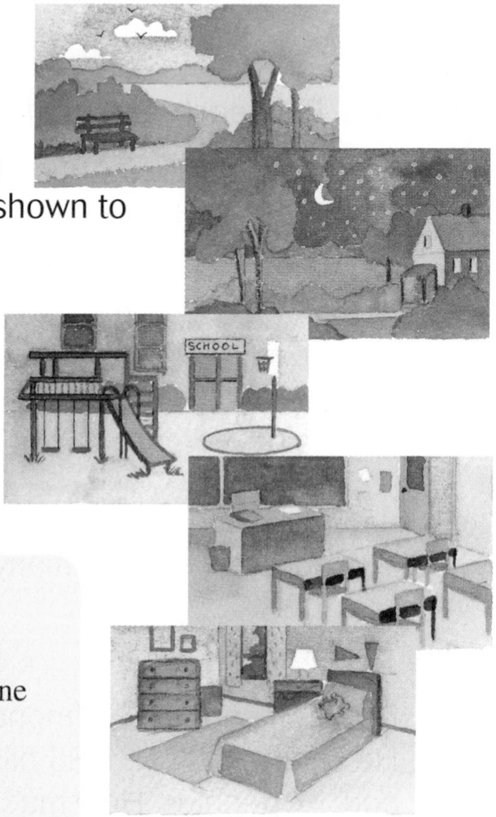

1. How many people are making costumes?

2. How many scenes are being painted?

Think and Discuss

MATH FOCUS

Choose the Operation

You can add to put groups together. You can subtract to find out how many more are in one group than in another. You can multiply to combine equal groups. You can divide to separate items into equal groups.

Reread the paragraph at the top of the page.

3. Which operation would you use to find the total number of people painting scenery? Explain why.

4. How many more people are painting scenery than making costumes? Which operation did you use to find the answer? Explain why.

5. Explain how you know whether to multiply or divide.

 Additional Standards: Mathematical Reasoning 1.2, 3.2 *(See p. 263.)*

Guided Practice

Alyssa and Peter are making programs and posters for the play. They want to make 100 programs for the ushers to hand out. They also need a total of 10 posters to place in stores around town.

1. Which operation would you use to find out how many programs and posters they are making?

a. Addition

b. Subtraction

c. Multiplication

2. Which number sentence tells you how many programs and posters they are making?

a. $100 - 10 = ■$

b. $100 \times 10 = ■$

c. $100 + 10 = ■$

3. Which operation would you use to find out how many more programs they are making than posters?

a. Addition

b. Subtraction

c. Division

4. Which number sentence tells you how many more programs they are making than posters?

a. $100 - 10 = ■$

b. $100 \div 10 = ■$

c. $100 + 10 = ■$

Independent Practice

The play tickets are finally on sale! So far 58 tickets have been sold. There are 42 tickets left to sell. Six people have promised to sell the rest of the tickets. Suppose they each sell the same number of tickets.

5. Which operation would you use to find out how many tickets each person will sell?

a. Subtraction

b. Division

c. Multiplication

6. Which number sentence tells you the number of tickets each person will sell?

a. $42 \div 6 = ■$

b. $42 - 6 = ■$

c. $58 \div 6 = ■$

7. Math Reasoning Suppose you wanted to know the total number of tickets. How would you solve the problem?

LESSON 7-4

Dividing by 8

California Content Standard *Number Sense 2.3 (🔑): Use the inverse relationship of multiplication and division to compute and check results.*

Warm-Up Review

1. 8×1
2. 8×3
3. 8×5
4. 8×8
5. Amber had 24 trading cards. Sophie had half the number of cards as Amber. If they put their cards together, how many cards would they have?

Math Link You know how to multiply by 8. Now you will use those multiplication facts to learn to divide by 8.

Example 1

A puppeteer uses 16 finger puppets to tell a story in 8 scenes. Each puppet appears in only 1 scene. The same number of puppets are used in each scene. How many puppets are in each scene?

$16 \div 8 = \blacksquare$ or $8\overline{)16}$ (quotient: ■)

Think: $8 \times \blacksquare = 16$
$8 \times 2 = 16$

So, $16 \div 8 = 2$, or $8\overline{)16}$ (quotient: 2).

There are 2 puppets in each scene.

More Examples

A. Find $72 \div 8$.

Think: $8 \times \blacksquare = 72$
$8 \times 9 = 72$

So, $72 \div 8 = 9$.

B. Find $8\overline{)40}$.

Think: $8 \times \blacksquare = 40$
$8 \times 5 = 40$

So, $8\overline{)40}$ (quotient: 5).

Guided Practice *For another example, see Set C on p. 288.*

Algebra Find each missing factor. Use it to help you divide.

1. $8 \times \blacksquare = 64$
$64 \div 8 = \blacksquare$

2. $8 \times \blacksquare = 56$
$56 \div 8 = \blacksquare$

3. $8 \times \blacksquare = 48$
$48 \div 8 = \blacksquare$

4. Beau has 16 red apples, 4 green apples, and 4 yellow apples. He needs to put an equal number of apples into 8 separate bags. How many apples should he put in each bag?

Additional Standards: Number Sense 2.8; Algebra and Functions 1.2, 1.3; Mathematical Reasoning 1.2, 2.2 (See p. 263.)

Independent Practice *For more practice, see Set C on p. 290.*

Algebra **Find each missing factor. Use it to help you divide.**

5. $8 \times ■ = 32$
$32 \div 8 = ■$

6. $8 \times ■ = 24$
$24 \div 8 = ■$

7. $8 \times ■ = 16$
$16 \div 8 = ■$

8. $8\overline{)16}$ **9.** $8\overline{)32}$ **10.** $8\overline{)48}$ **11.** $8\overline{)56}$ **12.** $8\overline{)24}$

13. $56 \div 8$ **14.** $32 \div 8$ **15.** $16 \div 8$ **16.** $48 \div 8$

Algebra **Write × or ÷ for each ●.**

17. 8 ● 8 = 64 **18.** 56 ● 8 = 7 **19.** 24 ● 8 = 3

20. 63 ● 9 = 7 **21.** 4 ● 2 = 2 **22.** 9 ● 2 = 18

23. 5 ● 8 = 40 **24.** 8 ● 4 = 32 **25.** 72 ● 8 = 9

26. A puppeteer is putting away 32 puppets in boxes. Each box holds 8 puppets. How many boxes does he use?

27. Each day there are 6 puppet shows. How many shows are there in 8 days?

Mixed Review

28. A gift shop sold 5,378 balloons in June and 4,192 balloons in July. How many more balloons did the shop sell in June than July?

29. $7\overline{)56}$ **30.** $6\overline{)36}$ **31.** $6\overline{)48}$ **32.** $7\overline{)49}$ **33.** $7\overline{)0}$

Test Prep **Choose the correct letter for each answer.**

34. (3-3) Julia was 3 feet 10 inches at the beginning of the school year. She grew 4 inches during the year. How tall was she at the end of the school year?

A 17 inches
B 44 inches
C 50 inches
D 59 inches

35. (5-2) Samantha bought 4 packages of juice boxes. Each package had 6 juice boxes. Which number sentence tells how many juice boxes Samantha had?

F $4 + 6 = 10$
G $4 \times 6 = 24$
H $6 \times 6 = 36$
J $30 \div 6 = 4$

Diagnostic Checkpoint

Find each missing factor. Use it to help you divide.

1. (7-1) $6 \times ■ = 36$
$36 \div 6 = ■$

2. (7-1) $6 \times ■ = 42$
$42 \div 6 = ■$

3. (7-1) $6 \times ■ = 18$
$18 \div 6 = ■$

4. (7-2) $7 \times ■ = 28$
$28 \div 7 = ■$

5. (7-2) $7 \times ■ = 14$
$14 \div 7 = ■$

6. (7-2) $7 \times ■ = 42$
$42 \div 7 = ■$

7. (7-4) $8 \times ■ = 40$
$40 \div 8 = ■$

8. (7-4) $8 \times ■ = 72$
$72 \div 8 = ■$

9. (7-4) $8 \times ■ = 64$
$64 \div 8 = ■$

Find each quotient.

10. (7-2) $7\overline{)35}$ **11.** (7-1) $6\overline{)36}$ **12.** (7-1) $6\overline{)42}$ **13.** (7-2) $7\overline{)49}$

14. (7-1) $6\overline{)30}$ **15.** (7-2) $7\overline{)0}$ **16.** (7-1) $6\overline{)6}$ **17.** (7-1) $6\overline{)48}$

18. (7-4) $8\overline{)24}$ **19.** (7-4) $8\overline{)40}$ **20.** (7-4) $8\overline{)16}$ **21.** (7-4) $8\overline{)72}$

22. (7-2) $21 \div 7$ **23.** (7-2) $63 \div 7$ **24.** (7-1) $54 \div 6$ **25.** (7-2) $42 \div 7$

26. (7-1) $18 \div 6$ **27.** (7-2) $56 \div 7$ **28.** (7-2) $28 \div 7$ **29.** (7-1) $12 \div 6$

30. (7-4) $72 \div 8$ **31.** (7-1) $24 \div 6$ **32.** (7-4) $64 \div 8$ **33.** (7-4) $56 \div 8$

34. (7-4) Forty students are being driven to the theater in vans. Each van holds 8 students. How many vans will be needed to transport all the students?

35. (7-2) Suppose there are 35 people dancing. They form 7 circles with the same number of people in each circle. How many people are in each circle?

36. (7-1) At a folk festival, 42 people dance in groups. If 6 people are in each group, how many groups are there?

37. (7-3) Cody collects paperback books. He has 36 science fiction books and 14 mystery books. How many books does Cody have in his collection? How many more science fiction books does Cody have than mystery books?

TEST PREP

Multiple-Choice Cumulative Review

Choose the correct letter for each answer.

1. **There are 5 sections of seats in the Division Street Theater. If 4 ushers work in each section, how many ushers are there?**

A 9 ushers **C** 20 ushers
B 15 ushers **D** 40 ushers

2. $4\overline{)32}$

F 4 **J** 32
G 8 **K** NH
H 16

3. **Kit plays a videotape of her favorite singing group. The tape has 9 songs. Each song lasts 5 minutes. How long is the tape?**

A 60 minutes
B 45 minutes
C 40 minutes
D 14 minutes

4. **27 ÷ 3**

F 3 **J** 12
G 6 **K** NH
H 9

5. **There are 126 post office boxes at the post office. What is 126 rounded to the nearest 10?**

A 100 **C** 130
B 120 **D** 200

6. **A theater manager divided 42 free tickets equally among 6 groups of students. How many tickets did each group get?**

F 6 tickets **H** 8 tickets
G 7 tickets **J** 9 tickets

7. **Dwane spent $63 on 7 theater tickets. How much did each ticket cost?**

A $7 **C** $56
B $9 **D** $70

8. **What is the value of the number 6 in 706,040?**

F 6
G 60
H 600
J 6,000

9. $8\overline{)40}$

A 8 **D** 4
B 6 **E** NH
C 5

10. **At the theater, the musicians sit on 56 chairs arranged in 8 equal rows. How many chairs are in each row?**

F 7 chairs **H** 9 chairs
G 8 chairs **J** 10 chairs

LESSON 7-5

Dividing by 9

California Content Standard *Number Sense 2.3 (🔑): Use the inverse relationship of multiplication and division to compute and check results.*

Warm-Up Review

1. 2×9
2. 9×5
3. 6×9
4. 9×9
5. A theater has 48 shadow puppets and 8 finger puppets. The puppets are displayed in groups of 8. How many groups of puppets are displayed?

Math Link You know how to multiply by 9. Now you will learn how to use these facts to help you divide by 9.

Example 1

The third-grade chorus is getting ready for their spring concert. They are making flower costumes. They need 9 petals for each flower. They have cut out 27 petals so far. How many flowers can they make?

$27 \div 9 = ■$ or $9\overline{)27}$ with ■ above

Think: $9 \times ■ = 27$
$9 \times 3 = 27$

So, $27 \div 9 = 3$, or $\overset{3}{9\overline{)27}}$.

They can make 3 flowers.

More Examples

A. Find $18 \div 9$.

Think: $9 \times ■ = 18$
$9 \times 2 = 18$

So, $18 \div 9 = 2$.

B. Find $9\overline{)63}$.

Think: $9 \times ■ = 63$
$9 \times 7 = 63$

So, $\overset{7}{9\overline{)63}}$.

Guided Practice *For another example, see Set D on p. 289.*

Algebra Find each missing factor. Use it to help you divide.

1. $9 \times ■ = 36$
$36 \div 9 = ■$

2. $9 \times ■ = 9$
$9 \div 9 = ■$

3. $9 \times ■ = 45$
$45 \div 9 = ■$

4. Julie had 18 baseball cards and 18 basketball cards. She can fit 9 cards on each page of her card album. How many pages can she fill?

Additional Standards: Number Sense 2.8; Algebra and Functions 1.2, 2.2; Mathematical Reasoning 1.2, 2.2 (See p. 263.)

Independent Practice *For more practice, see Set D on p. 291.*

Algebra Find each missing factor. Use it to help you divide.

5. $9 \times \blacksquare = 27$ **6.** $9 \times \blacksquare = 81$ **7.** $9 \times \blacksquare = 54$

$27 \div 9 = \blacksquare$ $81 \div 9 = \blacksquare$ $54 \div 9 = \blacksquare$

8. $9\overline{)45}$ **9.** $9\overline{)63}$ **10.** $9\overline{)18}$ **11.** $9\overline{)54}$ **12.** $9\overline{)0}$

Algebra Complete each table.

Rule: Divide by 9.

	Input	Output
	9	1
13.	36	
14.	54	
15.	72	

Rule: Divide by 7.

	Input	Output
	28	4
16.		5
17.		7
18.	63	

Rule: Divide by 8.

	Input	Output
	16	2
19.	48	
20.		7
21.	64	

22. There are 72 people in the chorus. They form 9 groups to practice. Each group has the same number of people. How many people are in each group?

23. Math Reasoning Suppose 15 people left the chorus and another 6 joined the chorus. Now how many people are in each group?

24. Mental Math What related multiplication fact would you use to help you divide $63 \div 9$?

Mixed Review

25. Jack bought 40 miniature figurines. They come in packs of 8. How many packs did Jack buy?

26. $8\overline{)48}$ **27.** $7\overline{)21}$ **28.** $8\overline{)64}$ **29.** $7\overline{)49}$ **30.** $8\overline{)0}$

Test Prep Choose the correct letter for the answer.

31. (2-4)

$$\begin{array}{r} 719 \\ +298 \\ \hline \end{array}$$

A 421 **D** 1,007
B 907 **E** NH
C 917

32. (2-8)

$$\begin{array}{r} 719 \\ -298 \\ \hline \end{array}$$

F 581 **J** 411
G 521 **K** NH
H 421

LESSON 7-6

Dividing by 10

California Content Standard *Number Sense 2.3 (Key): Use the inverse relationship of multiplication and division to compute and check results.*

Warm-Up Review

1. 10×3
2. 10×5
3. 10×8
4. 10×10
5. Megan took 28 trips on the ferry in June. In July, she took 6 more trips than in June. How many trips did she take on the ferry in the 2 months?

Math Link You know how to multiply by 10. Now you will learn to divide by 10.

Example 1

Trina is making beaded key chains for the school craft fair. Trina can use 10 beads on a key chain. Use the data to the right. How many green beaded key chains can Trina make?

Craft Beads

Color	Number
Red	80
Yellow	20
Blue	90
Black	100
Green	60

$60 \div 10 = \blacksquare$

Think: $10 \times \blacksquare = 60$

$10 \times 6 = 60$

So, $60 \div 10 = 6$.

Trina can make 6 green beaded key chains.

More Examples

A. How many yellow beaded key chains can she make?

$20 \div 10 = \blacksquare$

Think: $10 \times \blacksquare = 20$

$10 \times 2 = 20$

So, $20 \div 10 = 2$.

She could make 2 yellow beaded key chains.

B. How many black beaded key chains can she make?

$100 \div 10 = \blacksquare$

Think: $10 \times \blacksquare = 100$

$10 \times 10 = 100$

So, $100 \div 10 = 10$.

She could make 10 black beaded key chains.

Guided Practice

For another example, see Set E on p. 289.

Algebra Find each missing factor. Use it to help you divide.

1. $10 \times \blacksquare = 40$
   $40 \div 10 = \blacksquare$
2. $10 \times \blacksquare = 90$
   $90 \div 10 = \blacksquare$
3. $10 \times \blacksquare = 50$
   $50 \div 10 = \blacksquare$
4. How many more blue key chains can Trina make than yellow key chains?

Additional Standards: Number Sense 2.8; Algebra and Functions 1.2, 2.1(Key); Mathematical Reasoning 1.1, 1.2 (See p. 263.)

Independent Practice *For more practice, see Set E on p. 291.*

Algebra **Find each missing factor. Use it to help you divide.**

5. 10 × ■ = 30
30 ÷ 10 = ■

6. 10 × ■ = 10
10 ÷ 10 = ■

7. 10 × ■ = 70
70 ÷ 10 = ■

8. 80 ÷ 10 **9.** 40 ÷ 10 **10.** 0 ÷ 10 **11.** 90 ÷ 10

12. 60 ÷ 10 **13.** 50 ÷ 10 **14.** 20 ÷ 10 **15.** 100 ÷ 10

Use the data on page 276 to answer Exercises 16 and 17.

16. Trina gave 10 red and 10 blue beads to Maria. Now how many red key chains will Trina be able to make?

17. Trina mixed the green beads and the yellow beads. She doesn't care how many yellow or green beads are on each key chain, just as long as there are 10 total beads. How many key chains could she make?

Mixed Review

18. Sarah takes the subway 6 times per week. How many trips will she take in 7 weeks?

19. 64 ÷ 8 **20.** 9 ÷ 9 **21.** 54 ÷ 9 **22.** 32 ÷ 8

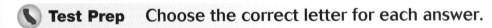

Test Prep **Choose the correct letter for each answer.**

Use the road mileage table to answer Exercises 23 and 24.

Distance Between Cities	
San Diego to Los Angeles	121 miles
Los Angeles to San Francisco	382 miles
San Francisco to Sacramento	88 miles

23. (2-4) Tom lives in Los Angeles. He drove to San Francisco to visit his friend. Then he drove back home. How many miles did Tom drive?

A 242 miles
B 382 miles
C 664 miles
D 764 miles
E NH

24. (2-8) On Monday, Mary drove from Los Angeles to San Francisco. On Tuesday, she drove from San Francisco to Sacramento. How many more miles did she drive on Monday than on Tuesday?

F 306 miles
G 294 miles
H 292 miles
J 261 miles
K NH

LESSON 7-7

Understand
Plan
Solve
Look Back

Problem-Solving Strategy:
Make a Table

California Content Standard *Mathematical Reasoning 2.3: Use a variety of methods, such as words, numbers, symbols, charts, graphs, tables, diagrams, and models, to explain mathematical reasoning. Also, Mathematical Reasoning 3.3 (See p. 263.)*

Warm-Up Review

1. 19 + 38 **2.** 96 − 89

3. 56 ÷ 8 **4.** 5 × 8

5. Jack has 3 boxes of markers. Each box has 8 markers. If Jack takes 2 markers out of each box, how many are still in the boxes?

Monica set up a training schedule for the bike-a-thon she entered. Each day she wants to ride 6 more laps around the track than she rode the day before.

On the first day, she rode 8 laps. On the second day, she rode 14 laps. If she follows the pattern in her schedule, how many laps will she ride on the seventh day?

Day	Number of Laps Ridden
First	8
Second	14
Third	20
Fourth	26
Fifth	32
Sixth	38
Seventh	44

Understand

What do you need to know?

You need to know that Monica rode 8 laps on the first day. Then you need to know that she always rides 6 more laps than she did the day before.

Plan

How can you solve the problem?

You can make a table like the one at the right.

Solve

List the number of laps Monica rides each day. Remember to add 6 laps to the day before.

Monica will ride 44 laps on the seventh day.

Look Back

Why is using a table helpful?

It can help you organize information so that it is easier to read.

 Additional Standard: Mathematical Reasoning 3.2 (See p. 263.)

Guided Practice

Make a table to solve the problem.

1. Lenny began with $8 in his bank account. Each week he receives $5 for doing his chores. If Lenny saves all the money, how much will he have after 6 weeks?

Weeks	Money
1	
2	
3	
4	
5	
6	

Independent Practice

Make a table to solve Exercises 2–4.

2. Mr. William's class is having a jump rope contest. Each jump rope team needs 3 students. How many students would be needed to make 4 teams? 6 teams? 8 teams?

Number of Teams	Number of Students
1	
2	
3	
4	
5	
6	
7	
8	

3. Eight teams started the contest. Half of the teams were eliminated in the first round. How many students are still in the contest?

4. **Math Reasoning** Suppose Mrs. Lopez's class wants to have their own jump rope contest. There are 22 students in the class. Are there enough students to have 8 teams?

Mixed Review

Try these or other strategies to solve each problem. Tell which strategy you used.

Problem-Solving Strategies

- *Work Backward*
- *Write a Number Sentence*
- *Use Logical Reasoning*
- *Make a List*

5. After the movie, the children went bowling. They spent $48 on lane fees. If each game cost $6, how many games did the children bowl?

6. Chris buys 3 sets of markers. Each set of markers is the same price. He pays with a $20 bill and receives $11 in change. How much does each set of markers cost?

Use Homework Workbook 7-7.

LESSON 7-8

Finding Missing Numbers

Algebra

Warm-Up Review

1. $16 \div 4$ **2.** $49 \div 7$

3. $72 \div 9$ **4.** $64 \div 8$

5. Layne bought 8 baseballs for $3 each. She paid with $30. How much change did she get?

California Content Standard *Algebra and Functions 1.1 ( ): Represent relationships of quantities in the form of mathematical expressions, equations, or inequalities.*

Math Link You know all the basic division facts. Now you will learn how to find missing numbers in equations like $35 \div \blacksquare = 7$ and $\blacksquare \div 3 = 4$.

Example 1

Find the missing number in this equation:
$35 \div \blacksquare = 7$.

Think: Use a related multiplication fact.

You know that $7 \times 5 = 35$.
So, $\blacksquare = 5$.

$7 \times 5 = 35$ and $35 \div 5 = 7$ are related facts.

Check: Since $35 \div 5 = 7$, the answer checks.

Example 2

Find the missing number in this equation:
$\blacksquare \div 3 = 4$.

Think: Use a related multiplication fact.

You know that $4 \times 3 = 12$.
So, $\blacksquare = 12$.

$4 \times 3 = 12$ and $12 \div 3 = 4$ are related facts.

Check: Since $12 \div 3 = 4$, the answer checks.

Guided Practice *For another example, see Set F on p. 289.*

Algebra Find each missing number.

1. $16 \div \blacksquare = 8$ **2.** $\blacksquare \div 4 = 6$ **3.** $27 \div \blacksquare = 9$ **4.** $\blacksquare \div 7 = 8$

5. Rob bought some stamps for his collection. He is not sure how many stamps he bought. He had 10 envelopes. Each envelope had 8 stamps. How many stamps did Rob buy?

Additional Standards: Number Sense 2.3 ( ); Algebra and Functions 1.2; Mathematical Reasoning 3.3 (See p. 263.)

Independent Practice *For more practice, see Set F on p. 291.*

Algebra Find each missing number.

6. ■ ÷ 5 = 8 **7.** 9 ÷ ■ = 3 **8.** 3 ÷ ■ = 3 **9.** ■ ÷ 2 = 6

10. 63 ÷ ■ = 9 **11.** ■ ÷ 4 = 7 **12.** ■ ÷ 6 = 6 **13.** 32 ÷ ■ = 4

14. 14 ÷ ■ = 7 **15.** 12 ÷ ■ = 2 **16.** ■ ÷ 3 = 8 **17.** ■ ÷ 7 = 8

Algebra Write a division sentence to solve each exercise.

18. Marcus bought a jar full of marbles at the school yard sale. He was not sure how many there were in total, so he separated them into piles of 5. He made 8 piles. How many did he buy?

19. Colton also bought a jar of marbles. He put his into piles of 10. He had 2 piles of red, 3 piles of blue, and 2 piles of mixed colors. How many marbles did he buy?

20. Math Reasoning How do you know that the missing divisor in 14 ÷ ■ = 7 is less than 3?

Mixed Review

Use the sign for Exercises 21 and 22.

Discount Store Sale	
CDs	$10
Mystery Collections	$ 9
Marker Sets	$ 3

21. Cale has $40. How many CDs could he buy at the discount store?

22. Bret has $27. How many mystery collections can he buy?

23. 80 ÷ 10 **24.** 54 ÷ 9 **25.** 50 ÷ 10 **26.** 81 ÷ 9

Test Prep Choose the correct letter for each answer.

27. How can you make 38¢ with the fewest number of coins?
(1-8)

A 

B 

C 

D 

28. What is the rule for the table?
(4-10)

F Multiply by 5.

G Divide by 5.

H Multiply by 3.

J Divide by 3.

Input	Output
0	0
3	9
5	15
6	18
9	27

LESSON 7-9

Understand
Plan
Solve
Look Back

Problem-Solving Application:
Using Operations

California Content Standard *Mathematical Reasoning 2.0: Students use strategies, skills, and concepts in finding solutions.*

Warm-Up Review

1. 19 + 18 **2.** 28 − 21

3. 9 × 2 **4.** 42 ÷ 6

5. Seven people get on the train at the first stop. At the second stop, 4 people get on the train and 2 others get off. At the third stop, 5 people get on the train and 3 people get off. How many people are on the train after the second stop?

The school open house schedule is shown at the right. The talent show follows lunch. Students have five minutes to perform each act. Fifteen minutes have been planned for introductions. How many acts can be in the talent show?

Open House	
Activity	**Time**
Parent-teacher meetings	9:00 A.M.–noon
Lunch	noon–1:00 P.M.
School Talent Show	1:00 P.M.–2:00 P.M.
Book Sale	2:00 P.M.–3:00 P.M.

Understand

What do you need to know?

You need to know how long the show lasts, the number of minutes for introductions, and the number of minutes for each act.

Plan

How can you solve the problem?

First find the total number of minutes the show will last. Then subtract 15 minutes for introductions. Finally, divide the remaining minutes by 5 to find the number of acts.

Solve

Step 1 1:00 P.M. to 2:00 P.M. = 60 min

Step 2 60 min − 15 min = 45 min

Step 3 45 ÷ 5 = 9 acts

There can be 9 acts in the talent show.

Look Back

What if the introductions lasted 20 minutes? How many acts could there be? Explain.

Additional Standards: Number Sense 2.8; Mathematical Reasoning 2.3 (See p. 263.)

Guided Practice

1. There are 9 acts in the talent show. Three of the acts do not include music. How many acts in the talent show do include music?

2. There are 6 students on stage tap-dancing. Seven more students join them. Then 3 students leave. How many students are dancing now?

Independent Practice

3. Marisa is performing in 3 acts. Each act lasts 5 minutes. For how many minutes will Marisa perform in the talent show?

4. Rich and Jess have a juggling act. Rich has 14 pins. Jess has 4 pins. They need to have the same number of pins to begin their act. How many pins should Rich give to Jess?

5. Jerome and Derek buy 2 hats, a set of juggling pins, and 3 funny ties for their comedy act. If they share the total cost equally, how much money will each boy have to pay?

Comedy Props	
Hat	$2.50 each
Ties	$2.00 each
Juggling Pins	$7.00 set

6. Fifteen minutes is set aside at the end of a talent show for comedy acts. The first 2 acts last 4 minutes each. The third act lasts 5 minutes. Is there enough time left for a 3-minute act? Explain why or why not.

Mixed Review

Use the chart to the right to answer Exercises 7–8.

Show Tickets	
Child under 6	$2
Student	$7
Adult	$9
Senior citizen	$4

7. The chart lists the ticket prices for the Division Street Theater show. You sell $49 worth of student tickets and $54 worth of adult tickets. How many of each kind of ticket do you sell?

8. If you buy the tickets in advance, you can save $1 on student tickets and $2 on adult tickets. How much would you spend if you bought 3 student tickets, 2 adult tickets, and 1 senior citizen ticket in advance?

Use Homework Workbook 7-9.

Diagnostic Checkpoint

Word Bank
factors
quotient
divisor
dividend

1. (7-2) The numbers that are multiplied to give a product are ________.

2. (7-1) In $18 \div 6 = 3$, the ________ is 3.

Find each missing factor. Use it to help you divide.

3. (7-5) $9 \times ■ = 18$
$18 \div 9 = ■$

4. (7-5) $9 \times ■ = 36$
$36 \div 9 = ■$

5. (7-5) $9 \times ■ = 45$
$45 \div 9 = ■$

6. (7-6) $10 \times ■ = 30$
$30 \div 10 = ■$

7. (7-6) $10 \times ■ = 70$
$70 \div 10 = ■$

8. (7-6) $10 \times ■ = 20$
$20 \div 10 = ■$

Find each quotient.

9. (7-5) $9\overline{)54}$

10. (7-6) $10\overline{)90}$

11. (7-6) $60 \div 10$

12. (7-5) $72 \div 9$

13. (7-5) $27 \div 9$

14. (7-5) $9\overline{)63}$

15. (7-6) $0 \div 10$

16. (7-5) $9\overline{)36}$

17. (6-3) $3\overline{)15}$

18. (6-6) $45 \div 5$

19. (7-5) $81 \div 9$

20. (6-5) $4\overline{)24}$

Algebra **Find each missing number.**

21. (7-8) $36 \div ■ = 6$

22. (7-8) $49 \div ■ = 7$

23. (7-8) $■ \div 9 = 6$

24. (7-8) $■ \div 6 = 7$

25. (7-8) $■ \div 4 = 8$

26. (7-8) $■ \div 3 = 9$

27. (7-8) $80 \div ■ = 8$

28. (7-8) $■ \div 5 = 0$

29. (7-8) $45 \div ■ = 9$

Solve.

30. (7-7) Kevin has collected 12 pounds of aluminum cans. He receives \$1 for every 2 pounds of cans he collects. How much money will he receive for 12 pounds of cans? 16 pounds? 22 pounds? Make a table to solve the problem.

31. (7-9) Davis, Shelby, and Colton collected gallon-sized plastic milk containers for a class project. Davis collected 7, Shelby 17, and Colton 12. The containers were divided equally among 6 teams of students. How many containers did each team get?

Chapter 7 Test

Find each quotient.

1. $7\overline{)49}$ **2.** $8\overline{)64}$ **3.** $6\overline{)42}$

4. $9\overline{)36}$ **5.** $8\overline{)72}$ **6.** $7\overline{)63}$

7. $6\overline{)54}$ **8.** $9\overline{)63}$ **9.** $10\overline{)40}$

Find each missing number.

10. 20 ÷ ■ = 5 **11.** ■ ÷ 9 = 9 **12.** 50 ÷ ■ = 5

13. ■ ÷ 9 = 3 **14.** 35 ÷ ■ = 7 **15.** ■ ÷ 6 = 4

16. 48 ÷ ■ = 6 **17.** ■ ÷ 7 = 8 **18.** ■ ÷ 7 = 10

Complete each table.

Rule: Divide by 9.

	Input	Output
	9	1
19.	27	
20.	36	
21.	81	

Rule: Divide by 6.

	Input	Output
	12	2
22.	24	
23.	42	
24.	54	

Rule: Divide by 8.

	Input	Output
	48	6
25.	24	
26.	40	
27.	64	

28. Mike and Sam are collecting aluminum cans and newspapers. They want to collect 50 pounds of cans and 80 pounds of newspapers. How many pounds of cans and newspapers do Mike and Sam want to collect? How many more pounds of newspapers will they have than cans?

29. Karen has $10 in her bank. Each week she receives $4 in allowance. If Karen saves all the money, how much will she have after 5 weeks? Make a table to solve the problem.

30. Matthew invited 6 friends to spend the night. Two of his friends had other plans and couldn't come. Matthew ordered 3 slices of pizza per person including himself. How many pieces of pizza did he order?

TEST PREP

Multiple-Choice Chapter 7 Test

Choose the correct letter for each answer.

1. **The 24 members of a school band travel in vans. Each van carries 6 passengers. How many vans are needed to carry all the band members?**

A 3
B 4
C 5
D 6

2. $9\overline{)54}$

F 4
G 5
H 6
J 7
K NH

3. **Carmen collected 48 pictures of famous people. She put 8 pictures on each page of a photo album. How many pages of the album did she fill?**

A 8 pages
B 7 pages
C 6 pages
D 5 pages

4. $7\overline{)35}$

F 5
G 6
H 7
J 8
K NH

5. **There are 45 seats in one part of a theater. The seats are arranged in 9 equal rows. How many seats are in each row?**

A 9 seats
B 7 seats
C 5 seats
D 3 seats

6. $70 \div 10$

F 7
G 10
H 70
J 80
K NH

7. **Find the missing number.**

$$\blacksquare \div 6 = 7$$

A 35
B 42
C 48
D 49
E NH

8. **A music teacher places her students into groups of 9. If she has 27 students, how many groups can she make?**

F 9 groups
G 7 groups
H 4 groups
J 3 groups

9. $6\overline{)30}$

A 4
B 5
C 6
D 7
E NH

10. Maria went to the beach for vacation. She was there for one week. During that week she collected 56 seashells. If she collected the same number of seashells each day, how many did she collect each day?

F 7 seashells
G 8 seashells
H 9 seashells
J 56 seashells

11. Simon bought two boxes of pencils. There were 14 pencils in one box and 16 pencils in the other. He gives each friend at his party 3 pencils. If he gave away all of the pencils, how many friends get pencils?

A 10 friends
B 9 friends
C 8 friends
D 7 friends

12. $40 \div 8$

F 8
G 6
H 5
J 4
K NH

13. Ninety used cars were parked in a used car lot. They were arranged in rows. Each row had 10 cars in it. How many rows of used cars were there?

A 9 rows
B 10 rows
C 90 rows
D 100 rows

14. A club is handing out fliers. So far, 28 have been handed out. Seven people have promised to hand out an equal number of the remaining 42 fliers. Which number sentence tells you the number of fliers each person will hand out?

F $70 \div 7$
G $70 - 28$
H $42 \div 7$
J $42 - 28$

15. At a school fun day, each grade participated in a treasure hunt. Grade 1 needed to collect 6 items. Grade 2 needed to collect 2 more items than Grade 1. Grade 3 had to collect 2 more items than Grade 2 and so on. How many items did Grade 6 need to collect?

A 6 items
B 10 items
C 16 items
D 20 items

Reteaching

Set A (pages 264–265)

Find $6\overline{)24}$.

Think: $6 \times \blacksquare = 24$
$6 \times 4 = 24$

So, $24 \div 6 = 4$.

Remember a missing factor can help you find a quotient.

1. $18 \div 6$ **2.** $6\overline{)6}$ **3.** $54 \div 6$

4. $6\overline{)48}$ **5.** $30 \div 6$ **6.** $6\overline{)12}$

7. $6\overline{)0}$ **8.** $42 \div 6$ **9.** $6\overline{)36}$

Set B (pages 266–267)

Find $35 \div 7$.

Think: $7 \times \blacksquare = 35$
$7 \times 5 = 35$

So, $35 \div 7 = 5$.

Remember you know how to multiply by 7. Now you can use those multiplication facts to divide by 7.

1. $7\overline{)14}$ **2.** $63 \div 7$ **3.** $7\overline{)42}$

4. $28 \div 7$ **5.** $0 \div 7$ **6.** $7\overline{)49}$

7. $7\overline{)7}$ **8.** $21 \div 7$ **9.** $56 \div 7$

Set C (pages 270–271)

Find $32 \div 8$.

Think: $8 \times \blacksquare = 32$
$8 \times 4 = 32$

So, $32 \div 8 = 4$.

Remember the answer in division is called the quotient.

1. $8\overline{)0}$ **2.** $8\overline{)40}$ **3.** $8\overline{)64}$

4. $16 \div 8$ **5.** $8 \div 8$ **6.** $24 \div 8$

7. $8\overline{)48}$ **8.** $8\overline{)72}$ **9.** $56 \div 8$

Set D *(pages 274–275)*

Find 36 ÷ 9.

Think: $9 \times \blacksquare = 36$
$9 \times 4 = 36$

So, $36 \div 9 = 4$.

Remember you know how to use 9 as a factor in multiplication. Use these facts to help you divide by 9.

1. $72 \div 9$ **2.** $45 \div 9$ **3.** $9\overline{)18}$

4. $9\overline{)27}$ **5.** $63 \div 9$ **6.** $0 \div 9$

7. $9\overline{)54}$ **8.** $9\overline{)81}$ **9.** $9\overline{)9}$

Set E *(pages 276–277)*

Find 40 ÷ 10.

Think: $10 \times \blacksquare = 40$
$10 \times 4 = 40$

So, $40 \div 10 = 4$.

Remember you know how to multiply by 10. Now you can use those multiplication facts to divide by 10.

1. $30 \div 10$ **2.** $60 \div 10$ **3.** $10\overline{)0}$

4. $10\overline{)10}$ **5.** $10\overline{)40}$ **6.** $10\overline{)90}$

7. $100 \div 10$ **8.** $50 \div 10$ **9.** $10\overline{)20}$

Set F *(pages 280–281)*

Find the missing number in this equation: $48 \div \blacksquare = 6$.

Use a related multiplication fact. You know that $6 \times 8 = 48$.

So, $\blacksquare = 8$.

Remember to see if your answer checks. Since $48 \div 8 = 6$, the answer checks.

1. $32 \div \blacksquare = 4$ **2.** $\blacksquare \div 3 = 9$

3. $\blacksquare \div 10 = 0$ **4.** $\blacksquare \div 9 = 5$

5. $30 \div \blacksquare = 3$ **6.** $18 \div \blacksquare = 2$

7. $56 \div \blacksquare = 7$ **8.** $\blacksquare \div 1 = 8$

9. $\blacksquare \div 8 = 6$ **10.** $63 \div \blacksquare = 9$

More Practice

Set A *(pages 264–265)*

Algebra **Find each missing factor. Use it to help you divide.**

1. $6 \times \blacksquare = 18$
$18 \div 6 = \blacksquare$

2. $6 \times \blacksquare = 30$
$30 \div 6 = \blacksquare$

3. $6 \times \blacksquare = 42$
$42 \div 6 = \blacksquare$

4. $6\overline{)24}$

5. $6\overline{)6}$

6. $6\overline{)18}$

7. $6\overline{)42}$

8. $6\overline{)12}$

9. $6\overline{)30}$

10. $6\overline{)36}$

11. $6\overline{)54}$

12. Suppose 30 musical instruments are shared equally among 6 classes. How many instruments would each class get?

Set B *(pages 266–267)*

Algebra **Find each missing factor. Use it to help you divide.**

1. $7 \times \blacksquare = 49$
$49 \div 7 = \blacksquare$

2. $7 \times \blacksquare = 28$
$28 \div 7 = \blacksquare$

3. $7 \times \blacksquare = 63$
$63 \div 7 = \blacksquare$

4. $35 \div 7$

5. $14 \div 7$

6. $28 \div 7$

7. 49×7

8. A dance instructor places 35 students into 7 groups. How many students are in each group if all the groups have an equal number of students?

Set C *(pages 270–271)*

Algebra **Find each missing factor. Use it to help you divide.**

1. $8 \times \blacksquare = 40$
$40 \div 8 = \blacksquare$

2. $8 \times \blacksquare = 48$
$48 \div 8 = \blacksquare$

3. $8 \times \blacksquare = 64$
$64 \div 8 = \blacksquare$

4. $8\overline{)0}$

5. $8\overline{)56}$

6. $40 \div 8$

7. $64 \div 8$

8. There are 32 costumes worn by 8 actors in a play. If each actor wears the same number of costumes, how many costumes does each actor wear?

Set D (pages 274–275)

Algebra Find each missing factor. Use it to help you divide.

1. $9 \times ■ = 36$
$36 \div 9 = ■$

2. $9 \times ■ = 63$
$63 \div 9 = ■$

3. $9 \times ■ = 45$
$45 \div 9 = ■$

4. $9\overline{)27}$ **5.** $9\overline{)54}$ **6.** $9\overline{)9}$ **7.** $9\overline{)72}$

8. $9\overline{)18}$ **9.** $1\overline{)9}$ **10.** $9\overline{)45}$ **11.** $9\overline{)36}$

12. Malik bought $63 worth of tickets to a play. If each ticket cost $9, how many tickets did he buy?

Set E (pages 276–277)

Algebra Find each missing factor. Use it to help you divide.

1. $10 \times ■ = 60$
$60 \div 10 = ■$

2. $10 \times ■ = 80$
$80 \div 10 = ■$

3. $10 \times ■ = 30$
$30 \div 10 = ■$

4. $60 \div 10$ **5.** $90 \div 10$ **6.** $0 \div 10$ **7.** $50 \div 10$

8. $10\overline{)50}$ **9.** $10\overline{)20}$ **10.** $10\overline{)70}$ **11.** $10\overline{)30}$

12. At a theater, there are 80 seats. Each row has 10 seats. How many rows are there?

Set F (pages 280–281)

Algebra Find each missing number.

1. $24 \div ■ = 8$ **2.** $16 \div ■ = 4$ **3.** $36 \div ■ = 9$ **4.** $72 \div ■ = 8$

5. $63 \div ■ = 7$ **6.** $■ \div 6 = 9$ **7.** $■ \div 10 = 4$ **8.** $35 \div ■ = 5$

9. $42 \div ■ = 6$ **10.** $■ \div 8 = 0$ **11.** $3 \div ■ = 1$ **12.** $■ \div 9 = 2$

13. Bart bought a bag of buttons for a craft project. He separated the buttons into piles of 6. He made 7 piles. Write a division sentence to find out how many buttons Bart bought.

TEST PREP

Problem Solving: Preparing for Tests

Choose the correct letter for each answer.

1. Chelsea and 3 of her friends each made 6 baskets during a basketball game. Each basket is worth 2 points. How many points did Chelsea and her friends make?

A 24 points
B 36 points
C 42 points
D 48 points
E NH

Tip

Decide what steps you need to do to solve the problem. Then decide on the order in which to do them.

2. One afternoon Kenny painted model planes. He painted from 12:45 P.M. until 4:30 P.M. He stopped once for a 15-minute break. What other information do you need in order to figure out how many planes Kenny painted?

F When Kenny took a break from painting
G How many unpainted planes Kenny had
H How long Kenny spent painting each plane
J How long Kenny painted before his break

Tip

Try to answer the question "How many planes did Kenny paint?" in order to see what information is missing.

3. Mr. Birch is making a display of soup cans in the supermarket. He puts 8 cans in the bottom row, 7 in the next row, and so on until there is 1 can in the top row. If he has 30 cans, how many more cans will he need in order to complete the display?

A 2 cans
B 6 cans
C 28 cans
D 36 cans
E NH

Tip

Try the strategy *Draw a Picture* to help you answer the question.

4. Tracy and Dan each have 2 cats. Sue and Jorge each have 3 cats. Which number sentence shows the number of cats the four friends have in all?

F 4×2

G $2 + 3$

H $2 \times 3 \times 2$

J $2 + 2 + 3 + 3$

---

5. Peter had 25 markers. He lost 3 of them and he gave 10 to a friend. Which number sentence shows how many markers Peter has now?

A $25 - 3 = \blacksquare$

B $25 - 10 = \blacksquare$

C $25 - 13 = \blacksquare$

D $25 + 3 + 10 = \blacksquare$

---

6. If today is November 4, what will the date be in 3 weeks?

F November 1

G November 7

H November 18

J November 25

---

7. Jordan has a piece of wood that is 24 feet long. He wants to divide it into 8 equal pieces. How many cuts will he need to make?

A 3 cuts

B 7 cuts

C 8 cuts

D 9 cuts

E NH

8. Raul went on a trip to North Carolina. He took 75 pictures on Friday, 48 pictures on Saturday, and 63 pictures on Sunday. Which is the best estimate of how many pictures Raul took on Saturday and Sunday?

F 100 pictures

G 110 pictures

H 170 pictures

J 180 pictures

K NH

---

9. Kristy is choosing 4 toys to buy at the toy store. The lowest-priced toy costs $2, and the highest-priced toy costs $5. What is a reasonable total for the cost of the 4 toys?

A Less than $8

B Between $8 and $20

C Between $20 and $24

D More than $24

---

10. Steve and Marta each chose a video to rent. The video Steve chose lasts 91 minutes. The video Marta chose lasts 68 minutes. *About* how much longer is the video that Steve chose?

F 20 minutes

G 30 minutes

H 90 minutes

J 160 minutes

Multiple-Choice Cumulative Review

TEST PREP

Choose the correct letter for each answer.

Number Sense

1. What number is the same as three hundred ninety-nine thousand, seven hundred seventy-seven?

A 39,777
B 339,977
C 399,777
D 777,399

2. Which figure does NOT represent $\frac{1}{2}$?

F 

H 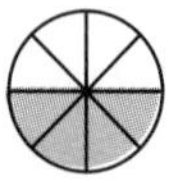

G 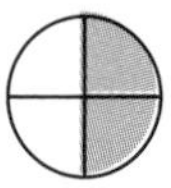

J 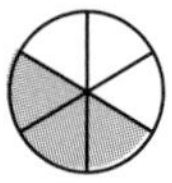

3. Which set of numbers is in order from *greatest* to *least*?

A	1,014	1,128	1,235	1,310
B	1,310	1,235	1,128	1,014
C	1,310	1,235	1,014	1,128
D	1,235	1,014	1,310	1,128

4. Which number is between 1,111 and 1,122?

1,111		1,122

F 15 **H** 1,115
G 115 **J** 1,151

5. Tom has 26 toy cars, 15 toy boats, and 9 model planes. Which number sentence could be used to find how many more cars Tom has than boats?

A 26 + 15 = ■
B 15 − 9 = ■
C 26 − 15 = ■
D 26 − 9 = ■

6. Tara and Pete had 135 comic books and 25 puzzle books. They sold 45 comic books to a collector. How many comic books did they have left?

F 90 **H** 160
G 95 **J** 180

7. There are 7 seats in each of 6 vans. How many seats are there in all?

A 13 **C** 36
B 23 **D** 42

8. 12 ÷ 2 = ■

F 3 **H** 6
G 4 **J** 9

Algebra and Functions

9. Which is the missing number in the number pattern?

35, 28, 21, ■, 7

A 10　　**C** 14
B 12　　**D** 16

---

10. Which number sentence belongs to the same family of facts as $2 \times 4 = 8$?

F $8 \div 4 = 2$
G $8 + 4 = 12$
H $4 \div 2 = 2$
J $8 - 4 = 4$

---

11. Which number line has stars on the whole numbers that are greater than 12 *and* less than 16?

A 

B 

C 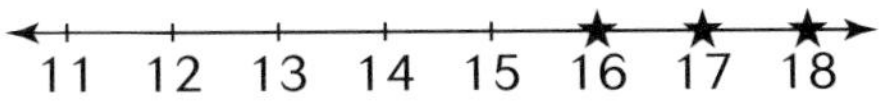

D 

---

12. Which object completes the pattern?

F 　　**H** 

G 　　**J** 

Measurement and Geometry

13. Julia made a doghouse for her dog, Skip. In which units did she measure the materials?

A Liters
B Inches
C Ounces
D Degrees Celsius

---

14. Stephanie started her homework at 6:45 P.M. She worked for 45 minutes. What time was it when she finished her homework?

F 7:00 P.M.
G 7:15 P.M
H 7:30 P.M.
J 7:45 P.M.

---

15. Six months ago Jane was 4 feet 6 inches tall. Now she is 4 inches taller. How tall is she now?

A 4 ft 8 in.
B 4 ft 10 in.
C 5 ft 2 in.
D 5 ft 4 in.

---

16. Which symbol makes the statement true?

10 grams ● 1 kilogram

F $<$
G $>$
H $=$
J $+$

CHAPTER 8

Geometry

- 8-1 Plane Figures
- 8-2 Lines, Segments, Rays, and Angles
- 8-3 Classifying Triangles Using Angles
- 8-4 Classifying Triangles Using Sides
- 8-5 Quadrilaterals
- 8-6 Problem-Solving Skill: Spatial Reasoning
- 8-7 Congruent Figures
- 8-8 Slides, Flips, and Turns
- 8-9 Problem-Solving Strategy: Find a Pattern
- 8-10 Perimeter
- 8-11 Area
- 8-12 Problem-Solving Application: Using Symmetry
- 8-13 Solid Figures
- 8-14 Volume

Diagnosing Readiness

In Chapter 8, you will use these skills:

A Plane Shapes

(Grade 2)

Name each plane shape.

1. 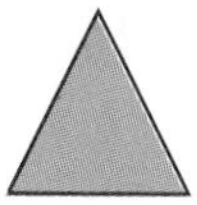

2. 

3. Sophie traced around the bottom of a soup can. What shape did she make?

B Corners and Sides

(Grade 2)

Write the number of sides and corners each plane shape has.

4. 

5. 

6. Manuel made a shape that had 4 corners and 4 sides. Two of the sides were 4 inches long and two of the sides were 3 inches long. What shape did he make?

C Solid Shapes

(Grade 2)

Name each solid shape.

7. 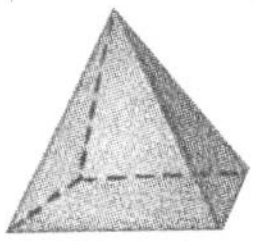

8. 

9. 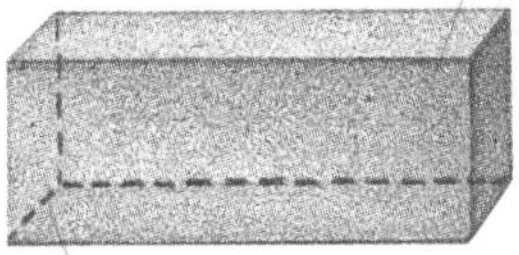

10. 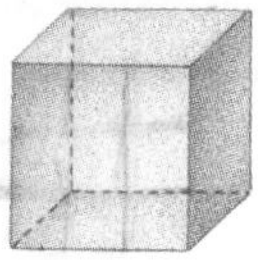

11. What solid shape does a baseball look like?

D Faces, Corners, and Edges

(Grade 2)

Name the solid shape each sentence describes.

12. It has no faces, corners, or edges.

13. It has 6 faces. All the faces are squares.

14. It has 1 face that is a square and 4 faces that are triangles.

E Congruent Figures

(Grade 2)

Are the figures the same size and shape?

15. 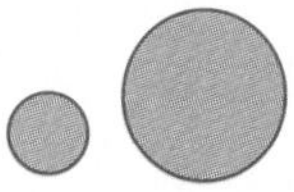

16. 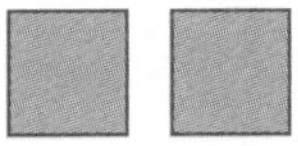

17. 

18. 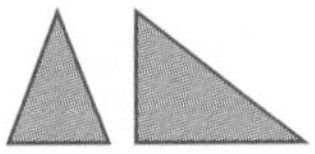

F Perimeter

(Grade 2)

How far is it around each figure?

19. 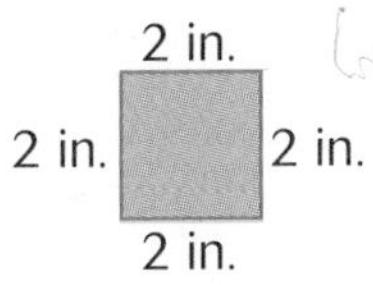

20. 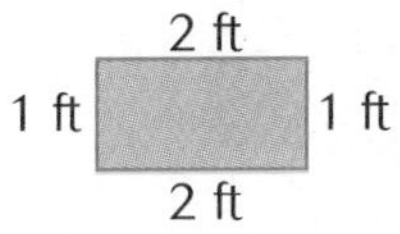

21. Brent made a vegetable garden. Its sides measured 5 feet, 3 feet, 5 feet, and 3 feet. How many feet is it around his garden?

To the Family and Student

Looking Back

In Grade 2, students learned how to describe and classify basic plane and solid geometric shapes (circle, triangle, square, rectangle, sphere, pyramid, cube, and rectangular prism).

Chapter 8

Geometry

In this chapter, students learn about characteristics and relationships of plane and solid figures. They will also learn about perimeter, area, and volume.

Looking Ahead

In Grade 4, students will describe the plane and geometric figures learned in Grade 3 in great detail.

Math and Everyday Living

Opportunities to apply the concepts of Chapter 8 abound in everyday situations. During the chapter, think about how geometry can be used to solve a variety of real-world problems. The following examples suggest just a few of the many situations that could launch a discussion about geometry.

Math and Hobbies You make a rectangular pillow. You need to buy lace to put around the edge. You want to buy 5 extra inches of lace. How much lace do you need?

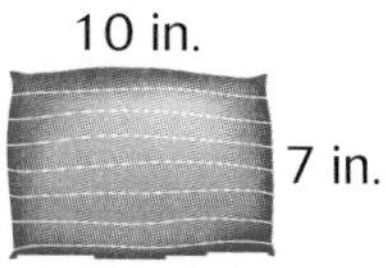

Math and Storage You have 2 large boxes in which you are going to store smaller shoe boxes. You can fit 9 shoe boxes in 1 large box. If each large box is the same size, how many shoe boxes can you fit in the 2 large boxes?

Math and the Department Store While at the department store you see many different three-dimensional figures. What did you see?

a. 

b. 

c. 

Math and Gardening In each square unit of your garden you can plant 1 petunia. How many petunias do you need to buy?

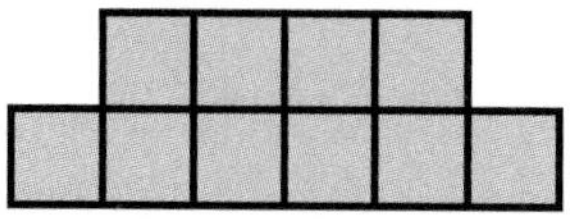

Math and Road Safety You try to identify some of the road signs you see on the way to school, just by their shape. What are the signs?

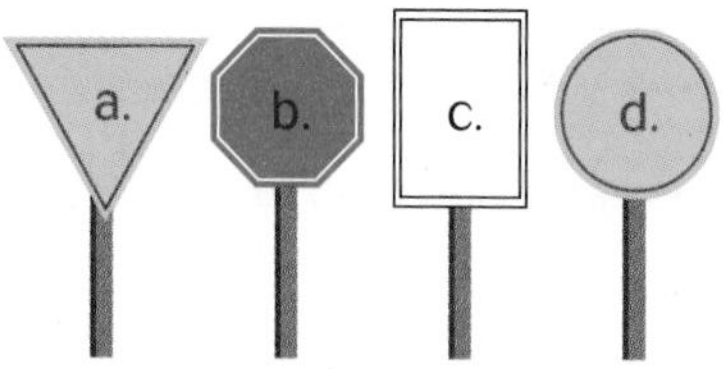

Math at Home Your brother's room is 8 feet wide and 10 feet long. Your room is 9 feet wide and 9 feet long. Who has the bigger room? What is the area of each room?

California Content Standards in Chapter 8 Lessons*

	Teach and Practice	Practice
Algebra and Functions		
2.2 Extend and recognize a linear pattern by its rules (e.g., the number of legs on a given number of horses may be calculated by counting by 4s or by multiplying the number of horses by 4).	8-9	
Measurement and Geometry		
1.2 (🔑) Estimate or determine the area and volume of solid figures by covering them with squares or by counting the number of cubes that would fill them.	8-11, 8-14	
1.3 (🔑) Find the perimeter of a polygon with integer sides.	8-10	
2.0 Students describe and compare the attributes of plane and solid geometric figures and use their understanding to show relationships and solve problems.	8-2, 8-8	
2.1 (🔑) Identify, describe, and classify polygons (including pentagons, hexagons, and octagons).	8-1	
2.2 (🔑) Identify attributes of triangles (e.g., two equal sides for the isosceles triangle, three equal sides for the equilateral triangle, right angle for the right triangle).	8-3, 8-4	
2.3 (🔑) Identify attributes of quadrilaterals (e.g., parallel sides for the parallelogram, right angles for the rectangle, equal sides and right angles for the square).	8-5	
2.4 Identify right angles in geometric figures or in appropriate objects and determine whether other angles are greater or less than a right angle.	8-2	8-3

	Teach and Practice	Practice
Measurement and Geometry		
2.5 Identify, describe, and classify common three-dimensional geometric objects	8-13	
2.6 Identify common solid objects that are the components needed to make a more complex solid object.	8-13	
3.3 (Grade 4) Identify congruent figures.	8-7	
3.4 (Grade 4) Identify figures that have . . . bilateral symmetry.	8-12	
Mathematical Reasoning		
1.1 Analyze problems by identifying relationships, distinguishing relevant from irrelevant information, sequencing and prioritizing information, and observing patterns.	8-6, 8-9	8-12
1.2 Determine when and how to break a problem into simpler parts.	8-6	
2.2 Apply strategies and results from simpler problems to more complex problems.	8-6	8-9, 8-11, 8-12
2.3 Use a variety of methods, such as words, numbers, symbols, charts, graphs, tables, diagrams, and models, to explain mathematical reasoning.		8-1, 8-5, 8-10, 8-13, 8-14
3.2 Note the method of deriving the solution and demonstrate a conceptual understanding of the derivation by solving similar problems.		8-9
3.3 Develop generalizations of the results obtained and apply them in other circumstances.		8-3, 8-7

* The symbol (🔑) indicates a key standard as designated in the Mathematics Framework for California Public Schools. Full statements of the California Content Standards are found at the beginning of this book following the Table of Contents.

LESSON 8-1

Plane Figures

California Content Standard *Measurement and Geometry 2.1( ): Identify, describe, and classify polygons (including pentagons, hexagons, and octagons).*

Warm-Up Review

Name the shape.

1. 

2. 

3. What comes next in the pattern?
△, ▽, △, ▽, ___, ___

4. A side of a rectangular picture frame measures 1 foot long. How long is this in inches?

Word Bank

plane figure
polygon
quadrilateral
pentagon
hexagon
octagon

Math Link You know how to identify a triangle, square, and rectangle. In this lesson, you will learn to identify other figures by looking at their sides and corners.

The **plane figures** below are all flat. These figures are also called **polygons**. They can be named by the number of sides and corners they have. A corner is where 2 sides meet.

Polygons

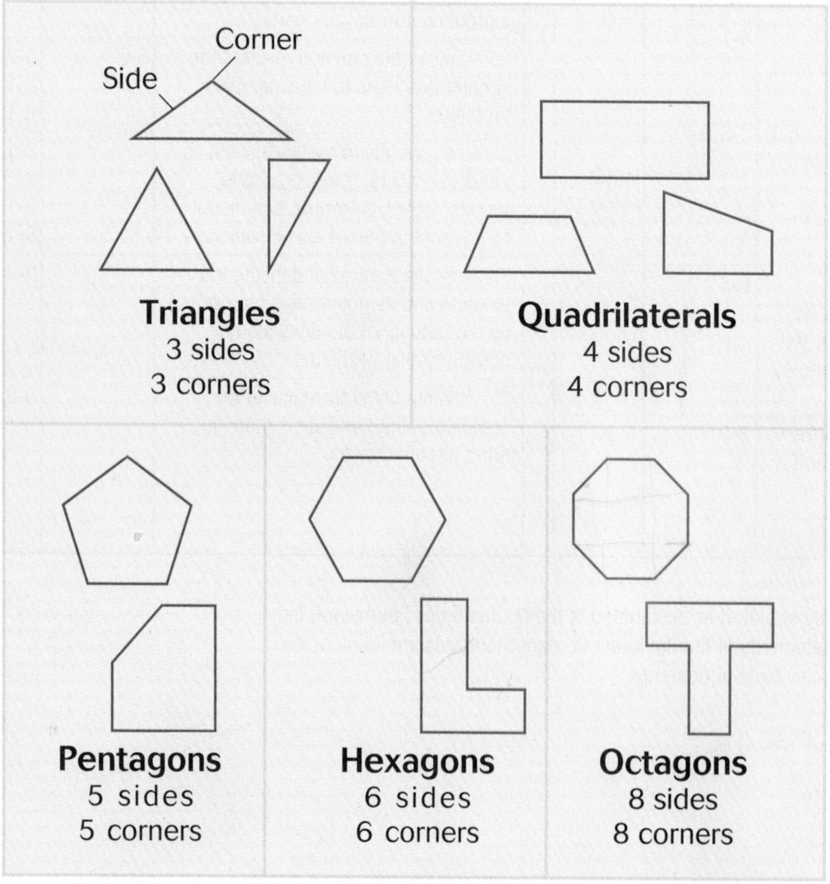

The number of sides and corners in a polygon are always the same.

 Additional Standard: Mathematical Reasoning 2.3 *(See p. 299.)*

Example 1

What is the name of the figure to the right?

Count the number of sides and corners.

It has 3 sides and 3 corners.

So, the figure is a triangle.

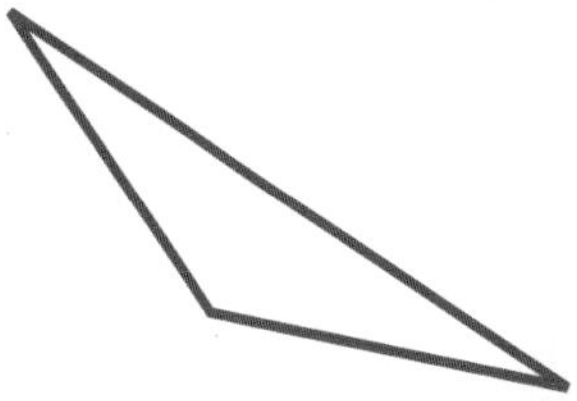

Example 2

What shape does the sign at the right look like?

Count the number of sides and corners.

It has 5 sides and 5 corners.

So, the shape of the sign looks like a pentagon.

Guided Practice *For another example, see Set A on p. 338.*

Name each figure.

1. 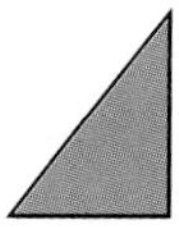

2. 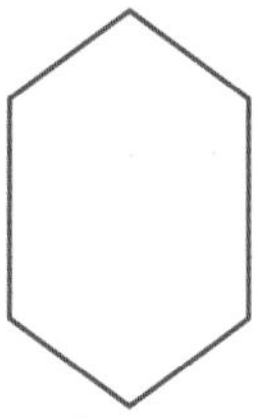

3. 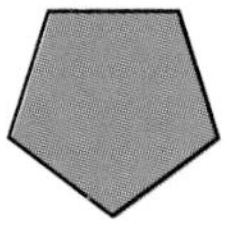

4. 

5. Look at the figure at the right.
What shapes do you see?

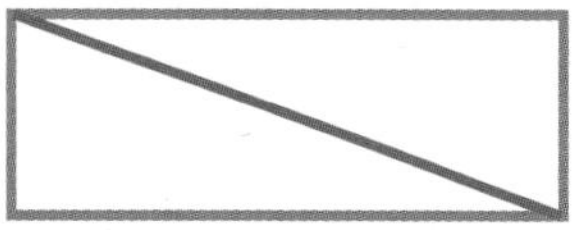

Independent Practice *For more practice, see Set A on p. 341.*

Name each figure.

6. 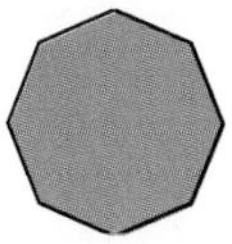

7. 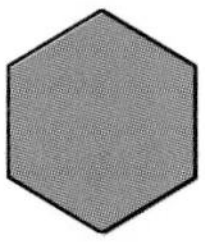

8. 

9. 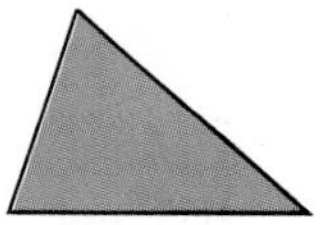

Name the shape of each object.

10. 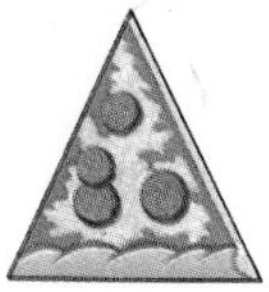

11. 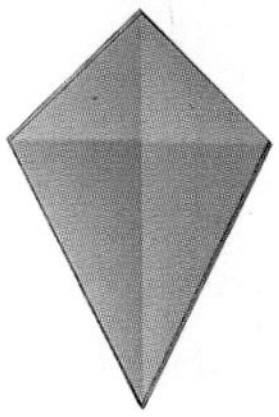

12. 

13. 

14. Many quilts use the same polygon over and over again. What polygon is in this quilt pattern?

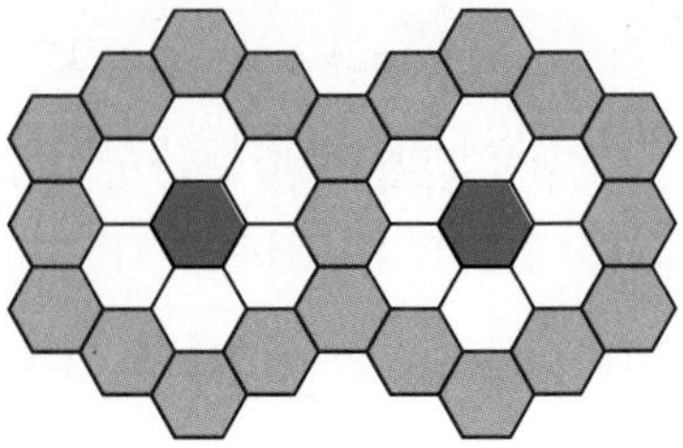

15. Sally's younger brother has a puzzle with pieces shaped like several different polygons. He has triangles, squares, rectangles, and pentagons. Which pieces are not quadrilaterals?

16. **Math Reasoning** George says, "A hexagon has 6 sides so I know that it also has 6 corners." Do you agree? Explain.

17. **Math Reasoning** Is a circle also a polygon? Explain.

Mixed Review

18. Jocelyn measured a rope and found that it was as long as 5 yardsticks. How many feet long was the rope?

19. Kim cut 200 small squares to make a quilt. She sewed 10 squares together to make a large rectangle. How many large rectangles can Kim make?

20. Randy bought 3 sheets of posterboard for $4. How much would he have to pay for 12 sheets of posterboard?

21. $70 \div 10$ **22.** $40 \div 10$ **23.** $620 + 332$ **24.** $8 + 400 + 39$

Algebra Find each missing number.

25. $5 \times ■ = 50$ **26.** $42 \div ■ = 7$ **27.** $18 \div ■ = 6$ **28.** $■ \times 6 = 36$

Test Prep Choose the correct letter for each answer.

29. (3-4) How many quarts are there in one gallon?

A 2 quarts
B 4 quarts
C 6 quarts
D 8 quarts
E NH

30. (4-9) A cup of yogurt costs $1. How much do 8 cups of yogurt cost?

F $0
G $1
H $8
J $8.10
K NH

 Use Homework Workbook 8-1.

LESSON 8-2

Lines, Segments, Rays, and Angles

California Content Standards *Measurement and Geometry 2.4: Identify right angles in geometric figures or in appropriate objects and determine whether other angles are greater or less than a right angle. Also, Measurement and Geometry 2.0* *(See p. 299.)*

Warm-Up Review

Tell the number of corners each figure has.

1. 

2. 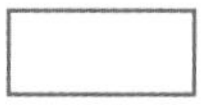

3. I have more sides than a rectangle. I have fewer corners than a hexagon. What shape am I?

Math Link You know how to identify plane figures. Now you will learn how to identify other types of geometric figures.

Word Bank

line
line segment
ray
parallel lines
intersecting lines
angle
right angle
acute angle
obtuse angle

Below are some geometric terms used in this chapter.

Line

straight path that goes on and on in both directions

Line segment

part of a line with two endpoints

Ray

part of a line with one endpoint that goes on and on in one direction

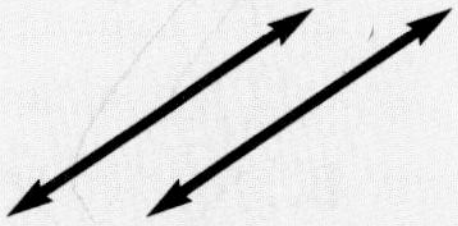

Parallel lines

lines that do not cross

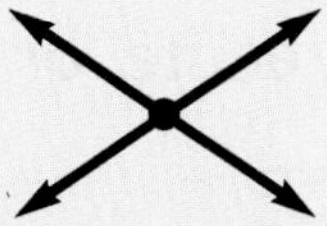

Intersecting lines

lines that cross at one point

An **angle** is formed when two rays meet. Below are three types of angles.

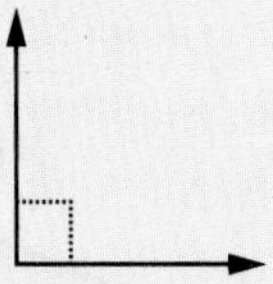

Right angle

angle that forms a square corner

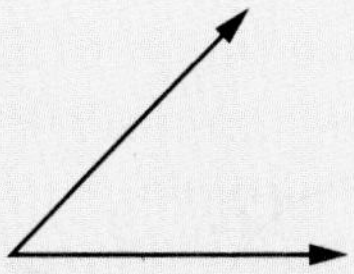

Acute angle

angle that is less than a right angle

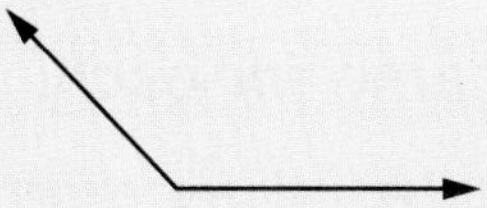

Obtuse angle

angle that is greater than a right angle

Example 1

Name the type of lines shown at the right.

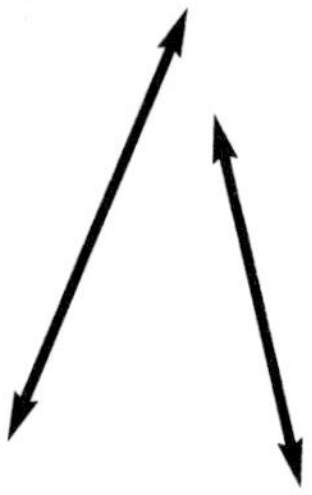

Remember that lines go on and on in both directions

If these two lines were extended, they would cross at one point.

So, these are intersecting lines.

Example 2

What kind of angle is shown in the picture at the right?

The angle forms a square corner.

So, it is a right angle.

Guided Practice *For another example, see Set B on p. 338.*

Write the name for each.

1. 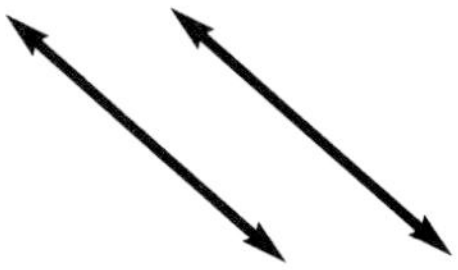

2. 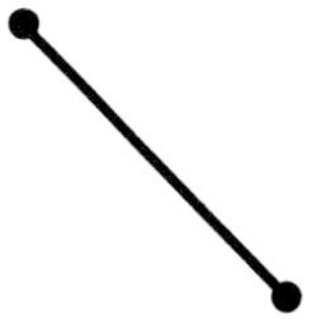

3. 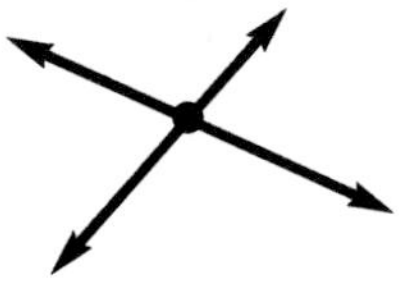

4. 

Name each angle as right, acute, or obtuse.

5. 

6. 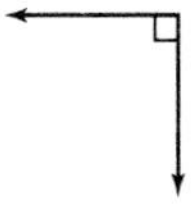

7. 

8. 

9. How many right angles are in a rectangle?

Independent Practice *For more practice, see Set B on p. 341.*

Write the name for each.

10. 

11. 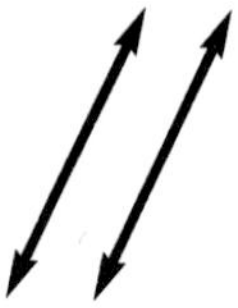

12. 

13. 

Name each angle as right, acute, or obtuse.

14. 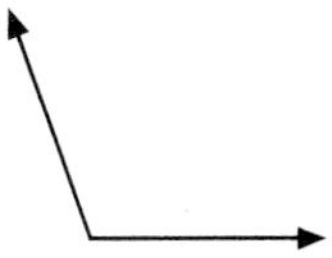

15. 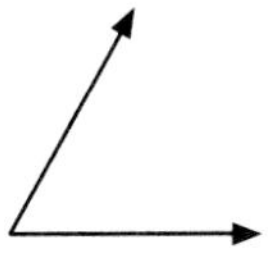

16. 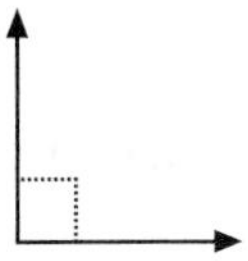

17. 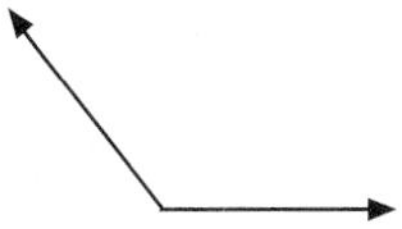

18. What kind of angle do the hands on the clock show?

19. What kind of angle will the hands on the clock show in 2 hours?

20. Name a time when the hands on a clock form a right angle.

21. Name a time when the hands on a clock form a line.

Mixed Review

22. You have a circle, a square, and a triangle. In how many ways can you arrange them in a row?

Name each figure.

23. 

24. 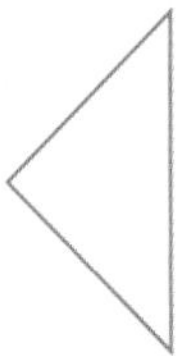

25. 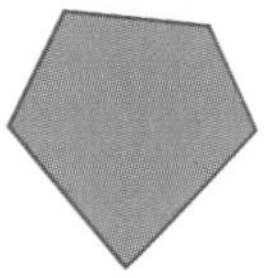

26. 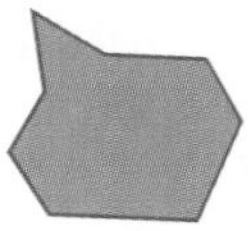

Algebra Find each missing number.

27. 50 ÷ ■ = 5 **28.** 24 ÷ ■ = 3 **29.** ■ ÷ 2 = 5

Test Prep Choose the correct letter for each answer.

30. (5-2) There are 8 rows of chairs with 6 chairs in each row. How many chairs are there in all?

A 14 chairs **B** 33 chairs **C** 48 chairs **D** 56 chairs

31. (2-7) Which is the best estimate of 98 − 52?

F 30 **G** 40 **H** 50 **J** 60 **K** NH

LESSON 8-3

Classifying Triangles Using Angles

Warm-Up Review

Name each angle as right, acute, or obtuse.

1. 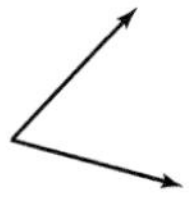

2. 

3. What kind of angles does a square have?

California Content Standard *Measurement and Geometry 2.2():*
Identify attributes of triangles (e.g., . . . right angle for the right triangle.)

Math Link In this lesson, you will use what you know about different types of angles to classify triangles.

Word Bank
right triangle
acute triangle
obtuse triangle

Triangles can be named by the kinds of angles that they have. Three different types of triangles are shown below.

Right triangle
one right angle

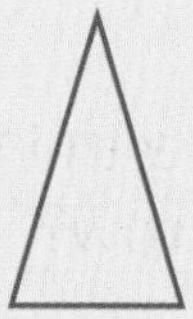

Acute triangle
three acute angles

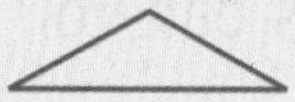

Obtuse triangle
one obtuse angle

Example 1

At the right, three California cities are connected by line segments that form a triangle. Name the triangle.

The triangle has one obtuse angle.

So, it is an obtuse triangle.

Example 2

What type of triangle is shown at the right?

The triangle has three acute angles. So, it is an acute triangle.

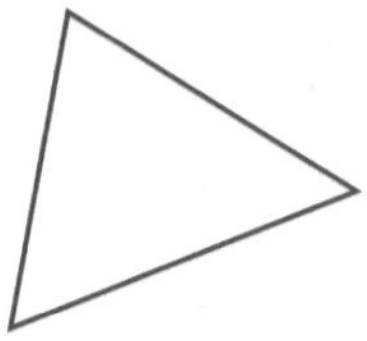

Additional Standards: Measurement and Geometry 2.4; Mathematical Reasoning 3.3 (See p. 299.)

Guided Practice *For another example, see Set C on p. 338.*

Name each triangle as right, acute, or obtuse.

1. 

2. 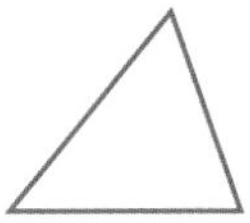

3. 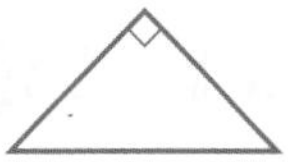

4. Math Reasoning A triangle has only two acute angles. Is this an acute triangle? Why or why not?

Independent Practice *For more practice, see Set C on p. 341.*

Name each triangle as right, acute, or obtuse.

5. 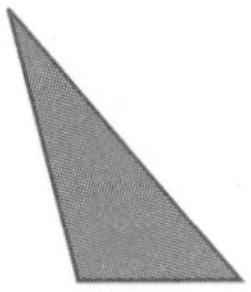

6. 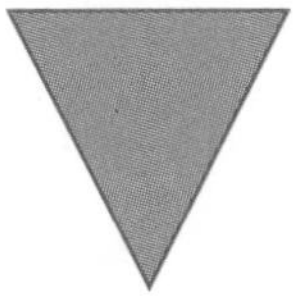

7. 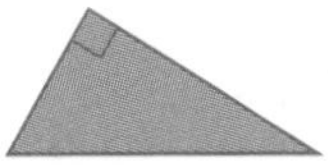

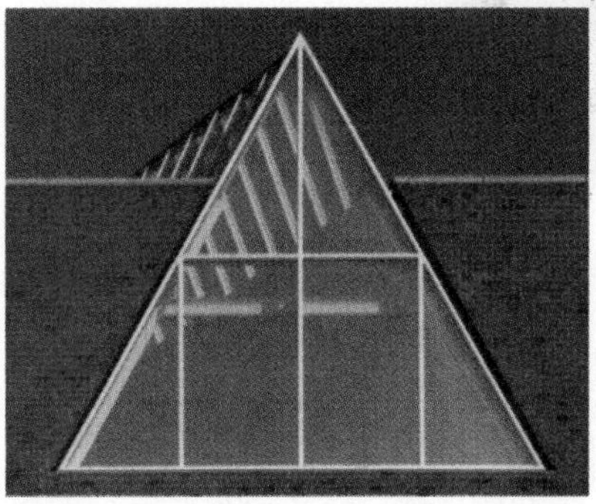

8. Are there any obtuse triangles in the photograph at the right? any acute angles?

9. How many right triangles can you find in the photograph?

Mixed Review

10. Algebra Find the missing number. 3,000 + ■ + 5 = 3,025

Name each angle.

11. 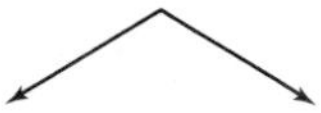

12. 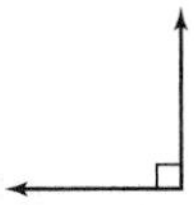

Name each figure.

13. 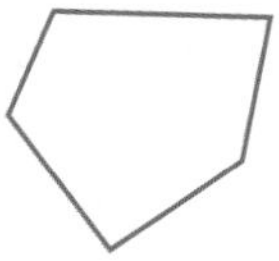

14. 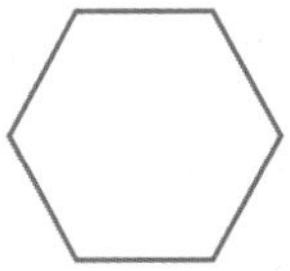

Test Prep **Choose the correct letter for each answer.**

15. Jack had 12 pennies, 3 dimes, and 2 quarters. How much money did he have?
(1-8)

A $0.55 **B** $0.92 **C** $1.02 **D** $1.32

16. Which is the best estimate for the length of a bed?
(3-3)

F 6 inches **G** 6 feet **H** 6 yards **J** 6 miles

LESSON 8-4

Classifying Triangles Using Sides

Warm-Up Review

Are all the sides of the shapes the same length?

1. 

2. 

3. How many obtuse angles does an obtuse triangle have?

California Content Standard *Measurement and Geometry 2.2(🔑): Identify attributes of triangles (e.g., two equal sides for the isosceles triangle, three equal sides for the equilateral triangle. . .).*

Math Link You know how to name a triangle by the types of angles it has. In this lesson, you will learn another way to name a triangle.

Word Bank

- equilateral triangle
- isosceles triangle
- scalene triangle

You can name the triangles by the lengths of their sides.

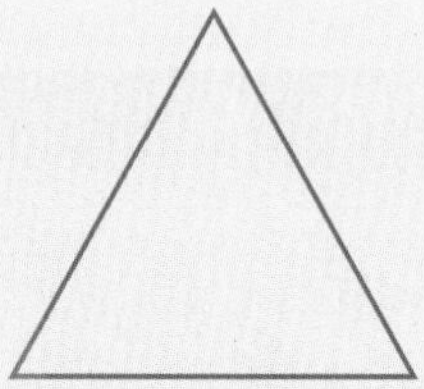	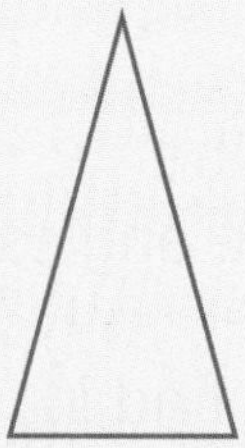	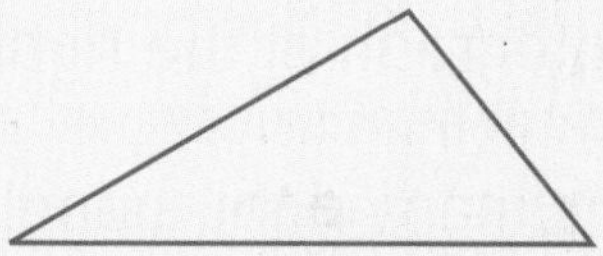
Equilateral triangle	**Isosceles triangle**	**Scalene triangle**
All sides are the same length.	At least two sides are the same length.	No sides are the same length.

Example

The photograph at the right shows triominos. Name the triangle outlined in purple as equilateral, isosceles, or scalene.

Each side of the triangle is the same length.

So, it is an equilateral triangle.

Guided Practice *For another example, see Set D on p. 338.*

Name each triangle as equilateral, isosceles, or scalene.

1. 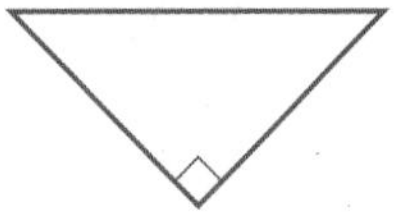

2. 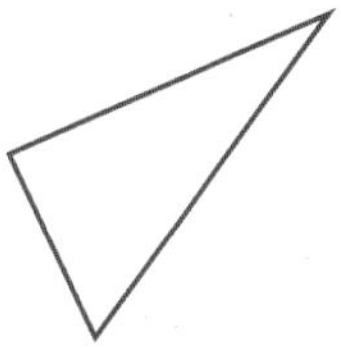

3. 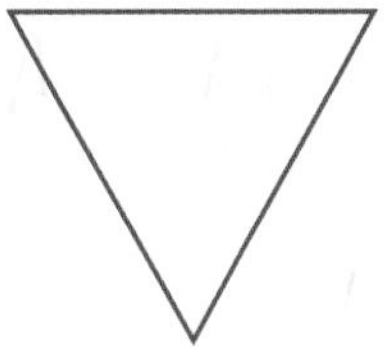

4. Two sides of an equilateral triangle each measure 5 inches long. How long is the third side?

Independent Practice *For more practice, see Set D on p. 341.*

Name each triangle as equilateral, isosceles, or scalene.

5. 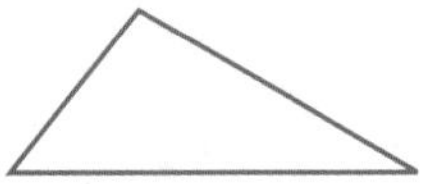

6. 

7. 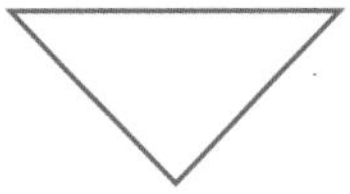

8. Look at the isosceles triangle at the right. What is the length of the third side?

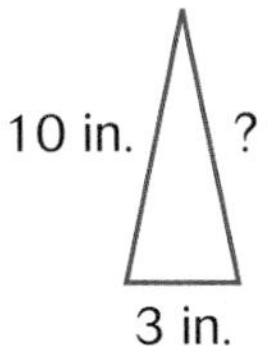

Mixed Review

9. A company has a triangle in its logo. Two of the angles are acute and one is obtuse. Is the triangle right, acute, or obtuse?

Name the angle or triangle as right, acute, or obtuse.

10. 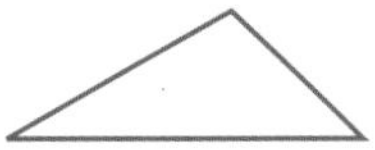

11. 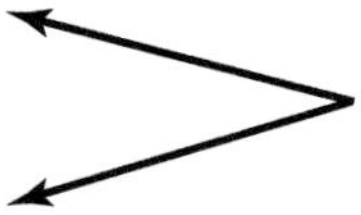

12. 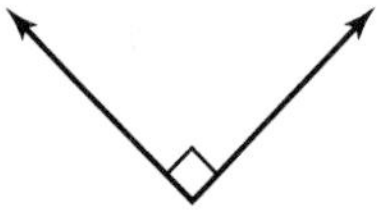

13. 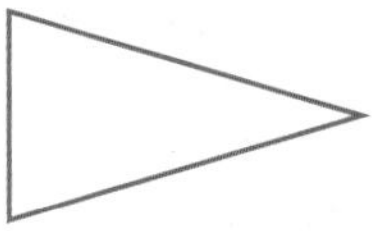

Test Prep Choose the correct letter for each answer.

14. Which multiplication fact describes the array?
(4-2)

A 3×5 **B** 4×4 **C** 4×5 **D** 3×4

15. There were 5 party favors in all for 5 guests. Each guest got the same number of favors. How many favors did each guest get?
(6-8)

F 0 favors **G** 2 favors **H** 1 favor **J** 5 favors

LESSON 8-5

Quadrilaterals

California Content Standard *Measurement and Geometry 2.3(🔑): Identify attributes of quadrilaterals (e.g., parallel sides for the parallelogram, right angles for the rectangle, equal sides and right angles for the square).*

Warm-Up Review

How many sides does each figure have?

1. 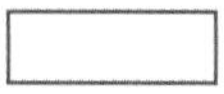
2. 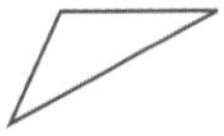

3. What type of lines are shown below?

Word Bank

parallelogram
rhombus

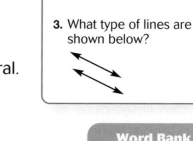

Math Link You know how to identify a quadrilateral. Now you will learn about special types of quadrilaterals.

You can name the quadrilaterals by the lengths of their sides and the sizes of their angles.

There are two pairs of parallel sides. Opposite sides are the same length.

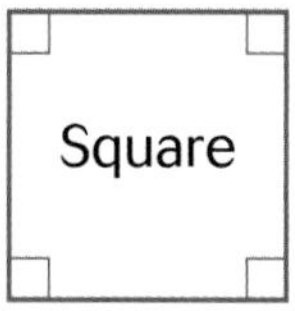

All sides are the same length. Opposite sides are parallel. There are four right angles.

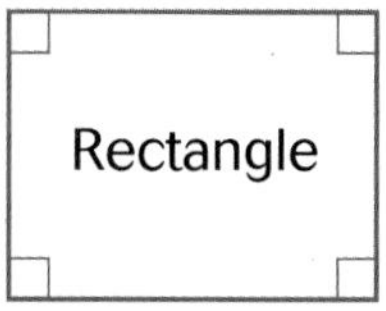

Opposite sides are the same length and parallel. There are four right angles.

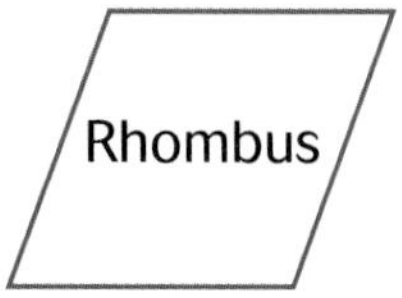

There are two pairs of parallel sides. All the sides are the same length.

Example

Name the quadrilateral shown.

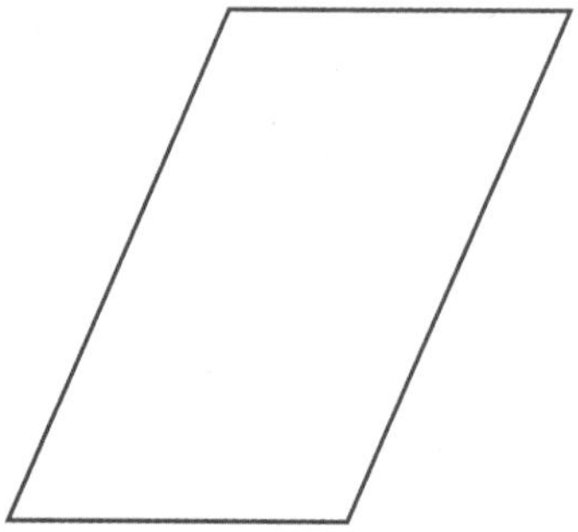

The figure has opposite sides that are the same length and parallel.

The figure has no right angles, so it is not a square or rectangle.

Its sides are not all the same length, so it is not a rhombus.

So, it is a parallelogram.

 Additional Standard: Mathematical Reasoning 2.3 *(See p. 299.)*

Guided Practice *For another example, see Set E on p. 339.*

Name each quadrilateral.

1. 

2. 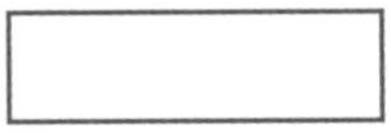

3. 

4. 

5. How do you know that the figure at the right is a rhombus? Explain.

Independent Practice *For more practice, see Set E on p. 342.*

Name each quadrilateral.

6. 

7. 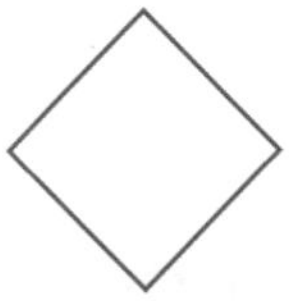

8. 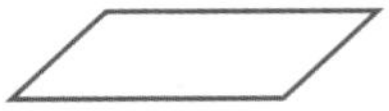

9. 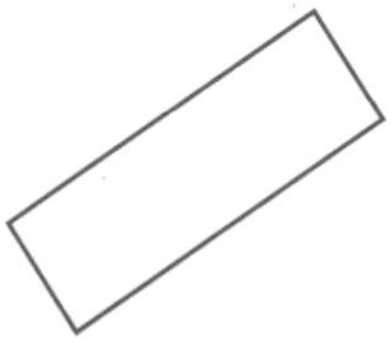

10. Greg hit a home run at the baseball game. The distance between each of the bases is 90 feet. What quadrilateral did Greg make when he ran around the bases?

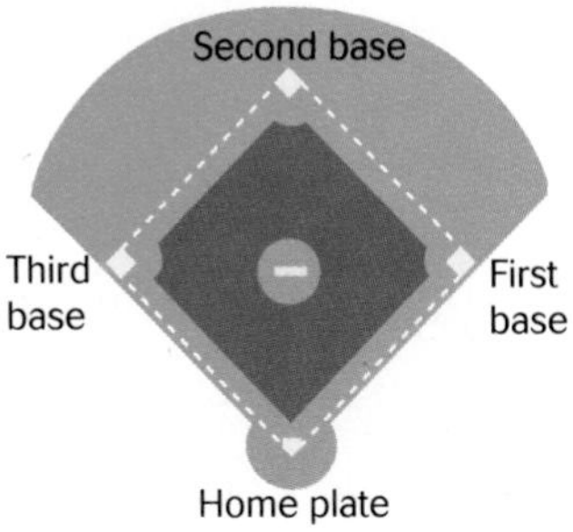

11. Math Reasoning Can a quadrilateral be both a square and a rectangle? Explain your answer.

Mixed Review

12. Two sides of an isosceles triangle measure 5 inches and 7 inches long. How long could the third side be?

13. I have 3 corners, 3 sides, and 3 acute angles. What shape am I?

Test Prep Choose the correct letter for each answer.

14. $4 \times 5 \times 2 =$
(5-9)

A 11
B 20
C 28
D 40
E NH

15. $503 - 394 =$
(2-8)

F 109
G 119
H 209
J 897
K NH

LESSON 8-6

Understand
Plan
Solve
Look Back

Problem-Solving Skill:
Spatial Reasoning

Warm-Up Review

1. How many sides does a quadrilateral have?
2. Is the triangle at the right equilateral, isosceles, or scalene?

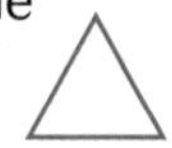

3. Carrots are sold in bunches of 6. How many carrots are in 5 bunches?

California Content Standards *Mathematical Reasoning 1.1: Analyze problems by identifying relationships . . . and observing patterns. Also, Mathematical Reasoning 1.2, 2.2 (See p. 299.)*

Read for Understanding

James looked at the figure at the right. Then he showed it to Annie and told her that there are 16 squares in it. Annie looked at the figure and said she could see more than 16 squares.

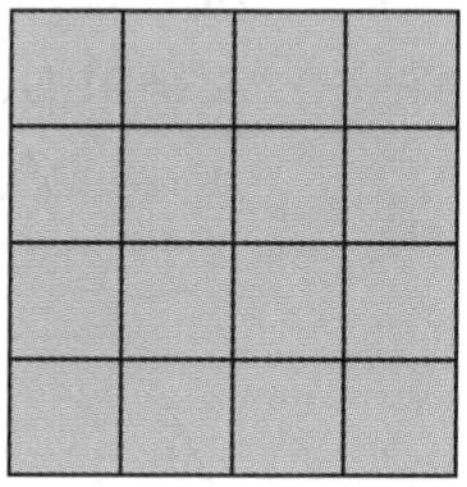

1. How many squares did James see in the figure?
2. How many squares did Annie see?

Think and Discuss

MATH FOCUS

Spatial Reasoning

If you look at a figure carefully, sometimes you can find geometric shapes and patterns. These shapes and patterns may be able to help you solve problems.

Look again at the figure at the top of the page.

3. How many squares of this size can you find?

4. How many squares of this size can you find?

5. How many squares of this size can you find?

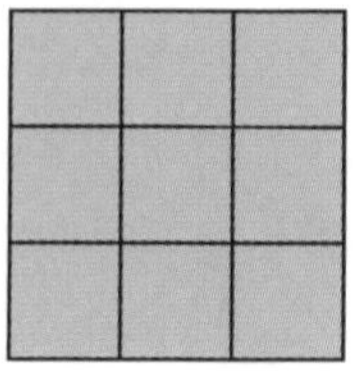

6. What is the biggest square you can find?
7. How many squares can you find in the figure?

Guided Practice

Use the figure at the right for Exercises 1–3.

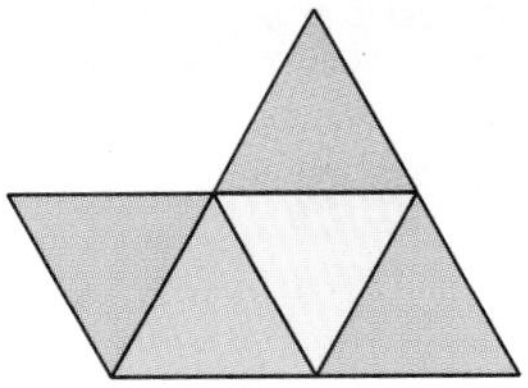

1. How many triangles are there in the design?

   a. 6

   b. 7

   c. 5

2. How many quadrilaterals are there in the design?

   a. 6

   b. 9

   c. 8

3. Which of these shows the above design from a different position?

   a. 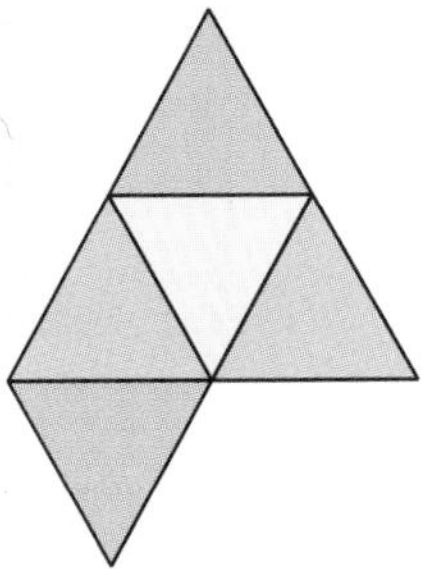 **b.** 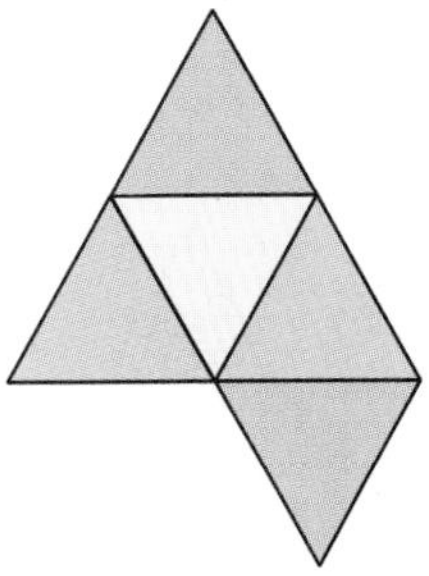 **c.** 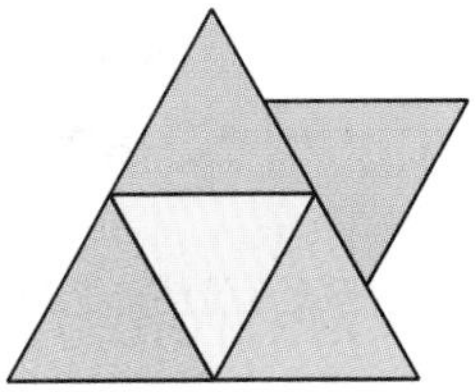

Independent Practice

Use the figure at the right for Exercises 4–7.

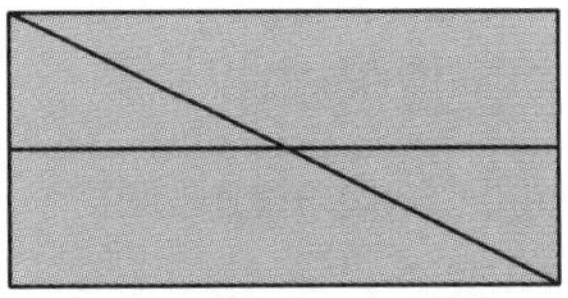

4. How many rectangles are there in the design?

   a. 4

   b. 3

   c. 5

5. How many triangles are there in the design?

   a. 2

   b. 5

   c. 4

6. How may triangles share the upper left corner of the figure?

   a. 2

   b. 3

   c. 4

7. How many rectangles share the left edge of the figure?

   a. 3

   b. 4

   c. 5

8. **Math Reasoning** Henna says she can make 9 rectangles with 6 craft sticks. Draw a picture to show how she could do it.

LESSON 8-7

Congruent Figures

California Content Standard *Measurement and Geometry 3.3, Grade 4: Identify congruent figures.*

Math Link You know how to identify different types of polygons. Now you will learn to identify polygons that are the same size and shape.

Warm-Up Review

1. Are both figures squares?

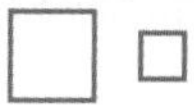

2. Are both figures obtuse triangles?

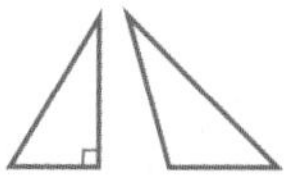

3. Jim mows 2 lawns each weekday. He mows 6 lawns each weekend day. How many lawns does he mow each week?

Figures with the same size and shape are called **congruent**.

Word Bank

congruent

Example 1

Look at this potato stamp design. Are the two stars made from this stamp congruent?

You may be able to tell just by looking at the stars whether or not they are congruent.

If not, you could trace one of the stars and place the tracing over the other star.

If it fits exactly, the stars are congruent.

Since the stars are the same size and shape, they are congruent.

More Examples

Are the figures in each pair congruent?

A.

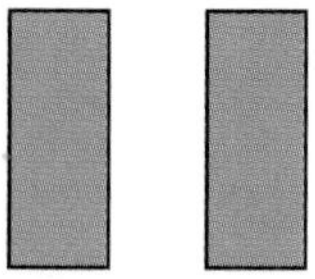

Congruent

B.

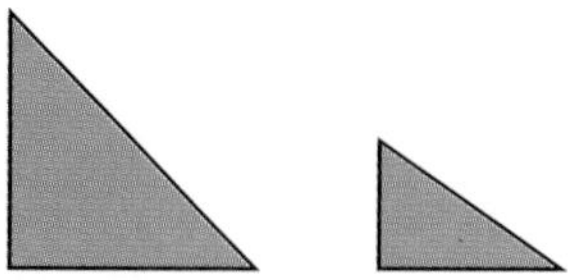

Not congruent

C.

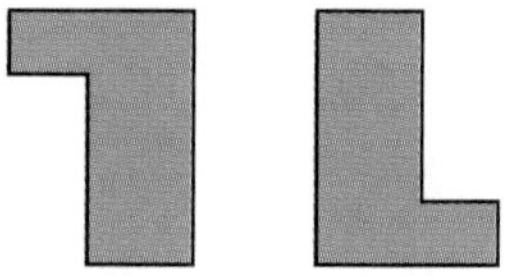

Congruent

 Additional Standard: Mathematical Reasoning 3.3 (See p. 299.)

Guided Practice *For another example, see Set F on p. 339.*

Are the figures in each pair congruent?

1. 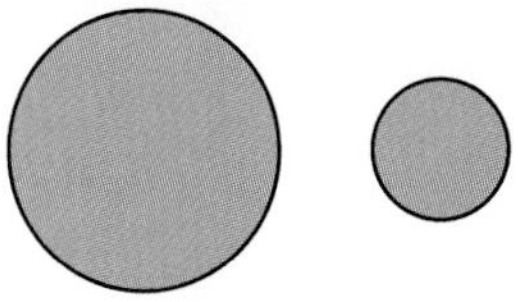

2. 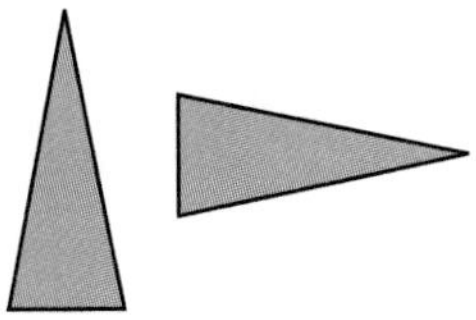

3. 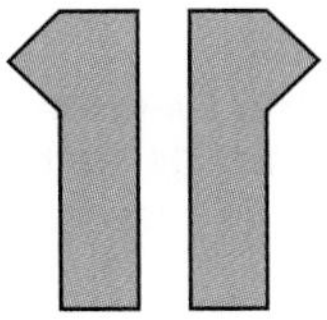

4. The square at the right is divided into two triangles. Are the triangles congruent?

Independent Practice *For more practice, see Set F on p. 342.*

Are the figures in each pair congruent?

5. 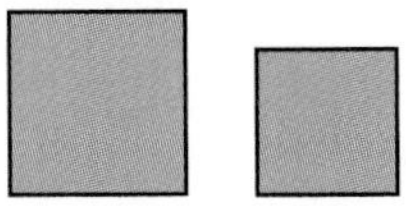

6. 

7. 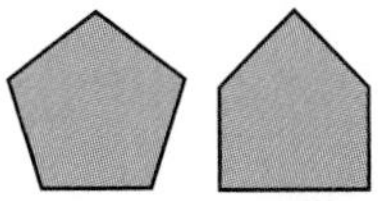

8. Math Reasoning Could a triangle and square ever be congruent? Explain your answer.

Mixed Review

9. Which of the figures at the right is a parallelogram?

A 

B 

Name each triangle as equilateral, isosceles, or scalene.

10. 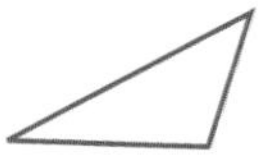

11. 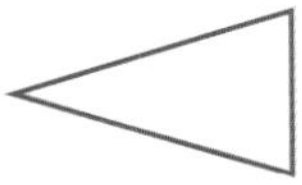

12. 

Algebra **Find each missing number.**

13. $3 \times ■ = 15$ **14.** $12 \div ■ = 4$ **15.** $22 - ■ = 15$

Test Prep **Choose the correct letter for each answer.**

16. $5 \times 10 =$
(4-5)

A 5 **B** 10 **C** 100 **D** 500 **E** NH

17. Which number is the least?
(1-5)

F 2,451 **G** 3,074 **H** 2,186 **J** 2,500 **K** NH

LESSON 8-8

Slides, Flips, and Turns

Warm-Up Review

Are the figures in each pair congruent?

1. 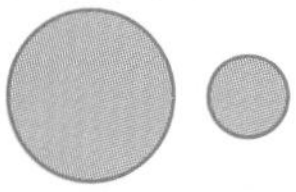

2. 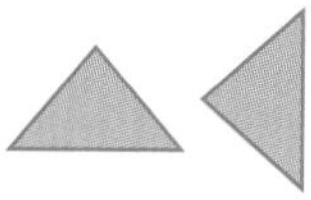

3. 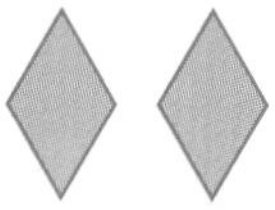

California Content Standard *Measurement and Geometry 2.0: Students describe and compare the attributes of plane . . . figures and use their understanding to show relationships and solve problems.*

Math Link You know how to identify congruent figures. Now you will learn different ways to move congruent figures.

Here are three different ways to move a figure.

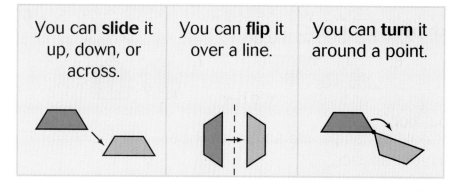

You can **slide** it up, down, or across.	You can **flip** it over a line.	You can **turn** it around a point.
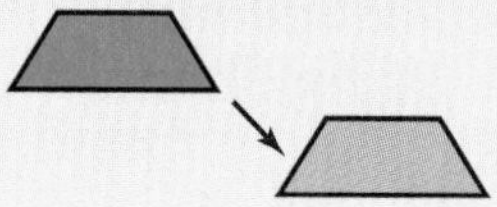	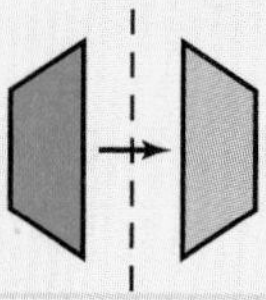	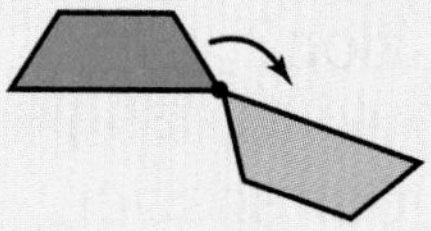

Word Bank

slide
flip
turn

In each box above, notice that the pair of figures is congruent.

Example

Does the diagram at the right show a slide, flip, or turn?

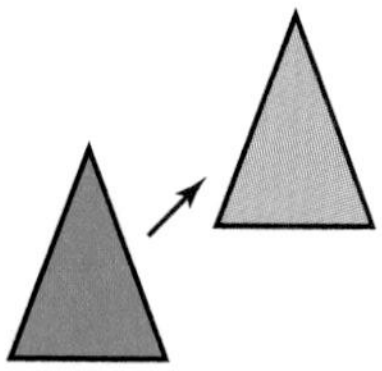

Compare the position of the two triangles.

The darker-colored triangle was moved up and over to a new position.

So, the diagram shows a slide.

Guided Practice *For another example, see Set G on p. 339.*

Write slide, flip, or turn for each diagram.

1. 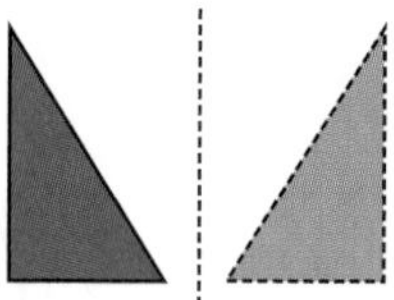

2. 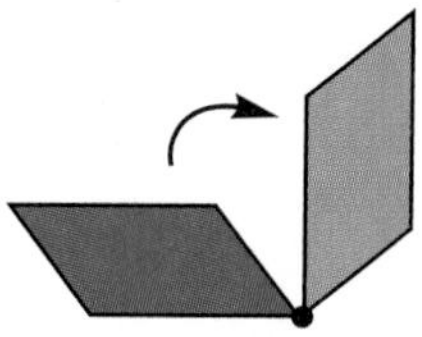

3. 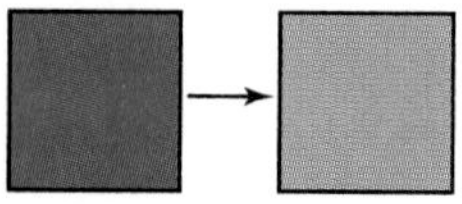

Independent Practice *For more practice, see Set G on p. 342.*

Write slide, flip, or turn for each diagram.

4. 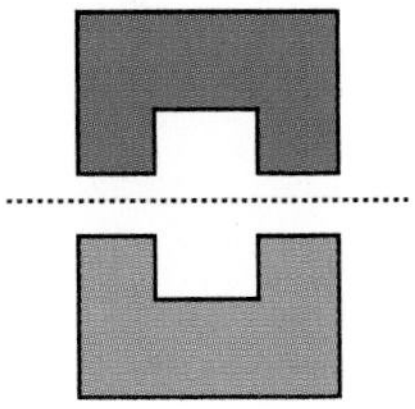

5. 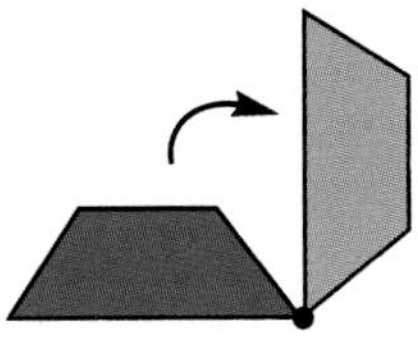

6. 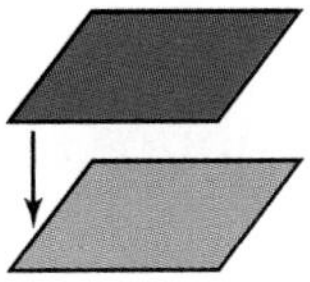

Use the diagram at the right for Exercises 7 and 8.

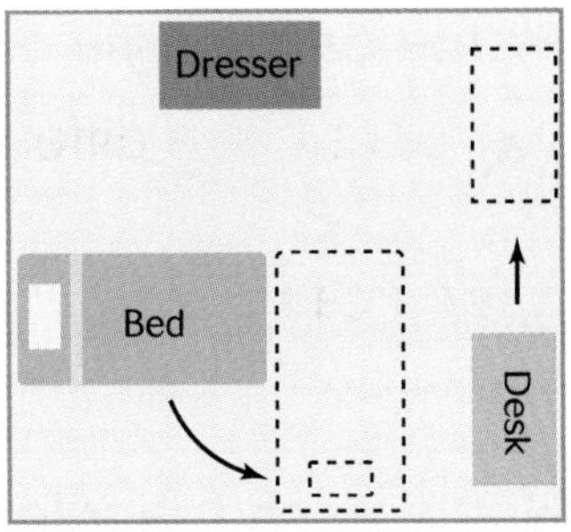

7. Muriel is rearranging her bedroom furniture. She wants to move her bed as shown. Will she use a flip, turn, or slide to move her bed to the new position?

8. Will Muriel use a slide, flip, or turn to move her desk to the new position?

Mixed Review

9. Are the figures at the right congruent?

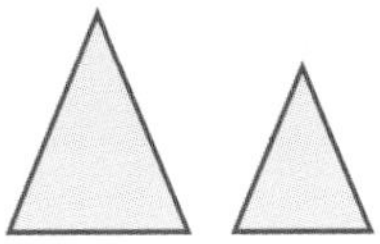

Name each quadrilateral.

10. 

11. 

12. 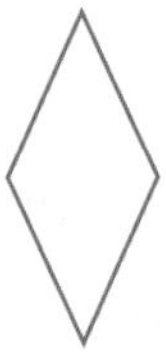

13. 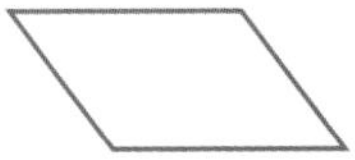

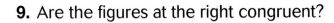

Test Prep Choose the correct letter for each answer.

14. (7-1) **Algebra** What is the missing number?

Input	12	24	30	42
Output	2	4	5	■

A 6

B 7

C 8

D 9

15. (1-1) What is the standard form for three thousand, six hundred twelve?

F 1,326

G 3,612

H 3,621

J 6,312

K NH

Diagnostic Checkpoint

Name each figure.

1. (8-1) 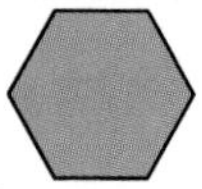

2. (8-1) 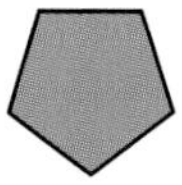

3. (8-5) 

Name each angle or triangle as right, acute, or obtuse.

4. (8-2) 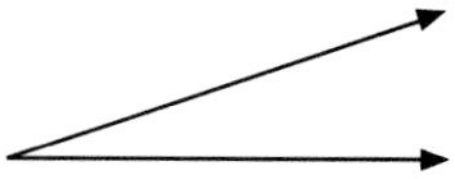

5. (8-3) 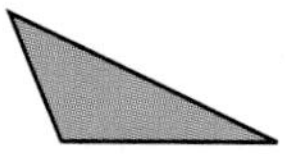

6. (8-3) 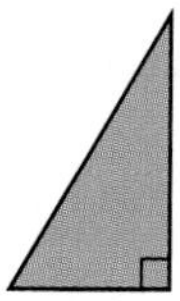

Name each triangle as equilateral, isosceles, or scalene.

7. (8-4) 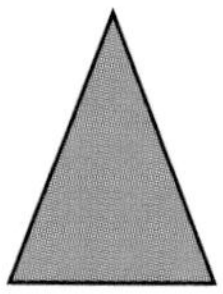

8. (8-4) 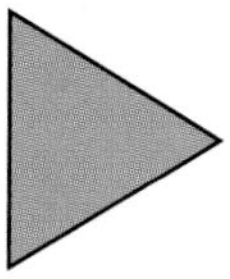

9. (8-4) 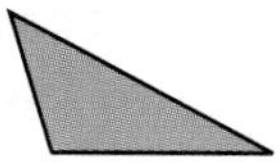

Are the figures in each pair congruent?

10. (8-7) 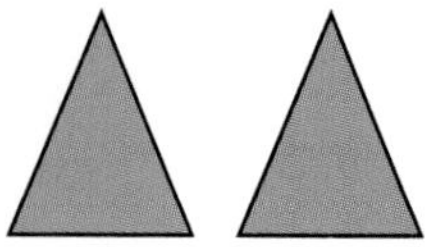

11. (8-7) 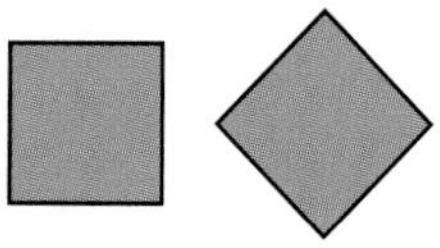

12. (8-7) 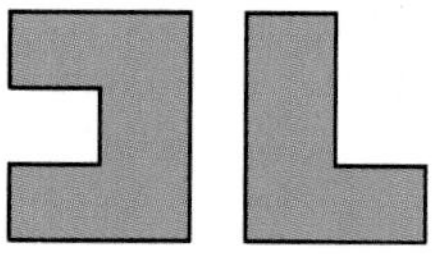

Write slide, flip, or turn for each diagram.

13. (8-8) 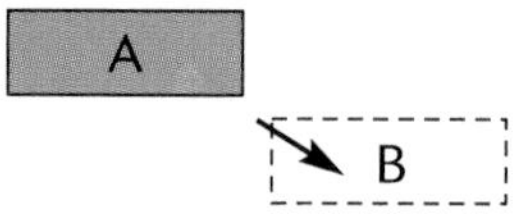

14. (8-8) 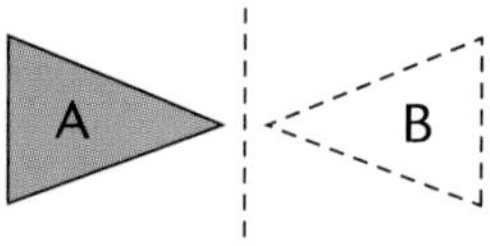

15. (8-8) 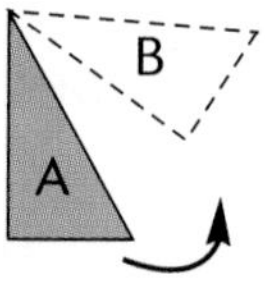

16. (8-6) How many triangles can you find in the shape at the right?

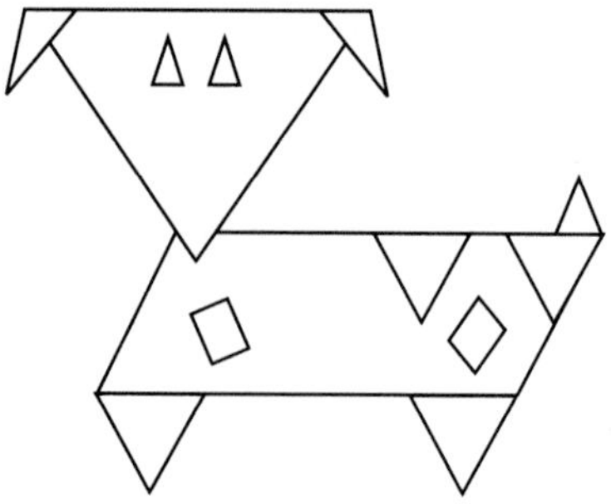

TEST PREP

Multiple-Choice Cumulative Review

Choose the correct letter for each answer.

1. What is the value of 6 in 326,479?

A 6 hundreds
B 6 thousands
C 6 ten-thousands
D 6 hundred-thousands

2. Terran delivers newspapers to earn extra spending money. She has already delivered 53 of the 98 papers she delivers each morning. How many more newspapers must she deliver today?

F 45
G 53
H 98
J 151

3. Which number makes this sentence true?

37 + ■ = 46

A 9 **C** 46
B 11 **D** 83

4. Which number sentence belongs in the same family of facts as $3 \times 7 = 21$?

F $21 - 3 = 18$
G $21 - 7 = 14$
H $21 \div 7 = 3$
J $21 + 7 = 28$

5.

$$\begin{array}{r} 563 \\ -\ 97 \\ \hline \end{array}$$

A 463 **C** 534
B 466 **D** 660

6. What is the missing number in the number pattern?

15, 20, 25, ■, 35, 40

F 28 **H** 30
G 29 **J** 31

7. Which names the same number as $17 + 6 + 12$?

A $1 + 7 + 6 + 12$
B $17 - 6 + 12$
C $17 + 12 + 6$
D $17 + 1 + 2 + 6$

8.

$$\begin{array}{r} 623 \\ +\ 158 \\ \hline \end{array}$$

F 465 **J** 781
G 681 **K** NH
H 771

9. The sides of a square are each 3 feet long. Find the perimeter.

A 3 feet **C** 9 feet
B 6 feet **D** 12 feet

LESSON 8-9

Understand
Plan
Solve
Look Back

Problem-Solving Strategy:
Find a Pattern

California Content Standards *Mathematical Reasoning 1.1: Analyze problems by . . . observing patterns. Also, Algebra and Functions 2.2 (See p. 299.)*

Warm-Up Review

Complete each pattern.

1. 19, 21, 23, ■, ■
2. 75, 80, 85, ■, ■
3. 100, 80, 60, ■, ■
4. Which numbers between 54 and 64 are odd?

Becky is making a necklace. Look at the beads she has put on the necklace so far. If she continues the pattern, what color will the 20th bead be?

Understand

What do you need to know?

You need to know the order in which the colored beads are put on the necklace.

Plan

How can you solve the problem?

You can **find a pattern** by looking at how the beads have been put on the necklace. Then continue the pattern up to the 20th bead.

Solve

Becky puts on 1 bead of each color, then 2 beads of each color, and then 3 beads of each color. She always puts the colors in the same order.

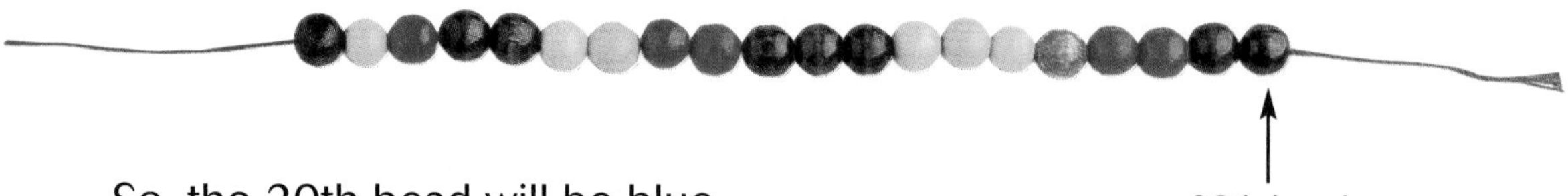

So, the 20th bead will be blue.

Look Back

If the beads were not put on in a pattern, could you still tell what color the 20th bead would be? Explain.

 Additional Standards: Mathematical Reasoning 2.2, 3.2 (See p. 299.)

Guided Practice

1. Daniel drew the pattern shown at the right. Draw the next two figures in the pattern.

2. Tom wrote the numbers 3, 6, 9, 12, and 15. If he continues the pattern, what are the next five numbers Tom should write?

Independent Practice

3. Nadine made the pattern at the right using plane figures. Draw the next four figures in the pattern.

4. Ms. Martin gave her students a number pattern. She said, "5, 10, 8, 13, 11, 16, 14." What are the next six numbers in her pattern?

5. Ellie wrote the following letters: A B B C D A B B C D A B B C D A B B. If she continues the pattern, what will the next four letters be?

Mixed Review

Try these or other strategies to solve each problem. Tell which strategy you used.

Problem-Solving Strategies

- *Work Backward*
- *Make a Table*
- *Make a List*
- *Write a Number Sentence*

6. Wendy recorded the number of shapes she found in the classroom. How many more squares than triangles did she find?

Shape	Number Found
Circle	𝍸 IIII
Triangle	𝍸 𝍸 I
Square	𝍸 𝍸 II

7. Amy went shopping for a new ski hat. The hats came in small, medium, or large. She had a choice of blue or red in any size. How many different size and color combinations did Amy have to choose from?

LESSON 8-10

Perimeter

California Content Standard *Measurement and Geometry 1.3(🔑): Find the perimeter of a polygon with integer sides.*

Warm-Up Review

1. 5 + 5 + 5 + 5 =
2. 30 + 15 + 30 + 15 =
3. 25 + 18 + 25 =
4. How many sides does a hexagon have?
5. Mark is 54 inches tall. Randy is 2 inches taller than Mark. How tall is Randy?

Word Bank

perimeter

Math Link You have learned that plane figures come in many shapes and sizes. In this lesson, you will learn how to find the distance around a plane figure.

The distance around a figure is called its **perimeter**.

Example 1

Luis wants to put a fence around his vegetable garden shown at the right. How much fencing should he buy?

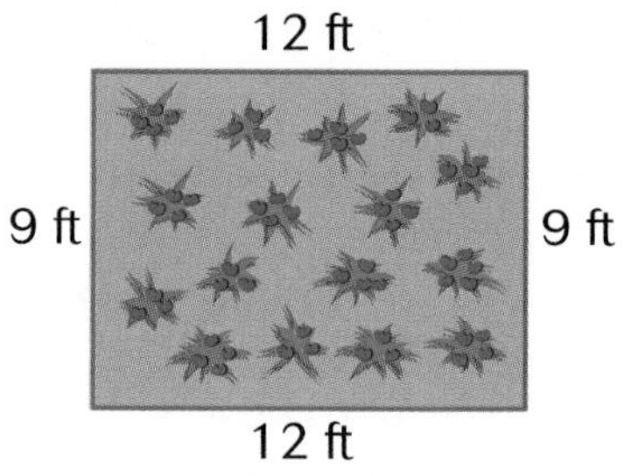

He needs to know the perimeter of his garden in order to determine how much fencing he should buy. To find the perimeter of his garden, add the length of the sides.

9 + 12 + 9 + 12 = 42 ft

So, Luis should buy 42 feet of fencing.

Example 2

Find the perimeter of the pentagon at the right.

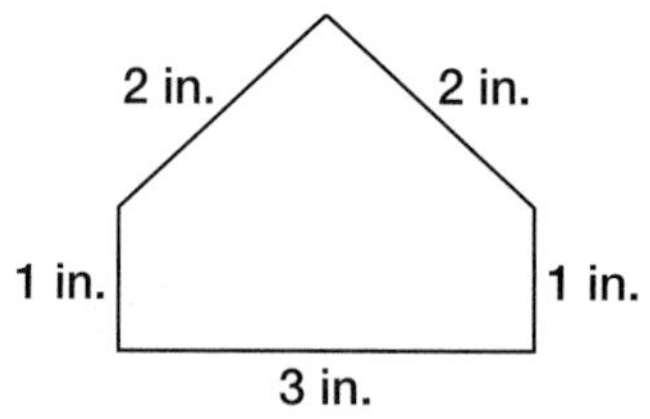

Add the lengths of the sides.
1 + 2 + 2 + 1 + 3 = 9 in.

So, the perimeter of the pentagon is 9 inches.

Guided Practice *For another example, see Set H on p. 340.*

Find the perimeter of each figure.

1.

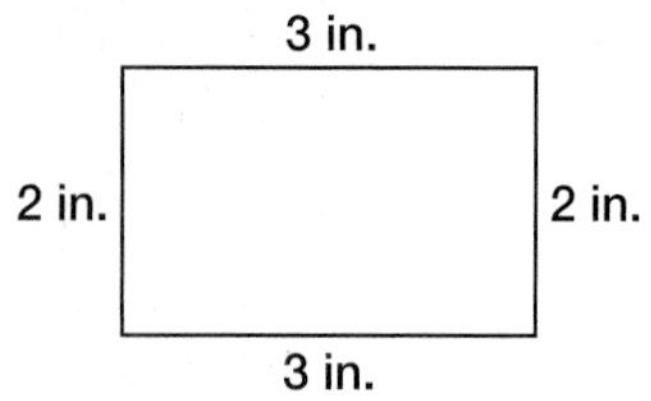

2.

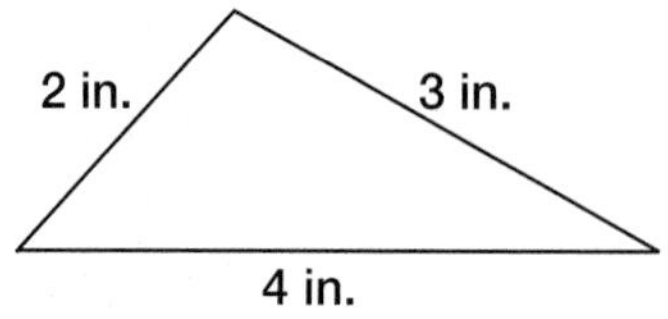

3.

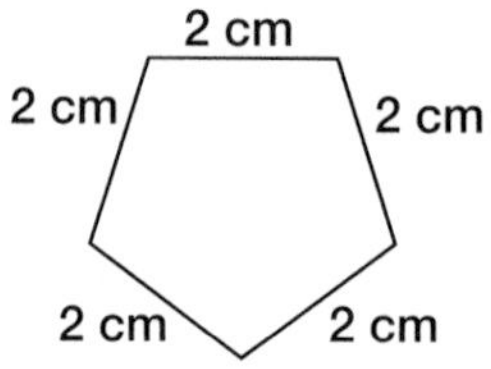

 Additional Standard: Mathematical Reasoning 2.3 (See p. 299.)

4. Lenny made a square picture. One side is 14 inches long. What is the perimeter of the picture?

Independent Practice *For more practice, see Set H on p. 343.*

Find the perimeter of each figure.

5. 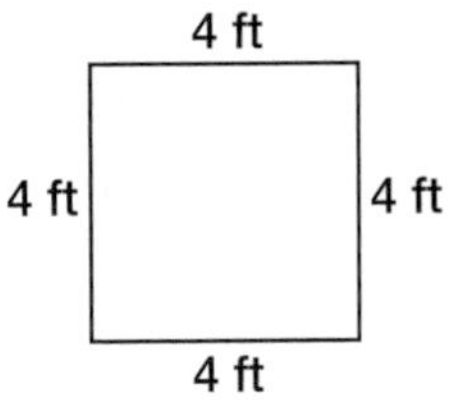

6. 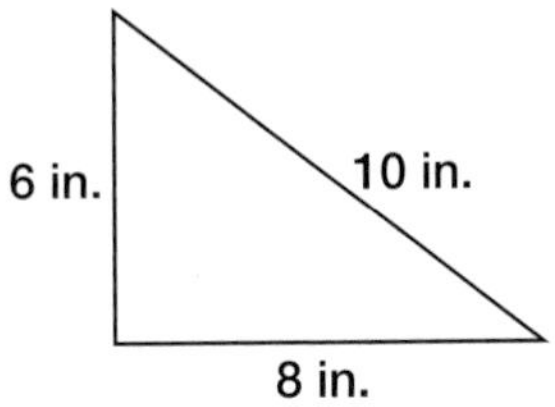

7. 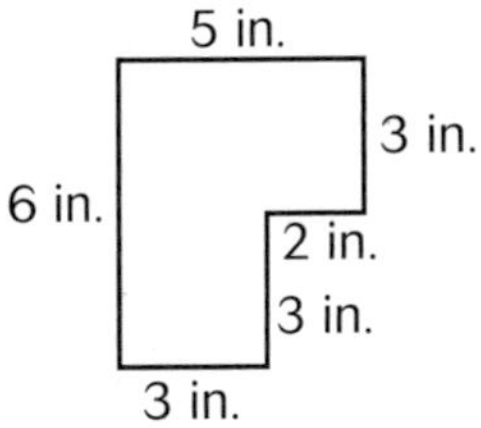

8. **Math Reasoning** The rectangle to the right has a perimeter of 18 units. Can you draw a different shaped rectangle with the same perimeter? Draw a rectangle to show your answer. Label the length of each side.

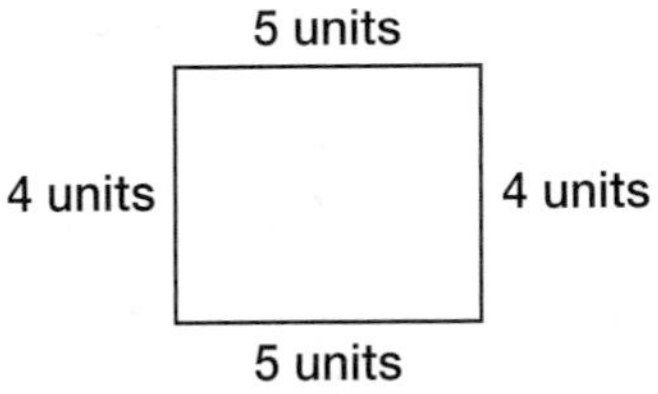

Mixed Review

9. A rose bush was 12 inches tall when it was planted. Now it is 4 feet tall. How many feet has the bush grown?

Write slide, flip, or turn for each diagram.

10. 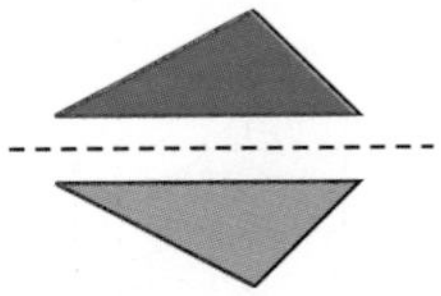

11. 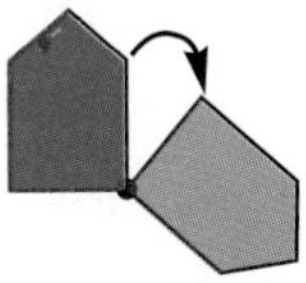

12. 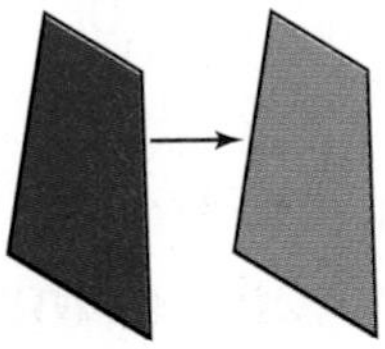

Are the figures in each pair congruent?

13. 

14. 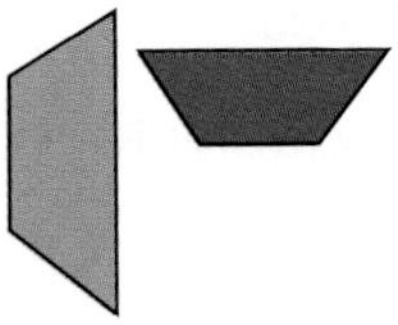

15. 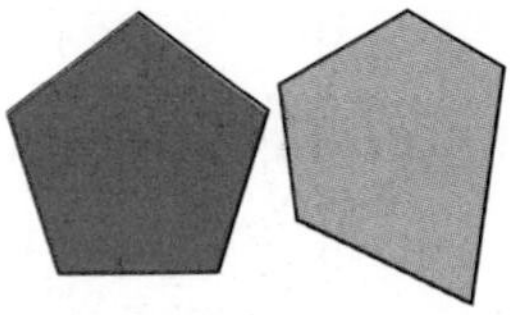

Test Prep Choose the correct letter for each answer.

16. (6-2) If 2 people can ride in each sled, how many sleds are needed for 14 people?

A 16 sleds **C** 7 sleds
B 12 sleds **D** 6 sleds

17. (4-7) Joanna walks to school 4 times per week. How many times does she walk to school in 7 weeks?

F 11 times **H** 32 times
G 28 times **J** 36 times

LESSON 8-11

Area

California Content Standard *Measurement and Geometry 1.2(🔑): Estimate or determine the area . . . of solid figures by covering them with squares. . ..*

Warm-Up Review

Write a multiplication sentence for each array.

1. 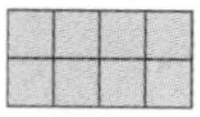

2. 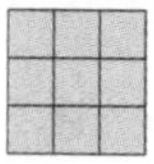

3. A square has sides that are 6 inches long. What is the perimeter of the square?

Math Link You know how to find the distance around a figure. Now you will learn how to measure the space inside a figure.

A **square unit** is a square with sides that are 1 unit long. The number of square units needed to cover a figure is called its **area**.

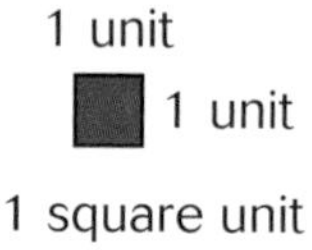

Word Bank

square unit
area

Example 1

Find the area of the shaded figure at the right in square units.

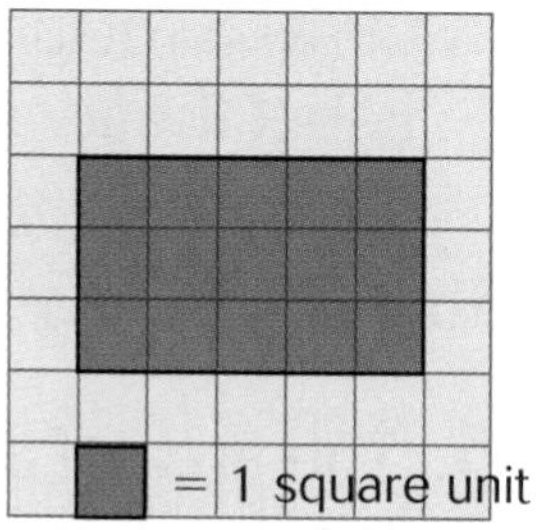

Count the number of squares inside the figure.

The area of the figure is 15 square units.

Example 2

Estimate the area of the shaded figure at the right in square units.

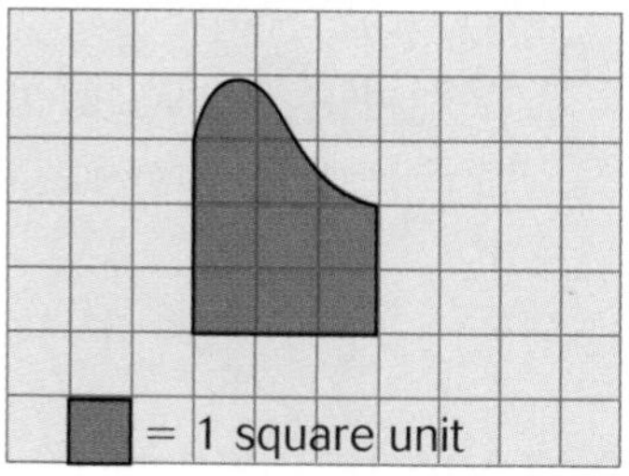

To help you estimate, you can think of two partly covered squares as one whole square.

Count the number of whole squares and partly covered squares inside the figure. There are 7 squares and 4 partly covered squares.

So, the area of the figure is about 9 square units.

Guided Practice *For another sample, see Set I on p. 340.*

Find each area. Write your answer in square units.

1. 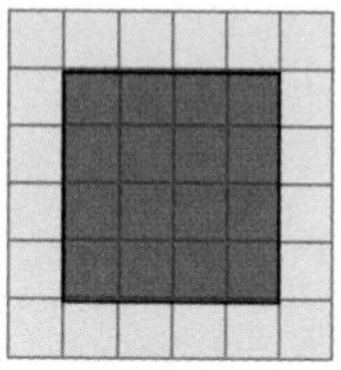

2. 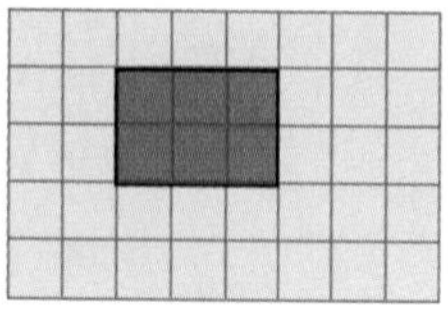

3. 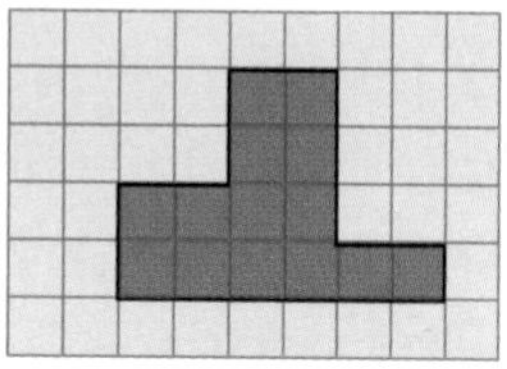

 Additional Standard: Mathematical Reasoning 2.2 (See p. 299.)

4. Which areas in Exercises 1–3 could be found by multiplying. Explain.

Independent Practice *For more practice, see Set I on p. 343.*

Find each area. Write your answer in square units.

5. 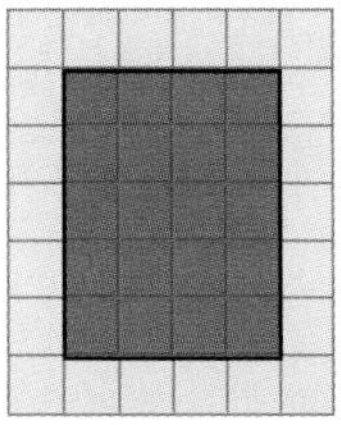

6. 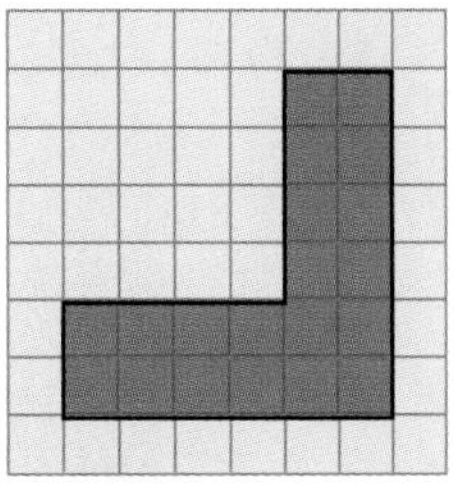

7. 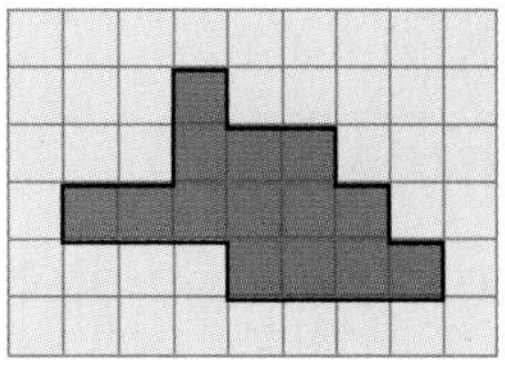

Estimate the number of square units in each figure.

8. 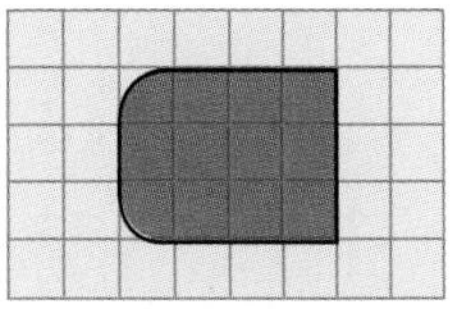

9. 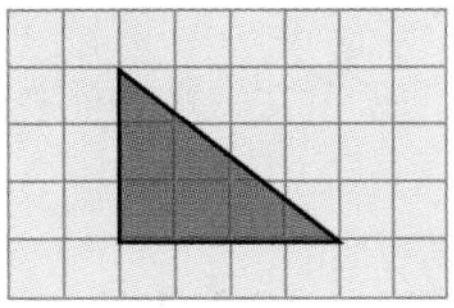

10. 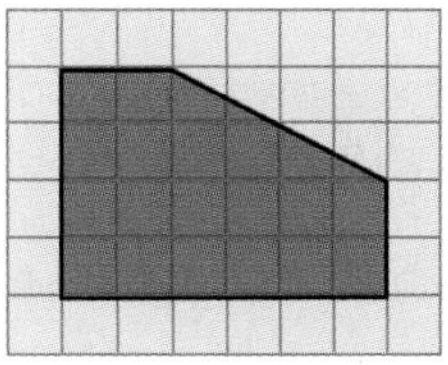

11. The area of a square is 9 square units. What is the length of each side?

Mixed Review

12. What is the perimeter of a rectangle with a length of 10 inches and a width of 8 inches?

Write slide, flip, or turn for each diagram.

13. 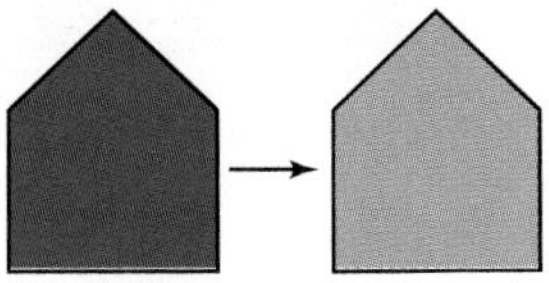

14. 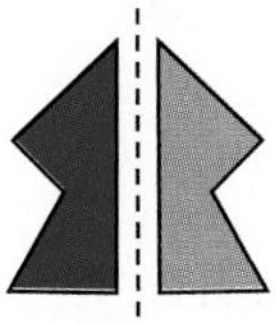

15. 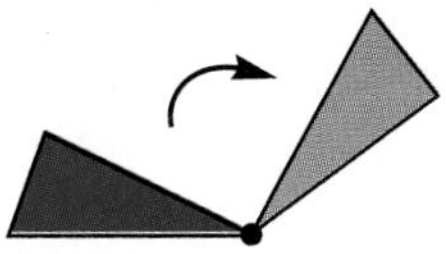

Test Prep **Choose the correct letter for each answer.**

16. $8 \times 4 =$
(5-3)

A 10 **B** 12 **C** 22 **D** 32 **E** NH

17. $35 \div 5 =$
(6-6)

F 6 **G** 7 **H** 8 **J** 9 **K** NH

LESSON 8-12

Understand
Plan
Solve
Look Back

Problem-Solving Application:
Using Symmetry

California Content Standard *Measurement and Geometry 3.4, Grade 4: Identify figures that have bilateral symmetry.*

Warm-Up Review

Are the shapes congruent?

1. 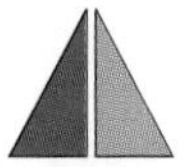

2. 

3. What fraction of the figure is shaded? 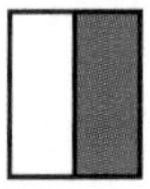

Example 1

Tina folded a red piece of construction paper in half. Then she cut out a heart as shown at the right. Is the heart that Tina made symmetrical?

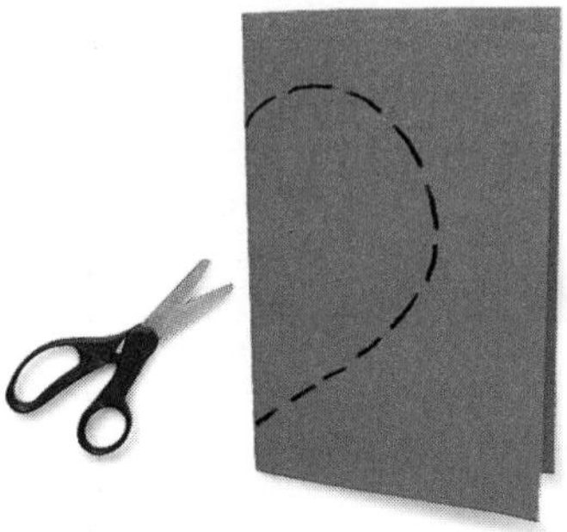

Word Bank

symmetrical
line of symmetry

Understand

What do you need to know?

You need to find out whether the heart is symmetrical. It is symmetrical if it can be folded so that one half of the heart fits exactly on the other half.

Plan

How can you solve the problem?

You can trace the heart and cut it out. Then fold the heart to see if one half fits exactly on the other half.

Solve

Trace the heart. The heart is symmetrical because it can be folded to form two congruent parts. A line that divides a figure into two congruent parts is a **line of symmetry**.

Look Back

Is the line along the fold of the paper a line of symmetry? Why or why not?

Additional Standards: Mathematical Reasoning 1.1, 2.2 (See p. 299.)

Guided Practice

1. A company wants to use a symmetrical shape for its logo. A design agency shows the company the shapes below. For which of the shapes is the dashed line a line of symmetry?

a. 

b. 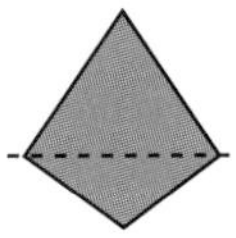

c. 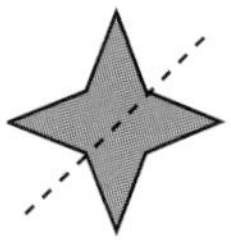

d. 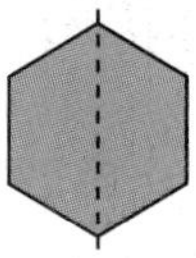

2. Thomas is cutting out the plane figures at the right for a class project. Which of the figures has at least one line of symmetry? more than one line of symmetry?

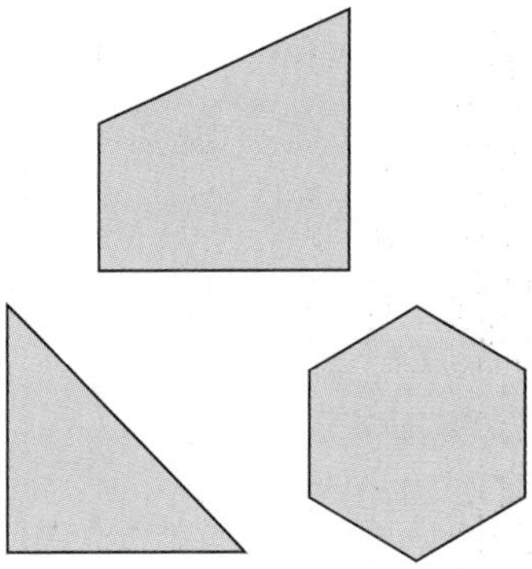

Independent Practice

3. Which figure below has no line of symmetry?

a. 

b. 

c. 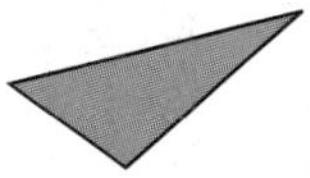

4. Half of the design at the right is missing. The dashed line is a line of symmetry. Trace the design and draw the other half.

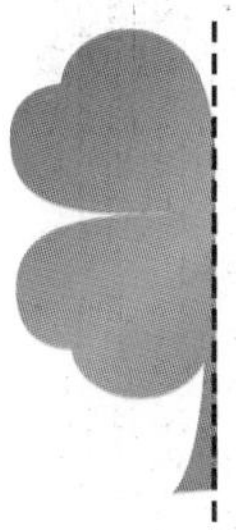

5. Paul wants to make a card out of a square. How many ways can he fold the card so that both sides match up exactly? Draw each way showing the line of symmetry.

Mixed Review

6. Maggie spent $12 on school supplies. She spent $4 on paper, $2 on colored pencils, $2 on glue, and the rest on a lunch box. How much did the lunch box cost?

7. There are 8 boats at Adventure Camp. If each boat can seat 4 campers, how many campers in all can the boats seat?

8. The sum of two numbers is 21. Their difference is 3. What are the numbers?

Use Homework Workbook 8-12.

LESSON 8-13

Solid Figures

Warm-Up Review

Name the figures.

1. 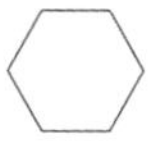

2. 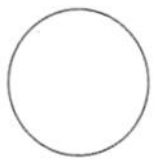

3. 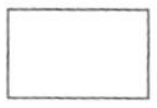

4. 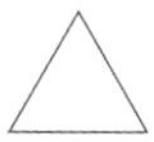

California Content Standard *Measurement and Geometry 2.5: Identify, describe, and classify common three-dimensional geometric objects . . .. Also, Measurement and Geometry 2.6 (See p. 299.)*

Math Link You know how to identify plane figures. Now you will use what you know about plane figures to help you identify other geometric figures.

Word Bank

solid figure
face
edge

Example 1

Look at the castle sculpture below. It is made up of **solid figures** like the ones below. Which of the solid figures below were used to make the tower on the top of the castle?

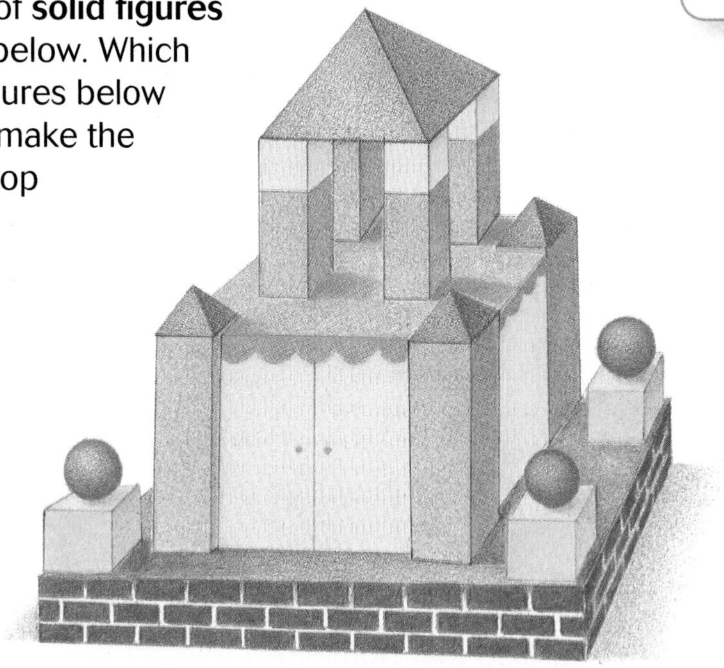

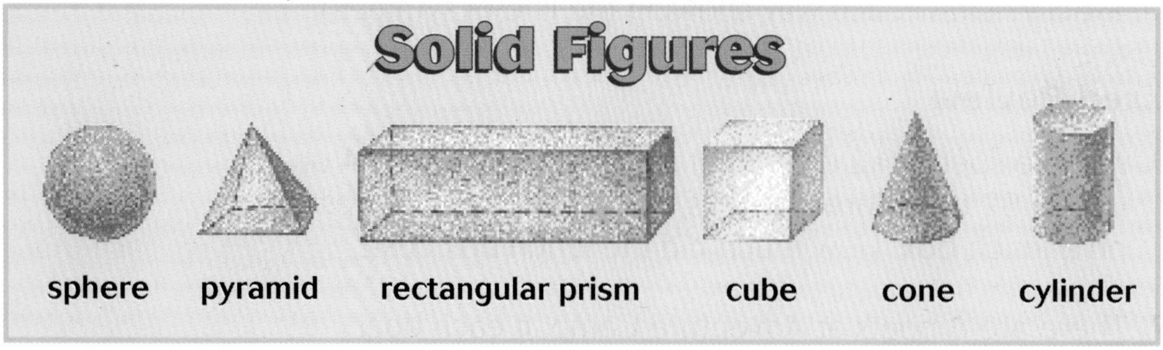

A pyramid was used to make the roof of the tower.

The columns were made from cubes stacked on top of rectangular prisms.

 Additional Standard: Mathematical Reasoning 2.3 (See p. 299.)

Many solid figures have **faces**, **edges**, or corners.

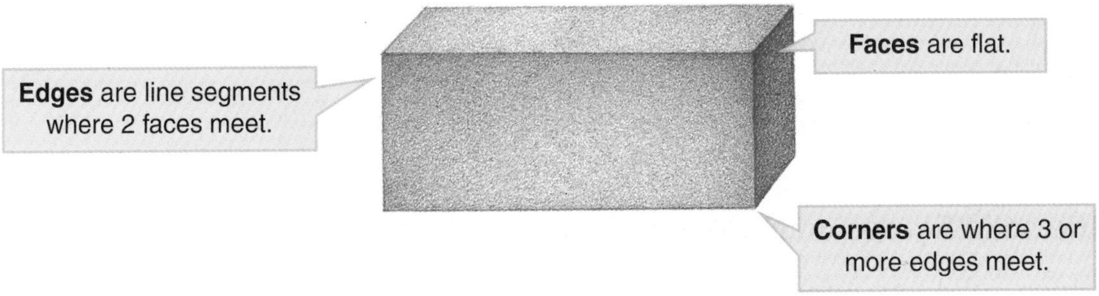
Edges are line segments where 2 faces meet.
Faces are flat.
Corners are where 3 or more edges meet.

Example 2

Which of the solids on page 328 have a face that is a square?

The cube, the rectangular prism, and the pyramid each have one or more faces that are squares.

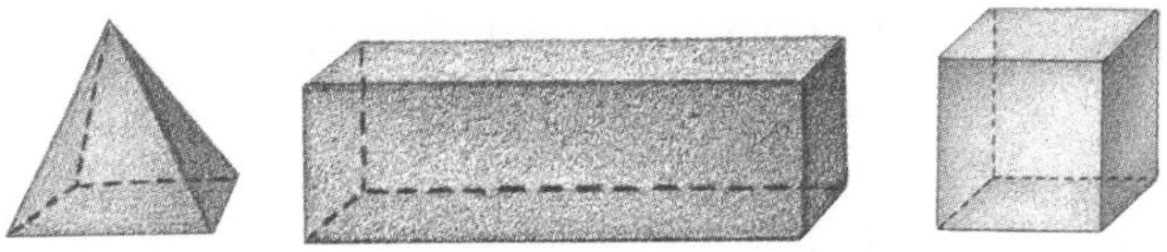

pyramid **rectangular prism** **cube**

Guided Practice *For another example, see Set J on p. 340.*

Name the solid figure that each object looks like.

1. 

2. 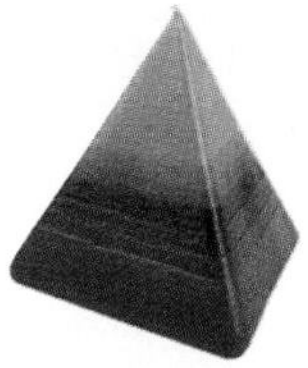

3. 

4. Sophie painted a box in the shape of a cube. She used a different color paint for each face of the box. How many colors did she use?

Independent Practice *For more practice, see Set J on p. 343.*

Name the solid figure that each object looks like.

5. 

6. 

7. 

Name the solid figures used to make each object.

8. 

9. 

10. 

Use the solid figures on page 328 for Exercises 11–14.

11. Which solid has 4 faces that are triangles?

12. Which solid has 6 faces that are squares?

13. Which solid has no flat surfaces?

14. Which solid has 1 flat surface?

15. Math Reasoning How is a rectangular prism like a cube? How is it different?

Mixed Review

16. Is the colored area in Figure A *the same as*, *greater than*, or *less than* the colored area in Figure B?

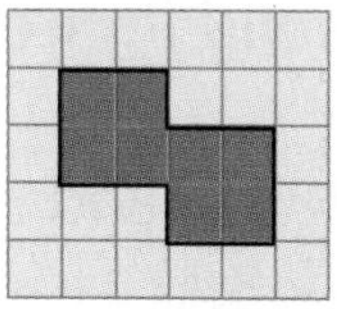

Figure A

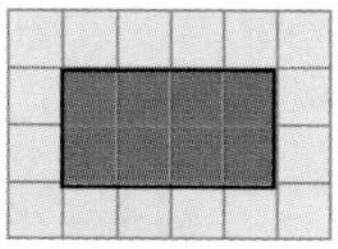

Figure B

Find the perimeter of each figure.

17. 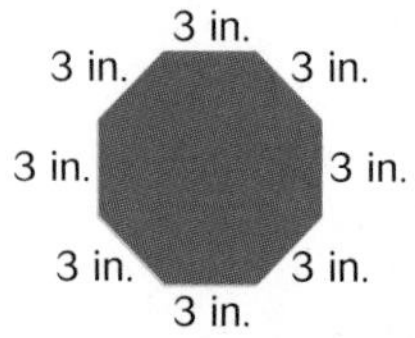

18. 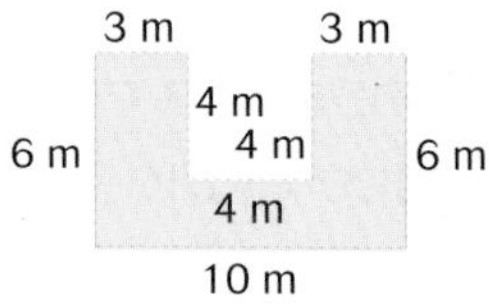

19. 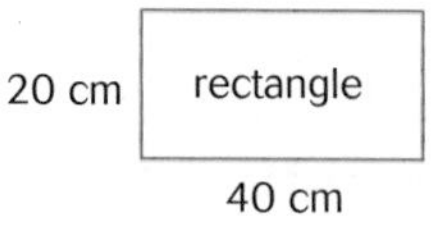

Algebra Write >, <, or = for each ●.

20. 8 + 14 ● 2 × 10 **21.** 36 ÷ 6 ● 15 − 9 **22.** 8 × 7 ● 9 × 6

Test Prep Choose the correct letter for each answer.

23. (4-4) At the school store, notebooks cost $2 each. How much do 7 notebooks cost?

A $9 **C** $12
B $11 **D** $14

24. (1-3) Round 1,284 to the nearest hundred.

F 1,200 **H** 1,300
G 1,290 **J** 1,384

LESSON 8-14

Volume

California Content Standard *Measurement and Geometry 1.2(🔑): Estimate or determine the . . . volume of solid figures . . . by counting the number of cubes that would fill them.*

Warm-Up Review

1. Find the area in square units.

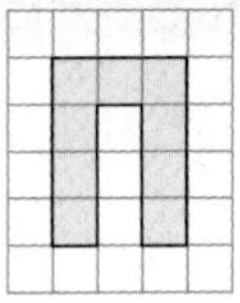

2. Identify the solid.

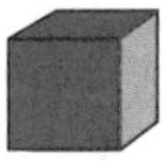

Math Link You know how to identify solid figures. Now you will learn how to measure the space inside solid figures.

The number of cubes needed to fill a solid figure is its **volume**. The volume of a solid figure is measured in **cubic units**.

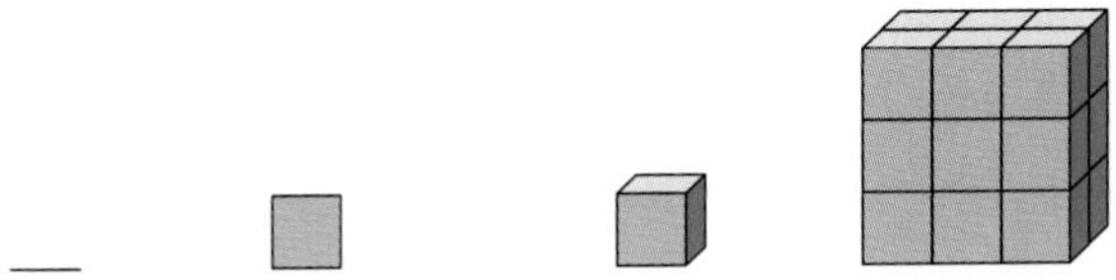

1 unit 1 square unit 1 cubic unit 18 cubic units

Example 1

Look at the cube and the empty box at the right. About how many cubic units would fill the box?

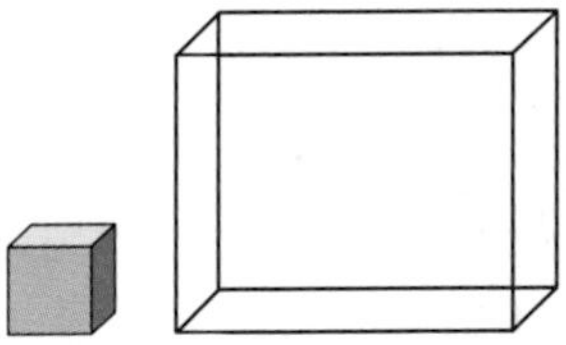

First, estimate how many cubes would fit in one layer. It looks like 2 rows of 4 cubes would fill one layer. So, 8 cubes would fit in one layer.

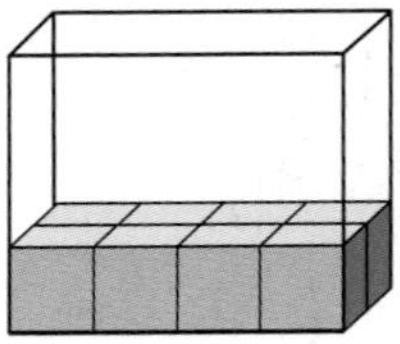

Then estimate how many layers would fill the box. It looks like 3 layers would fill the box.

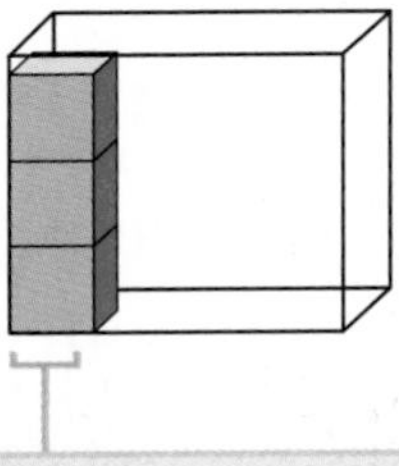

Multiply 3 layers times 8 cubes in each layer.
$3 \times 8 = 24$

Finally, multiply the number of layers by the number of cubes in one layer.

About 24 cubic units would fill the box.

Additional Standard: Mathematical Reasoning 2.3 *(See p. 299.)*

Example 2

What is the volume of the box below?

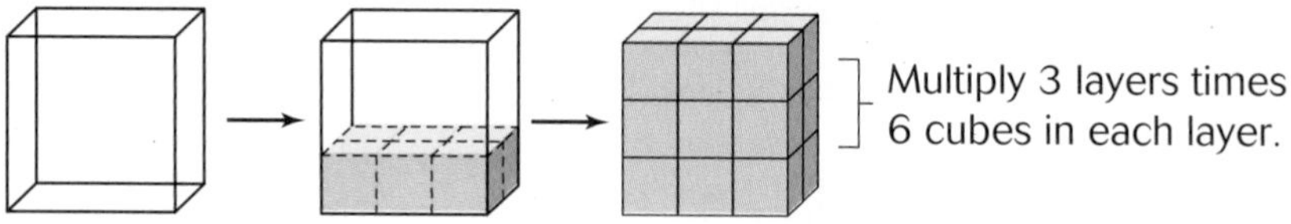
Multiply 3 layers times
6 cubes in each layer.

The box holds 3 layers of cubes. The first layer has 6 cubes. Although you cannot see all the cubes, you know that each layer has the same number of cubes.

So, the volume of the box is 18 cubic units.

Guided Practice *For another example, see Set K on p. 340.*

Estimate the volume of each figure in cubic units.

1. 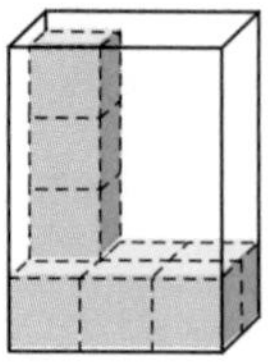

2. 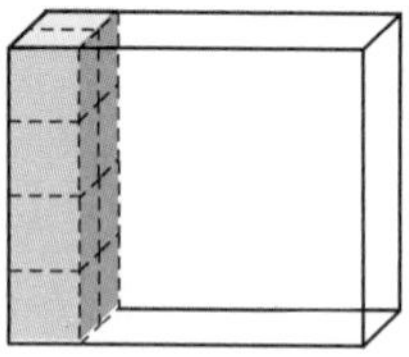

3. 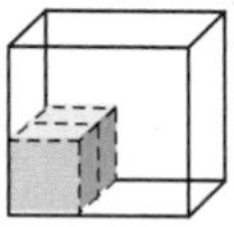

Find the volume of each figure in cubic units.

4. 

5. 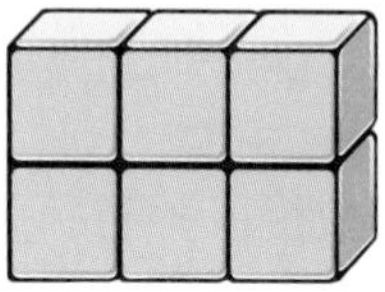

6. 

7. A box holds exactly 4 rows of 3 cubes. What is the volume of the box?

Independent Practice *For more practice, see Set K on p. 343.*

Estimate the volume of each figure in cubic units.

8. 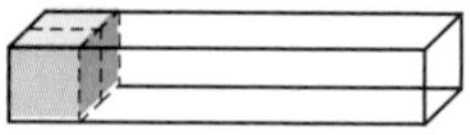

9. 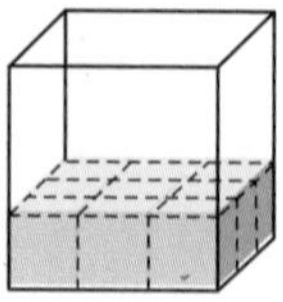

10. 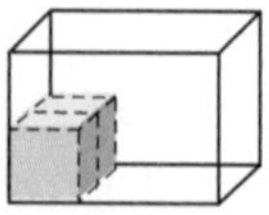

Find the volume of each figure in cubic units.

11. 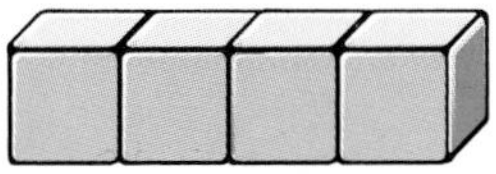

12. 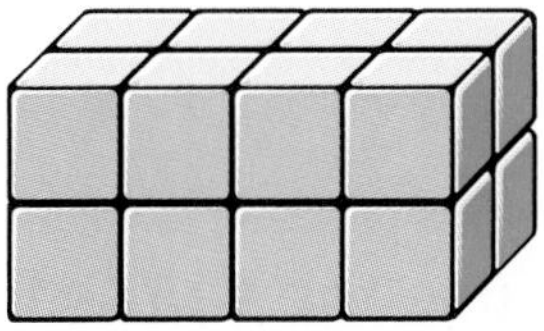

13. 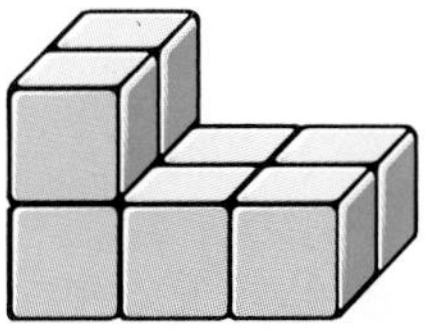

14. Math Reasoning Jay built both of the solid figures at the right with 9 cubes. Are the volumes of the two solids different? Explain.

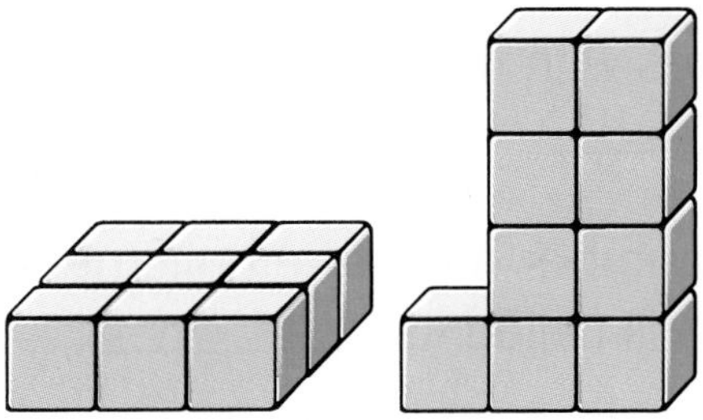

Mixed Review

15. Tim is going to cover the faces of the rectangular prism shown on the right with colored paper. What kind of plane figures will he need to cut from the colored paper?

Find the area of each shaded figure in square units.

16. 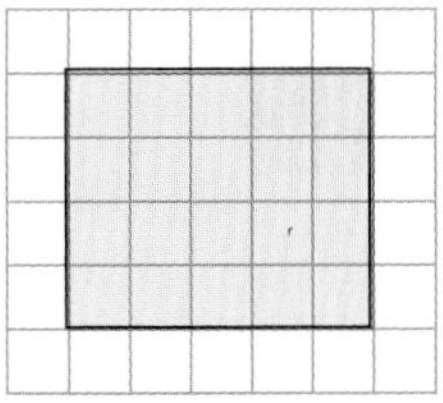

17. 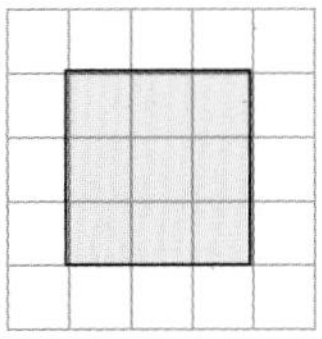

18. 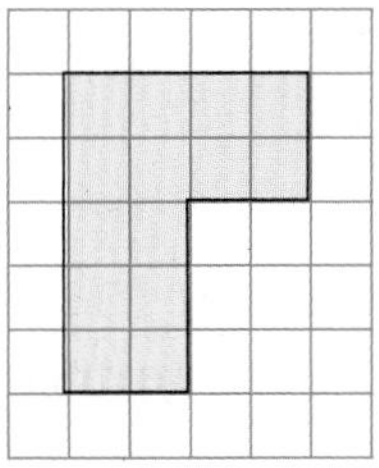

Test Prep **Choose the correct letter for each answer.**

19. Jill has 18 pencils. She wants to share them equally with a friend. How many pencils will the friend get?
(6-2)

A 9 pencils **C** 14 pencils

B 10 pencils **D** 22 pencils

20. Dale bought a map for $4.95 and a pin for $1.39. How much money did he spend?
(1-9)

F $3.56 **H** $6.24

G $5.34 **J** $6.34

Diagnostic Checkpoint

Complete. For Exercises 1–4, use the words from the Word Bank.

Word Bank
area
congruent
faces
perimeter
symmetrical
volume

1. (8-7) Figures with the same size and shape are __________.

2. (8-11) The number of square units needed to cover a plane figure is called its __________.

3. (8-14) The number of cubic units needed to fill a solid figure is called its __________.

4. (8-10) Find the perimeter of the figure.

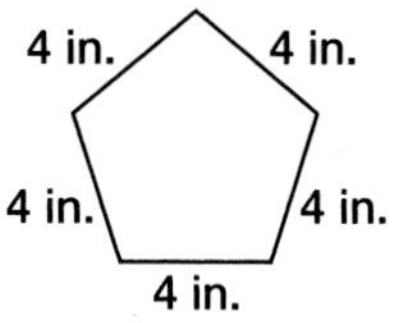

5. (8-11) Find the area of the figure. Write your answer in square units.

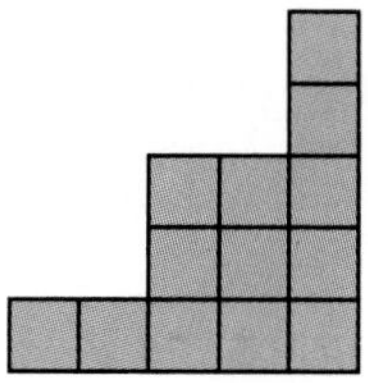

6. (8-12) Tell whether the dotted line is a line of symmetry.

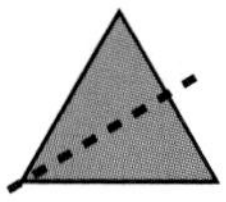

7. (8-13) Name the three-dimensional figure.

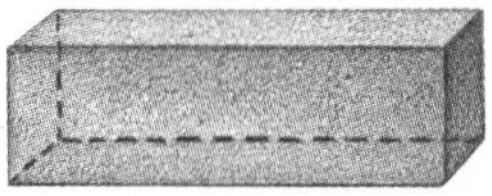

8. (8-14) Find the volume of the figure.

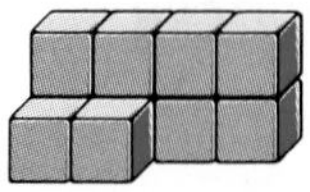

9. (8-9) Draw the next two shapes in the pattern.

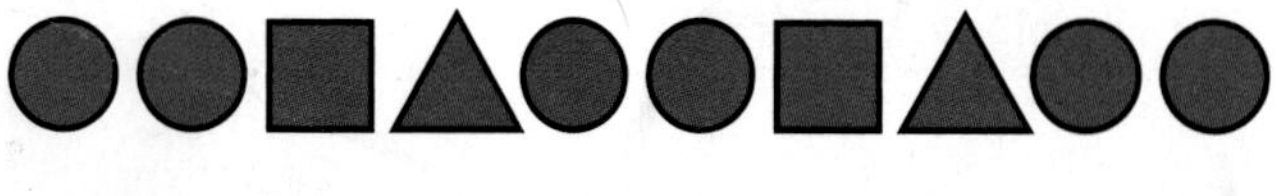

Chapter 8 Test

Name each figure.

1. 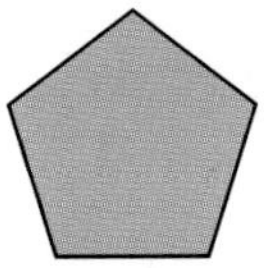

2. 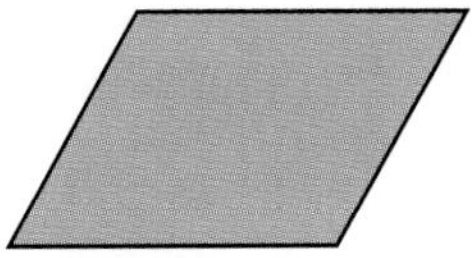

3. 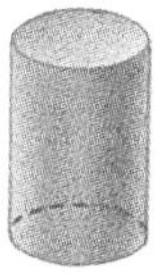

4. 

Name each angle as right, acute, or obtuse.

5. 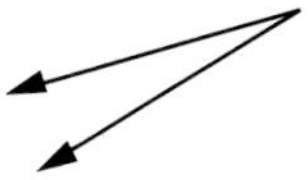

6. 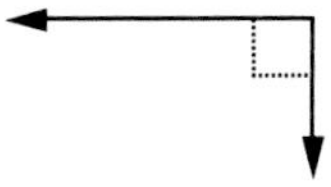

7. 

Name each triangle as right, acute, or obtuse. Then name each as equilateral, isosceles, or scalene.

8. 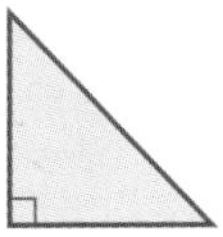

9. 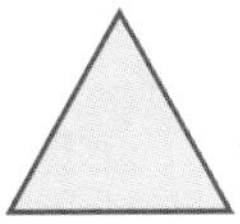

10. 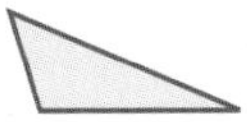

11. Are the pair of figures congruent?

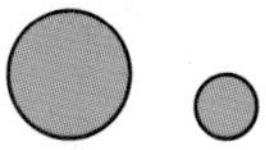

12. Is the red line a line of symmetry?

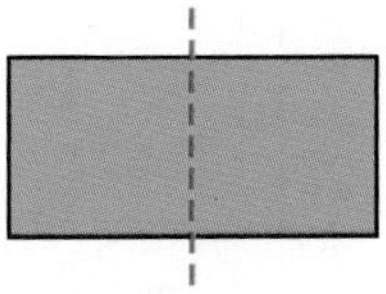

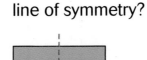

13. Does the picture show a slide, flip, or turn?

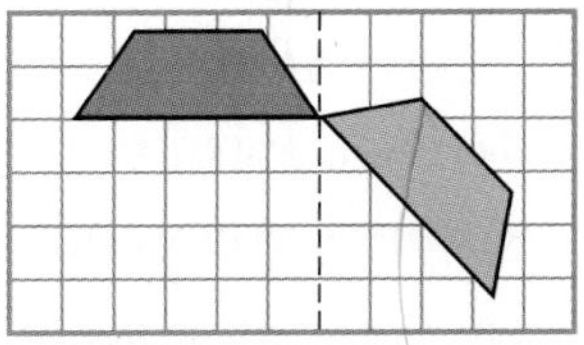

14. Find the perimeter.

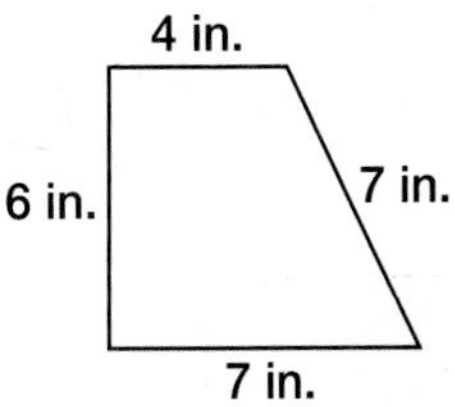

15. Find the area.

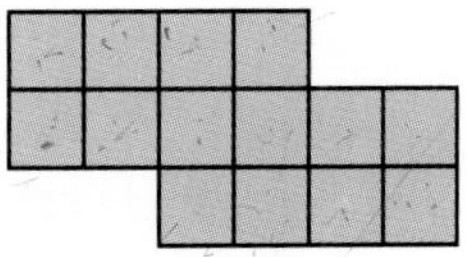

16. Find the volume.

17. Look at the figure below. How many triangles are there?

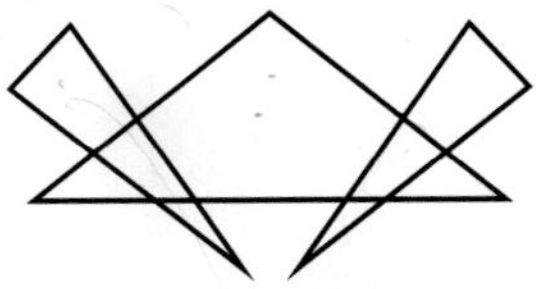

18. What is the color of the next tile in the pattern?

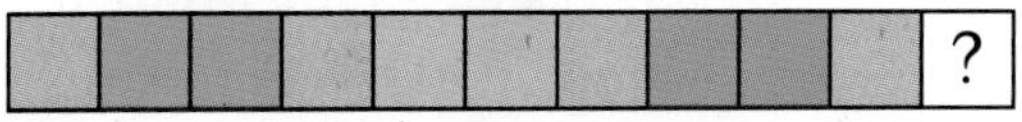

Multiple-Choice Chapter 8 Test

Choose the correct letter for each answer.

1. What is the name of this shape?

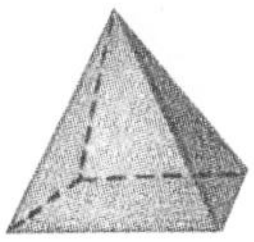

A cone
B cylinder
C pyramid
D triangle

2. Which two figures are congruent?

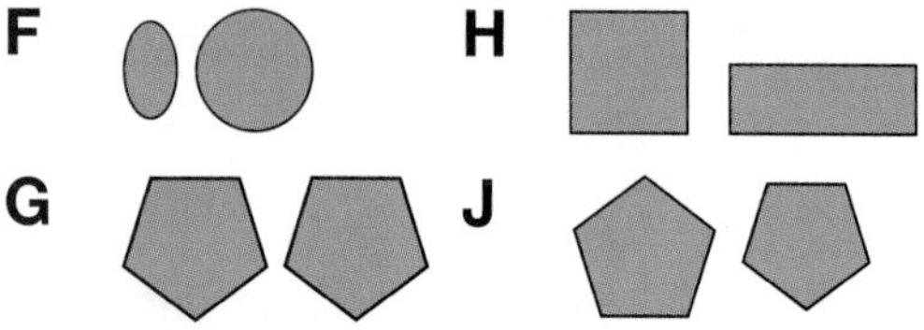

3. I have four sides that are the same length. I am not a square. Which quadrilateral am I?

A parallelogram
B rectangle
C rhombus
D square

4. Name the plane figure below.

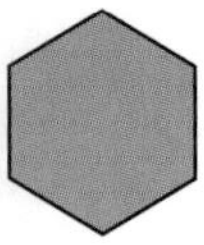

F circle
G hexagon
H pentagon
J octagon

5. What does the picture represent?

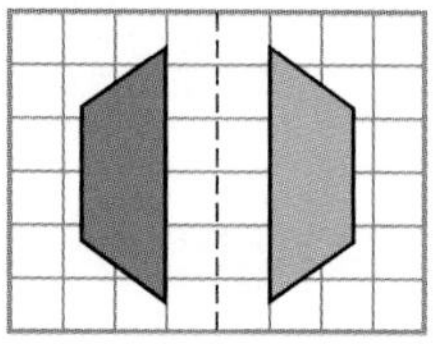

A a flip
B a line of symmetry
C a slide
D a turn

6. Which best describes the following angle?

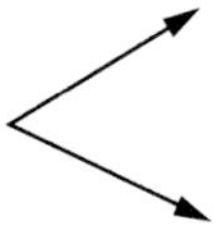

F acute
G equilateral
H obtuse
J right

7. Laura made a figure out of string. The sides measured 4 cm, 3 cm, and 4 cm. What type of figure did she make?

A equilateral triangle
B isosceles triangle
C quadrilateral
D scalene triangle

8. How many squares are in this figure?

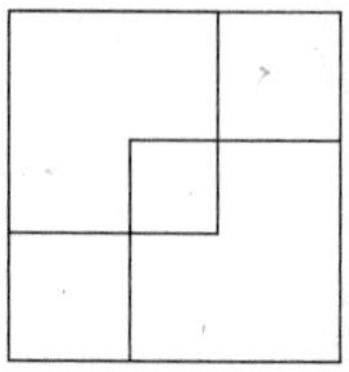

F 1
G 3
H 6
J 9

9. **Which picture shows a line of symmetry?**

A 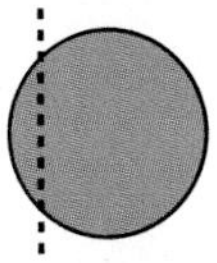

C 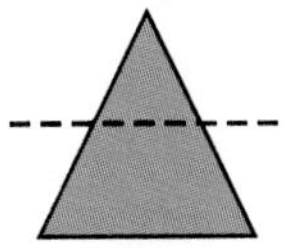

B 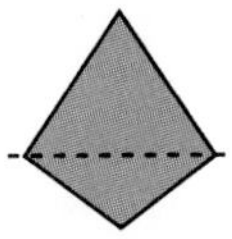

D 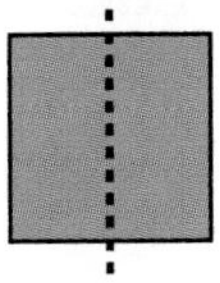

10. **What is the area of the figure below?**

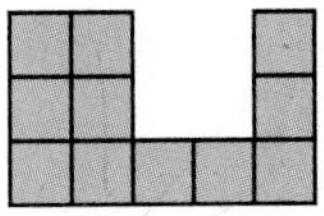

F 4 square units
G 11 square units
H 13 square units
J 15 square units

11. **Which best describes the triangle?**

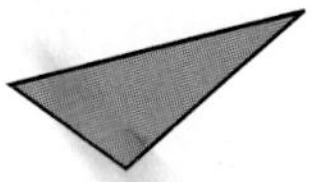

A right, isosceles triangle
B acute, scalene triangle
C obtuse, equilateral triangle
D obtuse, scalene triangle

12. **What is the volume of the following figure?**

F 6 cubic units
G 8 cubic units
H 10 cubic units
J 14 cubic units

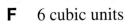

13. **What is the perimeter of the figure?**

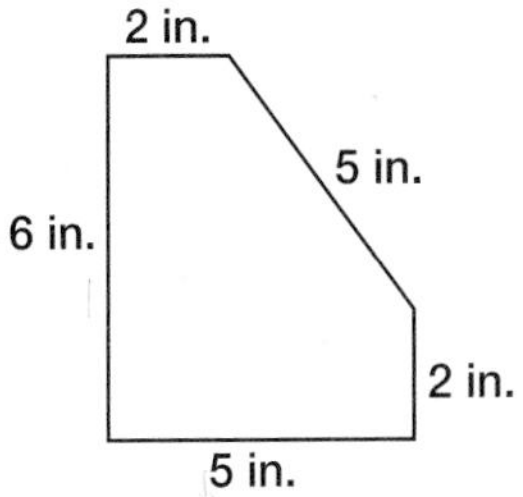

A 20 inches
B 18 inches
C 16 inches
D 14 inches

14. **Which color squares cover the least area?**

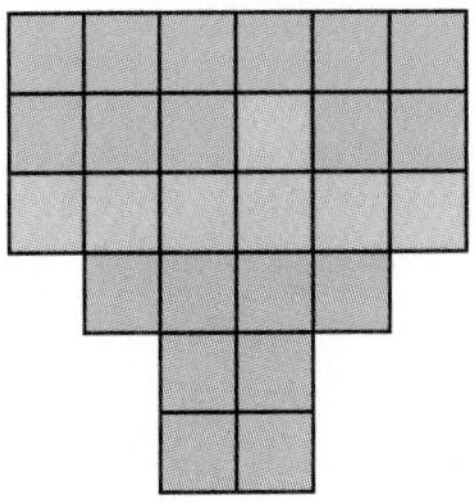

F green
G orange
H blue
J red

15. **Which number is next in the pattern below?**

1, 2, 4, 7, 11, 16, ▒

A 17
B 21
C 22
D 32

16. **I have 6 faces. Two of them are squares and 4 are rectangles. What am I?**

F cube
G cylinder
H pyramid
J rectangular prism

Reteaching

Set A *(pages 300–302)*

Name the figure.

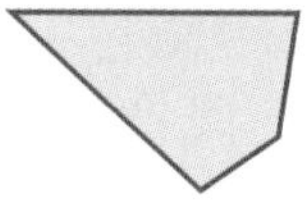

This shape has 4 sides and 4 corners. It is a quadrilateral.

Remember there are many different four-sided shapes, but they are all quadrilaterals.

Name each figure.

1. 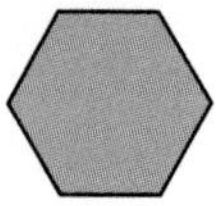

2. 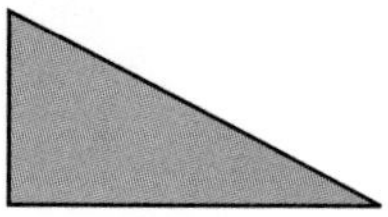

Set B *(pages 303–305)*

Name the angle as right, acute, or obtuse.

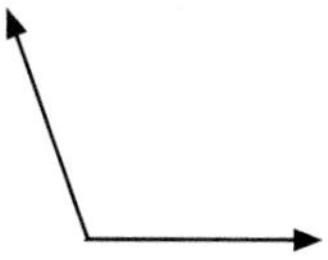

This is an obtuse angle because it is larger than the corner of a door.

Remember a right angle looks like the corner of a door. An acute angle is smaller than, and an obtuse angle is larger than, a right angle.

Name each angle as right, acute, or obtuse.

1. 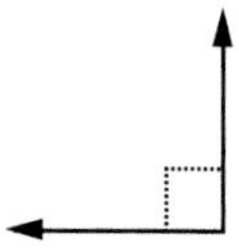

2. 

Set C *(pages 306–307)*

Is this triangle right, acute, or obtuse?

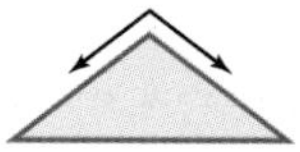

This triangle has an obtuse angle, so it is an obtuse triangle.

Remember to look first for a right angle, then an obtuse angle, and then acute angles.

Name each triangle as right, acute, or obtuse.

1. 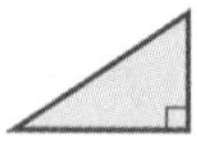

2. 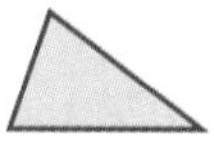

Set D *(pages 308–309)*

Is this triangle an equilateral, isosceles, or scalene triangle?

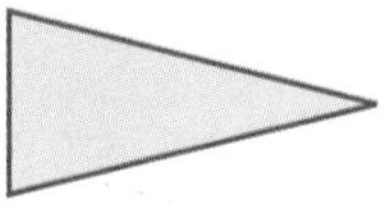

Two of the sides are the same length, so the triangle is an isosceles triangle.

Remember an equilateral triangle has all sides equal and a scalene triangle has no sides equal.

Name each triangle as equilateral, isosceles, or scalene.

1. 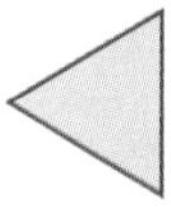

2. 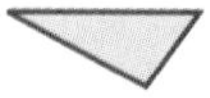

Set E (pages 310–311)

Name the quadrilateral.

This figure has right angles. Four sides are the same length. Opposite sides are parallel. This is a square.

Remember you can name quadrilaterals by the sizes of their angles and the lengths of their sides.

Name each quadrilateral.

1. 

2. 

3. 

4. 

Set F (pages 314–315)

Are the figures congruent?

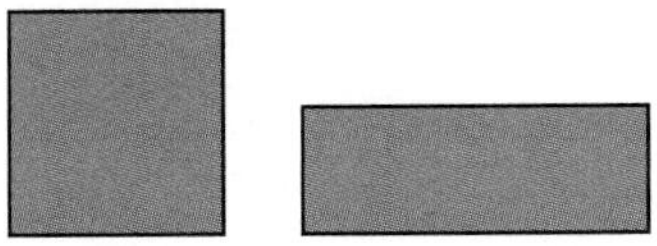

These are both quadrilaterals, but one is a square and one is a rectangle.

Remember congruent means two figures have the same size and shape.

Are the figures in each pair congruent?

1. 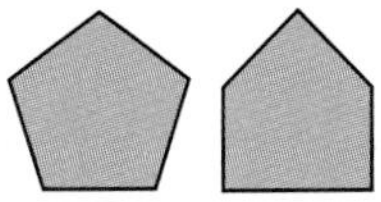

2. 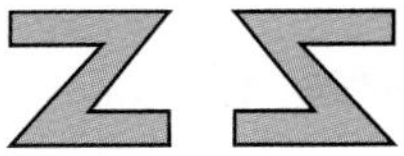

Set G (pages 316–317)

Write slide, flip, or turn for the diagram.

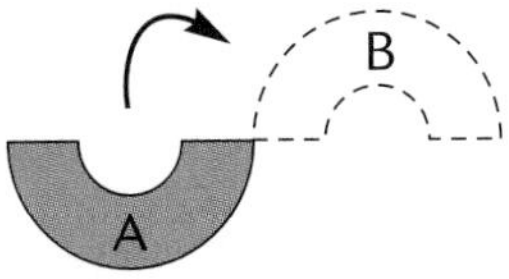

The two shapes are going in different directions. So it cannot be a flip or a slide. So the shape was turned.

Remember to be a flip you would actually have to pick up the shape and flip it over. The slide and turn do not have to be picked up.

Write slide, flip, or turn for each diagram.

1. 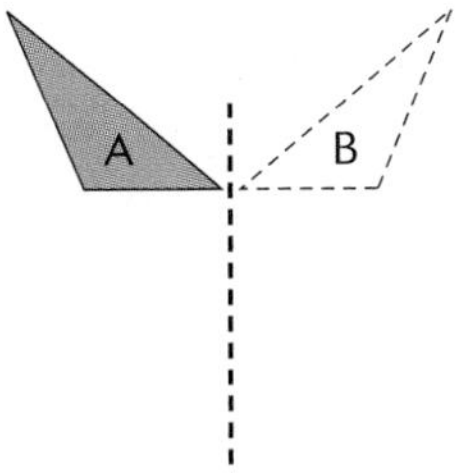

2. 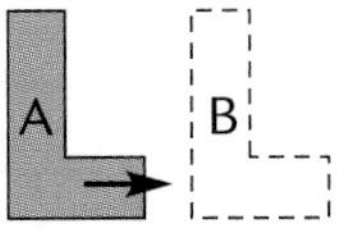

Reteaching (continued)

Set H *(pages 322–323)*

Find the perimeter of the figure.

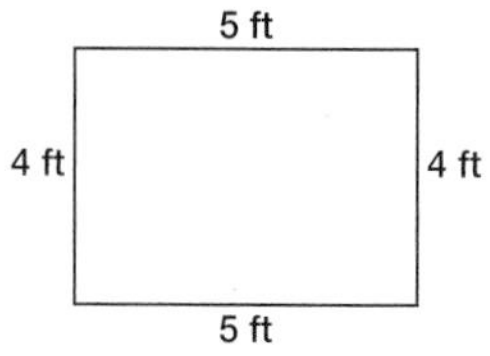

5 ft + 4 ft + 5 ft + 4 ft = 18 ft

The perimeter is 18 ft.

Remember to add all the lengths around the figure.

Find the perimeter of each figure.

1. 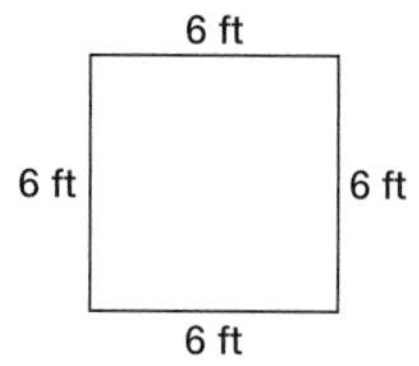

2. 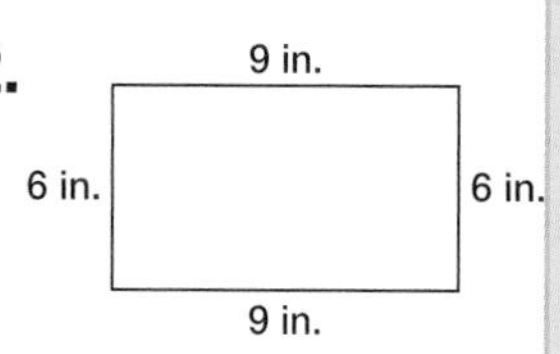

Set I *(pages 324–325)*

Find the area in square units.

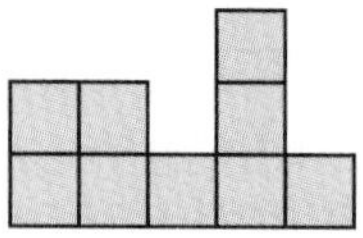

There are 9 squares.
The area is 9 square units.

Remember to label your answers in square units for area.

Find the area of each figure.

1. 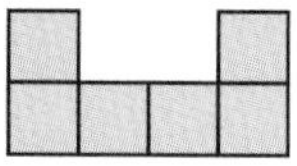

2. 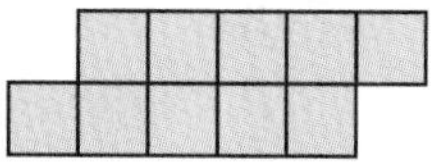

Set J *(pages 328–330)*

Name the solid figure that the object looks like.

The figure looks like a cylinder.

Remember a solid figure that has only flat surfaces has faces, edges, and corners.

Name the solid figure that the object looks like.

1. 

2. 

Set K *(pages 331–333)*

Find the volume of the figure in cubic units.

You can see 9 cubes.
One cube is hidden.

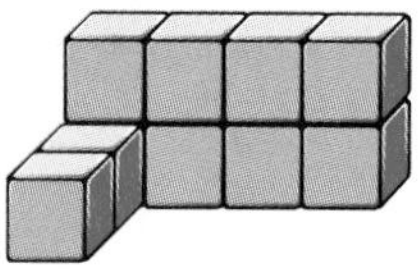

9 + 1 = 10

So, the volume is 10 cubic units.

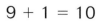

Remember to count the boxes that you can't see.

Find the volume of each figure in cubic units.

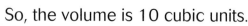

1. 

2. 

More Practice

Set A *(pages 300–302)*

Name each figure.

1. 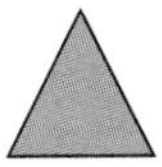
2. 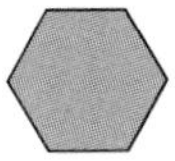
3. 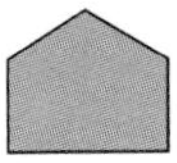
4. 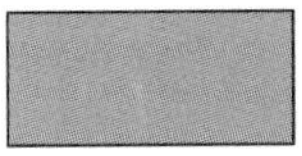

5. Andy cut out some squares. He counted 32 corners in all. How many squares did he cut out?

Set B *(pages 303–305)*

Name the angle as right, acute, or obtuse.

1. 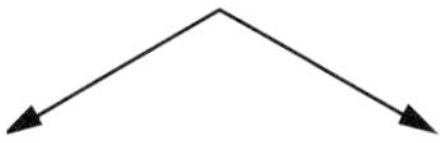
2. 
3. 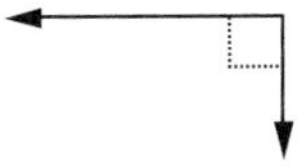
4. 

5. Edward looks at the clock. It shows 1:30. What type of angle does the clock show?

Set C *(pages 306–307)*

Name each triangle as right, acute, or obtuse.

1. 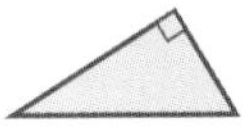
2. 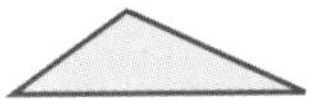
3. 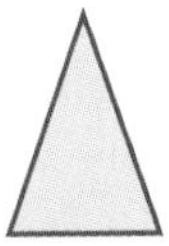
4. 

5. Lou folded a square in half to make a triangle. What type of triangle did he make?

Set D *(pages 308–309)*

Name each triangle as equilateral, isosceles, or scalene.

1. 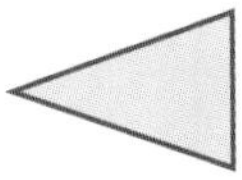
2. 
3. 
4. 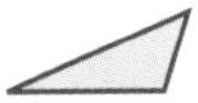

5. One side of an isosceles triangle is 8 cm. Another side of the isosceles triangle is 6 cm. What could be the length of the third side?

More Practice (continued)

Set E (pages 310–311)

Name each quadrilateral.

1. 

2. 

3. 

4. 

5. I have four sides. I have no right angles. Only my opposite sides are the same length. What quadrilateral am I?

Set F (pages 314–315)

Are the figures in each pair congruent?

1. 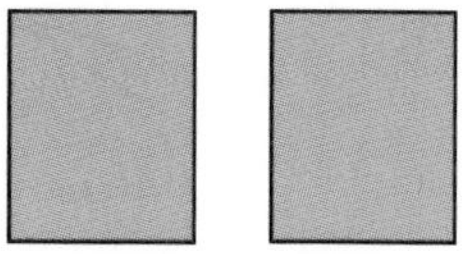

2. 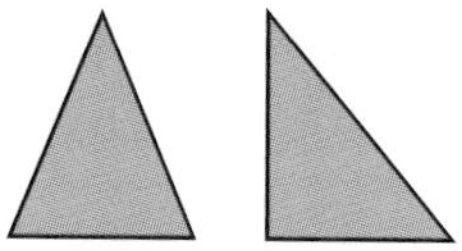

3. 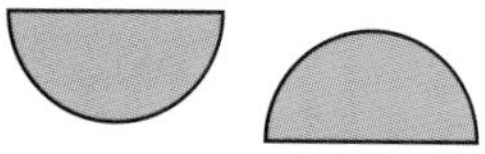

4. 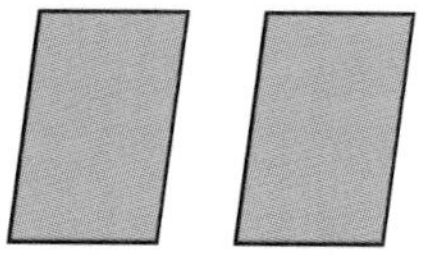

5. 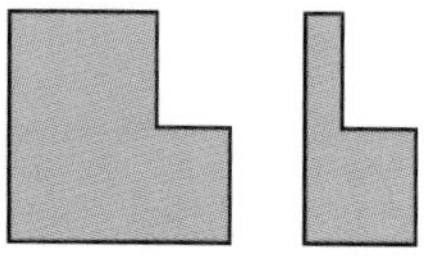

6. 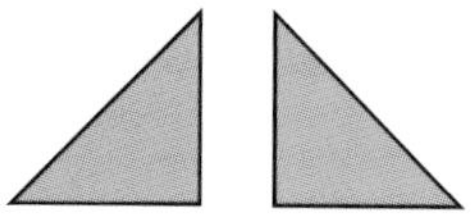

7. Corrina cut a piece of construction paper from one corner to the other (diagonal). Did she make 2 congruent figures? If so, what did she make?

Set G (pages 316–317)

Write slide, flip, or turn for each diagram.

1. 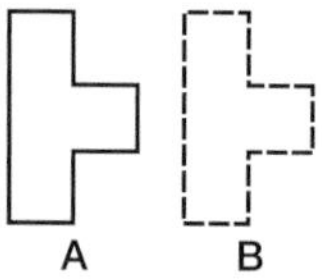

2. 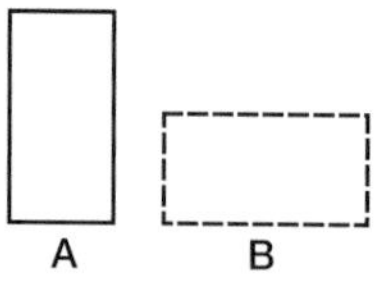

3. 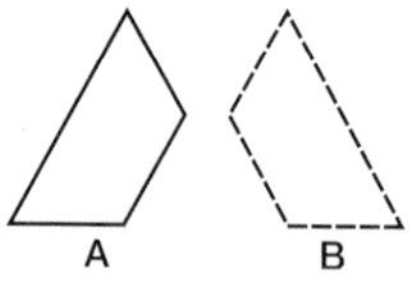

4. 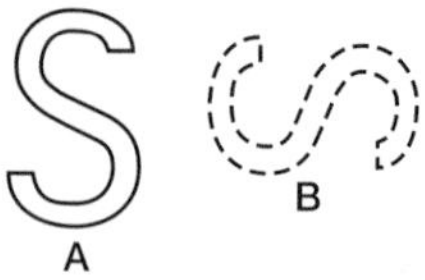

5. 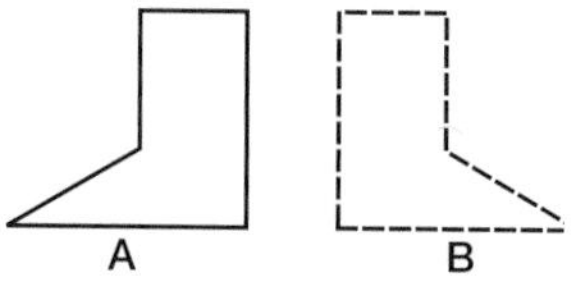

6. 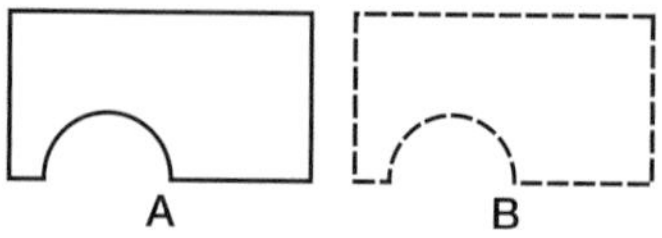

7. If you slide, flip, or turn a figure, will position A and position B always be congruent? Explain.

Set H (pages 322–323)

Find the perimeter of each figure.

1. 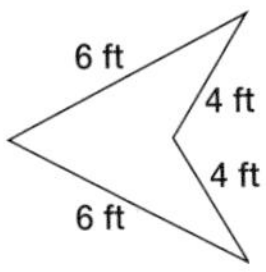

2. 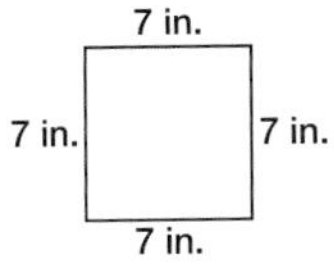

3. 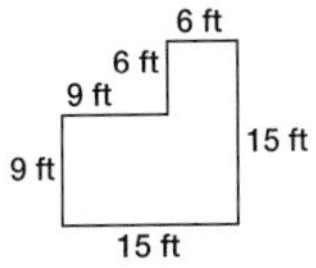

4. Quinta wants to fence in her rectangular-shaped garden. The length is 10 feet and the width is 8 feet. How much fence will she need?

Set I (pages 324–325)

Find the area of each figure in square units.

1. 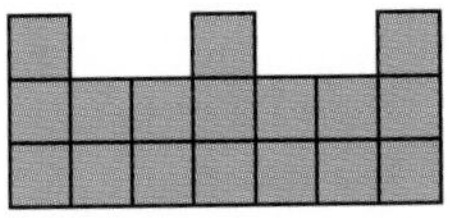

2. 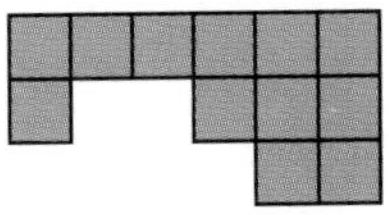

3. 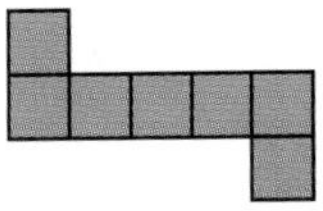

Set J (pages 328–330)

Name the solid figure that each object looks like.

1. 

2. 

3. 

4. Candice brought a cereal box, baseball, and soup can to school for a geometry lesson. Which object looks like a rectangular prism?

Set K (pages 331–333)

Find the volume of each figure in cubic units.

1. 

2. 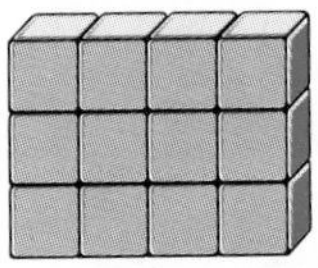

3. 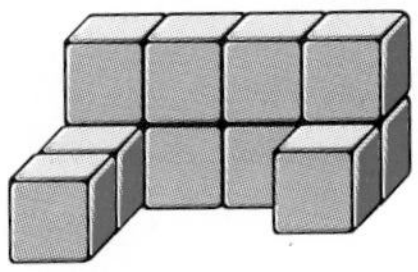

4. Al has 3 bags of cubes. Each bag has 9 cubes. He used all the cubes to build a rectangular prism. What is the volume of the rectangular prism he built?

Problem Solving: Preparing for Tests

TEST PREP

Choose the correct letter for each answer.

---

1. **Wendy made this drawing of a patio. Her dad plans to cover the patio with tiles. Which measurement should Wendy write for the missing length?**

A 7 ft
B 8 ft
C 16 ft
D 20 ft

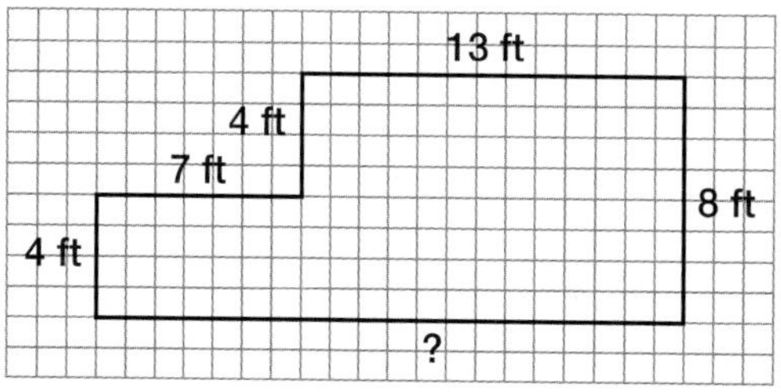

Tip

You need to use two of the lengths given to find the one length that is missing.

---

2. **A school library has 48 science magazines and 29 art magazines. *About* how many science and art magazines does the library have?**

F 60
G 70
H 80
J 90

Tip

Start by rounding each number to the nearest 10. Then decide whether to add or subtract the rounded amounts.

---

3. **Elena had a collection of toy cars. She gave half of her cars to her brother. Then she gave 5 of the cars she had left to a friend. Elena then had 12 cars left. How many cars did Elena have when she began?**

A 17
B 24
C 34
D 40

Tip

Try using the strategy *Work Backward* for this problem. Start with the 12 cars Elena has left.

4. **Kim and Laura each spent $4.25 for lunch. Tom spent $6.50 for lunch. How much did the three friends spend on lunch in all?**

F $2.25　　H $14.00
G $10.75　　J $15.00

5. **A city park has 3 bike trails. The Green Trail is the longest bike trail, and the Red Trail is the shortest bike trail. The Blue Trail is exactly 8 miles long. Which is a reasonable conclusion?**

A The Green Trail is less than 8 miles long.
B The Red Trail is less than 8 miles long.
C The Green Trail is shorter than the Red Trail.
D The Blue Trail is longer than the Green Trail.

6. **Angelo packed 3 suitcases for a trip to Dallas. The suitcases weighed 21 pounds, 29 pounds, and 32 pounds. *About* how much did the suitcases weigh altogether?**

F 75 pounds　　H 90 pounds
G 80 pounds　　J 100 pounds

7. **One side of a small square rug is 4 feet long. One side of a large square rug is 6 feet long. How much greater is the perimeter of the large rug?**

A 6 feet　　C 16 feet
B 8 feet　　D 24 feet

8. **Four students are collecting empty soda cans. Meg has more than Jo but fewer than Sid. Bart has the same number as Meg. Who has the greatest number of cans so far?**

F Meg　　H Sid
G Jo　　J Bart

Use the graph for Questions 9 and 10.

Mrs. Murray made the graph below to show the kinds of dogs that were in her dog show.

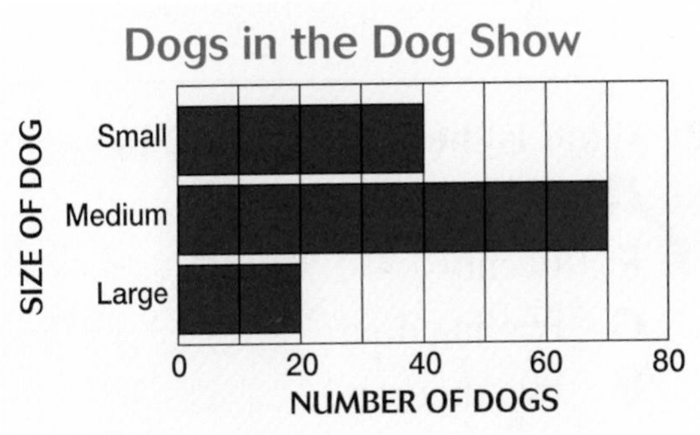

9. **How many small dogs and medium-sized dogs were in the dog show?**

A 10 dogs
B 50 dogs
C 60 dogs
D 110 dogs

10. **Mrs. Murray gave each dog a dog treat at the end of the show. How many dog treats did she give out?**

F 110 treats
G 120 treats
H 130 treats
J 140 treats

Multiple-Choice Cumulative Review

Choose the correct letter for each answer.

Number Sense

1. Which number is between 9,001 and 9,010?

9,001		9,010

A 9,009
B 9,011
C 9,090
D 9,101

2. What is the value of the 2 in 123,031?

F twenty
G two hundred
H two thousand
J twenty thousand

3. What number is the same as 60,000 + 2,000 + 500 + 30?

A 20,653
B 30,625
C 52,630
D 62,530

4. Which shaded region represents $\frac{1}{3}$ of the circle?

F 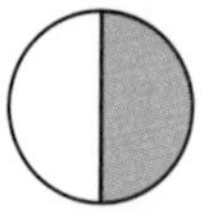
H 
G 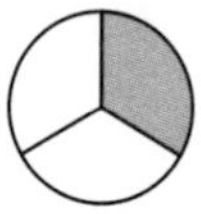
J 

Algebra and Functions

5. What is the missing number in the number pattern?

103, 106, 109, ■, 115

A 110
B 111
C 112
D 113

6. Look at the pattern of shapes. What shape goes in the empty space?

F 
H 
G 
J 

7. How many wheels would 4 freight trucks have?

Number of Freight Trucks	Number of Wheels
1	8
2	16
3	24
■	■

A 4
B 12
C 32
D 48

Measurement and Geometry

8. Look at the thermometer. What is the temperature?

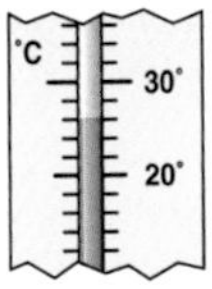

- **F** 20°C
- **G** 22°C
- **H** 26°C
- **J** 28°C

9. Look at the clock. What time will it be in 1 hour?

- **A** 9:20
- **B** 10:20
- **C** 4:45
- **D** 5:45

10. What is the *perimeter* of this figure?

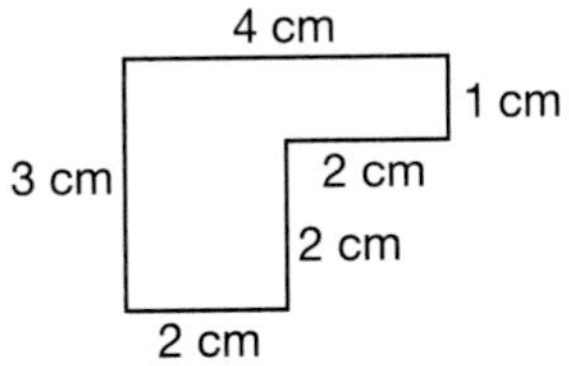

- **F** 14 cm
- **G** 12 cm
- **H** 10 cm
- **J** 6 cm

11. Susan's piano lesson starts at 3:30. It lasts for 30 minutes. When does her lesson end?

A 

C 

B 

D 

12. How many sides does a hexagon have?

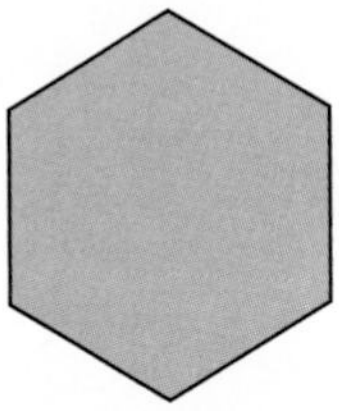

- **F** 4
- **G** 5
- **H** 6
- **J** 8

13. How many lines of symmetry does a square have?

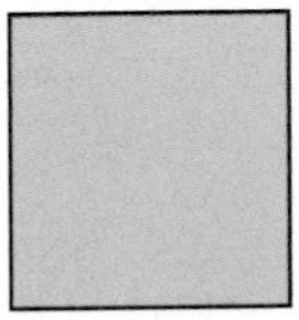

- **A** 2
- **B** 3
- **C** 4
- **D** 6

14. Which of these plane figures is a quadrilateral?

F 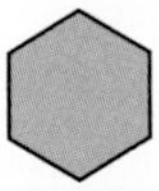

G 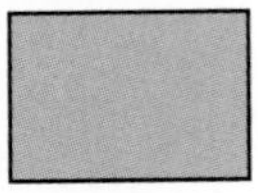

H 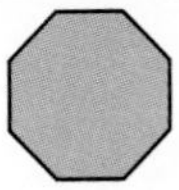

J 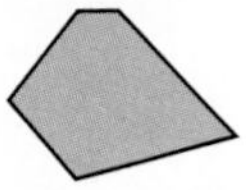

15. Which symbol makes the statement true?

10 cm ● 1 m

- **A** $>$
- **B** $=$
- **C** $<$
- **D** $\times$

CHAPTER 9

Multiplying Greater Numbers

Diagnosing Readiness

In Chapter 9, you will use these skills:

A Rounding

(pages 6–11)

Round to the nearest ten.

1. 63 **2.** 28

3. 47 **4.** 95

Round to the nearest hundred.

5. 627 **6.** 465

7. 392 **8.** 513

Round to the nearest thousand.

9. 1,235 **10.** 4,678

11. 5,519 **12.** 7,005

B Multiplication Facts

(Chapters 4 and 5)

13. 3×6 **14.** 5×9

15. 8×4 **16.** 6×7

17. 2×8 **18.** 5×1

19. 4×9 **20.** 7×7

21. Lou paid $6 for each rosebush and $4 for each bag of potting soil. How much did he spend if he bought 5 bags of potting soil and 4 rosebushes?

C Multiplying by 10

(pages 192–193)

22. 7×10

23. 3×10

24. 6×10

25. 9×10

26. Jennifer had 10 packages of stickers. Each package had 10 stickers. How many stickers does Jennifer have if she gave 8 stickers to Monica?

D Adding Whole Numbers

(pages 48–51)

27. $\begin{array}{r} 365 \\ +\ 28 \\ \hline \end{array}$

28. $\begin{array}{r} 528 \\ +\ 432 \\ \hline \end{array}$

29. $\begin{array}{r} 751 \\ +\ 609 \\ \hline \end{array}$

30. $\begin{array}{r} 3,549 \\ +\ 687 \\ \hline \end{array}$

31. $\begin{array}{r} 2,861 \\ +\ 1,343 \\ \hline \end{array}$

32. $\begin{array}{r} 8,542 \\ +\ 1,097 \\ \hline \end{array}$

33. The main floor of a theater has 565 seats. The balcony has 124 seats. How many seats does the theater have in all?

E Adding and Subtracting Money

(pages 50–51, 60–64)

34. $\begin{array}{r} \$5.63 \\ +\ 2.84 \\ \hline \end{array}$

35. $\begin{array}{r} \$12.30 \\ +\ 8.50 \\ \hline \end{array}$

36. $\begin{array}{r} \$12.91 \\ +\ 0.58 \\ \hline \end{array}$

37. $\begin{array}{r} \$9.53 \\ -\ 4.61 \\ \hline \end{array}$

38. $\begin{array}{r} \$20.00 \\ -\ 14.24 \\ \hline \end{array}$

39. $\begin{array}{r} \$17.06 \\ -\ 4.58 \\ \hline \end{array}$

40. $\begin{array}{r} \$19.95 \\ +\ 6.95 \\ \hline \end{array}$

41. $\begin{array}{r} \$16.58 \\ +\ 1.37 \\ \hline \end{array}$

F Multiplying Three Numbers

(pages 198–199)

42. $2 \times 0 \times 8$

43. $5 \times 2 \times 3$

44. $6 \times 8 \times 1$

45. $2 \times 4 \times 2$

46. $9 \times 1 \times 8$

47. $3 \times 2 \times 3$

48. Porter bought 2 cases of juice boxes. Each case had 4 packages. Each package had 6 juice boxes. How many juice boxes did Porter buy?

To the Family and Student

Looking Back

In Chapters 4 and 5, students learned how to multiply the basic facts.

$6 \times 7 = 42$

Chapter 9

Multiplying Greater Numbers

In this chapter, students will learn how to multiply two-, three-, and four-digit numbers by a one-digit number.

$6{,}329 \times 5 = 31{,}645$

Looking Ahead

In Grade 4, students will learn how to multiply by two-digit numbers.

$6{,}329 \times 53 = 335{,}437$

Math and Everyday Living

Opportunities to apply the concepts of Chapter 9 abound in everyday situations. During the chapter, think about how multiplication can be used to solve a variety of real-world problems. The following examples suggest just several of the many situations that could launch a discussion about multiplication.

Math at Home Last week your family washed 8 loads of clothes. At that rate, how many loads would your family wash in a year? (Note: There are 52 weeks in a year.)

Math and Nutrition A glass of fruit juice has 120 calories. If you drink a glass of juice every day, how many calories will you consume in a week from the juice?

Math at the Movie Theater Movie tickets cost $7.25 for adults and $5.75 for children. What would you pay for 2 adult tickets and 4 children's tickets?

Math at the Grocery Store Lean hamburger costs $3.69 per pound. You need 5 pounds to make chili. How much will the hamburger cost?

Math and Transportation You travel 32 miles each day going to and from your job Monday through Friday. How many miles do you travel in 1 week? How many in 6 weeks?

Math at Work You deliver 75 newspapers each day, Monday through Saturday. You deliver 115 newspapers every Sunday. How many newspapers do you deliver in 4 weeks?

Math at the Department Store A pair of shoes costs $26.99. How much would it cost for 3 pairs of shoes?

Math and Baking You can fit 18 biscuits on a pan. How many biscuits would you have if you made 4 pans of biscuits?

Math at Work You baby-sat for 4 hours each Saturday for 3 weeks. You were paid $6 per hour. How much money did you make altogether?

Math and Sports You play soccer after school twice per week. There are 15 soccer players on your team, and each one has 2 jerseys. How many jerseys does the team have altogether?

California Content Standards in Chapter 9 Lessons*

	Teach and Practice	Practice
Number Sense		
2.4 (🔑) Solve simple problems involving multiplication of multidigit numbers by one-digit numbers	9-1, 9-4, 9-6, 9-7	
3.3 (🔑) Solve problems involving addition, subtraction, multiplication . . . of money amounts in decimal notation and multiply . . . money amounts in decimal notation by using whole-number multipliers	9-8	9-6, 9-7
Algebra and Functions		
1.2 Solve problems involving numeric equations or inequalities.		9-7
1.3 Select appropriate operational and relational symbols to make an expression true		9-7
1.5 Recognize and use the commutative and associative properties of multiplication		9-4, 9-6

	Teach and Practice	Practice
Mathematical Reasoning		
1.1 Analyze problems by identifying relationships, distinguishing relevant from irrelevant information, sequencing and prioritizing information, and observing patterns.	9-2	9-3, 9-7, 9-8
2.0 Students use strategies, skills, and concepts in finding solutions.		9-8
2.1 Use estimation to verify the reasonableness of calculated results.	9-3	
2.2 Apply strategies and results from simpler problems to more complex problems.	9-5	
2.3 Use a variety of methods, such as words, numbers, symbols, charts, graphs, tables, diagrams, and models, to explain mathematical reasoning.		9-4
2.4 Express the solution clearly and logically by using the appropriate mathematical notation and terms and clear language; support solutions with evidence in both verbal and symbolic work.		9-4
2.5 Indicate the relative advantages of exact and approximate solutions to problems and give answers to a specified degree of accuracy.		9-3
3.1 Evaluate the reasonableness of the solution in the context of the original situation.		9-7
3.2 Note method of deriving the solution and demonstrate conceptual understanding of the derivation by solving similar problems.		9-2, 9-5

* The symbol (🔑) indicates a key standard as designated in the Mathematics Framework for California Public Schools. Full statements of the California Content Standards are found at the beginning of this book following the Table of Contents.

LESSON 9-1

Mental Math: Multiplication Patterns

Warm-Up Review

1. 3×4
2. 6×2
3. 3×9
4. 5×10
5. 9×8
6. 7×8
7. Max is 9 years old. He read 8 minutes each night for 6 nights in a row. How many minutes did he read in all?

California Content Standard *Number Sense 2.4(🔑): Solve simple problems involving multiplication of multidigit numbers by one-digit numbers. . ..*

Math Link You know how to find 3×2. Now you will learn to find products like 3×200.

Example 1

Find 3×200.

You can use a basic fact and patterns to help you find the product.

$3 \times 2 = 6$
$3 \times 20 = 60$
$3 \times 200 = 600$

Here's WHY It Works

$3 \times 2 = 6$	**$3 \times 20 = 3 \times 2$ tens $= 6$ tens $= 60$**	**$3 \times 200 = 3 \times 2$ hundreds $= 6$ hundreds $= 600$**

Example 2

Find 5×200.

$5 \times 2 = 10$
$5 \times 20 = 100$
$5 \times 200 = 1{,}000$

When the product of the basic fact includes a zero, that zero is not part of the pattern.

Guided Practice

For another example, see set A on p. 376.

Use basic facts and patterns to find each product.

1. $3 \times 3 = \blacksquare$
   $3 \times 30 = \blacksquare$
   $3 \times 300 = \blacksquare$
2. $4 \times 9 = \blacksquare$
   $4 \times 90 = \blacksquare$
   $4 \times 900 = \blacksquare$
3. $7 \times 2 = \blacksquare$
   $7 \times 20 = \blacksquare$
   $7 \times 200 = \blacksquare$
4. The gift shop bought 8 boxes of birthday cards. Each box had 200 cards. How many cards did the gift shop buy?

Independent Practice *For more practice, see Set A on p. 378.*

Use basic facts and patterns to find each product.

5. 6 × 2 = ■
6 × 20 = ■
6 × 200 = ■

6. 8 × 4 = ■
8 × 40 = ■
8 × 400 = ■

7. 5 × 7 = ■
5 × 70 = ■
5 × 700 = ■

Mental Math **Use mental math to find each product.**

8. 3 × 50 **9.** 4 × 70 **10.** 80 × 8 **11.** 5 × 700

12. 4 × 500 **13.** 400 × 6 **14.** 7 × 800 **15.** 700 × 9

16. Lisa had $4 worth of pennies in her piggy bank. How many pennies did she have in her bank?

17. Abe can type 100 words in 1 minute. How many words can he type in 5 minutes?

Mixed Review

18. A Ferris wheel ride costs $3. Jill, Mark, and Kishi each rode the Ferris wheel 2 times. How much did they spend altogether on Ferris wheel rides?

Name each solid figure.

19. 

20. 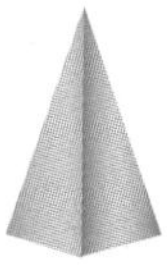

21. 

22. 

Find the volume of each solid in cubic units.

23. 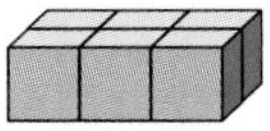

24. 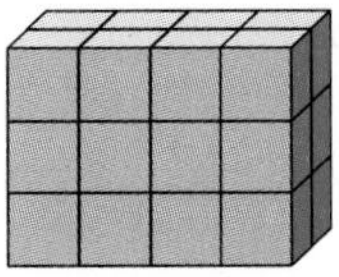

25. 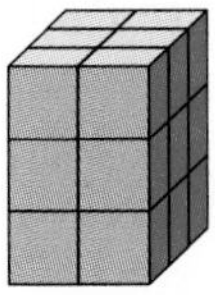

Test Prep **Choose the correct letter for the answer.**

26. **Algebra** Find the missing number. 6 + ■ = 21
(2-14)

F 5 **G** 15 **H** 25 **J** 27

LESSON 9-2

Understand
Plan
Solve
Look Back

Problem-Solving Skill:

Choose the Operation

Warm-Up Review

1. 8 × 9 **2.** 74 + 97

3. 64 ÷ 8 **4.** 67 − 25

5. 3 × 9 **6.** 143 − 68

7. A box of 24 crayons costs $2. How much do 5 boxes of crayons cost?

California Content Standard *Mathematical Reasoning 1.1(🔑): Analyze problems by identifying relationships, distinguishing relevant from irrelevant information, sequencing and prioritizing information, and observing patterns.*

Read for Understanding

The third-grade classes at Wildwood School are having a reading contest. Students record the number of minutes they read at home each night for one week. The goal for the entire third grade is to read a total of 2,000 minutes in one week. The totals for the first week are shown in the table at the right.

Reading Contest

Class	Minutes Read in First Week
Mrs. Hofstad	860
Mrs. Baker	650
Mr. Marshall	540

1. What kind of contest are the third-grade classes having?

2. How many minutes did Mrs. Baker's class read in the first week?

Think and Discuss

MATH FOCUS

Choose the Operation

You can add to put groups together. You can subtract to find out how many more are in one group than in another. You can multiply to combine equal groups. You can divide to separate items into equal groups.

Reread the paragraph at the top of the page.

3. Which operation would you use to find out if the third graders reached their goal the first week?

4. Did the third graders reach their goal the first week? Explain.

 Additional Standard: Mathematical Reasoning 3.2 *(See p. 351.)*

Guided Practice

Use the table on p. 354 for Exercises 1 and 2.

1. Which operation would you use to find out how many more minutes Mrs. Hofstad's class read than Mrs. Baker's class?

a. Subtraction

b. Addition

c. Division

2. Which number sentence tells you how many more minutes Mrs. Hofstad's class read than Mrs. Baker's class?

a. $860 - 650 = ■$

b. $860 + 650 = ■$

c. $860 - 540 = ■$

Independent Practice

The principal gave each third-grade class 5 tokens for each minute they read during the first week. The tokens can be used to purchase books or supplies for the class.

3. Which operation would you use to find out how many tokens the principal gave to each class?

a. Addition

b. Subtraction

c. Multiplication

4. Which number sentence tells you how many tokens the principal gave Mrs. Hofstad's class?

a. $860 \times 5 = ■$

b. $860 + 5 = ■$

c. $860 - 5 = ■$

The 3 third-grade teachers also kept track of how much they read during the week. Each read the same number of minutes the first week. Together they read a total of 450 minutes.

5. Which operation would you use to find out how many minutes each teacher read in the first week?

a. Addition

b. Multiplication

c. Division

6. Which number sentence tells you how many minutes each teacher read in the first week?

a. $450 + 4 = ■$

b. $450 \div 3 = ■$

c. $450 \times 3 = ■$

7. Math Reasoning Suppose the third-grade students and their teachers altogether have a goal to read for 2,600 minutes in one week. How many minutes did the students and their teachers read altogether in the first week? Did they reach their goal in the first week? Explain.

LESSON 9-3

Estimating Products

Warm-Up Review

1. 6×4
2. 4×300

Round to the nearest ten.

3. 35
4. 892
5. After lunch, 4 tractors took 8 students each on a hayride. The tractors drove 5 miles per hour. How many students went on the hayride?

California Content Standard *Mathematical Reasoning 2.1(🔑): Use estimation to verify the reasonableness of calculated results.*

Math Link You know how to multiply by multiples of ten. Now you will learn how to estimate a product by rounding one factor to a multiple of ten.

Example 1

Estimate 34×3.

34×3

rounds to

$30 \times 3 = 90$

To the nearest ten, 34 rounds to 30.

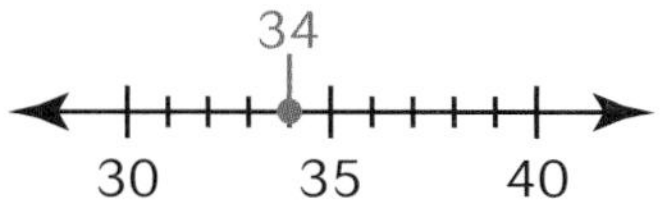

34×3 is about 90.

Example 2

Is 1,416 a reasonable answer for 472×3? Estimate to check.

Round 472 to the nearest hundred to get numbers you can multiply mentally.

472×3

rounds to

$500 \times 3 = 1{,}500$

To the nearest hundred, 472 rounds to 500.

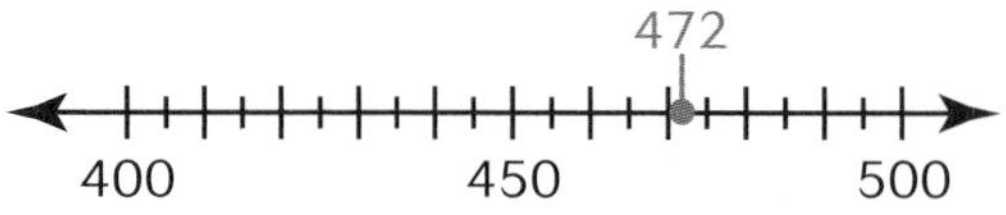

The answer is reasonable because 1,416 is close to 1,500.

Guided Practice *For another example, see Set B on p. 376.*

Round to the underlined place. Estimate each product.

1. $4 \times \underline{2}8$
2. $\underline{5}6 \times 2$
3. $\underline{2}85 \times 3$
4. $5 \times \underline{6}03$
5. Jana spends about $22 per month on pet food. About how much does she spend on pet food in 6 months?

 Additional Standards: Mathematical Reasoning 1.1, 2.5 (See p. 351.)

Independent Practice *For more practice, see Set B on p. 378.*

Round to the underlined place. Estimate each product.

6. $\underline{4}3 \times 6$ **7.** $2 \times \underline{3}7$ **8.** $\underline{3}8 \times 3$ **9.** $\underline{4}7 \times 5$

10. $\underline{1}75 \times 8$ **11.** $\underline{8}93 \times 4$ **12.** $2 \times \underline{1}36$ **13.** $7 \times \underline{4}29$

14. A bakery can make 21 cakes every day. About how many cakes can the bakery make in 5 days?

15. Math Reasoning The same bakery can make 288 rolls in an hour. Can the bakery fill an order for 2,500 rolls in an 8-hour day? Explain.

Mixed Review

16. It takes Jake 30 minutes to mow each lawn in his neighborhood. There are 9 lawns. How long does it take Jake to mow all 9 lawns?

17. 40×4 **18.** 20×7 **19.** 600×9 **20.** 200×5

Find the volume of each figure in cubic units.

21.
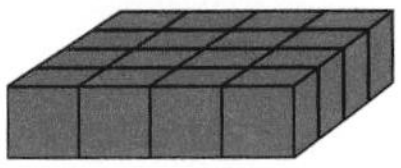

22.
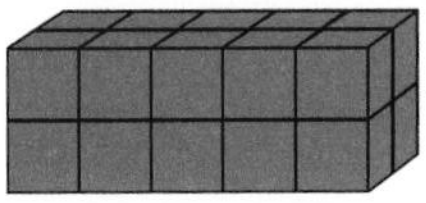

23.
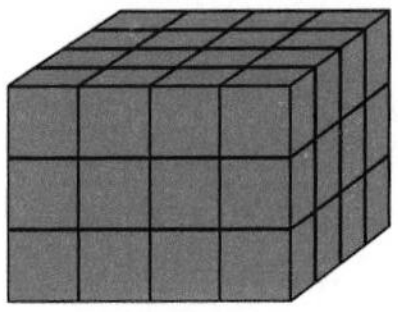

Test Prep **Choose the correct letter for each answer.**

24. (3-3) What is the distance from the top of the table to the ceiling in inches?

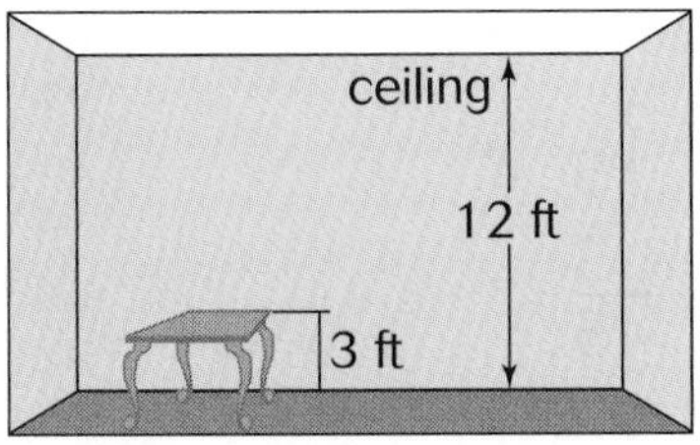

A 108 inches **C** 36 inches
B 98 inches **D** 9 inches

25. (8-10) What is the perimeter of the rectangle?

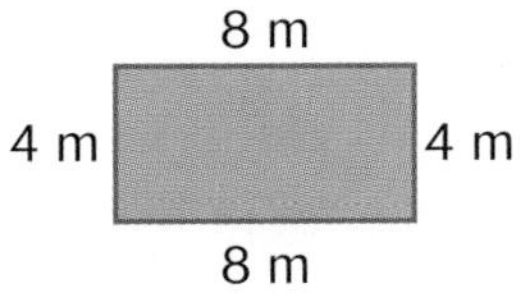

F 8 m **H** 24 m
G 12 m **J** 32 m

LESSON 9-4

Multiplying Two-Digit Numbers

Warm-Up Review

1. 4 × 3
2. 8 × 4
3. 3 × 5
4. 30 × 2
5. 40 × 5
6. 70 × 6
7. John mailed 12 letters each day for 3 days. On the 4th day, he mailed 5 letters. How many letters did he mail in all?

California Content Standard *Number Sense 2.4(🔑): Solve simple problems involving multiplication of multidigit numbers by one-digit numbers. . . .*

Math Link You know how to find 5 × 3. Now you will learn how to find products like 15 × 3.

Example 1

Cora kept track of the number of miles she biked each week for 4 weeks. She recorded her information in the table at the right. How many miles did she bike in the first 3 weeks?

Find 15 × 3.

Step 1 Think about 3 groups of 15.

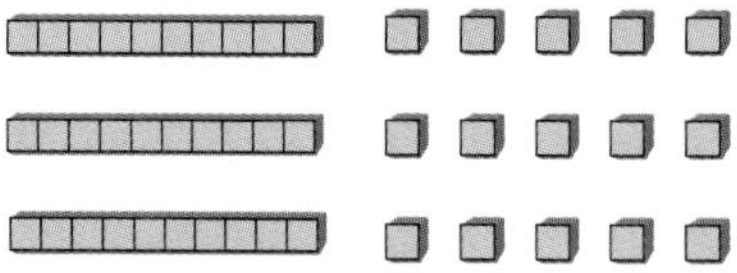

$$\begin{array}{r} 15 \\ \times\ 3 \\ \hline \end{array}$$

Step 2 Multiply ones.
3 × 5 ones = 15 ones
Regroup 15 ones as 1 ten 5 ones.

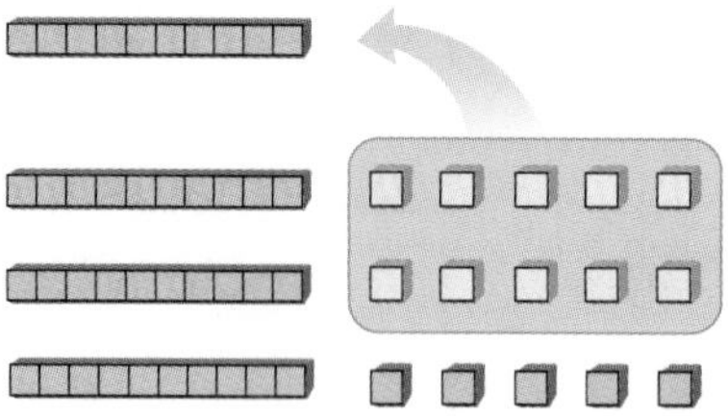

$$\begin{array}{r} {}^{1}\ \\ 15 \\ \times\ 3 \\ \hline 5 \end{array}$$

15 ones

Step 3 Multiply tens.
3 × 1 ten = 3 tens
Add the 1 regrouped ten.
3 tens + 1 ten = 4 tens

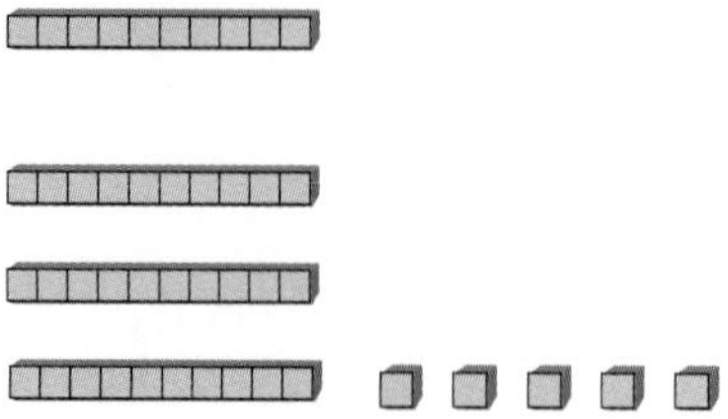

$$\begin{array}{r} {}^{1}\ \\ 15 \\ \times\ 3 \\ \hline 45 \end{array}$$

Cora biked 45 miles in the first three weeks.

Additional Standards: Algebra and Functions 1.5; Mathematical Reasoning 2.3, 2.4 *(See p. 351.)*

Example 2

Sometimes you need to regroup ones and tens when you multiply.

Find 23 × 6.

Step 1 Think about 6 groups of 23.

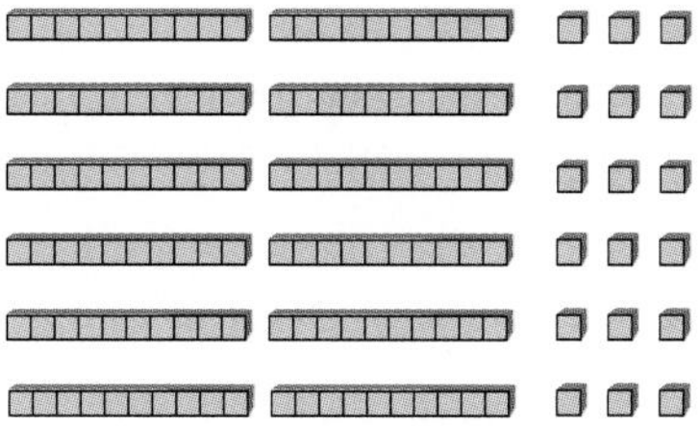

$$\begin{array}{r} 23 \\ \times\ 6 \\ \hline \end{array}$$

Step 2 Multiply ones.
6 × 3 ones = 18 ones

Regroup 18 ones as 1 ten 8 ones.

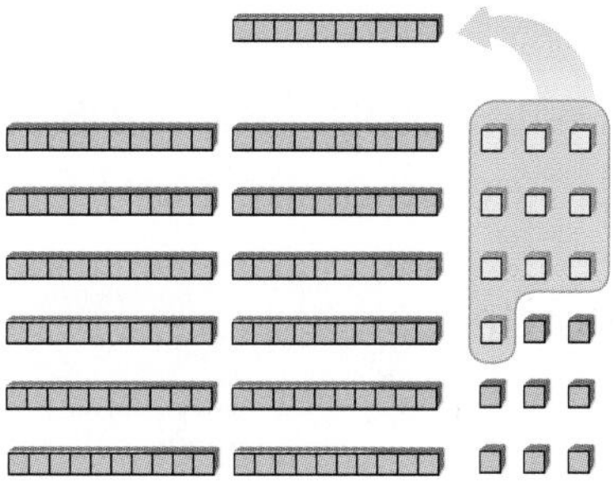

$$\begin{array}{r} ^{1} \\ 23 \\ \times\ 6 \\ \hline 8 \end{array}$$

18 ones

Step 3 Multiply tens.
6 × 2 tens = 12 tens

Add the 1 regrouped ten.
12 tens + 1 ten = 13 tens

Regroup 13 tens as 1 hundred 3 tens.

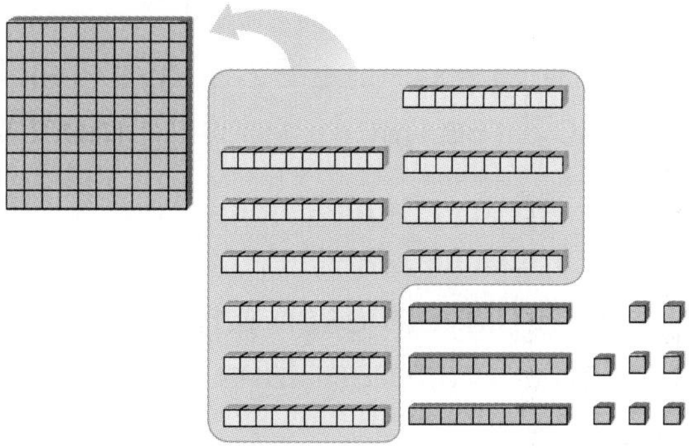

$$\begin{array}{r} ^{1} \\ 23 \\ \times\ 6 \\ \hline 138 \end{array}$$

13 tens

So, 23 × 6 = 138.

Guided Practice

For another example, see Set C on p. 376.

1. $\begin{array}{r} 13 \\ \times\ 4 \\ \hline \end{array}$ **2.** $\begin{array}{r} 36 \\ \times\ 2 \\ \hline \end{array}$ **3.** $\begin{array}{r} 42 \\ \times\ 3 \\ \hline \end{array}$ **4.** $\begin{array}{r} 29 \\ \times\ 4 \\ \hline \end{array}$

5. $\begin{array}{r} 43 \\ \times\ 5 \\ \hline \end{array}$ **6.** $\begin{array}{r} 51 \\ \times\ 4 \\ \hline \end{array}$ **7.** $\begin{array}{r} 72 \\ \times\ 6 \\ \hline \end{array}$ **8.** $\begin{array}{r} 88 \\ \times\ 7 \\ \hline \end{array}$

9. It takes 8 minutes to make a copy of a videotape. How long does it take to make 26 copies?

Independent Practice *For more practice, see Set C on p. 378.*

10. 14×6 **11.** 54×2 **12.** 27×3 **13.** 86×4 **14.** 53×7

15. 67×3 **16.** 45×4 **17.** 97×3 **18.** 80×2 **19.** 55×8

Use the sign to solve Exercises 20 and 21.

20. How much do 5 honey locusts and 8 dogwoods cost?

21. Tess paid for 2 trees with $200. She got $32 back in change. What trees did she buy?

Algebra **Multiply in any order.**

22. $8 \times 2 \times 5$

23. $7 \times 9 \times 3$

24. $6 \times 5 \times 7$

25. $4 \times 6 \times 6$

26. **Math Reasoning** Look at Exercise 22 above. Tell how you could multiply the three numbers using mental math.

Mixed Review

27. After a soccer game, 8 players each gave an autographed photo to 30 different fans. How many photos did they give away?

Mental Math **Use mental math to find each product.**

28. 400×2 **29.** 30×8 **30.** 6×50 **31.** 500×2

Round to the underlined place. Estimate each product.

32. $3 \times \underline{1}2$ **33.** $\underline{4}2 \times 4$ **34.** $\underline{7}3 \times 6$ **35.** $5 \times \underline{3}74$

Test Prep **Choose the correct letter for each answer.**

36. 2 c = ___?___ gal
(3-4)

A 4
B 6
C 8
D 12
E NH

37. **Algebra** Which three numbers make the statement true?
(5-10)
6 × ■ is less than 50.

F 6, 9, 12
G 5, 7, 9
H 6, 7, 8
J 0, 5, 10

 Use Homework Workbook 9-4.

Diagnostic Checkpoint

Use basic facts and patterns to find each product.

1. (9-1) $4 \times 2 = \blacksquare$
$4 \times 20 = \blacksquare$
$4 \times 200 = \blacksquare$

2. (9-1) $3 \times 5 = \blacksquare$
$3 \times 50 = \blacksquare$
$3 \times 500 = \blacksquare$

3. (9-1) $6 \times 7 = \blacksquare$
$6 \times 70 = \blacksquare$
$6 \times 700 = \blacksquare$

Round to the underlined place. Estimate the product.

4. (9-3) $4 \times \underline{5}8$

5. (9-3) $3 \times \underline{8}9$

6. (9-3) $5 \times \underline{6}2$

7. (9-3) $\underline{7}2 \times 5$

8. (9-3) $8 \times \underline{3}85$

9. (9-3) $\underline{2}93 \times 3$

10. (9-3) $\underline{1}17 \times 9$

11. (9-3) $5 \times \underline{8}29$

Find each product.

12. (9-4) $\begin{array}{r} 13 \\ \times\ 3 \\ \hline \end{array}$

13. (9-4) $\begin{array}{r} 24 \\ \times\ 3 \\ \hline \end{array}$

14. (9-4) $\begin{array}{r} 39 \\ \times\ 6 \\ \hline \end{array}$

15. (9-4) $\begin{array}{r} 27 \\ \times\ 2 \\ \hline \end{array}$

16. (9-4) $\begin{array}{r} 94 \\ \times\ 5 \\ \hline \end{array}$

17. (9-4) $\begin{array}{r} 62 \\ \times\ 7 \\ \hline \end{array}$

18. (9-4) $\begin{array}{r} 46 \\ \times\ 8 \\ \hline \end{array}$

19. (9-4) $\begin{array}{r} 85 \\ \times\ 4 \\ \hline \end{array}$

20. (9-2) It's the grand opening of Frontier Florists! Every day for 8 days they give away 50 roses. How many roses in all do they give away? What operation did you use?

21. (9-4) School T-shirts cost \$7. School shorts cost \$9. How much money will Mrs. Templeton's class need to raise if they want to buy 24 T-shirts and 24 shorts?

22. (9-3) Footballs sell for \$32 each. Would it be reasonable to say that \$200 would be enough to buy 8 footballs? Explain.

23. (9-1) Mr. Tillman wants to buy 6 calculators for his class. The cost for each calculator is \$20. How much money will Mr. Tillman spend?

24. (9-2) Jami baby-sat for 20 hours. If she worked for the same number of hours each day for 5 days, how many hours did she work each day? What operation did you use?

LESSON 9-5

Understand
Plan
Solve
Look Back

Problem-Solving Strategy:

Solve a Simpler Problem

California Content Standard *Mathematical Reasoning 2.2: Apply strategies and results from simpler problems to more complex problems.*

Warm-Up Review

1. 230 + 15 **2.** 293 − 59

3. 18 × 7 **4.** 40 ÷ 4

5. A square has a perimeter of 16 feet. What is the length of each side of the square?

Maria found a long rope that she wanted to have cut into 7 jump ropes. What is the least number of cuts needed to make the 7 jump ropes?

Understand

What do you need to find?

You need to find the least number of cuts necessary to make one rope into 7 ropes.

Plan

How can you solve the problem?

You can begin by **solving a simpler problem.**

Think about how many cuts are needed to make 2, 3, and 4 ropes.

Solve

For 2 jump ropes, you need 1 cut.
For 3 ropes, you need a second cut.
For 4 ropes, you need a third cut.

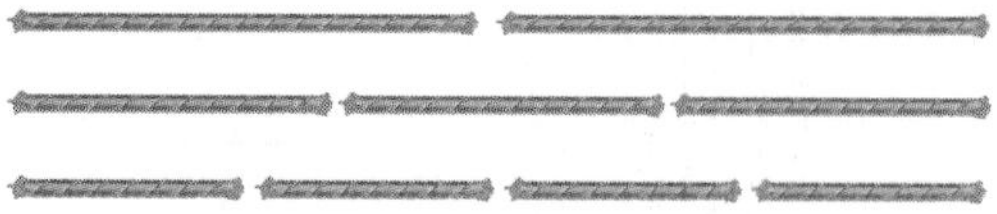

Organize your results in a table. Then, look for a pattern. The number of cuts needed is 1 less than the number of ropes made. So, 6 cuts are needed to make 7 ropes.

Number of of Cuts	Number of Jump Ropes
0	1
1	2
2	3
3	4
4	5
5	6
6	7

Look Back

Look for another pattern in the table. Does the pattern give the same results for 7 ropes?

 Additional Standard: Mathematical Reasoning 3.2 *(See p. 351.)*

Guided Practice

1. Mary Etta Proper wants to use her initials in her e-mail address. How many different combinations are possible if each letter is used only once?

2. A board was cut into 10 equal parts to make shelves. How many cuts were made?

Independent Practice

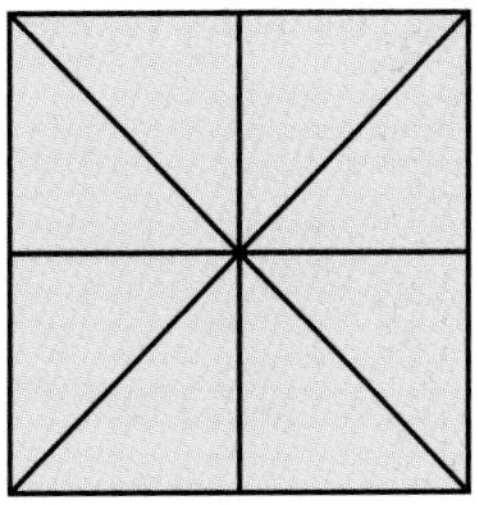

3. How many triangles can you find in the design to the right?

4. How many squares are in the design?

5. Every person at Lexi's party played tic-tac-toe with everyone else one time. If there were 4 people at the party, how many games of tic-tac-toe were played?

6. You are buying T-shirts to donate to a charity. T-shirts come in packages of 3 shirts for $7. How many T-shirts could you buy for $35?

Mixed Review

Try these or other strategies to solve each problem. Tell which strategy you used.

Problem-Solving Strategies

- *Write a Number Sentence*
- *Find a Pattern*
- *Make a List*
- *Use Logical Reasoning*

7. The cost of a table after a discount of $180 is $952. What was the original cost of the table?

8. The difference between two numbers is 20. Their sum is 40. What are the numbers?

9. Ben wrote these numbers: 10, 11, 13, 16, 20, 25. If he continues the pattern, what will the next 3 numbers be?

LESSON 9-6

Multiplying Three-Digit Numbers

Warm-Up Review

1. 11 × 4
2. 21 × 3
3. $15 × 8
4. 30 × 5
5. Kisha calls 6 of her friends on the phone. She talks to 4 friends for 12 minutes each and 2 friends for 8 minutes each. How long does she talk on the phone?

California Content Standard *Number Sense 2.4(🔑): Solve simple problems involving multiplication of multidigit numbers by one-digit numbers. . ..*

Math Link You know how to find 46 × 7. Now you will learn how to find products like 463 × 7.

Example 1

Find 137 × 2.

Step 1
Multiply ones.
2 × 7 ones = 14 ones

Regroup 14 ones as 1 ten 4 ones.

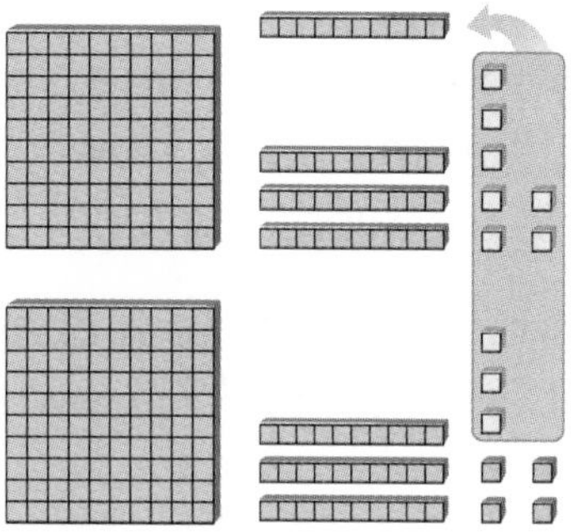

```
   1
  137   14 ones
×   2
    4
```

Step 2
Multiply tens.
2 × 3 tens = 6 tens

Add the 1 regrouped ten.
6 tens + 1 ten = 7 tens

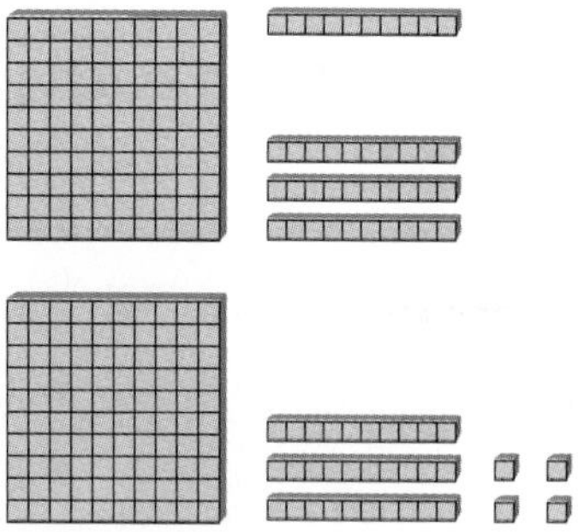

```
   1
  137
×   2
   74
```

Step 3
Multiply hundreds.
2 × 1 hundred = 2 hundreds

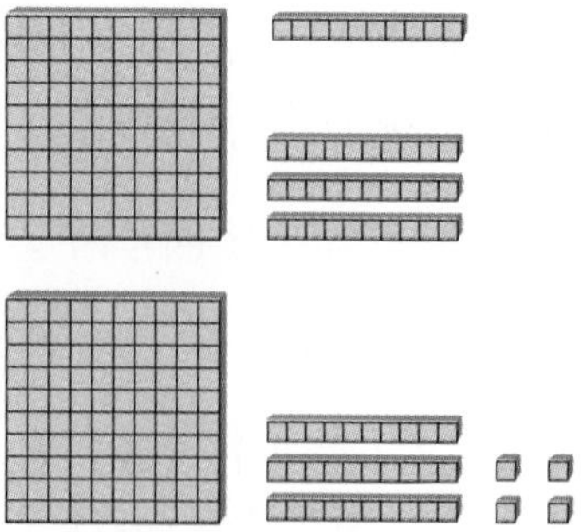

```
   1
  137
×   2
  274
```

So, 137 × 2 = 274.

Additional Standards: Number Sense 3.3(🔑); Algebra and Functions 1.5 *(See p. 351.)*

Example 2

Now that you know how to multiply three-digit numbers, you can multiply money.

Find $1.43 × 6.

Step 1
Multiply pennies.
6 × 3 pennies = 18 pennies

Trade 18 pennies for
1 dime 8 pennies.

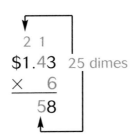

$$\begin{array}{r} \scriptstyle 1 \\ \$1.43 \\ \times \quad 6 \\ \hline 8 \end{array}$$

18 pennies

Step 2
Multiply dimes.
6 × 4 dimes = 24 dimes

Add the 1 dime.
24 dimes + 1 dime = 25 dimes

Trade 25 dimes for 2 dollars
5 dimes.

$$\begin{array}{r} \scriptstyle 2\ 1 \\ \$1.43 \\ \times \quad 6 \\ \hline 58 \end{array}$$

25 dimes

Step 3
Multiply dollars.
6 × 1 dollar = 6 dollars

Add the 2 traded dollars.
6 dollars + 2 dollars = 8 dollars

$$\begin{array}{r} \scriptstyle 2\ 1 \\ \$1.43 \\ \times \quad 6 \\ \hline \$8.58 \end{array}$$

So, $1.43 × 6 = $8.58.

When you multiply money, remember to use a dollar sign and a decimal point.

Guided Practice

For another example, see Set D on p. 377.

1. 134 × 3

2. $2.41 × 3

3. 452 × 3

4. $4.81 × 7

5. 324 × 0

6. Small water bottles cost $1.80 each and large water bottles cost $2.60 each. How much do 4 small water bottles cost?

7. There are 144 crayons in each box. How many crayons are in 6 boxes?

Independent Practice

For more practice, see Set D on p. 379.

8. 121 × 3
9. $6.23 × 2
10. 329 × 5
11. $5.99 × 1
12. 946 × 2

13. 385 × 5
14. $2.91 × 4
15. 488 × 4
16. $3.79 × 6
17. 876 × 6

18. 431 × 5 **19.** $3.84 × 2 **20.** 671 × 4 **21.** $263 × 4

22. Mental Math Find $3.00 × 7. **23. Mental Math** Find $1.11 × 5.

24. Algebra Find the missing number. 578 × ■ = 6 × 578.

Use the table at the right to answer Exercises 25 and 26.

25. How much will 6 pounds of deluxe mix and 2 pounds of safflower seeds cost?

26. How much more does one pound of safflower seeds cost than one pound of standard mix?

Bird Seed

Type of Seed	Price per pound
Standard Mix	$0.98
Deluxe Mix	$1.45
Safflower Seeds	$2.49

Mixed Review

27. The circus feeds its horses about 106 pounds of hay per day. About how much hay are the horses fed in a week?

28. 23 × 5 **29.** 46 × 8 **30.** 19 × 0 **31.** 73 × 4

Round to the underlined digit. Estimate each product.

32. $\underline{4}6$ × 4 **33.** $\underline{1}8$ × 8 **34.** $\underline{3}71$ × 4 **35.** $\underline{4}93$ × 3

Test Prep **Choose the correct letter for each answer.**

36. (1-1) A museum owns 1,403 paintings. What is this number in expanded notation?

A 1 + 4 + 3
B 100 + 40 + 3
C 1,000 + 400 + 3
D 1,000 + 400 + 30

37. (3-1) The rodeo starts at 11:30 A.M. It lasts 2 hours and 30 minutes. When does it end?

F 11:32 A.M.
G 11:50 A.M.
H 2:00 P.M.
J 2:30 P.M.

LESSON 9-7

Multiplying Greater Numbers

Warm-Up Review

1. 23 × 4 **2.** 98 × 7

3. 143 × 6 **4.** $2.53 × 2

5. A baseball bat that originally cost $8.46 is on sale for $6.50. How much will 4 bats cost on sale?

California Content Standard *Number Sense 2.4(🔑): Solve simple problems involving multiplication of multidigit numbers by one-digit numbers. . ..*

Math Link You know how to find 368 × 6. Now you will learn how to find products like 1,368 × 6.

Example 1

The chart below shows how many tickets can be sold at each city event center. This year's circus sold out 4 shows at Metro Auditorium. How many tickets were sold for the circus?

Find 1,954 × 4.

City Event Centers

Location	Seating Capacity
Oak Hill Theater	1,247
Jones Hall	968
River Arena	8,978
Metro Auditorium	1,954

Step 1 Multiply the ones. Regroup as needed.

$$\begin{array}{r} {}^{1}\\ 1{,}954 \\ \times \quad 4 \\ \hline 6 \end{array}$$

Step 2 Multiply the tens. Add any extra tens. Regroup as needed.

$$\begin{array}{r} {}^{21}\\ 1{,}954 \\ \times \quad 4 \\ \hline 16 \end{array}$$

Step 3 Multiply the hundreds. Add any extra hundreds. Regroup as needed.

$$\begin{array}{r} {}^{3\,21}\\ 1{,}954 \\ \times \quad 4 \\ \hline 816 \end{array}$$

Step 4 Multiply the thousands. Add any extra thousands.

$$\begin{array}{r} {}^{3\,21}\\ 1{,}954 \\ \times \quad 4 \\ \hline 7{,}816 \end{array}$$

So, 7,816 tickets were sold for the circus.

<u>Check</u> by estimating. 2,000 × 4 = 8,000. The answer is reasonable because 8,000 is close to 7,816.

Additional Standards: Number Sense 3.3(🔑); Algebra and Functions 1.2, 1.3; Mathematical Reasoning 1.1, 3.1 (See p. 351.)

Example 2

Tom and his two friends each bought front row seats to the basketball game at River Arena. With tax, each ticket cost $43.98. How much money did they spend in all for the tickets?

Find $43.98 × 3.

Step 1	Step 2	Step 3	Step 4
2 $43.98 × 3 4	2 2 $43.98 × 3 94	1 2 2 $43.98 × 3 194	1 2 2 $43.98 × 3 $131.94

Remember to show dollars and cents in the product.

So, the tickets cost $131.94.

<u>Check</u> by estimating. $40.00 × 3 = $120.00. The answer is reasonable because $120.00 is close to $131.94.

More Examples

A.
```
     1
 4,002
×    5
20,010
```

B.
```
 5 1
 3,820
×    7
26,740
```

C.
```
   2  2
 $67.19
×     3
$201.57
```

Guided Practice

For another example, see Set E on p. 377.

1. 5,656 × 2

2. 2,482 × 9

3. $60.38 × 4

4. 3,982 × 6

5. $81.20 × 4

6. A bike company made 2,576 bikes. How many tires did it need for the bikes?

7. Robby bought 3 backpacks at $21.68 each with tax. How much money did Robby spend on backpacks?

Independent Practice *For more practice, see Set E on p. 379.*

8. 2,413 × 3
9. \$35.92 × 8
10. 4,040 × 5
11. \$70.53 × 4
12. 1,128 × 7
13. 2,521 × 4
14. \$36.90 × 6
15. \$86.42 × 2
16. 3,499 × 5
17. \$78.50 × 5

Find each product. Use estimation to check your answer.

18. 4 × 4,102 **19.** \$22.34 × 6 **20.** 3,738 × 3

Algebra **Compare. Use >, <, or =.**

21. \$14.55 × 6 ● \$14.55 × 7 **22.** 3,600 × 9 ● 3,500 × 9

Use the table for Exercises 23 and 24.

23. What is the cost of 4 round-trip tickets with a 2-week advance purchase?

24. How much more do three 7-day advance purchase tickets cost than three 4-week advance purchase tickets?

Airline Tickets	
Advance Purchase	Cost for Round Trip
4 weeks	\$1,098
2 weeks	\$1,624
7 days or less	\$2,249

Mixed Review

25. Sophia's Garden Club planted 8 rows of tomato plants. They planted 12 plants in each row. How many tomato plants did the Garden Club plant?

26. 78 × 2
27. 59 × 7
28. 123 × 6
29. 462 × 8
30. 356 × 1

Test Prep **Choose the correct letter for each answer.**

31. (2-13) **Algebra** Which number makes the statement true?

■ + 7 is greater than 12.

A 1 **C** 5
B 4 **D** 6

32. (8-10) The perimeter of a rectangle is 14 feet. Two of the sides are 5 feet, and one side is 2 feet. What is the length of the fourth side?

F 2 feet **H** 5 feet
G 4 feet **J** 6 feet

LESSON 9-8

Understand
Plan
Solve
Look Back

Problem-Solving Application:
Using Money

California Content Standard *Number Sense 3.3(🔑): Solve problems involving addition, subtraction, multiplication . . . of money amounts in decimal notation and multiply . . . money amounts in decimal notation by using whole-number multipliers . . ..*

Warm-Up Review

1. $1.50 × 3
2. $3.25 + $1.50
3. Megan and her 2 friends went shopping. They each bought 2 new pairs of earrings that cost $8.95 each. How many pairs of earrings did they buy altogether?

Use the table at the right. Paul is going to rent a mountain bike. How much will it cost to rent a 15-speed mountain bike for 6 hours?

Bike Rentals	
10-speed	$4.50 per hour
15-speed	$6.25 per hour

Understand

What do you need to find?

You need to find out how much it will cost to rent a 15-speed mountain bike for 6 hours.

Plan

How can you solve the problem?

You can multiply the hourly rental price by 6 hours.

Solve

```
   1 3
  $6.25 ←— price per hour
×     6 ←— number of hours
 $37.50 ←— total cost
```

It will cost $37.50 to rent a mountain bike for 6 hours.

Look Back

How can you check your answer?

Use estimation to see if your answer is reasonable. $6.00 × 6 = $36.00. The answer is reasonable because $36.00 is close to $37.50.

Additional Standards: Mathematical Reasoning 1.1, 2.0 *(See p. 351.)*

Use the sign at the right for Exercises 1–5.

Additional Items For Sale	
bike helmet	$23.50
tire-tube repair kit	$4.50
gloves	$8.95
bike lock	$12.50
nutrition bar	$1.25
water bottle	$3.70

Guided Practice

1. How much money would you spend if you bought a water bottle and gloves?

2. How much money would you spend if you bought a lock and 3 nutrition bars?

Independent Practice

3. You have $20. How much will you have left if you buy gloves and a tire-tube repair kit?

4. You bought a helmet and one other item advertised at the right. Together the items cost $36.00. What was the other item that you bought?

5. You buy 4 nutrition bars, a helmet, and a bike lock. You pay for your items with three $20 bills. How much change should you get back?

Mixed Review

6. Ms. Richardson gave her students a number pattern. She wrote the numbers 1, 2, 4, 8, and 16 on the chalkboard. If she continues the pattern, what will the 10th number be?

7. Stan got home from school at 4:45 P.M. He talked to a friend for 10 minutes after school, then spent an hour at band practice, and afterward walked for 20 minutes to get home. At what time did the school day end?

8. Jeffrey spends $124.99 for a new snowboard and $48.50 for boots. How much money does Jeffrey spend?

9. Tasha has $55 in the bank. Each week she earns $10 raking leaves for her neighbors. She also receives $6 weekly from her parents for cleaning her room and helping with the dishes. If she saves all her money, how much will she have in 4 weeks?

Diagnostic Checkpoint

Complete. For Exercises 1–4, use the words from the Word Bank.

Word Bank
estimate
factors
multiply
product
quotient
rounding

1. (9-1) The answer in multiplication is called the ________.

2. (9-3) The numbers you multiply are called ________.

3. (9-3) If you round the numbers before multiplying them, your answer will be a(n) ________.

Find each product.

4. (9-6) $\begin{array}{r} 816 \\ \times \quad 5 \\ \hline \end{array}$

5. (9-6) $\begin{array}{r} \$2.13 \\ \times \quad 4 \\ \hline \end{array}$

6. (9-6) $\begin{array}{r} 328 \\ \times \quad 7 \\ \hline \end{array}$

7. (9-6) $\begin{array}{r} \$914 \\ \times \quad 5 \\ \hline \end{array}$

8. (9-7) $\begin{array}{r} \$27.19 \\ \times \quad 4 \\ \hline \end{array}$

9. (9-7) $\begin{array}{r} 8{,}039 \\ \times \quad 3 \\ \hline \end{array}$

10. (9-7) $\begin{array}{r} 5{,}620 \\ \times \quad 5 \\ \hline \end{array}$

11. (9-7) $\begin{array}{r} \$16.25 \\ \times \quad 6 \\ \hline \end{array}$

12. (9-6) $8.68 × 4

13. (9-6) 189 × 9

14. (9-7) $45.27 × 5

15. (9-7) 6,119 × 8

16. (9-8) A box of pecans costs $7.20. Beth has $21.36. How much more money does she need to buy 3 boxes?

17. (9-5) Tanner can make 5 birdhouses in 2 hours. How many birdhouses could he make in 8 hours?

18. (6-4) Paperback books cost $1.99. Hardback books cost three times as much. Marshall wants to buy 5 paperback books and 2 hardback books. How much money will he need?

19. (9-6) Each case has 144 oranges. How many oranges did the store order if it ordered 7 cases?

20. (9-5) Rena wants to plant tulips, pansies, and marigolds side by side. In how many different ways can she arrange the three types of flowers? List all the ways.

Chapter 9 Test

Use basic facts and patterns to help you multiply.

1. $5 \times 6 = ■$
$5 \times 60 = ■$
$5 \times 600 = ■$

2. $3 \times 7 = ■$
$3 \times 70 = ■$
$3 \times 700 = ■$

3. $6 \times 4 = ■$
$6 \times 40 = ■$
$6 \times 400 = ■$

Round to the underlined place. Then estimate each product.

4. $\underline{8}2 \times 7$ **5.** $\underline{3}6 \times 6$ **6.** $\underline{8}00 \times 5$ **7.** $\underline{9}43 \times 8$

Find each product.

8. 71×5 **9.** 248×6 **10.** 32×3 **11.** 356×4

12. $3{,}018 \times 5$ **13.** $\$2.99 \times 5$ **14.** $2{,}651 \times 4$ **15.** $\$22.88 \times 7$

16. $\$3.29 \times 6$ **17.** $3{,}210 \times 7$ **18.** 43×8

19. Tickets to the amusement park cost $35.50 each. Mr. Kelly has $200. Does he have enough to buy tickets for himself and 5 friends? Explain.

20. A complete soccer uniform costs $87. Estimate how much it will cost the Kirby family to buy uniforms for their 4 boys.

21. Each coloring book costs $2.39. You have $10. How much will you have left after buying 4 coloring books?

22. Amy is making costumes for a play. She can make 2 costumes in 7 hours. How many costumes can she make in 35 hours?

23. You did 20 sit-ups for 5 days in a row. Write a number sentence that tells how many sit-ups you did altogether.

TEST PREP

Multiple-Choice Chapter 9 Test

Choose the correct letter for each answer.

1. Estimate 5×62.

   A 30
   B 300
   C 3,000
   D 30,000

2. Find the product of 6×900.

   F 54
   G 540
   H 5,400
   J 54,000
   K NH

3. Which is the most reasonable estimate of 8×361?

   A 240
   B 320
   C 2,400
   D 3,200

4. Mercedes wants to buy 5 boxes of pencils. Each box has 12 pencils. Which operation should she use to find the total number of pencils?

   F Addition
   G Subtraction
   H Multiplication
   J Division

5. Ms. Nelson's class is making decorations for the school play. Each student is making 7 tissue flowers. If there are 24 students in Ms. Nelson's class, how many tissue flowers will there be?

   A 148 tissue flowers
   B 164 tissue flowers
   C 168 tissue flowers
   D 188 tissue flowers

6. Each section of the arena has 1,170 seats. There are 8 sections in the arena. How many seats are there in all?

   F 8,360 seats
   G 8,860 seats
   H 9,360 seats
   J 9,368 seats

7. Each bracelet cost $9.46. Nick bought a bracelet for his mother and one for each of his 2 sisters. How much did Nick spend?

   A $27.38
   B $28.38
   C $28.44
   D $28.68

8. Find the product of 4×617.

   F 2,448
   G 2,458
   H 2,461
   J 2,468
   K NH

9. $\begin{array}{r} 37 \\ \times\ 9 \\ \hline \end{array}$

A 263
B 273
C 333
D 2,763
E NH

---

10. $6 \times 3 \times 8 =$

F 144
G 168
H 192
J 216
K NH

---

11. **It is 326 miles from Leo's house to his grandmother's house. If Leo travels from his house to his grandmother's house round trip 3 times per year, how many miles will he travel?**

A 978 miles
B 1,826 miles
C 1,856 miles
D 1,956 miles

---

12. $5 \times \$26.05 =$

F $100.05
G $130.05
H $130.25
J $13,025.00
K NH

---

13. **Rose bought 48 apples. She needs to put 8 apples in each basket. What operation would you use to find the number of baskets needed for all the apples?**

A Addition
B Subtraction
C Multiplication
D Division

---

14. **Gwen can drive 10 miles in 15 minutes. How many miles could she drive in 1 hour?**

F 10 miles
G 15 miles
H 30 miles
J 40 miles

---

15. **Each package of paper has 500 sheets. How many sheets would you have if you bought 6 packages?**

A 30 sheets
B 300 sheets
C 3,000 sheets
D 30,000 sheets

---

16. $\begin{array}{r} \$5.67 \\ \times\ \ \ \ 4 \\ \hline \end{array}$

F $20.48
G $22.48
H $22.68
J $2,268.00
K NH

Reteaching

Set A (pages 352–353)

Find 7 × 500.

You can use basic facts and patterns to help you multiply multiples of 10.

7 × 5 = 35
7 × 50 = 350
7 × 500 = 3,500

Remember when the product of a basic fact includes a zero, that zero is not part of the pattern.

1. 5 × 80 **2.** 6 × 800

3. 9 × 300 **4.** 4 × 60

5. 3 × 20 **6.** 8 × 700

Set B (pages 356–357)

Estimate 4 × 93.

To the nearest ten, 93 rounds to 90.

4 × 93

rounds to

4 × 90 = 360

Remember that if the first digit to the right of the rounding place is a 5, you round up.

Round to the underlined place. Estimate each product.

1. $3 \times \underline{4}7$ **2.** $8 \times \underline{2}4$

3. $6 \times \underline{6}5$ **4.** $7 \times \underline{3}69$

5. $5 \times \underline{2}37$ **6.** $9 \times \underline{5}85$

Set C (pages 358–360)

Find 57 × 6.

Step 1 Multiply ones.

$$\begin{array}{r} {}^{4} \\ 57 \\ \times\ 6 \\ \hline 2 \end{array}$$

42 ones

Step 2 Multiply tens.

$$\begin{array}{r} {}^{4} \\ 57 \\ \times\ 6 \\ \hline 342 \end{array}$$

34 tens

Remember to regroup ones and tens when necessary.

1. $\begin{array}{r} 42 \\ \times\ 7 \\ \hline \end{array}$ **2.** $\begin{array}{r} 98 \\ \times\ 3 \\ \hline \end{array}$

3. $\begin{array}{r} 24 \\ \times\ 2 \\ \hline \end{array}$ **4.** $\begin{array}{r} 65 \\ \times\ 4 \\ \hline \end{array}$

5. $\begin{array}{r} 77 \\ \times\ 3 \\ \hline \end{array}$ **6.** $\begin{array}{r} 81 \\ \times\ 9 \\ \hline \end{array}$

Set D *(pages 364–366)*

Find 468 × 3.

Step 1 Multiply ones.

$$\begin{array}{r} {}^{2} \\ 468 \\ \times \quad 3 \\ \hline 4 \end{array}$$

24 ones

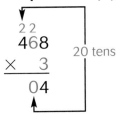

Step 2 Multiply tens.

$$\begin{array}{r} {}^{2\,2} \\ 468 \\ \times \quad 3 \\ \hline 04 \end{array}$$

20 tens

Step 3 Multiply hundreds.

$$\begin{array}{r} {}^{2\,2} \\ 468 \\ \times \quad 3 \\ \hline 1{,}404 \end{array}$$

14 hundreds

Remember to estimate to check if the product is reasonable.

1. 321 × 7
2. 824 × 5
3. $5.46 × 4
4. 685 × 6
5. 719 × 8
6. $4.43 × 5
7. 296 × 3
8. $8.60 × 9
9. 2 × 984
10. 632 × 6
11. 554 × 8
12. 3 × $5.17

Set E *(pages 367–369)*

Find $26.13 × 5.

$$\begin{array}{r} \$26.13 \\ \times \quad 5 \\ \hline \$130.65 \end{array}$$

Remember to show dollar and cents in the product when multiplying money.

1. 6,328 × 3
2. 1,698 × 4
3. $26.15 × 5
4. 8,064 × 9
5. 7,361 × 6
6. $12.88 × 7
7. $76.30 × 8
8. 4,343 × 3

More Practice

Set A *(pages 352–353)*

1. $80 \times 4 =$
2. $70 \times 4 =$
3. $500 \times 3 =$
4. $600 \times 8 =$
5. A window washer can clean 30 windows in 1 hour. How many windows can he clean in 8 hours?
6. A computer company sends 900 e-mail messages each day. How many e-mail messages does it send in a 5-day work week?

Set B *(pages 356–357)*

Round to the underlined place. Estimate each product.

1. $\underline{5}7 \times 4$
2. $\underline{9}5 \times 6$
3. $6 \times \underline{3}40$
4. $\underline{7}28 \times 9$
5. The Comet football team practices 3 hours at a time. There are 38 practices during the season. About how many hours does the team practice each season?
6. The Comet football team bought 7 new uniforms. The cost for each new uniform was $270. About how much did the team spend on new uniforms?

Set C *(pages 358–360)*

Find each product.

1. 95×6
2. 48×7
3. 52×4
4. 86×5
5. 93×8
6. 23×2
7. 73×3
8. 82×4
9. 14×5
10. 28×3
11. 2×42
12. 7×93
13. 24×4
14. 8×95
15. In-line skates sell for $62 a pair. Mr. Hui has $200. Does he have enough to buy 3 pairs of in-line skates? How do you know?

Set D (pages 364–366)

Find each product.

1. 422×5
2. 242×4
3. $\$2.23 \times 4$
4. 875×8
5. $\$4.19 \times 7$
6. 513×6
7. 757×3
8. $\$1.27 \times 5$
9. 377×9
10. $\$2.56 \times 7$
11. 3×239
12. 176×5
13. $\$3.28 \times 4$
14. $\$5.13 \times 7$
15. 326×4
16. $7 \times \$6.94$
17. 8×132
18. $\$7.19 \times 9$
19. A hospital cafeteria prepares 495 meals each day. How many meals are prepared in one week?

Set E (pages 367–369)

Find each product.

1. $6{,}205 \times 3$
2. $\$28.61 \times 8$
3. $4{,}528 \times 5$
4. $3{,}391 \times 4$
5. $\$19.75 \times 6$
6. $9{,}212 \times 7$
7. $\$38.15 \times 2$
8. $5{,}246 \times 9$
9. $4{,}290 \times 4$
10. $\$27.94 \times 3$
11. $2{,}056 \times 8$
12. $\$73.10 \times 9$
13. $\$23.86 \times 6$
14. $4 \times 3{,}392$
15. $\$46.66 \times 5$
16. $7 \times 3{,}234$
17. $3 \times 2{,}242$
18. $\$98.50 \times 2$
19. A car company needs to buy tires for 1,198 cars. How many tires will it need to buy?
20. The driving distance from San Diego, California, to Atlanta, Georgia, is approximately 2,140 miles. If Mr. Miller, a truck driver, made 3 trips from San Diego to Atlanta and back, how many miles did he drive?

TEST PREP

Problem Solving: Preparing for Tests

Choose the correct letter for each answer.

1. A computer club has 48 members. There are 26 girls in the club. Which number sentence could be used to find the number of boys in the club?

   A 50 + 30 = ■

   B 50 − 30 = ■

   C 48 + 26 = ■

   D 48 − 26 = ■

Tip

Think about the action in the problem and then see which operation matches that action.

2. Hal puts pictures of his four sisters on a shelf. Ann's picture is all the way on the left. Meg's picture is all the way on the right. Kay's picture is between Meg's and Jo's. Which is the order of the pictures from left to right?

   F Ann, Jo, Meg, Kay

   G Ann, Kay, Jo, Meg

   H Jo, Ann, Kay, Meg

   J Ann, Jo, Kay, Meg

Tip

Try using the *Use Logical Reasoning* strategy to solve this problem. Start listing the order of the pictures as you find new information.

3. Sarah bought 6 books at the book fair. Each book cost $2.99. She also bought 3 bookmarks that cost $1.15 each. She paid with a twenty-dollar bill and a five-dollar bill. How much money did she have left?

   A $2.06

   B $3.61

   C $4.61

   D $7.06

Tip

When more than one step is needed to solve a problem, you must decide both what to do and what order you should do it.

4. **Susan practiced the piano for 28 minutes on Saturday and 47 minutes on Sunday. About how much time did Susan practice on both days?**

F 40 minutes
G 50 minutes
H 70 minutes
J 80 minutes

---

5. **An airplane flying from Boston to Phoenix started with 113 passengers. The plane stopped in Dallas, where 15 people got on, and 23 people got off. How many passengers were on the plane then?**

A 75 passengers
B 105 passengers
C 121 passengers
D 151 passengers

---

6. **Nan spent \$1.50 on pens and \$2.00 on markers. She bought pencils that cost more than the pens but less than the markers. Which is a reasonable amount Nan might have spent on the pencils?**

F \$1.25
G \$1.50
H \$1.75
J \$2.00

---

7. **A toy store ordered 67 toy boats, 49 toy cars, and 82 toy airplanes. Which is the best way to estimate the total number of toys ordered?**

A $67 + 49 + 82 = \blacksquare$
B $70 + 30 + 80 = \blacksquare$
C $67 + 50 + 80 = \blacksquare$
D $70 + 50 + 80 = \blacksquare$

Use the graph for Questions 8–10.

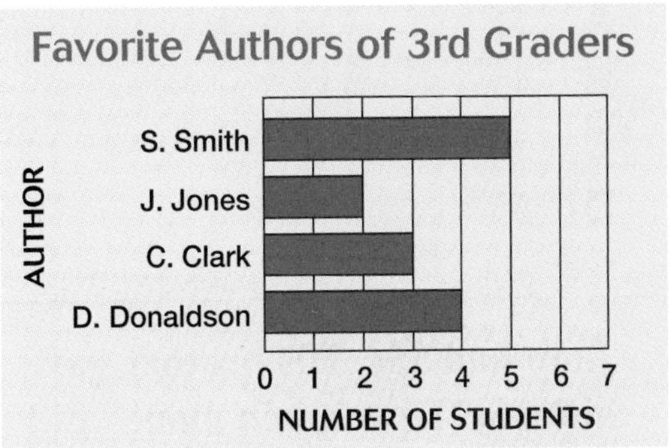

8. **How many students chose D. Donaldson?**

F 5
G 4
H 3
J 2

---

9. **How many more students chose S. Smith than chose C. Clark?**

A 2
B 3
C 4
D 5

---

10. **Which author was chosen most often?**

F S. Smith
G J. Jones
H C. Clark
J D. Donaldson

Multiple-Choice Cumulative Review

Choose the correct letter for each answer.

Number Sense

1. Look at the base-ten blocks. If 2 ▭ are added to the tens groups, what number will be shown?

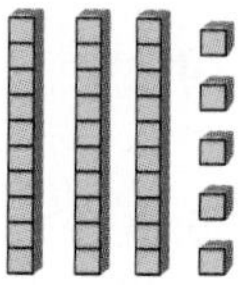

A 35
B 45
C 50
D 55

2. Juan had 55¢. His brother gave him 15¢. How much money did Juan have then?

F 40¢
G 45¢
H 65¢
J 70¢

3. Which is a set of even numbers?

A	6	9	12	18
B	8	10	24	39
C	6	12	16	28
D	3	7	9	15

4. Which number sentence is NOT correct?

F $36 > 32$
G $98 < 106$
H $202 < 201$
J $353 > 335$

Algebra and Functions

5. What two numbers make the statement true?

17 + ■ is greater than 25.

A 5, 6
B 7, 8
C 9, 10
D 8, 25

6. What is the missing number in the number pattern?

31, 34, 37, ■, 43, 46

F 38
G 40
H 41
J 42

7. Which number makes this sentence true?

$6 \times ■ = 42$

A 6
B 7
C 8
D 9

8. What operation makes the number sentence true?

72 ■ 8 = 9

F +
G −
H ×
J ÷

Measurement and Geometry

9. Which object is shaped like a sphere?

A 

C 

B 

D 

---

10. The soup can is the shape of a ________.

F pyramid
G sphere
H cone
J cylinder

---

11. How many corners does a triangle have?

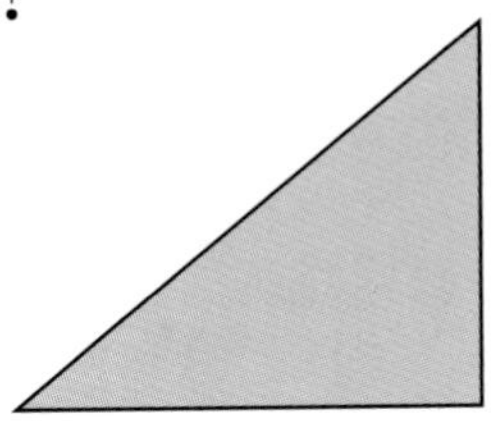

A 2
B 3
C 4
D 6

---

12. What number is inside the rectangle and outside the triangle?

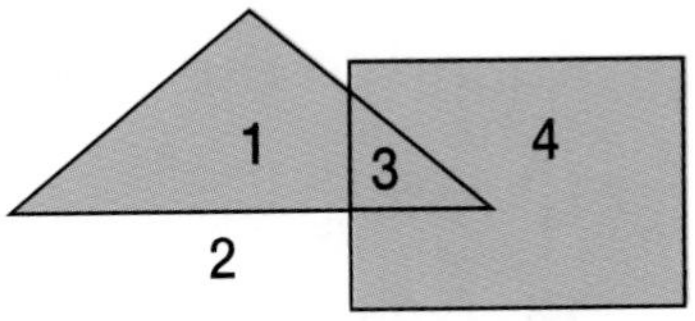

F 1
G 2
H 3
J 4

Statistics, Data Analysis, and Probability

Use the pictograph for Questions 13–15.

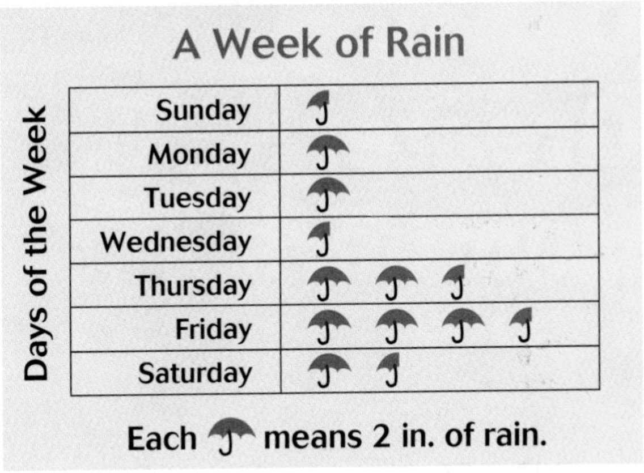

13. How many inches of rain fell on Monday?

A 1 inches
B 2 inches
C 3 inches
D 4 inches

---

14. Which day of the week had the most rain?

F Sunday
G Monday
H Friday
J Saturday

---

15. How many more inches did it rain on Thursday than on Wednesday?

A 2 inches
B 3 inches
C 4 inches
D 5 inches

CHAPTER 10

Dividing Greater Numbers

Diagnosing Readiness

In Chapter 10, you will use these skills:

A Subtraction

(pages 58–59)

1. $\begin{array}{r} 27 \\ -24 \\ \hline \end{array}$

2. $\begin{array}{r} 35 \\ -32 \\ \hline \end{array}$

3. $\begin{array}{r} 18 \\ -16 \\ \hline \end{array}$

4. $\begin{array}{r} 53 \\ -48 \\ \hline \end{array}$

5. $\begin{array}{r} 72 \\ -64 \\ \hline \end{array}$

6. $\begin{array}{r} 21 \\ -18 \\ \hline \end{array}$

7. Mary had 32 stickers. She gave 17 stickers to Tina. How may stickers does Mary have left?

B Rounding

(pages 6–8)

Round to the nearest ten.

8. 42 **9.** 65

10. 924 **11.** 308

Round to the nearest hundred.

12. 657 **13.** 418

14. 231 **15.** 875

16. A stereo costs \$347. What is the cost rounded to the nearest ten? nearest hundred?

C Multiplication Facts

(Chapters 4 and 5)

17. 6×4

18. 8×7

19. 3×9

20. 5×4

21. 2×6

22. 7×3

23. 8×4

24. 5×9

25. Megan had 4 packages of bagels. Each package has 6 bagels. How many bagels does Megan have in all?

D Multiplying by a One-Digit Number

(pages 358–360)

26. $\begin{array}{r} 27 \\ \times\ 3 \\ \hline \end{array}$

27. $\begin{array}{r} 92 \\ \times\ 8 \\ \hline \end{array}$

28. $\begin{array}{r} 52 \\ \times\ 4 \\ \hline \end{array}$

29. $\begin{array}{r} 35 \\ \times\ 5 \\ \hline \end{array}$

30. $\begin{array}{r} 48 \\ \times\ 9 \\ \hline \end{array}$

31. $\begin{array}{r} 29 \\ \times\ 6 \\ \hline \end{array}$

32. How many eggs would you have if you bought 8 dozen eggs?

E Multiplication Patterns

(pages 352–353)

33. $3 \times 4 = \blacksquare$
$3 \times 40 = \blacksquare$
$3 \times 400 = \blacksquare$

34. $6 \times 4 = \blacksquare$
$6 \times 40 = \blacksquare$
$6 \times 400 = \blacksquare$

35. $5 \times 8 = \blacksquare$
$5 \times 80 = \blacksquare$
$5 \times 800 = \blacksquare$

36. One package of bells has 20 bells. Mindy bought 3 packages. How many bells did she buy?

F Division Facts

(Chapters 6 and 7)

37. $12 \div 3$

38. $56 \div 8$

39. $54 \div 6$

40. $35 \div 5$

41. $21 \div 7$

42. $32 \div 4$

43. James has 63 marbles. He wants to share them equally among 7 friends. How many marbles will each friend get?

To the Family and Student

Looking Back	Chapter 10	Looking Ahead
In Chapters 6 and 7, students learned how to divide basic facts. 8 ÷ 2	**Dividing Greater Numbers** In this chapter, students will learn how to divide up to 4-digit numbers by one-digit numbers. 1,569 ÷ 3	In Grade 4, students will learn how to divide up to 5-digit numbers by one-digit numbers. 15,696 ÷ 9

Math and Everyday Living

Opportunities to apply the concepts of Chapter 10 abound in everyday situations. During the chapter, think about how division can be used to solve a variety of real-world problems. The following examples suggest just several of the many situations that could launch a discussion about division.

Math at the Grocery Store
At 3 apples for $1.59, how much would one apple cost?

Math at the Park You are going to have your birthday party at the park. There will be 22 people at your party. Each picnic table seats 6 people. How many picnic tables will you need so that everyone will have a place to sit?

Math and the Movies
Kasim's parents gave him and his 3 brothers $31 to go to the movies. They told the boys that they could spend the money left over from the tickets on snacks. The tickets were $6 each. How much did the boys have to spend on snacks?

Math at Home You are putting all your pictures into a photo album. Each page can hold 8 pictures. How many pages will you need if you have 128 pictures?

Math and Cooking Jenny brought 20 mini-muffins to a party. If each of the 6 people at the party ate 3 mini-muffins, how many were left for Jenny to take home?

Math at the Market Josh buys a six-pack of juice bottles for $4.50. How much does each bottle of juice cost?

Math and Hobbies You enjoy making friendship pins. You need 9 beads to make each pin. About how many friendship pins could you make with 350 beads?

Math and the Garden
James has 96 marigold plants in his garden. There are 8 rows of marigolds. If there are the same number of marigolds in each row, how many plants are in each row?

Math and Travel Your family goes on a road trip to visit historical sites. Each day you travel about the same number of miles. By the end of your vacation you have traveled 710 miles in 7 days. About how far did you travel each day?

California Content Standards in Chapter 10 Lessons*

	Teach and Practice	Practice
Number Sense		
2.0 Students calculate and solve problems involving addition, subtraction, multiplication, and division.	10-1	10-2, 10-7
2.3 (🔑) Use the inverse relationship of multiplication and division to compute and check results.		10-5, 10-6
2.5 Solve division problems in which a multidigit number is evenly divided by a one-digit number (135 ÷ 5 = __).	10-3,10-5, 10-6	
2.7 Determine the unit cost when given the total cost and number of units.	10-8	
2.8 Solve problems that require two or more of the skills mentioned above.	10-9	10-1
3.3 (🔑) Solve problems involving addition, subtraction, multiplication, and division of money amounts in decimal notation and multiply and divide money amounts in decimal notation by using whole-number multipliers and divisors.	10-8	
Algebra and Functions		
1.1 Represent relationships of quantities in the form of mathematical expressions, equations, or inequalities.		10-5, 10-8
1.3 Select appropriate operational and relational symbols to make an expression true (e.g., if 4 __ 3 = 12, what operational symbol goes in the blank?).		10-5, 10-8
2.2 Extend and recognize a linear pattern by its rules.		10-6

	Teach and Practice	Practice
Mathematical Reasoning		
1.0 Students make decisions about how to approach problems.	10-2	
1.1 Analyze problems by identifying relationships, distinguishing relevant from irrelevant information, sequencing and prioritizing information, and observing patterns.		10-8, 10-9
1.2 Determine when and how to break a problem into simpler parts.		10-5, 10-9
2.1 Use estimation to verify the reasonableness of calculated results.	10-4	
2.2 Apply strategies and results from simpler problems to more complex problems.		10-2, 10-7
2.4 Express the solution clearly and logically by using the appropriate mathematical notation and terms and clear language; Support solutions with evidence in both verbal and symbolic work.	10-1	10-6
2.5 Indicate the relative advantages of exact and approximate solutions to problems and give answers to a specified degree of accuracy.		10-4
3.2 Note the method of deriving the solution and demonstrate a conceptual understanding of the derivation by solving similar problems.	10-7	

* The symbol (🔑) indicates a key standard as designated in the Mathematics Framework for California Public Schools. Full statements of the California Content Standards are found at the beginning of this book following the Table of Contents.

LESSON 10-1

Dividing with Remainders

Warm-Up Review

1. 21 ÷ 7 **2.** 28 ÷ 4

3. 48 ÷ 6 **4.** 54 ÷ 9

5. Ms. Martin wants to put her students into groups of 4. There are 24 students in the class. How many groups of 4 will there be?

California Content Standards *Number Sense 2.0: Students calculate and solve problems involving . . . division. Also, Mathematical Reasoning 2.4.* *(See p. 387.)*

Math Link You know how to find 24 ÷ 4. Now you will learn to solve problems like 25 ÷ 4 in which there is a number left over after dividing.

Word Bank

remainder

Example 1

Sheri is a caterer. She had 25 apples. She put the same number of apples into each of 4 fruit baskets. How many apples did she put into each basket? How many apples were left over?

Find 25 ÷ 4.

So, she put 6 apples in each basket. There was 1 apple left over.

When dividing whole numbers, the number left over is the **remainder**. Here is how to record your work when you divide with a remainder.

Step 1

$$\begin{array}{r} 6 \\ 4\overline{)25} \\ 24 \end{array}$$

24 ← **Multiply: 6 × 4 24 apples are used.**

Step 2

R1 means there is a remainder of 1.

$$\begin{array}{r} 6\text{ R1} \\ 4\overline{)25} \\ \underline{-24} \\ 1 \end{array}$$

1 ← **Subtract: 25 − 24 1 apple is left over.**

Example 2

Find 14 ÷ 3.

Step 1

$$\begin{array}{r} 4 \\ 3\overline{)14} \\ 12 \end{array}$$

12 ← **Multiply: 4 × 3**

Step 2

$$\begin{array}{r} 4\text{ R2} \\ 3\overline{)14} \\ \underline{-12} \\ 2 \end{array}$$

2 ← **Subtract: 14 − 12**

 Additional Standard: Number Sense 2.8 *(See p. 387.)*

Guided Practice

For another example, see Set A on p. 414.

1. $2\overline{)7}$ 2. $9\overline{)30}$ 3. $9\overline{)27}$ 4. $21 \div 4$ 5. $53 \div 6$

6. Kenesha buys 3 books with a twenty-dollar bill. Each book costs the same amount. If she gets $2 in change, how much does each book cost?

Independent Practice

For more practice, see Set A on p. 416.

7. $2\overline{)11}$ 8. $4\overline{)12}$ 9. $5\overline{)21}$ 10. $6\overline{)17}$ 11. $9\overline{)61}$

12. $16 \div 7$ 13. $50 \div 6$ 14. $42 \div 7$ 15. $45 \div 8$ 16. $74 \div 9$

17. There are 24 students in the Ecology Club. They formed groups of 5 students to pick up litter. How many students were left over?

18. Carlos made 32 cups of soup and poured it into containers that held 6 cups each. How many containers did he fill? How many cups of soup were left over?

19. Natalie is organizing her art supplies. She has 61 crayons to put in boxes that hold 8 crayons each. How many boxes will she fill? How many crayons will be left over?

Mixed Review

20. Write *right angle, acute angle,* or *obtuse angle* to name the angle shown.

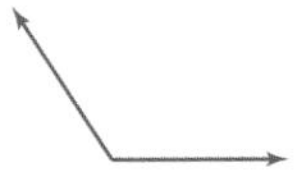

21. **Algebra** Find the missing number: ■ × 6 = 48.

22. 8 × 235 23. 4 × 652 24. 2,651 × 2 25. 5 × 1,897

Test Prep **Choose the correct letter for each answer.**

26. (8-10) One side of a square room is 12 feet long. What is the perimeter of the room?

A 16 feet **C** 36 feet

B 24 feet **D** 48 feet

27. (9-3) Mr. Lyles drives a school bus. Each day he drives 38 miles. About how many miles does he drive in 5 days?

F 40 mi **H** 200 mi

G 100 mi **J** 400 mi

LESSON 10-2

Understand
Plan
Solve
Look Back

Problem-Solving Skill:
Interpreting Remainders

Warm-Up Review

1. $3\overline{)25}$ 2. $8\overline{)18}$

3. $53 \div 7$ 4. $29 \div 5$

5. There are 6 granola bars in a box. Liselle has 3 boxes. She wants to give 2 bars to each friend. How many friends will get granola bars?

California Content Standard *Mathematical Reasoning 1.0: Students make decisions about how to approach problems.*

Read for Understanding

Use the diagram at the right. Mr. Wong's class is going on a field trip. There are 26 students going on the trip.

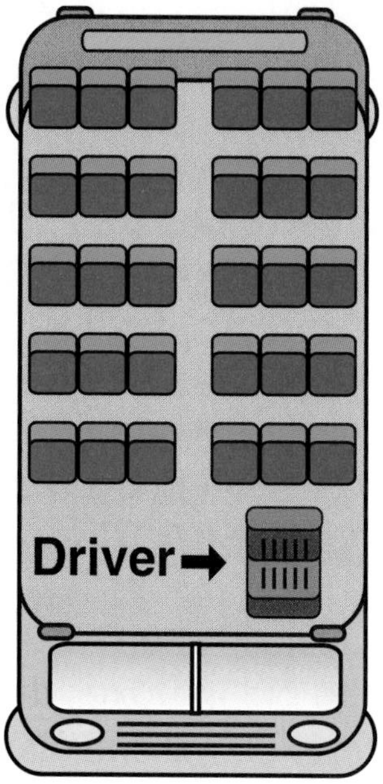

1. How many students can ride in each seat?
2. How many students are going on the trip?

Think and Discuss

MATH FOCUS

Interpreting Remainders

When you divide, a remainder can sometimes affect the answer. Sometimes when you have a remainder, you need to round the quotient up to the next number. Sometimes you need to use the remainder itself. Sometimes you can just drop the remainder.

Reread the paragraph at the top of the page.

3. How many seats are needed for just 2 students?
4. How many seats are needed for all 26 students?
5. Look back at your answer to Exercise 4. What did you do with the remainder to solve the problem?

Additional Standards: Number Sense 2.0; Mathematical Reasoning 2.2 *(See p. 387.)*

Guided Practice

Students on a camping trip need to carry flashlights. Each flashlight needs 5 batteries to work. If there are 47 batteries, what is the greatest number of flashlights that will work?

1. Which of the following could you do to solve the problem?
   a. You could find $47 \div 5 = 8$ R7.
   b. You could find $47 \times 5 = 235$.
   c. You could find $47 \div 5 = 9$ R2.

2. How should you use the remainder to solve the problem?
   a. Use it to round up the quotient, so the answer is 10 flashlights.
   b. Drop the remainder, so the answer is 9 flashlights.
   c. Use the remainder, so the answer is 9 R2 flashlights.

Independent Practice

Rob is packing snacks into boxes for a trip. He has 32 snacks. Each box holds 5 snacks. How many boxes does he need to pack all of the snacks?

3. Which should you do first to solve the problem?
   a. You should find $32 \div 5 = 6$ R2.
   b. You should find $32 - 5 = 27$.
   c. You should find $32 \div 5 = 5$ R7.

4. How should you use the remainder to solve the problem?
   a. Use it to round up the quotient, so the answer is 7 boxes.
   b. Drop the remainder, so the answer is 6 boxes.
   c. Use the remainder, so the answer is 6 R2 boxes.

5. **Math Reasoning** Would the number of boxes Rob needs change if he had 34 snacks? Why or why not?

LESSON 10-3

Mental Math: Division Patterns

Warm-Up Review

1. $8 \div 2$
2. $9 \div 3$
3. $12 \div 4$
4. $56 \div 7$
5. $45 \div 9$
6. $30 \div 6$
7. Marissa earned $35 for baby-sitting last week. If she earns $5 an hour, how many hours did she baby-sit last week?

California Content Standard *Number Sense 2.5: Solve division problems in which a multidigit number is evenly divided by a one-digit number . . ..*

Math Link You know how to find quotients like $6 \div 3$. Now you will learn how to find quotients like $60 \div 3$ and $600 \div 3$.

Example 1

A store received a shipment of 600 baseball cards in 3 boxes. Each box has the same number of baseball cards. How many baseball cards are in each box?

Find $600 \div 3$.

You can use a basic fact and patterns to help you find the quotient.

$6 \div 3 = 2$
$60 \div 3 = 20$
$600 \div 3 = 200$

Here's WHY It Works

$6 \div 3 = 2$	**$60 \div 3 = 6$ tens $\div 3$ $= 2$ tens $= 20$**	**$600 \div 3 = 6$ hundreds $\div 3$ $= 2$ hundreds $= 200$**

So, there are 200 baseball cards in each box.

Example 2

Find $4{,}000 \div 5$.

When the dividend of the basic fact includes a zero, that zero is not part of the pattern.

$40 \div 5 = 8$
$400 \div 5 = 80$
$4{,}000 \div 5 = 800$

Guided Practice

For another example, see Set B on p. 414.

1. $8 \div 2 = \blacksquare$
   $80 \div 2 = \blacksquare$
   $800 \div 2 = \blacksquare$
2. $9 \div 3 = \blacksquare$
   $90 \div 3 = \blacksquare$
   $900 \div 3 = \blacksquare$
3. $35 \div 7 = \blacksquare$
   $350 \div 7 = \blacksquare$
   $3{,}500 \div 7 = \blacksquare$
4. $40 \div 2$
5. $100 \div 5$
6. $180 \div 2$
7. $7{,}200 \div 9$

8. There are 240 students waiting to go on a field trip. The students are standing in groups of 8. How many groups of students are there?

Independent Practice

For more practice, see Set B on p. 416.

9. $4 \div 2 = \blacksquare$
$40 \div 2 = \blacksquare$
$400 \div 2 = \blacksquare$

10. $14 \div 7 = \blacksquare$
$140 \div 7 = \blacksquare$
$1{,}400 \div 7 = \blacksquare$

11. $30 \div 6 = \blacksquare$
$300 \div 6 = \blacksquare$
$3{,}000 \div 6 = \blacksquare$

12. $60 \div 2$ **13.** $80 \div 4$ **14.** $270 \div 9$ **15.** $320 \div 8$

16. $200 \div 4$ **17.** $160 \div 8$ **18.** $5{,}600 \div 7$ **19.** $2{,}800 \div 4$

20. There are 480 people attending a dinner. There are 8 people at each table. How many tables are there?

21. Mrs. Taba's class is 60 minutes long. She wants to divide her class time into 3 equal periods. How long will each period be?

22. A drama club with 8 members wants to sell 400 tickets to a play. If each member sells the same number of tickets, how many tickets will each person sell?

Mixed Review

23. Is the triangle shown at the right equilateral, isosceles, or scalene?

24. A playground is 100 yards long. How many feet is that?

25. $29 \div 5$ **26.** $37 \div 6$ **27.** $7 \times 1{,}258$ **28.** $2{,}096 \times 3$

Test Prep **Choose the correct letter for each answer.**

29. (5-3) **Algebra** Find the missing operation.

$5 \bullet 8 = 40$

A $+$
B $-$
C $\times$
D $\div$

30. (3-3) Which unit would you use to measure the distance a train will travel in one day?

F mile
G yard
H inch
J foot

LESSON 10-4

Estimating Quotients

California Content Standard *Mathematical Reasoning 2.1: Use estimation to verify the reasonableness of calculated results.*

Warm-Up Review

1. $60 \div 6$
2. $90 \div 3$
3. $400 \div 2$
4. $100 \div 5$
5. $210 \div 7$
6. $640 \div 8$
7. Round 816 to the nearest hundred.

Math Link You know how to find $40 \div 2$ and $320 \div 8$. In this lesson, you will use facts like these to help you estimate quotients.

Word Bank

compatible numbers

Example 1

Mike has 78 photographs to place in a photo album. He arranges the photos on each page as shown. About how many pages can he fill?

Estimate $78 \div 4$.

One way to estimate is to think of a number that is close to 78 that you can divide easily by 4.

To estimate:		Think:
$78 \div 4$	⟶	$80 \div 4$

80 is close to 78.

$80 \div 4 = 20$

So, he can fill about 20 pages.

In division, pairs of numbers such as 80 and 4 are called **compatible numbers**. Compatible numbers are easy to divide mentally and can be used to help you estimate.

Example 2

Estimate $362 \div 7$.

Think of a number that is close to 362 that you can divide easily by 7.

To estimate:		Think:
$362 \div 7$	⟶	$350 \div 7$

350 is close to 362.

$350 \div 7 = 50$

So, $362 \div 7$ is about 50.

 Additional Standard: Mathematical Reasoning 2.5 (See p. 387.)

Guided Practice *For another example, see Set C on p. 414.*

Estimate each quotient. Tell the numbers you used.

1. 64 ÷ 3 **2.** 73 ÷ 7 **3.** 38 ÷ 2 **4.** 725 ÷ 8 **5.** 430 ÷ 6

6. If Katie pours 88 cups of lemonade equally into 9 pitchers, about how many cups will be in each pitcher?

Independent Practice *For more practice, see Set C on p. 416.*

Estimate each quotient. Tell the numbers you used.

7. 43 ÷ 2 **8.** 92 ÷ 3 **9.** 51 ÷ 5 **10.** 79 ÷ 8 **11.** 96 ÷ 2

12. 286 ÷ 4 **13.** 260 ÷ 9 **14.** 345 ÷ 7 **15.** 112 ÷ 5 **16.** 798 ÷ 2

Use the portion of Debby's phone bill shown at the right for Exercises 17 and 18.

	Total Cost	Length of Call
Day	78¢	4 min.
Evening	43¢	4 min.

17. About how much did Debby pay each minute for the call she made in the evening?

18. About how much more each minute did Debby pay for the call she made during the day than the call she made in the evening?

19. **Math Reasoning** Would you use 240 ÷ 3 or 270 ÷ 3 to estimate 250 ÷ 3? Explain.

Mixed Review

20. **Algebra** Give 3 numbers that make the statement true: 9 + ■ is less than 14.

21. 31 ÷ 6 **22.** 27 ÷ 7 **23.** 80 ÷ 4 **24.** 270 ÷ 3

Test Prep **Choose the correct letter for each answer.**

25. (5-9) Which has the same product as 2 × 3 × 6?

A 2 × 9
B 5 × 6
C 6 × 6
D 2 × 19
E NH

26. (1-3) A printer costs $643. What is the cost rounded to the nearest ten?

F $650
G $640
H $630
J $600
K NH

Diagnostic Checkpoint

1. $4\overline{)15}$ *(10-1)*

2. $2\overline{)9}$ *(10-1)*

3. $7\overline{)22}$ *(10-1)*

4. $5\overline{)19}$ *(10-1)*

5. $3\overline{)17}$ *(10-1)*

6. $9\overline{)23}$ *(10-1)*

7. $8\overline{)18}$ *(10-1)*

8. $7\overline{)38}$ *(10-1)*

9. $6\overline{)41}$ *(10-1)*

10. $7\overline{)53}$ *(10-1)*

11. *(10-3)* 6 ÷ 3 = ■
60 ÷ 3 = ■
600 ÷ 3 = ■

12. *(10-3)* 72 ÷ 9 = ■
720 ÷ 9 = ■
7,200 ÷ 9 = ■

13. *(10-3)* 10 ÷ 2 = ■
100 ÷ 2 = ■
1,000 ÷ 2 = ■

14. 630 ÷ 9 *(10-3)*

15. 5,400 ÷ 6 *(10-3)*

16. 7,000 ÷ 7 *(10-3)*

17. 2,000 ÷ 5 *(10-3)*

Estimate each quotient. Tell the numbers you used.

18. 52 ÷ 5 *(10-4)*

19. 79 ÷ 2 *(10-4)*

20. 59 ÷ 3 *(10-4)*

21. 94 ÷ 9 *(10-4)*

22. 532 ÷ 6 *(10-4)*

23. 800 ÷ 9 *(10-4)*

24. 322 ÷ 4 *(10-4)*

25. 231 ÷ 3 *(10-4)*

26. *(10-2)* It takes 4 slices of cheese to make a sub sandwich. Mrs. Knoke bought a package of cheese with 38 slices in it. What is the greatest number of sandwiches that Mrs. Knoke can make?

27. *(10-1)* Science kits cost \$5. Sergei has \$34. How many science kits can Sergei buy? How much money would he have left over?

28. *(3-6)* Dorothy bought 2 books for \$4 each and a magazine for \$2.50. Her change was \$0.50. How much money did she give the salesperson?

29. *(10-4)* It will take Leslie 150 hours to paint her house. Leslie paints for 8 hours each day. About how many days will it take her to paint the house?

30. *(10-2)* Malik is displaying baseball cards in an album. He can fit 4 cards on a page, and he has 97 cards. How many pages does he need to display his baseball cards?

Multiple-Choice Cumulative Review

Choose the correct letter for each answer.

1. What is the value of the 6 in the number 9,068?

A 6 **C** 600
B 60 **D** 6,000

2. Last week 3,923 people visited the zoo. This week 2,837 people visited the zoo. How many fewer people visited this week than last week?

F 6,760 people
G 1,186 people
H 1,086 people
J 86 people
K NH

3. Which two numbers would make the statement true?

3 × ■ is less than 15

A 5 and 7 **C** 4 and 5
B 4 and 6 **D** 3 and 4

4. Which has the same product as 2 × 600?

F 4 × 400
G 3 × 400
H 4 × 200
J 3 × 40
K NH

5. Ivan bought a dozen pencils for \$0.12 each, 4 folders at \$0.49 each, and 2 notepads for \$1.59 each. All taxes are included. If he paid with a \$10 bill, how much change should he have received?

A \$3.42
B \$4.36
C \$4.42
D \$6.58

6. Find the perimeter of the figure.

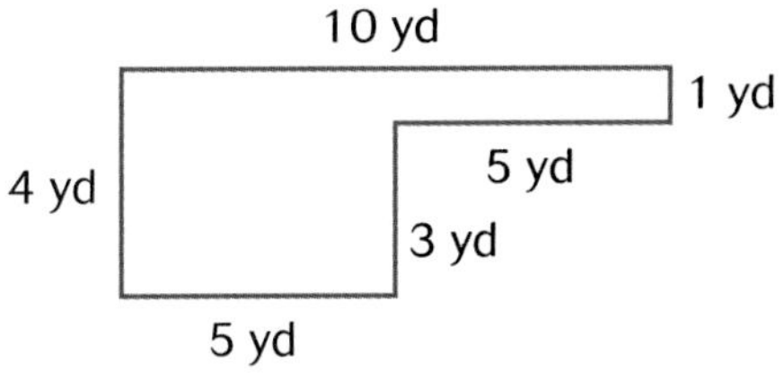

F 20 yards
G 23 yards
H 28 yards
J 32 yards

7. I have 4 right angles. All of my sides are the same length. Which shape am I?

A 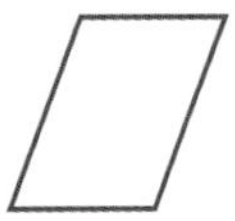
C 
B 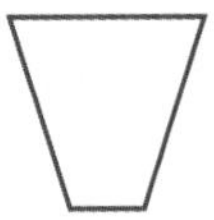
D 

LESSON 10-5

Dividing Two-Digit Numbers

California Content Standard *Number Sense 2.5: Solve division problems in which a multidigit number is evenly divided by a one-digit number . . ..*

Warm-Up Review

1. 13×4
2. 6×16
3. $72 =$ ■ tens ■ ones
4. $35 =$ 2 tens ■ ones
5. Carlton separated his postcard collection into 3 equal groups. He has 30 postcards. How many postcards did he put in each group?

Math Link You know how to find $60 \div 3$. In this lesson, you will find quotients like $57 \div 3$.

Example 1

Dawn has collected the old toys and games shown at the right for a sale at Washington School. She has 26 items divided equally among the boxes. How many items are in each box?

26	÷	2	=	■
total items		number of boxes		items in each box

Step 1 Think about dividing 2 tens 6 ones into 2 equal groups.

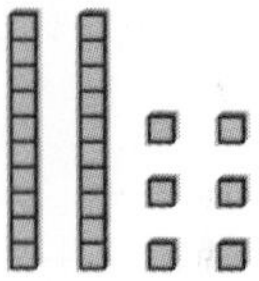

$2\overline{)26}$

Step 2 Divide 2 tens into 2 equal groups. There are no tens left over.

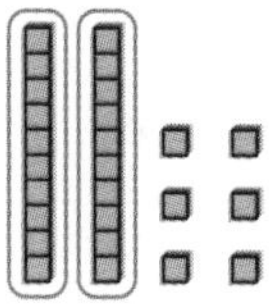

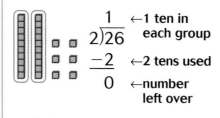

$$\begin{array}{r} 1 \\ 2\overline{)26} \\ -2 \\ \hline 0 \end{array}$$

←1 ten in each group
←2 tens used
←number left over

Step 3 Divide 6 ones equally among the 2 groups. There are no ones left over. So, $26 \div 2 = 13$.

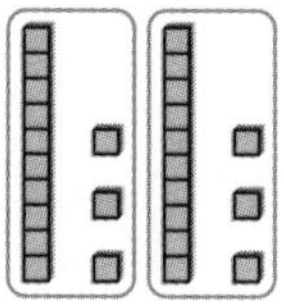

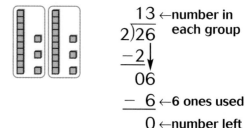

$$\begin{array}{r} 13 \\ 2\overline{)26} \\ -2\downarrow \\ \hline 06 \\ -\ 6 \\ \hline 0 \end{array}$$

←number in each group
←6 ones used
←number left over

<u>*Check*</u> your answer by multiplying the quotient and the divisor. Since $13 \times 2 = 26$, the answer is correct.

So, there are 13 items in each box.

Additional Standards: Number Sense 2.3(🔑); Algebra and Functions 1.1(🔑), 1.3; Mathematical Reasoning 1.2 *(See p. 387.)*

Example 2

Find 45 ÷ 3.

Step 1 Think about dividing 4 tens 5 ones into 3 equal groups.

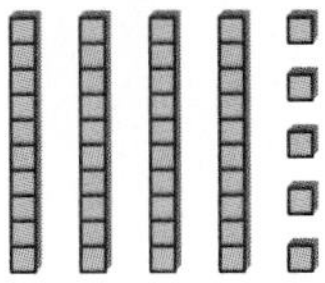

$3\overline{)45}$

Step 2 Divide 4 tens into 3 equal groups. There is 1 ten left over.

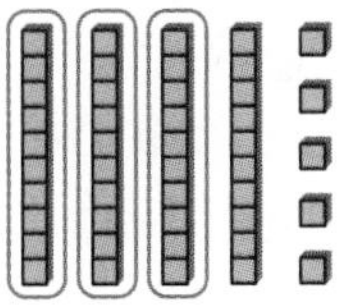

$$\begin{array}{rl} 1 & \leftarrow \textbf{1 ten in each group} \\ 3\overline{)45} & \\ \underline{-3} & \leftarrow \textbf{3 tens used} \\ 1 & \leftarrow \textbf{1 ten left over} \end{array}$$

Step 3 Regroup the 1 ten as 10 ones. Now there are 15 ones altogether.

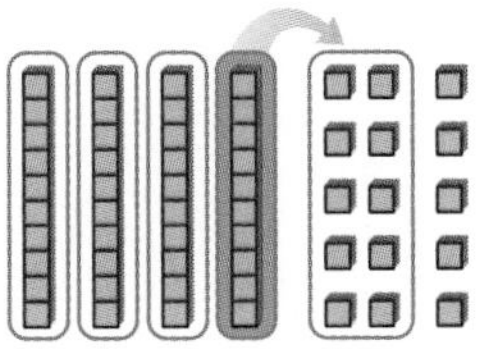

$$\begin{array}{r} 1 \\ 3\overline{)45} \\ \underline{-3}\downarrow \\ 15 \end{array}$$

Step 4 Divide 15 ones equally among the 3 groups. There are no ones left over.

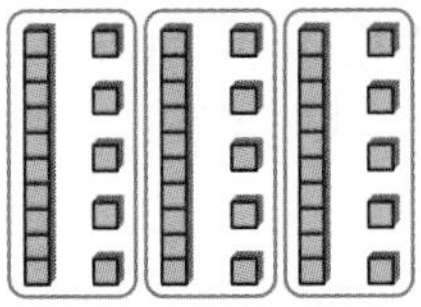

$$\begin{array}{rl} 15 & \leftarrow \textbf{number in each group} \\ 3\overline{)45} & \\ \underline{-3} & \\ 15 & \\ \underline{-15} & \leftarrow \textbf{15 ones used} \\ 0 & \leftarrow \textbf{number left over} \end{array}$$

Check your answer by multiplying. Since 15 × 3 = 45, the answer is correct.

Guided Practice

For another example, see Set D on p. 415.

1. $2\overline{)22}$ **2.** $3\overline{)36}$ **3.** $2\overline{)42}$ **4.** 51 ÷ 3 **5.** 68 ÷ 4

6. There are 54 exhibit areas divided equally among 3 floors of a museum. How many exhibit areas are on each floor?

Independent Practice

For more practice, see Set D on p. 417.

7. $2\overline{)26}$ **8.** $3\overline{)69}$ **9.** $2\overline{)36}$ **10.** $6\overline{)72}$ **11.** $4\overline{)84}$

12. 64 ÷ 2 **13.** 56 ÷ 4 **14.** 65 ÷ 5 **15.** 91 ÷ 7 **16.** 96 ÷ 8

Algebra Write >, <, or = for each ●.

17. 60 ÷ 3 ● 63 ÷ 3 **18.** 84 ÷ 2 ● 84 ÷ 4 **19.** 5 × 5 ● 75 ÷ 3

20. Janelle had 78 flowers. She put 6 flowers in each vase. How many vases did she fill?

21. Mrs. Edward's class checked out 87 books at the library. Each student checked out 3 books. How many students checked out books?

22. Pine Valley School used money it raised to buy 92 computers. They put 4 of the computers in the school library. The rest of the computers were evenly divided among the 8 computer labs. How many computers were put in each lab?

Mixed Review

23. The third graders bought 4 single tickets and 7 rolls of tickets. Each roll had 10 tickets. How many tickets did they buy in all?

24. Order from greatest to least: 2,004 2,400 2,012

25. Find the sum of $24 + 1{,}895 + 317$.

26. 500×3

27. $4 \times 2{,}000$

28. $250 \div 5$

29. $720 \div 8$

30. Estimate $91 \div 3$.

31. Estimate $572 \div 8$.

Test Prep **Choose the correct letter for each answer.**

32. (8-11) What is the area of the shaded part of the grid below?

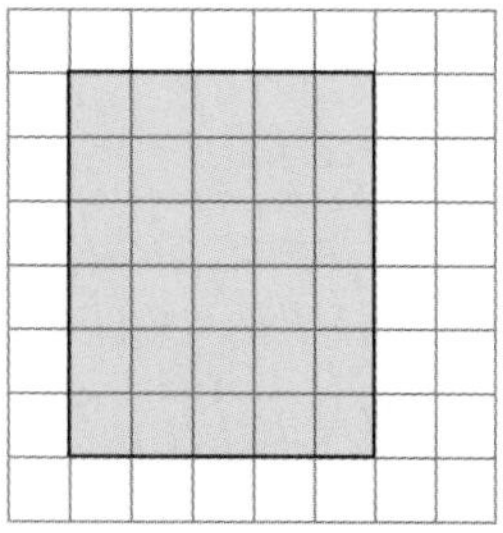

A 11 square units
B 30 square units
C 36 square units
D 64 square units

33. (8-14) What is the volume of the figure below?

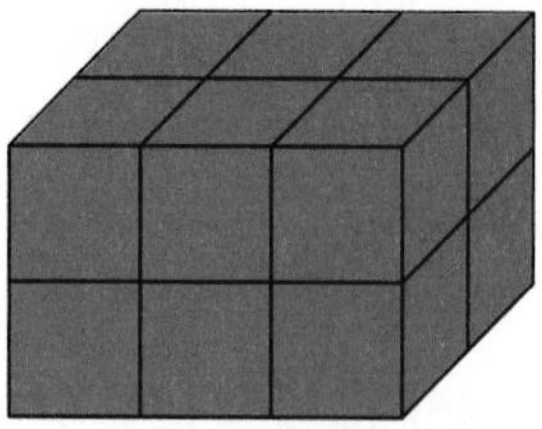

F 4 cubic units
G 6 cubic units
H 12 cubic units
J 18 cubic units

LESSON 10-6

Dividing Greater Numbers

Warm-Up Review

1. $42 \div 6$ **2.** $56 \div 7$

3. 324×4 **4.** 115×6

5. There are 57 third grade students in 3 classes. All 3 classes are the same size. How many students are in each class?

California Content Standard *Number Sense 2.5: Solve division problems in which a multidigit number is evenly divided by a one-digit number . . ..*

Math Link You know how to divide two-digit numbers. In this lesson, you will learn how to divide three- and four-digit numbers.

Example 1

Use the data at the right about Bridalveil Fall located in Yosemite National Park in California. Bridalveil Fall is how many times as high as a 5-foot-tall student?

Find $620 \div 5$.

Step 1 Decide where to start dividing. Check the hundreds first.

```
   1
5)620
```

Since 5 < 6, start with hundreds.

Step 2 Divide the hundreds. Then multiply, subtract, and compare. The difference must be less than the divisor.

```
   1
5)620
 -5      Multiply: 1 hundred × 5
  1      Subtract and compare: 1 < 5
                               ↑   ↑
                      difference   divisor
```

Step 3 Bring down the tens. Divide. Then multiply, subtract, and compare.

```
   12
5)620
 -5↓
  12
 -10     Multiply: 2 tens × 5
   2     Subtract and compare: 2 < 5
```

Step 4 Bring down the ones. Divide. Then multiply, subtract, and compare.

```
   124
5)620
 -5
  12
 -10↓
   20
  -20    Multiply: 4 ones × 5
    0    Subtract and compare: 0 < 5
```

Check by multiplying the quotient and the divisor. Since $124 \times 5 = 620$, the answer is correct.

So, the waterfall is 124 times as high as a 5-foot-tall student.

Additional Standards: Number Sense 2.3(key); Algebra and Functions 2.2; Mathematical Reasoning 2.4 *(See p. 387.)*

Example 2

Find 136 ÷ 4.

First, estimate using compatible numbers.
Think: 120 ÷ 4 = 30
Now find the exact answer.

Step 1 Decide where to start dividing. Check the hundreds first.

$4\overline{)136}$

Since 4 > 1, check the tens.
Since 4 < 13, start with tens.

Step 2 Divide the tens. Then multiply, subtract, and compare.

$$\begin{array}{r} 3 \\ 4\overline{)136} \\ -12 \\ \hline 1 \end{array}$$

−12 ← **3 tens × 4**
1 ← **1 < 4**

Step 3 Bring down the ones. Divide. Then multiply, subtract, and compare.

$$\begin{array}{r} 34 \\ 4\overline{)136} \\ -12\downarrow \\ \hline 16 \\ -16 \\ \hline 0 \end{array}$$

−16 ← **4 ones × 4**
0 ← **0 < 4**

<u>Check</u> by comparing the exact answer to the estimate.
34 is close to 30, so the answer is reasonable.

More Examples

You can use the same steps to divide a four-digit number.

A.

$$\begin{array}{r} 2{,}435 \\ 3\overline{)7{,}305} \\ -6 \\ \hline 13 \\ -12 \\ \hline 10 \\ -9 \\ \hline 15 \\ -15 \\ \hline 0 \end{array}$$

Check the thousands first. Since 3 < 7, start with thousands.

<u>Check</u>: 2,435 × 3 = 7,305

B.

$$\begin{array}{r} 432 \\ 5\overline{)2{,}160} \\ -20 \\ \hline 16 \\ -15 \\ \hline 10 \\ -10 \\ \hline 0 \end{array}$$

Check the thousands first. Since 5 > 2, check the hundreds. Since 5 < 21, start with hundreds.

<u>Check</u>: 432 × 5 = 2,160

Guided Practice *For another example, see Set E on p. 415.*

1. $5\overline{)580}$ **2.** $6\overline{)774}$ **3.** $9\overline{)459}$ **4.** 472 ÷ 8 **5.** 1,263 ÷ 3

6. Brad puts 128 stickers onto 4 pages. He puts the same number on each page. How many stickers are on each page?

Independent Practice *For more practice, see Set E on p. 417.*

7. $4\overline{)484}$ **8.** $6\overline{)546}$ **9.** $8\overline{)304}$ **10.** $9\overline{)747}$ **11.** $5\overline{)6{,}250}$

12. $672 \div 6$ **13.** $712 \div 8$ **14.** $504 \div 4$ **15.** $486 \div 9$ **16.** $4{,}318 \div 2$

Algebra **Follow each rule.**

Rule: Divide by 5.

	Input	Output
17.	320	
18.	315	
19.	310	

Rule: Divide by 3.

	Input	Output
20.	99	
21.	102	
22.	105	

Rule: Divide by 2.

	Input	Output
23.	184	
24.		142
25.	384	

26. There are 432 jars that need to be put in boxes. Each box holds 8 jars. How many boxes are needed?

27. **Math Reasoning** How do you know if $310 \div 5$ will have a 3-digit quotient or a 2-digit quotient? Explain.

Mixed Review

Use the data at the right for Exercises 28 and 29.

28. How much do 3 T-shirts cost?

29. Roy and Sue each want to buy a T-shirt and a pair of socks. How much money will each person save by buying them together?

30. $1{,}305 - 62$ **31.** $429 + 758$ **32.** $78 \div 6$ **33.** $84 \div 7$

34. Estimate $79 \div 4$. **35.** Estimate $513 \div 5$.

Test Prep **Choose the correct letter for each answer.**

36. Find the missing number: 2 ft = ■ in.
(3-3)

A 12 **B** 24 **C** 36 **D** 48

37. Jillian buys 3 notebooks with a ten-dollar bill. Each notebook costs the same amount. If she gets $1 in change, how much does each notebook cost?
(10-1)

F $1 **G** $3 **H** $6 **J** $9

LESSON 10-7

Understand
Plan
Solve
Look Back

Problem-Solving Strategy:
Choose a Strategy

Warm-Up Review

1. 3×50
2. 8×70
3. $42 \div 6$
4. $420 \div 6$
5. $48 \div 8$
6. $480 \div 8$
7. How much time has passed between 9:35 A.M. and 10:40 A.M.?
8. There are 8 bits in a byte of computer memory. How many bits are in 256 bytes?

California Content Standard *Mathematical Reasoning 3.2: Note the method of deriving the solution and demonstrate a conceptual understanding of the derivation by solving similar problems.*

Mrs. Ling buys 8 theater tickets for $560. All tickets are the same price. How much does each ticket cost?

Understand

What do you need to find?

You need to find the cost of each ticket.

Plan

How can you solve the problem?

You can **write a number sentence**, or you can **solve a simpler problem.**

Solve

Write a Number Sentence

560	÷	8	=	■
total cost of the tickets		number of tickets		cost of each ticket

So, $560 \div 8 = 70$

Solve a Simpler Problem

Think of 560 as 56×10.

If tickets cost $56 in all, you would divide $56 by 8. $56 \div 8 = 7$

Since tickets cost $560 in all, you would divide 560 by 8. $560 \div 8 = 70$

Each theater ticket costs $70.

Look Back

How can you check your answer?

Additional Standards: Number Sense 2.0; Mathematical Reasoning 2.2 *(See p. 387.)*

Try these or other strategies to solve each problem. Tell which strategy you used.

Problem-Solving Strategies

- *Make a Table*
- *Write a Number Sentence*
- *Find a Pattern*
- *Use Logical Reasoning*

Guided Practice

1. Together, Beth and Lee collect 31 moon rocks. Lee collects 3 fewer rocks than Beth. How many rocks do Beth and Lee each collect?

2. To get in shape, Nan set up the sit-up plan at the right. If she continues the pattern set on Monday, Tuesday, and Wednesday, how many sit-ups will she do on Friday?

Nan's Sit-Up Plan

Day	Sit-Ups
Monday	20
Tuesday	25
Wednesday	30

3. A wire on a space shuttle must be cut into 15 pieces. How many cuts will have to be made in order to have 15 pieces?

Independent Practice

4. In 1969, Neil Armstrong became the first person to set foot on the moon. How many years ago was that?

5. The moon helps cause the ocean tides on Earth. Suppose low tide is at 11:30 A.M. and high tide is at 5:45 P.M. How much time is there between low tide and high tide?

6. Dan buys 2 items at the space museum gift shop. The items cost a total of $18. One item is twice the price of the other item. What are the prices of the items?

7. Eight people are playing in a checkers tournament. Once a player loses a game, he or she is out of the tournament. How many games will be played before there is one winner left?

Use Homework Workbook 10-7.

LESSON

10-8 Dividing Money

Warm-Up Review

1. $\$3.50 \times 2$ **2.** $\$1.13 \times 4$

3. $250 \div 5$ **4.** $748 \div 4$

5. Does $672 \div 4$ have a two-digit or a three-digit quotient?

California Content Standards *Number Sense 3.3(🔑): Solve problems involving . . . division of money amounts in decimal notation and . . . divide money amounts in decimal notation . . . Also, Number Sense 2.7.* *(See p. 387.)*

Math Link You know how to find $945 \div 3$. In this lesson, you will do division problems like $\$9.45 \div 3$.

Example 1

Use the data in the picture at the right. Juanita's Garden Shop is having a sale on iris bulbs. What is the cost of one iris bulb?

$9.45	÷	3	=	■
total cost		number of bulbs		cost of each bulb

Step 1 Divide the way you would with whole numbers.

```
    3 15
 3)$9.45
 − 9
   04
  − 3
    15
  − 15
     0
```

Step 2 Show dollars and cents in the quotient.

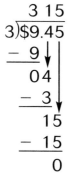

Dollars, Dimes, Pennies

```
  $3.15
3)$9.45
```

So, each iris bulb costs $3.15.

More Examples

A.

```
   $0.95
 5)$4.75
 − 4 5
     25
   − 25
      0
```

Remember to write a 0 in the dollars place when the quotient is less than $1.00.

B.

```
    $3.24
 4)$12.96
   −12
     0 9
    − 8
      16
     −16
       0
```


Additional Standards: Algebra and Functions 1.1(🔑), 1.3; Mathematical Reasoning 1.1 *(See p. 387.)*

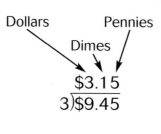

Guided Practice *For another example, see Set F on p. 415.*

1. $6\overline{)\$8.34}$ **2.** $7\overline{)\$8.47}$ **3.** $7\overline{)\$6.86}$ **4.** $3\overline{)\$15.48}$

5. A package of 5 erasers costs $1.30. A package of 8 pencils costs $2.40. What is the cost of each eraser?

Independent Practice *For more practice, see Set F on p. 417.*

6. $5\overline{)\$9.75}$ **7.** $6\overline{)\$9.48}$ **8.** $2\overline{)\$4.98}$ **9.** $9\overline{)\$2.34}$

10. $4\overline{)\$8.52}$ **11.** $3\overline{)\$6.48}$ **12.** $8\overline{)\$5.68}$ **13.** $2\overline{)\$35.16}$

14. Mental Math Find $8.00 ÷ 2. **15. Mental Math** Find $2.40 ÷ 6.

16. Algebra Write >, <, or =. $3.60 ÷ 3 ● $3.60 ÷ 4

17. A six-pack of juice boxes costs $3.72. What is the cost of each juice box?

18. A 6-ounce box of rice costs $2.28. How much does the rice cost per ounce?

Mixed Review

19. All the items on one table at a used toy store are on sale for $2 each. There are 4 old computer games and 3 old toy robots on the table. How much would it cost to buy all the items?

20. Order from greatest to least: 1,316 1,031 1,361

21. 85 ÷ 5 **22.** 98 ÷ 7 **23.** 652 ÷ 2 **24.** 261 ÷ 9

Test Prep **Choose the correct letter for each answer.**

25. Mr. Kogen bought 20 magazines for each classroom. There are 7 classrooms. How many magazines did he buy?
(9-1)

A 14 magazines **B** 27 magazines **C** 40 magazines **D** 140 magazines

26. 2,435 + 389 =
(2-5)

A 2,814 **B** 2,823 **C** 2,824 **D** 3,824 **E** NH

LESSON 10-9

Understand
Plan
Solve
Look Back

Problem-Solving Application: Using Operations

Warm-Up Review

1. 20 ÷ 5 **2.** 2 × $348

3. 84 + 26 **4.** 135 − 49

5. Miranda has 59 playing cards. Steven has 73 cards. How many more cards does Steven have than Miranda?

California Content Standard *Number Sense 2.8: Solve problems that require two or more of the skills mentioned above.*

Use the sign at the right. You want to go on several bus tours of Los Angeles. You sign up for 12 hours of tours. How much money will you spend?

Understand

What do you need to find?

First you need to find how many tours you will take. Then you need to find how much money you will spend on all the tours.

Plan

How can you solve the problem?

Divide 12 by 4 to find the number of tours you will take. Then multiply that number by the cost of each tour.

Solve

Step 1

12 ÷ 4 = 3 tours

Step 2

$$\begin{array}{r} \$64.50 \\ \times \quad 3 \\ \hline \$193.50 \end{array}$$

You will spend $193.50.

Look Back

How can you use addition to check your answer?

 Additional Standards: Mathematical Reasoning 1.1, 1.2 *(See p. 387.)*

Guided Practice

1. A group of 5 people hire a tour guide for $80. Each person shares the cost equally. How much does each person pay?

2. There are 76 people in line for a Ferris wheel. Each car can hold 4 people. How many cars will be needed so all the people in line can ride?

Independent Practice

3. A bus leaves the station with 38 people. It makes 2 stops. At the first stop, 23 people get on board. At the second stop, 15 people get on board. No one gets off at either stop. How many people are now on board?

4. One day a temperature of 430°C was recorded on the planet Mercury. Later the same day the temperature was 200°C. What was the difference between the two temperatures?

5. Leah phoned a friend in Europe. She spent $3.00 for a 5-minute phone call. If each minute costs the same amount, what was the cost for 1 minute? How much would it cost for 6 minutes?

6. Uranus was discovered in 1781. Neptune was discovered in 1846. How many years passed between the discovery of Uranus and the discovery of Neptune?

Mixed Review

Use the menu at the right for Exercises 7 and 8.

7. You pay for 6 bagels with a $5 bill. How much change do you receive?

8. You bought two items and paid with a one-dollar bill and 2 quarters. The cashier gave you 2 dimes in change. What did you buy?

Diagnostic Checkpoint

Word Bank
division
divisor
quotient
remainder
compatible numbers

1. (10-4) ______________________ are easy to divide mentally and can be used to help you estimate.

2. (10-1) When dividing whole numbers, the number left over is the ______________________.

3. (10-2) In $60 \div 3 = 20$, 20 is the ______________________.

4. (10-5) $4\overline{)48}$ **5.** (10-5) $3\overline{)63}$ **6.** (10-5) $2\overline{)82}$ **7.** (10-5) $2\overline{)36}$ **8.** (10-5) $4\overline{)64}$

9. (10-6) $3\overline{)639}$ **10.** (10-6) $5\overline{)735}$ **11.** (10-6) $4\overline{)348}$ **12.** (10-6) $3\overline{)642}$ **13.** (10-6) $8\overline{)3{,}848}$

14. (10-8) $8.48 ÷ 4 **15.** (10-8) $6.64 ÷ 8 **16.** (10-8) $50.54 ÷ 7

Algebra Write >, <, or = for each ●.

17. (10-5) $39 \div 3$ ● 13×3 **18.** (10-6) $126 \div 6$ ● $120 \div 6$

19. (10-7) Jordan swims 72 laps each week. She swims 4 days a week and swims the same number of laps each day. How many laps does she swim each day?

20. (6-7) The Pet Shop has 3 fish tanks. There are 18 fish in each tank. How many fish are there in all?

21. (10-8) Eric spent $46.50 for 6 tickets to a movie. How much did each ticket cost?

22. (10-9) David has 12 toy cars and 18 toy boats. He keeps all the toys in 6 boxes. Each box holds the same number of toys. How many toys are in each box?

23. (10-9) Last week, Susan did each of the jobs shown at the right once. She spent all the money she earned on 3 cans of tennis balls. How much did 1 can of tennis balls cost?

Job	Pay
Walk dog	$5
Do dishes	$3
Run errands	$4

Chapter 10 Test

1. $9 \div 3 = $ ■
$90 \div 3 = $ ■
$900 \div 3 = $ ■

2. $45 \div 9 = $ ■
$450 \div 9 = $ ■
$4{,}500 \div 9 = $ ■

3. $30 \div 5 = $ ■
$300 \div 5 = $ ■
$3{,}000 \div 5 = $ ■

Find each quotient and remainder.

4. $31 \div 6$ **5.** $29 \div 3$ **6.** $40 \div 6$ **7.** $57 \div 8$

Find each quotient.

8. $8\overline{)88}$ **9.** $3\overline{)93}$ **10.** $3\overline{)81}$ **11.** $5\overline{)90}$

12. $6\overline{)672}$ **13.** $5\overline{)235}$ **14.** $3\overline{)819}$ **15.** $4\overline{)8{,}644}$

16. $6.48 ÷ 3 **17.** $8.19 ÷ 9 **18.** $3.85 ÷ 7 **19.** $7.38 ÷ 6

Estimate each quotient. Tell the numbers you used.

20. $59 \div 6$ **21.** $570 \div 7$ **22.** $329 \div 8$

23. A package of 8 pencils costs $2.80. How much does each pencil cost?

24. Erica is making necklaces for her friends. Each necklace uses 9 beads. She has a package of 50 beads. What is the greatest number of necklaces she can make?

25. Phillip practices gymnastics the same number of hours each week. His weekly practice schedule is shown at the right. How many hours does he practice in 4 weeks?

Phillip's Practice Schedule

Day	Hours
Monday	2
Wednesday	2
Thursday	1
Saturday	4

Multiple-Choice Chapter 10 Test

Choose the correct letter for each answer.

1. **Mrs. Jackson has 23 students. She wants to put them in groups of 4 students. How many students will be left over?**

   A 3 students
   B 4 students
   C 5 students
   D 6 students

2. **Find 27 ÷ 5.**

   F 4 R7
   G 5 R2
   H 5 R3
   J 5 R7
   K NH

3. **Mrs. Perry wants to buy each student in her class an apple to take on the field trip. There are 9 apples in a bag. How many bags would she need to buy if she has 25 students in her class?**

   A 2 bags
   B 3 bags
   C 4 bags
   D 5 bags

4. **Find 540 ÷ 6.**

   F 9
   G 80
   H 90
   J 900
   K NH

5. **Doug has 320 rocks in his rock collection. He wants to put his rocks equally into 8 boxes. How many rocks should he put into each box?**

   A 4 rocks
   B 40 rocks
   C 400 rocks
   D 2,560 rocks

6. **Marcus has 128 bagels to put into bags. He needs to put 6 bagels in each bag. About how many bags will he fill?**

   F About 6 bags
   G About 10 bags
   H About 20 bags
   J About 30 bags

7. **Which is the most reasonable estimate of 650 ÷ 8?**

   A 60
   B 70
   C 80
   D 90

8. **Find 57 ÷ 3.**

   F 12
   G 18
   H 19
   J 20
   K NH

9. Which will give a quotient with 3 digits?

A 96 ÷ 3
B 175 ÷ 5
C 598 ÷ 2
D 783 ÷ 9

---

10. $3\overline{)7{,}896}$

F 2,232
G 2,292
H 2,632
J 2,732
K NH

---

11. There are 6 buses for 228 students. The same number of students will ride in each bus. How many students will ride in each bus?

A 36 students
B 37 students
C 38 students
D 40 students

---

12. Find $7.76 ÷ 8.

F $0.97
G $9.07
H $9.70
J $970
K NH

---

13. Which is the most reasonable estimate of 98 ÷ 5?

A 10
B 15
C 20
D 500

---

14. Denzel needs to buy notebooks for school. He finds the same type of notebooks at 4 different stores. At which store will he pay the least amount per notebook?

Store	Cost of Notebooks
A	3 for $3.95
B	2 for $2.40
C	$1.39 each
D	$1.19 each

F Store A
G Store B
H Store C
J Store D

---

15. Maria buys 6 bags of beads. Each bag has 32 beads. Maria wants to make 8 bracelets. Each bracelet will have an equal number of beads. How many beads can she put on each bracelet?

A 4 beads
B 5 beads
C 22 beads
D 24 beads

---

16. Find $21.72 ÷ 4.

F $5.43
G $5.48
H $54.30
J $54.80
K NH

Reteaching

Set A *(pages 388–389)*

Find 16 ÷ 3.

Step 1	Step 2
$\begin{array}{r} 5 \\ 3\overline{)16} \\ \underline{15} \end{array}$ ← Multiply: 5 × 3	$\begin{array}{r} 5\text{ R1} \\ 3\overline{)16} \\ \underline{-15} \\ 1 \end{array}$ ← Subtract: 16 − 15

Remember to include the remainder in your answer.

1. $8\overline{)76}$
2. $2\overline{)17}$
3. $5\overline{)39}$
4. $7\overline{)50}$
5. 15 ÷ 4
6. 32 ÷ 6

Set B *(pages 392–393)*

Find 1,800 ÷ 3.

18 ÷ 3 = 6
180 ÷ 3 = 60
1,800 ÷ 3 = 600

Find 300 ÷ 6.

30 ÷ 6 = 5
300 ÷ 6 = 50

Remember that sometimes you can use basic facts and patterns with zeros to help you divide greater numbers.

1. 16 ÷ 4 = ■
   160 ÷ 4 = ■
   1,600 ÷ 4 = ■
2. 40 ÷ 8 = ■
   400 ÷ 8 = ■
   4,000 ÷ 8 = ■
3. 60 ÷ 3
4. 210 ÷ 7
5. 1,600 ÷ 8
6. 2,700 ÷ 9

Set C *(pages 394–395)*

Estimate 349 ÷ 4.

Think of a number that is close to 349 that you can divide easily by 4.

360 is close to 349.

360 ÷ 4 = 90

So, 349 ÷ 4 is about 90.

Remember that you can use compatible numbers to help you estimate.

Estimate each quotient. Tell the numbers you used.

1. 53 ÷ 5
2. 89 ÷ 9
3. 208 ÷ 2
4. 359 ÷ 9

Set D *(pages 398–400)*

Find 84 ÷ 3.

$$\begin{array}{r} 2 \\ 3\overline{)84} \\ \underline{-6} \\ 2 \end{array} \qquad \begin{array}{r} 28 \\ 3\overline{)84} \\ \underline{-6\downarrow} \\ 24 \\ \underline{-24} \\ 0 \end{array}$$

Remember that you can check your answer by multiplying.

1. $3\overline{)87}$ **2.** $2\overline{)28}$

3. $4\overline{)92}$ **4.** $5\overline{)70}$

5. 78 ÷ 6 **6.** 96 ÷ 2

Set E *(pages 401–403)*

Find 976 ÷ 4.

First decide where to start dividing.

$$\begin{array}{r} 244 \\ 4\overline{)976} \\ \underline{-8\downarrow} \\ 17 \\ \underline{-16\downarrow} \\ 16 \\ \underline{-16} \\ 0 \end{array}$$

Remember that the quotient will have 2 digits if the hundreds digit of the dividend is less than the divisor.

1. $3\overline{)966}$ **2.** $8\overline{)648}$

3. $9\overline{)171}$ **4.** $5\overline{)365}$

5. $4\overline{)640}$ **6.** $8\overline{)984}$

7. $2\overline{)5{,}924}$ **8.** $6\overline{)7{,}326}$

Set F *(pages 406–407)*

Find $8.78 ÷ 2.

Divide money the way you would divide whole numbers.

$$\begin{array}{r} \$4.39 \\ 2\overline{)\$8.78} \\ \underline{-8\downarrow} \\ 07 \\ \underline{-6\downarrow} \\ 18 \\ \underline{-18} \\ 0 \end{array}$$

Remember to show dollars and cents in the quotient when dividing money.

1. $4\overline{)\$8.84}$ **2.** $5\overline{)\$6.60}$

3. $9\overline{)\$8.28}$ **4.** $6\overline{)\$7.20}$

5. $5.85 ÷ 3 **6.** $3.68 ÷ 8

7. $9.26 ÷ 2 **8.** $9.73 ÷ 7

More Practice

Set A *(pages 388–389)*

1. $5\overline{)23}$ 2. $6\overline{)35}$ 3. $2\overline{)19}$ 4. $7\overline{)38}$ 5. $4\overline{)28}$

6. $3\overline{)23}$ 7. $8\overline{)66}$ 8. $9\overline{)72}$ 9. $6\overline{)56}$ 10. $7\overline{)59}$

11. $15 \div 2$ 12. $19 \div 3$ 13. $28 \div 9$

14. Thomas has 36 bottles of water. He drinks 5 bottles each day. How many days will he be able to have 5 bottles of water? How many bottles will be left over?

Set B *(pages 392–393)*

1. $32 \div 8 = ■$
   $320 \div 8 = ■$
   $3{,}200 \div 8 = ■$

2. $54 \div 9 = ■$
   $540 \div 9 = ■$
   $5{,}400 \div 9 = ■$

3. $36 \div 6 = ■$
   $360 \div 6 = ■$
   $3{,}600 \div 6 = ■$

4. $80 \div 4$ 5. $600 \div 3$ 6. $120 \div 4$

7. $280 \div 7$ 8. $4{,}000 \div 8$ 9. $3{,}600 \div 9$

10. There are 180 students waiting to be put in teams for the spelling contest. Each team will have 6 students. How many spelling teams will there be?

Set C *(pages 394–395)*

Estimate each quotient. Tell the numbers you used.

1. $72 \div 7$ 2. $59 \div 3$ 3. $543 \div 6$ 4. $370 \div 9$

5. $572 \div 8$ 6. $179 \div 2$ 7. $228 \div 6$ 8. $154 \div 5$

9. $369 \div 4$ 10. $207 \div 7$ 11. $491 \div 8$ 12. $195 \div 9$

13. Talia read a 213-page book in a week. About how many pages did she read each day?

Set D (pages 398–400)

1. $7\overline{)77}$
2. $6\overline{)78}$
3. $5\overline{)60}$
4. $3\overline{)39}$
5. $5\overline{)90}$
6. $2\overline{)52}$
7. $4\overline{)76}$
8. $7\overline{)98}$
9. Dorothy has 42 stuffed animals. She wants to put the same number of stuffed animals on each shelf. She has 3 shelves. How many stuffed animals should she put on each shelf?

Set E (pages 401–403)

1. $3\overline{)342}$
2. $8\overline{)896}$
3. $3\overline{)105}$
4. $9\overline{)801}$
5. $2\overline{)550}$
6. $6\overline{)852}$
7. $5\overline{)900}$
8. $4\overline{)5{,}248}$
9. $948 \div 4$
10. $6{,}726 \div 6$
11. $7{,}569 \div 9$
12. Mrs. Flemming's class collected 184 cans during the can drive. Each student collected 8 cans. How many students are in the class?
13. If 295 boxes were loaded equally onto 5 trucks, how many boxes were put on each truck?

Set F (pages 406–407)

1. $5\overline{)\$9.25}$
2. $3\overline{)\$7.41}$
3. $9\overline{)\$3.87}$
4. $6\overline{)\$8.46}$
5. $2\overline{)\$1.78}$
6. $4\overline{)\$8.88}$
7. $8\overline{)\$9.52}$
8. $7\overline{)\$8.75}$
9. $3\overline{)\$2.25}$
10. $5\overline{)\$8.50}$
11. $\$6.36 \div 6$
12. $\$4.96 \div 4$
13. $\$18.26 \div 2$
14. Melanie bought a 6-pack of juice cans to take to the track meet. The 6-pack cost $3.54. What was the cost of each can?

Problem Solving: Preparing for Tests

Choose the correct letter for each answer.

---

1. Karolyn is ordering cheese pizza for herself and 4 friends. Each person wants 3 slices. Each pizza is sliced like below. How many pizzas should Karolyn order?

A 2 pizzas
B 3 pizzas
C 4 pizzas
D 5 pizzas

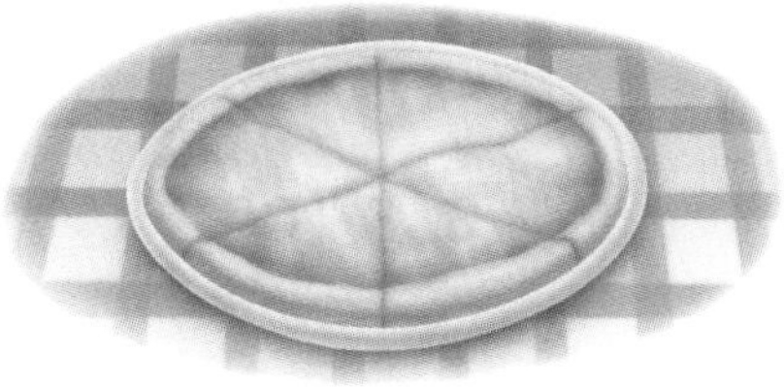

Tip
There is more than one step to this problem. Decide what the steps are and in what order they should be done.

---

2. Gina is planning a cookout for herself and 6 friends. She wants to have 3 hamburger buns for each person. Hamburgers come in different-sized packages. Which packages should she buy?

F 2 packages of 4 hamburger buns
G 3 packages of 4 hamburger buns
H 3 packages of 6 hamburger buns
J 4 packages of 6 hamburger buns

Tip
For this problem, you need to read all the answer choices in order to solve the problem.

---

3. Luis has a bag of 20 marbles. He wants to give an equal number of marbles to each of 4 friends. Which picture shows how he should divide the marbles?

A 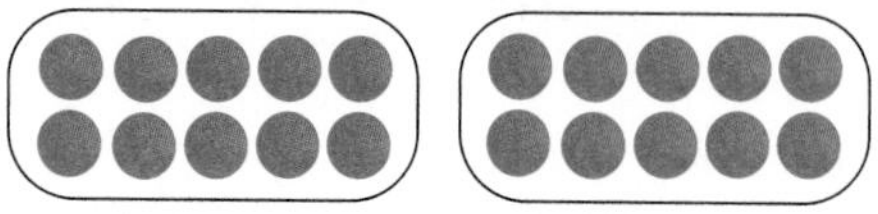

B 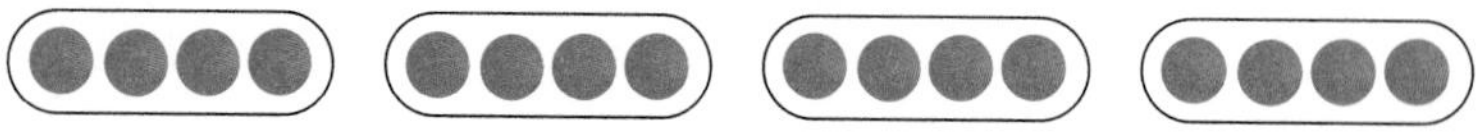

C 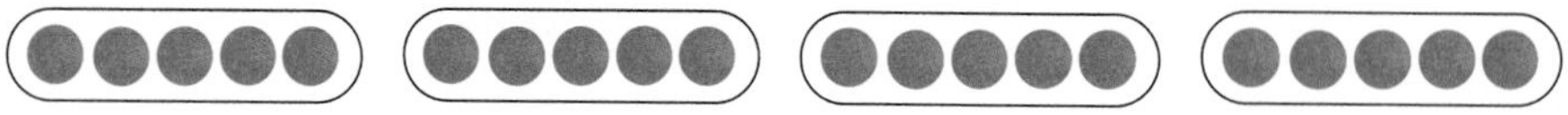

D 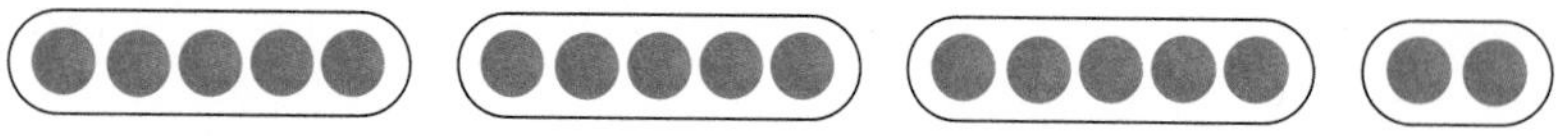

Tip
Since Luis has 4 friends, look for the answer that shows 4 groups. Then make sure that each group is equal.

4. **Jim bought 4 boxes of computer disks. There were 10 disks in each box. Each box cost $13. How many disks did Jim buy?**

F 9 disks
G 17 disks
H 27 disks
J 40 disks

---

5. **At the bike-a-thon, Cathy biked 74 laps around the track. Sam biked half that number. How many laps did the two friends bike?**

A 37 laps
B 101 laps
C 111 laps
D 148 laps

---

6. **Jon read 59 pages from his book on Monday. He read 22 pages on Tuesday. About how many pages did he read on Monday and Tuesday?**

F 90 pages **H** 70 pages
G 80 pages **J** 40 pages

---

7. **Ruth is 3 years younger than Vic. The sum of both their ages is 17. How old is Vic?**

A 7 years old
B 8 years old
C 10 years old
D 11 years old

8. **Pat got to school at 8:05 A.M. Fred arrived at 7:50 A.M. Nan was later than Fred, but earlier than Sue. Who would it be reasonable to say was the first to arrive?**

F Pat **H** Fred
G Nan **J** Sue

Use the graph for Questions 9–10

Ernie made the graph below to show how many hours he spent raking leaves last week.

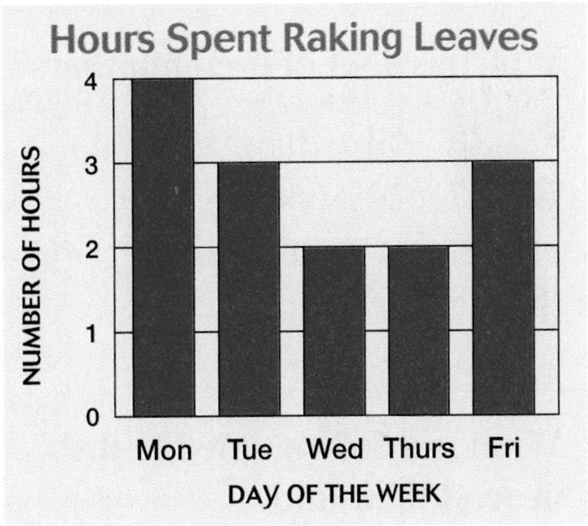

9. **Ernie makes $4.50 an hour. How much money did he make on Tuesday?**

A $9.00 **C** $13.50
B $12.00 **D** $18.00

---

10. **Ernie had planned to work only 10 hours last week. How many more hours did he work than he planned?**

F 1 hour **H** 3 hours
G 2 hours **J** 4 hours

TEST PREP

Multiple-Choice Cumulative Review

Choose the correct letter for each answer.

Number Sense

1. Which group of numbers is in order from *greatest* to *least?*

A	5,677	4,566	3,455	5,443
B	3,455	4,566	5,443	5,677
C	5,443	5,677	4,566	3,455
D	5,677	5,443	4,566	3,455

2. Which is a set of even numbers?

F	75	60	20	18
G	17	21	55	73
H	24	16	4	86
J	22	48	13	12

3. What is 6,562 rounded to the nearest thousand?

A 6,000
B 7,000
C 7,560
D 7,600

4. What number is the same as two thousand, one hundred thirty?

F 213
G 2,130
H 20,130
J 21,030

5. What multiplication fact does the picture show?

A $2 \times 2 = 4$
B $2 \times 3 = 6$
C $2 \times 7 = 14$
D $3 \times 6 = 18$

6. What is the quotient of $72 \div 9$?

F 7 H 9
G 8 J 10

7. A furniture factory can make 22 chairs in one hour. How many chairs can it make in 4 hours?

A 26 chairs C 66 chairs
B 44 chairs D 88 chairs

8. Sports World just received a shipment of hockey pucks. There are 396 pucks in each box. About how many pucks are there in 2 boxes?

F 800 pucks H 500 pucks
G 700 pucks J 400 pucks

Algebra and Functions

9. A pencil costs 15¢ at the school store. Two pencils cost 30¢, and 3 pencils cost 45¢. How much would 6 pencils cost?

   A 45¢
   B 50¢
   C 60¢
   D 90¢

10. What operation symbol would make the statement true?

    3 ▇ 4 = 12

    F $+$ **H** $\times$
    G $-$ **J** $\div$

11. If 3 times a number is 15, what expression could be used to find the number?

    A $15 \div 3$
    B $15 - 3$
    C 15×3
    D $15 + 3$

12. What is the missing number in the number pattern?
    75, 100, ▇, 150, 175

    F 110
    G 125
    H 130
    J 145

Statistics, Data Analysis, and Probability

Use the graph for Questions 13–15.

13. How many more days did it snow in February than in December?

    A 2 days
    B 4 days
    C 5 days
    D 6 days

14. How many days did it snow in March?

    F 3 days
    G 5 days
    H 6 days
    J 7 days

15. Which month had the fewest days of snow?

    A April
    B January
    C February
    D December

CHAPTER 11

Fractions and Decimals

Diagnosing Readiness

In Chapter 11, you will use these skills:

Ⓐ Comparing Numbers

(pages 14–16)

Compare. Write >, <, or = for each ●.

1. 6 ● 8 **2.** 15 ● 12

3. 36 ● 52 **4.** 19 ● 19

5. April has 18 yards of material. Jamie has 15 yards. Who has more material?

Ⓑ Ordering Numbers

(pages 14–16)

Order the numbers from least to greatest.

6. 6, 3, 0, 5

7. 12, 11, 26, 13

8. Mr. Hall's class is helping with a canned food drive. Dillon gave 12 cans, Hillary gave 15 cans, Mike gave 9 cans, and Tashina gave 19 cans. List the names in order from least to most number of cans given.

C Adding

(pages 48–51)

9. $8 + 9$

10. $3 + 6$

11. $36 + 29$

12. $57 + 15$

13. $\begin{array}{r} 136 \\ +824 \\ \hline \end{array}$

14. $\begin{array}{r} 369 \\ +289 \\ \hline \end{array}$

15. The basketball team scored 78 points their first game and 86 points their second game. How many points did they score in both games together?

D Subtracting

(pages 58–64)

16. $8-3$

17. $12-5$

18. $56 - 24$

19. $92 - 78$

20. $\begin{array}{r} 215 \\ -166 \\ \hline \end{array}$

21. $\begin{array}{r} 871 \\ -493 \\ \hline \end{array}$

22. The marching band has 104 members. 37 of the members are drummers. How many members are not drummers?

E Using Money

(pages 50–51, 60–61)

23. $\begin{array}{r} \$5.00 \\ -\ 3.29 \\ \hline \end{array}$

24. $\begin{array}{r} \$6.98 \\ +\ 2.63 \\ \hline \end{array}$

25. $\begin{array}{r} \$10.00 \\ -\ 7.82 \\ \hline \end{array}$

26. $\begin{array}{r} \$12.19 \\ +\ 16.87 \\ \hline \end{array}$

27. $\begin{array}{r} \$23.17 \\ -\ 18.09 \\ \hline \end{array}$

28. $\begin{array}{r} \$18.92 \\ +\ 0.86 \\ \hline \end{array}$

29. Layne bought a box of cereal for $3.19, a loaf of bread for $1.29, and a gallon of milk for $2.79. How much change will she get if she pays with a ten-dollar bill?

F Fractions

(Grade 2)

Write how many equal parts each figure is divided into.

30. 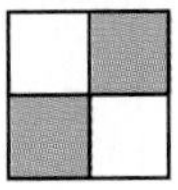

31. 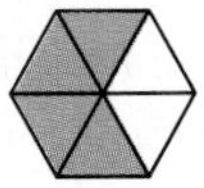

32. José folded a piece of notebook paper in half twice. How many equal parts did the paper have?

To the Family and Student

Looking Back	Chapter 11	Looking Ahead
In Grade 2, students learned how to find equal parts of shapes, and learned about simple fractions to twelfths.	**Fractions and Decimals** In this chapter, students will learn how whole numbers, simple fractions, and decimals relate. They will also learn how to compare, order, add, and subtract fractions and decimals.	In Grade 4, students will learn how to add and subtract mixed numbers and how to round decimals. They will also learn how to mark fractions and decimals on a number line.

Math and Everyday Living

Opportunities to apply the concepts of Chapter 11 abound in everyday situations. During the chapter, think about how fractions and decimals can be used to solve a variety of real-world problems. The following examples suggest just a few of the many situations that could launch a discussion about fractions and decimals.

Math and Art During art class you divided your paper into 6 equal parts. You colored 2 parts purple, 1 part blue, 1 part orange, and 2 parts red. What part of the paper did you color orange?

Math and Gardening Carol planted 100 flower seeds. Fifty out of 100 were daisies, 35 out of 100 were mums, and 15 out of 100 were pansies. Write a decimal to describe the part of the seeds planted for each flower.

Math and Food
You have $\frac{3}{5}$ of a granola bar. Your friend got $\frac{7}{10}$ of a granola bar. Who got more? Explain.

Math and Hobbies You collect marbles. You bought 12 marbles the last time you went to the toy store. Five of them were solid in color, the rest were multicolored. What fraction of the marbles were multicolored?

Math and Shopping At a department store, 0.1 of the shoppers buy designer clothes. What fraction of the shoppers do not buy designer clothes?

Math and Exercise
You walked $\frac{2}{3}$ of a mile. Your friend walked $\frac{1}{2}$ of a mile. How much farther did you walk?

Math and Money You saved $7.36 from your birthday. You got $5.25 for doing your chores. How much money do you have now?

Math and Transportation
8 out of 10 people travel to work by car, and the rest use public transportation. What decimal shows how many of the 10 people travel by car? by public transportation?

Math and Baking You are baking blueberry muffins for your class. The recipe makes 12 muffins. You need to double the recipe. If you needed $\frac{1}{3}$ cup sugar, how much would you need when doubling the recipe?

California Content Standards in Chapter 11 Lessons*

	Teach and Practice	Practice
Number Sense		
1.2 (Gr. 4) Order and compare whole numbers and decimals to two decimal places.	11-12	
1.5 (Gr. 4) Explain different interpretations of fractions, for example, parts of a whole, parts of a set, ...	11-1, 11-4	
1.7 (Gr. 4) Write the fraction represented by a drawing of parts of a figure; represent a given fraction by using drawings; and relate a fraction to a simple decimal on a number line.		11-1, 11-4
1.9 (Gr. 4) Identify on a number line the relative position of positive fractions, positive mixed numbers, ...	11-8	
2.0 (Gr. 4) Students extend their use and understanding of whole numbers to addition and subtraction of decimals.	11-13	
3.1 Compare fractions represented by drawings or concrete materials to show equivalency . . . (e.g., $\frac{1}{2}$ of a pizza is the same amount as $\frac{2}{4}$ of another pizza that is the same size; show that $\frac{3}{8}$ is larger than $\frac{1}{4}$).	11-2, 11-3	
3.2 (🔑) Add and subtract simple fractions (e.g., determine that $\frac{1}{8} + \frac{3}{8}$ is the same as $\frac{1}{2}$).	11-6, 11-7	
3.3 (🔑) Solve problems involving addition, subtraction . . . of money amounts in decimal notation	11-14	
3.4 Know and understand that fractions and decimals are different representations of the same concept (e.g., 50 cents is $\frac{1}{2}$ of a dollar, 75 cents is $\frac{3}{4}$ of a dollar).	11-10, 11-11	

	Teach and Practice	Practice
Algebra and Functions		
1.1 (🔑) Represent relationships of quantities in the form of mathematical expressions, equations, or inequalities.		11-2, 11-3, 11-5, 11-12
1.3 Select appropriate operational and relational symbols to make an expression true (e.g., if 4 ___ 3 = 12, what operational symbol goes in the blank?).		11-3, 11-12
Mathematical Reasoning		
1.1 Analyze problems by identifying relationships, distinguishing relevant from irrelevant information, sequencing and prioritizing information, and observing patterns.		11-1, 11-4, 11-6, 11-7, 11-13
2.0 Students use strategies, skills, and concepts in finding solutions.		11-5, 11-9, 11-14
2.3 Use a variety of methods, such as words, numbers, symbols, charts, graphs, tables, diagrams, and models to explain mathematical reasoning.	11-9	11-2, 11-11, 11-12
2.4 Express the solution clearly and logically by using the appropriate mathematical notation and terms and clear language; support solutions with evidence in both verbal and symbolic work.		11-3, 11-8, 11-11, 11-13
3.1 Evaluate the reasonableness of the solution in the context of the original situation.	11-5	11-14
3.2 Note the method of deriving the solution and demonstrate a conceptual understanding of the derivation by solving similar problems.		11-5, 11-9

*The symbol (🔑) indicates a key standard as designated in the Mathematics Framework for California Public Schools. Full statements of the California Content Standards are found at the beginning of this book following the Table of Contents.

LESSON 11-1

Fractions as Parts of a Whole

Warm-Up Review

1. 8 ÷ 2 **2.** 12 ÷ 2

3. 9 ÷ 3 **4.** 8 ÷ 4

5. Joe cut a sandwich into 6 equal pieces. He shared the sandwich equally with two friends. How many pieces of the sandwich did each person get?

California Content Standard *Number Sense 1.5 (Gr. 4): Explain different interpretations of fractions, for example, parts of a whole, ...*

Math Link You know how to divide regions into parts. Now you will learn how to name equal parts of regions.

Word Bank

fraction
numerator
denominator

Example 1

Martha divided her paper into 4 equal parts. She colored it as shown at the right. What fraction of the paper did she color orange?

You can use a **fraction** to tell how much of the paper she colored.

numerator ⟶ 1 ⟵ orange part
denominator ⟶ 4 ⟵ parts in all

So, Martha colored $\frac{1}{4}$ of the paper orange.

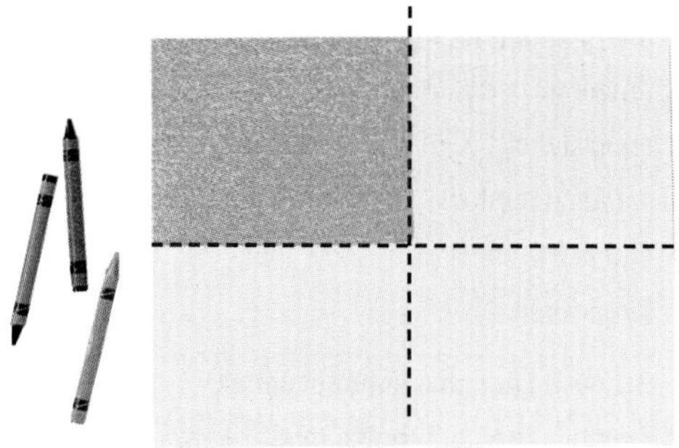

Example 2

Ian colored the paper strips as shown below. What fraction tells how much of each strip he colored?

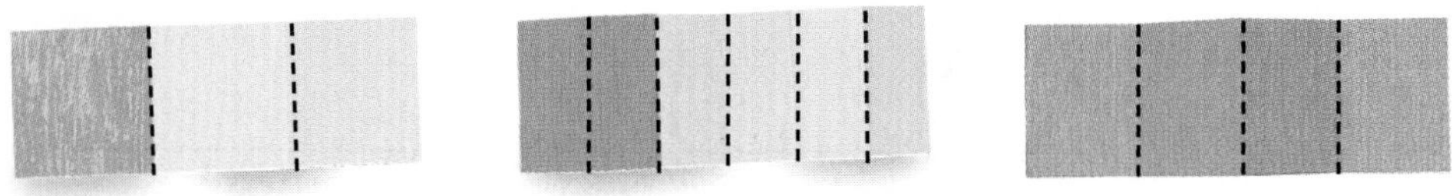

colored parts ⟶ 1
parts in all ⟶ 3
$\frac{1}{3}$

colored parts ⟶ 2
parts in all ⟶ 6
$\frac{2}{6}$

colored parts ⟶ 4
parts in all ⟶ 4
$\frac{4}{4} = 1$ whole

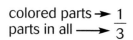

Additional Standards: Number Sense 1.7 (Gr. 4); Mathematical Reasoning 1.1 *(See p. 425.)*

Guided Practice *For another example, see Set A on p. 464.*

Write a fraction for the shaded part. Then write a fraction for the part that is not shaded.

1. 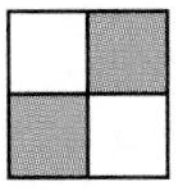

■ shaded parts
4 parts in all

2. 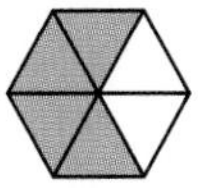

4 shaded parts
■ parts in all

3. 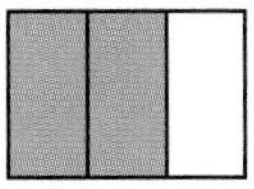

$\frac{■}{3}$

4. 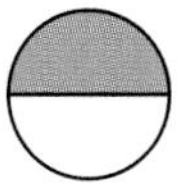

$\frac{1}{■}$

5. Jill divided a circle into 8 equal parts. She colored 4 parts red, 3 parts white, and 1 part yellow. What fraction of the circle did she color white?

Independent Practice *For more practice, see Set A on p. 467.*

Write a fraction for the shaded part.

6. 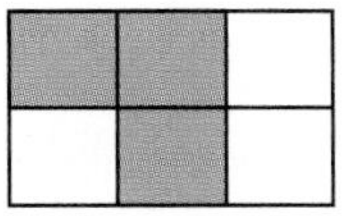

7. 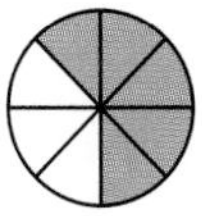

8. 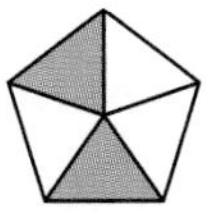

9. 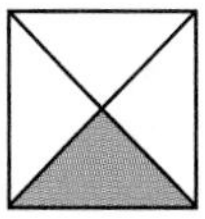

10. Mark folded his paper into 10 equal parts. He colored 4 parts blue and 3 parts red. What fraction of his paper did he color?

Mixed Review

11. Will has 180 marbles. He divides the marbles equally into 3 bags. How many marbles are in each bag?

12. $8 ÷ 2 **13.** $15 ÷ 5 **14.** 125 ÷ 5 **15.** 270 ÷ 3

Test Prep **Choose the correct letter for each answer.**

16. **Algebra** Which number makes the statement false? (2-13)

■ − 8 is greater than 2.

A 10
B 11
C 12
D 13

17. What is the value of 1,283 rounded to the nearest hundred? (1-2)

F 1,200
G 1,280
H 1,300
J 2,000
K NH

LESSON 11-2

Finding Equivalent Fractions

Warm-Up Review

Write *true* or *false* for each statement.

1. $2 + 3 = 5$
2. $7 - 4 = 1 + 2$
3. $5 \times 3 = 10 + 5$
4. $8 \div 2 = 4 \times 2$
5. Marta divided a circle into 4 equal parts. She colored 2 parts purple and 2 parts green. What fraction did she color green?

California Content Standard *Number Sense 3.1: Compare fractions represented by drawings or concrete materials to show equivalency . . . (e.g., $\frac{1}{2}$ of a pizza is the same amount as $\frac{2}{4}$ of another pizza that is the same size; . . .).*

Math Link You know what a fraction is. Now you will learn to use different fraction names to identify the same part of a region.

Example 1

One of the sandwiches at the right is cut into fourths. One is cut in half. How many fourths are equal to $\frac{1}{2}$? You can use fraction pieces to model the sandwiches. Show 1 whole, 2 halves, and 4 fourths.

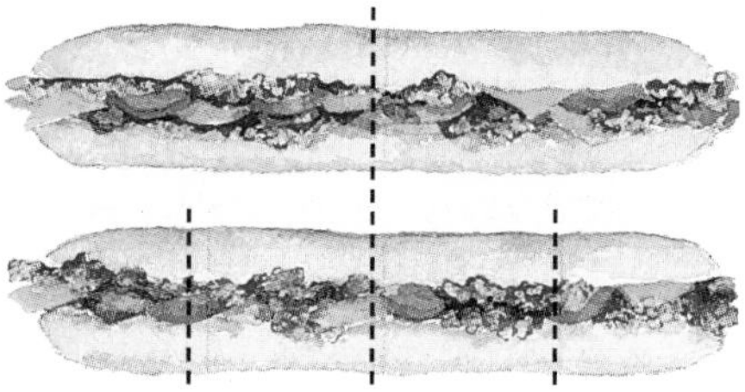

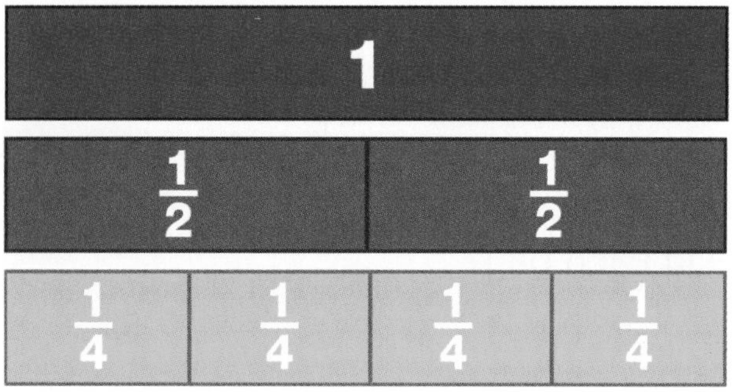

Word Bank

equivalent fractions

Two fourths are equal to $\frac{1}{2}$. Fractions that name the same parts of a whole are called **equivalent fractions**.

More Examples

Find equivalent fractions.

A. 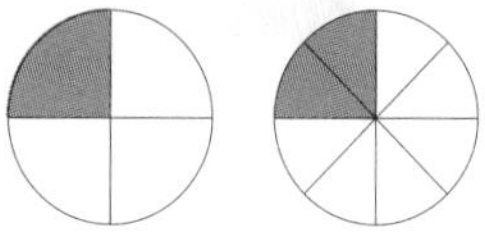

$\frac{1}{4} = \frac{2}{8}$

B. 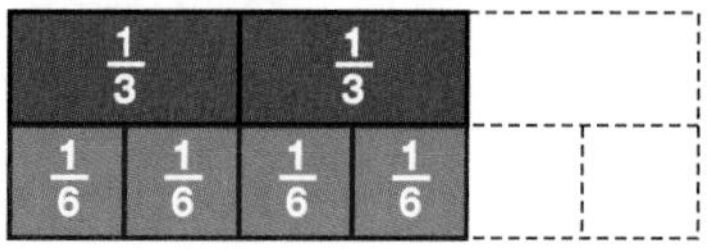

$\frac{2}{3} = \frac{4}{6}$

C. 

$\frac{3}{4} = \frac{9}{12}$

Additional Standards: Algebra and Functions 1.1 (key); Mathematical Reasoning 2.3 (See p. 425.)

Guided Practice *For another example, see Set B on p. 464.*

Find equivalent fractions. You may use fraction strips or fraction circles to help.

1.

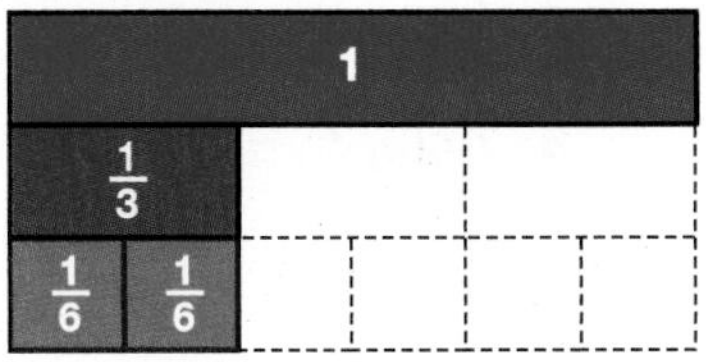

$\frac{\square}{3} = \frac{\square}{6}$

2.

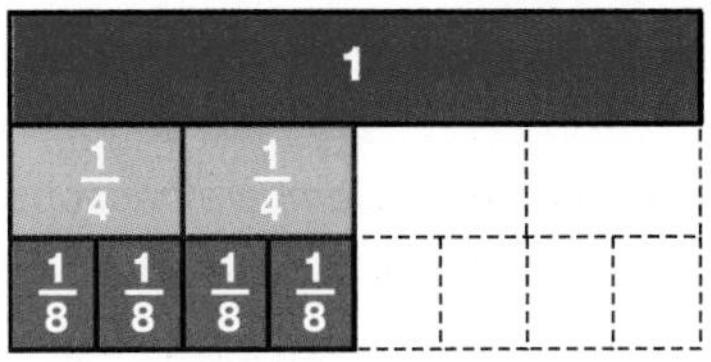

$\frac{\square}{4} = \frac{\square}{8}$

3.

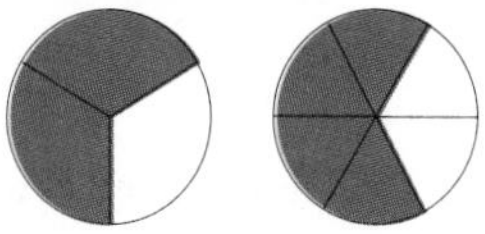

$\frac{\square}{3} = \frac{\square}{6}$

4. Arnie and Pat had equal-sized hoagies. Arnie ate $\frac{2}{4}$ of his hoagie. Pat ate $\frac{3}{6}$ of his. Who ate more? Explain.

Independent Practice *For more practice, see Set B on p. 467.*

Find equivalent fractions. You may use fraction strips or fraction circles to help.

5.

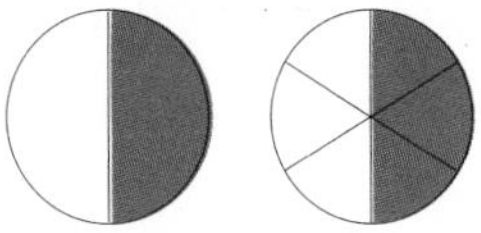

$\frac{1}{2} = \frac{\square}{6}$

6.

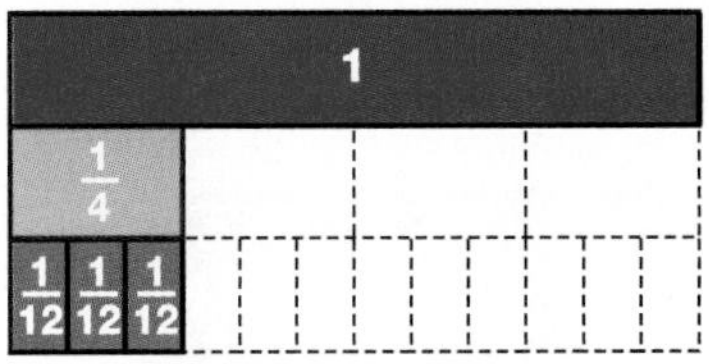

$\frac{1}{4} = \frac{\square}{12}$

7.

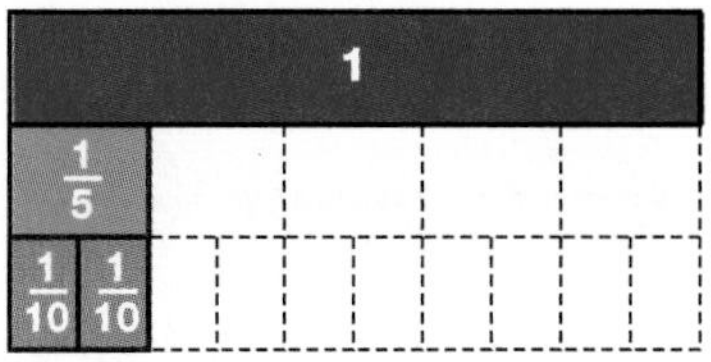

$\frac{1}{5} = \frac{\square}{10}$

8. Marnie found a beetle that was $\frac{3}{4}$ of an inch long. Elaine found a beetle the same length as Marnie's. How many eighths of an inch long is Elaine's beetle?

Mixed Review

9. Math Reasoning A striped tent is red and blue. Each color has an equal number of stripes. What fraction are red?

Test Prep **Choose the correct letter for each answer.**

10. (10-8) A box of 8 pencils costs $1.20. How much does each pencil cost?

A $0.20 **C** $0.12

B $0.15 **D** $0.10

11. (Gr. 2) Which number is NOT an even number?

F 80

G 45

H 36

J 12

LESSON 11-3

Comparing and Ordering Fractions

California Content Standard *Number Sense 3.1: Compare fractions represented by drawings or concrete materials to show equivalency . . . (e.g., $\frac{1}{2}$ of a pizza is the same amount as $\frac{2}{4}$ of another pizza that is the same size; show that $\frac{3}{8}$ is larger than $\frac{1}{4}$).*

Math Link You know how to find equivalent fractions. Now you will learn to compare fractions that are not equivalent.

Warm-Up Review

Are the fractions equivalent? Write *yes* or *no*.

1. $\frac{1}{2}$ and $\frac{2}{4}$
2. $\frac{3}{4}$ and $\frac{2}{3}$
3. $\frac{3}{6}$ and $\frac{2}{4}$
4. $\frac{1}{5}$ and $\frac{2}{3}$
5. A football game is divided into four equal parts called quarters. How many quarters are in the first half of the game?

Example 1

The spice rack is filled with ground spices. It is divided into 6 equal parts. Is there more red pepper or more ginger?

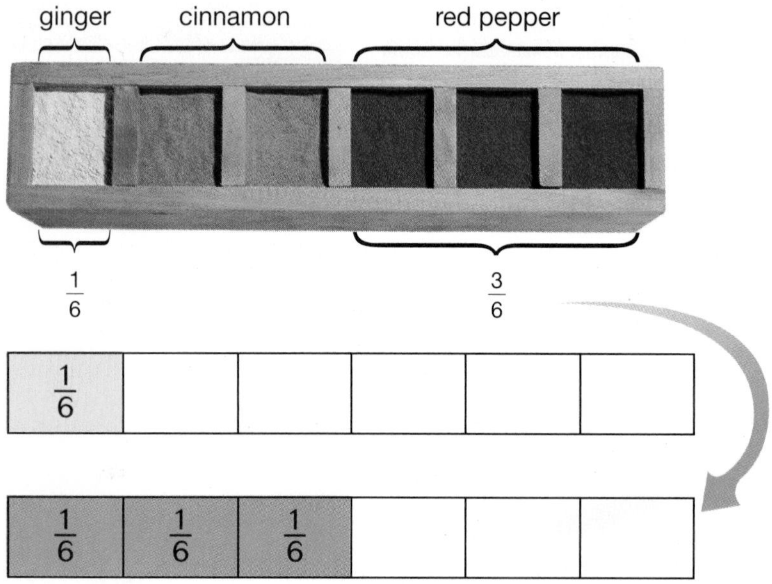

$\frac{1}{6}$ is less than $\frac{3}{6}$.

$$\frac{1}{6} < \frac{3}{6}$$

$\frac{3}{6}$ is greater than $\frac{1}{6}$.

$$\frac{3}{6} > \frac{1}{6}$$

There is more red pepper.

Additional Standards: Algebra and Functions 1.1, 1.3; Mathematical Reasoning 2.4 *(See p. 425.)*

Example 2

Arrange the fractions $\frac{1}{4}, \frac{1}{3}, \frac{1}{8}, \frac{1}{6}, \frac{1}{12}$ in order from least to greatest. Which is greater, $\frac{1}{3}$ or $\frac{1}{12}$?

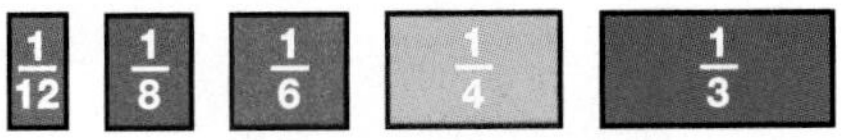

$\frac{1}{3}$ is greater than $\frac{1}{12}$.

More Examples

Compare. Write >, <, or = for each ●.

A. $\frac{1}{4}$ ● $\frac{3}{4}$

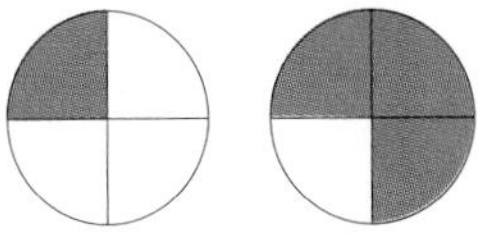

$\frac{1}{4} < \frac{3}{4}$

B. $\frac{1}{6}$ ● $\frac{1}{4}$

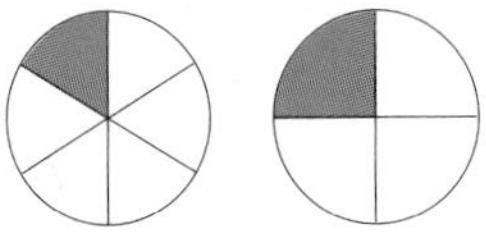

$\frac{1}{6} < \frac{1}{4}$

Guided Practice

For another example, see Set C on p. 464.

Algebra Compare. Write >, <, or = for each ●. You may use fraction strips or fraction circles to help.

1.

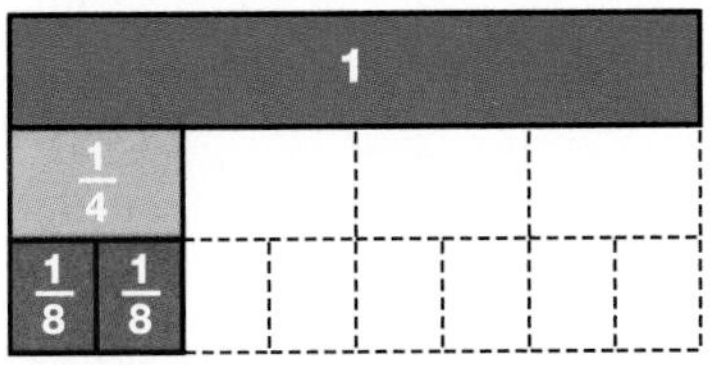

$\frac{1}{4}$ ● $\frac{2}{8}$

2.

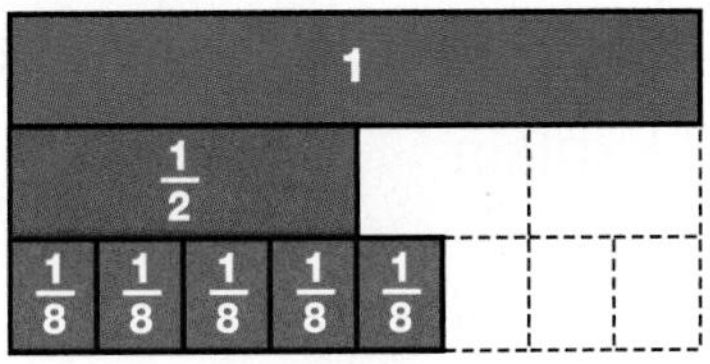

$\frac{1}{2}$ ● $\frac{5}{8}$

3.

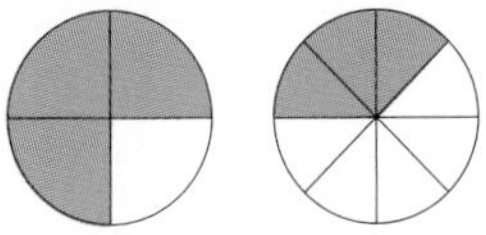

$\frac{3}{4}$ ● $\frac{3}{8}$

4.

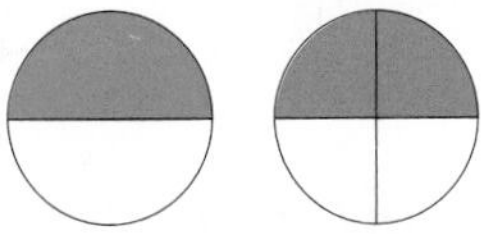

$\frac{1}{2}$ ● $\frac{2}{4}$

5. Samir and her friends made an apple pie. Samir ate $\frac{1}{4}$ of the pie, John ate $\frac{1}{8}$ of the pie, and Rani ate $\frac{1}{3}$ of the pie. Who ate the most pie?

Independent Practice *For more practice, see Set C on p. 467.*

Algebra **Compare. Write >, <, or = for each ●. You may use fraction strips or fraction circles to help.**

6. 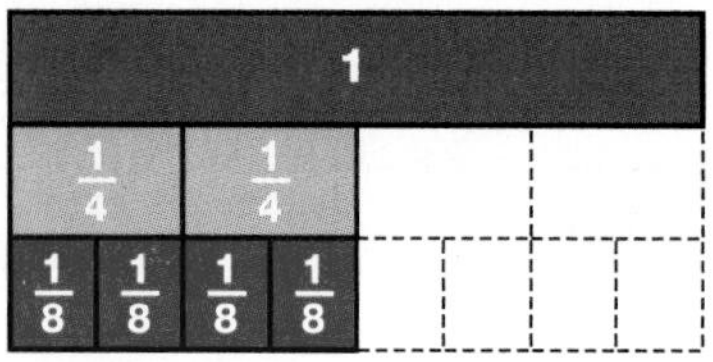

$\frac{2}{4}$ ● $\frac{4}{8}$

7. 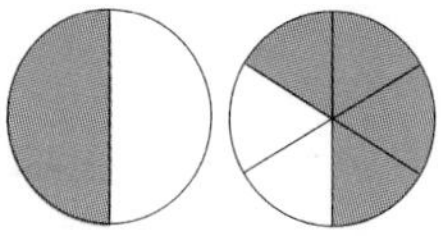

$\frac{1}{2}$ ● $\frac{4}{6}$

8. 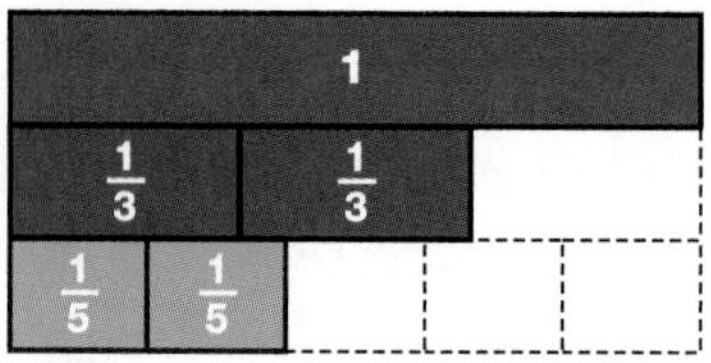

$\frac{2}{5}$ ● $\frac{2}{3}$

9. $\frac{1}{3}$ ● $\frac{1}{4}$

10. $\frac{1}{6}$ ● $\frac{2}{3}$

11. $\frac{2}{4}$ ● $\frac{2}{8}$

12. $\frac{1}{2}$ ● $\frac{3}{6}$

Arrange the fractions in order from least to greatest.

13. $\frac{1}{3}, \frac{1}{2}, \frac{1}{6}$

14. $\frac{1}{3}, \frac{1}{12}, \frac{1}{4}$

15. $\frac{1}{4}, \frac{3}{4}, \frac{1}{8}$

16. Ken bought a bag of 12 balloons. He filled $\frac{1}{3}$ of the balloons with water and $\frac{1}{2}$ of the balloons with air. Did he have more air-filled balloons or water-filled balloons?

17. **Math Reasoning** Which is greater, $\frac{1}{3}$ or $\frac{2}{3}$? Explain.

Mixed Review

18. Carla had $\frac{1}{2}$ dollar. Jamie had $\frac{5}{10}$ of a dollar. Who had more money? Explain.

Write a fraction for the shaded part.

19. 

20. 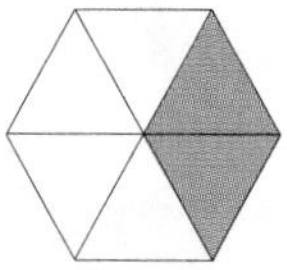

21. 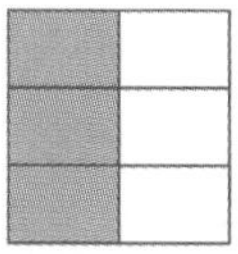

22. 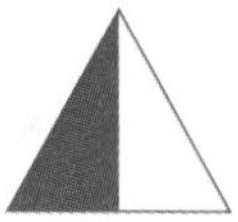

Test Prep **Choose the correct letter for each answer.**

23. (4-1) Find a multiplication sentence for the addition sentence
$3 + 3 + 3 + 3 = 12$.

A $3 \times 4 = 12$ **C** $12 \times 3 = 36$

B $3 + 4 = 7$ **D** $3 \times 13 = 39$

24. (1-8) Pete bought a juice drink. He gave the clerk 3 quarters. The clerk gave him a dime and a nickel back. How much did the juice drink cost?

F $0.90 **H** $0.60

G $0.70 **J** $0.50

TEST PREP

Multiple-Choice Cumulative Review

Choose the correct letter for each answer.

1. Which lists odd numbers only?

A 56 97 31 73
B 62 48 90 12
C 17 29 81 30
D 51 25 37 99

2. What is the missing number in the number pattern?

36, 44, 52, ■, 68

F 54
G 58
H 60
J 64

3. Which would be the best estimate for a temperature when you would be swimming?

A 32°F
B 56°F
C 89°F
D 212°F

4. Which lists the fractions from *least* to *greatest*?

F $\frac{1}{6}, \frac{1}{2}, \frac{3}{4}$
G $\frac{1}{2}, \frac{3}{4}, \frac{1}{6}$
H $\frac{3}{4}, \frac{1}{2}, \frac{1}{6}$
J $\frac{1}{2}, \frac{1}{6}, \frac{3}{4}$

5. Which represents $4 + 4 + 4 + 4 + 4$?

A 4×1
B 5×4
C $20 \div 5$
D $20 \div 4$

6. Which number makes the number sentence true?

3 × ■ = 600

F 2
G 20
H 200
J 2,000

7. Issac's school starts at 8:30 A.M. Math starts at 9:45 A.M. How much time passes between the start of school and math?

A 15 minutes
B 45 minutes
C 1 hour 15 minutes
D 1 hour 45 minutes

8. When you multiply a number by 1 you always get

F 1.
G an even number.
H an odd number.
J the other number.

LESSON 11-4

Fractions as Parts of a Set

Warm-Up Review

How many in each set are yellow?

1. 

2. 

3. 

4. There are 25 marbles in a bag. Ten are blue, 8 are green, and 3 are yellow. How many are *not* blue, green, or yellow?

California Content Standard *Number Sense 1.5 (Gr. 4): Explain different interpretations of fractions, for example, . . . , parts of a set . . ..*

Math Link You know how to use fractions to name equal parts of a region. Now you will learn to use fractions to name equal parts of a set.

Example 1

The ants are carrying 2 green leaves and 4 yellow leaves. What fraction of the leaves are green?

numerator ⟶ 2 ⟵ green leaves

denominator ⟶ 6 ⟵ total number of leaves

$\frac{2}{6}$ of the leaves are green.

More Examples

What fraction of each set is red?

A. 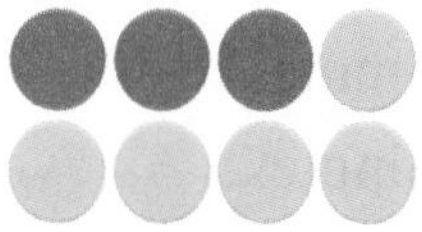

$\frac{3}{8}$ red counters / counters in all

So, $\frac{3}{8}$ of the set is red.

B. 

$\frac{5}{6}$ red counters / counters in all

So, $\frac{5}{6}$ of the set is red.

C. 

$\frac{10}{10}$ red counters / counters in all

So, $\frac{10}{10}$, or the whole set, is red.

Additional Standards: Number Sense 1.7 (Gr. 4); Mathematical Reasoning 1.1 *(See p. 425.)*

Guided Practice *For another example, see Set D on p. 465.*

Write a fraction to name the part of each set that is green.

1. 

2. 

3. 

4. 

5. Carrie bought 7 bananas. Three are ripe. What fraction of the bananas is not ripe?

Independent Pratice *For more practice, see Set D on p. 468.*

Write a fraction that names the part of each set that is red.

6. 

7. 

8. 

9. Jamal bought 5 oranges. He peeled 2 of them. What fraction of the oranges is peeled?

Mixed Review

10. The Earth's surface is made up of land and water. There is about $\frac{3}{4}$ water and $\frac{1}{4}$ land. Is there more land or water?

Find equivalent fractions.

11. 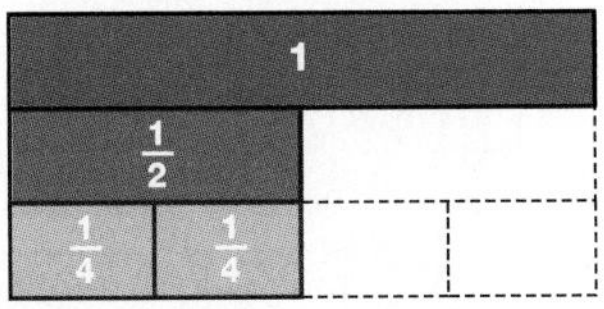

$\frac{■}{2} = \frac{■}{4}$

12. 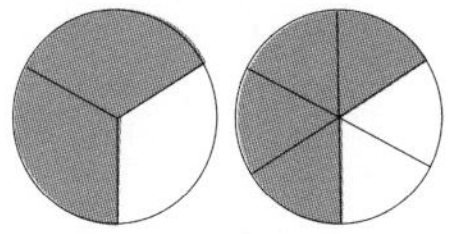

$\frac{■}{3} = \frac{■}{6}$

13. 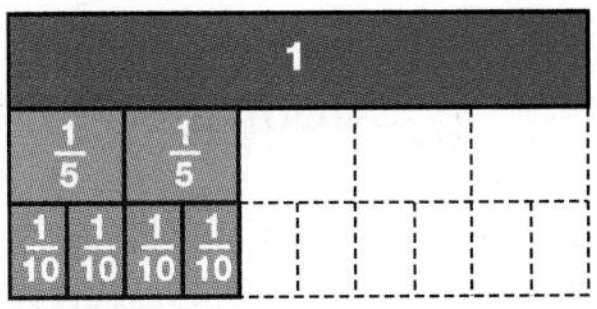

$\frac{■}{5} = \frac{■}{10}$

Test Prep **Choose the correct letter for each answer.**

14. (6-6) Joe is buying bags of soil. The soil comes in 5-lb bags. He needs 20 pounds of soil. How many bags should he buy?

A 10 bags **C** 4 bags

B 5 bags **D** 2 bags

15. Algebra (5-11) Find the missing factor.

$4 \times ■ = 28$

F 7 **H** 20

G 8 **J** 24

LESSON 11-5

Understand
Plan
Solve
Look Back

Problem-Solving Skill:
Reasonable Answers

Warm-Up Review

Are the estimates reasonable?

1. 525 + 300 is about 1,000.
2. 1,029 − 600 is about 400.
3. Jerry reads 6 pages per day from his book. He estimates that he can finish the last 120 pages in 12 days. Is his estimate reasonable?

California Content Standard *Mathematical Reasoning 3.1: Evaluate the reasonableness of the solution in the context of the original situation.*

Read for Understanding

Mr. O'Connell sells corn, tomatoes, and beans at a roadside stand. The stand is divided into 4 equal sections. The picture shows how he displays the vegetables.

1. How many equal sections are there?
2. Which two kinds of vegetables cover the same area?
3. Which vegetable covers the most area?

Think and Discuss

MATH FOCUS

Reasonable Answers

Whenever you answer a question, you should check that it is reasonable. Look at the facts that are given. Make sure your answer makes sense compared to the facts.

Reread the paragraph at the top of the page.

4. Is it reasonable to think that $\frac{4}{4}$ of the stand is used for corn? Explain why or why not.
5. Is it reasonable to think that $\frac{1}{4}$ of the stand could be used for corn? Why or why not?
6. Why is it helpful to check to make sure an answer is reasonable?

Additional Standards: Algebra and Functions 1.1; Mathematical Reasoning 2.0, 3.2 (See p. 425.)

Guided Practice

One morning, Dolores put 27 tomatoes on a table to sell. At the end of the day, 8 tomatoes were still on the table.

1. Is it reasonable to say that Dolores has 35 tomatoes left to sell?
   - **a.** Yes; she should have more tomatoes now than when she started.
   - **b.** No; she should have fewer tomatoes now than when she started.
   - **c.** No; she sold all her tomatoes.

2. Which number sentence shows how many tomatoes Dolores sold?
   - **a.** $27 + 8 = \blacksquare$
   - **b.** $27 - 8 = \blacksquare$
   - **c.** $27 \div 8 = \blacksquare$

3. Is it reasonable to say that Dolores sold about 20 tomatoes?
   - **a.** Yes; $27 - 8$ is about 20.
   - **b.** No; $27 + 8$ is greater than 20.
   - **c.** No; $27 \div 8$ is less than 20.

Independent Practice

Ernie bought two oranges of the same size at a roadside stand. He cut the first orange into 4 equal sections. He cut the second orange into 6 equal sections.

4. How many sixths are equal to $\frac{1}{2}$?
   - **a.** 6 sixths
   - **b.** 3 sixths
   - **c.** 2 sixths

5. How many fourths are equal to $\frac{1}{2}$?
   - **a.** 2 fourths
   - **b.** 3 fourths
   - **c.** 4 fourths

6. **Math Reasoning** Ernie gave 1 section of the first orange to Tina. He gave 1 section of the second orange to Robert. Is it reasonable to say that he gave a larger section of orange to Tina than to Robert? Why or why not?

7. Ernie still has three sections of the first orange and five sections of the second orange. Does he have more of the first orange or the second orange left? Explain.

Use Homework Workbook 11-5.

LESSON 11-6

Adding and Subtracting Fractions with Like Denominators

Warm-Up Review

1. $3 + 6$ **2.** $4 + 7$

3. $8 - 3$ **4.** $3 + 4$

5. $12 - 7$ **6.** $9 + 4$

7. When George was 3 years old he slept 12 hours per day. Now George is 10 years old and he sleeps 10 hours per day. How much less does he sleep now than when he was 3?

California Content Standard *Number Sense 3.2(🔑): Add and subtract simple fractions (e.g., determine that $\frac{1}{8} + \frac{3}{8}$ is the same as $\frac{1}{2}$).*

Math Link You know how to add and subtract whole numbers. Now you will learn to add and subtract fractions.

Example 1

Find $\frac{1}{3} + \frac{1}{3}$.

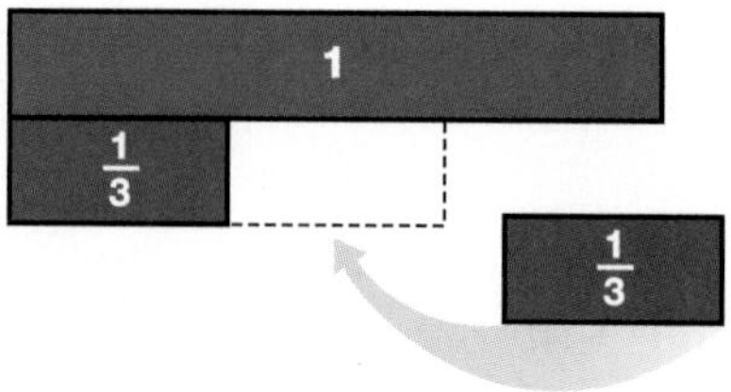

$\frac{1}{3} + \frac{1}{3} = \frac{2}{3}$ ← Add the numerators.
← Use the same denominator, thirds.

Since each fraction you're adding is in thirds, you can simply add how many thirds you have in all.

Example 2

Find $\frac{3}{4} - \frac{1}{4}$.

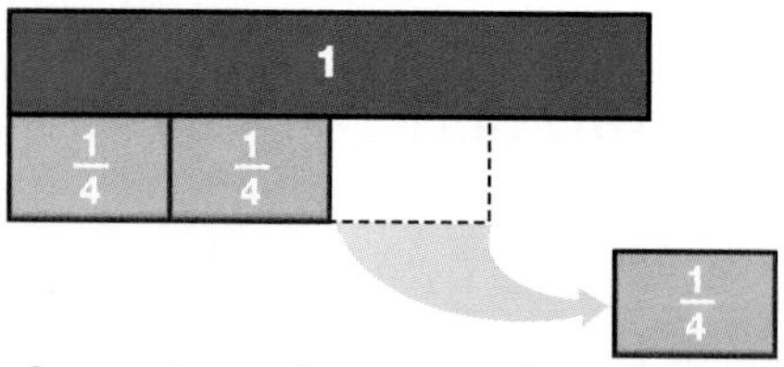

$\frac{3}{4} - \frac{1}{4} = \frac{2}{4}$ ← Subtract the numerators.
← Use the same denominator, fourths.

Since each fraction is in fourths, you can simply subtract out one-fourth from the three-fourths.

 Additional Standard: Mathematical Reasoning 1.1 (See p. 425.)

Guided Practice *For another example, see Set E on p. 465.*

Find each sum or difference. You may use fraction strips to help.

1.

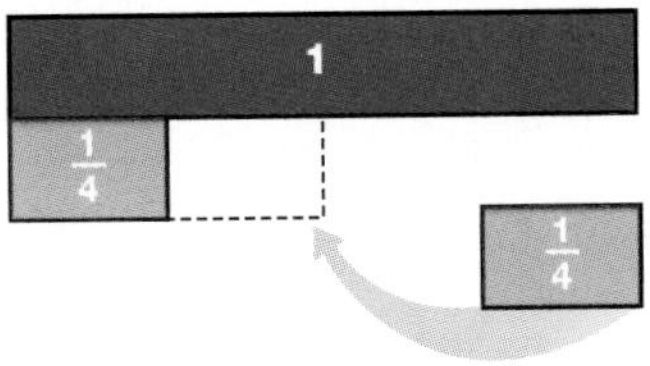

$\frac{1}{4} + \frac{1}{4}$

2.

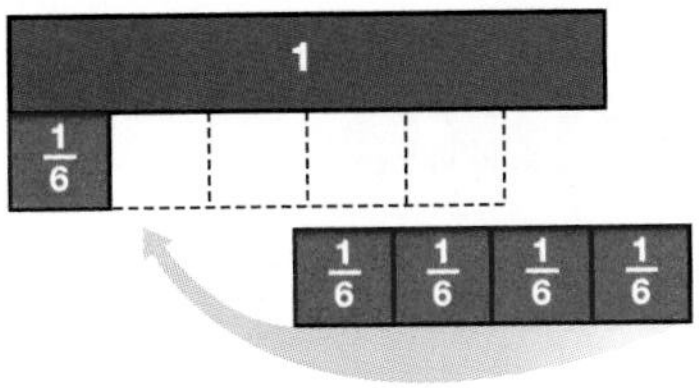

$\frac{1}{6} + \frac{4}{6}$

3.

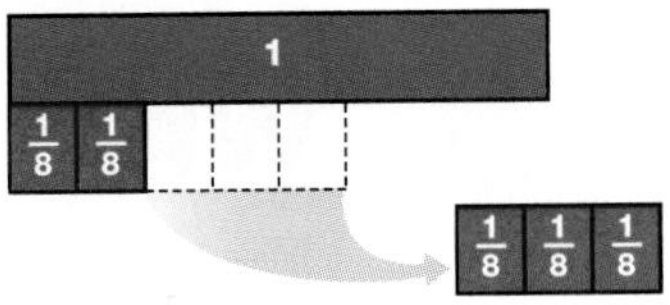

$\frac{5}{8} - \frac{3}{8}$

4. Emily can hold her breath for $\frac{2}{3}$ of a minute. Sean can hold his breath for $\frac{1}{3}$ of a minute. How much longer can Emily hold her breath than Sean?

Independent Practice *For more practice, see Set E on p. 468.*

Find each sum or difference. You may use fraction strips to help.

5. $\frac{5}{10} + \frac{4}{10}$ **6.** $\frac{3}{5} - \frac{1}{5}$ **7.** $\frac{7}{8} - \frac{3}{8}$ **8.** $\frac{3}{12} + \frac{4}{12}$

9. $\frac{7}{8} - \frac{2}{8}$ **10.** $\frac{3}{6} + \frac{2}{6}$ **11.** $\frac{6}{10} - \frac{3}{10}$ **12.** $\frac{4}{8} + \frac{3}{8}$

13. Elle knocked down 2 of the ten bowling pins on her first turn. She knocked down 4 more pins on her next turn. What fraction of the bowling pins did she knock down?

Mixed Review

14. Tim's cat had 10 kittens. Three of the kittens were males. What fraction of the kittens were females?

Compare. Write >, <, or = for each ●.

15. $\frac{1}{4}$ ● $\frac{3}{4}$ **16.** $\frac{2}{3}$ ● $\frac{1}{2}$ **17.** $\frac{3}{6}$ ● $\frac{1}{6}$ **18.** $\frac{1}{2}$ ● $\frac{1}{8}$

Test Prep Choose the correct letter for each answer.

19. Algebra Find the missing number.
(2-14)
$4 \times 3 = ■ - 15$

A 12 **C** 24
B 15 **D** 27

20. Which number is greater than 4,637?
(1-5)

F 4,630 **H** 4,640
G 4,603 **J** 4,600

LESSON 11-7

Adding and Subtracting Fractions with Unlike Denominators

Warm-Up Review

Tell if the fractions are equivalent. Write *yes* or *no*.

1. $\frac{2}{4}$ and $\frac{4}{6}$
2. $\frac{1}{3}$ and $\frac{3}{9}$
3. $\frac{2}{6}$ and $\frac{1}{3}$
4. $\frac{2}{12}$ and $\frac{1}{6}$
5. Joel asked 4 people which they liked better, reading or watching TV. Three people said they liked reading better. Is it reasonable to say that $\frac{3}{4}$ of the people he asked like reading better?

California Content Standard *Number Sense 3.2 (key): Add and subtract simple fractions (e.g., determine that $\frac{1}{8}+\frac{3}{8}$ is the same as $\frac{1}{2}$).*

Math Link You know how to add and subtract fractions that have the same denominators. Now you will learn to add and subtract fractions that have different denominators.

Example 1

Find $\frac{1}{2}+\frac{1}{4}$.

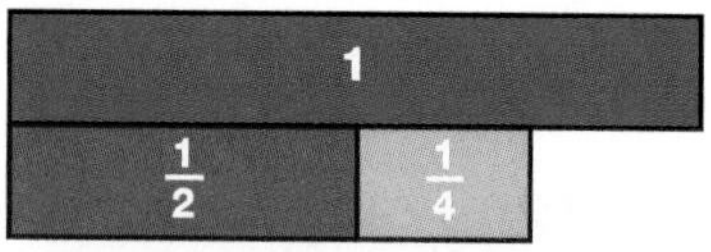

The denominators are different.

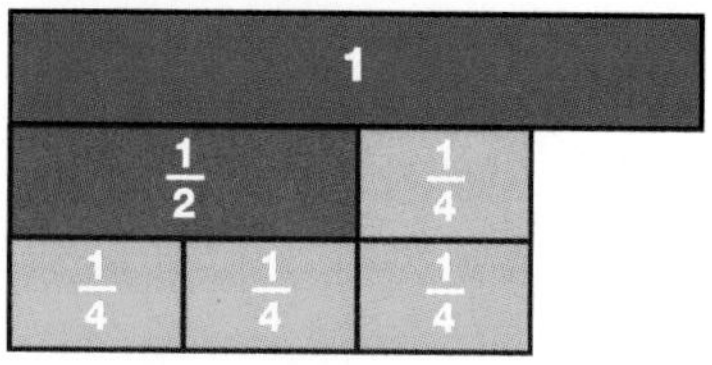

Find equivalent fractions with the same denominators.

$$\frac{2}{4}+\frac{1}{4}=\frac{3}{4}$$

Add the numerators and use the same denominator.

Example 2

Find $\frac{1}{2}-\frac{2}{6}$.

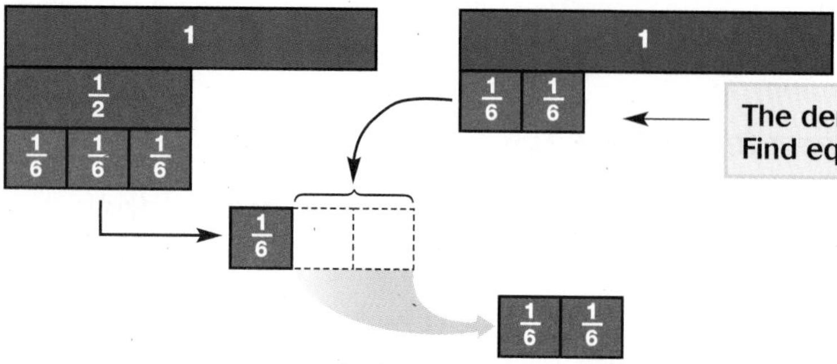

The denominators are different. Find equivalent fractions.

$$\frac{3}{6}-\frac{2}{6}=\frac{1}{6}$$

Subtract the numerators.
Keep the denominators the same.

 Additional Standard: Mathematical Reasoning 1.1 *(See p. 425.)*

Guided Practice

For another example, see Set F on p. 465.

Find each sum or difference. You may use fraction strips to help.

1. $\frac{1}{2} + \frac{1}{4}$ **2.** $\frac{1}{3} + \frac{1}{6}$ **3.** $\frac{3}{5} + \frac{1}{10}$ **4.** $\frac{1}{4} + \frac{3}{8}$

5. $\frac{3}{4} - \frac{1}{8}$ **6.** $\frac{4}{5} - \frac{1}{10}$ **7.** $\frac{5}{6} - \frac{1}{3}$ **8.** $\frac{1}{4} - \frac{1}{12}$

9. A recipe calls for $\frac{1}{2}$ cup powdered sugar and $\frac{1}{4}$ cup brown sugar. How much sugar is in the recipe altogether?

Independent Practice

For more practice, see Set F on p. 468.

Find each sum or difference. You may use fraction strips to help.

10. $\frac{1}{2} - \frac{1}{4}$ **11.** $\frac{3}{4} - \frac{1}{8}$ **12.** $\frac{4}{6} + \frac{1}{3}$ **13.** $\frac{3}{12} + \frac{2}{6}$

14. $\frac{7}{12} - \frac{1}{3}$ **15.** $\frac{3}{4} + \frac{1}{8}$ **16.** $1 - \frac{3}{4}$ **17.** $\frac{2}{6} + \frac{3}{12}$

18. Max read for $\frac{3}{4}$ of an hour. Janice read for $\frac{1}{2}$ of an hour. How much longer did Max read than Janice?

Mixed Review

19. Megan invited 12 friends to her party. Only 10 of her friends came to the party. Of the friends she invited, what fraction came to the party?

20. $\frac{2}{4} - \frac{1}{4}$ **21.** $\frac{5}{6} + \frac{1}{6}$ **22.** $\frac{5}{8} - \frac{2}{8}$ **23.** $\frac{7}{10} + \frac{1}{10}$

Test Prep Choose the correct letter for the answer.

24. (3-1) Gym class starts at 11:15 A.M. and lasts 40 minutes. What time does gym class end?

A 11:40 A.M. **B** 12:05 P.M. **C** 11:55 P.M. **D** 11:55 A.M.

25. (6-5) Tarik and 3 friends share 12 grapes equally. How many grapes does each person get?

F 3 **G** 4 **H** 6 **J** 12

LESSON 11-8 Understanding Mixed Numbers

California Content Standard *Number Sense 1.9 (Gr. 4) (🔑): Identify on a number line the relative position of positive fractions, positive mixed numbers, ...*

Math Link You know what whole numbers and fractions are. Now you will learn about numbers that are whole numbers and fractions together.

Warm-Up Review

True or false?

1. $6 > 3$
2. $\frac{1}{2} < \frac{2}{3}$
3. A vase holds $\frac{1}{2}$ red roses, $\frac{2}{8}$ white carnations, and $\frac{1}{4}$ yellow roses. Are there more red or yellow roses in the vase?

Example 1

The amount of water needed to make a loaf of bread is shown at the right.

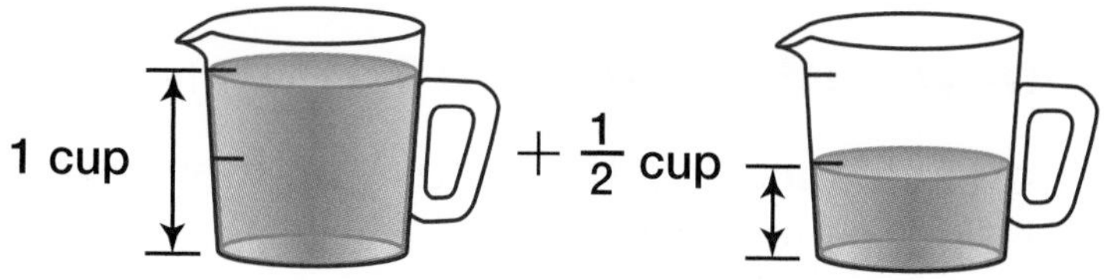

Write a mixed number for the amount of water needed to make a loaf of bread.

Word Bank

mixed number

1 cup + $\frac{1}{2}$ cup = $1\frac{1}{2}$ cups

It is read as one and one half cups.

The number $1\frac{1}{2}$ is a **mixed number**.

A mixed number is a whole number and a fraction.

More Examples

Write a mixed number for the length of each object.

A.

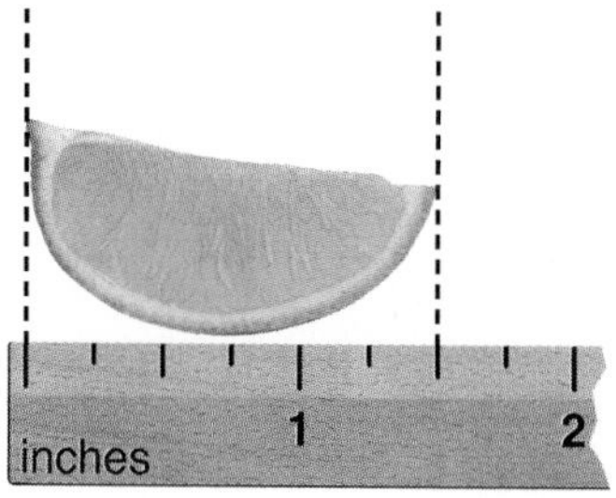

The lime measures $1\frac{1}{2}$ in.

B.

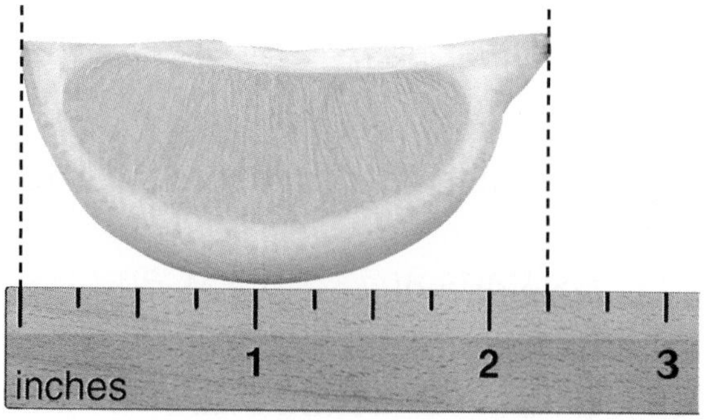

The lemon measures $2\frac{1}{4}$ in.

 Additional Standard: Mathematical Reasoning 2.4 (See p. 425.)

Guided Practice *For another example, see Set G on p. 465.*

Write a mixed number for the part that is shaded.

1. 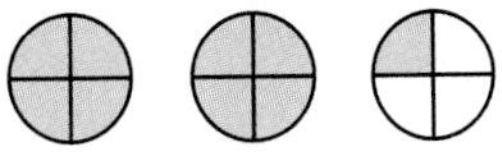

2. 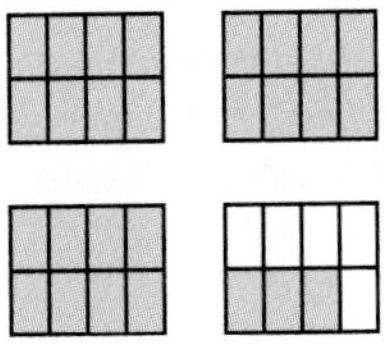

3. 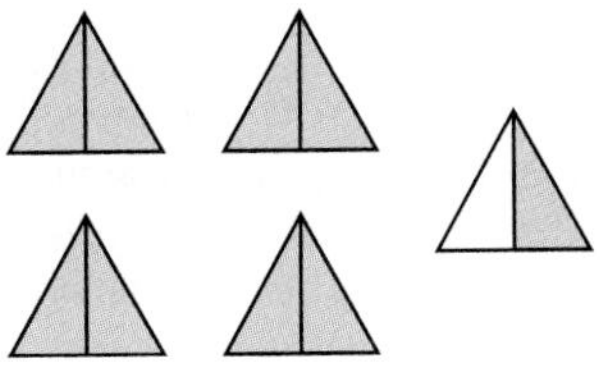

4. You need $1\frac{3}{4}$ teaspoons of food coloring. Is that closer to 1 teaspoon or 2 teaspoons?

Independent Practice *For more practice, see Set G on p. 468.*

Write a mixed number for the part that is shaded.

5. 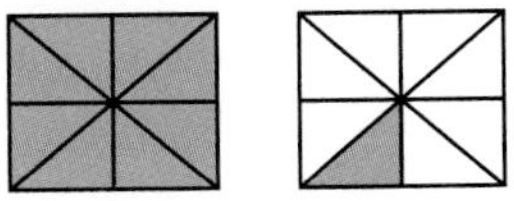

6. 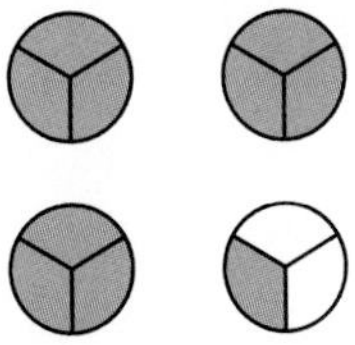

7. 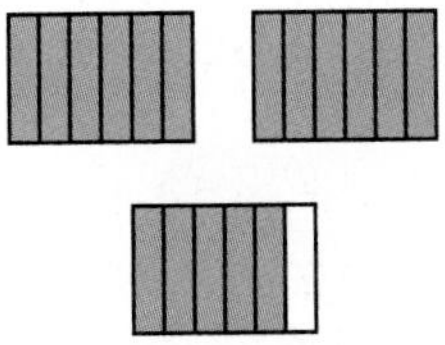

Measure each object to the nearest quarter inch.

8. 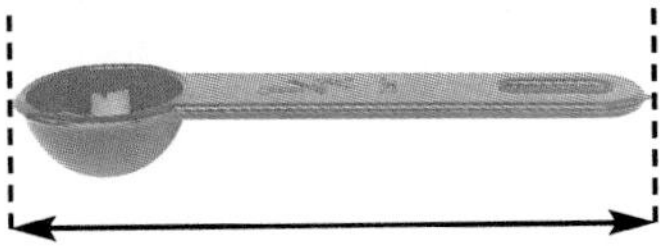

9. 

10. Math Reasoning Explain why $\frac{1}{2} + \frac{3}{4} = 1\frac{1}{4}$.

Mixed Review

11. Glen bought 6 boxes of crayons. Each box had 144 crayons. He gave 1 box to his friend Jan. How many crayons does he have left?

12. $\frac{2}{4} + \frac{1}{4}$ **13.** $\frac{2}{3} - \frac{1}{3}$ **14.** $\frac{1}{3} + \frac{1}{6}$ **15.** $\frac{3}{4} - \frac{5}{8}$

Test Prep **Choose the correct letter for each answer.**

16. (2-9) In June, there were 1,850 geese in the nature preserve. By fall, 1,160 had flown south. How many geese are left?

A 720 **C** 632

B 690 **D** 600

17. (10-5) **Algebra** Write $>$, $<$, or $=$ to make the statement true.

$56 \div 7$ ● $56 \div 8$

F $>$ **H** $=$

G $<$ **J** NH

LESSON 11-9

Understand
Plan
Solve
Look Back

Problem-Solving Strategy:
Draw a Picture

California Content Standard *Mathematical Reasoning 2.3: Use a variety of methods, such as words, numbers, symbols, charts, graphs, tables, diagrams, and models, to explain mathematical reasoning.*

Warm-Up Review

Draw a picture for each fraction or mixed number.

1. $\frac{3}{5}$
2. $1\frac{1}{2}$
3. $\frac{2}{3}$
4. $2\frac{1}{4}$
5. Ten apples fell off a tree. Three of them got bruised. How many of the apples did not get bruised?

Example

At the farmer's market, a farmer has 10 bags of potatoes to sell. Each bag weighs 10 pounds. Three of the bags contain red potatoes, 3 of the bags contain white potatoes, and the rest of the bags contain sweet potatoes. What fraction of the total bags of potatoes contain sweet potatoes?

Understand

What do you need to find?

You need to find what fraction of the total of the bags contain sweet potatoes.

Plan

How can you solve the problem?

You can **draw a picture** to show the information. Then you can use the picture to find the answer.

Solve

Draw 10 bags. Label each bag *red, white,* or *sweet.*

$\frac{4}{10}$ of the bags contain sweet potatoes.

Look Back

Check to make sure your drawing shows the correct facts from the problem.

 Additional Standards: Mathematical Reasoning 2.0, 3.2 *(See p. 425.)*

Guided Practice

1. There are 16 farmers selling food at the market. Only 5 of them are selling corn. What fraction of the farmers are selling corn?

2. Kate is selling 6 baskets of onions. She sold 4 baskets of them by noon. What fraction of the baskets of onions does she have left to sell?

Independent Practice

3. A farmer has 8 boxes of cabbage to sell at the market. She sells 3 boxes in the morning and 2 boxes in the afternoon. What fraction of the boxes of cabbage does she have left to sell?

4. Terry has 5 barrels full of nuts. He has 2 barrels of salted peanuts, 1 barrel of roasted peanuts, 1 barrel of pecans, and 1 barrel of walnuts. What fraction of these barrels contain peanuts?

Mixed Review

Try these or other strategies to solve each problem. Tell which strategy you used.

Problem-Solving Strategies

- *Work Backward*
- *Solve a Simpler Problem*
- *Use Logical Reasoning*
- *Write a Number Sentence*

5. Margo gives 2 free apples for every 6 apples that a person buys. If you buy 24 apples, how many free apples will you get?

6. Jonathan has some beanbag animals. He gives 3 animals to a friend and shares the rest equally with his sister. His sister gets 4 animals. How many animals did Jonathan have to begin with?

7. A farmer has 15 pounds of turnips. She sells 5 pounds. Later someone returns 2 pounds. How many pounds of turnips does she have left?

Diagnostic Checkpoint

Write a fraction for the shaded part. Then write a fraction for the part not shaded.

1. (11-1) 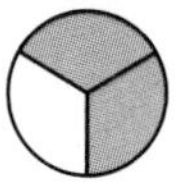

2. (11-1) 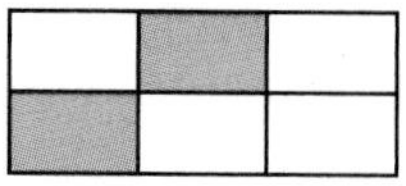

3. (11-1) 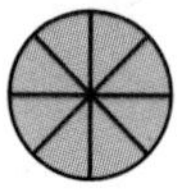

4. (11-1) 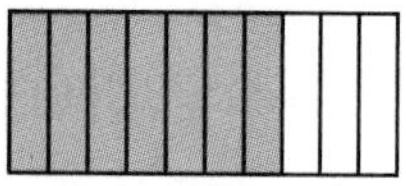

Write the equivalent fractions.

5. (11-2) 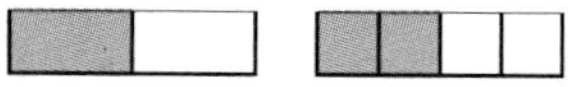

$\frac{1}{2} = \frac{■}{4}$

6. (11-2) 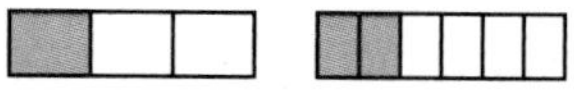

$\frac{1}{3} = \frac{■}{6}$

7. (11-2) 

$\frac{1}{4} = \frac{■}{8}$

Compare. Write >, <, or = for each ●.

8. (11-3) 

$\frac{3}{4}$ ● $\frac{3}{8}$

9. (11-3) 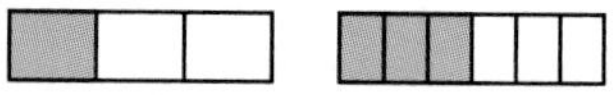

$\frac{1}{3}$ ● $\frac{3}{6}$

10. (11-3) 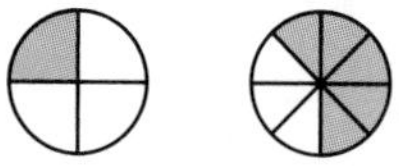

$\frac{1}{4}$ ● $\frac{5}{8}$

Write a fraction for the shaded part of each set.

11. (11-4) 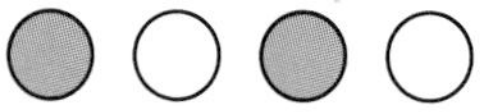

12. (11-4) 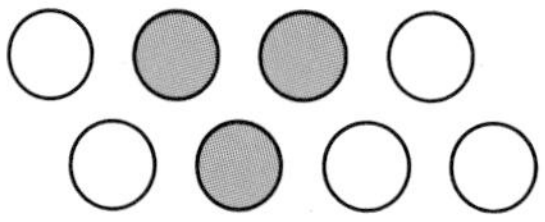

13. (11-4) 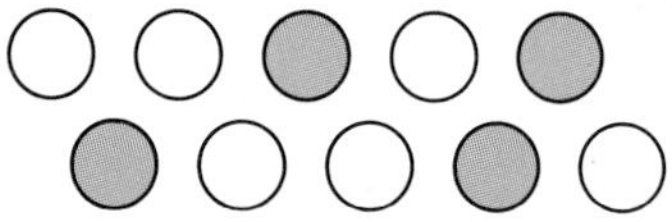

Find each sum or difference.

14. (11-6) $\frac{2}{5} + \frac{2}{5}$

15. (11-6) $\frac{8}{10} - \frac{6}{10}$

16. (11-7) $\frac{2}{10} + \frac{1}{5}$

17. (11-7) $\frac{1}{2} - \frac{1}{8}$

Write a mixed number for the part that is shaded.

18. (11-8) 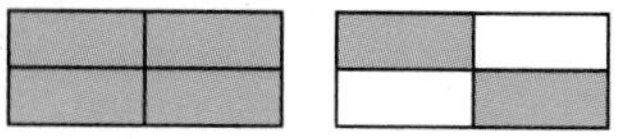

19. (11-8) 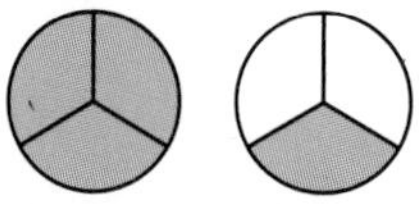

20. (11-8) 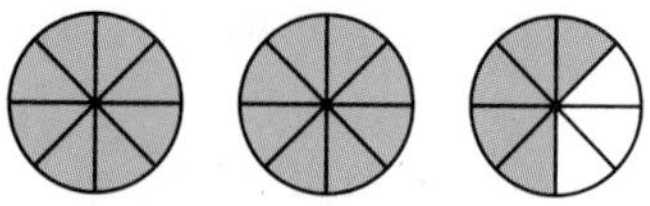

21. (11-9) Jeff bought 8 apples. Five of the apples were red and the rest were yellow. What fraction of the apples were red apples?

22. (11-5) After sharing with his friends, Billy has 17 baseball cards left out of 35 cards. Is it reasonable to say he gave away about 20 cards? Explain.

LESSON 11-10

Decimals in Tenths

California Content Standard *Number Sense 3.4: Know and understand that fractions and decimals are two different representations of the same concept (e.g., 50 cents is $\frac{1}{2}$ of a dollar, 75 cents is $\frac{3}{4}$ of a dollar).*

Warm-Up Review

Write a fraction to name the colored part of the region.

1. 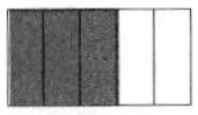

2. 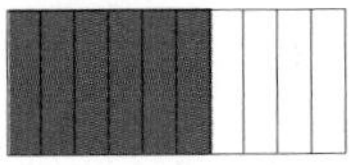

3. Mu Lan jogs 4 miles each day. Andy jogs half as far as Mu Lan each day. After a week, how many more miles has Mu Lan jogged than Andy?

Math Link You know how to write a fraction. Now you will learn to write fractions as decimals.

Word Bank

decimal
decimal point

Example 1

Look at the garden below. There are 10 equal rows or parts. How can you describe the bean section of the garden using fractions, decimals, and words?

$\frac{2}{10}$ is beans. $\frac{3}{10}$ is tomatoes. $\frac{5}{10}$ is corn.

The chart below shows the parts of the garden in fractions, decimals, and words. A **decimal** is a number with one or more places to the right of a **decimal point.**

ones		tenths
0	.	1

↑ decimal point

Plants	Fraction	Decimal	Words
green beans	$\frac{2}{10}$	0.2	two tenths
tomatoes	$\frac{3}{10}$	0.3	three tenths
corn	$\frac{5}{10}$	0.5	five tenths

So, the bean section can be described as $\frac{2}{10}$, 0.2, or two tenths of the garden.

Example 2

You can use fractions, decimals, and words to describe numbers greater than one. How can you describe the shaded parts of the grids?

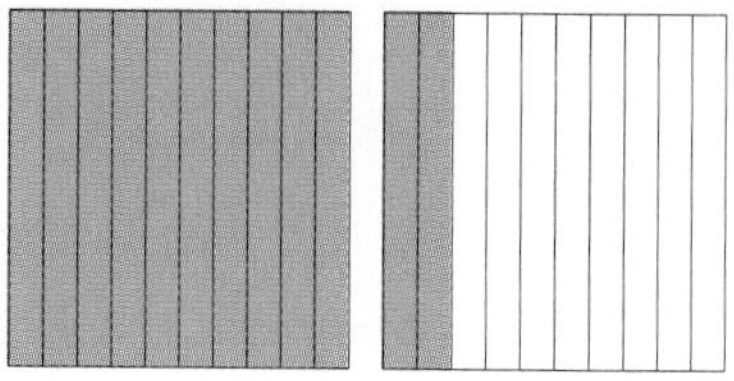

Fraction	Decimal	Words
$1\frac{2}{10}$	1.2	one and two tenths

Read the decimal point as "and".

So, $1\frac{2}{10}$, 1.2, or one and two tenths of the grids are shaded.

More Examples

What part of the shape is shaded?

A.

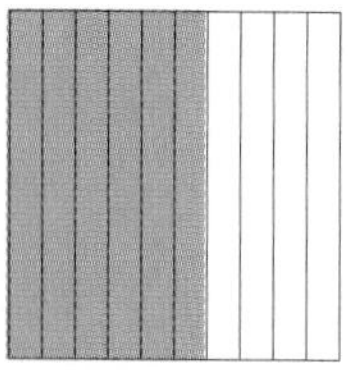

Fraction: $\frac{6}{10}$ Decimal: 0.6

Words: six tenths

B.

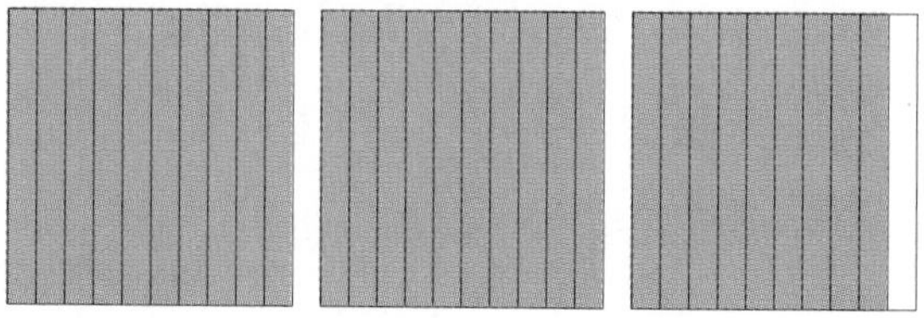

Fraction: $2\frac{9}{10}$ Decimal: 2.9

Words: two and nine tenths

Guided Practice

For another example, see Set H on p. 466.

Write a fraction and a decimal for the shaded part.

1.

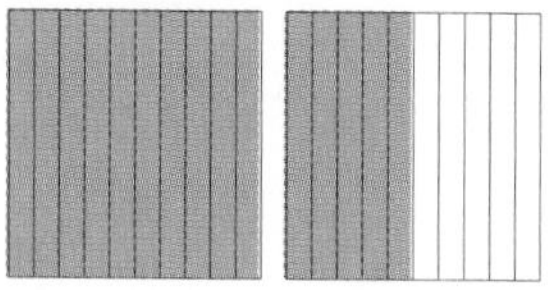

2.

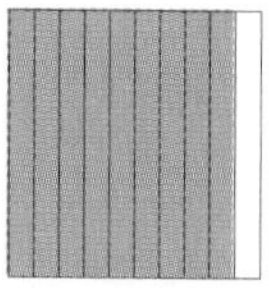

3.

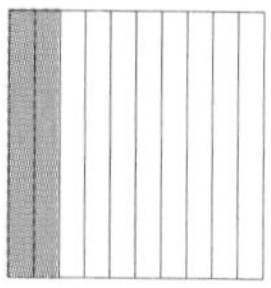

4. Seven out of 10 families recycle their magazines. Write a decimal for the part of the group of families that recycle.

5. At camp, 0.8 of the campers took swimming lessons. What fraction of the campers took swimming lessons?

Independent Practice *For more practice, see Set H on p. 469.*

Write a fraction and a decimal for the shaded part.

6. 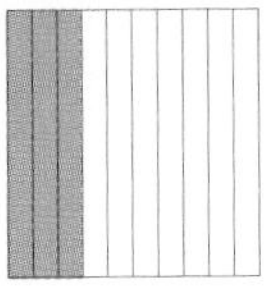

7. 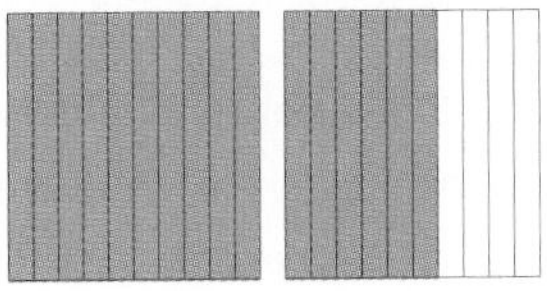

8. 

Write each as a decimal.

9. $\frac{4}{10}$ **10.** $\frac{9}{10}$ **11.** $1\frac{3}{10}$ **12.** $3\frac{7}{10}$

13. two tenths

14. one and four tenths

15. one tenth

16. five and six tenths

17. Draw a picture to show $\frac{4}{10}$. Then write the decimal shown by your picture.

Mixed Review

18. Sonja needs $\frac{1}{4}$ teaspoon of salt to make muffins and $\frac{1}{8}$ teaspoon of salt to make rolls. How much salt does she need altogether?

19. $\frac{2}{3} - \frac{1}{3}$ **20.** $\frac{1}{2} + \frac{1}{4}$ **21.** $\frac{3}{6} - \frac{1}{3}$ **22.** $\frac{3}{8} + \frac{1}{2}$

Write a mixed number for the part that is shaded.

23. 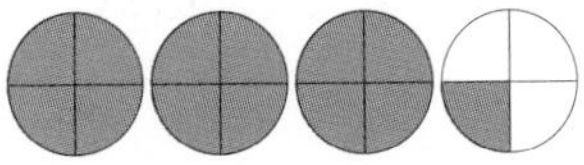

24. 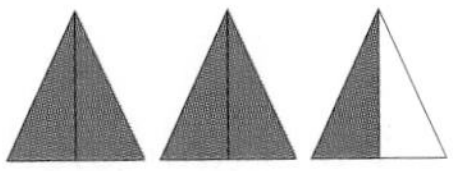

Test Prep **Choose the correct letter for each answer.**

25. (1-1) **Algebra** What missing number would make the number sentence 7,000 + ■ + 5 = 7,075 true?

A 700 **C** 70

B 500 **D** 7

26. (3-7) How long is the peanut?

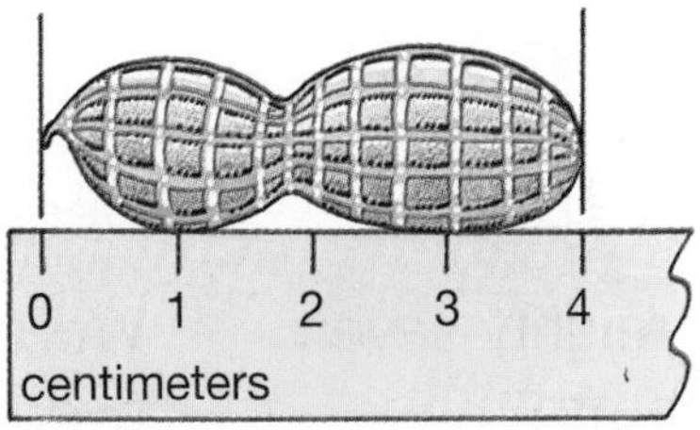

F 4 ft **H** 4 cm

G 4 in. **J** 4 mm

LESSON 11-11

Decimals in Hundredths

Warm-Up Review

Write a fraction as a decimal.

1. $\frac{7}{10}$
2. $\frac{3}{10}$
3. $1\frac{2}{10}$
4. $6\frac{9}{10}$
5. At a track meet, 0.8 of the students finished the race in less than 10 minutes. What fraction of the students finished the race in less than 10 minutes?

California Content Standard *Number Sense 3.4: Know and understand that fractions and decimals are two different representations of the same concept (e.g., 50 cents is $\frac{1}{2}$ of a dollar, 75 cents is $\frac{3}{4}$ of a dollar).*

Math Link You know how to write $\frac{8}{10}$ as a decimal. Now you will learn how to write fractions like $\frac{45}{100}$ as a decimal.

Example 1

The grid at the right has 100 squares. How can you describe the part of the grid that is green? What part of the grid is white?

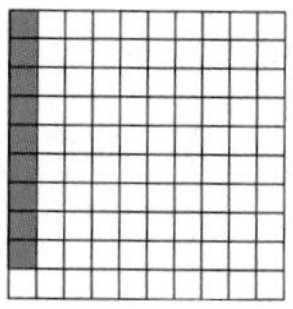

Color	Fraction	Decimals	Words
green squares	$\frac{9}{100}$	0.09	nine hundredths
white squares	$\frac{91}{100}$	0.91	ninety-one hundredths

0.09 of the grid is blue. 0.91 of the grid is white.

More Examples

Write a fraction and a decimal for the shaded part.

A.

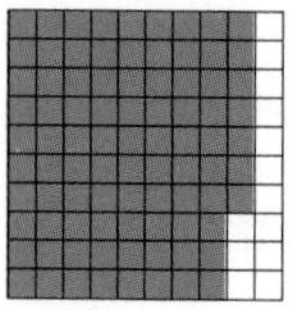

Fraction: $\frac{87}{100}$

Decimal: 0.87

Words: eighty-seven hundredths

B.

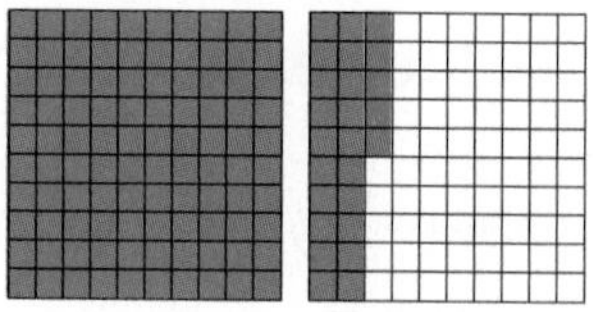

Fraction: $1\frac{25}{100}$

Decimal: 1.25

Words: one and twenty-five hundredths

C.

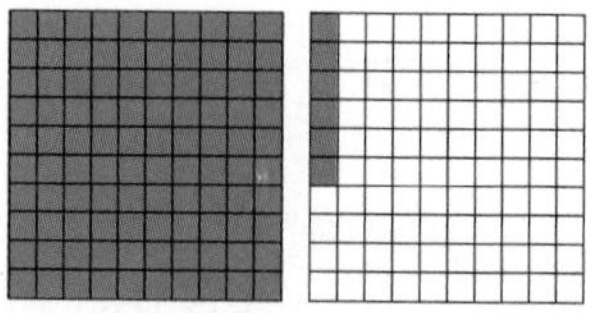

Fraction: $1\frac{6}{100}$

Decimal: 1.06

Words: one and six hundredths

 Additional Standards: Mathematical Reasoning 2.3, 2.4 *(See p. 425.)*

Guided Practice *For another example, see Set I on p. 466.*

Write each as a decimal.

1. $\frac{11}{100}$ **2.** $\frac{60}{100}$ **3.** $1\frac{51}{100}$ **4.** $\frac{12}{100}$ **5.** $\frac{42}{100}$ **6.** $1\frac{6}{100}$

7. A penny is $\frac{1}{100}$ or 0.01 of a dollar. Belinda has 28 pennies. How much money does she have? Write your answer using a dollar sign and decimal point.

Independent Practice *For more practice, see Set I on p. 469.*

Write each as a decimal.

8. $\frac{79}{100}$ **9.** $1\frac{8}{100}$ **10.** $\frac{90}{100}$ **11.** $\frac{9}{100}$ **12.** $\frac{25}{100}$ **13.** $1\frac{82}{100}$

What is the value of the digit 3 in each number?

14. 3.81 **15.** 0.53 **16.** 0.30 **17.** $1.32 **18.** $0.03

19. Math Reasoning Mark said that 0.20 is greater than 0.2 because 20 is greater than 2. Was he right? Explain.

Mixed Review

20. You need $5\frac{1}{8}$ yards of fabric. Is that closer to 5 yards or 6 yards?

Write each as a decimal.

21. $\frac{4}{10}$ **22.** $\frac{3}{10}$ **23.** $\frac{1}{10}$ **24.** $\frac{8}{10}$ **25.** $\frac{5}{10}$

Find each sum or difference. You may use fraction strips to help.

26. $\frac{5}{6} - \frac{2}{6}$ **27.** $\frac{2}{3} + \frac{1}{3}$ **28.** $\frac{3}{8} + \frac{4}{8}$ **29.** $\frac{3}{5} - \frac{1}{5}$

Test Prep Choose the correct letter for each answer.

30. Algebra Fill in the missing number to make the statement true.
(5-9)

$7 \times 5 \times 3 = 5 \times \blacksquare \times 7$

A 35 **C** 5

B 7 **D** 3

31. Ellen and her 4 friends divided up a bag of 16 plums equally. If they don't cut up any plums, how many will be left over?
(10-1)

F 3 plums **H** 1 plum

G 2 plums **J** 0 plums

LESSON 11-12

Comparing and Ordering Decimals

California Content Standard *Number Sense 1.2 (Grade 4) (key): Order and compare whole numbers and decimals to two decimal places.*

Warm-Up Review

Compare. Write >, <, or =.

1. $\frac{7}{10}$ ● $\frac{3}{10}$
2. $\frac{91}{100}$ ● $\frac{94}{100}$
3. $\frac{1}{2}$ ● $\frac{4}{8}$
4. Terry read 2 books a week for 8 weeks. Each book was 10 chapters long. How many books did Terry read in 8 weeks?

Math Link You know how to write fractions as decimals. Now you will learn how to compare and order decimals.

Example 1

Compare 0.34 and 0.31. Use >, <, or =.

Step 1 Line up the decimal points and write the numbers.

0.31
0.34

The decimal point separates the ones and the tenths.

Step 2 Start at the greatest place value. Compare the digits.

0.31

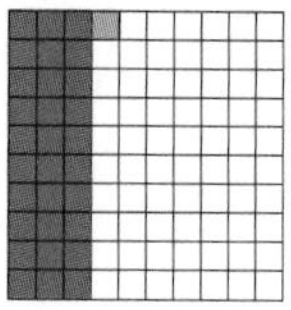

0.34

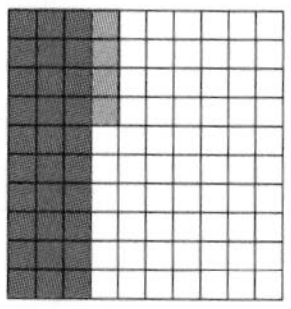

There are not any ones.

The tenths are the same.

Step 3 When the digits are the same, compare the next digit to the right.

0.31

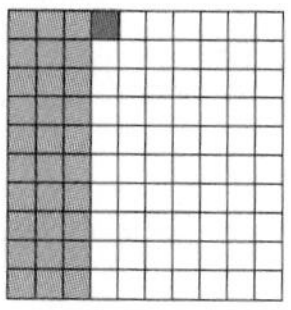

0.34

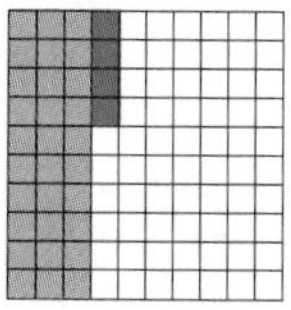

There are more hundredths in 0.34 than in 0.31.

So, 0.34 > 0.31.

More Examples

Compare. Use >, <, or =.

A. Compare 0.6 and 0.4.

0.6

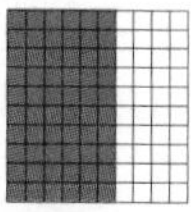

0.4

There are not any ones.

0.6 has more tenths than 0.4.

0.6 > 0.4

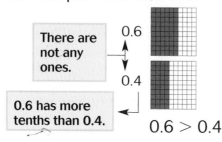

B. Compare 1.37 and 1.41.

1.37

1.41

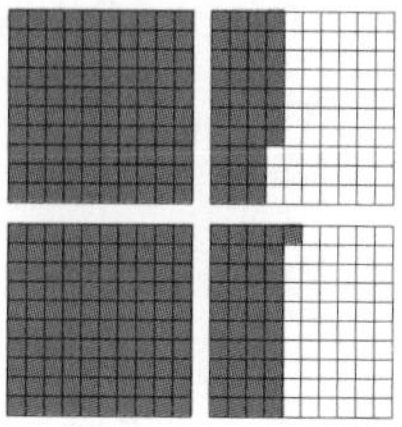

The ones are the same.

1.37 has fewer tenths.

1.37 < 1.41

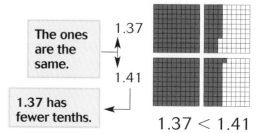

Additional Standards: Algebra and Functions 1.1, 1.3; Mathematical Reasoning 2.3 (See p. 425.)

Example 2

Order these numbers from *greatest* to *least.*

0.56 0.62 0.58

Line up the numbers by the decimal point. Then compare the numbers digit by digit, starting with the greatest place value.

0.56
0.62
0.58

There are no ones. 0.62 has the most tenths, so 0.62 is the greatest number.

Since 0.56 and 0.58 have the same tenths, compare the hundredths digits.

0.56
0.58

Since 8 hundredths is greater than 6 hundredths, 0.58 is the next greatest number.

The order of numbers from *greatest* to *least* is:

0.62 0.58 0.56

More Examples

Order the numbers from *greatest* to *least*.

A. 1.5, 1.3, 2.4

1.5
1.3
2.4

Since 2.4 has the most ones, it is the greatest number. The next number is 1.5 since it has more tenths than 1.3.

The numbers from *greatest* to *least* are 2.4, 1.5, 1.3.

B. 3.59, 2.58, 3.54

3.59
2.58
3.54

3.59 and 3.54 have the most ones. Since the tenths are the same, compare the hundredths. 3.59 has more hundredths.

The numbers from *greatest* to *least* are 3.59, 3.54, 2.58.

Guided Practice *For another example, see Set J on p. 466.*

Algebra Compare. Write >, <, or = for each ●.

1.

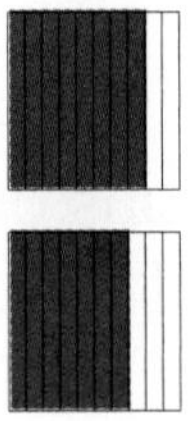

0.8 ● 0.7

2.

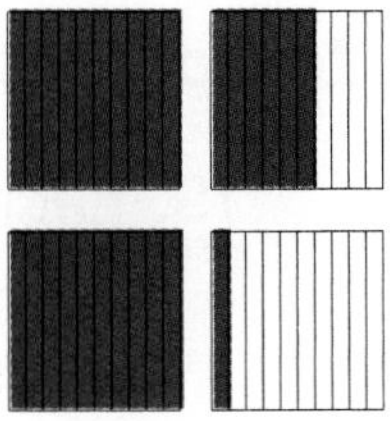

1.6 ● 1.1

3.

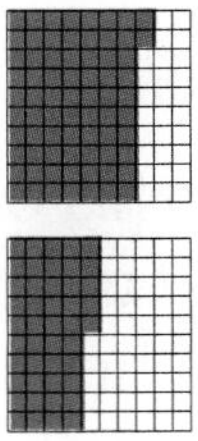

0.72 ● 0.45

4. Jamal is 1.4 meters tall. His older brother is 1.7 meters tall. Who is taller? Explain your answer.

Independent Practice *For more practice, see Set J on p. 469.*

Algebra **Compare. Write >, <, or = for each ●.**

5. 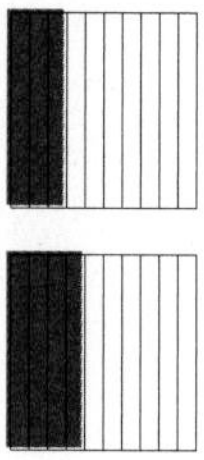

0.3 ● 0.4

6. 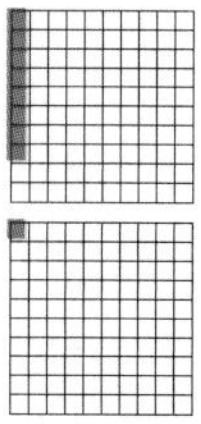

0.08 ● 0.01

7. 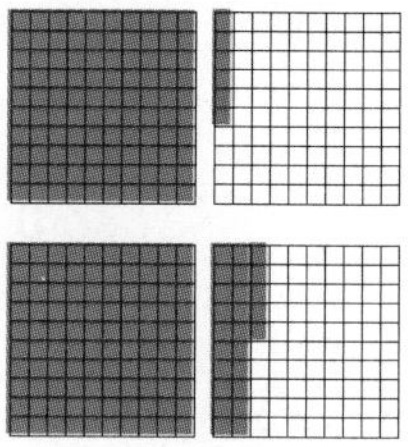

1.06 ● 1.25

Put the decimals in order from *greatest* to *least*.

8. 0.3, 0.1, 0.5

9. 2.6, 1.2, 2.3

10. 0.12, 0.48, 0.42

Use the table at the right for Exercises 11 and 12.

Wildwood Junior Olympics Long Jump Results

Students	Length
Malcolm	1.5 m
Peggy	1.3 m
Cynthia	1.7 m

11. Who had the longest jump?

12. List the students in order from longest jumper to shortest jumper.

Mixed Review

13. A milk crate holds 100 cartons in all. There are 9 cartons of chocolate milk. The rest are white milk. What decimal describes the part of the crate that holds white milk?

Write each as a decimal.

14. $\frac{3}{10}$

15. $\frac{64}{100}$

16. $\frac{7}{100}$

17. $\frac{8}{10}$

Test Prep **Choose the correct letter for each answer.**

18. (4-5) James rides his bike 3 miles to school. How many miles does he ride to school and home again in 5 days?

A 8 miles **C** 30 miles

B 15 miles **D** 45 miles

19. (5-5) Each day Ellie drinks 3 cups of water. How many cups of water does she drink in a week?

F 12 cups **H** 18 cups

G 15 cups **J** 21 cups

LESSON 11-13

Adding and Subtracting Decimals

Warm-Up Review

1. 38 + 59
2. 41 − 26
3. 309 − 125
4. 487 + 636
5. A radio costs $18. Batteries cost $1 each. How much do a radio and 4 batteries cost?

California Content Standard *Number Sense 2.0 (Grade 4): Students extend their use and understanding of whole numbers to the addition and subtraction of simple decimals.*

Math Link You know how to add and subtract whole numbers. Now you will learn to add and subtract decimals.

Example 1

Brad made a fruit salad using the watermelon, strawberries, and bananas shown below. How many pounds of melon and strawberries did he use in the salad?

Find 2.6 + 1.8.

Step 1
Show 2.6 and 1.8 using decimal models.

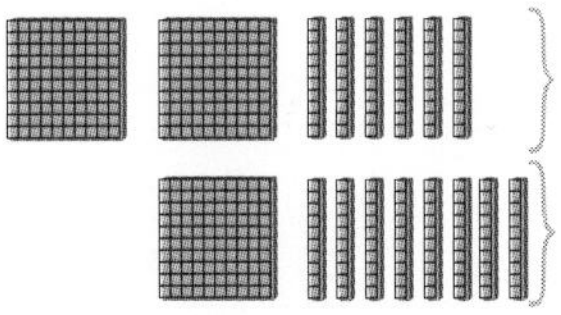

2.6

1.8

Step 2
Add tenths.
6 + 8 = 14 tenths
Regroup 14 tenths as 1 whole and 4 tenths.

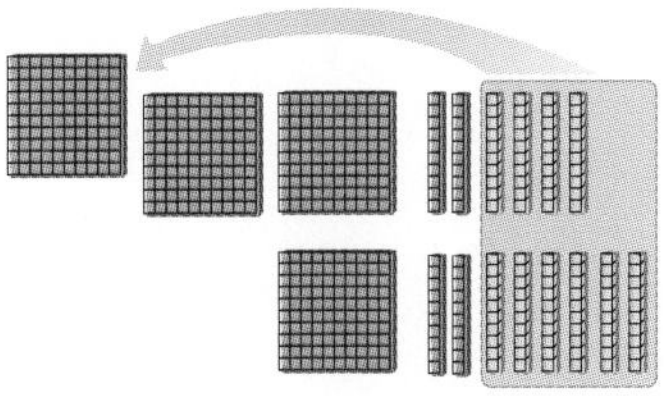

$$\begin{array}{r} ^{1} \\ 2.6 \\ +\ 1.8 \\ \hline 4 \end{array}$$

14 tenths

Step 3
Add ones.
1 + 2 + 1 = 4 ones

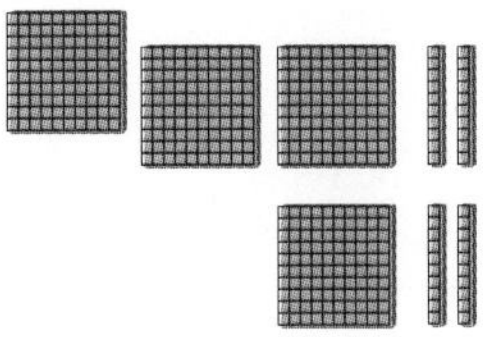

$$\begin{array}{r} ^{1} \\ 2.6 \\ +\ 1.8 \\ \hline 4.4 \end{array}$$

Place the decimal point.

Brad used 4.4 pounds of melon and strawberries.

Additional Standards: Mathematical Reasoning 1.1, 2.4 (See p. 425.)

Example 2

Use the fruit shown on the previous page. How many more pounds of bananas than strawberries did Brad use in his salad?

Find 3.2 − 1.8.

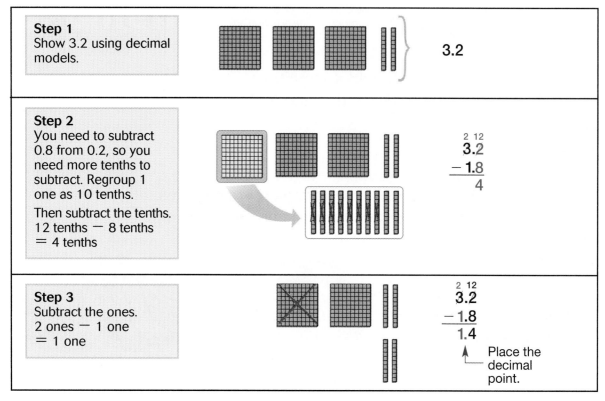

Step 1
Show 3.2 using decimal models.

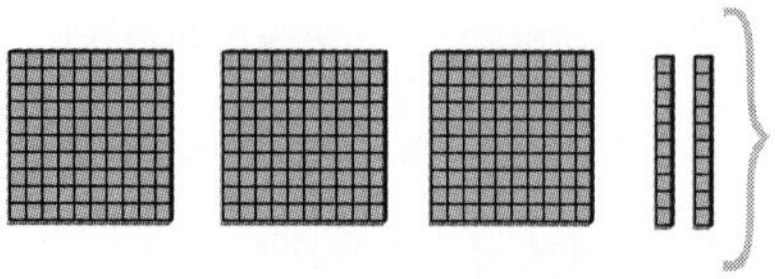

3.2

Step 2
You need to subtract 0.8 from 0.2, so you need more tenths to subtract. Regroup 1 one as 10 tenths.

Then subtract the tenths.
12 tenths − 8 tenths = 4 tenths

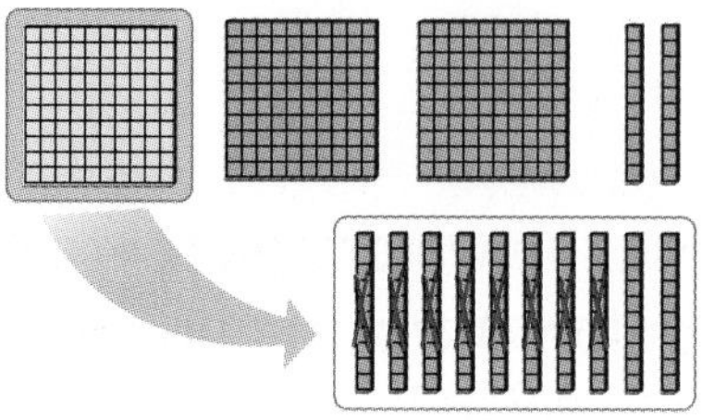

```
 2 12
 3.2
−1.8
   4
```

Step 3
Subtract the ones.
2 ones − 1 one = 1 one

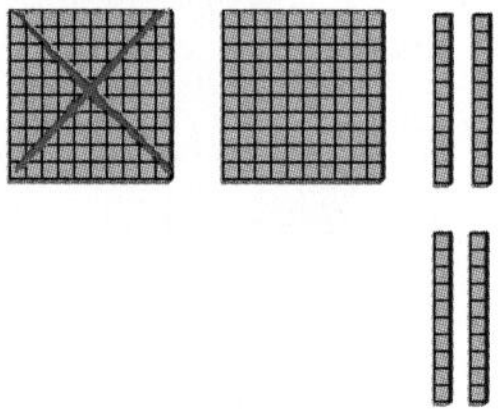

```
 2 12
 3.2
−1.8
 1.4
```

Place the decimal point.

Brad used 1.4 more pounds of bananas.

More Examples

When you add and subtract decimals to hundredths, add and subtract as you would with money.

A.

```
  1
 1.48
+2.34
 3.82
```

B.

```
 3 16
 4.65
−1.83
 2.82
```

Guided Practice *For another example, see Set K on p. 466.*

1. 2.3 + 0.1

2. 6.91 + 5.34

3. 3.1 − 1.1

4. 4.2 − 2.7

5. 2.63 − 1.91

6. Jana jogged 3.4 miles. Kelsey jogged 2.7 miles. How much farther did Jana jog than Kelsey?

Independent Practice *For more practice, see Set K on p. 469.*

7. $\begin{array}{r} 6.2 \\ +4.3 \\ \hline \end{array}$ **8.** $\begin{array}{r} 7.6 \\ -4.3 \\ \hline \end{array}$ **9.** $\begin{array}{r} 3.84 \\ +1.42 \\ \hline \end{array}$ **10.** $\begin{array}{r} 1.8 \\ -0.9 \\ \hline \end{array}$ **11.** $\begin{array}{r} 4.61 \\ -3.58 \\ \hline \end{array}$

12. $1.5 + 7.5$ **13.** $9.5 - 1.7$ **14.** $0.61 + 4.42$ **15.** $6.21 - 0.9$

16. Ms. Renner challenged her class to build the tallest stack of cards without it falling over. Group A's card stack measured 1.07 meters. Group B's card stack measured 0.98 meters. How much taller was Group A's card stack than Group B's?

17. Math Reasoning Sara rode her bike 0.7 mile to the store. Then she turned around and went home. When she returned home, she had ridden 1.5 miles altogether. Did she use the same route going back home? Explain.

Mixed Review

18. Juan had 100 trading cards. He gave 13 of them to a friend. What decimal describes the part of his trading card collection he gave to his friend?

Put the decimals in order from least to greatest.

19. 1.2, 1.8, 1.1 **20.** 0.93, 0.91, 0.86 **21.** 0.8, 0.3, 0.6

What is the value of the underlined digit in each number?

22. $0.\underline{5}6$ **23.** $1.9\underline{3}$ **24.** $\$4.\underline{8}0$ **25.** $0.\underline{0}7$

Test Prep **Choose the correct letter for each answer.**

26. (9-3) **Mental Math** Jamal earned $22.50 mowing lawns. If he earned this much each week, about how much money would he earn in 8 weeks?

A $80
B $100
C $120
D $160

27. (3-4) A sports drink is sold in 1-gallon bottles. How many cups of juice is that?

F 24 cups
G 16 cups
H 8 cups
J 4 cups

LESSON 11-14

Understand
Plan
Solve
Look Back

Problem-Solving Application:
Using Money

California Content Standard *Number Sense 3.3(🔑): Solve problems involving addition, subtraction, . . . of money amounts in decimal notation . . ..*

Warm-Up Review

1. 0.6 + 0.2

2. 1.9 + 0.3

3. 5.3 − 2.8

4. Ron bought a bag for \$4 and a book for \$8. How much change should he get from a \$20 bill?

Look at the menu at the right. Suppose you order a roast beef sandwich with Swiss cheese. If you pay with a \$5 bill, how much change will you get back?

SANDWICHES
Roast Beef........\$ 3.95
Turkey...........\$ 2.95
Ham..............\$ 2.55
Chicken Salad....\$ 2.95
Egg Salad........\$ 2.00
Tuna Salad.......\$ 2.95
EXTRAS
Swiss Cheese....\$0.65
Tomatoes........\$0.75
Peppers.........\$2.40

Understand

What do you need to know?

You need to know the price of a roast beef sandwich and Swiss cheese. You also need to know that you paid with a \$5 bill.

Plan

How can you solve the problem?

First add the cost of the sandwich and the cost of the cheese. Then subtract the total cost from the amount you paid.

Solve

Step 1

¹ ¹	
\$3.95	← Roast beef sandwich
+ .65	← Swiss cheese
\$4.60	← total cost

Step 2

4 10	
\$~~5~~.~~0~~0	← what you paid
− 4.60	← total cost
\$0.40	← change

You will get \$0.40 in change.

Look Back

How can you use subtraction to check your answer to Step 1 and addition to check Step 2?

For Step 1, subtract \$4.60 − \$0.65 = \$3.95.
For Step 2, add \$0.40 + \$4.60 = \$5.00.

 Additional Standards: Mathematical Reasoning 2.0, 3.1 *(See p. 425.)*

Guided Practice

Use the information at the right and on page 458 for Exercises 1–5.

1. Gary buys a chicken salad sandwich with tomatoes and peppers. He pays for the sandwich with a $10 bill. How much change should he get back?

2. Kenya orders 2 egg salad sandwiches with tomatoes and a pint of chili. She gives the salesperson $10. What is her change?

Independent Practice

3. Daryl has $7 to buy a roast beef sandwich with tomatoes. Is it reasonable to say he has enough money left to buy a pint of chili? Explain.

4. Joan orders a tuna salad sandwich with cheese. She gives the clerk three $1 bills and 2 quarters. How much more money does Joan owe?

5. Sherri wants to spend no more than $25 at the deli. She wants to order as much sesame chicken as she can. How many full pounds of sesame chicken can she buy? Explain.

Mixed Review

6. Bill is thinking of an odd number that is greater than 1,000 but less than 2,000. The number uses the digits 0, 1, 4, and 7 each once. The number has 4 hundreds. What is the number?

7. Tiana has boxes that hold 1 or 4 sweaters. She has 16 sweaters. In how many ways can she pack the sweaters?

8. Patty decides to buy candles for her mother. The candles cost $3 per pair. How many candles can Patty buy with $9?

Diagnostic Checkpoint

Complete. For Exercises 1–4, use the words from the Word Bank.

Word Bank
denominator
equivalent
hundredth
mixed number
numerator

1. In the fraction $\frac{4}{5}$, 4 is the ___?___.
(11-1)

2. The bottom number of the fraction is the ___?___.
(11-1)

3. One and one-third is a ___?___.
(11-8)

4. When two fractions are equal they are called ___?___.
(11-2)

Write a fraction and a decimal for the shaded part.

5. (11-10)
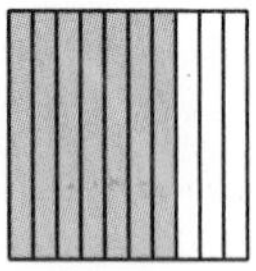

6. (11-10)
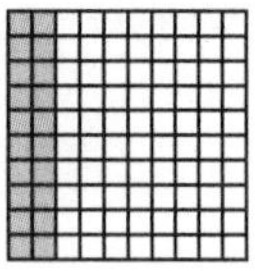

7. (11-11)
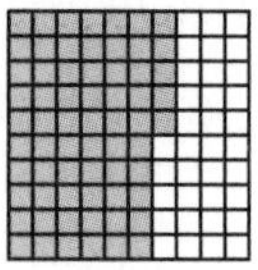

8. (11-11)
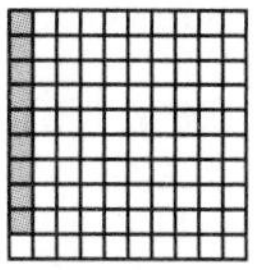

Write each as a decimal.

9. $\frac{8}{10}$ (11-10)

10. $\frac{10}{10}$ (11-10)

11. $\frac{4}{100}$ (11-11)

12. $\frac{58}{100}$ (11-11)

13. $1\frac{2}{10}$ (11-10)

14. three tenths (11-10)

15. twenty-seven hundredths (11-11)

Put the decimals in order from *greatest* to *least*.

16. 0.8, 0.1, 0.2 (11-12)

17. 0.53, 0.86, 0.68 (11-12)

18. 1.3, 1.2, 1.8 (11-12)

Find each sum or difference.

19. (11-13) $0.8 + 0.1$

20. (11-13) $2.65 - 1.32$

21. (11-13) $0.73 + 0.87$

22. (11-13) $1.4 - 0.8$

23. Han bought yogurt with 4 quarters and 3 dimes. How much money did he spend?
(11-14)

24. Flora and her mother used 100 squares of fabric to make a quilt. Forty-five squares are red. The rest are white. What part of the quilt is white? Write your answer as a fraction and a decimal.
(11-11)

25. Ruth ran 1.5 miles. Jackie ran 0.9 mile. Who ran farther? How much farther?
(11-12 & 11-13)

Chapter 11 Test

Write a fraction or mixed number for the shaded part.

1. 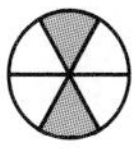

2. 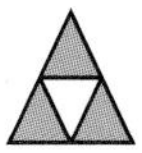

3. 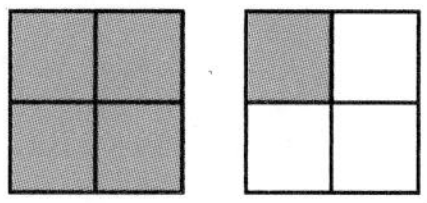

Write the equivalent fraction.

4. 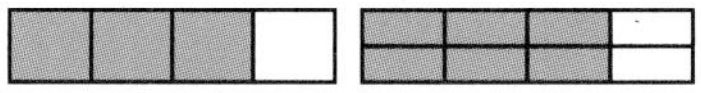

$\frac{3}{4} = \frac{\blacksquare}{8}$

5. 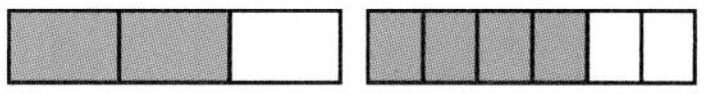

$\frac{2}{3} = \frac{\blacksquare}{6}$

Compare. Use >, <, or = for each ●.

6. 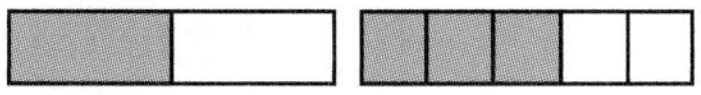

$\frac{1}{2}$ ● $\frac{3}{5}$

7. 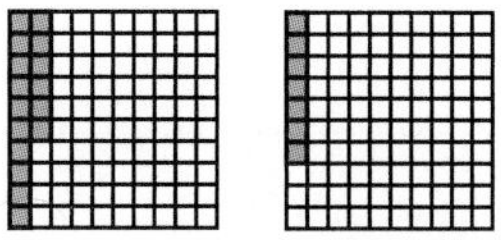

0.16 ● 0.07

Write in order from *greatest* to *least*.

8. $\frac{1}{4}, \frac{1}{2}, \frac{1}{3}$

9. 0.51, 0.48, 0.6

Write a fraction and a decimal for the shaded part.

10. 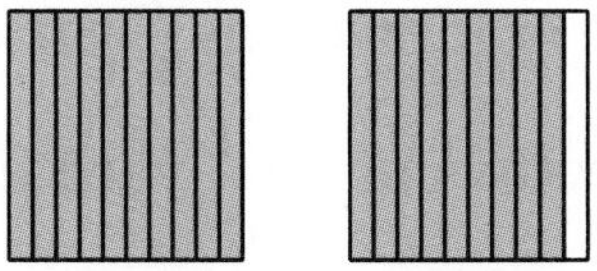

11. 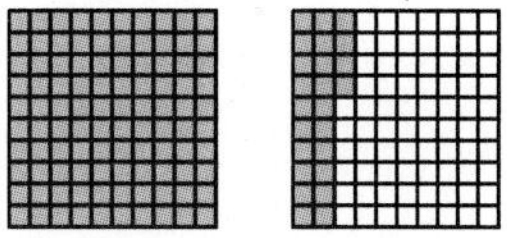

Find each sum or difference.

12. $\frac{2}{8} + \frac{5}{8}$

13. $\frac{3}{4} - \frac{1}{8}$

14. $\begin{array}{r} 0.82 \\ -0.57 \\ \hline \end{array}$

15. $\begin{array}{r} 2.3 \\ +2.75 \\ \hline \end{array}$

16. You had 12 cherries. You ate 5 and your friend ate 3. What fraction of the cherries is left?

17. Kendra buys 2 notebooks for $3.50 each and pays with a ten-dollar bill. What is her change?

18. Jill said that 0.6 is equal to 0.60. Is her statement reasonable? Explain.

Multiple-Choice Chapter 11 Test

Choose the correct letter for each answer.

1. What equivalent fractions are shown?

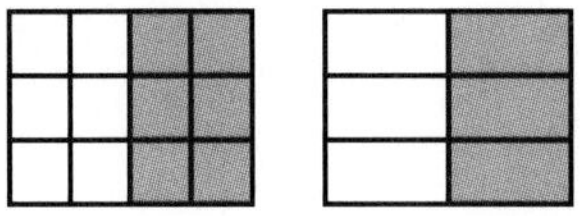

A $\frac{6}{12} = \frac{3}{12}$

B $\frac{6}{12} = \frac{3}{6}$

C $\frac{12}{16} = \frac{6}{3}$

D $\frac{1}{2} = \frac{1}{4}$

E NH

2. Find the decimal for $\frac{9}{10}$.

F 0.09
G 0.1
H 0.9
J 9.0
K NH

3. Find the sum of 3.5 + 0.2.

A 3.3
B 3.6
C 5.7
D 7.5
E NH

4. Which shows the decimals from *least* to *greatest*?

F 0.26, 0.39, 0.84, 0.01
G 0.01, 0.39, 0.26, 0.84
H 0.84, 0.39, 0.26, 0.01
J 0.01, 0.26, 0.39, 0.84

5. Carmen had a bagel she cut into 6 pieces. Liz ate 1 piece, Michael ate 3 pieces, and Carmen ate the rest. What fraction of the bagel did Carmen eat?

A $\frac{1}{6}$ **C** $\frac{3}{6}$

B $\frac{2}{6}$ **D** $\frac{4}{6}$

6. Marty rode his bike 2.8 miles on Monday, 3.1 miles on Wednesday, and 1.9 miles on Friday. Which would be a reasonable estimate for the number of miles Marty biked?

F 3 miles **H** 8 miles
G 6 miles **J** 12 miles

7. The piece of fabric was $\frac{7}{8}$ yard long. Dorothy cut off $\frac{1}{4}$ yard to use on her quilt. How much material was left?

A $\frac{1}{8}$ yard **C** $\frac{5}{8}$ yard

B $\frac{4}{6}$ yard **D** $\frac{9}{8}$ yards

8. Find the decimal for $1\frac{3}{10}$.

F 0.3 **J** 130
G 1.03 **K** NH
H 1.3

9. **Find the mixed number for the shaded part.**

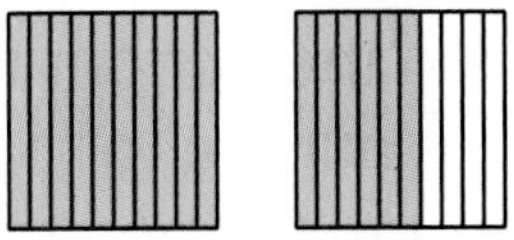

A $\frac{4}{10}$

B $1\frac{4}{10}$

C $1\frac{6}{10}$

D 60

E NH

---

10. **Find the decimal for seventy-six hundredths.**

F 0.70

G 0.76

H 7.6

J 76

K NH

---

11. **Find the fraction for the number of red apples.**

A $\frac{5}{15}$

B $\frac{5}{10}$

C $\frac{10}{15}$

D $\frac{15}{5}$

E NH

---

12. **Which shows the fractions in order from *least* to *greatest*?**

F $\frac{3}{4}, \frac{1}{3}, \frac{1}{5}$

G $\frac{1}{3}, \frac{1}{5}, \frac{3}{4}$

H $\frac{1}{3}, \frac{3}{4}, \frac{1}{5}$

J $\frac{1}{5}, \frac{1}{3}, \frac{3}{4}$

13.

Park Bike Trials

Trails	Length (miles)
Creek Trail	5.6
Pond Trail	3.8
Oak Trail	2.7
Flower Trail	4.1

How much longer is Flower Trail than Pond Trail?

A 0.3 mile

B 1.3 miles

C 1.7 miles

D 7.9 miles

---

14. **Find the sum of $\frac{3}{12}$ and $\frac{4}{12}$.**

F $\frac{1}{12}$

G $\frac{7}{12}$

H $\frac{12}{12}$

J $\frac{7}{24}$

K NH

---

15. **A hot dog costs $1.68. Cheese is an extra $0.50, and chili is an extra $0.75. How much would it cost for a hot dog with chili and cheese?**

A $2.18

B $2.43

C $2.93

D $3.18

---

16. **Find the fraction for the shaded part.**

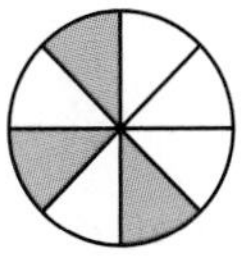

F $\frac{3}{8}$

G $\frac{5}{8}$

H $\frac{8}{5}$

J $\frac{8}{3}$

K NH

Reteaching

Set A *(pages 426–427)*

Write a fraction for the shaded part.

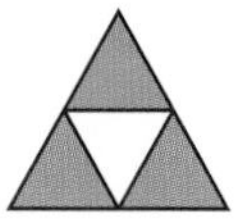

3 ← shaded parts
4 ← parts in all

So, $\frac{3}{4}$ of the triangle is shaded.

Remember the number of parts in all goes on the bottom (denominator) and the number of parts shaded goes on the top (numerator).

Write a fraction for the shaded part. Then write a fraction for the part not shaded.

1. 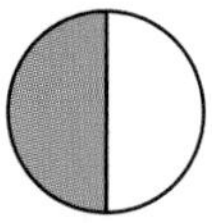

2. 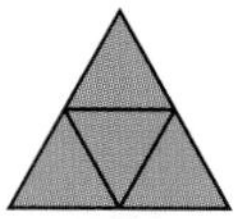

Set B *(pages 428–429)*

Write the equivalent fraction.

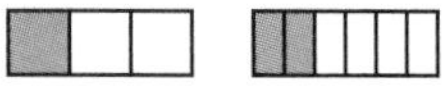

$\frac{1}{3} = \frac{\blacksquare}{6}$

Both the rectangles are the same size.

The shaded parts are the same size.

So, $\frac{1}{3} = \frac{2}{6}$ are equivalent fractions.

Remember equivalent fractions are the same parts of a whole.

Write the equivalent fraction.

1. 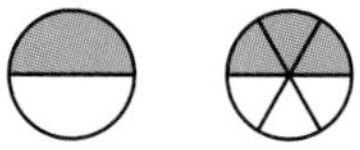

$\frac{1}{2} = \frac{\blacksquare}{6}$

2. 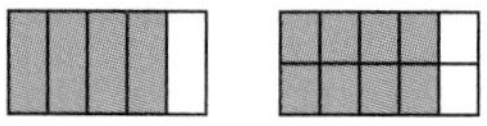

$\frac{4}{5} = \frac{\blacksquare}{10}$

Set C *(pages 430–432)*

Compare. Write >, <, or = for each ●.

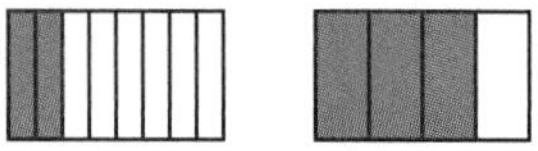

$\frac{2}{8}$ ● $\frac{3}{4}$

The picture that has $\frac{3}{4}$ shaded is more than the one with $\frac{2}{8}$ shaded.

So, $\frac{2}{8} < \frac{3}{4}$.

Remember if the denominators are the same, you can compare the numerators. You can use fraction strips or fraction circles to help.

Compare. Write >, <, or = for each ●.

1. $\frac{4}{5}$ ● $\frac{5}{5}$

2. $\frac{2}{3}$ ● $\frac{1}{3}$

3. $\frac{3}{8}$ ● $\frac{3}{6}$

4. $\frac{2}{5}$ ● $\frac{4}{10}$

5. $\frac{1}{4}$ ● $\frac{2}{8}$

6. $\frac{5}{6}$ ● $\frac{1}{3}$

Set D (pages 434–435)

What fraction of the apples are green?

$\frac{3}{4}$ ← green apples / ← total number of apples

So, $\frac{3}{4}$ of the apples are green.

Remember the number of total objects goes on the bottom (denominator).

Write a fraction to name the part of each set described.

1. red plums

2. purple grapes

Set E (pages 438–439)

Find $\frac{4}{8} + \frac{2}{8}$.

Step 1 Add the numerators.

$\frac{4}{8} + \frac{2}{8} = \frac{6}{}$

Step 2 Use the same denominators.

$\frac{4}{8} + \frac{2}{8} = \frac{6}{8}$

Remember when the denominators are the same, add or subtract only the numerators.

1. $\frac{7}{10} - \frac{3}{10}$

2. $\frac{5}{8} + \frac{2}{8}$

3. $\frac{2}{6} + \frac{3}{6}$

4. $\frac{3}{4} - \frac{2}{4}$

Set F (pages 440–441)

Find $\frac{4}{6} - \frac{1}{3}$.

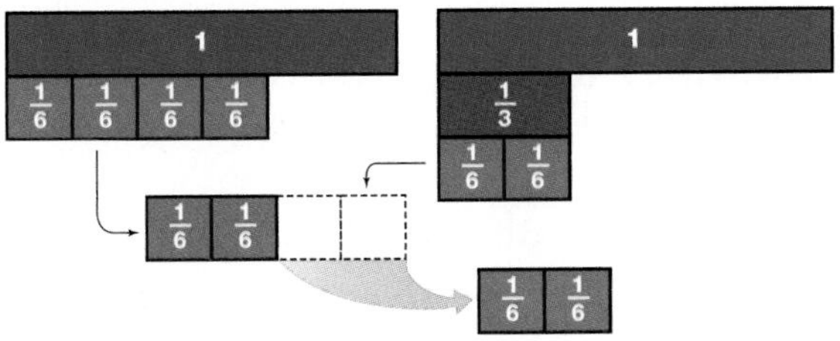

$\frac{4}{6} - \frac{2}{6} = \frac{2}{6}$

Remember when the denominators are different you must first find an equivalent fraction to make the denominators the same.

1. $\frac{3}{4} - \frac{3}{8}$

2. $\frac{2}{8} + \frac{2}{4}$

3. $\frac{4}{10} + \frac{2}{5}$

4. $\frac{5}{6} - \frac{1}{3}$

Set G (pages 442–443)

Write a mixed number for the part that is shaded.

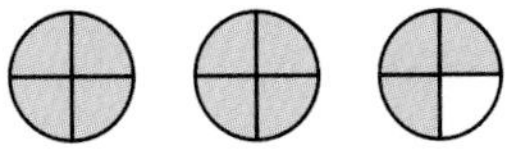

2 circles and $\frac{3}{4}$ of a circle are shaded. So, the mixed number is $2\frac{3}{4}$.

Remember to include the whole numbers in your mixed number.

Write a mixed number for the part that is shaded.

1.

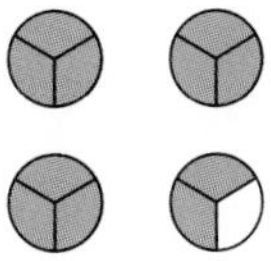

2.

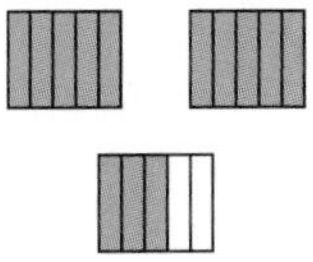

Reteaching (continued)

Set H *(pages 447–449)*

Write a fraction and a decimal for the shaded part.

0.5 or $\frac{5}{10}$ of the grid is shaded.

Remember to include a decimal point between the ones and tenths.

Write a fraction and a decimal for the shaded part.

1. 

2. 

Set I *(pages 450–451)*

Write a fraction and a decimal for the shaded part.

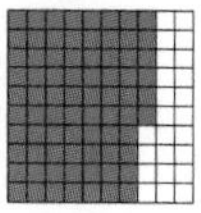

0.76 or $\frac{76}{100}$ of the grid is shaded.

Remember that each grid shows hundredths, so your answer must be to the hundredths place.

Write a fraction and a decimal for the shaded part.

1. 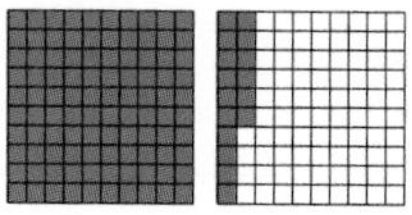

2. 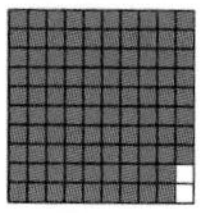

Set J *(pages 452–454)*

Put the decimals in order from *least* to *greatest*.

0.61 0.29 0.30

0.29 ← least
0.30
0.61 ← greatest

Remember to compare numbers starting with the greatest place value.

Put the decimals in order from *least* to *greatest*.

1. 0.3, 0.1, 0.5 **2.** 1.6, 1.4, 1.5

Set K *(pages 455–457)*

Find the sum of 3.6 and 2.9.

Step 1 Add the tenths. Regroup.

$$\begin{array}{r} \scriptstyle 1 \\ 3.6 \\ +\ 2.9 \\ \hline 5 \end{array}$$

15 tenths

Step 2 Add ones. Place decimal point.

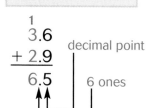

$$\begin{array}{r} \scriptstyle 1 \\ 3.6 \\ +\ 2.9 \\ \hline 6.5 \end{array}$$

decimal point
6 ones

Remember to always line up and place your decimal point in the answer.

Find the sum or difference.

1. $\begin{array}{r} 2.8 \\ +3.9 \\ \hline \end{array}$ **2.** $\begin{array}{r} 8.12 \\ -2.41 \\ \hline \end{array}$

More Practice

Set A *(pages 426–427)*

Write a fraction for the shaded part. Then write a fraction for the part not shaded.

1. 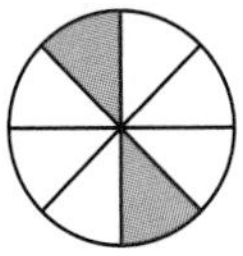

2. 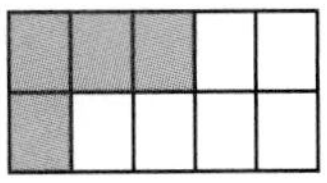

3. 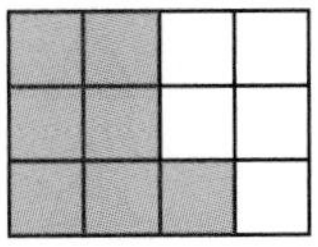

4. 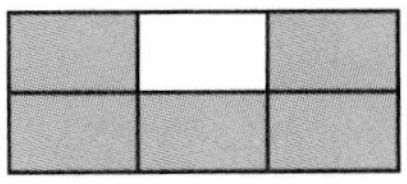

5. Ireland's flag is separated into 3 equal parts. One part is green. One part is orange. One part is white. What fraction of the flag is white?

Set B *(pages 428–429)*

Write the equivalent fraction.

1. 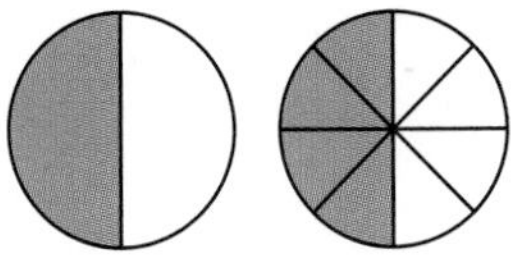

$\frac{1}{2} = \frac{■}{8}$

2. 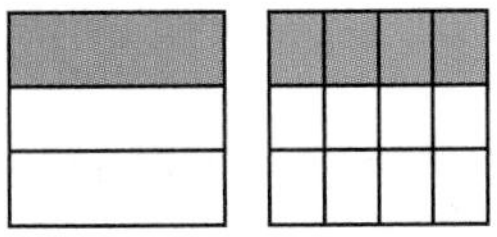

$\frac{1}{3} = \frac{■}{12}$

3. 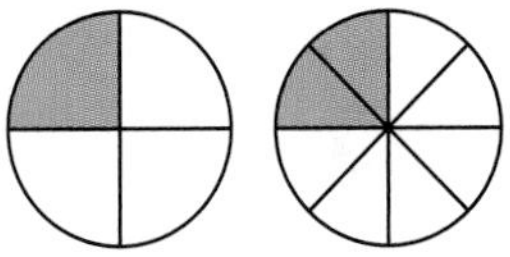

$\frac{1}{4} = \frac{■}{8}$

4. Tania ate $\frac{2}{8}$ of her sandwich. Mark ate the same amount of his sandwich. How many fourths did Mark eat?

Set C *(pages 430–432)*

Compare. Write >, <, or = for each ●.

1. 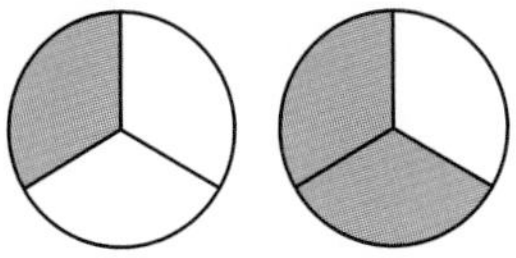

$\frac{1}{3}$ ● $\frac{2}{3}$

2. 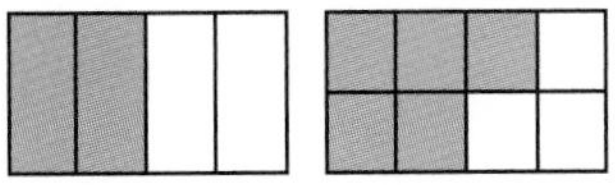

$\frac{2}{4}$ ● $\frac{5}{8}$

3. 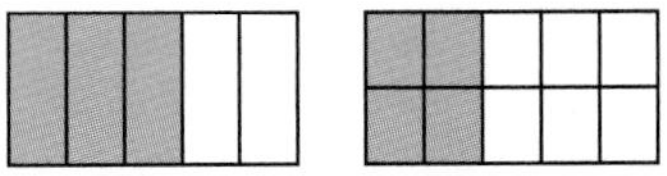

$\frac{3}{5}$ ● $\frac{4}{10}$

4. Anna and Pedro each made the same number of pies for a bake sale. Anna sold $\frac{2}{3}$ of her pies. Pedro sold $\frac{2}{6}$ of his pies. Who sold more?

More Practice (continued)

Set D (pages 434–435)

Write a fraction that names the part of each set that is green.

1. 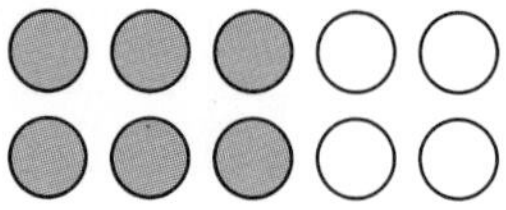

2. 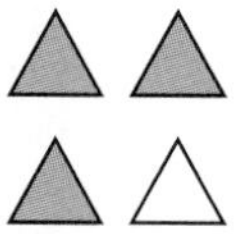

3. 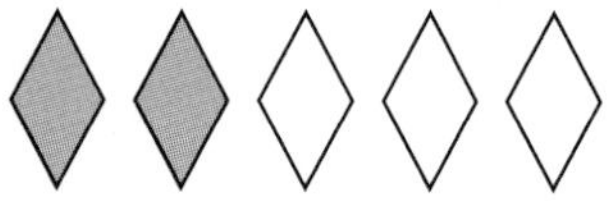

4. Jamal has 12 marbles. Three are blue, 5 are yellow, and 1 is green. The rest are red. What fraction of the marbles are red?

Set E (pages 438–439)

Find each sum or difference.

1. $\frac{2}{8} + \frac{4}{8}$
2. $\frac{3}{4} - \frac{1}{4}$
3. $\frac{4}{5} - \frac{2}{5}$
4. $\frac{3}{10} + \frac{5}{10}$
5. Katrina used $\frac{3}{8}$ yard of material on a pillow. She also used $\frac{2}{8}$ yard of material on a vest. How much material did she use?

Set F (pages 440–441)

Find each sum or difference.

1. $\frac{3}{4} - \frac{1}{12}$
2. $\frac{1}{3} + \frac{4}{6}$
3. $\frac{1}{2} + \frac{1}{8}$
4. $\frac{2}{3} - \frac{1}{6}$
5. Marcus ate $\frac{4}{6}$ of a bagel. Billy ate $\frac{10}{12}$ of his bagel. How much more did Billy eat?

Set G (pages 442–443)

Write a mixed number for the part that is shaded.

1. 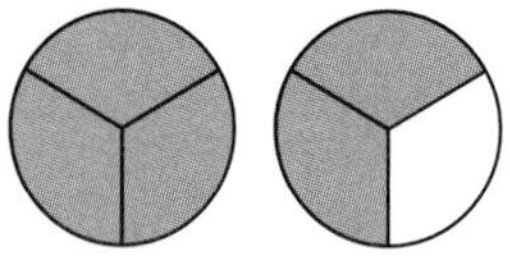

2. 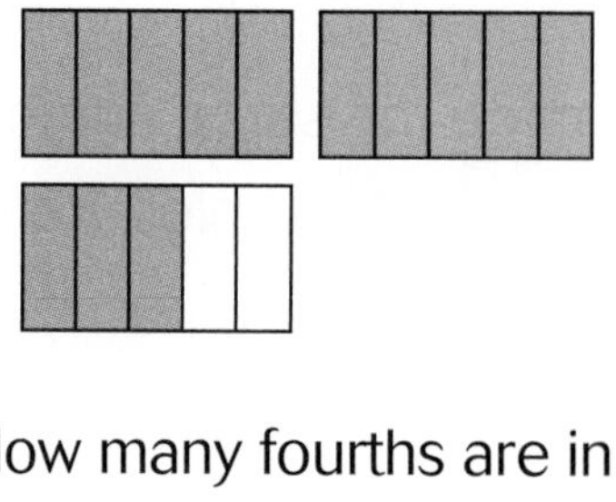

3. 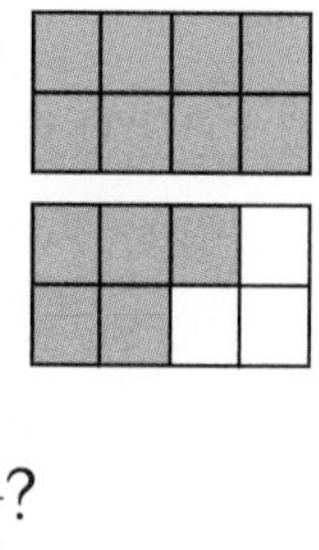

4. Bill has $1\frac{3}{4}$ cups of flour. How many fourths are in $1\frac{3}{4}$?

Set H (pages 447–449)

Write a fraction and a decimal for the shaded part.

1. 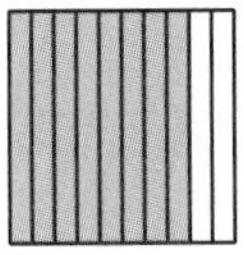

2. 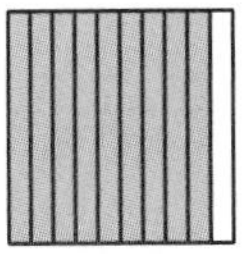

3. 

4. 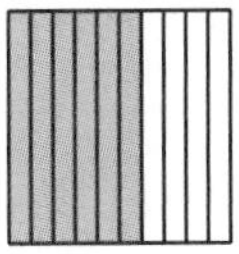

5. Yolanda folded a sheet of paper into 10 equal parts. She colored 2 parts orange, 3 parts green, and 1 part blue. She left the rest white. Write the decimal that shows how much she left white.

Set I (pages 450–451)

Write a fraction and a decimal for the shaded part.

1. 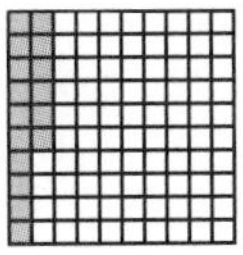

2. 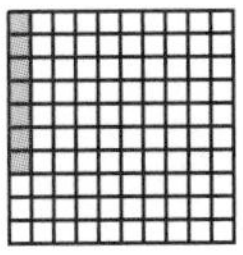

3. 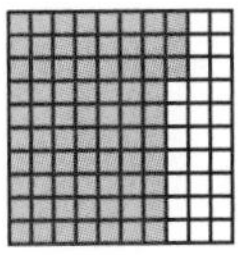

4. 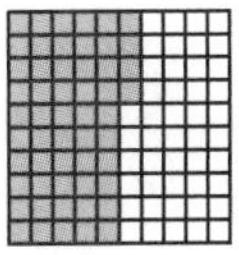

5. Brenda has 7 dimes and 15 pennies. How much money does she have? Write your answer using a dollar sign and decimal point.

Set J (pages 452–454)

Put the decimals in order from *greatest* to *least*.

1. 0.3, 0.2, 0.9
2. 4.8, 2.6, 6.2
3. Kenyatta ran 0.63 mile. Melissa ran 0.58 mile, and Hunter ran 0.61 mile. Who ran the farthest distance? Who ran the shortest distance?

Set K (pages 455–457)

1. $\begin{array}{r} 4.6 \\ +3.9 \\ \hline \end{array}$

2. $\begin{array}{r} 3.8 \\ -2.4 \\ \hline \end{array}$

3. $\begin{array}{r} 7.4 \\ -1.7 \\ \hline \end{array}$

4. $\begin{array}{r} 9.35 \\ +2.86 \\ \hline \end{array}$

5. $\begin{array}{r} 3.32 \\ -0.79 \\ \hline \end{array}$

6. Carlos rode his bicycle 0.6 mile to the store. Then he rode it 0.5 mile to friend's house. How many miles did he ride?

TEST PREP

Problem Solving: Preparing for Tests

Choose the correct letter for each answer.

---

1. Karen cut a string into 15 equal pieces. How many cuts did she make?

A 13 cuts

B 14 cuts

C 15 cuts

D 16 cuts

> **Tip**
>
> Try the strategy *Draw a Picture* to solve this problem. Draw a piece of string and make lines to show the cuts.

---

2. At a toy store, Ms. Jackson bought 23 green balls, 49 yellow balls, 18 kites, and 41 puzzles. How many balls did Ms. Jackson buy altogether?

F 26 balls

G 72 balls

H 90 balls

J 131 balls

> **Tip**
>
> Read the question carefully and decide what information you need to answer it.

---

3. Jake made blueberry muffins. His sisters ate 4 of the muffins and his mom ate 1 of the muffins. If there were 22 muffins left, which number sentence could you use to show how many muffins Jake made?

A $22 - 4 = \blacksquare$

B $22 + 4 = \blacksquare$

C $22 - 5 = \blacksquare$

D $22 + 5 = \blacksquare$

> **Tip**
>
> Start by figuring out how many muffins were eaten. Use what you find to eliminate some of the answer choices.

4. Potato salad costs $2.98 per pound at the store. Hal wants to buy 3 pounds of potato salad. Which is the best estimate of how much Hal will pay?

F $3 **H** $8

G $6 **J** $9

5. There are 30 students in Terry's class. Ten students are reading books. The rest of the students are writing stories. Which is a reasonable conclusion?

A More students are reading than writing.

B More students are writing than reading.

C The same number of students are reading **and** writing.

D Some students are not reading **or** writing.

6. Devon spent $3.28 on paper, $1.15 on pens, and $2.94 on stamps. How much money did he spend on paper and pens?

F $7.37 **H** $4.43

G $6.22 **J** $2.13

7. Jodi is older than Tyler. Sam is younger than Tyler. Which is a reasonable conclusion?

A Jodi is younger than Sam.

B Jodi is older than Sam.

C Tyler is younger than Sam.

D Sam is older than Jodi.

8. On Monday, a department store had 40 pillows for sale. On Tuesday, the store sold 1 pillow. The day after, it sold 2 pillows. The next day, it sold 3 pillows. If this pattern continues, how many pillows will be left by the end of the day on Saturday?

F 20 pillows

G 25 pillows

H 30 pillows

J 34 pillows

Use the chart for Questions 9 and 10.

Mr. Gómez made the chart below to show how many model sports cars he has in his shop.

Model Sports Cars in Stock

	White	Black	Red
Small	80	60	115
Large	125	35	55

9. Which kind of car does Mr. Gómez have the most of?

A Small, black sports cars

B Small, white sports cars

C Large, red sports cars

D Large, white sports cars

10. How many more red cars than black cars does Mr. Gómez have?

F 20

G 55

H 75

J 175

TEST PREP

Multiple-Choice Cumulative Review

Choose the correct letter for each answer.

Number Sense

1. **There were 7 glasses, 5 bowls, and 10 plates for sale at a yard sale. How many plates and bowls were for sale?**

A 12 **C** 17
B 15 **D** 22

2. **Wendy read 67 pages of a book. Ellie read 32 pages. *About* how many more pages did Wendy read than Ellie?**

F 20 **H** 40
G 25 **J** 100

3. **Pablo had 34 football cards and 24 baseball cards. His father gave him 47 more football cards. How many football cards did Pablo have then?**

A 20 **C** 81
B 25 **D** 91

4. **Cindy puts 8 photos on each page of her photo album. If she fills 9 pages of her album, how many photos are in her album?**

F 17 photos
G 18 photos
H 72 photos
J 81 photos

Measurement and Geometry

5. **Look at the hair clip. Which unit should be used to measure the *length* of the clip?**

A centimeters **C** meters
B kilograms **D** milliliters

6. **If it is 11:00 now, what time will it be in 2 hours?**

F

H

G

J

7. **At 9:00 A.M., the temperature was 60°F. By 2:00 P.M., the temperature had risen 15°F. What was the temperature at 2:00 P.M.?**

A 15°F **C** 75°F
B 45°F **D** 90°F

8. **Gayle drove 123 kilometers to visit her grandmother. How many *meters* is that? (Hint: 1 km equals 1,000 m.)**

F 1,230,000 m **H** 1,230 m
G 123,000 m **J** 123 m

Measurement and Geometry

9. Which does NOT show a line of symmetry on a figure?

A 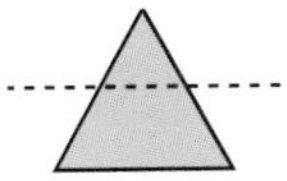

C 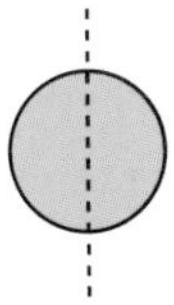

B 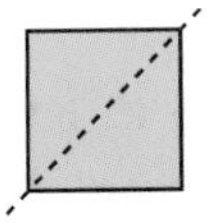

D 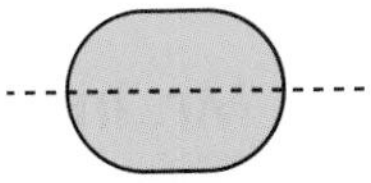

10. How many corners does the figure have?

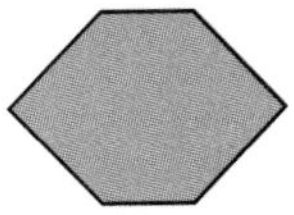

F 4 **H** 8
G 6 **J** 10

11. Which letter has a line of symmetry?

A D **C** P
B R **D** Q

12. Which number is inside the square and outside the circle?

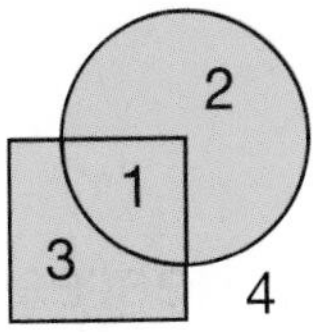

F 1 **H** 3
G 2 **J** 4

Statistics, Data Analysis, and Probability

Use the graph for Questions 13–16.

This graph shows the number of hours 5 students practice piano each week.

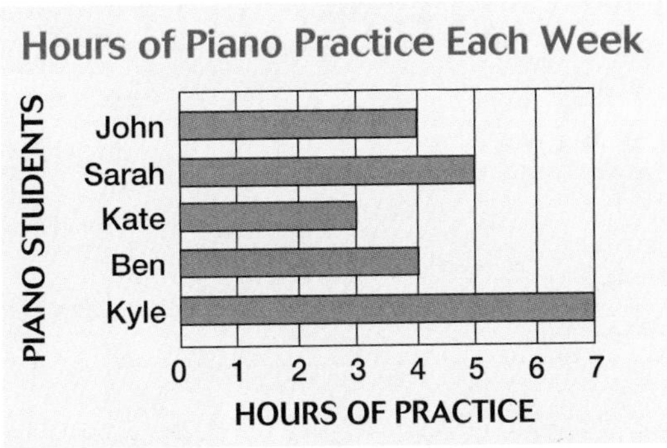

13. How many hours does Kyle practice each week?

A 3 **C** 6
B 4 **D** 7

14. Which student practices the least each week?

F John **H** Kate
G Sarah **J** Ben

15. Who practices the same number of hours as Ben?

A Kyle **C** Sarah
B Kate **D** John

16. How many more hours does Sarah practice than Kate?

F 1 **H** 4
G 2 **J** 8

CHAPTER 12

Data, Graphs, and Probability

Diagnosing Readiness

In Chapter 12, you will use these skills:

A Recording Data from a Survey

(Grade 2)

Mr. Ingram's class is keeping track of the weather. Their information is below.

The Weather	
Sunny	𝍸 𝍸 |
Cloudy	𝍸 |
Rainy	|||

1. How many days were cloudy?

2. How many days were sunny?

B Rounding Numbers

(Grade 2)

Round to the nearest ten.

3. 38 **4.** 52

5. 85 **6.** 49

Round to the nearest hundred.

7. 349 **8.** 570

9. 278 **10.** 701

C Probability

(Grade 2)

11. If you roll a cube numbered 1 through 6, what are the possible numbers that you could roll?

12. You toss a coin. What are the possible sides it could land on?

D Making Predictions

(Grade 2)

Use the data from the table to answer Exercises 13 and 14.

Number of Times Each Color Was Picked	
Color	**Picks**
Red	9
Blue	15
Green	0
Yellow	8

13. Which color do you think you would pick next?

14. Which color do you think you would not pick next?

E Using a Bar Graph

(pages 68–69)

Use the bar graph to answer Questions 15–19.

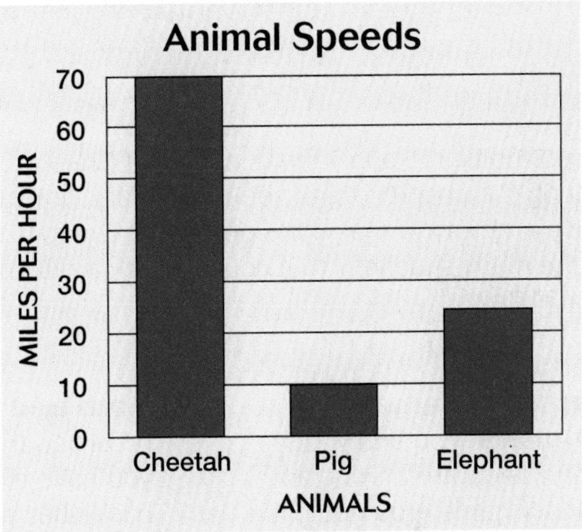

15. Which animal runs the slowest?

16. Which animal runs the fastest?

17. Which animal can run 25 miles per hour?

18. How fast does a pig run?

19. How much slower is a pig than a cheetah?

To the Family and Student

Looking Back

In Grade 2, students learned ways to record data and use probability. In Chapter 2 of this book, students learned how to read a bar graph.

Chapter 12

Data, Graphs, and Probability

In this chapter, students will learn to read data in tables, graphs, line plots, and grids. Students will also learn to list probabilities, outcomes, and predictions.

Looking Ahead

In Grade 4, students will continue recording and reading data in various types of graphs. They will also continue to use probability to solve problems.

Math and Everyday Living

Opportunities to apply the concepts of Chapter 12 abound in everyday situations. During the chapter, think about how data, graphs, and probability can be used to solve a variety of real-world problems. The following examples suggest just a few of the many situations that could launch a discussion about data, graphs, and probability.

Math and Games with Spinners You and your friend Todd are playing a spinner game. You get to move 1 space if you spin yellow. Todd moves a space if he spins blue. During the game, you spin 5 yellows in a row. Todd says the game is unfair. Look at the spinner for the game below. Is Todd correct?

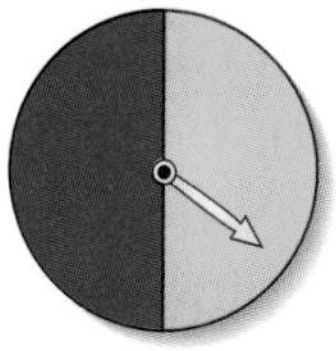

Math and Taking Turns You and your friend both want to play the same video game. Your friend says, "If I flip this coin and it lands on heads, you will go first." What are the possible outcomes of flipping the coin?

Math and Sports You have recorded the number of points you have made in the last 15 basketball games.

Number of Points Made

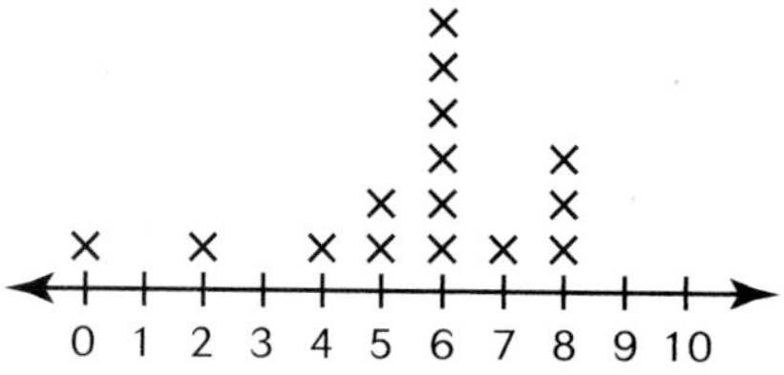

If you had to predict how many points you were going to make in the next game, what would be your prediction?

Math and the Weather It has been raining at your house for the last 3 days. You want to go to your friend's house. Your dad says you can go if it stops raining in the next 30 minutes. Is it likely or unlikely that you will be able to go?

Math and Field Trips Your class voted on where they wanted to go on their field trip. Here are the results.

<table>
<tr><th>Place</th><th>Votes</th></tr>
<tr><td>Zoo</td><td>𝍸 ||||</td></tr>
<tr><td>Ice Skating</td><td>||||</td></tr>
<tr><td>Science Museum</td><td>𝍸 ||</td></tr>
<tr><td>Aquarium</td><td>𝍸 |||</td></tr>
</table>

From the results, where will your class go on your field trip?

California Content Standards in Chapter 12 Lessons*

	Teach and Practice	Practice
Statistics, Data Analysis, and Probability		
1.0 Students conduct simple probability experiments by determining the number of possible outcomes and make simple predictions.	12-9	
1.1 (Grade 2) Record numerical data in systematic ways, keeping track of what has been counted.	12-1	
1.1 Identify whether common events are certain, likely, unlikely, or improbable.	12-6	
1.1 (Grade 4) Formulate survey questions; systematically collect and represent data on a number line; and coordinate graphs, tables, and charts.	12-4	
1.2 (🔑) Record the possible outcomes for a simple event (e.g., tossing a coin) and systematically keep track of the outcomes when the event is repeated many times.	12-7	
1.3 (🔑) Summarize and display the results of probability experiments in a clear and organized way (e.g., use a bar graph or line plot).	12-8	
1.3 (Grade 4) Interpret one- and two-variable data graphs to answer questions about a situation.	12-3	
1.4 Use the results of probability experiments to predict future events (e.g., use a line plot to predict the temperature forecast for the next day).	12-8	

	Teach and Practice	Practice
Mathematical Reasoning		
2.1 Use estimation to verify reasonableness of calculated results.		12-2
2.2 Apply strategies and results from simpler problems to more complex problems.		12-9
2.3 Use a variety of methods, such as words, numbers, symbols, charts, graphs, tables, diagrams, and models, to explain mathematical reasoning.	12-5	12-2, 12-9
2.5 Indicate the relative advantages of exact and approximate solutions to problems and give answers to a specified degree of accuracy.	12-2	
3.1 Evaluate the reasonableness of a solution in the context of the original situation.		12-1, 12-3, 12-6, 12-8
3.2 Note the method of deriving the solution and demonstrate a conceptual understanding of the derivation by solving similar problems.		12-2, 12-5
3.3 Develop generalizations of the results obtained and apply them in other circumstances.		12-1, 12-7, 12-8, 12-9

* The symbol (🔑) indicates a key standard as designated in the Mathematics Framework for California Public Schools. Full statements of the California Content Standards are found at the beginning of this book following the Table of Contents.

LESSON 12-1

Organizing Data

California Content Standard *Statistics, Data Analysis, and Probability 1.1 (Grade 2): Record numerical data in systematic ways, keeping track of what has been counted.*

Warm-Up Review

1. 5, 10, 15, 20, ■, ■, ■

Compare. Use >, <, or =.

2. 96 ● 98

3. 6×19 ● 8×12

4. Tashina bought 3 bags of apples. Each bag had 2 dozen apples. Four of the apples were bad. How many good apples did she have?

Math Link You know how to organize data into tables, bar graphs, and pictographs to show information. Now you will organize data in a tally chart.

All the pieces of information you collect are called **data**. A **tally chart** is a chart used to record data.

Word Bank

data
tally chart
tally marks

Example 1

Mr. Johnson asked students in his class to name their favorite recess game. Each student's choice is shown at the right. Use the data he collected to make a tally chart.

Our Favorite Recess Games

tag	tag	hopscotch
kickball	kickball	tag
tag	kickball	kickball
jump rope	kickball	jump rope
hopscotch	jump rope	tag
tag	kickball	kickball

Use **tally marks** to record the data.

| means 1 vote.
𝍸 means 5 votes.

Count the tally marks and write the number for each game.

Example 2

Use the tally chart. How many more students chose kickball as their favorite recess game than chose hopscotch?

Think: 7 students chose kickball and 2 students chose hopscotch.
$7 - 2 = 5$ students.

So, 5 more students chose kickball than chose hopscotch.

Our Favorite Recess Games

Game	Votes
tag	𝍸 |
hopscotch	||
jump rope	|||
kickball	𝍸 ||

Count 5, then 6, 7.

Additional Standards: Mathematical Reasoning 3.1, 3.3 (See p. 477.)

Guided Practice *For another example, see Set A on p. 504.*

1. Copy and complete the tally chart. Use the data to help. The votes for "Morning" have already been counted.

2. Which time of day had the most votes? Which time of day had the least number of votes?

Our Class's Favorite Times of Day

evening	morning
afternoon	afternoon
afternoon	morning
evening	morning
afternoon	afternoon

Our Favorite Times of Day

Time of Day	Tally
Morning	|||
Afternoon	
Evening	

Independent Practice *For more practice, see Set A on p. 507.*

Use the data at the right to answer Exercises 3–6.

3. Make a tally chart to record the information.

4. Which season got the most votes? Which season got the least number of votes?

5. How many more students chose summer than winter?

6. **Math Reasoning** Mark said the class likes warmer months more than colder months. Is his statement reasonable? Explain.

Our Class's Favorite Seasons

fall	summer
summer	winter
fall	summer
spring	summer
summer	spring
summer	summer

Mixed Review

7. Jason rode his bike 0.8 mile. Mike rode 1.3 miles. Tom's chain fell off his bike and he only rode 0.08 mile. List these distances from least to greatest.

8. 1.8 + 3.6 **9.** 5.3 − 2.1 **10.** 4.2 + 3.9 **11.** 6.1 − 0.8

Test Prep **Choose the correct letter for the answer.**

12. Which number shows the decimal two and three tenths?
(11-10)

A 2.03 **B** 2.3 **C** 20.3 **D** 23.0

LESSON 12-2

Understand
Plan
Solve
Look Back

Problem-Solving Skill:

Is an Estimate Enough?

Warm-Up Review

Round each number to the nearest hundred.

1. 863 **2.** 289

3. 331 **4.** 546

5. Robin found 28 shells. Marshall found 46 shells. About how many more shells did Marshall find?

California Content Standard *Mathematical Reasoning 2.5: Indicate the relative advantages of exact and approximate solutions to problems and give answers to a specified degree of accuracy.*

Read for Understanding

The third-grade Recycling Club collects soda cans around school. When at least 400 cans have been collected, the club takes them to a recycling center. The table at the right shows the number of cans the club has collected in the last 4 weeks.

Number of Cans We Have Collected

Week	Number of Cans
Week 1	89
Week 2	96
Week 3	102
Week 4	75

1. How many cans does the club collect before taking them to a recycling center?

2. How many cans did the club collect each week?

Think and Discuss

MATH FOCUS

Is an Estimate Enough?

Sometimes an estimate is all you need to solve a problem. If you are asked if there is enough of something, often you just need to estimate.

Reread the paragraph at the top of the page.

3. Would you estimate or find an exact answer to find the total number of cans that the Recycling Club has collected?

4. Does the club have enough cans to take to the recycling center? How could an estimate help you decide?

5. Why can it be helpful to estimate to find answers?

 Additional Standards: Mathematical Reasoning 2.1, 2.3, 3.2 *(See p. 477.)*

Guided Practice

A company orders special recycled paper. The paper comes in cartons of 4,750 sheets. Each carton costs $65.00.

1. Which of these problems needs an exact answer to be solved?

- **a.** Is $200 enough to pay for 2 cartons of paper?
- **b.** How much do 2 cartons of paper cost?
- **c.** Will 2 cartons be enough to buy if the company needs 7,250 sheets of paper?

2. Which of these problems can be solved by using an estimate?

- **a.** How much do 5 cartons of paper cost?
- **b.** How many sheets are there in 2 cartons?
- **c.** Will 2 cartons be enough to buy if the company needs 8,000 sheets of paper?

Independent Practice

The Royal Recycling Center can start to recycle paper every time it has 1,500 pounds of paper. The table at the right shows the number of pounds of paper collected in 2 days.

Pounds of Paper Collected

Day	Pounds
Day 1	882
Day 2	492

3. Which number sentence could you use to estimate how much paper the center has?

- **a.** $882 + 492 = ■$
- **b.** $900 + 500 = ■$
- **c.** $900 - 500 = ■$

4. Which number sentence would you use to find exactly how much paper the center has?

- **a.** $882 + 492 = ■$
- **b.** $900 + 500 = ■$
- **c.** $882 - 492 = ■$

5. Math Reasoning Can you estimate to find out if the center has enough paper to begin recycling? Why or why not?

Use Homework Workbook 12-2.

LESSON 12-3

Line Plots

California Content Standard *Statistics, Data Analysis, and Probability 1.3 (Grade 4): Interpret one- and two-variable data graphs to answer questions about a situation.*

Warm-Up Review

Write whether each statement best describes a bar graph, a pictograph, or both.

1. Uses symbols to show data.
2. Uses bars to show data.
3. Compares data.

Word Bank

line plot
cluster

Math Link You know how to read information from a bar graph, a pictograph, and a tally chart. Now you will learn to read information from a line plot.

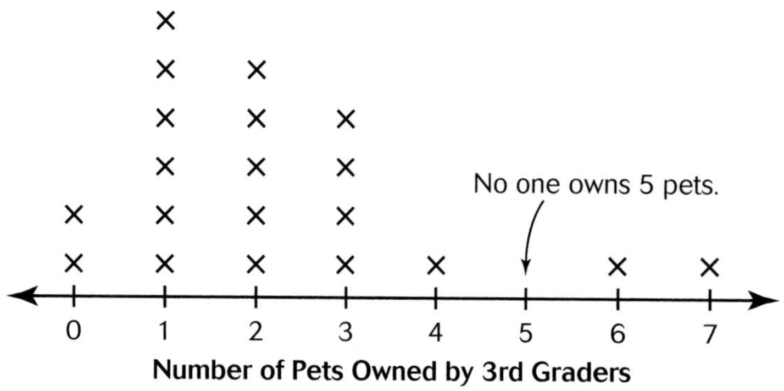

A **line plot** shows data along a number line.

A line plot uses an **X** to show data. Here each X stands for one student.

A **cluster** is a large group of Xs around 1 or more numbers.

Example 1

Read the line plot. What is the most number of pets owned?

Since the largest number with an **X** is 7, the most number of pets owned is 7.

More Examples

A. What is the most common number of pets owned?

Since the number with the most number of Xs is 1, the most common number of pets owned is 1.

B. Does the data form any cluster? If so, where?

Since most of the data is around 1 through 3, the data forms a cluster around 1–3 pets owned.

 Additional Standard: Mathematical Reasoning 3.1 (See p. 477.)

Guided Practice *For another example, see Set B on p. 504.*

Use the line plot to the right to answer Exercises 1–3.

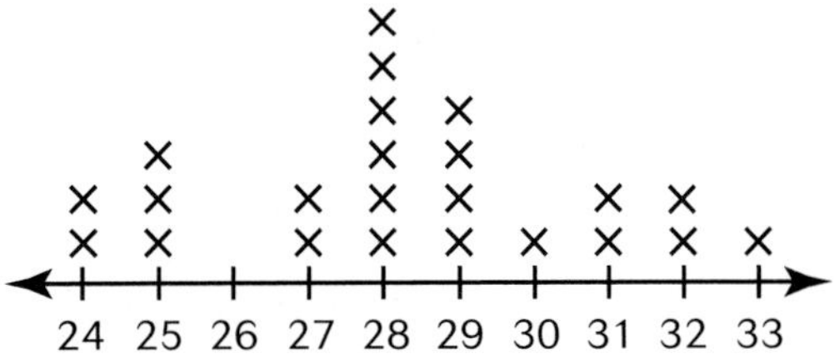

Distances Jumped by 3rd Grade Students (inches)

1. What is the mode (the most common distance jumped)?

2. How long was the shortest jump?

3. Does the data for distances jumped form any clusters? If so, where?

Independent Practice *For more practice, see Set B on p. 507.*

Use the line plot to answer Exercises 4–7.

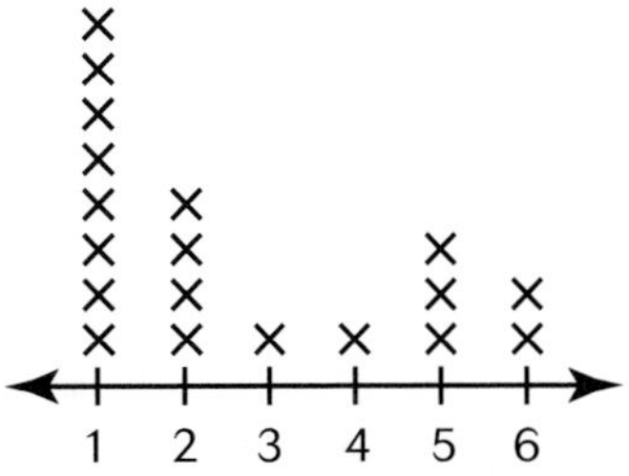

Distances Students Ride to School (miles)

4. How many students ride the bus for 2 miles?

5. How far do most students ride the bus?

6. What is the range (the greatest distance minus the least distance)?

7. Math Reasoning Reece rides 4 miles to school. He says that most students have a similar distance to ride to school. Is Reece's statement reasonable?

Mixed Review

8. Use the data from p. 479, Exercise 1 to answer the question. How many more people voted for afternoon than morning?

9. $6.3 - 2.7$ **10.** $8.1 + 1.3$ **11.** $6.3 - 0.3$ **12.** $4.4 + 4.4$

Test Prep **Choose the correct letter for each answer.**

13. $\frac{1}{4} + \frac{2}{3} =$
(11-7)

A $\frac{11}{12}$ **B** $\frac{10}{12}$ **C** $\frac{3}{7}$ **D** $\frac{3}{4}$

14. $8 \times 293 =$
(9-6)

F 1,624 **G** 2,244 **H** 2,344 **J** 20,344

LESSON 12-4

Reading Graphs with Ordered Pairs

California Content Standard *Statistics, Data Analysis, and Probability 1.1 (Grade 4): Formulate survey questions, systematically collect and represent data on a number line, and coordinate graphs, tables, and charts.*

Warm-Up Review

Use the array to answer each question.

1. How many dots are in each row?
2. How many rows are there?
3. How many dots are there in all?

Math Link You know how to gather information from a bar graph, pictograph, tally chart, and line plot. Now you will learn to gather information using locations.

Word Bank

ordered pair

Example 1

This grid map shows where different kinds of trash are collected at a recycling center. Where is glass recycled?

- Start at 0.
- Go 5 spaces to the right.
- Go 3 spaces up.

Glass is recycled at the **ordered pair** (5, 3). An ordered pair gives the location of a point on a graph.

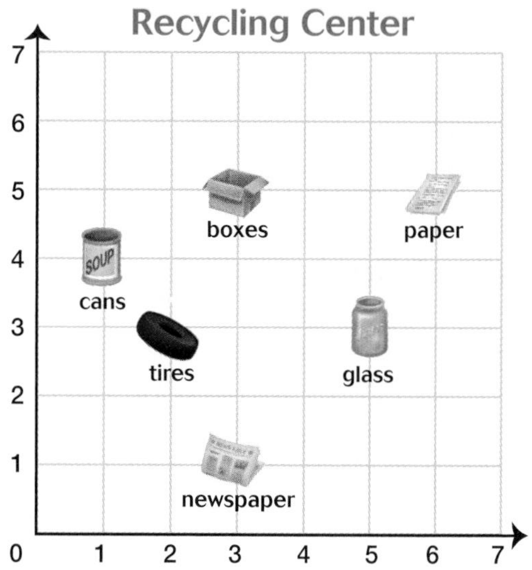

Example 2

What is recycled at (1, 4)?

- Start at 0.
- Go 1 space to the right.
- Go 4 spaces up.

Cans are recycled at (1, 4).

Guided Practice *For another example, see Set C on p. 505.*

Use the grid above for Exercises 1–5.

1. What is recycled at (3, 1)?

2. What is recycled at (6, 5)?

3. Where are boxes recycled?

4. Where are tires recycled?

5. Suppose plastics is 3 spaces above glass. What ordered pair would name the plastics' location?

Independent Practice *For more practice, see Set C on p. 508.*

Use the grid at the right for Exercises 6–13.

Write the ordered pair for each trash bin.

6.  **7.**  **8.** 

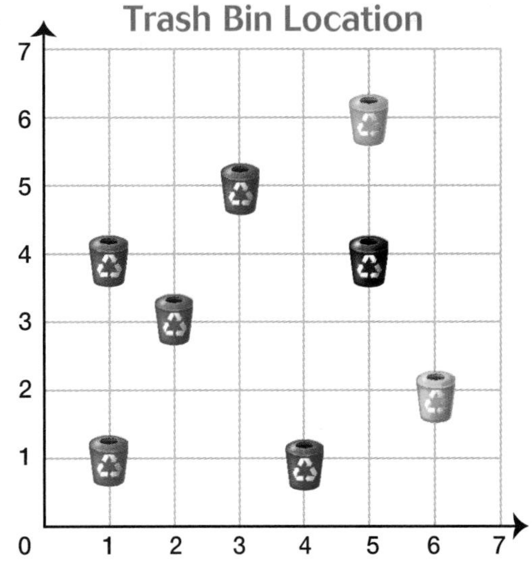

What color of bin is found at each ordered pair?

9. (6, 2) **10.** (5, 4) **11.** (1, 1)

12. Suppose a gray bin is 2 spaces to the right of the green bin. What ordered pair would name the gray bin's location?

13. Suppose you put a pink bin at (5, 3). What bin would be 3 spaces to the left of the pink bin?

Mixed Review

14. Make a tally chart to record the information at the right.

Our Favorite Subject		
Math	Social Studies	Reading
Spelling	Math	Math
Math	Math	Science
Science	Reading	Science
Reading	Spelling	Math

15. Tyler collected $292 for the local library. Jake collected $318. Write a number sentence to estimate how much money the boys collected.

Use the line plot from p. 482 to answer Exercises 16 and 17.

16. How many more students have 1 pet than have 3 pets?

17. How many students don't have any pets?

Test Prep **Choose the correct letter for each answer.**

18. *(11-11)* What is the value of the 5 in 2.35?

A fifty

B five

C five tenths

D five hundredths

19. *(8-4)* Rickey made a figure out of clay. There were 3 sides. All the sides were different lengths. What figure did he make?

F quadrilateral

G equilateral triangle

H isosceles triangle

J scalene triangle

LESSON 12-5

Understand
Plan
Solve
Look Back

Problem-Solving Strategy:
Make a Graph

California Content Standard *Mathematical Reasoning 2.3: Use a variety of methods, such as words, numbers, symbols, charts, graphs, tables, diagrams, and models, to explain mathematical reasoning.*

Warm-Up Review

1. 0, 2, 4, 6, ▒, ▒
2. 0, 3, 6, 9, ▒, ▒
3. Cheri kept track of rainy days in summer.

Month	Rain
June	卌
July	|||
August	卌 卌

How many days did it rain in June and July?

Tory's class is voting on a project to help our planet. Four people want to plant trees, 7 people want to collect trash, 8 people want to donate used toys, 6 people want to recycle bottles, and 4 people want to learn how to save water.

How could Tory organize the data? Which project is the most popular?

Understand

What do you need to find?

You need to find a way for Tory to organize the data. Then you need to find which project got the most votes.

Plan

How can you solve the problem?

You can **make a bar graph** to organize the data. Then you can compare the bars to see which project is most popular.

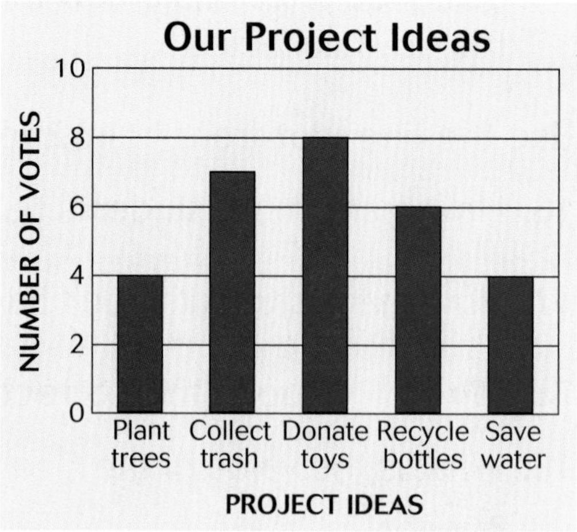

Solve

Make the bar graph as shown. Be sure to label the graph.

The "Donate toys" bar is the tallest. So, it is the most popular project.

Look Back

Could you have made a pictograph to organize and compare the data? Explain how.

 Additional Standard: Mathematical Reasoning 3.2 (See p. 477.)

Use the chart for Exercises 1–4.

Guided Practice

Kinds of Toys	Number of Toys Collected
Stuffed animals	𝍸 ||
Games	𝍸 |||
Dolls	𝍸 |
Trucks	||||
Sporting goods	𝍸 𝍸 |

1. Eric and his classmates decided to collect used toys to give away. Eric made the tally chart at the right to record the number of toys the class has collected so far. Make a bar graph to organize Eric's data.

Independent Practice

2. Which kind of toy was collected the most? the least?

3. Becky wants to make a list of the kinds of toys collected in order from least to most. How should she order her list?

4. Suppose the class collects 5 more games and 2 more dolls. How will that change your answers for Exercise 2?

Mixed Review

Try these or other strategies to solve each exercise. Tell which strategy you used.

Problem-Solving Strategies

- *Use Logical Reasoning*
- *Work Backward*
- *Find a pattern*
- *Write a Number Sentence*

5. A class collects 4 cans on Monday, 8 cans on Tuesday, and 16 cans on Wednesday. If this pattern continues, how many cans will be collected on Friday?

6. Laura counts 8 glass bottles and 15 cans in the class recycling bin. How many more cans than glass bottles are in the recycling bin?

7. **Math Reasoning** Laura puts some glass bottles in an empty class recycling bin. Later 5 bottles are taken out for a project. At the end of the day, Jonna puts 3 new bottles in the bin and says that now there are 15 bottles in the bin. How many bottles did Laura put in the bin?

Use Homework Workbook 12-5.

Diagnostic Checkpoint

Use the information at the right for Exercises 1–3.

1. Make a tally chart to record the information shown at the right.
(12-1)

2. Make a bar graph to organize the data.
(12-5)

3. Which color got the most votes? Which color got the least votes?
(12-1)

Our Class's Favorite Color	
Mike—red	Adam—red
Beau—blue	Joey—green
Jamie—green	Alan—red
Ashley—red	Frank—blue
Josh—red	Chanell—green
Michelle—blue	Chris—red
Sophie—yellow	Dillon—red

Use the line plot at the right to answer Exercises 4–6.

4. What was the most number of free throws made?
(12-3)

5. What was the least number of free throws made?
(12-3)

6. How many players made 7 free throws?
(12-3)

Number of Free Throws Made by the Stars

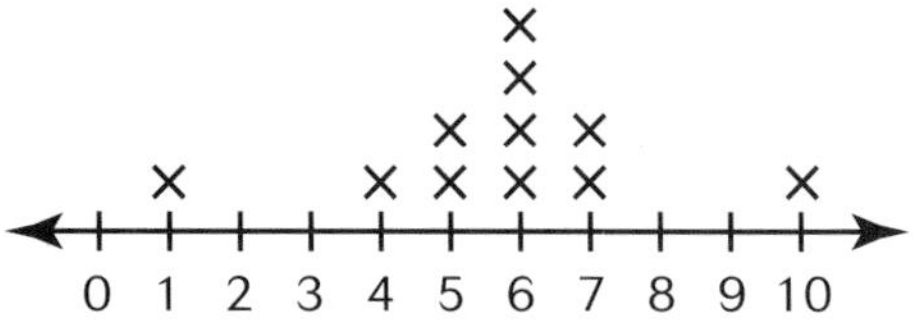

Use the grid at the right for Exercises 7–11. Write the ordered pair that names the location for each cabin.

7. Lost Trail
(12-4)

8. Big Pine
(12-4)

What cabin is found at each ordered pair?

9. (4, 1) (12-4) **10.** (1, 3) (12-4) **11.** (3, 4) (12-4)

Cabin Location

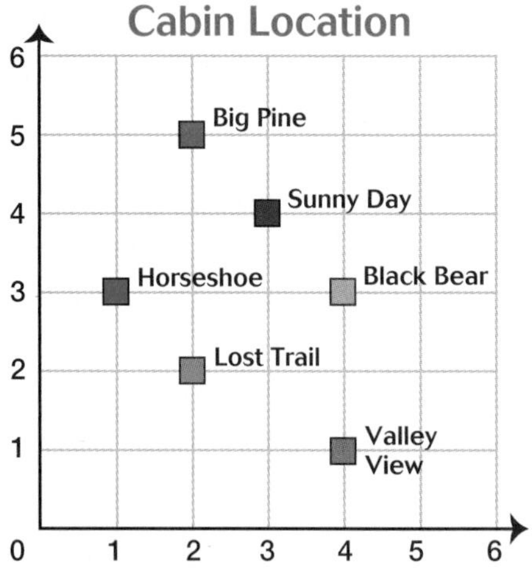

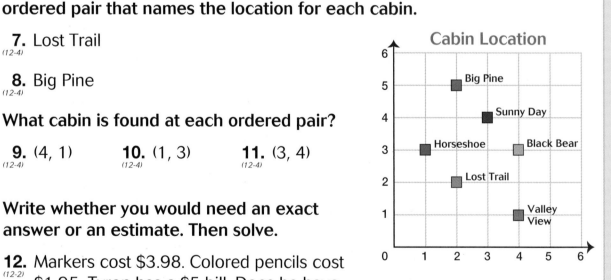

Write whether you would need an exact answer or an estimate. Then solve.

12. Markers cost \$3.98. Colored pencils cost \$1.95. Tyron has a \$5 bill. Does he have enough money to buy both the items?
(12-2)

TEST PREP

Multiple-Choice Cumulative Review

Choose the correct letter for each answer.

1. Frank has more than 50 toy cars. He also has 17 toy trucks. Which of these is reasonable for the total number of toy vehicles Frank has?

A 30 vehicles
B 50 vehicles
C 60 vehicles
D 70 vehicles

2. Which number sentence can help you find 63 ÷ 9 = ■?

F $63 + 9 = 72$
G $63 - 9 = 54$
H $9 \times 7 = 63$
J $9 \times 63 = 567$

3. Mary bought 5 bags of beads. In each bag there were 8 beads. Each bag cost $6. How many beads did Mary buy?

A 6 beads
B 30 beads
C 40 beads
D 48 beads

4. On clean-up day, Andy found 3 fewer cans than Steve found. Together, they collected 17 cans. How many cans did Steve find?

F 8 cans
G 9 cans
H 10 cans
J 11 cans

5. Which of the following means the same as 9 × 8?

A 9×6
B 8×8
C 7×6
D 8×9

Use the graph for Questions 6 and 7.

Lisa made the graph below to show how many hours she spent baby sitting last week.

6. Lisa makes $4.50 an hour. How much did she earn altogether on Saturday and Tuesday?

F $31.50
G $18.00
H $13.50
J $12.00

7. Lisa planned to work 20 hours last week. How many fewer hours did she work than she had planned?

A 2 hours
B 3 hours
C 5 hours
D 6 hours

LESSON 12-6

Understanding Probability

California Content Standard *Statistics, Data Analysis, and Probability 1.1: Identify whether common events are certain, likely, unlikely, or improbable.*

Math Link You know how to estimate using data from events. Now you will learn to describe the chance that an event will happen.

Probability tells the chance that something will happen. Some events are **certain** to happen. Others are **impossible**.

certain

Tuesday follows Monday.

impossible

A tree can run.

Many events are possible. A **likely** event is one with a good chance to happen. An **unlikely** event is one that probably won't happen.

likely

It is raining somewhere.

unlikely

School will close early today.

Example 1

Is it *certain* or *impossible* that the sun will rise in the east tomorrow?

The sun always rises in the east, so it is certain that it will rise in the east tomorrow.

Example 2

Is it *likely* or *unlikely* that you will win a bike today?

Winning a new bike probably won't happen, so it is unlikely that you will win one today.

Warm-Up Review

Estimate.

1. 358 + 232
2. 986 − 211
3. 2 × 71
4. 5 × 283
5. Janet folded a piece of paper into 6 equal parts. She put stars in 2 parts, and she put dots in the rest. What fraction of the paper has dots?

Word Bank

probability
impossible
certain
likely
unlikely

 Additional Standard: Mathematical Reasoning 3.1 *(See p. 477.)*

Guided Practice *For another example, see Set D on p. 505.*

Write whether each is impossible or certain.

1. A person is sleeping somewhere.

2. A turtle will learn to fly.

Write whether each is likely or unlikely.

3. All the books in the library will be checked out.

4. Milk will be served at school cafeterias.

Independent Practice *For more practice, see Set D on p. 508.*

Write whether each is impossible or certain.

5. You can be in two different places at the same time.

6. Water will become ice if it is frozen.

Write whether each is likely or unlikely.

7. You will find a ten-dollar bill today.
8. You will win a trip to Australia.

9. **Math Reasoning** Reid says, "It is likely to rain in our town every day." Do you agree or disagree? Explain.

Mixed Review

10. Use the grid map from p. 484. Suppose you found a plastic recycling spot 3 spaces up and 5 spaces to the left of glass. What ordered pair would name the location?

11. Use the line plot from p. 483. How many students jumped 29 inches?

Test Prep Choose the correct letter for each answer.

12. $\frac{9}{12} - \frac{4}{12} =$ (11-6)

A $\frac{5}{12}$
B $\frac{13}{12}$
C $\frac{13}{24}$
D 5
E NH

13. Which number belongs in the box? (3-3)

1 yard = ■ feet

F 1
G 3
H 12
J 36
K NH

LESSON 12-7

Listing Outcomes

California Content Standard *Statistics, Data Analysis, and Probability 1.2 (key): Record the possible outcomes for a simple event (e.g., tossing a coin) and systematically keep track of the outcomes when the event is repeated many times.*

Warm-Up Review

List the color that is more likely to be picked.

1. 5 yellow, 2 blue
2. 3 orange, 1 purple
3. 1 red, 4 yellow
4. Marcella had 87 stickers. She put 9 on each of 9 envelopes. How many stickers did she have left over?

Math Link You know there are different ways to describe the probability something will happen. Now you will learn how to predict the probability of something happening.

Word Bank

outcome

Example 1

Look at the spinner. There are 3 possible outcomes of a spin. The spinner could land on red, yellow, or green.

What is the probability that the spinner lands on red? on green? on yellow?

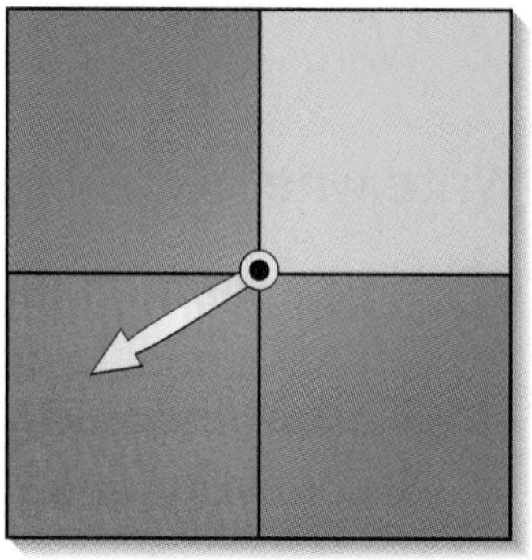

Think: Each space is the same size. There are 2 green spaces but only 1 red space and 1 yellow space.

The probability of spinning red is 1 out of 4.

The probability of spinning green is 2 out of 4.

The probability of spinning yellow is 1 out of 4.

Example 2

Vernon spun the spinner 40 times. His results are shown in the table at the right.

Why do you think Vernon spun green more than red and yellow?

Color	Probability	Outcome
Red	1 out of 4	𝍸 𝍸 |
Green	2 out of 4	𝍸 𝍸 𝍸 𝍸
Yellow	1 out of 4	𝍸 ||||

Think: The probability of spinning green is greater than the probability of spinning yellow or red.

So Vernon's results reflect the greater probability of spinning green.

 Additional Standard: Mathematical Reasoning 3.3 *(See p. 477.)*

Guided Practice *For another example, see Set E on p. 506.*

Toss one coin to complete Exercises 1 and 2.

1. What is the probability of landing on heads? on tails?

One Coin Toss		
Toss	**Probability**	**Outcome**
Heads		
Tails		

2. Toss your coin 20 times. Copy and complete the table at the right to keep track of your tosses.

3. Did the outcome of your 20 tosses come close to matching the probability of landing on heads or tails? Explain.

Independent Practice *For more practice, see Set E on p. 509.*

Toss two coins to complete Exercises 4–6.

4. What is the probability of tossing both heads? both tails? 1 head, 1 tail?

Two Coin Toss		
Toss	**Probability**	**Outcome**
Both Heads		
Both Tails		
1 Head, 1 Tail		

5. Toss your coins 20 times. Copy and complete the table at the right to keep track of your tosses.

6. **Math Reasoning** If you tossed your coins 1 more time, what result would you expect? Explain.

Mixed Review

7. Robin says, "I am certain it will rain tomorrow." Do you agree or disagree? Explain.

Use the grid for Exercises 8 and 9.

8. What shape is at (2, 3)?

9. What shape is at (3, 2)?

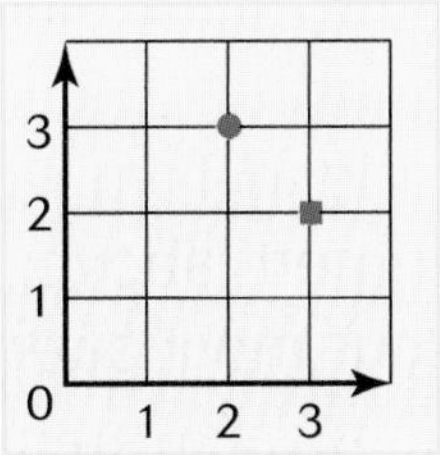

Test Prep Choose the correct letter for the answer.

10. Round 6,495 to the nearest thousand.
(1-3)

A 7,000 **B** 6,500 **C** 6,000 **D** 5,500

LESSON 12-8

Displaying Probability Data and Making Predictions

Warm-Up Review

For 1–3, write *likely* or *unlikely* for each event if you toss a cube numbered 1–6.

1. Toss a 1, 2, 3, or 4.

2. Toss a 6.

3. Toss a 1.

4. Janice has a bag with 4 red apples and 1 green apple. If she takes an apple without looking, what color do you think it will be?

California Content Standards *Statistics, Data Analysis, and Probability 1.3 (🔑): Summarize and display the results of probability experiments in a clear and organized way (e.g., use a bar graph or a line plot). Also, Statistics, Data Analysis, and Probability 1.4.*

Math Link You know how to use data to solve problems. Now you will use data to make predictions.

Example 1

You have two cubes numbered 1 through 6. Suppose you toss both cubes 30 times, and each time you record the sum of the numbers. What is the most common sum?

One way you could display the results of a probability experiment is on a line plot.

Toss Results	
Sum	**Tosses**
2	|
3	
4	||
5	||
6	𝍸
7	𝍸 |
8	𝍸
9	|||
10	||
11	|||
12	|

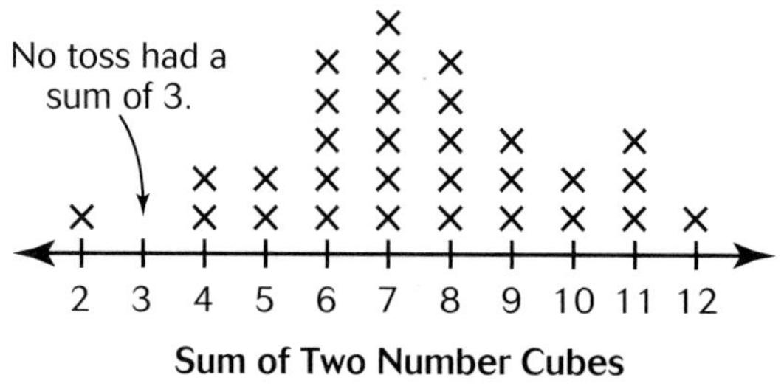

Think: The sum of 7 has the most **X**s.

So, 7 is the most common sum.

Example 2

Your friend Tom wants to repeat the number cube experiment above. What sum or sums could he expect to occur most often?

Think: The line plot clusters around the sums 6–8.

So, Tom could expect tosses of 6–8 to occur most often.

 Additional Standards: Mathematical Reasoning 3.1, 3.3 *(See p. 477.)*

More Examples

A. Jan spun a spinner with red, blue, and yellow sections 20 times. She recorded her results and then displayed them in a bar graph. What is the least common color she spun?

Spinner Results	
Color	**Spins**
Red	𝍸 𝍸
Blue	||
Yellow	𝍸 |||

She spun red 10 times, blue 2 times, and yellow 8 times. So, blue is the least common color she spun.

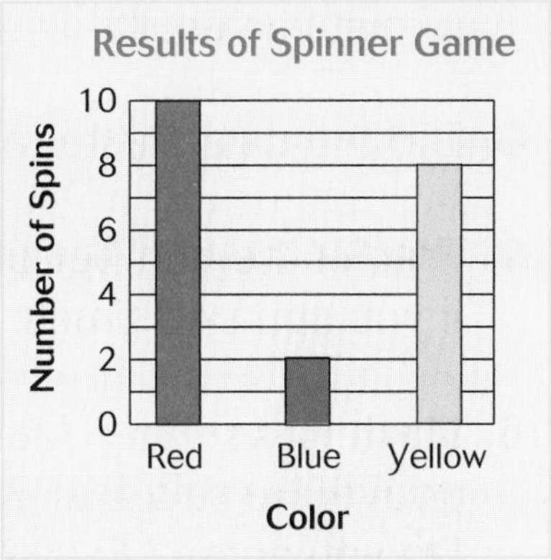

B. If Jan repeats the spinner game, predict which color she will land on least often.

Since she landed on blue only 2 times in the first game, you can predict that she'll land on blue least often in the next game.

Guided Practice *For another example, see Set F on p. 506.*

1. Copy the spinner and tally chart shown at the right and below.

Spinner Results	
Color	**Spins**
Blue	
Green	
Red	

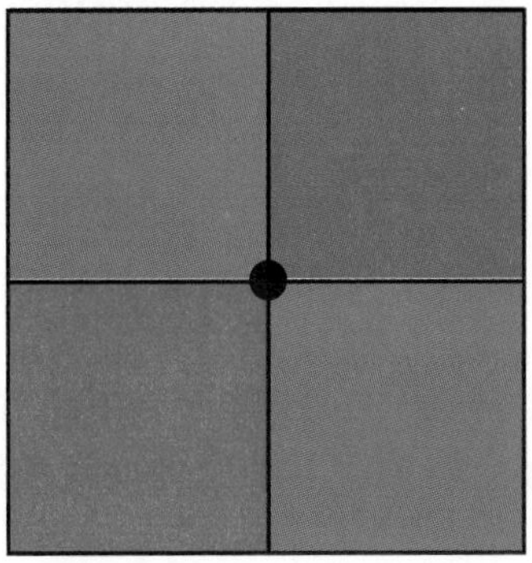

2. Use a pencil and paper clip to make spins on the spinner. Spin the spinner 10 times. Record your data in your chart.

3. Copy and complete the bar graph at the right.

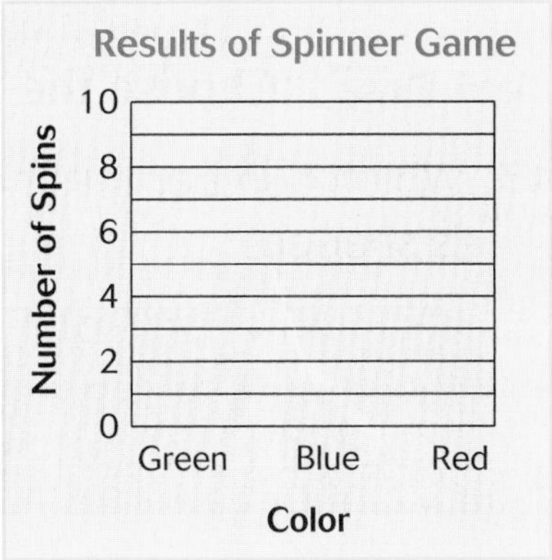

4. What color did you spin most often? least often?

5. If you repeated the 10 spins, what color would you expect to spin most often?

Independent Practice *For more practice, see Set F on p. 509.*

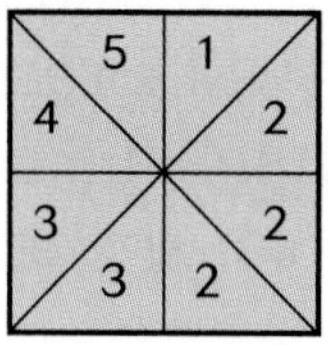

6. Make another spinner the same size as in Exercise 1. Divide the spinner into 8 sections and number like the square at the right.

7. Make a tally to record 20 spins. Copy and complete the line plot at the right to display results.

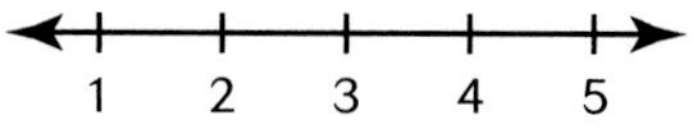

Spinner Results

8. Did the data cluster around any numbers?

9. Predict the number of spins for each number if you spun 40 times.

10. **Math Reasoning** Matt spun mostly 2s with the spinner above. He said that 2s would always be spun the most. Do you agree? Explain.

Mixed Review

11. Why would it be impossible to roll two number cubes labeled 1 through 6 and get a sum of 1?

12. List all the outcomes you could get when rolling a cube labeled 1 through 6.

Use the grid at the right to write each ordered pair for Exercises 13–16.

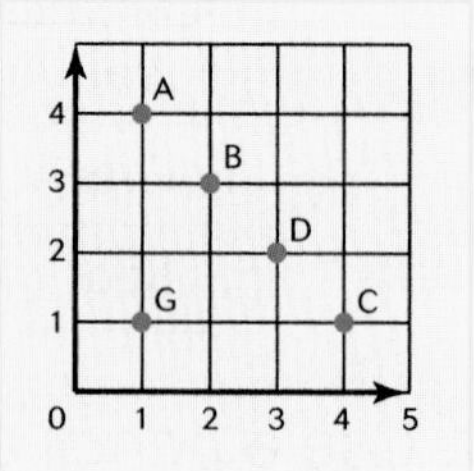

13. A　　14. B　　15. C

16. Which letter is located at (1, 1)?

Test Prep **Choose the correct letter for each answer.**

17. Which number tells how much is shaded? (11-10)

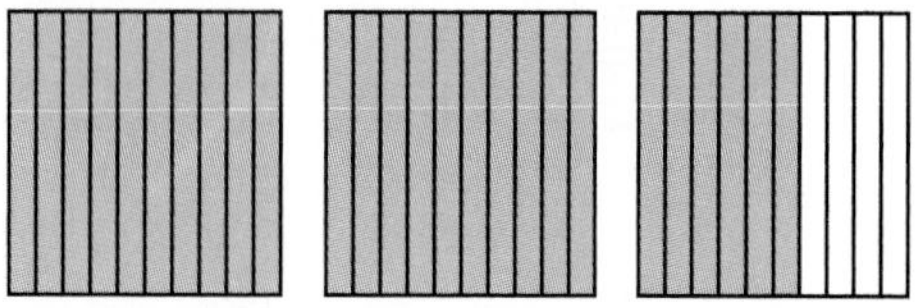

A 26.0　　**C** 2.6

B 2.66　　**D** 2.06

18. $3{,}628 \times 4 =$ (9-7)

F 13,512

G 14,512

H 14,812

J 24,512

K NH

TEST PREP

Multiple-Choice Cumulative Review

Choose the correct letter for each answer.

1. **What is the value of 5 in the number 153,409?**

A 50
B 500
C 5,000
D 50,000

2. **Jenny buys a book for $7.75. She pays with a $10 bill. Which shows the amount of change Jenny gets back?**

F 2 nickels, 2 dimes, 2 one-dollar bills
G 2 nickels, 1 dime, 2 one-dollar bills
H 1 quarter, 2 one-dollar bills
J 1 nickel, 2 dimes, 1 one-dollar bill

3. **Which is NOT a multiple of 5?**

A 54 **C** 70
B 60 **D** 75

4. **A square room has a perimeter of 32 feet. How long is one side of the room?**

F 3 feet
G 6 feet
H 9 feet
J 12 feet
K NH

5. **Use the fraction models. Which number belongs in the ■?**

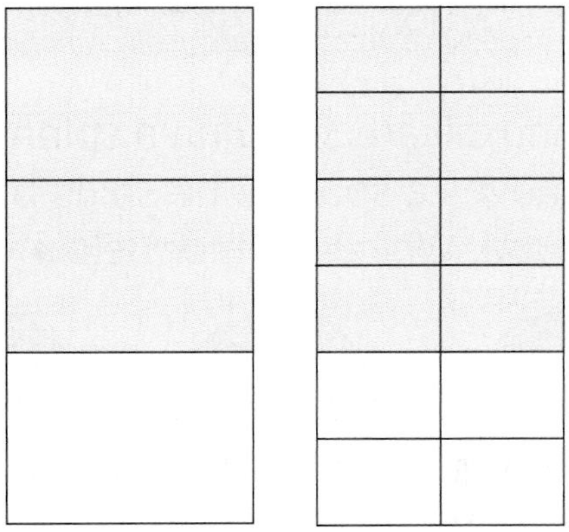

$\frac{2}{3} = \frac{\blacksquare}{12}$

A 2 **D** 8
B 3 **E** NH
C 6

6. **Which number shows the decimal five and three tenths?**

F 53.0
G 50.3
H 5.3
J 5.03

7. **Which shape am I? I have 4 sides. None of my angles are right angles.**

A 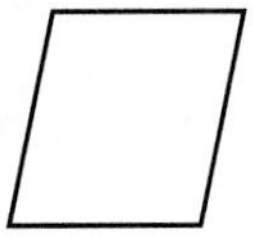 **C** 

B 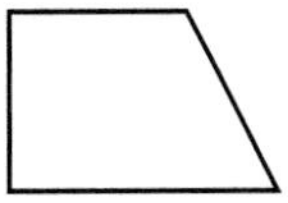 **D** 

LESSON 12-9

Understand
Plan
Solve
Look Back

Problem-Solving Application:

Fair and Unfair Games

Warm-Up Review

Write *certain, likely, unlikely,* or *impossible.*

1. A pig will grow wings and fly.
2. March comes before April.
3. Someone will make an A on one assignment.

California Content Standard *Statistics, Data Analysis, and Probability 1.0: Students conduct simple probability experiments by determining the number of possible outcomes and make simple predictions.*

Ben and Jill are spinning a spinner to play the Forest Game. Ben moves a space if he spins blue. Jill moves a space if she spins red. Which spinner below would make the game fair?

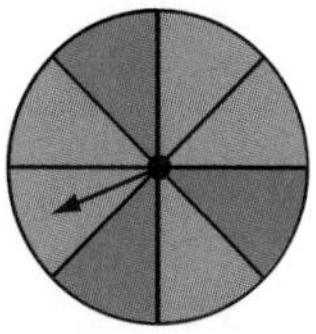

Spinner A

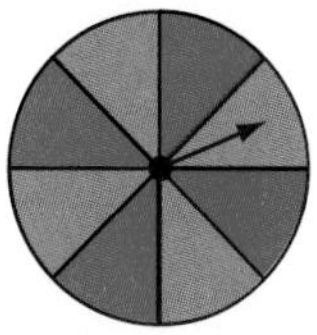

Spinner B

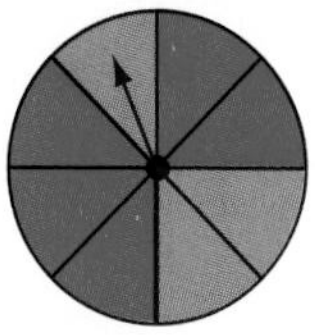

Spinner C

Forest Game

First player to reach FINISH wins!

Understand

What do you need to find?

You need to find the spinner that is equally likely to land on red or blue.

Plan

How can you solve the problem?

You can count the spaces on each spinner to find the one that has the same number of red and blue spaces.

Solve

Spinner A	Spinner B	Spinner C
3 blue spaces 5 red spaces	4 blue spaces 4 red spaces	5 blue spaces 3 red spaces

Spinner B would make the game fair.

Look Back

Explain which spinner gives Ben an unfair chance to win.

 Additional Standards: Mathematical Reasoning 2.2, 2.3, 3.3 *(See p. 477.)*

Use the spinners at the right to solve Exercises 1–4.

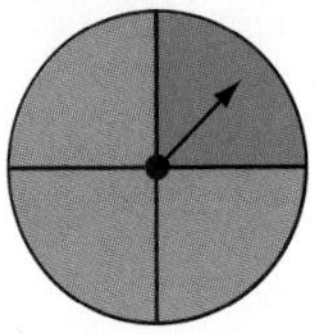

Spinner D

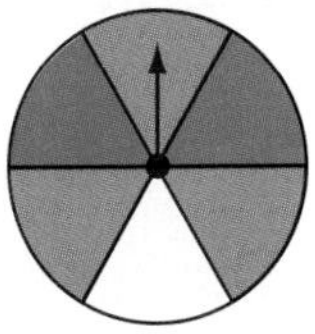

Spinner E

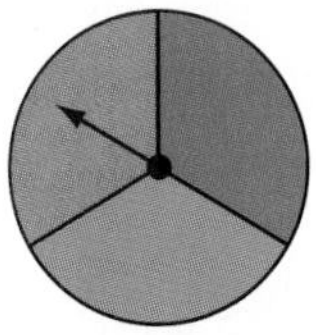

Spinner F

Guided Practice

1. Suppose you play the Forest Game with Spinner D. Would you be more likely to win if you were the blue player or the red player? Is this a fair spinner to use?

2. Suppose you want to play the Forest Game with Spinner E. One space needs to be filled in with red or blue. Which color should be used to make the spinner fair?

Independent Practice

3. Daisy and Hector are playing the Forest Game with Spinner F. Daisy is the red player and Hector is the blue player. Who do you think is more likely to win, Daisy or Hector? Tell why.

4. Suppose 3 people want to play the Forest Game together. Which spinner should they use if they want the game to be fair?

5. **Math Reasoning** Suppose you and a friend play the Forest Game 20 times with a fair spinner. How many games do you think each of you will win? Can you tell ahead of time exactly how many games each of you will win? Explain your thinking.

Mixed Review

6. How many lines of symmetry does the rectangle have?

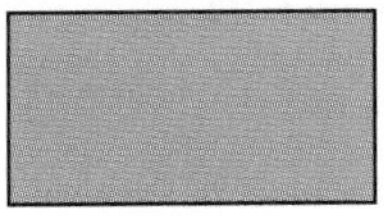

7. Laura planted tulips along the fence. She planted them in this order: red, yellow, white, purple, purple, white, yellow, red, red, yellow, and white. What are the next three colors if she keeps this pattern?

8. What combination of cans and glass items is worth 75¢? Describe two possible combinations.

Diagnostic Checkpoint

Word Bank
certain
impossible
outcome
probability
unlikely

Complete. For Exercises 1–3, use the words from the Word Bank.

1. The chance that something will happen is called ___?___.
(12-6)

2. The result of an experiment is called an ___?___.
(12.7)

3. When there is no chance that something will happen it is ___?___.
(12-6)

Write whether each event is *likely, unlikely, certain,* or *impossible.*

4. You eat 16 oranges a day.
(12-6)

5. People eat breakfast before noon.
(12-6)

6. January has 31 days.
(12-6)

For each spinner, name all the possible outcomes. Then write the probability of spinning each outcome.

7. (12-7)

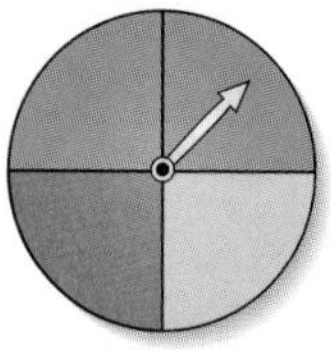

8. (12-7)

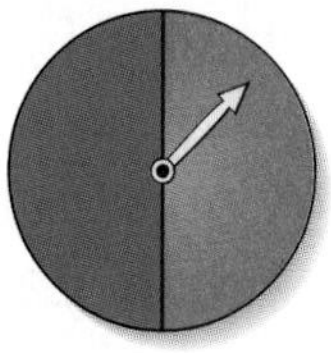

9. (12-7)

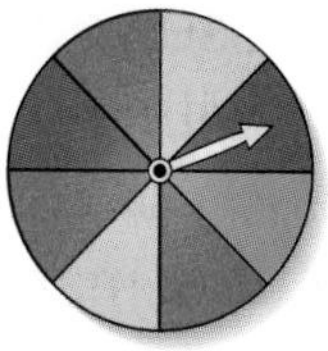

10. (12-7)

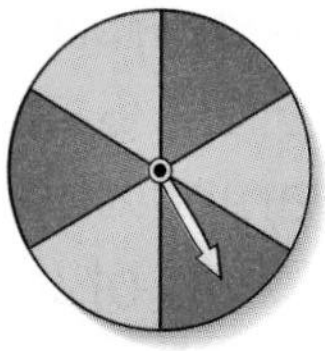

Use the bar graph at the right for Exercises 11 and 12.

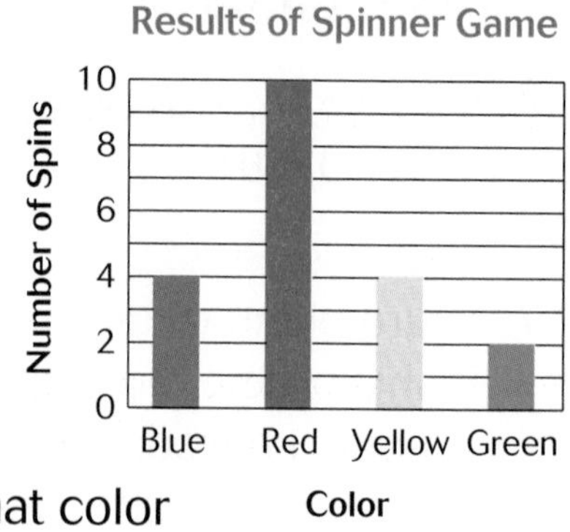

11. On which color did the spinner stop least often?
(12-8)

12. If the game is repeated, what color is likely to be spun most often? Explain.
(12-8)

Use the spinners from Exercises 7–10 to answer Exercises 13 and 14.

13. Suppose you used the spinner in Exercise 7. What color would be more likely to win, red, yellow, or green? Is the spinner fair?
(12-9)

14. Which spinners are fair spinners?
(12-9)

Chapter 12 Test

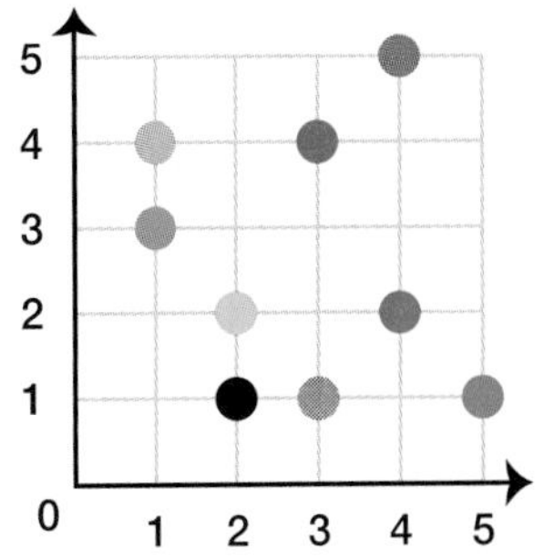

Write the ordered pair for each color.

1. purple **2.** blue

What color is found at each ordered pair?

3. (3, 4) **4.** (1, 4)

Use the line plot to answer Exercises 5 and 6.

5. What was the most common number of books read?

6. How many students read more than 17 books?

Books Read in One Month in Room 6

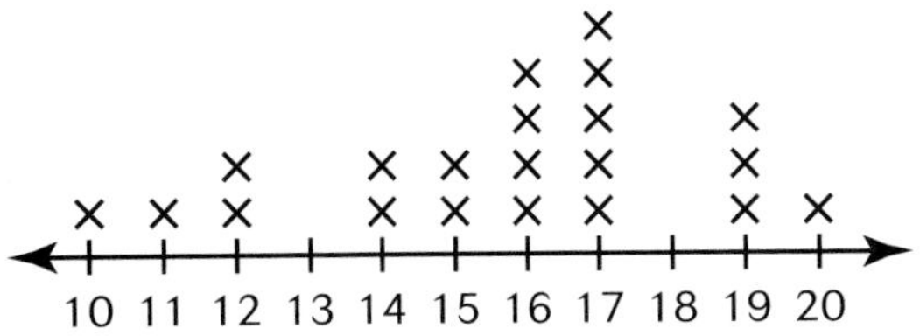

Terrance spun a spinner 20 times. His results are listed.

7. Make a tally chart to record the outcomes from Terrance's spins shown at the right.

8. Use the number of tallies in your tally chart to make a bar graph to organize Terrance's data.

Colors Terrance Spun			
Red	Blue	Red	Blue
Green	Red	Green	Red
Green	Green	Green	Green
Green	Green	Blue	Green
Blue	Green	Green	Green

9. If Terrance spun the spinner 20 more times, predict which color you think he will spin the most.

10. From the results of Terrance's spin, do you think this is a fair or unfair spinner?

Write whether the event is likely, unlikely, certain or impossible.

11. The sun will set.

12. You will be asleep at 2:00 A.M.

13. Name all the possible outcomes of a spin. Then write the chance of spinning each outcome.

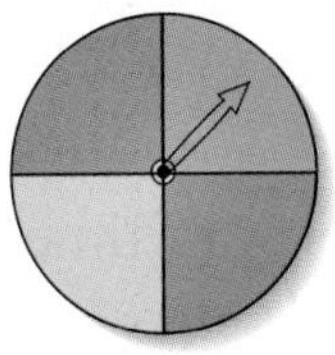

14. Savanna has 38 beads. Minta has 21 beads. The craft they want to make needs 50 beads. Do the girls have enough beads to do the project? How could an estimate help you decide?

Multiple-Choice Chapter 12 Test

Choose the correct letter for each answer.

1. **What is the probability of landing on green on the spinner below?**

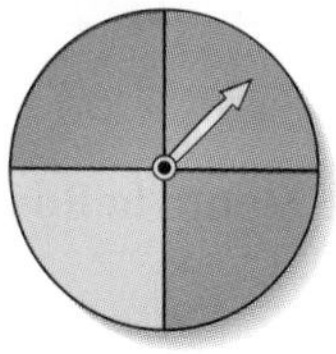

A 1 out of 3
B 2 out of 3
C 1 out of 4
D 2 out of 4

2. **Courtney spun a spinner that had 3 equal sections—red, green, and yellow. The bar graph shows her results. How many times was the spinner spun altogether?**

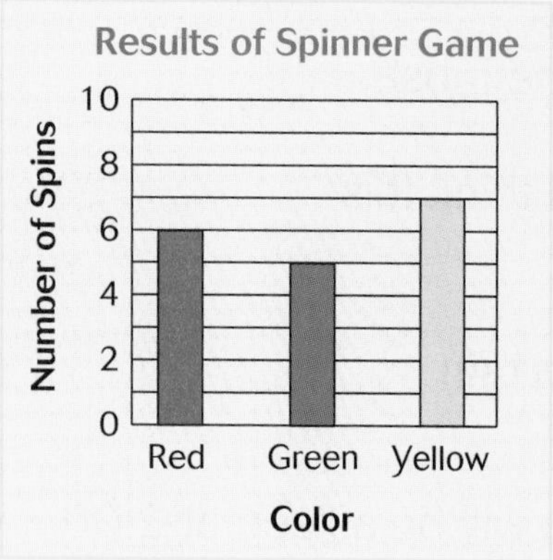

F 17 times
G 18 times
H 19 times
J 20 times

3. **The line plot shows the results of a poll of 10 students. Predict how many students out of 20 would say they study 3 nights per week.**

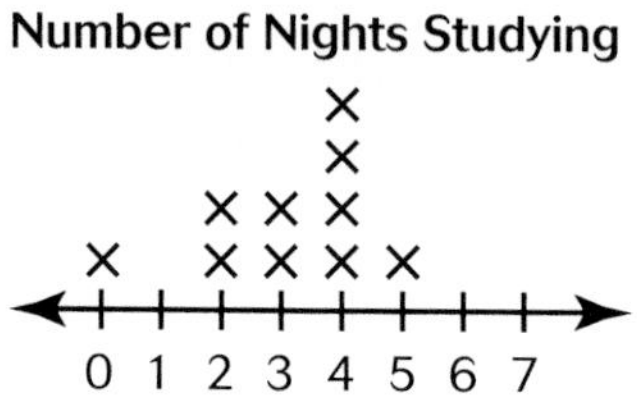

A 1 student
B 2 students
C 3 students
D 4 students

4. **Use the line plot in Exercise 3. How many students study 4 nights per week?**

F 1 student
G 2 students
H 3 students
J 4 students

5. **Mrs. North's class is selling calendars to raise money for their class field trip. For every calendar they sell, they get to keep $5. Which of these problems can be solved using an estimate?**

A Will 32 calendars be enough if they need $150?
B How much did Melanie raise if she sold 10 calendars?
C How many calendars did they sell if they made $15?
D How much money will they get if they sell 62 calendars?

6. **What ordered pair names the letter C?**

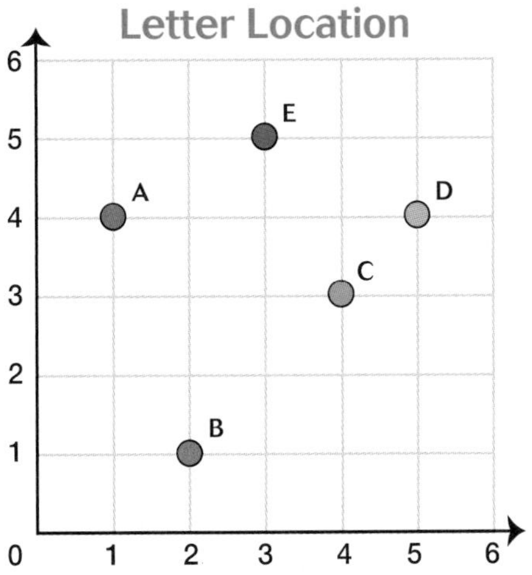

F (4, 3) **H** (4, 4)
G (3, 4) **J** (3, 3)

7. **The tally chart below has a mistake in it. How can the tally chart be fixed to show the data below?**

Favorite Sandwich			
Ham	Turkey	Cheese	Ham
Cheese	Ham	Turkey	Cheese
Ham	Cheese	Ham	Ham

Favorite Sandwich

Type	Votes
Ham	⊮ |
Cheese	⊮
Turkey	||

A Add 1 tally mark for ham.
B Take away 1 tally mark for cheese.
C Add 1 tally mark for cheese.
D Take away 1 tally mark for turkey.

8. **Which bar on the bar graph below does NOT represent the data in the tally chart below?**

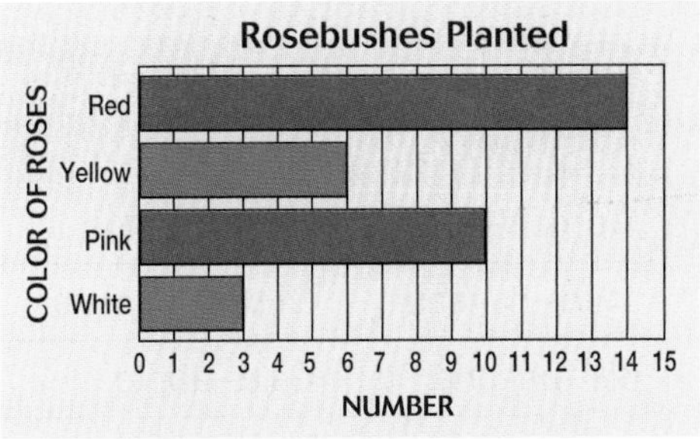

Rosebushes Planted

Color	Number
Red	⊮ ⊮ ||||
Yellow	⊮ |
Pink	⊮ ⊮
White	||

F Red **H** Pink
G Yellow **J** White

9. **Which spinner is fair?**

A
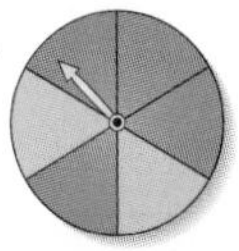
C
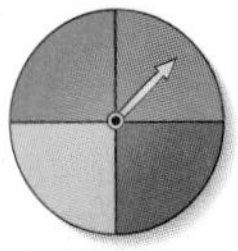
B
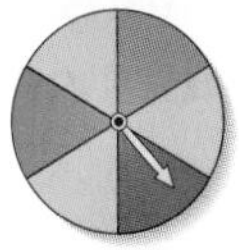
D
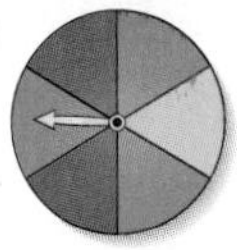

10. **Which of the events is certain?**

F You will eat lunch at noon.
G It will rain tomorrow.
H July follows June.
J Horses can fly.

Reteaching

Set A *(pages 478–479)*

Make a tally chart to record the information below.

Mrs. Dunbar's Class' Favorite Fruit	
Morgan—orange	Tyler—orange
Jake—banana	Dustin—banana
Bill—banana	Cale—apple
Angela—apple	Bret—orange
Julia—orange	Brittany—apple
Matt—banana	Zack—banana
LeeJay—banana	Melissa—orange
Tashina—apple	Cheyenne—orange

Mrs. Dunbar's Class' Favorite Fruit	
Orange	𝍸 |
Banana	𝍸 |
Apple	||||

Remember to put tally marks in groups of 5. This makes counting much easier.

1. Make a tally chart to record the information below.

Our Class' Favorite Meal			
Dinner	Lunch	Lunch	Breakfast
Lunch	Breakfast	Lunch	Dinner
Breakfast	Dinner	Breakfast	Dinner
Breakfast	Dinner	Dinner	Dinner
Breakfast	Lunch	Breakfast	Breakfast

2. Which meal got the most votes?

3. Which meal got the least votes?

4. How many fewer votes did dinner get than breakfast?

Set B *(pages 482–483)*

Use the line plot. How many students have no brothers or sisters?

Number of Brothers or Sisters

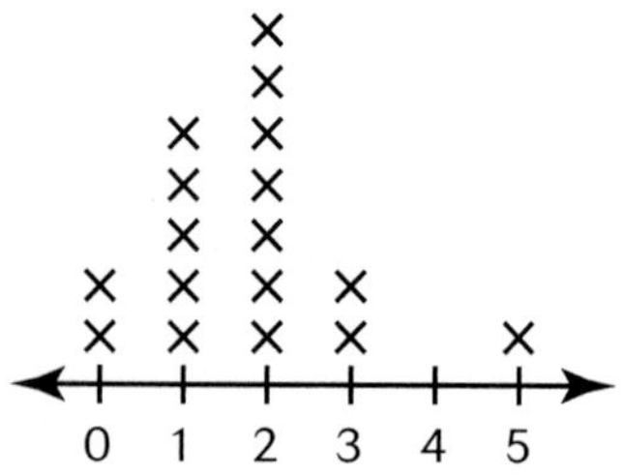

There are 2 **X**s above the 0. So, 2 students have no brothers or sisters.

Remember each **X** represents one student.

Use the line plot at the left to answer Exercises 1–3.

1. How many students have 3 brothers or sisters?

2. What is the most common number of brothers or sisters?

3. Does the data form any clusters?

Set C (pages 484–485)

Use the grid below. What place is located at (5, 3)?

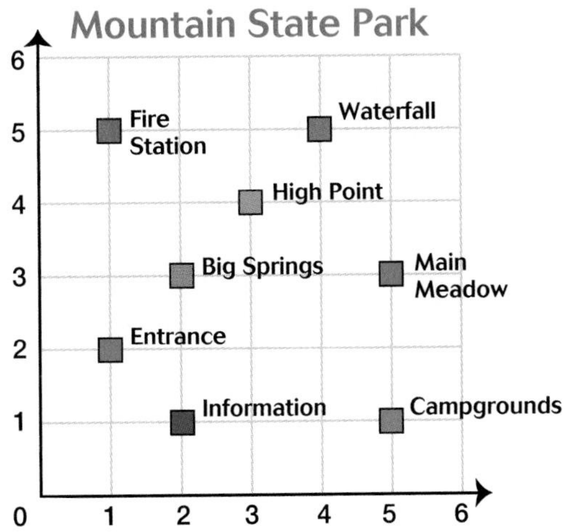

- Start at 0.
- Go 5 spaces to the right.
- Go 3 spaces up.

Main Meadow is located at (5, 3).

Remember when writing an ordered pair, the number of spaces to the right is listed first. The number of spaces up is listed second.

Use the grid at the left for Exercises 1–8.

Write the ordered pair for each place at Mountain State Park

1. Fire Station **2.** Entrance

3. Waterfall **4.** High Point

What place is found at each ordered pair?

5. (2, 1) **6.** (5, 1)

7. (2, 3) **8.** (4, 5)

Set D (pages 490–491)

Would it be likely or unlikely that you will go outside tomorrow?

Since you usually go outside, it is likely that you will tomorrow.

Is it certain or impossible that you can jump over the school?

Since you can only jump a few feet, it is impossible to jump over the school.

Remember for an event to be likely, there must be a good chance for it to happen.

Write whether each is *likely, unlikely, certain,* or *impossible.*

1. You will be awake at 8:30 A.M.

2. You will win a trip to Africa.

3. Fish are in the ocean now.

4. A dog will read out loud.

Reteaching (continued)

Set E *(pages 492–493)*

Name the possible outcomes of picking a cube. Then write the probability of each outcome.

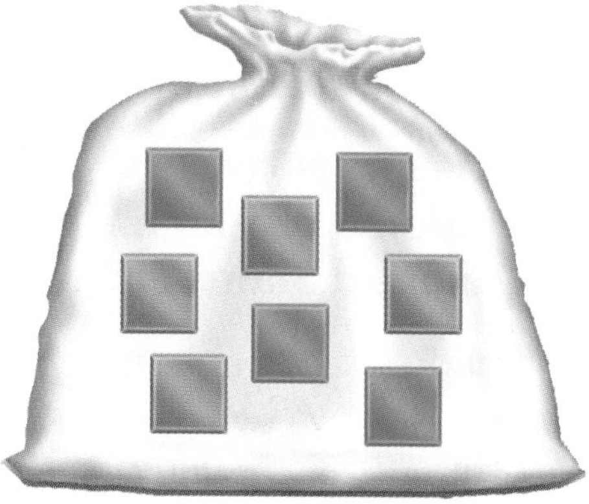

The only colors of cubes in the bag are blue and green. So, the outcomes are blue and green.

There are 8 cubes total; 4 blue and 4 green. So, the chances are: 4 out of 8 green and 4 out of 8 blue.

Remember outcomes list the options in words, and probabilities are listed with numbers.

Name all the possible outcomes. Then write the probabilities of each outcome.

1. 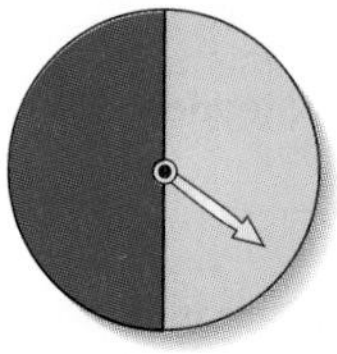

2. 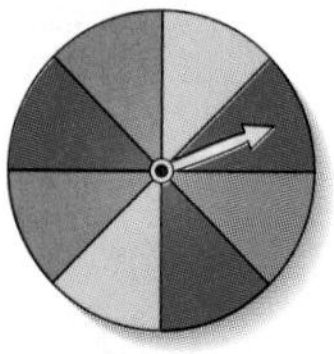

3. 

4. 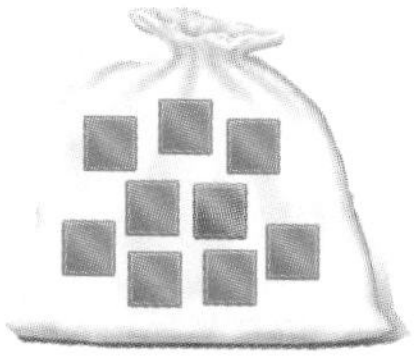

Write the probability of each event happening if you toss a cube numbered 1 through 6.

5. Tossing a 3.

6. Tossing an odd number.

Set F *(pages 494–496)*

Use the bar graph. Which color did the spinner land on most often?

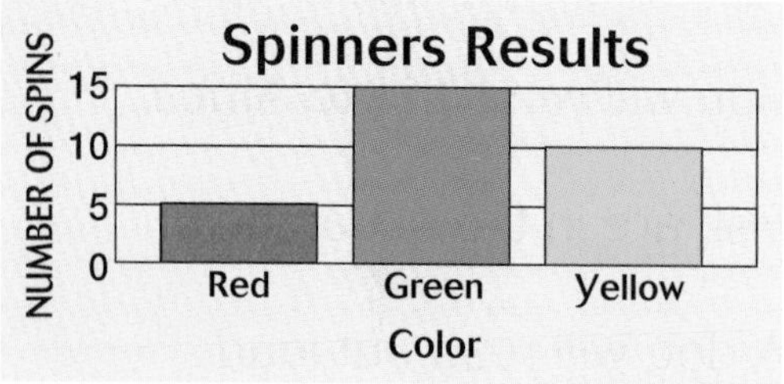

The bar that is the tallest is green. So, the spinner landed on green the most.

Remember a prediction is a guess you make based on data given to you.

Use the bar graph at the left for Exercises 1–3.

1. What does each bar on the graph show?

2. Which color did the spinner land on least often?

3. If you repeat this game, predict which color you think the spinner will land on most often.

More Practice

Set A (pages 478–479)

1. Make a tally chart to record the information shown at the right.

2. Which park received the most votes?

3. Which parks received more than 5 votes?

4. How many more students voted for Yellowstone than for the Grand Canyon?

5. How many students voted?

Favorite National Parks	
Tony–Grand Canyon	Porter–Yellowstone
Annette–Big Bend	Katy–Grand Canyon
Margo–Yellowstone	Marty–Yellowstone
Linda–Yellowstone	Allie–Big Bend
Jennifer–Grand Canyon	Vernon–Yellowstone
Heidi–Yellowstone	Erin–Big Bend
Ricky–Big Bend	Greg–Big Bend
Don–Yellowstone	Heather–Grand Canyon
Chuck–Big Bend	Suzanne–Yellowstone
Lacy–Grand Canyon	

Set B (pages 482–483)

Use the line plot to answer Exercises 1–6.

1. What was the most common grade on the spelling test?

2. How many students made a 90 on the spelling test?

3. What grades did no students make from the grades given?

4. How many more students made a 100 on the spelling test than made a 75?

5. Do the data form a cluster?

6. How many students took the spelling test?

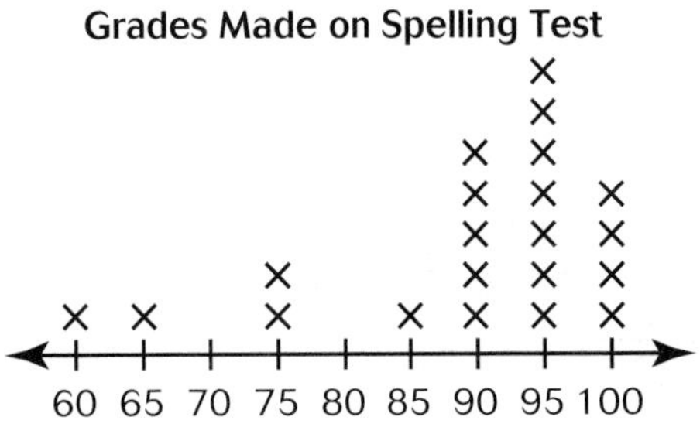

More Practice (continued)

Set C *(pages 484–485)*

Use the grid for Exercises 1–10.

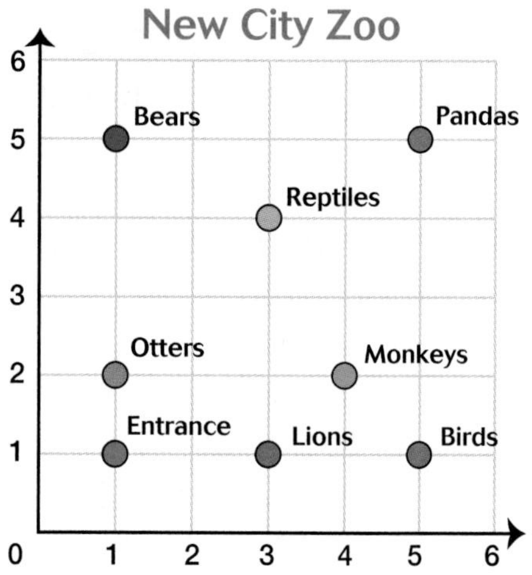

Write the ordered pair for each animal.

1. Reptiles **2.** Monkey

3. Birds **4.** Bears

What is found at each ordered pair?

5. (3, 1) **6.** (5, 5)

7. (1, 1) **8.** (1, 2)

9. Misha found the zebras 2 spaces below the pandas. What ordered pair names where the zebras are?

10. Which is closer to the entrance, reptiles or monkeys?

Set D *(pages 490–491)*

Write whether each is *certain* or *impossible*.

1. A brick will float in water.

2. A person is walking somewhere.

3. The sum of 5 and 5 is 10.

4. The product of 6 and 7 is 13.

Write whether each is *likely* or *unlikely*.

5. It will snow in Los Angeles this year.

6. There will be clouds in the sky this week.

7. You will find a ten-dollar bill today.

8. You will be awake at 1:25 A.M.

Set E *(pages 492–493)*

Name all the possible outcomes. Then write the probability of each outcome.

1. 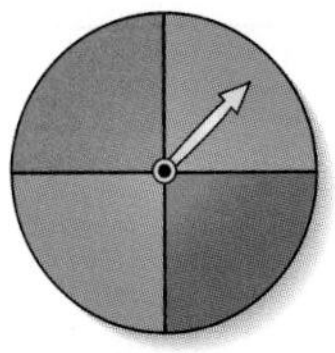

2. 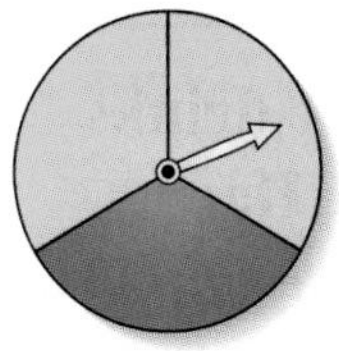

3. 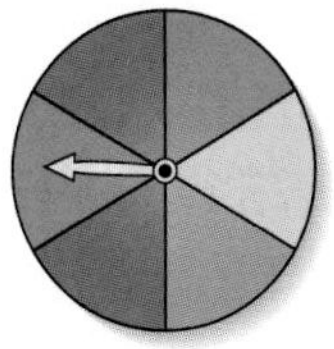

Write the probability of each event if you tossed a cube numbered 1 through 6.

4. Tossing a 6

5. Tossing a number less than 4

6. Tossing a 5 or 1

Set F *(pages 494–496)*

Use the bar graph for Exercises 1–4.

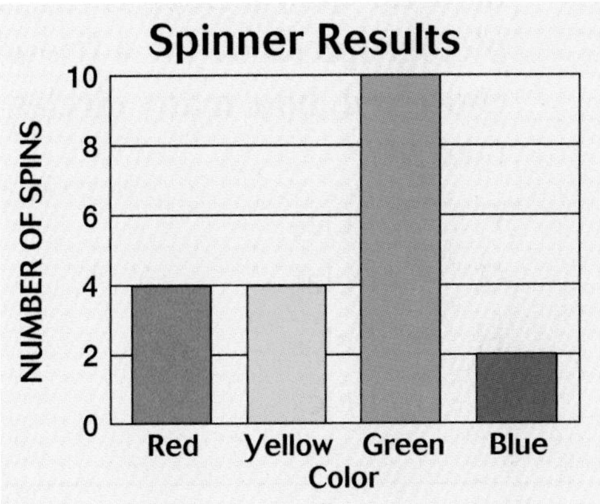

1. What does the bar graph show?

2. Which color was spun the most?

3. Which colors were spun the same number of times?

4. If you repeated this game, predict which color you think will be spun the least.

You have 5 cards numbered 0 through 4. Suppose you pick 2 cards, and each time you record the sum of the numbers. Use the line plot for Exercises 5–8.

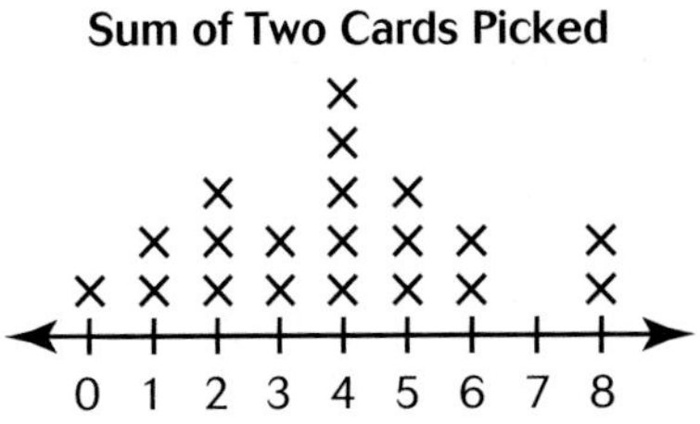

5. What does the line plot show?

6. How many times was the sum of 7 picked?

7. Which sums were picked twice?

8. If you repeat this activity, predict which sum you think will be picked the most.

TEST PREP

Problem Solving: Preparing for Tests

Choose the correct letter for each answer.

1. **Small drinks cost $1.15 each. Large drinks cost $0.75 more than small drinks. Harry bought 4 large drinks. About how much money did Harry spend on drinks?**

A $5
B $8
C $10
D $12

Tip

First find the price of one large drink. Then estimate the price of 4 large drinks.

2. **Kate made a pictograph to show her friends' favorite colors. Each circle she drew on the pictograph stood for 4 friends. If 20 friends chose red, how many circles should Kate make for red?**

F 4 circles
G 5 circles
H 6 circles
J 7 circles

Tip

Try the *Draw a Picture* strategy to solve this problem. Draw a circle for every 4 friends.

3. **Rich made a poster showing different leaves. He put 8 leaves in the first row, 10 leaves in the second row, and 12 leaves in the third row. If he continues this pattern, how many leaves will he use for the first 6 rows?**

A 36 leaves
B 60 leaves
C 72 leaves
D 78 leaves

Tip

Use one of these strategies to solve this problem.

- *Draw a Picture*
- *Find a Pattern*
- *Make a List*

4. **Suppose you buy 4 plants that cost $3 each. Which number sentence shows the change you would get from $20?**

F $20 − $3 = ■

G $20 − $4 = ■

H $20 − $7 = ■

J $20 − $12 = ■

5. **Kim is 52 inches tall. Her brother is 61 inches tall. Which is the best estimate of the difference in their heights?**

A 5 inches **C** 20 inches

B 10 inches **D** 110 inches

6. **Tim, Bob, Jon, Ann, and Ike were waiting in line at a shop. Ann is third. Bob is in front of Ike. Tim is behind Jon. Which of these is reasonable for the order of the 5 friends?**

F Jon, Ann, Bob, Ike, Tim

G Bob, Ike, Ann, Jon, Tim

H Tim, Bob, Ann, Ike, Jon

J Jon, Ike, Ann, Bob, Tim

7. **Marnie says her phone number has all even digits. Each digit is used twice. Which of these numbers could be Marnie's phone number?**

A (246) 814-6483

B (246) 824-6086

C (204) 805-4269

D (204) 824-6086

8. **Hannah buys 3 bags of hamburger rolls for a picnic. Each bag has 6 rolls. During the picnic, 16 of the rolls are eaten. Which shows how many rolls Hannah bought?**

F 18 − 16

G 3 × 6

H 16 − 6

J 3 + 6 + 16

Use the graph for Questions 9 and 10.

The graph shows how many books students read last month.

9. **How many students read five or more books last month?**

A 15 students

B 20 students

C 30 students

D 40 students

10. **How many students read fewer than three books last month?**

F 65 students

G 70 students

H 80 students

J 110 students

Multiple-Choice Cumulative Review

Choose the correct letter for each answer.

Number Sense

1. What is the sum of 234 and 789?

   A 555
   B 913
   C 1,023
   D 1,203

2. Jon has 3 remote-control cars and 2 remote-control trucks. Each toy uses 2 batteries. How many batteries does Jon need for the remote-control cars?

   F 4 batteries **H** 7 batteries
   G 6 batteries **J** 10 batteries

3. Peg used 100 yellow blocks, 35 blue blocks, and 125 red blocks to build a house. How many blue and red blocks did Peg use?

   A 135
   B 160
   C 225
   D 260

4. Carl has 4 packs of baseball cards. Each pack has 5 cards. How many baseball cards does Carl have?

   F 9 baseball cards
   G 10 baseball cards
   H 16 baseball cards
   J 20 baseball cards

Algebra and Functions

5. What is the missing number in the number pattern?

   0, 7, 14, ■, 28, 35

   A 7 **C** 21
   B 20 **D** 27

6. Which figure should NOT be grouped with the others?

   F  **H** 
   G 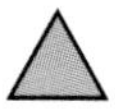 **J** 

7. Which number makes this sentence true?

   $36 \div ■ = 9$

   A 3
   B 4
   C 7
   D 9

8. Which names the same number as 7×3?

   F $7 - 3$
   G $7 + 3$
   H $3 + 7$
   J 3×7

Measurement and Geometry

9. Which figure is congruent to (has the same size and shape as) the figure in the box?

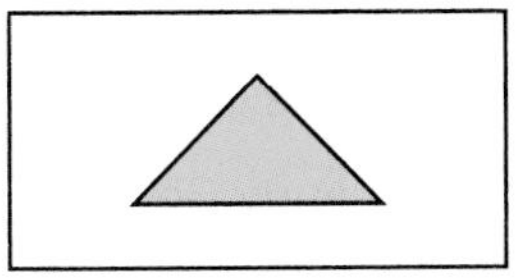

A 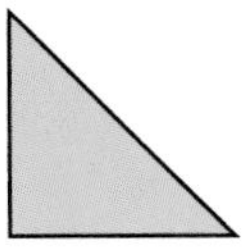

C 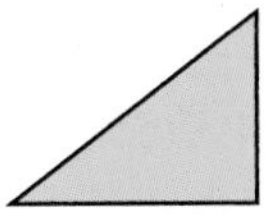

B 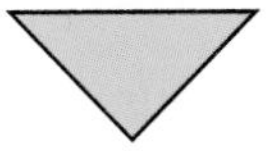

D 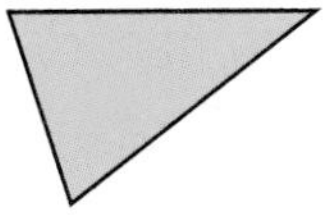

10. Which shows a line of symmetry?

F 

H 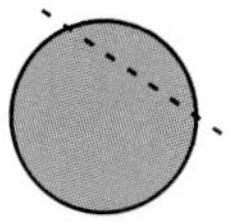

G 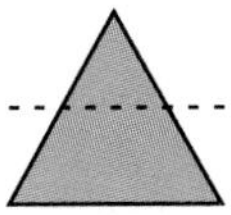

J 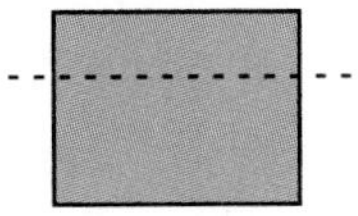

11. How many sides does a rectangle have?

A 1
B 2
C 3
D 4

Statistics, Data Analysis, and Probability

12. Which number is inside the circle but outside the square?

F 1
G 2
H 3
J 4

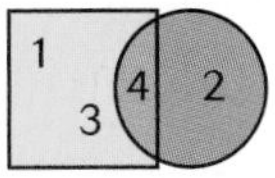

13. If you spun the spinner below 20 times, which color would you probably land on most often?

A green
B blue
C red
D yellow

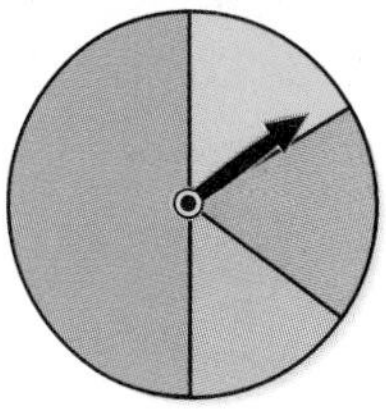

14. Look at the spinner in Exercise 13. How many possible outcomes are there?

A 2
B 4
C 6
D 8

15. If you pick one tile, what color will you most likely pick?

F green
G red
H blue
J yellow

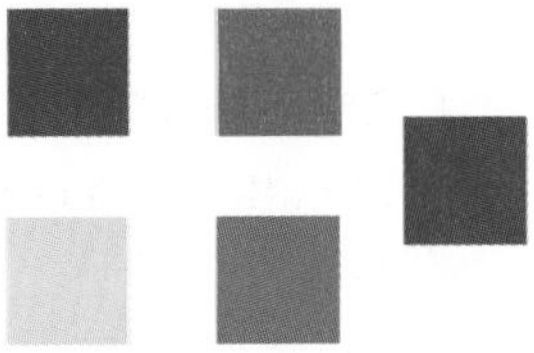

Credits

Photographs

All photographs owned by Scott Foresman unless listed here.

Front Cover and Back Inset: Carr Clifton; Front and Back Cover Background: Graham Chalmers/Panoramic Images

14: Lee Rentz/RENTL/Bruce Coleman Inc.

21: Steve Kaufman/Corbis

44: Robert Maier/Animals Animals/Earth Scenes

114: Frank Siteman/Stock Boston

307: Steve Rosenthal

401: ©Joseph Sohm/Visions of America, LLC/PictureQuest

Illustrations

2: George Hamblin

4: Carla Kiwior

8, 11, 42: Reggie Holladay

53-73: Chris Pappas

94, 100: George Hamblin

102, 105: Burgandy Beam

114, 117: George Hamblin

132: Reggie Holladay

134: George Hamblin

163: Linda Howard

166: Reggie Holladay

176, 186: George Hamblin

192: Rick Ewigleben

196: George Hamblin

198: Burgandy Beam

212: Carla Kiwior

268: Burgandy Beam

386, 390: George Hamblin

394: Chris Pappas

403: Gary Krejca

406: Chris Pappas

408, 409: George Hamblin

428: Burgandy Beam

434: Reggie Holladay

449: Chris Pappas

490: Mike Dammer

Additional Resources

Tables

Measures—*Customary*

Length

1 foot (ft) = 12 inches (in.)
1 yard (yd) = 3 feet or 36 inches
1 mile = 1,760 yards, or 5,280 feet

Weight

1 pound (lb) = 16 ounces (oz)

Capacity

1 pint (pt) = 2 cups
1 quart (qt) = 2 pints
1 gallon (gal) = 4 quarts

Measures—*Metric*

Length

1 centimeter (cm) = 10 millimeters (mm)
1 meter (m) = 100 centimeters
1 kilometer (km) = 1,000 meters

Mass

1 kilogram (kg) = 1,000 grams (g)

Capacity

1 liter (L) = 1,000 milliliters (mL)

Time

1 minute (min) = 60 seconds (s)
1 hour (h) = 60 minutes
1 day (d) = 24 hours
1 week (wk) = 7 days

1 month (mo) = 28 to 31 days, or about 4 weeks
1 year (yr) = 12 months, or 52 weeks, or 365 days

Money

1 penny = 1 cent (¢)
1 nickel = 5 cents
1 dime = 10 cents

1 quarter = 25 cents
1 half-dollar = 50 cents
1 dollar ($) = 100 cents

Symbols

=	is equal to
>	is greater than
<	is less than
. . .	and so on
10¢	ten cents
$1.60	one dollar and sixty cents
6:45	six forty-five
°C	degree Celsius
°F	degree Fahrenheit

Test-Taking Tips

Follow Instructions

- Listen carefully as your teacher explains the test.

Budget Your Time

- Do the questions in order if you can.
- If a question seems very hard, skip it and go back to it later.

Read Carefully

- Watch for extra information in a problem.
- Watch for words like *not*.
- Be sure to answer the question asked.

Make Smart Choices

- **Estimate** when you can so that you have a better idea what the answer might be.
- **Eliminate** answer choices that are not reasonable or are clearly wrong.
- **Check** an answer that you *think* is correct by working backward.

Mark Answers Correctly

- If you are using a "bubble" answer sheet or a gridded response form, be careful to match each question number with the correct number of the answer row.
- If you skip a question, be sure to leave that question's answer space blank.

Glossary

A

acute angle An angle that is less than a right angle. (p. 303)

acute triangle A triangle with three acute angles. (p. 306)

angle Two rays with a common endpoint. (p. 303)
Example:

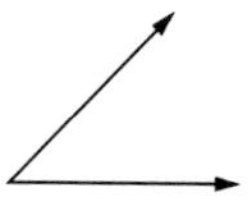

area The number of square units needed to cover a figure. (p. 324)

array An arrangement of objects or numbers in rows and columns. (p. 139)
Example: ★★★★★★
★★★★★★
★★★★★★

B

bar graph A graph with bars of different lengths to show information. (p. 68)

breaking apart A mental math strategy used to make addition and subtraction of numbers easier. (p. 65)

C

capacity The amount a container can hold. (p. 100)

centimeter (cm) A metric unit used to measure length. 100 centimeters equal 1 meter. (p. 107)

certain event An event that is sure to happen. (p. 490)

cluster A large group of **Xs** around one or more numbers on a line plot. (p. 482)

commutative (order) property of multiplication Two numbers may be multiplied in any order to give the same product. (p. 188)

compatible numbers Numbers that make mental math computation easier and can be used to help you estimate. (p. 394)

compensation A mental math strategy used to make computation easier. (p. 66)

cone A solid figure with one circular flat surface and one curved surface that forms a point. (p. 328)
Example:

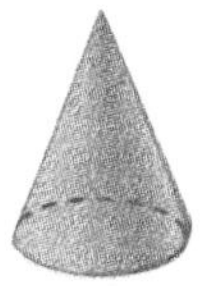

congruent Having the same size and shape. (p. 314)

corner A point where two sides of a plane figure meet. Also a point where more than two faces of a solid figure meet. (p. 329)
Example:

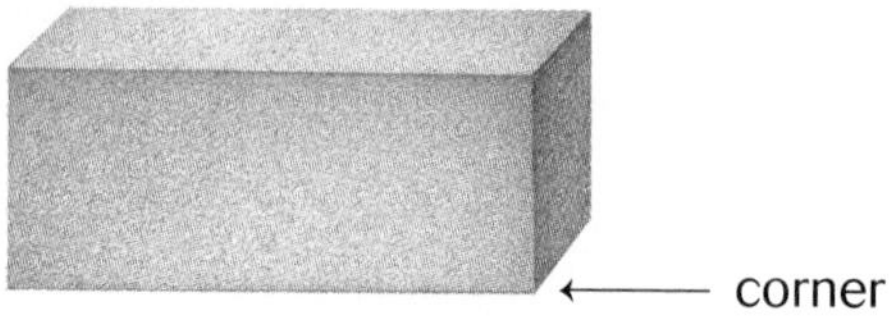

cube A solid figure with six congruent square faces. (p. 328)

Example:

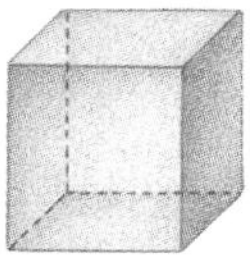

cubic units The units used to measure the volume of a solid figure. (p. 331)

cup (c) A customary unit used to measure capacity. 1 cup equals 8 ounces. (p. 100)

cylinder A solid figure with two flat surfaces that are shaped like congruent circles. (p. 328)

D

data Information that is collected. (p. 478)

decimal A number with one or more places to the right of the decimal point. (p. 447)

decimal point The dot used to separate dollars from cents and ones from tenths. (p. 447)

decimeter (dm) A metric unit used to measure length. 1 decimeter equals 10 centimeters. (p. 107)

degrees Celsius (°C) A metric unit used to measure temperature. (p. 114)

degrees Fahrenheit (°F) A customary unit used to measure temperature. (p. 114)

denominator The number below the fraction bar. (p. 426)

difference The answer in subtraction. (p. 55)

digit Any of the symbols 0, 1, 2, 3, 4, 5, 6, 7, 8, 9 used to write numbers. (p. 4)

divide To separate a number of items into groups of equal size. (p. 226)

dividend The number to be divided. (p. 226)

division An operation on two numbers that results in a quotient. (p. 226)

divisor The number by which another number is to be divided. (p. 226)

doubles Any number that is the sum of two of the same numbers or the product of a number and two. (p. 182)

E

edge The segment where two faces of a solid figure meet. (p. 329)

Example:

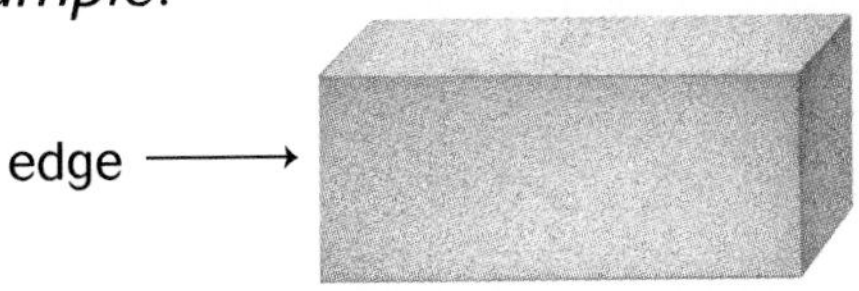

elapsed time The amount of time that has passed. (p. 92)

equation A number sentence with an equal sign. May have a missing number. (p. 72)

Glossary

equilateral triangle A triangle in which all sides are the same length. (p. 308)

equivalent fractions Fractions that name the same number. (p. 428)

estimate To give an approximate rather than an exact answer. (p. 12)

expanded form A number written as the sum of the value of its digits. (p. 4)

expression Numbers combined with one or more operations. May have a missing number. (p. 70)

F

face If a solid figure has only flat surfaces, each surface is a face. (p. 329)
Example:

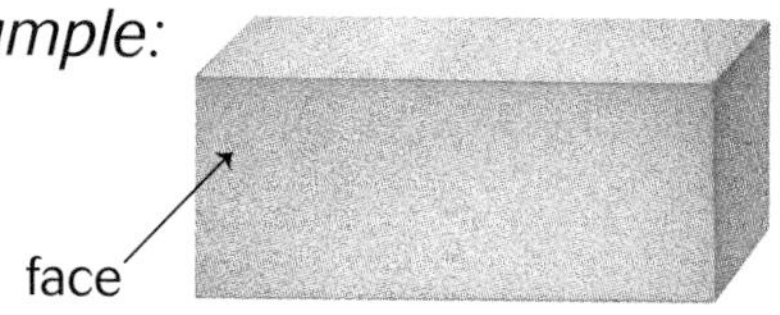

factors The numbers that are multiplied to give a product. (p. 136)

fair game A game in which all players have an equal chance of winning. (p. 498)

flip To pick up and turn over a figure. (p. 316)

foot (ft) A customary unit used to measure length. 1 foot equals 12 inches, also an Ancient Egyptian unit of measure equal to a human foot. (p. 96)

fraction A number that names part of a region or part of a group. (p. 426)
Example:

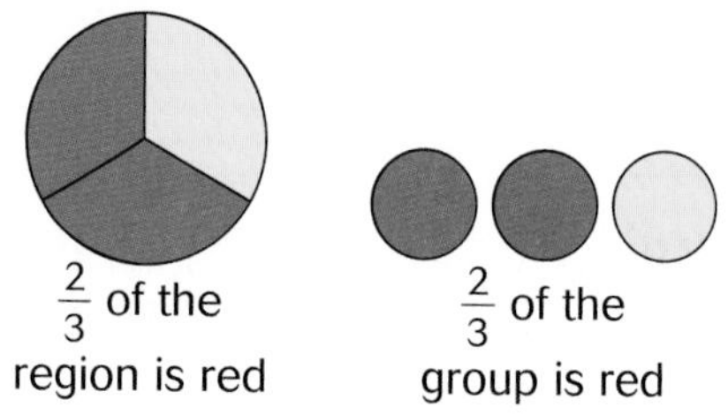

front digit The digit in the place with the greatest value, used for front-end estimation. (p. 56)

front-end estimation A method using only the front-end digits to estimate sums, differences, products, and quotients. (p. 56)

G

gallon (gal) A customary unit used to measure capacity. 1 gallon equals 4 quarts. (p. 100)

gram (g) A metric unit used to measure how heavy an object is. 1,000 grams equal 1 kilogram. (p. 112)

greater than (>) The symbol used to compare two numbers when the greater number is written on the left. (p. 14)

grouping (associative) property of multiplication You can change the grouping of factors and the product will be the same. (p. 198)

H

hexagon A plane figure with six sides and six corners. (p. 300)

hundredth One or more of one hundred equal parts of a whole. (p. 450)

I

impossible event An event that cannot happen. (p. 490)

inch (in.) A customary unit used to measure length. 12 inches equal 1 foot. (p. 96)

input/output table A table with a rule that tells what to do to the *input* number to get the *output* number. (p. 158)

intersecting lines Lines that cross at one point. (p. 303)

inverse operations Operations that undo each other: addition and subtraction; multiplication and division. (p. 42)

isosceles triangle A triangle with at least two sides that are the same length. (p. 308)

K

kilogram (kg) A metric unit used to measure how heavy an object is. 1 kilogram equals 1,000 grams. (p. 112)

kilometer (km) A metric unit used to measure length. 1 kilometer equals 1,000 meters. (p. 107)

L

less than (<) The symbol used to compare two numbers when the lesser number is written on the left. (p. 14)

likely event An event with a good chance to happen. (p. 490)

line A straight path that goes on in both directions. (p. 303)

line plot A graph that shows data along a number line. (p. 482)

line segment Part of a line with two endpoints. (p. 303)

line of symmetry A line on which a figure can be folded so that both sides match. (p. 326)
Example:

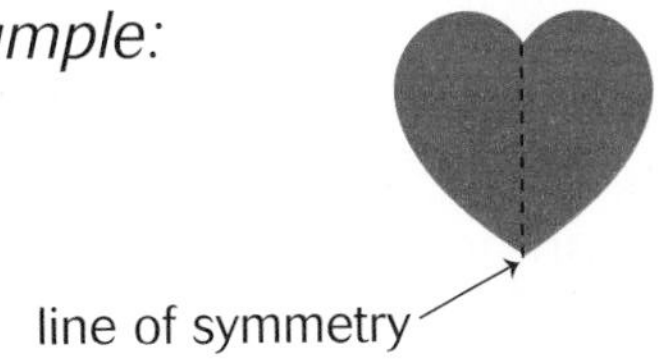

liter (L) A metric unit used to measure capacity. 1 liter equals 1,000 milliliters. (p. 110)

M

meter (m) A metric unit used to measure length. 1 meter equals 100 centimeters. (p. 107)

Glossary

mile (mi) A customary unit used to measure length. 1 mile equals 5,280 feet. (p. 96)

milliliter (mL) A metric unit used to measure capacity. 1,000 milliliters equal 1 liter. (p. 110)

mixed number A number written as a whole number and a fraction. (p. 442)

multiplication An operation on two or more numbers called factors to find a product. (p. 136)

multiplication property of one The product of 1 and any number is the number itself. (p. 156)

N

numerator The number above the fraction bar in a fraction. (p. 426)

O

obtuse angle An angle that is greater than a right angle. (p. 303)

obtuse triangle A triangle with one obtuse angle. (p. 306)

octagon A plane figure with eight sides and eight corners. (p. 300)

ounce (oz) A customary unit used to measure weight. 16 ounces equal 1 pound. (p. 102)

outcome A result of a probability experiment. (p. 492)

P

parallel lines Lines that do not cross. (p. 303)

parallelogram A quadrilateral in which there are two pairs of parallel sides and opposite sides are the same length. (p. 310)

pentagon A plane figure with five sides and five corners. (p. 300)

perimeter The distance around a figure. (p. 322)

pictograph A graph that shows information by using pictures. (p. 206)

pint (pt) A customary unit used to measure capacity. 1 pint equals 2 cups. (p. 100)

plane figure A geometric figure whose points are all in one plane. (p. 300)

polygon A plane figure named by its number of sides and corners. (p. 300)

pound (lb) A customary unit used to measure weight. 1 pound equals 16 ounces. (p. 102)

probability The chance that something will happen. (p. 490)

pyramid A solid figure whose base is a plane figure and whose faces are triangles with a common corner. (p. 328)

product The answer to a multiplication problem. (p. 136)

property of one for multiplication The product of any number and 1 is the number. (p. 156)

Q

quadrilateral A plane figure with four sides and four corners. (p. 300)

quart (qt) A customary unit used to measure capacity. 1 quart equals 4 cups. (p. 100)

quotient The answer in a division problem. (p. 226)

R

ray Part of a line with one endpoint that goes on and on in one direction. (p. 303)

rectangle A quadrilateral in which opposite sides are the same length and parallel. There are four right angles. (p. 310)
Example:

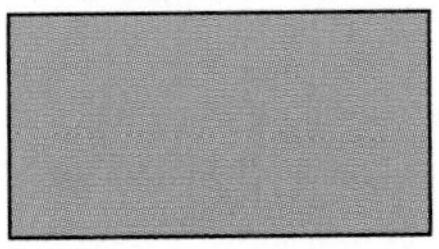

rectangular prism A solid figure whose faces are all rectangles. (p. 328)
Example:

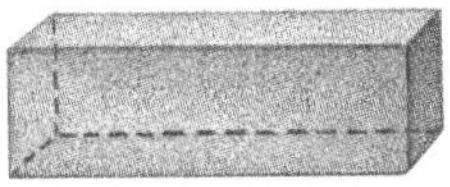

regrouping To use 1 ten to form 10 ones; 1 hundred to form 10 tens; 12 tens to form 1 hundred and 2 tens and so on. (p. 48)

remainder The number that is left after dividing. (p. 388)

rhombus A quadrilateral in which there are two pairs of parallel sides and all sides are the same length. (p. 310)

right angle An angle that forms a square corner. (p. 303)
Example:

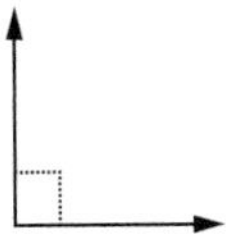

right triangle A triangle with one right angle. (p. 306)

rounding Expressing a number to the nearest ten, hundred, thousand, and so on. (p. 6)

S

scalene triangle A triangle with no sides that are the same length. (p. 308)

side A line segment that is part of a plane figure. (p. 300)

slide Moving a figure up, down, or across without picking it up. (p. 316)

solid (space) figure A geometric figure whose points are in more than one plane. (p. 328)

sphere A solid figure shaped like a round ball. (p. 328)

square A quadrilateral with all sides the same length. Opposite sides are parallel and there are four right angles. (p. 310)

Glossary

square number The product of two equal whole number factors. (p. 179)

square unit A square with sides that are 1 unit long. (p. 324)

standard form A number written with commas separating groups of three digits. (p. 4)

symmetrical Two figures that match exactly when folded on a line of symmetry. (p. 326)

symmetry A plane figure has symmetry if it can be folded along a line so that the two parts match exactly. (p. 326)

T

table Method used to organize data. (p. 278)

tally chart A chart used to record data. (p. 478)

tally marks Marks used to record data. (p. 478)

triangle A plane figure with three sides and three corners. (p. 300)

turn Moving a figure around a point. (p. 316)

U

unfair game A game in which each player does not have the same probability of winning. (p. 498)

unlikely event An event that probably won't happen. (p. 490)

V

volume The number of cubic units needed to fill a solid figure. (p. 331)

W

word name A name for a number that uses words rather than digits. (p. 4)

Y

yard (yd) A customary unit used to measure length. 1 yard equals 3 feet. (p. 96)

Z

zero property of division Zero divided by any number except 0 is 0. You cannot divide by 0. (p. 244)

zero property of multiplication The product of any number and zero is zero. (p. 156)

Index

Index

Index

Index

Index

Index

Index

Index

Index

Index

Index

Index

Index

S

Index

Index